# PARABLE AND POLITICS IN EARLY ISLAMIC HISTORY

# Parable and Politics in Early Islamic History

## THE RASHIDUN CALIPHS

Tayeb El-Hibri

COLUMBIA UNIVERSITY PRESS
*NEW YORK*

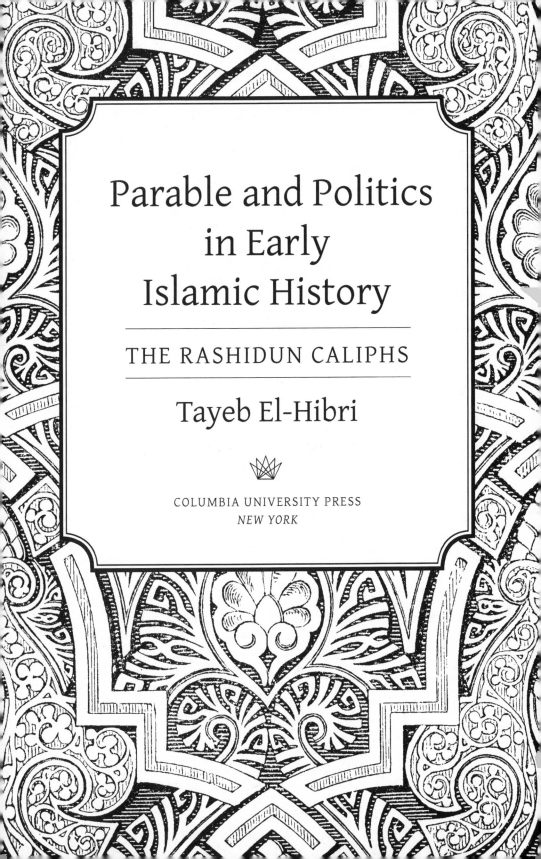

Columbia University Press
Publishers Since 1893
New York Chichester, West Sussex

Library of Congress Cataloging-in-Publication Data
EL-Hibri, Tayeb.
Parable and politics in early Islamic history : the Rashidun caliphs / Tayeb El-Hibri.
p. cm.
Includes bibliographical references and index
ISBN 978-0-231-15082-8 (cloth : alk. paper) — ISBN 978-0-231-52165-9 (ebook)
1. Islamic Empire—History—622–661—Historiography. 2. Caliphs—Islamic Empire—Historiography. 3. Caliphate—Historiography. 4. Prophets—Islamic Empire—Historiography. 5. Islam and politics—Islamic Empire—Historiography. 6. Islamic parables—Islamic Empire—History. 7. Historiography—Political aspects—Islamic Empire. 8. Historians—Islamic Empire—History. I. Title.

DS38.16.E425 2010
909′.1—dc22

2010009473

∞
Columbia University Press books are printed on permanent and durable acid-free paper.
This book is printed on paper with recycled content.
Printed in the United States of America
c 10 9 8 7 6 5 4 3

# Contents

# Preface

The study of the classical Islamic heritage remains something central not just for specialists of medieval history but also for those who study the modern Islamic world. Topics such as the caliphate, the division between Shīʿī and Sunnī, and the overall relevance of events and contentions that happened nearly fourteen centuries ago once again form crucial areas for reexamination and introspection. Even the casual reader of introductory writings on Islam can suddenly find himself forced to go beyond understanding the Qur'ān and the story of the Prophet to having to know about the reigns of the first four caliphs (Abū Bakr, ʿUmar, ʿUthmān, and ʿAlī), who succeeded him in the years 632–661, the period known as the Rāshidūn caliphate (lit. "the Rightly Guided Rulers"). The narrative of the expansion of the Islamic state into Sasanid Persia and the Byzantine empire, the idealized ascetic profiles of the early caliphs (who were also once companions of the Prophet), and the story of the sudden onset of succession crisis and civil war that followed the assassination of the third caliph, ʿUthmān, and the accession of ʿAlī are not mere political transitions folded in time but topics that continue to stir both passionate reverence and deep division in modern Islamic society.

The triumphant political careers of the Prophet and his successors, unlike the situation of Judaism and Christianity, have given this history a life of its own, and almost added understanding it in a particular way as an article of faith. Hence the Shīʿa sect would have no identity without its advocacy for the higher stature of the Hāshimite family of the Prophet generally, and ʿAlī and the line of *imāms* among his descendants more particularly, when compared to the other companions of the Prophet and their descendants, while for the Sunnīs the faith would equally be diminished without the high reverence accorded to the first two caliphs specifically, Abū Bakr and ʿUmar, and the collective importance of all the companions as a symbol of the collectivity of the community (the *jamāʿa*) more generally later. To debate the biographies of the early caliphs is therefore not analogous to writing the history of Roman Caesars but more like tracking the careers of the apostles of Jesus had they ever gone on to experience a cycle of political rise and decline. The dynasties of the Umayyads (661–750), based in Damascus, and the ʿAbbāsids (750–1258), based in Baghdad, would each lay claim to the titles of caliph and Commander of the Faithful, but a convention of religious authenticity among Sunnīs defines only the Rāshidūn—and for the Shīʿa only ʿAlī—as the true caliphs. All later rulers are monarchs who had become removed from the utopian lifestyle of the early society of Medina.

Each of the two Islamic sects has long approached this history with firm conviction regarding one or the other of the two versions of how the dispute over the succession began and developed. The Shīʿa believe that ʿAlī was deliberately wronged by the other companions when he was repeatedly passed over for the succession and later given the chance only after leadership of the community became a thankless task on the eve of a brewing conflict. To the Shīʿa this was not only an affront to a more erudite and puritanical individual—a veritable *imām*—but almost a deliberate conspiracy against the very family of the Prophet (the Hāshimites) to prevent them from holding leadership. And ʿAlī's tragedy would only accelerate later, when he had to deal with overzealous followers, the Khārijites, who turned against him and became some of his staunchest opponents.

Sunnīs, however, believe that this Shīʿī version of events falls somewhere between an exaggeration of ʿAlī's importance and a complete conspiracy fantasy. The first two caliphs are viewed by Sunnīs as having been more senior than ʿAlī, with their own other important ties to the Prophet, and as crucial framers of the *sunna* (tradition) of the Prophet (sometimes *sunna* is directly associated with the Prophet, but at other times just with the first caliphs and the companions—and thus only indirectly recognized as authoritative custom). The first caliphs, and to an even greater extent their more junior associates, such as Ibn 'Abbās and 'Abdallāh b. 'Umar, are equally viewed as crucial for the frame of *ḥadīths* (lit. "sayings of the Prophet") that underlie the Sharī'a.

A lot of the divergence in the religious concepts and institutions of Sunnīs and Shī'īs therefore emanates from that initial disagreement over who should have succeeded the Prophet and what really happened on the eve of his death—debates that created such a sudden rift in the community afterward. The present study revisits this original issue in religious and historical sources and argues for an alternative reading of this history as a largely parabolic cycle of literary narrative. Despite the seeming fragmentation of accounts about the first four caliphs, whether in *ḥadīths* or in historical stories, it is shown that these once formed a unified story with a particular plot line, with intertextual connections that conveyed a variety of allusive meanings about a political, polemical, or moralizing issue. These meanings would have been challenging but still accessible to an audience of the early Islamic period, which was steeped in the techniques of rhetorical argumentation and evocation. Such audiences were conscious of the potential layers of meaning in discussing issues and equally in command of learning across different cultures and their frames of presentation (Judaic, Christian, Arabic, Persian, folkloric, etc.). This awareness about the literary potential of caliphal history would gradually recede in importance in the ninth century with the emergence of different orthodoxies, Sunnī and Shī'ī, that narrowed the use of history to a mere factual reporting to support one official version or another. As the subsequent chapters will show, however, the partisan Sunnī and Shī'ī depictions of history or of historical characters both basically drew on the same collection of narratives. The emergent picture in this study will be that of an originally well-structured drama of strong and weak points for each central character—rather than one of a completely favorable or unfavorable image for one character over another.

All was not a fictional construct, however. While the pivotal political events and polarizations that happened in the Rāshidūn caliphate are true as told, it is in the description of the details of this history (dealing with the motives of characters, argumentations, or portrayals of strategy, to name but a few areas) that we find the literary construction. One could almost read the story of 'Alī's career within this frame, for example, to resemble that of a poetic Moses, where the image of the biblical character is adapted to a political context, and adjusted to confront new challenges. ʿAlī is therefore similarly challenged in dealing with a mix of wavering lieutenants and with a feisty community of followers. His quest to consolidate his caliphal control, while political, is also infused with strong arguments (or interpretations, according to Sunnīs) for the religious legitimacy of his actions.

The sources on which Muslim narrators drew in crafting these historical stories, best exemplified in the Chronicle of Ṭabarī, were varied. Sometimes they drew directly on precursor biblical accounts, at other times they worked with modified versions of these accounts, and in other instances they crafted their compositions in intense rhetorical dialogue within the already formed Islamic textual tradition (including the growing collection of legal dicta or commentaries that spanned *ḥadīth* as much as the Qur'ān). Dialogue in the historical texts, however, did not happen only in response to a previous episode in ancient legend but sometimes in response to events that happened forward in time (in the eighth and ninth centuries—during the Umayyad and ʿAbbāsid periods when the chronicle narratives were taking their final literary form). The Rāshidūn caliphs were always being depicted and judged in complex networks of relations to other monarchal characters, showing how different leaders addressed similar questions about the tensions between the imperatives of religious law and ideals from secular principles. The present study accomplishes this revisionist reading of the early medieval Islamic chronicles in a way that challenges both the traditional versions of Sunnī and Shīʿī Islam and the established academic synthesis of early Islamic history.

The background of research for this study rests on a variety of contributions from books and articles that laid the foundations in Islamic studies for traditional and revisionist scholarship. I have indicated all of these in the bibliography, but special credit must go to revisionist studies done within the past two to three decades, more often in religious studies than in Islamic history and frequently outside the latter field altogether. The beginning of the inquiry, however, was historical and undertaken with the aim of making the task of Islamic historical writing a more credible one for other potential specialists. Making use of conclusions in the fields of religious and literary studies and bridging these methods to the timid overviews composed about early Islamic history will be an increasingly necessary task in the future for making more credible judgments about a chronicle such as Ṭabarī's and other historical writings around his time more generally. This study differs from other revisionist writings in another respect as well, in having begun with the 'Abbāsid period and moved backward in time to the caliphate of the Rāshidūn, unlike many which have traditionally addressed the Rāshidūn period without attention to the narratives outside of its chronological frame. The fact that most of the classical writers dealing with early Islamic history began their first documented work in the middle of the eighth century has long been known, but few have ever bothered to take into account the political, cultural, and religious interests of the 'Abbāsid period, especially between 750 and 861, in projecting a certain type of historical representation on the earlier period of Islamic history. It is hoped that here as well this study will provide an alternative path of revisionist research that will invite others who work on the history of the early period or on issues of Islamic law or Arabic literature to better explore and incorporate issues of historical context.

Research for this project spanned a variety of digressions over the past several years. I am first and foremost indebted to the University of Massachusetts, Amherst, for having provided the time, funding, and availability of books that made this study possible. Specific credit is due to the Office of the Vice Chancellor for Research Development, the dean of the faculty of the College of Humanities and Fine Arts, and to John Mullin and Nigar Khan, the dean and associate dean respectively of the Graduate School. I am also grateful for a membership in 2003 at the School of Historical Studies at the Institute for Advanced Study in Princeton, which provided additional support during a sabbatical year as well as access to the library collections of Princeton University. Various scholars there and elsewhere were encouraging about the reliable prospects for such research—if only one were able to find the evidence from the texts. It is hoped that readers will find sufficient proof in this study for why I believe it more worthwhile to study the Islamic chronicles as texts of representation than as factual testimonies preserved in time.

# GENEALOGICAL CHART

## KINSHIPS OF THE CALIPHS IN CLAN OF QURAYSH

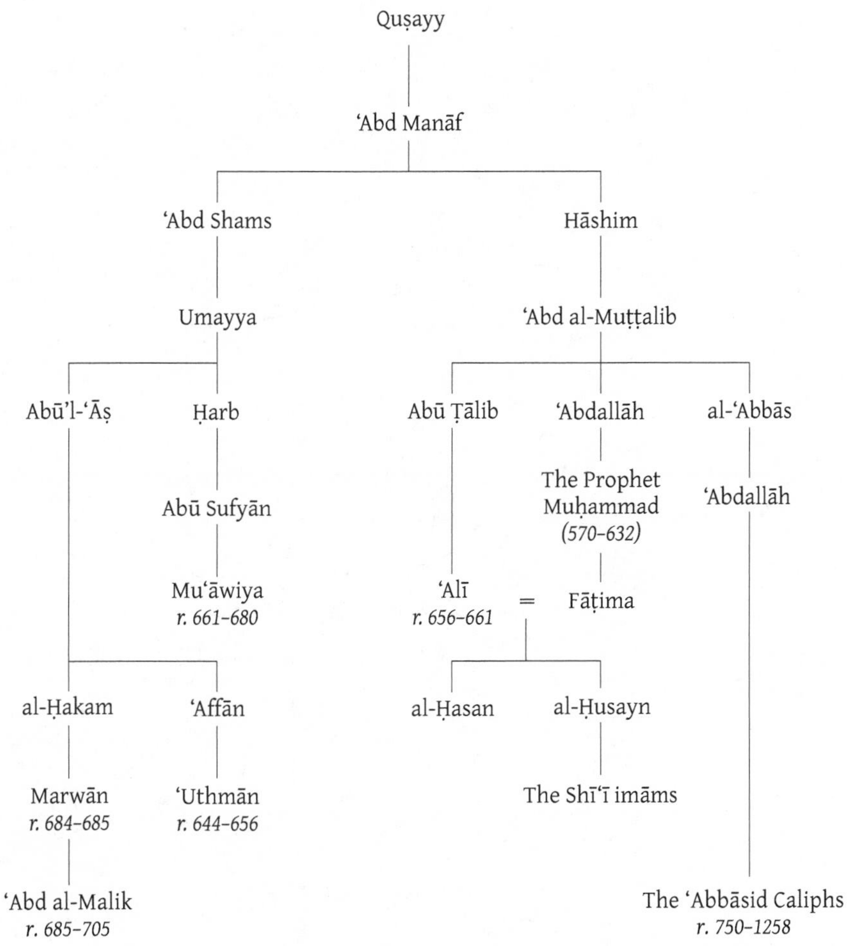


The first caliph, Abū Bakr (r. 632–634), meets the Hāshimites in genealogy at the grandparent of Quṣayy, Murra b. Kaʿb b. Luʾayy, while ʿUmar (r. 634–644) meets them at Kaʿb b. Luʾayy.

# PARABLE AND POLITICS IN EARLY ISLAMIC HISTORY

## CHAPTER ONE

# Introduction

The starting point for any investigation of early Islamic historiography has to be study of the stories, and specifically the stories of prophets. From its very beginning, Islam viewed itself as a continuation of earlier monotheistic messages and conceived of Muḥammad's life as another chapter of dialogue between a messenger and his people. The battle that biblical figures as diverse as Noah, Abraham, Moses, and Jesus had earlier fought on behalf of monotheism and imminent redemption found its conclusion in Arabia in the early seventh century and, to Muslims, was ultimately fulfilled by the victory of Muḥammad and his companions over the polytheists, and the conquest of Mecca.

In the Qur'ān, the basic highlights of Muḥammad's life and success are recounted in broad-brush strokes that parallel the depiction of the lives of earlier prophets. Here the long and detailed accounts in the Books of Genesis, Exodus, and Samuel that describe with vivid drama and biographical detail the lives of the Patriarchs, Moses, David, and Solomon, are no longer to be found. The Qur'ān reduces the stories of each of these individuals to a main theme, focusing in every case less on personal flaws and moral crises than on the fulfillment of religious promise and triumph over tribulation. Shifts and turns in the biblical biographies appear to have been understood in the Qur'ān on esoteric and abstract levels but were not repeated in concrete form.[1] The Qur'ān seems to allude more to the mystery of change in time, human nature, and the continuing dialogue between man and God. The principles that shaped the parables in various biblical books are indirectly evoked in the Qur'ān through poetic statements that appreciate the art and irony of existence and the tragic lot of man. Biblical tales appear removed from any fixed context, in time or locale, and only rarely does one find some slip of too much information (as in the cases of Joseph and Solomon).

The Qur'ān uses a number of terms to refer to these stories: "*naba'*," "*ḥadīth*," "*qaṣaṣ*," but perhaps most significantly "*mathal*." Used mostly to describe naturalistic phenomena and how the process of life and decay is governed by divine guidance, this term is also applied to the historical sphere of nations and prophets. *Mathal*, roughly to be translated as "parable," does not refer to a mere succession of facts but to the whole mystery by which God unfolds a cyclical process or a drama, which in the case of prophets and nations describes how the dispossessed are lent victory and the confident holders on power are subverted. The process rests on an artful interplay between patterns of behavior and anomaly, and interactions in life (both visible and sublimated) that lead to unusual turns in fortune for central figures. And through these plots, contradictions, and shifts one is led to recognize the poetic progress of divine justice through the earthly sphere. The same moral is applicable to different settings; whether it is the Jacob saga, the story of Joseph and his brothers, or the interactions of Moses and Pharaoh, all are viewed as parables with a common thread.

Understanding the vicissitudes of the parabolic narrative, or the divine novel (*mathal*), was probably the prime vocation of seers from biblical to postbiblical times and likely led some to craft stories that paralleled received parabolic structures. This exercise of pirating the modes of divine parables and adapting them to characters and issues anchored in later realities must have prevailed well into early Islamic times among Jews and Christians who lived in Arabian environments. The Qur'ān indirectly criticizes this group of individuals, who engaged in "narrating parables" (*ḍarb al-mathal*) as a form of religious debate,[2] and insists that divine stories are the "fairest of stories" (*aḥsan al-qaṣaṣ*)—in reference to the purged narratives of prophetic lives as recited by Muḥammad.[3] The Qur'ān follows up by discouraging believers from storytelling, too much memorializing of ancestors (*dhikr al-ābā'*), or parsing or interpreting stories (*ta'wīl*).[4]

The Qur'ānic reticence on telling stories in general, and prophetic stories in particular, did not, however, prevent Jewish and Christian converts after Muḥammad's death from developing the tradition of religious storytelling anew.[5] In a region stretching across the Fertile Crescent and spanning communities with a culturally cosmopolitan milieu of Greek, Arab, and Persian legend, a unique form of Abrahamic syncretism emerged in the eighth and ninth centuries that extended the frontiers of Islamic legend on many different fronts: exegetical, historical, and literary. These converted masters of storytelling not only revived the memory of biblical accounts in exegetical literature but crafted a whole new saga for the life of Muḥammad, his companions, his Hāshimite relations, and his successors in a trajectory that continued the biblical style of novelistic and parabolic accounts. The extended narrative of Islamic history now centered around a new peak in human history: the conception of Muḥammad as the Messenger of God and the seal of the Prophets who brought about the ushering in of a new cosmic cycle. Muḥammad is shown to have been, while he was alive, both successful in establishing stable political control, and adept at forging compromise at times of crisis, whether between the Medinans and Meccans or among individual followers ('Alī, Abū Bakr, 'Umar, and Khālid, as well as 'Āisha and her peers).

It is after the Prophet's death, however, that old patterns of biblical tragedy come back in full color. The central issue around which discord occurred was the question of succession, which would divide the community between those who favored allegiance to successors from the family of the Prophet, particularly 'Alī, and those who looked back to the political leaders of the pre-Islamic era as the more worthy candidates (the clan of Banū 'Abd Shams, from whom 'Uthmān and the Umayyad dynasty came). For the years immediately following the death of the Prophet, little is known about this division. The short two-year reign of the first caliph, Abū Bakr, is described in the chronicles as a time when Meccan and Muslim insecurity about rival Arabian tribes and pretender prophets was the central priority for action. Thus the circumstances of Abū Bakr's swift succession to the Prophet and the Hāshimite protest of this are relegated to the background, overshadowed by the higher religious objectives of seeking to reestablish unity and remain faithful to the message of Muḥammad (the reported initial codification of the text of the Qur'ān and the caliph's keeping the first Muslim incursion into Syria on track are represented as key manifestations of the community's loyalty to Islam during this time). Similarly, in 'Umar's reign the lingering rift over caliphal succession gets overshadowed by the story of 'Umar's merits as an equitable, pious, and ascetic leader, as well as by the dramatic account of the Muslim confrontation with the Sasanid and Byzantine empires. The successful Islamic conquest of the Sasanid empire provides a central image that is implicitly used to affirm the righteousness of the second caliph's reign, irrespective of the adequacy of his original grounds for inheriting the caliphate.

Through his combination of charisma, pious example, and vigilant attention to the details of government, 'Umar is shown to be adept both at forging a new confederation of tribal support similar to the one created by Muḥammad earlier and at maintaining this unity even as the community expanded outside Arabia. The trouble with the succession, however, is finally fully evoked during the transitions to the rule of the third and fourth caliphs, 'Uthmān and 'Alī. Tensions during 'Uthmān's reign translate into an open conflict that leads to his sudden assassination in Medina (purportedly by a band of outside invaders from Egypt and Kufa, but more likely by elements within Medina itself), and then in the ensuing double civil war that the fourth caliph, 'Alī, had to fight, first against a coalition of companions led by 'Āisha that claimed sympathy for 'Uthmān, and then against the governor of Syria, Mu'āwiya, who claimed a right to political opposition on the basis of his (i.e., Mu'āwiya's) kinship to the third caliph. The civil war between 'Alī and Mu'āwiya, which eventually stabilized in a stalemate between two Islamic centers of power in Syria and Iraq, simultaneously spawned an internal conflict in 'Alī's camp against the schismatic sect of the Khārijites, members of which eventually assassinated the caliph in A.H. 40/A.D. 661.

The narrative of this early Islamic period, known as the Rāshidūn caliphate, has tended to be divided in traditional Muslim perception into a phase of triumph, under the first two caliphs, and one of sedition and civil war, under the latter two. While Abū Bakr's and 'Umar's caliphates are thus viewed as times of unity, loyalty to leadership, and conquest, the times of 'Uthmān and 'Alī are considered marred by sociopolitical dissent, questionable behavior by rulers, and disarray in government (especially in the relations between the center and the provinces). This portrayal of a clear division between a perfect age and a phase of decline is, however, more a form of religious representation than one of actual historical fact, even if some elements of the story may be real. Perhaps an interesting way to examine the shaping of historical narrative within a religious rhetoric can be found in the way narrators describe the path toward *fitna* in ʿUthmān's reign and afterward. *Fitna* (a temptation or trial) was the religious term used to refer to an inexplicable moment of failure whose motives and/or responsibility was uncertain (whether entirely placed on the individual or on a divinely ordained event). Whether intended as a trial for the individual's or the community's faith or as something that holds other goals, the problem of *fitna* is never fully explained in religious rhetoric. Nevertheless, in narratives ranging in topic from the fall of Adam and Eve to the fall of ʿUthmān, the reader can find linkages in the Islamic valuation of change (sexual, political, and moral). Why a turn happened in the community's fortunes toward the middle of ʿUthmān's reign is a subject that forms a dilemma for rich discussion.[6]

The transition to *fitna* is never directly interpreted in the sources, but the various narratives that make up the accounts of the Rāshidūn caliphs provide diverse reasons for the motives for this change. The expansion of the community outside Arabia, contact with the temptations of the conquered lands and Persian culture, competition over wealth, jealousies, a drifting from the simple lifestyle of Arabia, and the relaxing of the law and its restrictions and penalties all form key reasons for changes in the behavior of the community. The second caliph is said to have warned the companions against participating in the campaigns outside Arabia,[7] to confirm the tendentious message in the chronicles that the new lands will bring about the undoing of the early piety and split the community into sects. Thus, far from being the gift of a religious triumph, the conquests are cast in the chronicles as an impetus for temptation.[8]

But along with this view of predestined events and the religious frame for rationalizing the causes of discord comes a great focus in the sources on particular developments in ʿUthmān's reign that are viewed as main reasons for the deterioration that subsequently occurred. Ṭabarī's narratives of events in ʿUthmān's reign, for instance, dwell extensively on the disagreement that occurred in Kufa over the equitable division of booty and the tension between the provincial leaders and the caliph's governor. These events are portrayed as occurring simultaneously with growing trends of religious innovation (*bidaʿ*) and opinions (*ra'y*), some of which are associated with the policies of ʿUthmān. The caliph's own religious interpretations are characterized as *ta'wwul* (analogical interpretations or simply personal exegesis) and sometimes branded as *taḥrīf* (a distortion of the text of the law or of the sacred religious practice). At other times the innovation is traced to the margins of the community, where a different strand of excessive religiosity (*ghuluww*) is attributed to a group known as al-Saba'iyya (followers of a semi-legendary figure, 'Abdallāh b. Saba', who is reported to have been an ardent devotee of 'Alī), and another attributed to the overzealousness of some companions of the Prophet (such as Abū Dharr, 'Ammār, and Ibn Mas'ūd).

At the same time that they survey these developments, the narratives also place considerable secular blame on the style of the third caliph's rule as a catalyst for disaster. The sources rebuke 'Uthmān through the words of his critics for moral and political failings, such as his favoring of his kinsmen in political appointments, his weakness in reining in their indulgencies, and his general failure to know what was happening in his name (as evidenced by the hegemony of Marwān b. al-Ḥakam in Medina and the use of the caliphal seal for treacherous or oppressive policies). Much in this representation is meant to contrast with 'Umar's more scrutinizing and stringent approach to affairs of state. 'Umar had ruled more like a shepherd than a king, and his officials are represented more as legatees of a religious master and keepers of a covenant than as political commanders. Everything about 'Umar's government had depended on the continued functioning of a certain moral economy of relationships between the capital and the provinces in a kind of great chain of being.[9]

This network of virtuous interaction gets undermined during 'Uthmān's reign. 'Uthmān's famous defense that his appointments of relatives represented a form of pious filial action, along with his general attitude of stubbornness about changing his policies, made his errors not only a political issue but also a religious infraction and misinterpretation. And similarly the community followed suit in a spirit of indulgence that imitated the behavior of 'Uthmān's officials, if not 'Uthmān himself. Hence, Ya'qūbī would describe in a specialized work, *Mushākalat al-Nās li-zamānihim*, how various companions set out to make fortunes during 'Uthmān's reign, building villas and mansions in Medina and the provinces in a way that, the historian suggests, could not have happened had the leader not given license to such ambitious displays of wealth. Ya'qūbī states about 'Uthmān:

> 'Uthmān was known for his forbearance, generosity, advancing his kinsmen and family, and ambitious spending [*ittikhādh al-amwāl*]; and people emulated his practices [*fa-imtathala al-nās fi'lahu*]. He built a home in Medina on which he spent a large sum of money by constructing it of stone and putting teakwood on its doors. He also acquired properties in Medina, springs, and herds of camels [*wa ittakhadha amwālan wa 'uyūnan wa iblan*].

Ya'qūbī then comments about the companions, saying,

> During 'Uthmān's time, the companions of the Messenger of God acquired great properties and built houses [*ittakhadha aṣḥābu rasūl allāh al-amwāl wa banū al-dūr*]. Al-Zubayr built his famous house in al-Basra, where there were many markets and commerce, and constructed other houses in Kufa, Egypt [Fuṣṭaṭ], and Alexandria. His fortune totaled fifty thousand dinars. Besides this, he left a thousand mares and a thousand slaves. Ṭalḥa also built houses and had estates to the value of one hundred thousand dinars . . . and left behind great wealth in gold and silver. 'Abd al-Raḥmān b. 'Awf also built himself a large and spacious house. He used to have a thousand camels and a hundred mares. A fourth of his wealth was estimated at eighty-four thousand dinars. Sa'd b. Abī Waqqās also constructed a house in Medina . . . and [another companion] al-Miqdād built a castle [*qaṣr*] at al-Jurf [near Medina]; put stucco on it both inside and out, and put balconies on it. No one had done this in the time of 'Umar. They only did this after he died.[10]

On another level, however, as mentioned above, the origin of *fitna* is represented as something that predated both the conquests and 'Uthmān's reign, and had more to do with the lingering tensions in the community over how the first succession to the Prophet had ended. Abū Bakr's succession to the caliphate is alternately represented in the sources as a religious approximation from the act of his leading the prayer, an accident, or—in secular terms—a result of circumstances that combined the clever use of coercion and craft by the Quraysh. Whatever the real reasons were, the event caused the shift in succession away from the family of the Prophet and the creation of a tension between the

Hāshimites and the Quraysh. With ʿAlī as the emblem of Hāshimite dispossession, the Saqīfa episode was viewed as kicking off a new Islamized version of the old rivalry between the Banū Hāshim and the Banū ʿAbd Shams. ʿAlī stood as the enduring victim of jealousy, the primordial blow against Adam, whose cause would come to attract all disgruntled groups, from the Saqīfa down to Ṣiffīn. To various narrators, the succession dilemma thus stood at the center of the Islamic historical narrative. Narrators not only tried to portray the rivalry between the Muhājirūn and the Anṣār as a precursor of the future rivalry between the Meccan-Syrian federation of tribes and the bedouin and Iraqi partisans of ʿAlī, but they also gave the dispute a predestined, ancestral root: the Hāshimite vs. Quraysh (Umayyad) rivalry was seen as mirroring the biblical rivalry between the lines of Jacob and Esau.[11]

## *ḤADĪTH* AND HISTORY

Whatever the original crisis in ʿUthmān's reign was—be it tension over the succession, division of the conquered lands, or religious issues—it appears clear that from ʿUthmān's time onward the companion community was immersed in a mortal fight over political power. The scene of the leading companions engaged in bitter civil war barely two decades after Muḥammad's death posed a moral dilemma to orthodox writers of the ninth century, who generally sought to look on the Prophet's companions with unquestioning reverence as supporters of the early message. Viewing the companions as exemplars of the proper practice of the ritual and the law was a crucial matter for religious writers, who relied on the companions as transmitters of *ḥadīth*s and as individuals who knew best the ways, or "*sunna*," of the Prophet. In light of this, *ḥadīth* scholars tried to ignore the turbulent history of ʿUthmān's and ʿAlī's reigns, opting instead to emphasize only the flattering portions of companion biographies during the Sīra (the biography of the Prophet) and the first two caliphates. And just as the biblical prophets were purged of error in the doctrine of *ʿiṣmat al-anbiyā*ʾ, a similar doctrine of *ʿadālat al-ṣaḥāba* emerged that downplayed negative evaluations of the companions and shielded them from blame for the conflicts that occurred.[12] Within this frame, conflict was blamed on outside instigators, while the companions were portrayed as having acted in good faith, however controversial their actions were, and in the end each met redemption through death or repentance of his error and thus rediscovered their early unity. The whole chapter was thus a divine trial, according to the orthodox view, that ought not to be parsed or evaluated with prejudice for one party over another.[13]

This apologetic attitude toward reading companion history is known to form the overt layer for understanding Ṭabarī's history of the civil war, according to its most prominent component narrative, which is reported by Sayf b. 'Umar, a version of history that R. S. Humphreys has dubbed the "Sunday School" version because it seems to downplay the political responsibility of the companions.[14] The apologetic on behalf of the companions is even more dramatically pronounced, however, in the much-reduced role in *ḥadīth* literature for historical accounts about the companions. Evidence for this can quickly be gleaned by contrasting the seeming disconnection between a chronicle such as that by Ṭabarī and the *ḥadīth* compilations of Bukhārī, Muslim, and others. The former gives detailed stories about the Rāshidūn caliphs and the companions, while the latter ignore this information, with a few exceptions that deal with issues of necessary religious value (either ritualistic, legalistic, or polemical). Such a division in the selection of accounts by *ḥadīth* compilers, however, was a purely institutional tool dating to the later ninth century, when *ḥadīth* had become a developed field that dominated religious ideology and social attention. That earlier generations saw things differently can partly be discerned in the great resemblance between portions of historical narratives and *ḥadīth* accounts (in episodes such as the Prophet's last days, the Saqīfa story, and the Shūrā succession to 'Umar). Historical accounts, it therefore often seems, belonged to an earlier (or different) climate of parabolic narration, which as mentioned earlier continued the tradition of biblical storytelling with a different focus, on the lives of the companions.

In spite of this distance between historical narratives and *ḥadīth/sunna* accounts, there remains in the *ḥadīth/sunna* accounts considerable material that seems in origin to have been a commentary on the very troubled *fitna* narrative of the Rāshidūn caliphate that canonical writers rejected. Far from reading a continuously rising tide of righteous behavior and triumph, certain *ḥadīth*s point to a coming cycle of change,[15] and even show the Prophet predicting that this change (i.e., conflict) will come from within the community rather than from without. As one *ḥadīth* puts it,

"I do not fear that you (my community) will become polytheists after I die, but that you will compete for this world."[16] In essence, the voice of rebuke for the companions can be found in the midst of as orthodox a compilation of tradition as that of Bukhārī.[17] Sometimes the warning is put in a more circumspect manner, in anecdotal information that bears more than one meaning, such as in a story after the Battle of Uḥud, when the Prophet reportedly declared that he would bear witness (presumably for the virtue) of those who fell in that battle (*ha'ulā' ashhadu 'alayhim*). When Abū Bakr then asked, "Aren't we like them, O Messenger of God, as we converted like they did, and fought like they have [*a-lasnā bi-ikhwānihim aslamnā ka-mā aslamū wa jāhadnā ka-mā jāhadū*]?," the Prophet replied: "Yes, but I do not know what you will do after my death [*balā wa lakin lā adrī mā tuḥdithūna ba'dī*]."[18] *Ḥadīth* compendia are generally redacted to avoid any overtly negative comments on the companions' political history and their conflicts. But once the thread of general rebuke is recognized, it can be found to form a completely different layer for reading texts and relating the religious and historical sources of the ninth century. Perhaps the most resonant image that *ḥadīth* uses to decry the political actions of the companions comes in a remarkable exchange between the Prophet and God on the Day of Judgment.

When the Prophet prepares to welcome his companions in the afterlife, according to *ḥadīth*, he will find himself prevented from receiving them. When he inquires as to why this is happening, the answer will come: "You do not know what they did after you. They have altered their behavior."[19] This is the basic conclusion in several *ḥadīth*s, but in one version the Prophet feels some blame for what has happened and declares: "Then I say as the saintly servant [*al-'abd al-ṣāliḥ*]: 'I was among them for the time you knew . . .,' "[20] borrowing the famous apologetic reply of Jesus in the Qur'ān. The Qur'ān recounts the latter reply in the context of a similar dialogue between God and Jesus concerning another problem, namely how Christians came to attribute divinity to Jesus and Mary.[21] When Islamic narrators portrayed Muḥammad as borrowing the language of Jesus in apologizing for the companions, they were clearly hinting that the damage caused by the conflict over succession to the caliphate after the Prophet died was equivalent in travesty to the evolution of the doctrine of the trinity after Jesus' death.

It seems clear from these *ḥadīth*s that the basic scheme of the stories about the companions was heavily influenced by a biblical model of writing and that this process of historical writing developed simultaneously with that of *ḥadīth* writing, and sometimes before it. With the community set adrift as a result of the succession conflict and the civil wars after 'Uthmān's reign, narrators crafted a history of the Rāshidūn that was influenced by biblical narration, portraying continuity in tribulations and transformations.[22] As one of the aforementioned *ḥadīths* shows, a comparison was sometimes made between the error of discord over the succession in Islam and the Christian disputes over Jesus and his crucifixion. However, at other times the scheme of comparison, perhaps the more prominent one in Ṭabarī's history, highlighted similarities between the Muslim civil war and the story of the Israelites in sedition and adrift after the incident of the golden calf, the event that led to their wandering in the desert for forty years (*al-tīh*).[23]

The failure of the Islamic community to agree on a successor to the Prophet and to cohere politically is a problem that would only increase further on in time with the transition from the Rāshidūn caliphs to the Umayyad dynasty. The problem of dissent and division, however, is viewed not as something unique to the Muslim community but as the natural lot of newly emergent nations or states. Islamic tradition portrays the historical cycle of the Rāshidūn caliphate and its passage to a phase of rivalry, jealousy, and abandonment of the righteous way (left undefined as it related to the issue of political succession) as typical of what can be termed historical *sunna* or the *sunna* of nations (i.e., the normal pattern of transition).[24] In its eventual divisions and rivalries, the Muslim community was portrayed as adhering to the pattern described by the Prophet.[25]

The *ḥadīth* that has the Prophet declare "You shall follow the patterns of those before you" (i.e., toward a process of decline) merits appreciation as a historical commentary rather than as a statement of religious admonishment. The possibility that this *ḥadīth* described a historical process and did not merely advise about the need for religious puritanism needs, however, to be combined with a better appreciation of the fact that historical narrators portray the Rāshidūn caliphate as resembling the received understanding of rise and fall in Jewish history or, rather, the fragmentation of the religion and the nation into sects and heresies (*aḥzāb wa shiya'*). While information that establishes such a comparison is scarce, there is enough evidence in sources such as those gathered by Balādhurī, Ṭabarī, Ibn Sa'd, and various *ḥadīth* compendia to make the case for continuity in this underlying frame, one in which the caliphs are viewed as playing the role that the prophets did in the Israelite state,[26] and the chronology of the Islamic state was similarly set in equal measure to the cycle of messianic Jewish and Christian history.

Thus, the golden age of the caliphate was perceived as lasting for thirty-five years after the time of the Hijra (the migration to Mecca), until civil war broke out, and this seems synchronous with the duration in Judeo-Christian history between the death of Jesus and the Roman destruction of Jerusalem after the Jewish revolt of A.D. 66–70.[27] Islamic historical narratives seem to have appropriated here a biblical chronology of a terrestrial cycle of cataclysm in which the death of Jesus (replaced in Islam by the murder of John the Baptist) began a cycle of redemptive trial for the community that defined the closure of its history.[28] While in the Judeo-Christian chronology this history began with the death of a prophet, in Islam it was timed as beginning with the murder of the third caliph, ʿUthmān, and the eventual sack of Medina was made equivalent to the sack of Jerusalem.[29] There are various perceptions of the consequences of this event, which Islamic traditionists closely compare to their understanding of Judeo-Christian history. In immediate terms, the murder is viewed as setting in motion a cycle of conflict that resulted in significant destruction to the community and could possibly explain the emergence of an authoritarian, monarchical state such as that of the Umayyads.[30] However, other traditions read greater eschatological implications into the third caliph's overthrow, setting it as the first of a sequence of events that would conclude with the second coming of Jesus, as per the tradition that stated, "The first of the cataclysms is the attack on ʿUthmān, and its final one is the emergence of the imposter of Jesus [*al-dajjāl*]."[31]

To appreciate Ṭabarī's scheme for constructing the *fitna* as a parabolic myth in Islamic history, the reader must be familiar with the mythic descriptions the chronicler gives of the last days of the Israelite kingdom in A.D. 66–70, particularly of a divine declaration to Jeremiah that enumerates the transgressions that will bring to Jerusalem its undoing. Various aspects dealing with the process of *fitna* history—the social groups that undergo the tribulation as well as the actual failings—are described here in vivid terms. The cycle of this history is then completed with the arrival of an outside monarchal power (Bukhtnassar) that seals the end of a nation that was hitherto protected by divine grace. Although the failings of the Rāshidūn period (specifically in ʿUthmān's time) are not described as openly as those of the Israelite period, significant overlap is shown, including the qualities of *bidaʿ* (innovations that part ways with tradition), *taghyīr al-sunan* (altering the tradition), *baṭar* (ingratitude and dissatisfaction with existing bounty), the overthrow of caliphs, and the use of religious charity revenues (*zakāt*) to subsidize family interests, which ʿUthmān justified as "*al-ṣila*" (pious filial support). Equally elliptical but nevertheless related are the social groups that are targeted by this divine tribulation. In the ancient period, the divine declaration to Jeremiah names specific groups (*al-aḥbār*, the rabbis; *al-qurrā'*, the reciters of the sacred text; *al-abnā'*, lit. "the sons" [descendants of the prophets]; and *al-mulūk*, the princely class) and admonishes each for a certain failing. The *aḥbār* manipulate the law for their personal ends, the *qurrā'* use religion and the temples for worldly gain rather than charitable causes, and the *abnā'* have joined in this scene of chaos, greed, and disobedience, ignoring the righteous ways of their forebears (*al-ābā'*) and the lesson of how their obedience to the laws brought them victory. Such a picture is not spelled out in detail for the Rāshidūn period in a divine declaration, but there are echoes of these warnings and problems in the speeches of all the Rāshidūn caliphs (including ʿUthmān).[32]

In his first speech after acceding to the caliphate, Abū Bakr seems to be referring to the example of the Israelites when he addresses the community, saying: "So compete in putting off your appointed times [*fa-sābiqū fī muhali ājālikum*], before your appointed times surrender you to the interruption of [your] works, for there once was a people who forgot their appointed times and became neglectful of the trust to do the [good] deeds—beware being like them [*fa-iyyākum an takūnū amthālahum*]. Be forewarned by [your deceased] fathers and sons and brothers [*wa iʿtabiru bi'l-ābā' wa'l-abnā' wa'l-ikhwān*]."[33] The message is stated more emphatically in another version of the speech: "Be forewarned by whoever among you has died, and think of those who were before you. Where were they yesterday, and where are they today? Where are the tyrants, and where are those who were renowned for fighting and victory in the fields of war? Time has abased them. . . . Where are the kings who tilled the earth and cultivated it? They have perished. . . . The deeds [they did] are [still reckoned] their works, but the world is the world of others. We remained after them; and, if we take warning from them, we will be saved, but if we are deceived by them, we will be like them [*fa-in naḥnu i'tabarnā bihim najawnā wa in ightararnā kunnā mithlahum*]. . . . Between God, Who has no associate, and between [any] one of His creatures there is no means of access by which he He may grant him grace or divert evil from—unless it be through obedience to Him."[34]

'Uthmān later repeats the same theme about the cycles of nations that Abū Bakr describes,[35] and confirms in another speech the use of ancient history as a frame of reference, when he describes the shift from the pastoral lifestyle of the Israelites to their later political and urban environments. In a letter to his governors, 'Uthmān declares: "To proceed: God has commanded the *imāms* to be shepherds [*ru'āt*]; He did not command them to be tax collectors [*jubāt*]. Indeed, at the inception of this community, they were made shepherds and not tax collectors [*inna ṣadra hādhihi al-umma khuliqū ru'āt, lam yukhlaqū jubāt*]. But your *imāms* are surely on the verge of becoming tax collectors rather than shepherds. If they turn out thus, then modest manners, integrity, and good faith will come to an end [*fa-in 'ādū kadhalika inqaṭa'a al-ḥayā' wa'l-amāna wa'l-wafā'*]."[36] What makes 'Uthmān's speeches different, however, is that they contain the expectation of transgressions that will set in motion a cycle of change for the Islamic polity.[37] 'Uthmān is not only anxious about changes to come (some of which involve his own policies and those of his governors), but he also enumerates innovations and changes that are usually recognized in *ḥadīth* as those that brought about the undoing of the righteous path of the Israelites earlier.[38]

While the caliphs leave the comparative theme between the Arabs and the Israelites on the level of abstraction and treat it as a matter of general religious foreshadowing, other characters that have a Jewish identity later establish the comparison more specifically, once the decline sets in. The main examples of this cautioning voice are Ka'b al-Aḥbar and 'Abdallāh b. Sallām. As noted above, 'Abdallāh b. Sallām was a vocal critic of the companions who challenged 'Uthmān. When he described Medina as a city guarded by angels and spoke of the punishment that had befallen earlier nations when they overthrew their prophets and caliphs, Ibn Sallām was clearly working from a biblical model. Ka'b al-Aḥbār is described as expressing similar forebodings about the *fitan* that lie in store for the community at the end of 'Umār's reign, and in fact he applies the comparative theme in admiration of 'Umar well ahead of the discussion of *fitan*. Ka'b al-Aḥbār, who reportedly sought out Medina and converted to Islam in the reign of 'Umar, functions a lot like Salmān al-Fārisī in the

Sīra, where there is the famous story about his wanderings in search of the final prophet in Syria, until he was guided by various ascetics and monks to Medina, where he converted at the hands of the Prophet. Later, after the conquest of the Sasanid empire, the cycle of Salmān's role is fulfilled when he is appointed by 'Umar as governor of Ctesiphon. Much as Salmān's story is an idealization of a national representative for Persia, Ka'b is a national representative of the Jews and plays a similar role in linking Israelite history with Islam. During 'Umar's famous trip to Jerusalem to gain the surrender of the city in A.H. 15/A.D. 637, and in the Islamic rediscovery of the temple's sanctuary grounds, Ka'b confirms the inevitability of Islamic conquest. While celebrating the arrival of 'Umar and his clearing of the temple grounds, Ka'b tells him: "O Commander of the Faithful, five hundred years ago a prophet predicted what you have done today."[39] To Ka'b, 'Umar's ascetic image and his strict application of the law are equally foretold in the scripture. What the story of the conquest of Jerusalem yields here is the image of 'Umar as a celebrated conqueror whose political achievement was so great—not just to Muslims but also to Jews, who viewed him as a liberator in Jewish history after a period of tribulation—that he came to be represented in messianic terms that are reminiscent of the way the Persian king Cyrus was represented in the sixth century B.C.[40] Ka'b, to a greater extent than Salmān, now declares the official transfer of the messianic mission from the Jews to the Arabs, as Jeremiah and Berechiah did when they recognized Ma'ad b. 'Adnān as the ancestor of the final prophet and thus set out to rescue him from the Babylonian invasion of Arabia.[41]

Toward the end of 'Umar's reign, just before the assassination story, Ka'b al-Aḥbār makes another appearance, this time foretelling the imminent end of 'Umar's reign, an event which Ka'b again finds foretold in the Bible. The occasion provides yet another moment of celebration of 'Umar's conquest of Jerusalem. The story of 'Umar's death provides a whole cluster of lamenting prophecies that tell of the beginning of a winding down in the cycle of Islamic history.[42] As for Ka'b, he is ready afterward to follow the next "orthodox" path of Islamic history, which recognizes the legitimacy or inevitability of Mu'āwiya's eventual succession as caliph. Ka'b predicts Mu'āwiya's succession as he did 'Umar's, although without any fanfare of biblical anticipation and without any particular enthusiasm (perhaps because Mu'āwiya represented the phase of the outside authoritarian ruler, now incorporated in the community's history).[43] Other *ḥadīth* writings in the same polemical context also have Ka'b predict the rise of Syria and declare praise for its people, as the eventual dock of the early Islamic state.[44] In other words, a narration that seemed highly orthodox in *ḥadīth* literature after the omissions and redaction had a strongly parabolic basis of biblical reformulation going back to the representational legend of 'Umar's messianism and the emergence of a caliphal authority that combined religious and temporal authority.[45] In a similar way, the movement toward dissent and decline during the *fitna* of the early Islamic state was viewed as a reenactment of an earlier pattern among the Jews and Christians.[46] The logic of both histories was viewed as belonging to the same religious philosophy: the community can fulfill its destiny only when it remains faithful to its covenant.

In establishing a pattern of analogy and prediction, Ka'b al-Aḥbār, 'Abdallāh b. Sallam, and other sages are quoted often as referring to a previous source, which they name "*al-kitāb al-awwal*."[47] Although this may well be a broad reference to the Bible, it can also be a moralizing construction that refers to the moral, astronomical, and historical patterns that their (or their narrators') predictions drew upon.[48] Ibn Sallām is certainly the Jewish convert who is better received in Islamic tradition than others, especially in light of prophetic *ḥadīth*s that designate him as the scholar of the Israelites and a man destined for paradise.[49] But even this does not help him during the final crisis of 'Uthmān's reign, when he is reprimanded and labeled again as a Jew by the opposition for his defense of 'Uthmān's legitimacy and for citing the prophesying traditions about the endangerment of Medina as a blessed city. The direct analogies that Ka'b and Ibn Sallām make during the *fitna*, scarce and of mixed Judeo-Christian provenance as they may be, however, gradually come to a halt, and the trail of biblical commentary runs cold. Political commentaries and those that deal with predictions of historical cycles are from then on reduced drastically in the historical narrative, and indeed are altogether banished to a different, little-respected genre of *ḥadīth*s identified as religious lore about the portents of the hour and the final judgment (*al-malāḥim wa'l-fitan*), a kind of Islamic apocrypha that combines historical commentaries with eschatological stories. What little discernibility there does remain for direct Jewish influences on the formation of the traditional texts becomes scattered and shuffled in the orthodox tradition, while the reference point for reporting the precursor Israelite lore—Arabized, Islamized, expanded, and transformed in exegesis—becomes ʿAbdallāh b. ʿAbbās.[50] Ibn ʿAbbās' primary contribution, however, no longer deals with casting opinions about the Rāshidūn caliphs, although there are significant stories on this subject, but instead is traditionist in nature and meant to glorify the role of the ʿAbbāsid family from the time of the Sīra until the rise of the ʿAbbāsid dynasty. The task of the historian of the Rāshidūn period, therefore, becomes more challenging and without a recognizable frame after the dissolution of the caliphate in Medina. Retrospective evaluations of the cycle of Rāshidūn history are then left to be analyzed as a religious-moral question.

## TOWARD A NEW METHOD FOR RĀSHIDŪN HISTORY

In spite of its importance as the period of foundation of the faith, the establishment of the Islamic empire, and the genesis of the earliest political controversies and sects, the history of the Rāshidūn caliphate has been relatively neglected in recent decades. This was not always the case. In the later nineteenth century and up until the period of World War I and its aftermath, the history of the early caliphate attracted the primary attention of Islamic scholars. After the editing of major medieval Islamic texts, such as the chronicle of Ṭabarī, the biographical dictionary of Ibn Saʿd, and various *ḥadīth* compendia, Western Orientalists eagerly sought to synthesize the narrative of the early Islamic state, down to the most detailed event and anecdote. There were various motives for this approach. The most obvious was that writing political history was considered in those days to be the main method for academic inquiry in various fields of history. But there were other motives that were more particular to the Orientalist relation to the Islamic world, ranging across diverse factors that reckoned with the political and cultural challenge that the Islamic world represented to Western colonialism.[51]

In that climate the complete narrative of the early Islamic caliphate was soon put in place, and this work became the reference point for other studies about Islamic law, institutions, and society. Perhaps even more noteworthy from a modern historian's vantage point is the degree to which this historical narrative has been considered the standard version of the history of the early Islamic period, a situation that has not been challenged until recently.[52] The reasons for this uniformity are varied. They include such factors as the limited amount of information that the Islamic chronicles provide about the early caliphate, the limitations of the academic paradigm, in which historians were more preoccupied with the accumulation of facts rather than with developing a source-critical sense in their reading, and last but certainly not least the intangible factor that Westerners wanted to believe that historical events and stories about the motives and actions of key historical personalities were completely accurate—that history occurred in exactly the ways described in the texts.

The unstated assumption behind such a credulous reading of early Islamic history was not only that once the miracles stopped with the biography of the Prophet, what followed constituted a plausible story about the behavior and actions of the caliphs, but more importantly that Muslims (and Arabs in particular) behave in exactly the ways that the texts describe.[53] However repetitive the accounts sometimes became, and however fantastic the religious prose appeared, nothing could dissuade the Orientalist sensibility from its desire to believe in historical fact. Thus the story of contention over the succession of Abū Bakr at the Saqīfa was considered plausible because it was seen as accurately reflecting the temperaments and emotions of tribesmen; the evocation of religious statements (whether Qur'ān or *ḥadīth*) in argumentations was viewed as likely to have happened because that is how believers argue, and 'Alī could make a mountain of sophisticated literary speeches and still have an audience of historians who believed that he in particular and the Arabs in general could deliver a spontaneous marathon of artful literary treatises at the drop of a hat.

More recent historians have also not departed much from the traditional credulous approach to reading history, yet these historians have remained timid about criticism for a whole different set of reasons. In part they were deferring to the pioneering philological achievement of their predecessors. But a more important factor is that these scholars have been working under a uniquely modern academic constraint, which is the compartmentalization of Arab and Islamic studies. Many Islamic historians did not venture far in critical readings because they did not consider *ḥadīth* and Qur'ānic exegesis to be directly relevant to historical research, and did not realize that the answers about one historical phase can only be reached through studying another. The narrative of the Rāshidūn caliphate, therefore, has been viewed as completely removed from 'Abbāsid history. This reality greatly diminished the chances of finding textual parallels in the chronicles and exploring alternative meanings based on a new set of referrent connections and with a different appreciation for literary art and religious logic.

This situation has begun to change recently, under the influence of a growing debate between the "credulous" and the "skeptical" approaches to Islamic history. The credulous approach in this case places significant belief in the historicity of Islamic traditions about the past, and the skeptical approach ranges from placing some trust in the historicity of this tradition to complete rejection. The debate has occurred among historians as well as among religious studies specialists, and it is far from being resolved, especially since the skeptics have so far been unsuccessful in offering a coherent alternative explanation for the coalescence of Islam in the early period and the rapid formation of the Islamic state.[54]

Among historians, a persistent stumbling block in the debate has been the continuing belief that critical study of the historical tradition has to begin with a focus on the identities of the various historical reporters who contributed to the early Islamic chronicles, and has also to center on recovering an earlier phase of historical testimony that predated their final compilation. This analysis of the concept of *isnād* (chain of transmission) is widely known to form a rich background for the accounts of the early Islamic period. The names of the main reporters of Islamic history are well known: Ibn Isḥāq (d. A.H. 151/A.D. 768), Wāqidī (d. A.H. 207/A.D. 823), 'Umar b. Shabba (d. A.H. 264/A.D. 877), Sayf b. Umar (A.H. 184/A.D. 800), Abū Mikhnaf (d. A.H. 157/A.D. 774), and Madā'inī (d. A.H. 228/A.D. 843). The attempts of historians to declare one narrator more reliable than another and to discern bias have taken up considerable attention. The criteria of bias have been wide ranging: a narrator could be more pro-Shī'ī than another, more biased toward a region or a tribe, or more prone to report legend than history. While this exercise of verification does not always follow the judgments of traditional *ḥadīth* scholars, as is evident in biographical dictionaries, it tends to apply a modern style of academic inquiry to the traditional method of *ḥadīth* criticism. The deductive conclusion from the preoccupation with the veracity of some early reporting is that the present shape of the historical tradition is a result of generations of layering of reports that were once much simpler.[55]

The possibility that historical narratives in many instances could have been attributed to particular narrators at a later time, such as in the latter part of the early 'Abbāsid caliphate, has never been explored (although the same critique of *ḥadīths* as religious texts attributed from a later period has been a standard analytic concept from Goldziher onward). This seems a necessity, however, given the fact that the historical fabric of a text such as Ṭabarī's chronicle appears consistent in rhetorical style and language, whether it is reporting on the caliphate of the Rāshidūn or on the early 'Abbāsids. Either certain later narrators emulated the style of the early history perfectly, which seems impossible from the perspective of a literary evaluation of the text—since a break can be discerned when it occurs, such as in the later Sāmarrā period—or the text was composed collectively at a later moment in time. Thus the efforts of modern historians to attribute particular qualities such as biases to the diverse narrators, as the guiding aspect to the historical substance of their reports in the chronicles, have not been entirely effective, given that these qualities can often be found across different accounts.[56] The answer must therefore be sought in a different approach that appreciates the meanings of these narratives outside the context of their attribution and takes into account their interconnectedness.

An important recent contribution in this direction has been the work of J. Wansbrough, which argues for a new reading of Islamic texts in a referential way, and as another example of salvation history that continues from a biblical paradigm.[57] Wansbrough's work, however, centered mainly on the examples of Ibn Isḥāq's *Sīra* and al-Wāqidī's *Maghāzī*—texts that generally described a process of religious triumph—but did not delve into the more varied history of the Islamic caliphate afterward.[58] His study, entitled *The Sectarian Milieu*, has the merit of proposing the use of literary typology for analyzing religious texts. It is not clear, however, that the explanations he proposed were the ones initially intended by the narrators, and his neglect of questions of political and historical context in the seventh–ninth centuries generally (and the early 'Abbāsid period particularly) further undermined the utility of his premises and conclusions.[59] Nevertheless, his conclusions about the need for a literary analysis of the Islamic texts, along with other historical critiques, challenged the traditional reception of the early Islamic historical narrative and motivated the revisionist debate further. Since that time, however, and in spite of the need for more source-critical assessments of chronicles and historical texts, the debate has often been fixated on seeking a new interpretation of the story of Islam's beginning. Some of the attitudes in this new historicist trend have become almost a cliché (the need for more archaeology, the late aspect of some primary sources, and the at times variant accounts in non-Muslim sources), even if little has been done to uncover more hard evidence or to make good on the call for more textual analysis.

Interestingly, amid all of this one aspect of this revisionist enterprise has become almost a new dogma: namely, the notion that the key period for the crystallization of the faith occurred in the reign of ʿAbd al-Malik. A lot has been made of the fact that the Islamic religious credo makes its first complete appearance on coinage in ʿAbd al-Malik's reign, regarding the function of the Dome of the Rock as a monument for declaring the religious triumph of Islam over other faiths, and about the possibility that early Islamic legal traditions reflected contemporary Umayyad legal practice that was suddenly turned into religious *sunna*. The chaotic scene between the times of ʿUthmān and ʿAbd al-Malik, with their various messianic and sectarian movements championing political causes, has been viewed as the background not only for the Umayyad consolidation of political power, but also for their final discovery of Islam and a systematic program to organize a coherent Islamic ideology.[60]

Although the subject of Islam's early historical formation is too broad to examine in detail here, the aforementioned historical conclusions about ʿAbd al-Malik warrant some attention, if only because they highlight the continued relevance of the traditional narrative generally, and the reliance on *isnād* more particularly. Aside from their speculative arguments, based mainly on the absence of historical evidence, a large part of the energy of the revisionist historical position, which built up the centrality of the Umayyads and argued that early Islamic tradition reflects Umayyad political interests and practices, comes from J. Schacht, who hypothesized an Umayyad-centered chronology for Islamic law that ignores the possibility of a more active ʿAbbāsid role at a later period.[61] Schacht's assumption partly suffered from his failure to recognize the interconnectedness among the various core spheres of Islamic religious source material (legal, *ḥadīth*, exegetical, and historical traditions), all of which display not only a key prominence for the ʿAbbāsids, but also a certain ʿAbbāsid style for mediating the orthodox image of other Sunnī tradition (i.e., a particular way of deploying the names of Abū Hurayra,

'Āisha, Ibn 'Umar, and others in the orthodox tradition).[62] But the bane of Schacht and others who placed emphasis on the Umayyads as organizers of the faith has ironically been none other than credulity in certain Sunnī traditions attributed to Sa'īd b. al-Musayyib (d. A.H. 94/A.D. 713), Ibn Jurayj (d. A.H. 150/A.D. 767), al-Sha'bī (d. A.H. 103/A.D. 721), and al-Zuhrī (d. A.H. 124/A.D. 742), which present what seem to be sneaking facts about the Umayyads as having been the first to organize aspects of Islam. These include: the refining of the codification of the text of the Qur'ān (along with grammatical systematization), the writing down of traditions (not just *ḥadīth* but other reports about the companions), and the establishment of a normative picture of certain ritualistic practices.[63]

What completely eluded revisionist historians who placed much stock in those traditions that establish the Umayyad importance in codifying all manner of religious tradition is that these traditions are very likely to have been attributed to the Umayyads by the 'Abbāsids or orthodox religious scholars working during the 'Abbāsid period. The Umayyad rulers mattered to the 'Abbāsid caliphs as kings (and as Arab kings, a point of not any minor importance) who were exercising their right or duty to safeguard the tradition. And the Umayyad rulers mattered to later Sunnī scholars of the eighth and ninth centuries as an early point for connecting religious chronology. Al-Zuhrī's contemporaneity with the followers of the companions, as well as with the caliphs, who wielded the authority to institutionalize religious tradition, as they purportedly did by promoting the writing down of *ḥadīth* and lore about the companions, played a vital role in bridging the Rāshidūn period with the 'Abbāsids. The history of the Umayyads, along with the Rāshidūn, according to this study, therefore, was represented according to political, legal, and rhetorical/artistic concerns that were prevalent in the early 'Abbāsid period. It was in fact Wāqidī rather than al-Zuhrī who gave the main shape to early Islamic history, and it was Hārūn al-Rashīd rather than 'Abd al-Malik who patronized this enterprise that aimed at systematizing Islamic religious and historical textuality.[64] The process was projected backward upon al-Zuhrī, who was idealized as a pioneer of *ḥadīth* writing, much as the narrative attributed to him was a construction of a certain way of narrating the controversies of earlier *fitna*s and of communicating issues of polemic, legitimation, and artful allusion on a variety of levels.

Although the present study is not mainly aimed at redating historical traditions to the 'Abbāsid period, this issue will be an implicit conclusion accompanying the more central topic of trying to determine the original meanings of the narratives of the Rāshidūn caliphate and their original frame of construction and reference. An earlier study on the 'Abbāsid period was crucial in guiding the new possibilities for reexamining the story of the Rāshidūn caliphs in a new light.[65] The hypothesis established there—that the texts were not a product of layering but represented a unity of composition that had a discernible set of meanings—is extended here. The literary-critical approach that was earlier applied to the narratives of the 'Abbāsid caliphate will find here additional evidence for the use of evocative intertextuality in Islamic historiography, as well as the possibility of a unity in scheme and plot line that goes beyond the mere repetition of topoi. By scrutinizing various levels of commentary in a wide range of historical narratives, this study also proposes types of political, moralizing, and religious allusion in the text that go beyond the traditional Western impression of a set of supposed Islamic themes that underlie the chronicles (*nubuwwa*, *futūḥ*, *fitan*, *siyar*, etc.).

That the 'Abbāsid period provides the key angle for representing the history of the Rāshidūn is a topic that should warrant greater recognition and analysis in the future. Although the 'Abbāsid caliphs were neither transmitters of *ḥadīth* nor considered in the rank of the companions of the Prophet, the story of the Rāshidūn addressed many political, moralistic, religious, and legalistic themes that would have mattered above all to 'Abbāsid society in the first half of the ninth century. Questions such as how to define the scope of central caliphal rule and how to reduce the messianic component of the 'Abbāsid revolution of A.H. 132/A.D. 750 and make the principle of a Hāshimite imamate consistent with a legally centered and *ḥadīth*-based orthodoxy were issues that resonated with antecedent problems in the Rāshidūn caliphate. The problem of the succession crisis after Hārūn al-Rashīd, and al-Ma'mūn's rise to power after the civil war of A.H. 196–198/A.D. 811–813, were also events with precedents in the Rāshidūn caliphate and were therefore broached in the narratives in intertextual ways from the Rāshidūn to the 'Abbāsid periods.

The 'Abbāsid period also left its polemical and religious imprint on Rāshidūn historiography in other ways. The Miḥna that the caliph al-Ma'mūn imposed in A.H. 218/A.D. 833 in an attempt to privilege the Mu'tazili school of rationalist and speculative theology over the customary religious culture of *ḥadīth* scholars resulted in an orthodox backlash after the lifting of the Miḥna in A.H. 234/A.D. 848. Afterward, traditionalist scholars not only placed the primary emphasis on *ḥadīth* as a foundation for religious dogma, law, and exegesis, but also succeeded in making the caliphs patronize the new orthodoxy. The confrontation between the Mu'tazila and the traditionalists (usually identified with the Ḥanbalī school of Sunnī Islam) was a bitter and momentous one that affected all fields of Islamic religious science. The victims of the orthodox backlash were not only the Mu'tazila faction and their rationalist method of speculative theology (*kalām*); it reached farther to affect the method of Ra'y, the hitherto well-regarded school of Ḥanafī Islam, and even Qiyās—the limited comparative exercise of analogical reasoning which al-Shāfi'ī pioneered—which also suffered some tarnish. All this is relevant to the study of the Rāshidūn because Ṭabarī's historical narratives often seem to weave an important thread of contention over the issue of whether it is wise (or even practicable) to rely exclusively on *sunna* and *ḥadīth* to the exclusion of Ra'y and Qiyās.

It was probably during the period when the 'Abbāsid caliphate was based at its capital in Sāmarrā (A.H. 221–276/A.D. 836–891) that the debate over all these issues would have flourished. That was a time of steadfast alliance between the state and the emergent class of traditionalist "'ulamā." The third century A.H. had begun with a spectacular phase of contention between the Mu'tazila and the traditionalist scholars but had quickly turned into a period of coordination and systematization of religious sciences according to traditionalist standards. The reduction of the Mu'tazila's role as purveyors of official interpretations of the faith was one key result of this conflict, and the reshaping of the 'Abbāsid imprint in Islamic history was another. The 'Abbāsids had begun their rule with some very defining actions, such as the foundation of a new capital, the invention of an 'Abbāsid messianic image that competed with the imamate of the 'Alids, and patronage for an official account of the life of the Prophet known as the Sīra (composed by Ibn Isḥāq). However, in the aftermath of the civil war that brought al-Ma'mūn to power and the Miḥna, the interests of traditionalist scholars and caliphs quickly and irrevocably diverged. And although al-Mutawakkil had done his best to salvage a relation of cooperation and sympathy between the 'Abbāsid court and the "'ulamā," it was very clear that this relation was defined by the "'ulamā" rather than by the caliphs, as it had been in the days of al-Manṣūr. The importance of the 'Abbāsid image in history was reduced to the contributions of 'Abdallāh b. 'Abbās to the narration of religious traditions (in terms of *ḥadīth*, exegesis, and literary heritage). The 'Abbāsids were no longer viewed as supreme *imāms* who ruled by virtue of being God's chosen caliphs, the anointed-relations of the Prophet, and individuals endowed with an understanding of mystical gnosis. Rather, in the post-Miḥna period they came to be viewed mainly as political leaders whose religious authority was symbolic and consisted of lending official support for one orthodox opinion or another. One may not discern this reduction of 'Abbāsid prominence quickly in the work of Balādhurī and others who referred reverently to the dynasty as "*al-dawla al-mubāraka*" (the blessed dynasty), but the changed attitude and priorities can be partly discerned in the fact that Balādhurī compiled an even more extensive volume about the Umayyads in his work *Ansāb al-Ashrāf*, even though he wrote with 'Abbāsid patronage. Umayyad history, as well as that of the Rāshidūn and the conquests, was clearly being crafted in a final version of official history that did not privilege the 'Abbāsids over the Umayyads according to a singular criteria, but related both, as well as other phases of the early caliphate, to a range of moralizing and religious criteria whose complexity has yet to be fully appreciated by modern historians.

CHAPTER TWO

# Abū Bakr

## *The Moment of Confirmation*

### THE DEATH OF THE PROPHET

The death of the Prophet in A.D. 632 did not come about suddenly. It followed a gradual fever that grew for days after Muḥammad had moved into the house of ʿĀisha, where he decided to spend his last days. He was brought there leaning on ʿAlī and al-ʿAbbās, the two chiefs of what would one day be viewed as the main branches of the Hāshimite family, the ʿAlid and the ʿAbbāsid. However, there are few reports about any interaction between him and members of his family once he was settled in ʿĀisha's house: ʿAlī, al-ʿAbbās, ʿAbdallāh b. al-ʿAbbās, or even Fāṭima, his daughter. Here the historian quickly notes that the story being reported in the chronicles is heavily structured to foster interaction between Muḥammad and the companions who would one day become the points of reference of Jamāʿī-Sunnī Islam: Abū Bakr, ʿUmar, and ʿĀisha. The physical distance between the Prophet and his kinsmen, the Hāshimites—the family viewed as the gravity center of Shīʿī sympathies—helped to legitimize three ideological messages in one image: that Muḥammad (or more correctly, memory of him) was becoming the sacred trust of the community and not just his family, that the *ḥadīth*s of ʿĀisha were now trustworthy by her proximity to him,[1] and that the rule of the first Rāshidūn was legitimate because it emerged from such a setting. The location of Muḥammad's death was thus a tool of political and religious legitimacy that formed both the reference point of an official history and a foundation for the *ḥadīth*-linked principles of Islamic law.

The only direct interaction and blessing given by Muḥammad in his final hours to a companion was to Usāma b. Zayd, son of his former adopted son, Zayd b. Ḥāritha, who was preparing to depart leading the first Islamic army of conquest against the Byzantines in Syria.[2] The sources describe the Prophet, weakened by illness, giving gestures of blessing only to the eighteen-year-old commander. Death had been drawing closer for days, and Muḥammad had prepared himself for it, instructing the community on some last points of ritual and, in a unique request, demanding an unusual final ablution to be performed whereby the companions were asked to pour water on him from seven different wells.[3] These were unusual rites for what was clearly an extraordinary death. Later Islamic memory, entwined with contemporary idealizations of Muḥammad, looked back on this event and saw hints that this was a signal closure of a messianic career, not only marking the completion of a paradigm of prophecy but encompassing a path of victory that carried cosmic overtones. Muḥammad had already proclaimed this in his final pilgrimage speech when he said: "Time has completed its cycle [and is] as it was on the day that God created the heavens and the earth [*inna al-zamān qad istadāra ka-hay'atihi yawma khalaqa allāhu al-samāwāt wa'l-arḍ*]."[4] This speech, made at the pilgrimage known as "*ḥijjat al-wadā*ʿ" (the Farewell Pilgrimage), provides a high point in his preachings, symmetrical perhaps with Jesus' Sermon on the Mount, and invites the historian of religion to examine how Muslims in the seventh century represented Muḥammad with a parallel messianic reverence, albeit in contrary fortune. Whereas one (Jesus) had resigned himself to being conquered, another had now become a conqueror.

The Islamic conquest of Mecca, a city with an ancient and central religious status among various cults in Arabia, must have led many to exaggerate the significance of Muḥammad's conquests, especially of Mecca, as a prelude to the conquest of the world.[5] Others projected Muḥammad's success into the future, seeing him to be potentially immortal,[6] with some cautioning that the deceased prophet should not be buried because he might come back to life.[7] Possibly in deference to such hopes, the community did in fact wait until Muḥammad's fingers began to turn blue before beginning preparations for the funeral rites.[8]

This aggrandizing view of Muḥammad as a messianic leader has been preserved in fragments of evidence in the sources, most notably in the words of ʻUmar, who famously declared that Muḥammad had not died but merely departed (in spirit) to encounter the Divine, as Moses had done, and that he would return in forty days. ʻUmar threatened to kill anyone who claimed Muḥammad had died.[9] Abū Bakr, as is well known, is remembered for chastising ʻUmar for expressing this view. Yet Abū Bakr himself uttered a no less messianic and esoteric view of Muḥammad at that juncture as well. As the first companion allowed to lift the veil from the deceased Prophet's face and bid him farewell, Abū Bakr declared cryptically, "With my father may you be ransomed, and with my mother! Indeed, you have tasted the death which God had decreed for you. No [other] death will ever overtake you."[10]

This remark by Abū Bakr has not traditionally attracted much attention, but if words in Ṭabarī's work were meant to be parsed with a cyclical view of history, and with the legacies of previous monotheistic prophets in mind, then Abū Bakr's words can be seen as forming a surreal comment on the Prophet's biography and its place in history. Always a keen interpreter of dreams and the abstractions of reality, as we shall see below, Abū Bakr in a sense implied that Muḥammad was the final incarnation of prophecy, as he both embodied and finally triumphed over all the tribulations that biblical prophets, patriarchs, seers, and kings had endured before. Consonant with this view, the final prophet was considered to have no remaining links of an earthly nature after his death, either with his family—which was forced to surrender all claim to his material inheritance—or his companions, including Abū Bakr, whose proximity to Muḥammad is heightened in the historical tradition only to be limited in a *ḥadīth* at the end, "Were I to choose a companion [*khalīl*], it would be Abū Bakr."[11] Abraham had been dubbed "*khalīl al-Raḥmān*" before, but in the terrestrial domain Muḥammad allowed no room for such proximity.

## THE AMBIGUOUS SUCCESSION

The death of the Prophet put in place one of the greatest dilemmas and mysteries in Islamic history: why did the founder of a religion with a clear past of political experience, evidenced best in letters of summons sent to foreign leaders exhorting them to embrace Islam, not name a successor? With the abundance of *ḥadīth* literature on a variety of topics, it is surprising that Muḥammad would not have considered this to be an important issue worthy of commentary. The key sources of Islamic history contain lengthy accounts about the conquests, delegations, and interactions in Muḥammad's lifetime but no clear word, or even contested word, on the succession. This silence was most likely not one of deletion or omission, as Shīʿī Muslims believe happened, but one deliberately crafted in the historical-*ḥadīth* accounts that dealt with the final days of the Sīra so that there remained a gaping field for the community to disagree—for trial (*fitna*)—after its master had passed away. Silence on this issue probably indicated equality among the companions on one level, but it also held other critical meanings, such as the complexity of comparing a group with diverse attributes of religious merit; it also opened the way for the inexplicable path of Hāshimite tragedy that began with ʿAlī's loss of the first succession. The ambiguity of whom Muḥammad wanted to lead the community was therefore left in part as an exercise to be deciphered. It was left for the believer to read political statements in signs, extrapolate from certain episodes, and sometimes even resign himself to the fact that the Hāshimite family, in its ʿAlid branch, was not destined to rule.[12]

Traditional Muslim readings of Abū Bakr's succession preserve faint signs of this original scheme of parabolic complexity by admitting the absence of Muḥammad's clear designation and seeking to adapt political meaning through shadow actions. The story of how Abū Bakr was designated by the Prophet to lead the community in its congregational prayers in the final days of the Sīra represents a prime example of how one type of religious duty would get interpreted as a sign of political favor for succession to the office of first caliph as well. The Sunnī perception of Abū Bakr's political precedence over other companions was not based only on this event, however. There were other components, such as pious memory of Abū Bakr as the first convert and his companionship with the Prophet during the Hijra.[13] And later, the Saqīfa event would add another dimension, relating to secular aspects of political skill used to enhance the image of the political worthiness of the Muhājirūn in general and Abū Bakr in particular.

## *The Issue of Leading the Prayer*

The Sunnī view of history has long held that it was Muḥammad's action of designating Abū Bakr to lead the prayer that provided a sign of the Prophet's desire to see him succeed to the caliphate. This view, however, draws only on a partial reading of one version of the events that took place. Ṭabarī's chronicle includes four versions of what the Prophet was going to do, as evidenced in the following reports.

1. The first version declares that when the Prophet's illness grew severe, he asked his companions, "Give me [pen and paper] so that I may write a document for you and you will never go astray after me [*i'tūnī aktubu kitāban lā taḍillū ba'dī abadan*]."[14] The companions wrangled over what he had said, as some started saying to others: "What is the matter with him? Is he starting to hallucinate [*mā sha'nuhu, a-hajar*]?" When they asked him to repeat, he gave up on them and reportedly muttered three wishes, which were, first, that they expel the polytheists from Arabia, and second that they give presents to the [Arab] delegations as he used to; the narrator claims to have forgotten the third! (This is taken by some as an omission of the order to have 'Alī succeed him.)

This version already evokes for the reader the range of meanings to which such accounts are open. When we see the companions suspecting infirmity in the Prophet, it is not clear if this is because he was simply asking to write (when he is traditionally viewed as illiterate), or whether he was trying to add to the Qur'ān (which Muslims were urged to consider already complete), or whether he just wished to name a successor (which could not have been allowed to be revealed in so straightforward a manner).[15] It is also worth noting that in this version Ṭabarī sets the dialogue between the Prophet and the collectivity of the community, thus making them question together the Prophet's desire to put something in writing. The word used to reflect their challenge, "*qālū*" (they said), can quickly slide by as being part of the normal course of narration, when in fact it greatly reflects Ṭabarī's choice to tone down the responsibility for this questioning. If an error was being committed in this exercise, then Ṭabarī was clearly trying to make it seem somewhat forgivable by virtue of the fact that it was the whole group that got the wrong impression (if indeed it was a "wrong" action). In texts other than those given by Ṭabarī, the responsibility for the challenging statement is more specifically attributed to ʿUmar, which seems to fit an original context for the story.

Other versions of this account, given in *ḥadīth* literature, can open up meanings that are even more suggestive about the context of composition of this text and the connection between historical and *ḥadīth* literature. In Bukhārī's version of the event, for example, we read that it was ʿUmar who started the rumor about the Prophet's infirmity, saying: "ʿThe Prophet has been weakened by his illness. You should all now abide by the Qurʾān. The Book of God shall suffice us' [*inna al-nabiyya qad ghalaba alayhi al-wajaʿ wa ʿindakum al-qurʾān, ḥasbunā kitāb allāh*] . . . Those who were at the Prophet's house [at the time] then got into a dispute, and argued with one another [*fa-ikhtalafa ahlu al-bayt, fa-ikhtaṣamū*]."[16] Since ʿUmar was the main architect of Abū Bakr's succession at the Saqīfa and was generally held responsible in Shīʿī Islam for steering the succession away from ʿAlī, this account indicates ʿUmar's role in setting the boundary on what Muslims are supposed to listen to from the Prophet. In essence, according to ʿUmar (the Sunnī view), the Prophet begins to hallucinate when he is about to set the succession in favor of ʿAlī. This designation of ʿAlī is not explicit, but it comes across in the clarification often given on the "matter forgotten" by the narrator, and it must have been well known as an aside in medieval times.[17]

While ʿUmar is not mentioned in Ṭabarī's account as the one who initiated the hallucination rumor (the rumor being assigned collectively to the companions),[18] the reader can read ʿUmar's manipulation of the situation as the first step in a growing literary drama that would build up a story of emergent discord among the successors. If there is a kernel of fact in these accounts, it is about ʿUmar's bias against the ʿAlids (since ʿUmar did not designate ʿAlī later for the third succession), which is worked now in this earlier scene as evidence of ʿUmar's earlier aversion to having ʿAlī succeed. In earlier times, during the Sīra, ʿUmar was famous for his questioning of the Prophet, an exercise that often brought forth divine concurrence (*muwāfaqāt*; see chapter 3) through explicit mention by the Prophet. The more controversial nature of such an early bias by ʿUmar against ʿAlī on the matter of succession (see chapter 7), however, made it necessary to reduce ʿUmar's personal responsibility for this "*muwāfaqa*" and let the record of future Rāshidūn history prove his judgment right.

Thus the story of the Prophet's aborted will kept the story of succession open, but it also provided the context for fulfilling later ninth-century Islamic expectations, some of which were pro-'Umar and Sunnī. This happened in two different ways. In a secular way, 'Umar's declaration, "*ḥasbunā kitāb allāh* [the book of God shall suffice us]," made it permissible for a Sunnī mind to ignore commands from the Prophet on secular matters such as succession if it appeared that he was taking an unwise step, such as placing 'Alī above other, more skilled companions in the office of leadership. And, in a religious way, 'Umar's declaration resonated with importance as the wisdom of a caliph best known in the Sharī'a for the cases of *muwāfaqāt*. Closely related to this latter point is, for example, the Prophet's purported command to expel polytheists (especially Christians and Jews) from the Arabian Peninsula. This command, like much of the detailed ordinances of Islamic law, clearly reflects a projection from the mid ninth-century when traditionists living in an age of a weakened 'Abbāsid caliphate made up for that politically fragmented institution with bravado claims against Christians and Jews that were back-projected to the time of the Sīra and the Rāshidūn. 'Umar's purported toughness against Christians and Jews was here also attributed in *ḥadīth* to the Prophet, in order to serve a later polemical purpose on behalf of Sunnī ideology that focused on what 'Umar was imagined to have favored.

2. The second version, related by 'Abdallāh b. Ka'b b. Mālik, claims that Ibn 'Abbās advised 'Alī to ask the Prophet whom he would appoint as successor. However, 'Alī, fearing that the Prophet might not offer him the succession, refused to do this.[19] "It seems to me that the Messenger of God will die from this illness," al-'Abbās told 'Alī, "for I know the look on the faces of 'Abd al-Muṭṭalib's sons when they approach death. So return to the Messenger of God, and ask him who will get this authority. If it is to be with us, we shall know that, if it is to be with others, he will command accordingly and entrust [that person] with us." In answer, 'Alī said: "By God, if we asked the Messenger of God and he denied it to us, the people will never give it to us. By God, I will never ask the Messenger of God [. . . *lā as'alahā rasūl allāh abadan*]."[20]

This version, focusing exclusively on debate within the Hāshimite household and alluding to the future 'Abbāsid inheritance of the caliphate after a long history of defeat for 'Alid pretenders to the throne, shows a missed opportunity at the hour of Muḥammad's death to solve the matter with a declaration. The burden of failure is directly attributed to 'Alī in this account. Continuing to live out the unlucky, beleaguered fortune that he often brought on himself by faulty inaction, pride, or wrong counsel as well as by damage inflicted by others, 'Alī is shown as somewhat too prideful to ask the Prophet to make him a clear successor. The whole issue branches from a complex representation of 'Alī in the sources as an unwitting counterpart to Muḥammad, living through experiences parallel to his cousin's as well as those of the biblical prophets, except 'Alī continuously faces failure.[21] The exchange between al-'Abbās and 'Alī is also open to other interpretations, such as that here the progenitor of the 'Abbāsid branch of the Hāshimite family was daring the 'Alid patriarch to see in which branch the Prophet would designate the succession and showed that 'Alī feared he would lose to the 'Abbāsids. In spite of the difficulty of comparing the merits of different branches of the Hāshimite family, the 'Abbāsid voice in the sources never wasted an opportunity to show that its attitude toward politics was wiser than the 'Alids', and to stake out an anachronistic position in the early controversies over succession to rule.[22]

3. According to a third version, related by 'Āisha, the Prophet asks that Abū Bakr be told to lead the prayer. In this version of events, widely popular for the way it casts an implicit commentary on women's role in politics, 'Āisha is portrayed as trying to discourage the Prophet from his wish by describing her father as "a tender-hearted man [*innahu rajulun raqīq*]." "I fear," she tells Muḥammad, "that if he stood in your place, he might not be able to bear [the idea of taking your place]." When the Prophet repeats his order, 'Āisha again resists, repeating the same reason, until finally the Prophet grows agitated and declares: "You [i.e., 'Āisha, but referring to women in general] are like Joseph's women companions [*ṣawāḥibāt Yūsuf*];[23] order Abū Bakr to lead the prayer!"[24] Abū Bakr thus came to lead the prayer temporarily. Then, when the Prophet felt well enough on his last day to perform the prayer and entered the mosque, Abū Bakr, who happened to be leading the prayer, tried to yield his position to the Prophet, but the latter motioned him (*ashāra, awma'*) to stay where he was. The Prophet then sat next to him, and Abū Bakr continued to lead the prayer (*kāna Abū Bakr yuṣallī bi-ṣalāti al-nabiyy*).[25]

This version is widespread in the sources and has gained the most popularity in later histories not only because it shows the Prophet repeating his demand to have Abū Bakr lead the prayer, in a strong signal of entrusting him with the most important task in community life, but also because this version shows 'Āisha in her best mode of intrusive behavior, resisting the wisdom of even a Prophet to have her will dominant in the household. The account provides rich hints of what signs Sunnīs upheld as proof of Muḥammad's preference for the political succession, and it puts in place a stereotype about the detrimental effects of female intrusion in the political sphere.

'Āisha's desire to relieve her father of the task of leading the prayer may well have been grounded in her knowledge of Abū Bakr's "tender-heartedness" or even weakness when it came to protecting the memory of Muḥammad, as the account overtly suggests. If Abū Bakr were to begin weeping upon remembering the Prophet's absence, 'Āisha argued, he could well cast a shadow of grief over the whole congregation, leading it to falter in performing the ritual and thus (implicitly) invalidating its prayer (*iftitān*). As 'Āisha was a well-known purveyor of *ḥadīth* and an arbiter of proper Islamic habits from her years of association with Muḥammad, the account can therefore sensibly depict 'Āisha as anxious about the religious welfare of the community. However, 'Āisha's alternately feisty, goofy, and wily personas in the sources make it possible that her suggestions to the Prophet involve more underlying meanings than simple piety. Ṭabarī's accounts, often bearing a range of messages on morality, political strategy, and wisdom, may here be telling us something different, perhaps about 'Āisha's wish to unseat Abū Bakr. For elsewhere we are told that 'Āisha also feared that the congregation, accustomed to the Prophet leading the prayer, would not tolerate another person replacing him and might turn on this person with negative sentiments.[26] Characterizing Abū Bakr as "tender-hearted," therefore, although easy to corroborate from other images of Abū Bakr's personality, would have also served to show 'Āisha's own guileful way of saving her father from the negative sentiment of the crowd. The moral of the story would still confirm the impression that women can act in a way that is oblivious to sound political strategy, but it also adds an element suggesting their deviousness in approach.[27]

4. Among the various versions given about how Abū Bakr came to lead the prayer, one in particular deserves closer attention, for it runs counter to the other accounts and throws considerable uncertainty on the directness of the prayer designation. This version, related by Ibn 'Abbās, runs as follows:[28]

> The narrator (al-Arqam b. Shuraḥbīl) asked Ibn 'Abbās: "Did the Messenger of God make a will?" "No," he replied. I asked, "How was that?" He replied: The Messenger of God asked for 'Alī, but 'Āisha said, "[I wish] you had asked Abū Bakr!" Ḥafṣa said, "[I wish] you had asked for 'Umar!" So all of them gathered before the Messenger of God. He asked them to disperse, for he would call them if there should be any need, and they went away. [At another time] the Messenger of God asked whether the time for prayer had drawn close. They said, "Yes." When he ordered that Abū Bakr should lead the people in prayer, 'Āisha said, "He is a delicate man, so order 'Umar." He did that, but 'Umar replied, "I will not lead while Abū Bakr is present." So Abū Bakr led [them in prayer]. The Messenger of God got some relief [from the pain], so he went out [to the mosque]. When Abū Bakr heard his movement, he stepped backward, so the Messenger of God pulled at his [Abū Bakr's] clothes [*jadhaba thawbahu*], asking him to stand in his place. He sat down [near Abū Bakr] and recited from where Abū Bakr had left off.[29]

The sequence of events here deserves close scrutiny. Contrary to versions that make Abū Bakr the designated *imām* of prayer from the start, the Prophet here begins by asking for 'Alī to undertake this action. 'Āisha, renowned for her animosity toward 'Alī, objects and enters in a duet of opposition with another notoriously selfish wife of the Prophet, Ḥafṣa, 'Umar's daughter, who wishes to have her father take that honor.[30] With two women fighting over his head to have their candidates lead, the Prophet is here shown yielding in exasperation, abandoning his original wish and allowing 'Umar to lead the prayer. Then, however, it is 'Umar who concedes the leadership of the prayer to Abū Bakr. Muḥammad does not know that this change has happened until he shows up at the mosque on a day when he feels healthy and sees Abū Bakr. The account concludes in the same way as the others, with Muḥammad signaling that Abū Bakr (even more strongly, *jadhaba*) should stay in his position.

Among all of Ṭabarī's narratives on the Prophet's last days, this account brings us closest to a designation of 'Alī as successor. The accidental motion of events in this account is typical of the stylized stories of early Islam, which drew on similar patterns from the biblical tradition. The important first message here is that the Prophet actually preferred 'Alī, but because of either the machinations of his wives or the pressure of the community, Muḥammad gave in and left the matter to the community. In the end, even Abū Bakr is shown as having been designated not by the Prophet but by 'Umar, who in general dominates the scene of the Saqīfa and Abū Bakr's designation to the caliphate afterward. These tussles between Abū Bakr and 'Umar over prayer leadership are themselves full of purpose and must not be ignored. When 'Umar refuses to lead the prayer in place of Abū Bakr, the reader notes the way the narrator foreshadows 'Umar's later deference to Abū Bakr at the Saqīfa of Banū Sā'ida, when once again 'Umar refuses to stand ahead of Abū Bakr in leadership. Nothing in the account of the Saqīfa, as we shall see below, refers to Abū Bakr having been designated to lead the prayer. However, the two episodes mirror one another closely in centering on a deferent exchange between the two Meccan chiefs.

The lack of commentary by Ṭabarī on the accounts he presents leaves the mention of 'Alī lost among the various reports. The focus shifts further when other sources, such as Ibn Sa'd, make the Abū Bakr–'Umar exchange the real center of further discussion and embellishment. Ibn Sa'd gives two versions of the story that make 'Umar lead the prayer, versions that are based on entirely different chains of narration than those Ṭabarī used, although both go back to Ibn 'Abbās. In the first of Ibn Sa'd's versions, Abū Bakr starts to lead the prayer when suddenly he falters from grief. Here, the muezzin goes over to the Prophet's house with a request for another *imām*. "Tell the Prophet, peace be upon him," the man says to the Prophet's wife, "to designate another man to lead the prayer, for Abū Bakr has proven weak [*qad iftutin*]." Ḥafṣa responds to this urgent matter on her own with the command: "Let 'Umar lead the prayer until the Prophet passes away." The congregation obeys the command, not knowing its origin. However, when 'Umar sounds the call to prayer, the Prophet hears it and asks: "Whose voice is this making the *takbīr*?" "'Umar b. al-Khaṭṭab," his wives say, and they explain to him what happened to Abū Bakr. The Prophet answers: "You are verily the companions to Joseph's women. Order Abū Bakr to lead the prayer, for [I am certain] had he [Abū Bakr] not designated him, the crowd would not have obeyed ['Umar]."[31]

This account confirms the standard themes about the scheming women, the delicate manner of Abū Bakr, and the overall importance of the prayer leader as a symbol of community leadership. However, the Prophet's concluding remark that the people would not have obeyed 'Umar had he not been designated by Abū Bakr, regardless of how much stronger a personality 'Umar has, anticipates 'Umar's succession to Abū Bakr as second caliph and shows the Prophet approving both the first succession of Abū Bakr and 'Umar's later succession. Muḥammad's statements here reflect a later Sunnī ideology in full bloom, as they essentially articulate support for 'Umar's succession and on the whole stress the precedence of *al-shaykhān* (Abū Bakr and 'Umar) above 'Alī, especially the more controversial precedence of 'Umar over 'Alī.

The second related account given by Ibn Sa'd stresses the Sunnī argument from another angle. Here we are told that the Prophet ordered a certain 'Abdallāh b. Zam'a b. al-Aswad to order the congregation to hold the prayers but did not tell him who should lead the prayer. Ibn al-Aswad says: "So I went forward, and then I ran into a group of people with whom I don't speak. When I came across 'Umar, I didn't think it useful to seek anyone beyond him, while at the same time Abū Bakr was absent. So I said to him ['Umar]: 'Lead the people in the prayer.' Now, 'Umar was a man of a sonorous voice [*mujhiran*], so when he took his place and made the *takbīr*, the Messenger of God, peace be upon him, heard his voice and sticking his head out of the window of his room said: 'No! No! No! Let the son of Ibn Abī Quḥāfa [Abū Bakr] lead the prayer!' He was saying all this with anger. 'Umar then came forth and said to 'Abdallāh b. Zam'a [*sic*][32] 'Did the Messenger of God, peace be upon him, order you to command me [to lead the prayer]?' 'No,' I said. 'Umar answered: 'I had believed that when you commanded me, you were ordered to do so by the Messenger of God. And had I believed differently, I wouldn't have led the people in prayer.' Ibn Zam'a then said: 'When I didn't run into Abū Bakr I thought you were more worthy of leading the prayer than others.'"[33]

This version, unlike the previous one, does not include Abū Bakr as a designated *imām* from the start, and the account's reference to a group of people with whom the narrator does not speak may be an oblique reference to the Hāshimites, the 'Alid partisans, or the Anṣār. The account is no doubt steered to Sunnī advantage, as it stresses the importance of 'Umar. However, it is clearly in dialogue with the original account of Ṭabarī cited above. The Prophet's angry interruption of the prayer to ensure that Abū Bakr was leading it pushes the Sunnī bias in favor of Abū Bakr to its ninth-century heights, when numerous polemical debates on the relative merits of the first four caliphs, and the comparison between 'Alī and the other companions in particular, stressed the superiority of Abū Bakr (*tafḍīl*) over the other companions. The overtly Sunnī thrust of this account argues that the Prophet would go as far as invalidating a prayer rite not presided over by Abū Bakr if he was present but ignored.

The Sunnī bias in these latter anecdotes is to be expected from Ibn Sa'd, whose work reflects redactions and additions that make the stories seem intended to praise Abū Bakr and 'Umar over the other companions (especially 'Alī). Ṭabarī did not share this binary view of early Islamic history, however, and his version reflects this when he includes narratives that stress the plight of 'Alī. And later the chronicler will develop this theme further when he recounts extensively stories about the 'Alid tragedies, reflecting thereby a measure of sympathy for their dilemma. In spite of this sympathy, however, Ṭabarī was ultimately a Jamā'ī-Sunnī, and therefore could not overlook the enduring success of the community around the memory of the companions and the emerging caliphate of the Rāshidūn. He probably was not alone in harboring such a mixed historical attitude, and found commonalities with other writers of universal chronicles, such as Ya'qūbī, who had a stronger Shī'ī-centered focus but accepted the importance of the first two caliphs and balanced it with the merits of the Hāshimite *imāms*.

The ambiguity in Abū Bakr's grounds for succession is clearer therefore in Ṭabarī. According to Ṭabarī, the Prophet's intentions may have been inclined toward Abū Bakr in some accounts but toward 'Alī in others, but at any rate they never went beyond the trope of prayer imamate to reach official investiture for caliphal succession.[34] And the whole question of Abū Bakr's primacy came down in the end to a single gesture: whether the Prophet beckoned, pushed, or pulled his companion to remain in his place in order to complete the prayer ritual. *Ḥadīth* texts that borrowed this story—in part to provide some closing scenes for the Sīra—tended on the whole to position it within a ritualistic context, giving it a sedate meaning related to what one can or cannot do in prayer: for example, that the congregation, surprised at an event (such as the sudden appearance of the Prophet) should merely say, "*subḥān allāh*," or that a leader of a prayer is allowed to step back, as Abū Bakr did. Like Ibn Sa'd, however, later *ḥadīth* scholars sometimes did not know what the stories they were transmitting were truly about, and in their effort to build a legalistic frame, they redacted from anecdotes and ended up losing the moral meanings of these stories.

We can explore this further by examining the issue of gestures. The account of Abū Bakr's stepping back when the Prophet showed up may seem a simple ritualistic matter, as we mentioned above, but if the Arabic wording used to describe this scene is examined closely, the reader can find some unusual potentials for alternative meaning. The adjectives used in Bukhārī's version to describe Abū Bakr's retreat (*raji'a al-qahqarā*)[35] are vivid in describing the physical scene. In another version, the wording is even stronger "*nakaṣa Abū Bakr 'alā 'aqibayhi*,"[36] an expression used in the Qur'ān to describe how Satan reneges on false promises he gives to the unbelievers.[37] The latter phrasing in particular gives the account an unsavory religious baggage that could have been easily avoided with a less stylized phrasing.

Narrators did more than give artful flourish in how they phrased accounts. They indulged in various types of innuendo that subverted the surface meanings of the text. In this case, the alternative meanings could include that Abū Bakr was retreating on an abstract level from something—perhaps from his loyalty to the Hāshimite family—and that the Prophet was prodding Abū Bakr to stay committed to the covenant that the early community had made. This message is corroborated in Bukhārī's other *ḥadīth*, which uses the phrasing "*raji'a al-qahqarā*." The wording is meant to evoke a more straightforward *ḥadīth* given elsewhere by Bukhārī, which contains a sad characterization of how the community has fallen behind on its commitment. When the Prophet reportedly asks God to grant favor to the companions on judgment day, the answer comes that Muḥammad cannot have this. "You do not know what they have done after you passed away," the answer comes, "they have retreated [*raji'ū al-qahqarā*]."[38] Both accounts of Abū Bakr's retreating during the prayer and this latter account were undoubtedly crafted by the same voice and intended to carry a intertextual link that meshed the physical with the abstract. Abū Bakr's action in prayer had a meaning beyond simple surprise at the Prophet's appearance. It meant that he was about to renege on his original loyalty by giving away the rights of 'Alī for succession. And while collective responsibility is given to the companions for regression during the *fitna*, the primary cause behind this can be traced to the dispossession of 'Alī, which the prayer scene was alluding to. All of this nuance in literary form and dramatic character, however, gets lost when the account becomes *ḥadīth*, and what would have been a story with multilayered meaning defying quick interpretation becomes by the time of the later ninth century a binding indication of Abū Bakr's succession.

## *Calming the Crowds*

Perhaps the strength of the depiction of Abū Bakr as the natural candidate for succession derives more from his famous actions in calming the crowds at the tumultuous moment of Muḥammad's death than from any official designation. Here a whole new set of narratives follows in Ṭabarī, describing how Abū Bakr handled the anger and chaos in the community. 'Umar had declared, as mentioned above, that the Prophet did not die but had sojourned on a spiritual retreat, like Moses did for forty days, and he accused all those who denied Muḥammad's death of being hypocrites.[39] At that critical juncture, in order to head off further chaos, Abū Bakr made his famous public announcement in the mosque. After saying his farewell words to Muḥammad, Abū Bakr entered the mosque amid the conflicting voices and declared from the pulpit: "Whoever worships God, God is alive and immortal; whoever worships Muḥammad, Muḥammad is dead." Abū Bakr then recited the verse: "Muḥammad is only a messenger; and many a messenger has gone before him. So if he dies or is killed, will you turn back on your heels? He who turns back on his heels will do no harm to God; and God will reward the grateful."[40, 41] This declaration dampened all the frustration and silenced 'Umar, who said along with other believers: "It is as if we had never heard this *āya* before."[42]

At that perilous hour, Abū Bakr showed himself not only as a wise elder of a tribal society, an attribute for which he had been known since before the rise of Islam, but also as a responsible religious leader who now sought to calm the religious anxiety of the crowd rather than fan the flames of division as al-Sāmirī had done after the temporary departure of Moses. In a context where Abū Bakr could have used the Qur'ān to foster anxiety or sectarianism to his advantage, he opts to use a verse of the Qur'ān for reconciliation by equalizing all those present. Here it was undoubtedly the intended message of the narrator to show how Abū Bakr used his knowledge of the Qur'ān (as a *qāri'*) in a way that strongly contrasts with the future use of the Qur'ān by 'Alī, and even more the Qurrā' and the Khārijites (as well as those calling for *al-amr bi'l-ma'rūf wa'l-nahy 'an al-munkar*, such as the Saba'iyya), in a zealous and divisive way. Indeed, it is interesting that 'Alī, the only potentially serious rival voice to Abū Bakr, is conveniently distanced from this scene by the narrators, as if to prevent him from spoiling the occasion with a gaff about prophetic *waṣiyya* or other formal religious right for inheriting the Prophet's leadership. 'Alī's whereabouts are thus unconvincingly contrived when narrators say that 'Alī was absent from the emerging scene of succession planning because he was busy, along with the Hāshimite family, preparing the Prophet's body for burial. If Abū Bakr had just bid farewell to the Prophet, and we accept that this scene of calming the crowds and the succession deliberations at the Saqīfa all happened sequentially on the same day, then surely the Prophet's body could not have been so far away from where Abū Bakr was, and the funeral preparations could not have happened so quickly. In fact, 'Alī is deliberately effaced not just at this scene when Abū Bakr announces the death of the Prophet, and in the subsequent scene of the Saqīfa, but is equally absent all the way until the beginning of discord in 'Uthmān's reign (with the exception of the Shūrā scene) in both word and deed. This serves not only to keep the spotlight on Abū Bakr and 'Umar as anchors of the community's attention and to show their leadership merits, but also to link 'Alī's emergence with political trouble more generally.[43]

This scene of transition, describing the calming of the crowds, is generally overshadowed by the attention of historians to the Saqīfa episode, which follows, but the transition moment is just as critical with its political and religious allusions: allusions about what did not happen, not just what did happen. Thus we should note that in the aftermath of 'Umar's famous declaration of denial of the Prophet's death, Abū Bakr's public remarks were directed as much toward 'Umar as to any future zealous or factional movement. After all, it was 'Umar who had declared in the last days of the Prophet that the community should not press him for an answer about caliphal succession, interrupting visits to the Prophet at the critical moment, and saying "The Book of God shall suffice us [*ḥasbunā kitāb allāh*]." This was in a way a foreshadowing of the future Khārijite attachment to the Qur'ān at the Taḥkīm, and may explain the reasons for the Khārijite affinity to 'Umar of which Ṭabarī later speaks. In light of this, Abū Bakr's stance just before the Saqīfa was a lesson for 'Umar about the shaping of a *jamā'a* now led by the collectivity of the companions, at the head of which stood Abū Bakr.[44] Anyone who was going to oppose the *jamā'a*, as will later happen (from the Anṣār to the Khārijites), was thus reenacting the type of sedition that occurred in Jewish and Christian history, and thus stood outside the pale of orthodoxy.

## *The Saqīfa Incident*

Barely had Abū Bakr brought calm to the mosque in Medina when a herald came rushing in to tell the leading Muhājirūn what was happening at the other end of town. The Anṣār had reportedly gathered under the leadership of Sa'd b. 'Ubāda to name one of their own as successor to the Prophet. This was the beginning of the so-called Saqīfa of Banū Sā'ida incident (*ḥadīth* al-Saqīfa), which was to bring about a confrontation between the Anṣār, represented by Sa'd, and an emerging triumvirate of the Muhājirūn, represented by Abū Bakr, 'Umar, and Abū 'Ubayda b. al-Jarrāḥ, and which would split the Sunnī and Shī'ī factions down the centuries. Conventional views on the incident do not hide the discord and bitterness evident in the rivalry between the two camps but generally settle for showing Abū Bakr gaining the backing of the Muhājirūn and eventually the entire community on account of his position as the eldest among the earliest companions.

However, much as the circumstances surrounding Abū Bakr's leadership of the prayer are murky, the events that led to his accession to the caliphate at the Saqīfa are ambiguous and laden with allusive messages. A rich variety of accounts exists, and these differ on what happened in the episode: who said what, what pressures were used, and how 'Umar and the opposition differed from each other. It is not clear, for instance, if the division that occurred was between the Anṣār and the Muhājirūn, between the Anṣār and the Quraysh in general (i.e., the Meccan elite predating Islam), or between a nascent pro-'Alī party (backed by the Anṣār) and a pro-Meccan (anti-Hāshimite) party. Some accounts frame the demands of the Anṣār in the famous slogan, "A commander from us and a commander from you [*minnā amīr wa min quraysh amīr*]," while others show them backing Sa'd b. 'Ubāda, the chief of the Khazraj faction among the Anṣār. Still a third version states that they wanted 'Alī to become leader. We will examine the range of these opinions below.

Whatever the circumstances, all accounts concur in showing the key role that Abū Bakr played in healing the rift between the factions and reuniting the *jamā'a* with sober counsel and kind words. Acting in a manner reminiscent of Muḥammad, Abū Bakr is shown defusing political ambitions and stressing the legacy of shared experience between the Muhājirūn and Anṣār in supporting the Prophet. When the Anṣār contend that they are more deserving of the caliphate because they had been the ones who first defended Islam when it was persecuted by the Meccans, Abū Bakr gives a conciliatory answer, recounting the fine qualities of the Anṣār and the Prophet's praise of them, before proposing that Quraysh be allowed to lead.[45]

The actual words of Abū Bakr are not preserved in the account, but the reader needs little prodding to recognize that this scene is a virtual repeat of the Prophet's famous speech after the Battle of Ḥunayn, when the Anṣār clamored (also at a physical distance from the leader's headquarters) over the division of the booty, arguing that the Prophet had treated them unfairly by favoring the Meccan converts with better shares. At the time, we are told, Muḥammad went over to the Anṣār and delivered a famous speech that justified his actions as a goodwill gesture to late converts (*al-mu'alafatu qulūbuhum*) while admitting his everlasting indebtedness to the Anṣār's help in defending the faith.[46] The similarity of the events underlying the different plots between the Anṣār camp and the Meccans (Quraysh), between events in the mosque and in the palace, as it were, becomes a running topos in the depiction of several episodes of rivalry between the pro-'Alid vs. the pro-Meccan parties (compare with the later conflict between 'Aqīl b. Abī Ṭālib and 'Ubaydallāh b. Ziyād in Kufa). This device of depiction may well have once contained a theatrical element, as the situation suggests that these events were probably meant to be staged as acting pieces and not just recited.

In all events, Abū Bakr also assumes at the Saqīfa a posture of wisdom and religious abnegation that connects him with Muḥammad's leadership qualities rather than revealing him displaying an independent strategy as a new caliph. Abū Bakr in one sense legitimizes the rule of Quraysh and articulates ninth-century views on the caliphate more than he defends his rights or those of any of the companions to rule. Whether centering on the Anṣār or 'Alid claims for the caliphate, the debate at the Saqīfa is ultimately more a polemical piece than actual history, reflecting ninth-century debates on whether non-Arabs (represented by the Medinan party), Persian converts in general, have the right to partake in ruling the Islamic state or whether the merits of Quraysh established its continuous political primacy.[47] The 'Alid cause in early Islam, while possibly true, becomes more the instrument of later debates and an object of Sunnī and Shī'ī memory rather than actual history.

To appreciate the range of meanings that this incident evokes, it is essential to survey all its possible versions.

1. Ṭabarī provides five versions of this event. Two directly connect with the emergence of the verse about Muḥammad's death and relate how Abū Bakr dampened potential sedition. In the first, we are told, Abū Bakr, after saying farewell to the Prophet, stepped out to the crowd and affirmed the eternity of the faith and the mortality of the Prophet and recited the verse: "Muḥammad is only a messenger; and many a messenger has gone before him. So if he dies or is killed, will you turn back on your heels? He who turns back on his heels will do no harm to God; and God will reward the grateful."[48] With this he answered religious skepticism about the prophet's mortality and quieted 'Umar, who had till that moment denied Muḥammad's death. The same narrative says that the Anṣār had meanwhile gathered at the Saqīfa to pledge the *bay'a* for Sa'd. When Abū Bakr heard of this, Ṭabarī relates, he went to that location, accompanied by 'Umar and Abū 'Ubayda, and inquired what the Anṣār were doing. "What is this [*mā hādhā*]?" he inquired. "Let's have a ruler from us and a ruler from you [*minnā amīr wa minkum amīr*]," they said. Abū Bakr answered, "Commanders shall come from our ranks, and vizirs from yours."[49] Then, with the gracious bestowal from a prophet, he nominated his companions, saying: "It makes me content to present you [as a leader] one of these two men: 'Umar or Abū 'Ubayda [*innī qad raḍiyutu lakum aḥada hādhayn al-rajulayn*]." He followed up with the assertion that the Prophet had once referred to Abū 'Ubayda as "*amīn al-ḥaqq*." 'Umar here interrupted and pushed for Abū Bakr's leadership, telling the Anṣār: "Who among you would be agreeable to leave Abū Bakr, whom the Prophet gave precedence?" and he gave him the oath of allegiance. The same account adds that "the Anṣār, or some of them, then said, 'We will not give the oath of allegiance [to anyone] except 'Alī [*lā nubāyi'u illā 'Aliyyan*].' "[50]

An appended report from another authority (stating clearly that this happened after the Saqīfa *bay'a*) says that 'Umar came to the house of 'Alī, where Ṭalḥa, al-Zubayr, and men of the Muhājirūn had gathered and held back from giving the *bay'a* to Abū Bakr, and shouted to them to come out and pledge allegiance. "By God, either you come out to render the oath of allegiance [to Abū Bakr], or I will set the house on fire," 'Umar said.[51] Zubayr, acting within the well-known chivalrous and heroic parameters of his personality, stepped out, sword in hand, but then he stumbled on something and the sword fell, allowing others to take it away!

This account summarizes the main picture of division between the Muhājirūn and the Anṣār and shows Abū Bakr towering over other voices with his prophet-like decree. His phrasing (*qad raḍiytu lakum*) derives from divine language mediated earlier in similar expressions by Muḥammad and is clearly meant to associate both prophet and successor in religious discourse and posture. The reference to ʿAlī later seems more like an afterthought to the account at the end. The segment professing pro-ʿAlid support is meant to discredit the Hāshimite/ʿAlid claim for the caliphate, not only because it was the Anṣār that were professing support for him, but even more because al-Zubayr's withholding of the *bayʿa* for Abū Bakr and the call for ʿAlī are timed to come *after* the nomination and the first steps to Abū Bakr's *bayʿa* had been taken. Ultimately, this made al-Zubayr's actions subversive to the collectivity of the community rather than simply an offense to the triumvirate of Abū Bakr, ʿUmar, and Abū ʿUbayda.

2. An even longer version of these events also appends the Saqīfa incident to the recitation of the Qur'ānic verse about the Prophet's death and also stresses that the companions had not heard that verse before. Then, with a loaded turn of phrase (*idh jāʾa rajulun yasʿā*),[52] the narrative describes how a messenger came with news of what the Anṣār were getting set to do at the Saqīfa (i.e., elect one of their own as caliph), but then oddly adds a remark for the messenger that may contradict their apparent aim. "They are saying, 'A commander from us and a commander for Quraysh.' "[53] Abū Bakr and ʿUmar then set out (Abū ʿUbayda is omitted) to deal with them. When they arrived, ʿUmar tried to start talking but, as in the prayer scene, 'Abū Bakr overshadows him. The narrator says:

> Abū Bakr spoke and did not leave out anything that was either revealed about the Anṣār or was said by the Messenger of God with regard to their fine qualities. He said: "You know that the Messenger of God said, 'If the people took one way and the Anṣār another, I would take the Anṣār's path.' O Saʿd [b. ʿUbāda], you know that the Messenger of God said, while you were sitting [*wa anta qāʿidun*], that the Quraysh were the masters of this authority. The righteous follow their kind, and the wicked follow theirs." Saʿd replied, "You have spoken the truth [*ṣadaqta*]. We are the viziers and you are the rulers." ʿUmar said, "Stretch out your hand, O Abū Bakr, so that I may give you the oath of allegiance." Abū Bakr replied, "Nay, rather you, O ʿUmar. You are stronger than I [to bear the responsibility]." ʿUmar was indeed the stronger of the two. Each of them wanted the other to stretch his hand

> so that he could strike the bargain with him. ʿUmar stretched Abū Bakr's hand, saying, "My power is for you with your power," and the people gave their oath of allegiance. They demanded confirmation of the oath, but ʿAlī and al-Zubayr stayed away. Al-Zubayr drew his sword [from the scabbard], saying, "I will not put it back until the oath of allegiance is rendered to ʿAlī [*lā yubāyaʿ illā ʿaliyy*]." [When] this news reached Abū Bakr and ʿUmar, the latter said, "Seize the sword of al-Zubayr and strike it on a stone!" It is stated that ʿUmar rushed [to the scene], brought them forcibly [while] telling them that they must give their oath of allegiance willingly or unwillingly [*la-tubāyiʿān wa antumā ṭāʾiʿān aw la-tubāyiʿān wa antumā kārihān*]. So they rendered their oath of allegiance.[54]

This account best represents the objective of showing Abū Bakr bridging the different points of view with minimum tension and casts ʿAlī and al-Zubayr as the odd dissidents in the affair, rather than Saʿd b. ʿUbāda. We also see here a clear division of roles and attitudes between the sensitive, lenient style of Abū Bakr, as he reminds the Anṣār, who are shown either to have forgotten the importance of Quraysh or to have become misguided, and the coercive approach of ʿUmar, as he attempts to suppress dissident opinions by vehemently pursuing ʿAlī and al-Zubayr for their defiance. ʿUmar's retort, "*la-tubayiʿān*," not only contrasts with Abū Bakr's language and mildness, but gives a flash forward to the future Umayyad use of pressure to extract political allegiance from the Hāshimite family. ʿUmar's future appointment of Muʿāwiya as governor of Syria, an action that in itself will be cited by the Umayyads as a sign of the second caliph's confidence in them (see chapter 5), becomes the link that bridges two characters (ʿUmar and Muʿāwiya) in their view that coercion is a permissible tool to maintain cohesion in the *jamāʿa*.

To maintain a measure of decorous rivalry among the leading companions, especially the caliphs (Abū Bakr, ʿUmar, and ʿAlī), ʿUmar is not allowed to display as great a hostility toward ʿAlī as he does towards al-Zubayr. Throughout, the latter bears the brunt of the reaction that responds in kind to his tempestuous nature, often referred to as "*kāfir al-ghaḍab*," and to his tendency to resort to arms at the smallest sign of dispute. This clearer hostility toward al-Zubayr is further facilitated by the frequent doubt cast on his political motives. Readers familiar with al-Zubayr's later biography would recognize his image as one who frequently switched sides in the first civil war, depending on who gave him greater honor, allying himself at one point with ʿAlī in the hope that the latter would assign him important political rank, and then abandoning him when this did not materialize.[55] This version of the Saqīfa, therefore, shows how closely narrators related events and interactions here with the later images and positions of companions (both on ʿUmar's side and on al-Zubayr's). One must be familiar with developments during the civil war to see how the behavior of the actors here confirms or exacerbates issues and attitudes from one period to another.

This version in Ṭabarī deserves close scrutiny for the way it taps into a Jamāʿī-Sunnī sensibility, best reflected in *ḥadīth*, and into other historical narratives. The roles that Saʿd b. ʿUbāda and al-Zubayr assumed in this account bore some unique connections to some orthodox messages, even as al-Zubayr was reprimanded and ʿUmar was broadsided for his coercive behavior in politics in general. In contrast to traditional accounts favored in *ḥadīth* compendia that show ʿUmar's fight to be mainly with Saʿd b. ʿUbada rather than with the more well-known Muhājirūn companions such as al-Zubayr and ʿAlī, Saʿd's image here seems considerably tamed as the burden of opposition shifts to al-Zubayr. Saʿd b. ʿUbāda is shown telling Abū Bakr "*ṣadaqta*," in confirmation of the caliph's name "*al-ṣiddīq*," and the Anṣār seem hardly to be an obstacle. There is a reason behind this painting of Saʿd as open to reconciliation in this account. In a small detail, we see Abū Bakr tell Saʿd that he was "sitting" when the Prophet spoke of the leadership of Quraysh (*qāla wa anta qāʿidun*). This detail makes no sense except in reference to the *ḥadīth* "*al-qāʿidu fī al-fitna khayrun min al-qāʾimi bihā*." In fact, with the mention at the outset of the account, "*idh jāʾa rajulun yasʿā*," we can see how both of these phrases referred to the famous *ḥadīth* about *fitan* (civil wars) that would be frequently invoked later on. The *ḥadīth* in question stated: "He who is sleeping in the *fitna* is better than one who is seated [*al-qāʿid*], and the one seated in it is better than the one standing in *fitna* [*al-qāʾim fīhā*], and the one standing superior to the one riding with it [*al-sāʿī bihā*]."[56] The *ḥadīth* surveys a range of actions (*nawm* [sleeping], *quʿūd* [sitting], *qiyām* [standing], and *saʿiy* [running or riding]), which are utilized in shaping this story and others to send important messages. The Saqīfa account here invokes two types of action in times of *fitna* (*quʿūd* and *saʿiy*), and this version shows how the words and actions (appearance) of Saʿd b. ʿUbada were consistent: namely, he is conciliatory while seated.

The use of the *ḥadīth* in question, however, did not end with the depiction of Sa'd, but spilled over into the depiction of al-Zubayr's final loss to 'Umar. When 'Umar ordered people at the end to "seize the sword of al-Zubayr and strike it on a stone," 'Umar was being made to fulfill the final command in the above-mentioned *ḥadīth*. According to a well-known version preserved by Muslim and others, the Prophet orders that when the times of the *fitna* arrive, a believer should abandon the scene of conflict and tend to his camels, sheep, or land. When someone asks the Prophet, "And what if a man did not have camels, sheep, or land?" the answer was: "Then he should take hold of his sword and strike till it is blunt on a stone."[57] The linkage between the Prophet's advice and what 'Umar was doing becomes clear as we see a narrator trying to bring a *jamā'ī* closure to al-Zubayr's performance during the Saqīfa, even though he was undergoing this communion involuntarily. The relation between this *ḥadīth* and the Saqīfa account also points to the way such historical *akhbār* sometimes developed in response to *ḥadīth*s and Qur'ānic formulas, and how in this instance the narrator's characterization of the Saqīfa episode as a *fitna* was communicated through a careful arrangement of the behavior of Sa'd b. 'Ubāda and al-Zubayr.

3. For readers who may still be skeptical of Abū Bakr's primacy for succession and the consensus on his *bay'a*, Ṭabarī adds a third narrative from the renowned transmitter Sayf b. 'Umar that gives a compact and direct Sunnī characterization of what the *bay'a* and its opposition meant. Sayf here has a certain 'Amr b. al-Ḥurayth ask Sa'īd b. Zayd: "Did you witness the event of the death of the Messenger of God, peace be upon him?" "Yes," the man answers, and the first adds: "When was Abū Bakr given the *bay'a*?" "The day the Messenger of God, peace be upon him, died," he adds. "They feared that the day might pass without them being in agreement [*karihū an yabqū ba'ḍa yawmin wa laysū fī jamā'a*]."[58] "Did anyone oppose him [Abū Bakr]?," 'Amr then asks. "No. Only apostates or those about to apostize. Verily, what a day that was when God saved them from the Anṣār." Finally the questioner asks: "Did any of the Muhājirūn hold back on giving the *bay'a*?" "No, the Muhājirūn came in succession to offer their *bay'a*."[59]

Brief as it may be, this account summarizes more bluntly what the preceding two versions try to put more delicately: shying away from the *bay'a* of Abū Bakr was tantamount to Ridda, and the Anṣār were on the verge of causing a huge sedition. However, this implication raises a problem. For if Ridda is equated with not giving loyalty to Abū Bakr, where does Sayf place the actions of Fāṭima and 'Alī, neither of whom agreed to the *bay'a*? It may be that Sayf's Jamā'ī-Sunnī voice, originating in the later environment of the ninth century, did not consider the *bay'a* of women as mandatory, and in any event Fāṭima's death soon after these events defused her leverage in backing 'Alī. However, Sayf, while hostile to those withholding the *bay'a*, seems to accommodate 'Alī's delay in coming on board by describing the procession of the Muhājirūn to give the *bay'a* in a slow pace as a natural event (*tatāba'ū*). That 'Alī gave in six months later to Abū Bakr therefore could sound as acceptable within this frame of delay as those who gave *bay'a* on the day of the Saqīfa. Once 'Alī consented to Abū Bakr, moreover, anyone who continued championing his cause was viewed as performing an action of subversion against the community as well as something that broke with 'Alī's wishes, such as the faction known as al-Saba'iyya would do with excessive reverence for 'Alī but without his consent.

It is important to note here that, even though the previous versions do not draw the link with the Ridda explicitly, they do so implicitly in terms of style. When we hear the narrator, for example, say that the call of the Anṣār was for "*minnā amīr wa min quraysh amīr*" (a commander from us and a commander from you), the reader would have noted the echo in this statement of the Ridda apostates of the Banū Ḥanīfa, whose slogan would have rung harmonious here: "*minnā nabiyy wa minkum nabiyy*" (a prophet from us and a prophet from you).[60]

If the first two accounts serve mostly to legitimize Abū Bakr's declaration of a Qur'ānic verse, to downplay the visible opposition of the Anṣār and to quickly heal potential rifts, a fourth narrative furnishes a far more detailed account titled: "*ḥadīth* al-Saqīfa." This account (along with another lengthy version by Abū Mikhnaf [see appendix 1]) provides a centerpiece that is more extensive and wide-ranging than the preceding versions. No details are spared in these accounts to honor Abū Bakr and 'Umar and no holds are barred to bring down the Anṣār and other opponents. They are perfect examples of the raw stories that Ṭabarī did not flinch from telling, but which others such as Ibn Sa'd withheld.

4. 'Abdallāh b. 'Abbās is the narrator here, but he mainly reports a subsidiary version told by 'Umar, who describes the story of the Saqīfa as a follow up on how he came to remind the community of the penalty for adultery verse and how its ordinance became official. Ibn 'Abbās begins

by saying how he was on the pilgrimage at Minā when 'Abd al-Raḥmān b. 'Awf dropped by to tell him of a small event that had occurred that day. "I was with the Commander of the Faithful today," said Ibn 'Awf, at a time well into the reign of 'Umar, "when I heard someone say, 'When the Commander of the Faithful dies, I will give *bay'a* to so and so.' 'Umar then said to us, 'Tonight I shall speak to the public and warn them of this crowd [*ha'ulā' al-rahṭ*] who want to seize matters into their hands [the 'Alids].'" He goes on:

> I [i.e., Ibn 'Awf] then said, "O Commander of the Faithful, the pilgrimage brings together the riffraff and the rabble [*ru'ā' al-nās wa ghawghā'uhum*]; they are the ones who will dominate over your assembly. I am afraid lest you should say something today which they might neither heed, nor remember, nor put in its context and spread everywhere; so wait until you come to Medina, [which is] the place of refuge [*dār al-hijra*] and a seat of the *sunna*. [There] you can confer privately with the Messenger of God's companions, both the emigrants and the Anṣār.[61] You can say what you will with firmness [*mutamakkinan*]; they will retain your words and interpret them properly." He [i.e., 'Umar] replied, "By God, I will do it at the first opportunity I get in Medina."

When the crowd arrived in Medina and Friday prayer time came, the narrator describes how he confided to Sa'īd b. Zayd that "the Commander of the Faithful will say something today from this pulpit which he has not said before." . . . 'Umar [then] stood up. He praised God, extolled Him and said, "Now then: I want to say something which has been decreed that I should say. He who takes heed of it, will understand it and remember it. Let him relate it wherever he goes . . . God sent Muḥammad with truth and revealed the book to him. The verse concerning the stoning [of adulterers] was among [the verses] which were revealed to him. The Messenger of God stoned [adulterers], and we stoned them after him. I am afraid that as time passes some people might say that they do not find stoning in God's book, and [thereby] they might go astray by forsaking an obligatory act [*farīḍa*] revealed by God. We used to say: 'Do not detest your ancestors [*lā targhabū 'an ābā'ikum*], for it is infidelity to do so.'"[62]

"It has reached me that some one of you said, 'If the Commander of the Faithful is dead, I will give the oath of allegiance to so-and-so.'[63] Let a man not deceive himself by saying that the oath of allegiance given to Abū Bakr was an event that happened without consideration [*falta*]. Admittedly it was so, but God averted its evil. There is none among you like Abū Bakr to whom people would have submitted. It is our information that when God took His prophet, 'Alī, al-Zubayr, and those who were with them stayed away from us in the house of Fatima; the Anṣār, all of them stayed away from us; and the Muhājirūn gathered round Abū Bakr. I told him that we should go to our brethern the Anṣār, so we rushed off, making for them. Two pious fellows who had been present at Badr met us, asking where we were going. When we told them that we were going to our brothers the Anṣār, they asked us to go back and to decide the affair among ourselves. We replied, 'By God, we will go to them.' We came to them as they had gathered in the hall of the Banū Sā'ida. In their midst was a man enwrapped in a cloak. When I asked who he was and what was his position, they said that he was Sa'd b. 'Ubāda and that he was ill. Then a man from them stood up. After he had praised God he said, 'We are the Helpers [al-Anṣār] and the squadron of Islam, while you, O men of Quraysh, are a family of our Prophet who have come to us journeying leisurely in search of herbage and sustenance.' ['Umar] said: 'When I saw that they wanted to cut us off from our root and wrest authority from us, I wanted to make a speech I had composed in my mind. As I used to treat Abū Bakr with gentle courtesy to some extent, [and considered] him more sober and gentler than me, I conferred with him about [the speech]. When I wanted to speak, he said, 'Gently!' so I did not like to disobey him. He stood up, praised God, extolled Him and did not leave anything [from his speech], which I myself had composed in my [own] mind if I had spoken, but that he expressed, or [expressed it] in a better way [than I would have done]."

"He said: 'Now then: O men of the Anṣār, you deserve all the fine qualities that you have mentioned about yourselves, but the Arabs will not recognize this authority except in this clan of Quraysh, for they represent the best in lineage and standing. It makes me content to offer you one of these two men; render your oath of allegiance to any one of them you like.' [Thus saying], he took hold of my hand and that of Abū 'Ubayda b. al-Jarrāḥ. By God, I liked everything he said except the last words. I would have preferred myself to be sent forward and my head struck off—if it were not considered a sin—rather than be appointed a ruler over a people of whom Abū Bakr was one.

"After Abū Bakr had finished his speech, a man of the Anṣār stood up, saying, 'I am their much rubbed little rubbing post and their little palm tree loaded with fruit. Let us have a ruler from us and another from you, O men of Quraysh.' ['Umar] said, 'Voices rose and clamorous speech waxed hotter. I feared [total] disagreement, so I said to Abū Bakr, 'Stretch out your hand [so that] I may give you the oath of allegiance.' He did so and I gave [him] the oath of allegiance; the Muhājirūn followed and then the Anṣār. [In so doing] we jumped on Sa'd b. 'Ubāda so someone said that we had killed him. I said, '[May] God kill him!' By God, nothing was mightier than rendering the oath of allegiance, no agreement would be hammered out later. It was either to follow the Anṣār in what we did not like, or else to oppose them, which would have led to disorder [*fasād*]."[64]

This account is typical of a master *khabar* told on the authority of an 'Abbāsid. It begins with one issue, meanders on to several others, and then finally ends in a different place. Ibn 'Abbās here uses 'Umar to convey the Sunnī view and establishes several ideological or legal points. Whereas in the previous versions we have examined how the discussion of succession arose as a follow up to the account of Abū Bakr's declaration of the Qur'ānic verse concerning Muḥammad's death, this account assumes a parallel scheme when 'Umar begins with the declaration of the adultery verse before moving on to describe the succession story.[65] Clearly, the story of Abū Bakr's reciting of the verse before moving on to settle the succession dispute at the Saqīfa became a classic story form that inspired this version, since here 'Umar commands obedience to the lost adultery verse before talking about the succession. The action proposed by 'Umar became most binding when it got bracketed by two events: the immediate passing of the Prophet and the emerging idea of a consensus in the community about giving *bay'a* to Abū Bakr.

Whereas Abū Bakr's speech when he calmed the crowds used a Qur'ānic verse for the purpose of unifying the community behind one prophetic leadership, 'Umar is represented attempting a similar exercise of unification, however, on a point of law. To overcome the problem of a missing verse and underscore a prophetic link, 'Umar positions himself as an elder of the community implicitly capable of issuing binding religious injunctions comparable to the more formal Qur'ānic laws (hence 'Umar's assertion: *lā targhabū 'an ābā'ikum fa-innahu kufr*). To make his new injunction synonymous with religious ordinances based on the consensus of the community rather than with *ḥadīth* or the Qur'ān and to lend it historic authenticity, ʿUmar sets about recounting the Saqīfa story, thus highlighting how Sunnī consensus was forged on that occasion and that he and Abū Bakr had religious primacy in the community. The Ibn ʿAbbās version of the Saqīfa thus made it impossible to accept the injunction against adultery without accepting the Sunnī view of Abū Bakr's greater merit for the first succession.

This message is underscored by ʿUmar's indirect rebuke of those who wish that ʿAlī would become caliph after the Prophet or that he could still succeed immediately after ʿUmar. As always, the disenfranchisement of ʿAlī is never addressed to ʿAlī directly. ʿUmar targets instead the potential followers of ʿAlī (*lā yaghurrana aḥadakum an yaqūla inna bayʿata Abī Bakr kānat falta*), stressing in his speech that no one present in the congregation of the mosque where ʿUmar was speaking (including ʿAlī) was superior in religious merit to Abū Bakr. ʿUmar enhances this assertion by declaring himself unworthy of leading a crowd of which Abū Bakr was a member. The statement is richly self-deprecating, as we saw earlier in ʿUmar's attitude regarding prayer leadership, but it is also self-serving in that it lends legitimacy to Abū Bakr's designation of ʿUmar as second caliph. Having put Abū Bakr at the top of the religious hierarchy, ʿUmar made his rule and partriarchal legal tradition (such as the penalty for adultery, *āyat al-rajm*) as binding as the rule of Muḥammad himself. Those who opposed ʿUmar's legal rulings would be categorized as infidels by the mere fact that they opposed the ancestors.[66]

We see therefore the complex and interdependent legitimation taking place in ʿUmar's proclamations, which encompass legal as well as political issues. The account also demonstrates tangentially ʿUmar's effectiveness as a strategist, one who accepts the counsel of his advisors and waits to be among his supporters before taking a risky step. ʿUmar is careful not to announce his declaration before going to Medina, and he heeds the advice of Ibn ʿAwf about the danger of the rabble (*ruʿāʿ*). To the general reader, Ibn ʿAwf's caution here seems out of context, but it will be remembered later how similar "*ruʿāʿ*" (i.e., ʿAlid loyalists) were accused of having stirred up trouble in Kufa for ʿUthmān's governor, Saʿīd b. al-ʿĀṣ, and how a part of that opposition came in response to ʿUthmān's alleged attempt to modify the religious ritual. The same parameters of the caliph and the *jamāʿa* confronting dogmatic, Hāshimite-centered opponents were to be used in describing two different contexts of opposition, one of a sedition that failed and another that brought civil war (see chapter 5).

More central to the account was the attempt to undermine the authority of the Anṣār and their leader and to extol the Muhājirūn (i.e., the Meccans). This was done by pinning 'Umar's wrath in this account on Sa'd b. 'Ubāda rather than 'Alī. Sa'd, as we saw, remains unreconciled to Abū Bakr, unlike in the previous version, despite Abū Bakr's admonishment. In 'Umar's version of the events, there may even be some parody applied in the description of Sa'd when we see him depicted as wrapped up (*muzzamil*) and lying down sick. The original image of "*muzzamil*" emerged, as would have been well known, in reference to Muḥammad, who used to undergo convulsions and fevers associated with moments of occultic revelation and thus used to be wrapped up by his family in the earlier days of Qur'ānic revelation. This image was coined and preserved in a Qur'ānic verse (*sūrat al-muzzamil*), and while it has a serious value in the Sīra, it lacks a parallel meaning when applied to Sa'd b. 'Ubāda and shows there an ironic twist meant to critique the pretensions of the Anṣār leader, or worse, to put him on par with some of the Ridda prophets who met death while in that situation.[67] The parallel cited earlier between the slogan of the Anṣār and the slogan of the Ridda folk (*minnā nabiyy wa minkum nabiyy*) corroborates the existence of a linkage behind these narratives, even if the narrators seem widely different.

'Umar gives full rein to his combative instincts in this account and shows no qualms about suppressing dissidents from the Qurashī position, whether the Anṣār or others are behind it. Indeed, 'Umar's angry gestures and statements here were meant as deterrents not only to Sa'd and the Anṣār, who are not present in this account, but also to 'Alī and the 'Alids. Sa'd bears the brunt of the attack because he is traditionally portrayed as having an attitude of snobbery (*zahw*) and had already been rebuked by the Prophet on the day of the conquest of Mecca for wanting to exact punishment on the Meccan people (with the famous slogan "Today shall be an epic day [*al-yawma yawmu al-malḥama*]").[68] The situation of the Saqīfa placed each character within an assigned role and produced an outcome that was a mix of design and accident. This is the version given by Ṭabarī, which is by far the most vivid and explicit of all the Saqīfa scenes. Ibn Sa'd and other, more *ḥadīth*-minded writers, however, generally avoid describing the severe discord among the companions (first here, then at the *shūrā* for 'Uthmān's succession), especially when it concerns a conflict between 'Umar and 'Alī or the story of the attack on Fāṭima's house. These stories get heavily sanitized in *ḥadīth* compendia, ending up as descriptions of a virtual agreement on Abū Bakr. Yet even a staunch Sunnī such as Bukhārī cannot help but tip his cards and show that he drew on Abū Mikhnaf (by referring to al-Ḥubāb b. al-Mundhir's opposition) in including an abridged account of the Saqīfa in his work.[69]

5. Abū Mikhnaf's version of the Saqīfa resembles the one attributed to Ibn 'Abbās, but, unlike the latter's, it does not use the narrative to convey a legal injunction ('Umar's ordinance on the penalty for adultery). Rather, the text is mainly about a historical episode and the way events (through poor judgment or fate) turned against the Anṣār after an initially promising beginning. Unlike the previously examined versions, Abū Mikhnaf's version is disconnected from the episode of the Prophet's death, the denial and chaos that surrounded it, and the announcement of the verse "*wa mā Muḥammad illā rasūl . . .*"—all events that tend to be described as coinciding in occurence in order to show the resolve of Abū Bakr's leadership in defusing several aspects of a crisis that could have ended Islam's political future. This fifth version is separated from all these issues and placed by Ṭabarī after the close of the Sīra with the mention of various dates given for the Prophet's death. The major difference between this version and the others, however, lies in its beginning, where Sa'd b. 'Ubāda is quoted as giving a fairly lengthy declaration of why he thought the Anṣār should inherit the caliphate. The declaration is then followed by the near unanimous agreement of the Anṣār on making a bid for the caliphate (with the important message here about the involvement of the Aws even in making this claim), and the somewhat sudden and fatal expression of doubt on what was clearly a matter of sound strategy (*al-ra'y*) devised by Sa'd.

Sa'd's opening speech is worth examining in full for the unique, and blunt, message it delivers on why he views the Anṣār as more worthy of the succession. In broad terms it gives a commentary not just on how the Anṣār viewed themselves but on how historians viewed their fluctuating fortune both during the Sīra and afterward through the reign of 'Alī. And, the speech includes a frank message of displeasure about how they were sidelined in history. This was not new to the Anṣār, who had earlier conveyed the same message after the Battle of Ḥunayn. Whereas in earlier times, however, it seemed that the Prophet had brought this sentiment under control, on the occasion of the Saqīfa the statement comes out in the open again, rebellious now not just for the possibility of leadership by Muhājirūn such as Abū Bakr and ʻUmar, but for their lot of submission during the Sīra as well. Hence we find how the declaration neglects to use a deferential language that would have remembered the gift of the Islamic message or the recognition that Islam's victory was first and foremost a result of divine help and favor. Instead, Saʻd highlights the political and earthly role of the Anṣār as something that decided the future of Islam, and hints with little equivocation that the Prophet, not to mention Quraysh, owed them (i.e., the Anṣār, and probably more specifically the Khazraj) something. Missing from this picture of imminent conflict among the companions is any spirit of equality or religious self-abnegation that would have been typical during the *ghazwas*, and indeed would briefly resurface under ʻUmar's reign at the battles of Qādisiyya, Yarmūk, and Nihāwand. The account therefore appears as highly practical and political rather than religious or hagiographic.

Saʻd's speech goes as follows:

> Company of the Anṣār! You have precedence in religion and merit [*lakum sābiqa fī'l-dīn wa faḍīla*] in Islam that no [other] tribe of the Arabs can claim. Muḥammad remained ten-odd years in his tribe, calling them to worship the Merciful and to cast off idols and graven images, but only a few men of his tribe believed in Him, and they were able neither to protect the Apostle of God, nor to render His religion strong, nor to divert from themselves the oppression that befell them all; until, when He intended excellence for you, He sent nobility to you and distinguished you with grace [*sāqa ilaykum al-karāma wa khaṣṣakum bi'l-niʻma*]. Thus God bestowed upon you faith in Him and in His Apostle, and protection for him and his companions, and strength for him and his faith, and battle [*jihād*] for his enemies. You were the most severe people against his enemies who were among you, and the most troublesome to his enemies who were not from among you, so that the Arabs became upright in God's cause, willingly or unwillingly, and the distant one submitted in abject humiliation, until through you God made great slaughter in the earth for His Apostle [*athkhan . . . li-rasūlihi bikum al-arḍ*], and by your swords the Arabs were abased for him. When God took (the Prophet to Himself), he was pleased with you, consoled by you. [So] keep [control of] this matter to yourselves, to the exclusion of others, for it is yours and yours alone.[70]

They answered him all together, "Your opinion is right, and you have spoken correctly. We will not diverge from your opinion, and we shall put you in charge of this issue [*qad wuffiqta fī'l-ra'y wa aṣabta fī'l-qawl wa lan na'dū mā ra'ayta wa nuwallīka hādhā al-amr*]. For indeed, you are sufficient for us and satisfactory to whoever is righteous among the believers." But then they began to debate among themselves [*thumma innahum tarāddū al-kalām baynahum*], and [some] said, "What if the Muhājirūn and the first companions of the Apostle of God resist and say, 'We are his kinsmen, protectors, and are the Muhājirūn and the first companions of the Messenger of God. So why do you dispute this matter with us after him?' [Another] group of (the Anṣār) said, "Then we should say, 'Let us have a leader from among ourselves, and you a leader from among yourselves,' for we should never be satisfied with less than this leadership." When Sa'd b. 'Ubāda heard this, he said, "This is the beginning of weakness [*hādhā awwal al-wahn*]."

This opening segment of the Saqīfa incident is generally omitted by *ḥadīth*-minded historians who favor viewing the Anṣār's claim as an accidental event that occurred in a temporary vacuum of the Quraysh from the political scene. Sa'd's actions, according to such a redacted version, involved no speech and there was no well-rationalized and competitive bid to seize the caliphate. Abū Mikhnaf's account shows, however, that the episode of a caliphal bid was part of an elaborate narrative that connected across time (involving both the Quraysh and the Anṣār), and that only in later times did *ḥadīth* collectors make use of the *isnād* tool to parcel out portions of the narrative that could have served an orthodox purpose while ignoring other messages and purposes of the original master text. The above segment depicts the Anṣār at a moment when they were on the verge of bouncing back into historical prominence. The unified pledge that they give to Sa'd b. 'Ubāda is a moralizing lesson of the need for quick and unified political action if a goal is to be achieved. This is a message that a later historian such as Miskawayh would have appreciated as a lesson in *tadbīr* (political planning). However, no sooner is this snapshot of unity taken than someone utters a word of doubt and worry, and then all the energy that the Anṣār had garnered in the introductory preparation for their political bid slowly begins to dissipate. Sa'd points to this, as if he is a commentator on the account when he says, "This is the beginning of weakness" (*hādhā awwal al-wahn*). Because of their old jealousies, the Aws and the Khazraj were unable to go forward and make a unified claim for a state.

Muḥammad's experiment of uniting the Aws and the Khazraj at the moment they converted and gave him the *bay'a* thus remained a unique moment in history. And, for all their pains in saving the Quraysh in earlier times, Abū 'Ubayda would reprimand the Anṣār for their claim to leadership by telling them, "O company of the Anṣār, you were the first who helped and strengthened, so do not be the first to substitute and change for the worse [*innakum awwala man naṣara wa āzar fa-lā takūnū awwala man baddala wa ghayyar*]." The statement was meant to set in motion a perception of the Anṣār as the paradigm of the transforming nation, who are about to experiment with seditious bids—implicitly among these is the backing of 'Alī's cause, and bring about the ominous disputes that the Prophet had warned might happen to the community one day. Meanwhile, Islam's true future was to remain with the tribe of Quraysh, which, as later narratives would show (see Mu'āwiya's speeches later), was divinely selected to be in a position of political leadership and the unchallenged guardian of the faith.

## THE INHERITANCE OF THE PROPHET

The debate over the succession to Muḥammad casts several allusive threads in the narratives of Ṭabarī. We have seen the leadership of the prayer and Abū Bakr's calming of the crowds as two different means by which the first caliph's legitimacy as successor was constructed. The Saqīfa incident was the final episode in a string of events meant to confirm Abū Bakr's precedence above other Muhājirūn and the Anṣār. With the different kinds of merit that the Rāshidūn caliphs commanded in the Islamic view, the argument for Abū Bakr's precedence ultimately rested, if the Saqīfa is to be believed, on the historical accident of 'Alī's absence from the scene. While Sunnism could draw at times on direct statements from the Prophet that position Abū Bakr above other companions, this was by no means a favorite approach since it could exact a heavy moral and methodological price. Aside from putting down other Rāshidūn companions (especially 'Alī) on an arbitrary basis, it demanded *isnād* preferences that could undermine the edifice of *ḥadīth* transmission more broadly. Thus, on the whole, the issue of succession priority remained tied to the elaborate story of the Saqīfa, and the focus was placed on who was at the Saqīfa rather than who was not. Within this frame, ʿAlī is then viewed as simply having been at the wrong place at the wrong time when deliberations over the succession were happening.[71] And, having missed that political auction, ʿAlī had no right to reopen the debate, an action that would have been read as a revocation of a binding agreement reached by the community, even if the procedure of caliphal selection was imperfect (a "*falta*," in the famous word used by ʿUmar). To put Abū Bakr's *bayʿa* in doubt therefore could undermine the *jamāʿa* and be viewed as an invitation for sedition. So Abū Bakr's leadership became synonymous with the birth of a unified community in Medina, where all challengers, whether Anṣār or others, were viewed by the established system as embittered rivals.

And yet, despite of the overtness of pro-*jamāʿī* sentiments in these texts, Ṭabarī does not entirely silence the wrong done to ʿAlī. The chronicler includes, for example, narratives that broach the issue of succession from an ʿAlid/Hāshimite-sympathizing angle. In one instance, Fāṭima sets about advocating the right of ʿAlī and does this in a somewhat elliptical way when she demands her right to inherit a famous piece of property from her father, namely the famous estate of Fadak in the former Jewish colony of Khaybar, which was Muḥammad's share of the booty after the conquest of that oasis. As a concrete question of inheritance, the Fadak issue has a very real-life feel to it and may sound like a purely legal issue set within a historical frame.[72] However, in reality the Fadak issue was a symbolic device used by narrators to allude to Fāṭima's (and the Hāshimites') claim to inheriting the Prophet's legacy and leadership (both political and religious). In placing her demand, Fāṭima does not argue her need for income from that estate, but merely demands her rightful share from the inheritance of the deceased. "Is it right that you should inherit your father, Abū Quḥāfa, but I do not inherit mine?" she embarrassingly asks Abū Bakr. In Ṭabarī's version of this exchange, Abū Bakr maintains a straight face and simply answers: "I have heard the Messenger of God say, 'Our [i.e., the prophets'] property cannot be inherited, and whatever we leave behind is alms [i.e., to be given in charity]' [*mā tarknā fa-huwa ṣadaqa*];"[73] thus settling the issue with a *ḥadīth*. However, in Yaʿqūbī's account of the same episode, Fatima repeats the same question several times, until Abū Bakr begins weeping.[74] In a different version, Ṭabarī shifts the demand for Fadak from Fāṭima to ʿAlī and makes Abū Bakr weep in response to ʿAlī, who invokes the argument of *qaraba* (kinship) instead of focusing on Fadak. Ṭabarī describes how ʿAlī, seeking reconciliation with Abū Bakr, invited the latter to confer with him. Ready to accept compromise, and over all the objections of ʿUmar, Abū Bakr went to ʿAlī while the latter was gathered with the Banū Hāshim. ʿAlī then told Abū Bakr: "It is neither denial of your good qualities nor an attempt to detract from the bounty which God has given you that prevented us from giving you the oath of allegiance, but the fact we considered was that we have a right in this authority which you have monopolized." ʿAlī then mentioned his relationship with the Messenger of God and the rights of Banū Hāshim. He continued speaking until Abū Bakr wept.[75]

Whether it was Abū Bakr's accession to the caliphate or his refusal to yield the estate of Fadak to Fāṭima that pushed ʿAlī and his wife to withhold *bayʿa* from the first caliph is not clear. But the sources agree that Fāṭima held very strong feelings on this issue, stopped talking to Abū Bakr, and even shunned him (*hajarathu*). When she died six months later, she still had not given the caliph the *bayʿa*, and Abū Bakr left it for ʿAlī to lead the funeral prayer over her at an odd hour of the night and did not announce the event (*lam yuʾdhin bihā*).[76] All this bitterness could not have been over just a piece of real estate. Fadak was clearly a metaphor for the lands of the caliphate. The Prophet had declared, "He who inherits the wealth, inherits allegiance as well [*yarith al-walāʾ man yarith al-māl*],"[77] and narrators were cognizant of this when they crafted the feud between Abū Bakr and Fāṭima.[78] Sunnī tradition could not let this dispute derail Abū Bakr's political legitimacy, even if it meant inheritance laws had to be changed to the extent that a sole surviving daughter of a deceased man would not be allowed to gain the majority share of inheritance from her father as her kin. Shīʿī law by contrast opts for the opposite. This division between Sunnī and Shīʿī practice has persisted in laws of civil status into the modern period.[79]

The story of conflict between Abū Bakr and Fāṭima is interesting for the way it came to represent a case of legal example on inheritance even though it originally emerged as a historical trope. What makes the incident especially remarkable is that it overthrew the paradigm of female silence that Sunnism tried to establish on other fronts. In contrast to the demure and withdrawn piety with which tradition paints Fāṭima's image in order to counterbalance the much-criticized political assertiveness of ʿĀisha during the civil war, Fāṭima suddenly comes across as a political challenger. Her uncharacteristically blunt confrontation with Abū Bakr complicated a story generally focusing on rivalry among companions with comparable credentials. Fāṭima's direct descent from the Prophet made the clash an embarrassment to companions who stood to later Muslim society like an antecedent collectivity of the *ʿulamā'*, who respected the honor of the prophetic family (particularly in its ʿAlid branch) even if they didn't recognize them as political and religious *imāms*. As a result narrators tapped into Sunnī rationalization of this matter in later times by devising both a legal and a social/tribal response to Fāṭima's argument. The first they achieved by discrediting Fāṭima's assertions on a technicality—that the testimony of a woman needed another one to make it valid—and the second they achieved by arguing that the tribal inheritance of leadership does not pass from father to daughter, but through the uncle (thus the ʿAbbāsid claim of inheriting the Hāshimite leadership was viewed as more credible than inheritance through the line of Fāṭima). The ʿAbbāsids were more than willing to join in this conspiracy later on, since it strengthened their claims to Hāshimite leadership and their position as regards the religious views of the Sunnī scholars.

By couching his rejection on the grounds of *ḥadīth* (*mā tarknā fa-huwa ṣadaqa*), Abū Bakr, or more accurately Sunnī Islam, accomplished several aims. The *ḥadīth* showed that the word of a companion (Abū Bakr in this case) was more authoritative than the demand of Fāṭima, and in the dialogue of the two the narrative undermined the idea of the authority of the Hāshimite *imām* (prophetic authority) and its corollary, that the *imām*'s/Hāshimite's authority was binding and transferable in the Prophet's line.[80] Instead, the legacy of the Prophet had become collective and tied to his statements. Who is speaking these *ḥadīth*s is important, but only so long as those speakers are companions who are the focus of Jamāʿī-Sunnī Islam.[81] The "Fadak *ḥadīth*," almost as much as the Qur'ānic verse recited by Abū Bakr upon the death of the Prophet, helped declare the finality of Muḥammad's prophethood, undermined Shīʿī ideas about the authority of esoteric knowledge harbored by the descendants of the Prophet, and declared in effect a separation between religious and political authority.

## THE NEW CALIPH

Whatever the circumstances of his succession to the Prophet, Abū Bakr's hold on power quickly grew. In spite of a variety of wars with other tribes around the peninsula in Yemen, Najd, and Oman, Abū Bakr succeeded in extending his power. In this he was helped by several factors, most notably the fact that to most Arab tribes, despite gripes and rivalries with Islam, Abū Bakr's regime was essentially the rule of the old Meccan elite, which had always commanded prestige in Arabia, although it had never sought to assert political hegemony prior to Islam. Abū Bakr was also helped in his enterprise by the fact that he had a number of talented commanders and offspring of former Meccan chiefs implementing his program of conquest and control. Khālid b. al-Walīd, al-Muhājir b. Abī Umayya al-Makhzūmī, 'Ikrima b. Abī Jahl, 'Amr b. al-'Āṣ, Yazīd b. Abī Sufyān, and Khālid b. Sa'īd b. al-'Āṣ, as well as the companions, provided a rotating leadership that reinforced the old Meccan authority with new Medinan circles of supporters.[82]

Unfortunately, we have little reliable information on how Abū Bakr charted his policies, envisaged the conquests, or handled Muslim and Arabian oppositions. The sources mainly depict his political resolve as an extension both of the firmness of his religious faith, and of his desire to preserve the last commands of the Prophet. Several instances are marshalled to illustrate this attitude, including the caliph's refusal to negotiate or make truce with the apostates (especially those who refused to pay the *zakāt*), his decisiveness in going ahead with sending the army the Prophet had prepared for an expedition against Syria even when those troops were becoming necessary for the Ridda war, and, finally, his refusal to replace the young leader of the Syrian campaign, Usāma b. Zayd, with a more experienced or senior leader. In all this, Abū Bakr is shown to have been steadfast in keeping the last actions of the Prophet in place, even if they were superseded by events, and in defending the unity of the religious mission without compromise. Thus, even if the caliph himself did not show physical strength, his resolve was a sufficient reason to his followers for confidence (as the later tradition famously describes him: "weak as regards himself, but strong in matters of faith [*ḍa'īfun fī nafsihi, qawiyyun fī amri allāh*]").[83] The third caliph, 'Uthmān, could have learned an important lesson from this type of leadership.

That an Arab campaign was launched against Syria at that time is probably a historical fact. It is the context of the casting of this event's story and the exaggeration of the expedition's centrality, however, that are open to question. In the way narrators emphasize the beginning of this wave of conquest, and in their portrayal of Abū Bakr's attentive preparation of that campaign, it seems as though there was something significantly different at the time between invading Syria and invading Iraq. That Abū Bakr was being portrayed as keeping faithful to the will of the Prophet has already been noted, but it is also likely that this story may reflect a layer of ninth-century orthodox affinity to Syria. Taking into account the staunch resistance of that province to the Miḥna, and its growing role in pushing out 'Alid and Shī'ī influences from the caliphal center at Baghdad, it is very likely that the narrative of the Syrian conquest was meant to show the early selection of the new province as the seed for a future emergence of political authority for the community outside Arabia (see chapter 7).

## THE PERSONALITY OF ABŪ BAKR

When one turns to evaluating the personality of Abū Bakr, the evidence continues to be less necessarily factual than religiously representational. In this context, such characterization is done mainly through a comparison of Abū Bakr and 'Umar, who are diametrically opposite in temperament and style. 'Āisha's description of her father as "*rajulun raqīq*" contrasts heavily with 'Umar, who is frequently depicted in physical fights.[84] The Prophet himself enhanced this comparison when he once reportedly described them as the human parallel to the contrasting roles of the angels Michael and Gabriel: the first is described as descending with divine mercy, while the other is the bearer of divine punishment.[85] On another occasion, the comparison is made with prophets who represented opposite temperaments. When asked what should be done with the prisoners of battle after the first Islamic victory at Badr, Abū Bakr advised that they be spared, while 'Umar proposed that they be put to death, which prompted the Prophet to comment: "God softens the hearts of men [in some instances] so that they become softer than milk, and God hardens the hearts of men [at times] so that they become harder than stones. Abū Bakr, you are like Abraham, who said, 'Whoso followeth me, he verily is of me. And whoso disobeyeth me—Still thou art Forgiving, Merciful.'[86] And Abū Bakr, you are [also] like Jesus, who said, 'If though punish them, lo! They are thy slaves, and if thou forgive them they are thy slaves. Thou, only Thou art the Mighty, the Wise.'[87] You 'Umar, are like Noah, who said, 'My Lord! Leave not one of the disbelievers in the Land.'[88] And you are like Moses, who said, 'Our Lord! Destroy their riches and harden their hearts so that they believe not till they see the painful doom.'[89]'[90]

The images projected in these comparisons are not incidental but reflect the core bedrock out of which narrators sculpted the range of actions and temperament of these two men before and after their conversion to Islam. Character, to Ṭabarī, as to other classical writers, did not change with changing religious belief. Archaic ideas about the astrological, moral, and class-related aspects of the individual lingered on from Greek into Islamic times and coexisted with new religious beliefs in the historiography of the period. Only the will and direction of the individual were controlled by a new belief, and not the natural impulse. Thus Abū Bakr's more sober, patient, and tolerant attitude is evident from the Sīra days, much as 'Umar's hotheaded anger and stubbornness in observing the old ways date back to the Jāhiliyya. 'Umar's staunch opposition to his sister when she converted to Islam continued into his reign, when he became a rough ruler and an ardent proponent of religious laws molded in his image.

While the depiction of an opposition to 'Umar formed one layer of representing Abū Bakr's personality, another was the similarity of the first caliph to the Prophet himself. The two greatly resemble one another in temperament, mood, and general style in handling debates and crises, and in passing judgments on matters. Abū Bakr's speech is sparse and measured, just like Muḥammad's, and his belief in Islam is depicted as a kind of epiphany followed by a trustful belief, similar to Muḥammad's initial belief in Islam through the context of revelation.[91] This is unlike, for example, 'Umar's more legalistic approach to religion. In matters of political planning and strategy as well, Abū Bakr displays some parallels to the consultative style of the Prophet (as do other caliphs in varying degrees), evoking in *majlis*-style discussions with various advisors and companions a similarity to how the Prophet himself related to his companions.

However, it is in the religious sphere that the sources enhance the nuances of Abū Bakr's comparison with the Prophet. There are significant similarities in their temperament and manner of reflection on the religious faith, which allow for a pairing of the two in such a way that the Prophet seems to carry on a spiritual dialogue with Abū Bakr that he did not have with other companions. Woven into the wider context of the Sīra, the companionship of Abū Bakr and the Prophet becomes a journey of mutual support that is analogous to the Islamic depiction of the relation between Hārūn and Moses. Certain images show this borrowing from the Moses saga, for instance, when Abū Bakr speaks at one point in the confrontation with the Meccans in the early days of Islam like the lone believer whom the Qur'ān speaks of in Pharaoh's family.[92] However, the wider range of this comparison becomes evident when we note the high number of stories that describe Abū Bakr as an individual with a unique ability to interpret dreams,[93] and with the ability to appreciate the language of prophecy more generally (*muṣaddiq*), much as Yūsuf was before, and is referred to in the Qur'ān as "*Yūsuf al-Ṣiddīq*."[94]

This unusual dialogue between Muḥammad and Abū Bakr combined with the event of their hijra later invited narrators to harmonize a greater level of association between their biographies, wherein the two lived an equal number of years (63),[95] and died from similar causes. One version, stating that the first caliph was poisoned by a meal offered to him by the Jews and that this poison took a full year for its effect to be fatal, has a parallel in the Sīra.[96] Another, more widely accepted version, however, states that the cause of their deaths was a severe fever. In the case of Abū Bakr, the story states that he was afflicted with a fever after bathing on a very cold day and remained ill for fifteen days.[97] Abū Bakr, like Muḥammad, was unable to lead the congregational prayer, and for fifteen days 'Umar stood in his place,[98] thus evoking another parallel with the Prophet, though this similarity still did not make 'Umar the official nominee of Abū Bakr for succession. There are also parallel descriptions of a slow decline in each man's health, occasional fainting, a scene of consultation with companions over succession, and the presence of 'Āisha beside both men in their closing hours—all meant to draw a parallel between the Prophet and Abū Bakr. And finally, the resemblance is completed when Abū Bakr commands that all his belongings, few as they were, be given to the community rather than passing as inheritance to his children.[99]

## SUCCESSION, DEATH, AND RETROSPECTION

We have thus far examined various scenes in Abū Bakr's life as constructs of representation. There remains the closing chapter of Abū Bakr's life, which equally deserves a revisionist analysis. Not surprisingly, the cluster of accounts here deals with the theme of succession, where once again there is a rich religious and literary allusion involved in its composition. To introduce the nature of the new problem of veracity, the story of Abū Bakr's death is recounted in different contexts in Ṭabarī's chronicle. We read about it once in the account of poisoning cited above, another in a more prolonged description tied to the succession issue, and finally in a brief interlude during vivid descriptions of the military campaigns. Here there is even a more detailed division in chronology as to whether the caliph died while the Arab army in Syria was at the gates of Damascus or while preparing for the famous battle of Yarmuk in Jordan.

The intention in the latter context was to convey the anxiety of the caliph over the future of the community engaged in war and his resolve to press ahead against the empires (as was done earlier during the Ridda) rather than to address the issue of succession. In his typical firm style at times of crisis, Abū Bakr tells 'Umar:

> Listen, O 'Umar, to what I say to you, then act according to it. I hope to die on this day of mine, . . . If I die, do not by any means let the evening enter before you have summoned the men [to go] with al-Muthannā [to Irāq] . . . Do not let any catastrophe at all, even if it is great, keep you from the matter of your religion and your Lord's counsel. You saw what I did on the day the Messenger of God died, and the people were never stricken with the like of it. By God, if I were to weaken in the affair of God and the affair of His Messenger, He would abandon me and punish me, so that Medina would be consumed by fire. If God grants victory to the commanders in Syria, return the troops of Khālid to Irāq, for they are its people, the governors of its affairs alone, and the people of violence and courage against the enemy.[100]

This speech stresses the importance of leadership continuity and gives a sense of the urgency of pressing forward. It appeals to a ninth-century Muslim sense of nostalgia for a reliable ruler who is able to combine religious commitment with political resolve to safeguard the abode of Islam.

Though Abū Bakr and 'Umar would have been known through *ḥadīth* literature as primarily men of religious erudition, this story in Ṭabarī is meant to show their awareness of the importance of matters of strategy as well. A line of analogy to the Prophet was included in this story as well, since Abū Bakr's resolute command for dispatching al-Muthannā was meant to provide a parallel to the Prophet's earlier resolve in sending Usāma's army (his famous words: "*anfidhū ba'tha Usāma*"). More importantly, we should note how in spite of the context of planning the campaign after his reign, Abū Bakr does not discuss the matter of caliphal succession either before or after this command. Rather, the discussion of this topic happens separately, in more domestic accounts—in that social and homey setting in which the Saqīfa incident and the Prophet's final days were placed before.

The succession of the second caliph tends to be viewed by historians, and even by narrators from the medieval period, as a straightforward designation by Abū Bakr (with the range of examples being: the Prophet appointed no one, Abū Bakr appointed a successor, and 'Umar left it for consultation among a group of six people). The event of 'Umar's designation is certainly favored in the traditional religious view, not only as a firm step from the first caliph but also as a sign that confirms 'Umar's religious knowledge and excellence, and allows the religious authority of the two leaders (Abū Bakr and 'Umar) to be closely linked. Later, when he was installed in power, 'Umar's political legitimacy in Sunnī memory derives its energy less from any act of designation than from a flood of praising traditions that detail his ascetic, egalitarian, and attentive manner of rule.

With all this said, however, the circumstances of 'Umar's succession, or the ways narrators discuss it, are more complex than the way modern historians have tended to believe. The account of how 'Umar was selected does not occur as a straightforward announcement from Abū Bakr to the companions but rather spans several steps and interactions that are informative in all their details. As before at the Saqīfa, this story begins with the conspicuous absence of 'Alī from the list of nominees and those being consulted by Abū Bakr about the succession. 'Alī's absence from consideration (not to mention the historical delay in his becoming caliph) perhaps formed an awkward issue for narrators, but it probably gave them a welcome opportunity for devising texts that were as artfully allusive as they were apologetic for Abū Bakr. As the following reading will show, there is an implicit regret in these narratives about 'Alī's loss and an attempt to distance Abū Bakr from direct responsibility for the appointment of 'Umar, and the awkward task thus of preferring one companion over another.

Ṭabarī devotes a separate section to recounting the narratives connected with this event of succession, and they stand less as linear components leading to the assured succession of 'Umar than as pronouncements of proper caliphal (or kingly) attention to strategizing succession, which in Abū Bakr's case culminate with a key ambiguity surrounding the final choice of a successor. These steps, along with their content can be classified as follows:

1. *The intent.* Ṭabarī's account opens with a description of how Abū Bakr privately consulted with 'Abd al-Raḥmān and 'Uthmān about the merits of 'Umar, on the assumption that 'Umar was to be named caliph. The account is typical of the consultative style generally assigned to the Prophet, Abū Bakr, and 'Umar (later, 'Umar does the same, but more extensively).[101] The gesture shows the humility of the leader as he defers to other opinions, and at the same time depicts him as an astute statesman who is feeling out the potential for opposition to a pending choice. The narrator here tells us that Abū Bakr summoned 'Abd al-Raḥmān and asked him, "Inform me about 'Umar," to which Abd al-Raḥmān responded, "O successor of God's Messenger, he is by God a better man than your opinion of him. But there is a roughness in him." To this Abū Bakr responds, "That is because he sees me as mild (*raqīqan*). If I entrust him with the affair he would leave behind much of his present behavior." Then the caliph summoned 'Uthmān and posed the same question, which 'Uthmān answered by saying: "My knowledge about him is that what he does in private is better than what he shows openly." Abū Bakr accepted these answers and asked both men to keep the discussion secret.[102] As a literary set piece, the account is rich in stylistic nuance, but its core thrust shows that the business of state, or making important decisions in general, is best done in stealth. It brings to mind similar pivotal decisions taken at an unknown hour of the night in other eras of Islamic history, such as Hārūn al-Rashīd's private discussion of how to plan the overthrow of the Barmakid family. The pattern of the caliph's questioning, argumentation, and determination is repeated across time, making the story structure the same in Rāshidūn or 'Abbāsid times. The account

does not end with the caliph's decision to designate 'Umar for succession, but it evokes his general intent and greatly polishes the merits of 'Umar to show his worthiness for succession. One should also note that the gist of Abū Bakr's praise of 'Umar centers on secular moral criteria, not religious judgment.

2. *Official designation.* In the next account, Abū Bakr reportedly addresses the people from his quarters (*ashrafa 'alā al-nās min kanīfih*) while standing beside Asmā' b. 'Umays, whose hands were said to be tattooed (*mawshūmat al-yadayn*).[103] The caliph declares: "Will you be satisfied with whom I have left as [my] successor over you? For, by God, I do not shun the effort [to reach] the best opinion, nor have I appointed a relative (*mā ālawtu min jahd al-ra'y wa la wallaytu dhā qarāba*). I have designated 'Umar b. al-Khaṭṭāb as my successor; therefore hear him and obey."[104] The reader is again shown that the choice of 'Umar is a product of sound evaluation (*jahd al-ra'y*), while future critics of 'Uthmān are silenced by the fact that the caliph resorted to no kin tie in making this decision. Although seemingly rhetorical, the caliph's question to the crowd preserves a sense of tribal consultation and collective religious involvement. The account's focus is ultimately less on Abū Bakr's declaration than on the agreement to abide by the choice. A variant, subsidiary version of this account has 'Umar as the one carrying his official investiture document to the public and ordering the crowd to abide by what the caliph has declared in it (Abū Bakr is absent from the scene).[105]

3. *The ambiguous succession.* The most critical scene, however, draws on the discussion Abū Bakr has in the first account with 'Uthmān, but here the caliph falls short of declaring 'Umar's designation himself. The way this account is crafted is worth examining closely. The narrator relates the following:

> Abū Bakr summoned 'Uthmān in private [*khāliyan*] and said to him: "Write: 'In the Name of God, the Compassionate, the Merciful. This is what Abū Bakr b. Abī Quḥāfa, has enjoined on the Muslims. Now then . . .'" Then he [Abū Bakr] fainted, and 'Uthmān continued writing: "Now then [*ammā ba'd*], I have designated 'Umar b. al-Khaṭṭāb as caliph upon you, and I have not found better than him." Then Abū Bakr came back to consciousness and asked 'Uthmān to read what he wrote, which he did. Abū Bakr then made the *takbīr*, and said: "I see that you were afraid that the people would quarrel if I died suddenly after I fainted!"

> [ʿUthmān] said: "Yes," and Abū Bakr concluded: "May God reward you kindly for the sake of Islam and its people!" Abū Bakr, the narrator adds, "confirmed the designation from that occasion."[106]

Reported via a chain of narrators entirely different from the first account, this third account nevertheless represents a sophisticated continuum with the first account. ʿUthmān, in narrative 3, picks up where he and the caliph left off in narrative 1. In narrative 1, ʿUthmān gave his favorable opinion of ʿUmar, and Abū Bakr promised that he would have chosen ʿUthmān had he skipped ʿUmar (*law taraktuhu mā ʿadawtuka*), and wished that ʿUmar would not accept the succession for his own wellbeing. Abū Bakr's odd remarks here (forecasting ʿUthmān's later succession) are usually overlooked, but they are significant for showing us the tendentious Sunnī perspective of the future, expecting the accession of ʿUthmān as third caliph, in the crafting of this account. On the surface, this segment affirms how the first three caliphs were the prime choices for succession, now that Abū Bakr has here given his blessings not only to ʿUmar, but to ʿUthmān as well. However, the artful dimension of the account is more important than the polemical, since the account is loosely concluded and crafted. Abū Bakr declares his preference for ʿUmar and leaves it for ʿUthmān in narrative 3 to fill in ʿUmar's name, even though there is no reason in this narrative to see Abū Bakr's grounds for preferring ʿUmar, which we noted earlier. In narrative 3, ʿUmar's hasty nomination is merely a security measure meant to thwart potential sedition (as happened at the Saqīfa) rather than a step based on a unanimous agreement on ʿUmar's superiority. In light of this careful crafting, one could then argue that Abū Bakr was probably being distanced from the decision for succession in the third account, as he merely comes back from the realm of the unconscious (like the dead peering into the world of the living) to see who would succeed him and what potential dangers this nomination would forestall momentarily. It is ʿUthmān who is centrally self-served by this nomination of ʿUmar for succession, and thus he is made to carry it out.

However, while ʿUthmān is the companion present in both accounts (1 and 3) of the dialogue with Abū Bakr, ʿAbd al-Raḥmān b. ʿAwf, although absent in narrative 3, is implicitly linked to this decision process as well. Here one should digress to recall the famous story that is set after ʿUmar's assassination, when the six companions appointed to head the *shūrā* for appointing the third caliph end up dependent on ʿAbd al-Raḥmān b. ʿAwf. It is well known that ʿUmar put Ibn ʿAwf at the head of this *shūrā* and gave him special status to tip the scale if a vote came to a tie.[107] More significant was what happened at the critical final hour at the *shūrā*, when ʿAbd al-Raḥmān b. ʿAwf privately summoned the leading candidates for succession, ʿAlī and ʿUthmān (in the best precedent for the Taḥkīm), and asked them how they would chart their policy if they became rulers. "Will you, ʿAlī, give me your oath of office based on God's Book, the practice of His Prophet, and the deeds of Abū Bakr and ʿUmar?" ʿAbd al-Raḥmān asked, to which (ʿAlī) replied, "Indeed no, but [only] based on my own effort in all this and in accordance with my own ability." When asked the same question by ʿAbd al-Raḥmān, ʿUthmān answered in the affirmative, thus confirming in the best Sunnī form the status of the first two caliphs as supplementary models for prophetic Sunna.[108]

That crucial account is almost identical to a portion of narrative 1 in which Abū Bakr questions ʿUthmān and Ibn ʿAwf about the merits of ʿUmar. Ibn ʿAwf's role in that account anticipates his role as a referee rather than making him a realistic candidate to the caliphate in narrative 1, and for this reason it is ʿUthmān who ends up drafting Abū Bakr's charter of succession and who evokes the discussion of the possibility that ʿUmar's name would thwart a dispute (*ikhtilāf*). With his retrospective knowledge of the danger of *fitna*, ʿUthmān is used by the narrator (now commentator) to provide ʿUmar as a solution, based as much on his earlier discussion with Abū Bakr before as on lessons ʿUthmān learned from his own tumultuous caliphate later on and his regret that he had not been as authoritative as ʿUmar.[109] Abū Bakr's acceptance of ʿUthmān's independent initiative in naming ʿUmar for succession can ultimately be read as the first caliph's endorsement of the third caliph's enterprising style (although limits are set on this in narrative 2, where the first caliph repudiates the role of nepotism in the process of naming a successor [i.e., that ʿUthmān was in error to appoint kinsmen to positions of political power; Abū Bakr's words: *mā ālawtu min jahd al-raʾy wa lā wallaytu dhā qarāba*]).[110]

4. *The broad retrospection.* Thus far the reader can note that much of the focus in the narrative is on discussing the succession and the merits of ʿUmar, rather than on giving a frequent and unequivocal designation of ʿUmar. Ṭabarī and other compilers, such as Ibn Saʿd, often included a

plethora of narratives repeating the same fact if it was a popular one. However, in a fourth narrative, to be examined next, Abū Bakr's words are sparse and generally evasive. Here the image we have is of Abū Bakr lying ill in his final hours and talking to Ibn 'Awf. The latter tries to comfort the caliph by saying, "You have indeed become purified (*bāri'an*)." Abū Bakr asks, "Do you think so?" "Yes," Ibn Awf answers. Abū Bakr then makes a general statement reflecting on the succession, without naming his designee, and prophesies the dangers of the future:

> I have entrusted your affairs to him who I feel is the best of you. Each of you is inflamed with anger by that, for each wants the succession to be his instead. You have seen that the world has opened up. And verily it shall open up [further] until you adopt curtains of silk and pillows of silk brocade, and come to find it [as] painful to lie on Adharī wool as anyone of you now is pained to sleep on thorns. By God, that any of you be brought forth to have his head struck off without a reason of penalty for a mortal sin would be better for him than plunging into the depths of this life. You will be the first to lead the people astray tomorrow [*wa antum awwalu ḍālin bi'l-nāsi ghadan*], so that you will turn them from the way to right and left. O guide of the way, it is either the light of dawn or evil [*innamā huwa al-fajr aw al-bajr*].[111]

These comments reflect a foreknowledge of the civil war that will follow the conquests that peak in the reign of 'Uthmān, and they show Abū Bakr's disinterest in worldly affairs and his intermingling of knowledge of present and future. To alleviate the impression that Islam totally discredits the vocation of political rule, Ibn 'Awf is made to compensate by advising that some experiments of leadership are actually virtuous activities. He tells Abū Bakr, "Calm down, may God have mercy on you, for this will only cause a relapse in your condition. . . . We have not known you to desire other than the good. You have not ceased to be a righteous man and one who sets matters aright. You do not grieve for anything from this world [*wa anta lā ta'sā 'alā a-dunyā min shay'*]."[112] This is a consoling voice that future caliphs, most notably the 'Abbāsids, will never hear again (instead their lot is rebukes from ascetics and *ḥadīth* scholars). And much as speeches of rebuke provided a hinge for confrontation, this speech by Ibn 'Awf serves as an impetus for Abū Bakr to build an even more self-deprecating commentary that reflects on his own achievements, judging their worth in light of the future. His final words run as follows:

> Indeed, I do not grieve for anything from this world, except for three [things] which I did that I wish had left aside, three that I left aside which I wish I had done, and three about which I wish I had asked God's Messenger. As for the three that I wish I had left aside, I wish that I had not thrown open the house of Fāṭima to reveal something, even though they had locked it with hostile intent. I wish that I had not burned al-Fuja'a al-Sulamī and that I had quickly killed him or forbearingly let him go. I wish on the day of Saqīfat Banī Sā'ida, that I had thrown the matter upon the neck of one of the two men [meaning 'Umar and Abū 'Ubayda] so that one of them would have become the Commander [of the Faithful] and I would have been his minister [*wazīr*]. As for those I left aside, I wish that on the day I was brought al-Ash'ath b. Qays as a prisoner I had cut off his head, for I imagine that he does not see any evil but that he helps it along. I also wish, when I sent Khālid b. al-Walīd to fight the people of apostasy, that I stayed at Dhū al-Qaṣṣa, so that if the Muslims had triumphed, they would have triumphed, but if they had been defeated, I would have been engaged or [provided] reinforcement. Furthermore, I wish when I sent Khālid b. al-Walīd to Syria, that I had sent 'Umar b. al-Khaṭṭāb to Iraq; thereby, I would have stretched forth both of my hands in God's path. [He stretched forth both his hands.] I also wish that I had asked God's Messenger with whom the government rests, so that no one would contend about it. I wish I had asked him whether the Anṣār had a share in the government. I wish I had asked him about the inheritance of the brother's daughter and the paternal aunt, for I have some doubts in my mind about the two of them.[113]

Abū Bakr's three wishes in each category can easily be construed by the general reader as ordinary regretful comments. However, this final declaration provides a synopsis for the reader of the thorny issues that haunted the earlier succession and that would give rise to further problems. In various categories—political history, military strategy concerning the conquests in Syria and Iraq, and religious schism—the reader sees a unique perspective on what the first caliph considered to have been detrimental lapses, or more accurately, the agonized response to constructed tragic action. For here the boundaries between significant historical facts and constructed narratives with religious and political bearings become entwined in a form of reporting and commentary that assumes a high level of spiritual sophistication, drawing on complex Qur'ānic forms of parabolic allusion. Given the representation of Abū Bakr's profile as a contemplative personality with a penetrating vision into future eventualities, his discourse is less that of a caliph than that of a religious seer. His view breaks binary boundaries of past and present to encompass the future as well and thus draws arcs of alternative chains of events that would have corrected a range of flawed actions.

This unconventional profile of behavior may well have been modeled by narrators on the Qur'ānic depiction of the famous itinerant clairvoyant companion of Moses (often referred to as al-Khiḍr), whose actions on a fateful journey defied logic and the morality of the here and now in favor of better future results. Tied to the boundaries of knowledge that was circumscribed by the present and the physical senses, Moses became incensed when his companion drilled a hole in the hull of a ship on which he was traveling, killed a boy unknown to them along the way, and wasted time building a wall in an anonymous locale. But in every instance, after his protests, Moses was told by this companion how such an action would thwart a future threat or make a future virtuous outcome possible. The ship was made defective because its owners were coming to the shores of a king who seized all perfect vessels; the child was killed because he would become a menace to his parents; and the wall was reconstructed because it hid in its foundation a treasure that belonged to two young orphans who could only survive in the future if their treasure was secure. Thus, while human knowledge of the present demanded one course of action, divine prescience demanded another. In the end, after giving these explanations to Moses, who little understood the wisdom of such actions until they were explained, al-Khiḍr broke off his companionship with Moses, saying, "This is the interpretation of that thou couldst not bear patiently."[114]

The moral in the Qur'ānic story is clear: one can either live by concrete reality, acting on what seems right in the present, or opt for retrospective insight after history has unfolded. Whereas Moses and al-Khiḍr form the two poles of religious appreciation and knowledge, debating views from the present and the future, Abū Bakr carries on the dialogue with himself. Having been represented as a master dream interpreter,

Abū Bakr is portrayed drawing on this knowledge to evaluate his own career as caliph, and to anticipate the more controversial future readings of his actions in light of later developments. The moments of illness and near-death had value in religious thought as occasions for epiphany, and thus the first caliph seeks forgiveness from God and offers an apology to the community (and to the Hāshimites) for having ruled and been partly responsible for what was to come. The lines of hidden insight are given to Abū Bakr not only because of his association with dreams, but through a dramatizing twist on his role of companionship to the Prophet. The picture of the traveling companions—Moses and al-Khiḍr across the sea, Muḥammad and Abū Bakr on the Hijra—allowed for the perfect parallel of two journeys of holy men, one undertaken for knowledge, and another for salvation.

The question then remains: what was Abū Bakr regretting in this bizarre statement? The caliph's deep regret about actions he took reveals his awareness of worse outcomes to emerge out of these lapses. Fāṭima's house should not have been violated, the reader can hypothesize, because it emboldened the future opponents of the third caliph, 'Uthmān, to attack his house.[115] One would note that the emotional reaction ascribed to Fāṭima when 'Umar and his cohorts broke down her door is not unlike that ascribed to Nā'ila, 'Uthmān's wife, as she attempted to defend 'Uthmān against the attackers later on. More critically, and consistent with the 'Alid theme of events, Abū Bakr was regretting the fact that the attack on Fāṭima's house set a precedent of aggression on the Hāshimite household and thus paved the way for future pressures applied by the Umayyads on the 'Alids so the former could gain the *bay'a* whether the 'Alids liked it or not. The imperative of abiding by the *jamā'a* (a frame that accommodated Umayyad and 'Abbāsid rule as de facto caliphates and made opposition to them a form of sedition) had opened the way for a cruel and relentless war by the rulers in Damascus and Baghdad on the descendants of 'Alī for withholding the *bay'a*. Ultimately, Abū Bakr, while accepting the need for a caliphate, was indirectly criticizing the Sunnī imperative of obeying authority at any price, as he viewed the caliphate as a defective institution. Had he not believed that, he would not have wished that he had let 'Umar or Abū 'Ubayda succeed instead.

The regret shown by Abū Bakr over having spared al-Ash'ath b. Qays after his capture at the end of the Ridda war possibly hints at the caliph's foreknowledge of the detrimental role that this tribal chief would play in undermining the leadership of 'Alī later and perhaps even a foreknowledge of the longer-lasting damage that the Ash'ath family would bring. It is well known how al-Ash'ath brought ruin to 'Alī's cause by insisting that the latter cease a military advance just prior to victory at Ṣiffīn and by declaring himself in favor of the Taḥkīm and of having the incompetent Abū Mūsā al-Ash'arī represent 'Alī at the Taḥkīm. This combination of events, more than anything, undermined 'Alī's momentum and emboldened the Khārijites to become more intransigent. Abū Bakr's regret, therefore, is wide-ranging but still tied to the misfortunes of 'Alī and the tragic breakup of the community. Sparing al-Ash'ath was a lamentable event not only because of this man's folly, but also because of the detrimental effects his posterity would have in the future. For when the time of the tragedy of Ḥusayn arrives, Ṭabarī presents a sensitive narrative that shows Muḥammad b. al-Ash'ath's role as a wavering supporter of Ḥusayn in Kufa, while his grandson, 'Abd al-Raḥmān b. Muḥammad b. al-Ash'ath, performs the critical gesture of betrayal that brings doom to the cause of Ḥusayn. The historical depiction in Abū Bakr's regretful words was therefore heavily dependent on the Qur'ānic paradigm of Moses and al-Khiḍr and an exercise of historical interpretation (*ta'wīl*) that gave away the true meaning of the texts.

Abū Bakr and the Prophet finally part ways in their last hours. Whereas Muḥammad declared that the world had come to a new beginning at *ḥijjat al-wadā'*, highlighted victory as the moment of closure in prophetic messages, and left the political future of the community uncertain, Abū Bakr took some controversial steps that set the community on an ever-widening path of division and coercive rule. Although their biographies share some points of resemblance, it is clear that narrators sought to show that the first caliphate represented something less than the Sīra. While Abū Bakr represented the example of the innately wise believer (*mu'min āl fir'awn*), and his companionship to the Prophet was an improvement on that of Hārūn toward Moses, with the first caliph's suppression of the Ridda and early devotion to the security of the community, Abū Bakr's conflict with the Hāshimites over the issue of succession established that the history of tribulation was to begin anew after the Prophet.

CHAPTER THREE

# 'Umar b. al-Khaṭṭāb

## *A Saga of Law and Conquest*

The name of Abū Bakr is usually paired in Sunnī Islamic doctrine with that of the second caliph, 'Umar, and together the two are well known as "*al-shaykhān*" (the two sages) in *ḥadīth* collections. Their practices and sayings are generally viewed as setting standards of religious behavior, and as second in authority only to Muḥammad's. No other companion, including 'Alī, is viewed as more excellent in merit than these two, and Sunnī jurists level harsh criticisms against those who detract from the *tafḍīl* (high ranking) of the two caliphs.[1] *Ḥadīth*s that praise Abū Bakr and 'Umar are considered an article of faith and can be found in the same legal texts that prescribe the rules on ritual purity, prayer, pilgrimage, and other religious rites. Whether Muḥammad made all of the praiseful comments about Abū Bakr and 'Umar that are attributed to him is doubtful, as is the case for many *ḥadīth*s. The historical context of ninth-century Baghdad, Basra, and Kufa, with their social and religious environments divided between Sunnīs (especially Ḥanbalīs) and Shī'īs, was no doubt crucial in shaping polarized Muslim perceptions of the early caliphate and its key personages.

### THE LAW

The images of the first two caliphs formed important and central points of orthodox reference in later Islamic tradition, although they seem to have diverged considerably in role and function. Whereas Abū Bakr represented the experience of belief as a leap of faith and trust in the call of the word and inspiration, 'Umar represented the experience of belief as an observation of the law and organizing norms. Unlike the case of Abū Bakr's dreamy profile, tradition paints 'Umar as a companion who is more involved in concrete reality and the day-to-day affairs of the community. To 'Umar, religion is a concrete social experience existing within boundaries defined by the law, where the rights (*ḥuqūq*) and limits (*ḥudūd*) are divinely ordained, and it is the observance of the law (fulfillment of the covenant, *'ahd, mithāq*), rather than a mere acceptance of the message, that determines the success or downfall of the community. The political and the legal are therefore closely related according to this definition, and the task falls on the caliph ("*al-sulṭān al-'ādil*") to ensure that the community, as his flock, does not go astray (the qualities of *tabdīl* and *taghyīr*).

In describing 'Umar's reign, the medieval chronicles attribute an extensive list of innovations to him, all of which carry a structural, organizing character. Along with the administrative dimension of 'Umar's reign there is an attribution of a legalistic emphasis. 'Umar's attention to a wide range of organizing rules (prohibitions, the penal code, social interaction) are illustrated in various stories set in his reign that illustrate examples and applications of these regulations. However, 'Umar is also shown as having been concerned with these issues since Muḥammad's time. Throughout the Sīra, exegetical narratives portray 'Umar as the touchstone of curiosity who elicited divine revelations dealing with the law or elaborations of religious accounts. The mix of these issues varies in the sources, but they almost always include the injunctions that prohibited the drinking of wine, the veiling of women, the demarcation of strong lines between believers and nonbelievers (as relating to the *munāfiqūn*), and strict observance of punishments (especially for adultery and wine drinking). The classic format of how such rules purportedly originated portrays 'Umar expressing extra religiosity and wondering, for example, whether wine is completely prohibited or hoping that women would be sheltered away from men, and that, in response, relevant Qur'ānic verses emerged. This process, which happened on a wide range of instances, and tends to touch several verses with a socially organizing character (particularly in *sūrat al-aḥzāb*), is known as the "*muwāfaqāt*," or concurrence between divine guidance and 'Umar's opinion.[2] The phenomenon on the whole raises the question of why these ideas (which are not all legalistic) were attributed to 'Umar rather than to another companion.

It is tempting to read in the cases of *muwāfaqāt* positive historical evidence of a second layering of Muḥammad's message with actual additions by 'Umar dealing with social norms. Stories about 'Umar's familiarity with biblical texts could impel the historian to hypothesize an early date for the incorporation of Judaic material that became staples of the Sharī'a.[3] However, in all likelihood the connection of 'Umar's name with these juristic innovations is a later attribution dating to early 'Abbāsid times. In an exercise that mirrors the anecdotal elaboration that explains the occasions of revelation of considerable material in the Qur'ān, later traditionists used the name of 'Umar in a similar manner to set the context of issues that occasioned the emergence of some verses. With 'Umar's name probably already associated with strong asceticism, egalitarianism, and zealousness as well as the politically useful feature of anti-'Alid attitude (evident in the passing over of 'Alī for succession), historical narrators in the eighth and ninth centuries worked under a lucky confluence of features that gave 'Umar's life the potential for what amounted in *ḥadīth* terms to a second Sīra. The exact circumstances in which this religious image of 'Umar was shaped are murky. But it is reasonable to assume that the exercise was heavily linked to the name of Ibn 'Abbās and most likely occurred in Iraq in the early ninth century, where various religious additions (Jewish, Christian, and Manichean) were incorporated into Islam and played a role in shaping Islamic law, exegesis, and historical narratives.

Whatever the origin of the Islamic legalistic rules in general and 'Umar's cases of *muwāfaqāt* in particular, the historical texts project an image of 'Umar as the keeper of the law, and this image appears woven in literary ways and with various intentions into the saga of 'Umar. A modern reading of 'Umar's biography must therefore begin with an appreciation of this orthodox emphasis in the various accounts. 'Umar's image as arbiter of the law is best exemplified in the tradition that describes his opinion as "*al-ḥaqq*" (the righteous position). Muḥammad is frequently reported as saying, "God placed righteousness in the mouth of 'Umar [*waḍa'a al-ḥaqqa 'alā lisāni 'Umar*]," [4] and "righteousness after me will lie with 'Umar, whatever he says [*al-ḥaqqu ba'dī ma' 'Umar aynamā kān*)."[5] Whereas the Prophet had turned to Abū Bakr for his skill in *ta'wīl* (interpretation), in the case of 'Umar, the Prophet emphasized 'Umar's *'ilm* and *fiqh* (jurisprudential knowledge): "If the knowledge of the Arabs was placed in one scale, and 'Umar's in another, the *'ilm* of 'Umar would prove the more weighty," the Prophet is reported as saying[6] in a *ḥadīth* that is a sure variation on a similar one regarding the faith (*imān*) of Abū Bakr.[7] Another companion would add that 'Umar's knowledge seemed as if it equaled nine-tenths of religious knowledge.[8] Muḥammad is said to have commented, "Were there to be a prophet after me, it would be 'Umar,"[9] but a less daring *ḥadīth* stresses inspiration by saying, "Every [religious] community had its inspired men in the past, and if any were to be in my nation it would be 'Umar."[10]

'Umar's mental world appears to be circumscribed by the law. Religious action for him was defined by boundaries of law that reflected either principles of equity and restraint (as was his ascetic bent) or the unquestioned code received from previous prophets. Questioning or interpreting the law was as dangerous as ignoring it, not least because it emboldened personal ambition, and the duty of authority was to ensure abidance within the community. 'Umar held a low view of human nature, somewhat akin to a Hobbesian view, and considered authority and the law to be necessary tools for keeping individual rights protected and on a straight path.

Closely related to this image of 'Umar as a guardian of the law is his frequent representation in the sources as an authoritarian, somewhat angry character. The depiction of 'Umar's heavy-handed style generally goes back to anecdotes about him during the Sīra of the Prophet, when 'Umar is portrayed as having started out as a sworn enemy of the new faith, like Paul in Christianity, who showed unrelenting hostility to new converts.[11] Evidence is scarce about 'Umar in this period, however, and such a tempestuous depiction was mainly intended to bolster his role as caliph (and in legal matters in general), when his strictness in applying the law, meting out punishments, and deprecating officials served edifying religious themes. Thus, from the start, "*haybat*" 'Umar (a quality roughly to be defined as presence) is cast as having an awe-inspiring quality,[12] and this caliph's anger with unruly officials and transgressors becomes the apotheosis for divine wrath—as Muḥammad would say, "The anger of 'Umar is something grave [*ghaḍabu 'Umar shay'un kabīr*]." The angel Gabriel reportedly declared to Muḥammad that 'Umar's satisfaction is a decree and his anger is glory ("*riḍāhu ḥukm wa ghaḍabuhu* 'izz").[13] The expression of severe authority was one extremity in the depiction of 'Umar as he gets characterized as "*shadīdun fi'l-ḥaqq*" (strict in pursuing truth and applying the law). Thus, the caliph would be depicted scolding important governors and commanders for their ambition and wealth with blows from his famous *darra* (whip), as he would family members and servants in his household. But at the same time, there was another extremity in his behavior, which was his compassion toward the weak and disenfranchised in the community.[14]

Moving between these two extremes of severity and compassion, later Muslim narrators constructed a fully human representation of 'Umar's character in every aspect of his life. The realism in depictions of 'Umar's inquisitive character, his turns of mood, his skepticism about people's motives, and his attitudes that show him at times confident and threatening but at others regretful and contrite, content, or simply gazing in reflection, all put his personality in a class by itself. 'Umar is a complete dramatic personality, fully existing within the parameters of reality and yet aiming to hold life at bay. This is certainly a far cry from 'Alī, whose image of one-dimensional piety and unchanging tone make his biography lack a real-life quality. 'Alī's straight-faced appearance, sober reflection on the world, and high-flying wisdom was fine for philosophers and mystics, but it made him little relevant to the everyday life of an average Muslim in ninth-century Baghdad or Damascus. The character of 'Umar, in contrast, spoke with a human relevance.

The caliph's religiosity and strict moral example are cast as the core model that kept the community faithful to principles and turned his reign into a divinely guided era. The many stories about his behavior and statements defy a historian's attempts to place them in a historical context, and can only show how this literature was meant to illustrate timeless messages of moral, social, and religious significance. That all the significant Arab battles against the Byzantines and the Sasanids are packed into the decade-long reign of 'Umar is also not to be viewed in strict historical terms. Conquest and ordinary behavior in Medina and various locales are not isolated subjects in the Islamic chronicles, but rather closely entwined and interdependent. These pivotal achievements, taking place after the erasure of the Ridda and the reuniting of Arab tribal solidarity, are shown as singularly symbolic of the miraculous in 'Umar's life and rule. And to this frame of embellished legend one can add the extensive attribution to 'Umar of various innovations that carry a structural, organizing character. Among these are the invention of the Hijrī calendar; the establishment of dīwans, taxation (*kharāj*) laws, and stipend levels of the conquerors; and the creation of new garrison cities in Basra, Kufa, Fusṭāṭ, and other locations.[15] While some of these innovations, such as building the new cities, were rooted in his reign, it is unlikely that all the administrative innovations depicted by such ninth-century writers as Abū Yūsuf in *Kitāb al-Kharāj* were created during the reign of 'Umar. It is more likely that ninth-century Sunnī jurists answered contemporary economic questions about the taxation of the agricultural lands of the Sawād in Irāq by attributing certain principles to the Rāshidūn caliphs, especially 'Umar. Like the name of Khusraw Anushirwan, 'Umar's name became an all-purpose touchstone for imagined idealized practices.[16] Both caliphs and jurists in later 'Abbāsid times shaped memories of the second caliph to provide a reference for the negotiating of legitimate political practice.

This memory of 'Umar from later times interacted with other idealizing perceptions of 'Umar by Christians and Jews from early times, who saw in him an unusual ruler guided by a mysterious force of destiny. 'Umar's conquest of Jerusalem was viewed by Christians in Syria opposed to the Church of Constantinople, and Jews—previously forbidden by the Byzantines from entering the city—as a political if not a religious redeemer. In a world constantly living on edge with the cataclysmic struggle between the Byzantines and the Sasanids in the early seventh century, expectations of a messianic figure were rife in Jewish and splinter Christian communities. 'Umar's extraordinary victories, combined with his ascetic reputation, must have sufficiently attracted the sympathy of outsiders to Islam, who viewed him in chiliastic terms as a redeemer, giving him the title "*al-fārūq*." His reign was viewed as the end of times, and it was believed that its end would bring about the apocalypse.[17] It was of little import that 'Umar came from Arabia or that the origin of Islam was tied to an Arabian prophet. To Jews of the time, what was good for Arabs at that hour was good for all Semites.[18] Islamic sources are not averse to divulging that it was "*ahl al-kitāb*" (the People of the Book) who first called the second caliph "*al-fārūq*."[19] However, where ambiguity arises in the sources is over what 'Umar's end signified. For, just as Christians and Jews saw the death of 'Umar as signifying the end of time, to the Arabs, especially when viewed after decades of civil strife of the mid seventh-century, the end of 'Umar's reign would mark the last moment of tranquility before the flood gates of civil war would open. 'Umar, therefore, has figured in history as a point of intersection of political and religious expectations, historical memory, and polemic.

## 'UMAR'S BIOGRAPHY AND ITS THEMES

The extant biography of 'Umar comprises a collection of *akhbār* and *ḥadīth* reports that appear carefully selected in the works of Ibn Sa'd, Balādhurī, and Ṭabarī. In spite of their commonalities, these sources do show some divergences in form if not in substance. Ibn Sa'd and Balādhurī, for example, essentially provide the same biographical entry on 'Umar, focusing less on historical topics than on religious themes (by recounting episodes of ascetic and legally pious behavior). The biographical format they provide consists of clearly distinct segments of *akhbār* in the following sequence: the story of 'Umar's conversion, an intermittent and carefully narrow phase of 'Umar's advice to the Prophet, the story of 'Umar's role in the succession of Abū Bakr, some stories about dealing with the effects of conquests (rather than the conquests themselves), stories about the caliph's asceticism, interaction with different officials and the arrangement of the *shūrā*, and finally a long and very carefully planned scene of the caliph's assassination. All later biographies derive their biographies of 'Umar from this essential framework, which provided a point of reference for jurists and *ḥadīth* scholars as much as for historians.[20]

Ṭabarī's biographical scheme stands in a class by itself, if only because his annalistic approach forced him to place anecdotes about the caliph under a specific year, whether dealing with 'Umar's conversion, the subject of the conquests, the organization of government, or the disputes over succession and tensions among the companions. This contextualized approach makes Ṭabarī seem more credible than other writers. However, a repeated reading of Ṭabarī shows the skeletal remains of a literary structure in 'Umar's biography that tied together the words and actions of carefully placed characters over a period of time with a beginning and an end. The historical length of 'Umar's reign and the memory of its momentous events allowed considerable space to build a drama of interaction among personalities, with plots both on the grand political/military level and the personal, mundane level. Despite minor differences in the various accounts, in the end all the different stories about 'Umar's reign come together to form a cohesive tale that can be appropriately termed the 'Umar saga or romance. Like other medieval romance tales, it chronicles a dialogue between the personal and universal (both political and religious), a clash of moral and religious imperatives; it wrestles with lingering flaws from a previous age and produces new ones. How Ṭabarī constructed a range of narratives to convey a process of clash and synthesis in history is a question that lies at the center of his interest in both Rāshidūn and Persian history. With the ideals of community, conviction, and equality present in one camp, and those of statecraft, strategy, and social organization present in the other, Ṭabarī was going to build up the story of 'Umar as the central drama for this epic struggle between two cultures.

On its surface, the organization of Ṭabarī's chronicle of this era may appear straightforward and mainly concerned with a set of obvious themes, such as *futūḥ* (conquests), *siyar* (lore), and *fitan* (civil strife within the community).[21] A distinction, however, needs to be made between the obvious level of recounting tales and the more indirect and allusive process of historical commentary. Medieval readers with an eye for inference and the seemingly unlikely correlation of accounts from different eras and with an awareness of a range of issues lying beneath the surface of any account would have approached the biography of 'Umar as a text that is unified with other accounts given by Ṭabarī for other periods. Characters and their actions during the conquest phase would be viewed by such readers as related to similar actions by the same characters or others during Ṭabarī's accounts of the later civil wars. The two phases would have been tied together by a set of religious, political, or moral issues that generated historical debate. Thus the biography of 'Umar provides a key example of Ṭabarī's approach, where the themes that are addressed indirectly shape his whole historical purpose behind the gathering of all these accounts into one book. We will explore here a set of themes that formed the foundation stones for an ironic and allusive debate in Ṭabarī's biography of 'Umar.

## *The Arab Body Politic*

One of the most easily overlooked themes in 'Umar's biography is the emphasis on "Arabism" as the defining feature of the Islamic state. This

Arabism is not to be perceived as a real ideological or nationalist affinity that existed in 'Umar's time, but rather as a social and cultural label that narrators used in describing a cycle of historical change that will be explained shortly. Throughout the descriptions of key Islamic battles on the Persian front (the Bridge, al-Qādisiya, and others), Ṭabarī provides vivid evocations of Arab imagery and literary expressions that are unmatched in similar situations on the Byzantine front. Images of the simple bedouin discovering in awe the riches of the world through the luxuries of Persian food, fine garments, and a new lifestyle are replete in the conquest narratives. Equally prevalent is the romanticized memory of the intrepid Arab horseman, who with a heroic spirit characteristic of the Jahiliyya days displays a musing poetic mind that is ever sensitive to the shadow of mortality and ready to deliver a spontaneous war song (*irtijāz*) to proudly reminisce about the deeds of his family and clan and hence immortalize their name through his final exploits. As such, conquest serves a historian's enterprise of literary and heroic nostalgia for an Arab culture long lost after the establishment of the 'Abbāsid empire, as much as it allows a basic recounting of reports of important battles.

At first this Arabo-centered depiction may not seem misplaced, given that the early Muslim conquerors were Arabs. Descriptions of how the various Arab tribes that had fought each other in the Ridda wars only a few years earlier rejoined forces later and waged a successful war against the Sasanids can seem the inevitable reflection of the historical record. However, a closer look at the sources shows that the focus on the Arabs in 'Umar's reign is more contrived than a mere reporting of events. A range of statements made by 'Umar in various anecdotes about his reign show a distinct bias in favor of the Arab element (as opposed to a broad category of outsiders—*mawālī, 'ajam, furs*), and the caliph's vision of the ideal Islamic state casts it as an Arab entity.[22]

The most glaring evidence of this bias surfaces during the scene of 'Umar's assassination, when the caliph, upon learning from his companions that his assassin was not an Arab, reportedly declared, "Thanks be to God that He did not make my killer someone who prayed to God even once," and added, "I knew the Arabs would not kill me [*mā kānat al-'arab li-taqtulanī*]."[23] He then berated Ibn 'Abbās for having enticed the *mawālī* to enter the peninsula and told him, "I used to caution you and your father about the danger of attracting these to Medina."[24] He said this at a time when al-'Abbās was said to be the biggest owner of slaves in Medina.

When Ibn 'Abbās offered to stop this trend, 'Umar told him in clear frustration, and possibly with a promise of things to come, "Now that they have prayed to the same *qibla* and learned your language!"[25] (i.e., now that they have converted to Islam).

These odd remarks, along with the unsual story of 'Umar's death, which will be examined below, are especially striking for using the terms "Arabs" and "Islam" interchangeably, even at a time when Christian Arabs were participants in the campaigns of conquest.[26] It is also noteworthy that, in spite of his pious depiction in the sources, 'Umar is never portrayed as having an interest in converting foreigners to Islam, even though he frequently issues guidelines on how to accept the surrender of towns and the submission of individual subjects.[27] To 'Umar, the association of Arabs and Islam is so central that the very fate of Islam in response to temptation and change is tied to the effect of change on the Arab lifestyle and behavior.

The Arabs are viewed by 'Umar not as a class of rulers at an early stage in history but as the very society of Islam. Their pre-Islamic geopolitical affinity continues to define their bond under Islam, and their ancient enmity toward the Sasanid empire continues to animate their struggle, as does their zeal for the faith. These old parameters also explain 'Umar's hesitance to expand the conquests beyond the culturally Arab lands of the Fertile Crescent (hence the initial aversion to conquering Egypt, venturing across the sea, and pushing into the Iranian heartland in the movement known as "*al-insiyāḥ*"). Guarding the Arab community, therefore, represents to 'Umar guarding the security of the faith. In 'Umar's view, any drastic change in the Arab mode of life threatens to influence the outlook of the religious community.

And here the reader is treated to an unusual extension to 'Umar's view of his community of subjects when he writes to his commanders and governors cautioning that they preserve the traditional lifestyle of the desert-bound Arabs (making the term "Arab" synonymous with "bedouin") and goes as far as creating a simile between the ecological conditions that affect the well being of the Arab and those that affect the camel. When 'Umar received word from Iraq that the Arabs had fallen ill and changed their color after settling there, he reportedly wrote to the governor, Sa'd, inquiring about what caused this change. "It must be the swamps of the area," Sa'd wrote back. 'Umar responded by saying: "The Arabs can only feel at home in a land that makes good grazing for the camel and the sheep"[28] and ordered him to send out Salmān to scout a location for a settlement close to sea and the hinterland.[29] This is to this day the apocryphal background that supposedly led to the establishment of the towns of Kufa and Basra. And elsewhere 'Umar extended the simile from biological to psychological when he made the camel symbolism cover issues of temperament and manner: "The Arabs are like a haughty camel following a leader, so let its leader be careful how to guide it. By God, I shall keep it on the straight path."[30] A long and complex history, therefore, links the fortunes of Islam and the circumstances of the Arab conquerors together. Social and economic influences on the Arab community are therefore viewed as capable of altering its cultural outlook and thus presage trends of moral temptation and change. The Arabs here become just another community in history that has presided over a perfect age and is about, like its predecessors, to experience a phase of sedition.

Not only the community is depicted in wholly Arab terms; even more, 'Umar is richly represented throughout his life as personifying in word and deed patterns of behavior that are quintessentially Arab, or even bedouin. In the way he leads a simple lifestyle in dress and diet, the way he speaks roughly with people in general and transgressors in particular, one finds in him a personification of a certain style and temperament that is exclusively bedouin and that will be romanticized later by the 'Abbāsid caliphs, not only for being straightforward but also for harkening back to the Arab ancestors, after the age of Persian domination and social integration set in. No other companion among the Rāshidūn caliphs shows a style that remotely resembles 'Umar's, even though they all grew out of the same social milieu in Mecca. There is more than a standard stress in the sources on 'Umar's alertness and vigor as a charismatic leader. There are rough edges, short spans of tolerance, and an overkill of reaction that is meant to stereotype 'Umar in a rustic bedouin way.[31] This would come to serve not only as a key to the wider scheme of the Arab nature of his rule, but would also shed light on the mentality and misguided use of these qualities later by the Khārijites, who are repeatedly represented as originating from a milieu of uncouth *a'rāb*, (bedouins usually associated with the loosely organized region of central Arabia) and of looking back on 'Umar with nostalgia as their model during their arguments with 'Alī.[32]

All this stress on the Arab theme leads one to ask: Why was 'Umar portrayed in this particular way, and what segment of narrators or current of thought would have benefited from or sought to craft this imagery? The answer has more to do with the Persian social and cultural milieu of Islamic society in the ninth century than it does with the seventh century. The romanticized and limiting parameters on the Arabism of 'Umar's reign reflect the view from Baghdad in later times, when the reign of 'Umar would come to be viewed as a moment of critical flux for the Islamic state, a moment when the rigid hierarchy of the Persian state was replaced by an egalitarian and cohesive new society. Reports of 'Umar's Arab ways of behavior were meant to function as extensions to the memory of the Sīra and to illustrate a new social *sunna* that debated monarchical and cultural values of the Sasanid state. 'Umar's Arabo-centered style was also tied to a dialogue that narrators tried to establish between his symbolic role and that of 'Alī, as we shall examine below.

### *The Persian Theme: Sasanid Persia as an Errant State*

In equal measure to his focus on Arabian tribal themes, Ṭabarī's chronicle shows a heavy preoccupation with Iranian affairs. Ṭabarī's recounting of events in the Sasanid period follows the same rich storytelling mode that he uses in writing about Islamic history. He includes details on Sasanid rulers, providing texts of imperial proclamations, speeches, and edicts laden with a moralizing language that would have been culturally accessible to a medieval Islamic society. The story of Sasanid political history was probably also viewed as interacting closely with the history of divine revelations. Political history examined secular themes relating to government, hierarchy, and wise strategy, while religious stories explored the periodic voice of revelation that stood in dialogue with the fortunes of the Iranian state, always transforming the latter yet never destroying it. Just before the arrival of Islam, Ṭabarī and Dīnawarī describe at length prosperous and tumultuous phases in the Sasanid polity under the beleaguered ruler Khusraw Parviz, who could be considered a counterpart to the caliph 'Uthmān. From a phase of stability, we see the accidental transition in Parviz's jealous rivalry with a virtuous yet misunderstood governor of Khurāsān, Bahram Chubin; then follows treachery, rebellion by kinsmen, reconquest, and eventual regicide, which set the Iranian state on a downward course of chaos, incompetent leadership, and vanity.

One senses from the drift of Ṭabarī's narratives that the Arab conquest of Iran not only represented the fulfillment of a religious promise for the Arabs, but also an inevitable judgment of history for the Sasanid state. With the coming of Islam, the Iranian state was on the verge of a correcting turn that would pave the way for its eventual revival. The standoff between the powerful and overconfident Sasanid army and a weak coalition of Arabian tribes recasts the confrontation between Pharaoh and the Israelite tribes—and the result is meant to be seen as just as miraculous as the earlier event even if the reporting sounds realistic. Narrators of the conquests were fond of describing the wealth and exotic booty acquired from victories on the Persian front in a way that finds no parallel in accounts of victories on the Byzantine front. The narrative of the conquest builds to its peak when we see the Arab army performing prayer in the White Palace of Khusraw and reciting the verse, "How many gardens and fountains they left, and a bountiful, noble station. And what prosperity they rejoiced in! Even so; and We bequeathed them upon another people."[33] Suddenly the promise of the afterlife and the promise in this world seem to converge at that hour. And when the caliph 'Umar in Medina soon afterward informs the community of this victory and begins to show apprehension of how wealth and victory can provide a source of temptation and sedition for the community, we get the impression that the story of Iran's conquest is finished long before Yazdajird meets his final fall, which would actually come about in the reign of 'Uthmān. The notion of a full Sasanid surrender was probably assigned to 'Umar's reign in the sources because he represented the ideal ruler whose justice and equity earned him the image of "*al-sulṭān al-'ādil*" in later Islamic memory. The second caliph's appeal was thus anchored not only in his pious behavior, but also in his reviving of sound government practice, political hierarchy, and the bonds of community loyalty. As such, this caliph synthesized the ranks of emperor and religious leader and thus conflated the cosmic mysteries of both characters under a new state.[34]

However, even 'Umar was not immune to the early Islamic conception of history as cyclical, punctuated by turning points of temptation and fall. Success contained within it the seeds of sedition, and the wealth of conquests would soon lead the new conquerors down a path of jealousy and rivalry that 'Umar warned would lead to division in the community and the turning away of divine favor.[35] On various occasions he repeated this, most notably when news of the conquest of Khurāsān and the fall of Yazdajird came. At that juncture he declared, in a tone not unlike the Prophet's at *ḥijjat al-wadā'*, "Do not change your ways, lest God replace you with other people [*lā tubbaddilū fa-yastabdil ghayrakum*]." These words were no doubt crafted by narrators to be in dialogue with the Qur'ānic verse that reads, "If you turn away, He will substitute another people instead of you, then they will not be your likes [*yastabdil qawman ghayrakum thumma lā yakūnū amthālakum*]."[36] Later, Sunnī thinkers would go a step farther in interpreting this Qur'ānic verse, saying that the reference to "another people" meant the Persian nation, which would become the new guardian of the Islamic mission.[37]

The theme of Iranian revival in the Islamic historical narratives was not only tied to the corrupting influence of wealth on the Arab conquerors. It was also tied to the growth of the Hāshimite cause in Iran and the growth of the *ḥadīth* spirit in Iranian society. The region of Khurāsān would serve as the regional nucleus for these two diverse currents (one Shī'ī, another Sunnī) that sometimes overlapped and on the whole gave Khurāsān a mythical image as the new base of the Islamic message. Khurāsānī support for the Hāshimite revolt against the Umayyads is usually the main claim to fame of this region, but it should not be forgotten that all four *ḥadīth* scholars who resisted al-Ma'mūn's Miḥna program came from Marw, including the eminent Aḥmad b. Ḥanbal, and that all the arbiters of the *ḥadīth* canon in the later ninth-century came from that region as well. The centrality of the Iranian converts in the shaping of Islam's fortunes was therefore not lost on historical narrators, who wove political, religious, and *shu'ūbī* (nationalist) factors in telling the story of the Rāshidūn caliphate and conquests.

### *The Succession Theme: The Silent Rivalry with 'Alī*

The choice of 'Umar as the prime leader to whom Persia submitted, as we have said, was partly connected to the orthodox image of this caliph in later times, but the heavy association of Persia's conquest with 'Umar's name is probably tied to an issue that may seem an altogether different topic, namely the controversy over succession to the caliphate and over whether the Hāshimites (i.e., Alī) ought to have been selected for the caliphate rather than another companion (Abū Bakr, 'Umar, and 'Uthmān) who was viewed as more excellent in Sunnī Islam. The dispute takes on special significance when the image of 'Umar is considered, since he played the critical role at the Saqīfa of Banū Sā'ida, as we saw earlier, by pushing Abū Bakr forward for leadership and stamping out dissent. Although the main clash of that incident lay between the Muhājirūn and the Anṣār—and in particular between 'Umar and Sa'd b. 'Ubāda—the shadow of 'Alī's victimization there is hard to miss, even without his active involvement. Throughout those first years of succession, Persia was still Sasanid, while any Islamic preoccupation with a war outside Ḥijāz lay with the Ridda wars. Yet, insofar as Persia in general (and Khurāsān in particular) will later rise as the chief patron of the 'Alid and Hāshimite cause and will be remembered as acting in a historical role parallel to that of the Anṣār in early times, those early events in the succession dispute were not, in the long term, marginal to Persia's political involvement on the 'Alid side, nor to its eventual resurgence during the 'Abbāsid revolution. An 'Alid-Persian tie in the narratives and an 'Umar-Arab one formed a division that permeates throughout the early history.[38]

'Umar and 'Alī each appear as a patron of one camp and as apprehensive about anything associated with the other side, as if in wary anticipation of how the *a'rāb* (Khārijites) would undermine the 'Alid caliphate and of how Khurāsānīs would torpedo the 'Umarī structure that gave rise to the Arabo-Umayyad state. 'Umar, for example, speaks of "*al-a'rāb*" as the source of the Arabs and the lifeline of Islam ("*aṣl al-'Arab wa māddat al-Islām*"), and he strongly advises proper treatment of the Arab constituency.[39] 'Alī, by contrast, shows a greater affinity to issues that deal with Persia. This duality of positions surfaced when news of the conquest of Khurāsān reportedly reached 'Umar. When al-Aḥnaf b. Qays, a future ally of 'Alī during the civil war, wrote to 'Umar about this conquest, the caliph was described as becoming unhappy with the news and saying, "Would that I had not sent an army to that region. Would that there was between us and them a sea of fire." This reaction prompted 'Alī to comment, "And why is that, O Commander of the Faithful? This is indeed an occasion for celebration (*inna dhalika la-mawḍi' surūr*)." 'Umar then said, "The People [of Khurāsān] will burst forth [from that region] on three occasions, and they will be destroyed on the third. I prefer that this should happen to its own people rather than to the Muslims."[40] On a previous occasion, 'Alī is also made to link 'Umar with the Arabs. When 'Umar consulted the companions on whether he should lead the Islamic army at Qādisiyya, 'Alī cautioned against this, saying, "Were the Persians (*al-a'ājim*) to see you in the battlefield, they would then say to each other, 'This is the king of the Arabs and the lifeline of the Arabs ('*hādhā amīr al-'Arab wa aṣl al-'Arab*').' And then they would be more persistent and ferocious in the fight to reach you."[41] Had the Islamic chronicles been written more as factual recordings than as storytelling, the reference to 'Umar as "*amīr al-'Arab*" could have been interpreted as historically real, but in the thick of an allusive discourse, 'Alī's words imagining what the Persians would say really reflects how a pro-Persian view from later times sought to limit 'Umar's actual leadership with a touch of irony. 'Alī on that occasion may have been offering sound advice, but this advice was also made to imply that 'Umar was commander of the "Arabs" ("*amīr al-'Arab*"), but not truly of the "non-Arabs," who were being anticipated as the future community of Islam (or of 'Alī).

Once we recognize the symbolic association of 'Umar with the Arabs and 'Alī with the Persian converts, then the whole relation of 'Alī with 'Umar and the early caliphate has to be reexamined and stretched beyond the boundaries of 'Umar's reign. The two personalities maintained their national associations long before the conquest of Persia or the support of the *mawālī* for the 'Alid cause at Ṣiffīn and beyond. 'Umar and 'Alī represented different political programs tied to the question of how the caliph's office was to be defined—whether in religious terms, as a successor to the Prophet, hence making the caliph (a descendant within the Prophet's family) the religious guide of the community without any particular attachment to one group over another, or in political terms, as the senior representative of a community that prophecy had left behind, thus explaining the focus on the Muhājirūn and Arabia's Arab community (which dealt with Muḥammad in his lifetime) as the holders of political authority. Only when we bind the religious controversy over caliphal succession with the national anticipation of the expansion of Islam beyond Arabia into Persia does the entire reported debate about succession to the Prophet become intelligible.

On the surface, relations between 'Umar and 'Alī are portrayed as cooperative. 'Alī, as is well known, acts out the role of counselor to 'Umar, giving occasional sound advice, as he did just before Qādisiyya. However, even with this alleged closeness, 'Alī appears on the whole throughout this period as a coerced or silenced figure. His absence in the reigns of Abū Bakr and 'Umar (except in the dispute with Abū Bakr over the early succession and the advice to 'Umar on whether to lead the conquests in person) is glaring in the narratives,[42] and one can only interpret this as a deliberate literary strategy meant to silence his claims to the caliphate in the years of the first two Rāshidūn and thus to avoid a head-on clash between 'Alī and the two leading companions. Still, evidence can be pieced together to show that narrators did intend to communicate, beyond the surface Sunnī reading, a certain degree of tension and conflict between 'Umar and 'Alī.

To discern this subtext, one must read 'Umar's actions indirectly. At the Saqīfa of Banū Sā'ida, for example, 'Umar's main fight was with Sa'd b. 'Ubāda and the Anṣār, who according to one version supported the 'Alid claim for succession. Whether the Anṣār-'Alid link is true or not, there is no doubt that in suppressing the dissent of Sa'd b. 'Ubāda, 'Umar was indirectly rebuking 'Alī for refusing to partake in the *bay'a*.[43] 'Umar's exaggerated reaction also reflects the militancy of the later ninth-century Sunnī attitude toward dissent from the *jamā'a*, specifically Shī'ism, and is meant to undermine any notion of a Shī'ī messianic view of the caliphal office. *Shūrā* had had its hour, but in the end the unanimity of the *jamā'a* had to rule.

For his part, 'Alī is not shown explicitly endorsing the Anṣār or any other specific candidate at the Saqīfa. He seems like an unwitting participant in a predestined plan that was constantly pushing him away from his right to test his religious resolve and pose a trial for the community. However, when 'Uthmān is selected as caliph by another *shūrā* after 'Umar's death, the deliberate drive to push 'Alī aside becomes very obvious. 'Abd al-Raḥmān b. 'Awf had reenacted at that *shūrā* a role similar to 'Umar's earlier role at the Saqīfa, and there was no more doubt that a succession story was being cooked to serve Sunnī aims and beliefs. At that juncture we finally hear 'Alī commenting in exasperation, "*khida'tun wa ayyu khid'a*" (what a deception this has been), in reference to how the succession had been lost.

Open enmity between 'Umar and 'Alī is absent in the sources, but one finds it in the margins, whether through the symbolic national affiliation we spoke of or through statements and unusual attitudes expressed toward secondary actors and well-known protégés on opposite sides of the Sunnī-Shī'ī fence. When later in his life 'Alī challenges 'Ubaydallāh b. 'Umar to a duel at the Battle of Ṣiffīn, 'Ubaydallāh, after having sought out a champion for the duel, refuses to confront 'Alī. When 'Alī returned to his camp, his son Muḥammad then commented, "Father, you put yourself in the face of that sinner [*al-fāsiq*]? Why, even if his father were in his place, I would have guarded you from deigning to fight him." To this 'Alī replies, "My son, let us not say but what is good about his father."[44] The message here is that 'Alī, who has suppressed negative feelings toward 'Umar, is now disclosing these feelings in a way that is supposedly only corrective of his son's manners rather than being political in substance.

For his part, 'Umar is made to vent his anti-'Alid hostility on historical actors who became some of the most ardent supporters of 'Alī later on, such as 'Ammār b. Yāsir and 'Abdallāh b. Budayl, long before these two showed signs of turning to one side or the other. In a dispute between a delegation of the people from Kufa and their disputed governor 'Ammār, 'Umar sides strongly with the Kufans, accusing 'Ammār of lying, and takes their word as grounds for dismissing him from the governorship.[45] Although 'Umar's appeasement of the Kufans was not new, as he did something similar for Sa'd b. Abī Waqqāṣ a year earlier,[46] 'Umar's rough treatment of 'Ammār is noticeably harsh and is meant no doubt to show the lack of affinity between supporters of 'Alī and 'Umar in general. 'Umar's treatment of 'Abdallāh b. Budayl also reflects the deliberate deprecation of a future 'Alid supporter.[47] These instances stand in stark contrast to 'Umar's gentle treatment of individuals who later became 'Alī's enemies, such as Ziyād b. Abīhi, al-Mughīra b. Shu'ba, and even Mu'āwiya.[48]

Other elliptical swipes between 'Umar and 'Alī are worked into representations that date much farther back than the Rāshidūn era. During the time of the Prophet, we know for instance that 'Alī appears in much greater proximity and favor to the Prophet than 'Umar. At the Battle of Uḥud, we read the unflattering note that 'Umar was one of those who retreated in battle ("*wa kāna min man inkashafa yawma uḥud min man ghufira lahu*").[49] And at the Battle of Khaybar, Ṭabarī relates how, on the day before the battle, the Prophet announced that he would give his banner the next day to someone beloved to God and His prophet. The narrator says: "When that day came, Abū Bakr and 'Umar each hoped it [the banner] would be his," with the narrator using an Arabic phrasing that is significantly unflattering to the first two caliphs: "*fa-taṭāwala lahā Abū Bakr wa 'Umar.*" But then the banner was given to 'Alī.[50]

## *The Theme of Wise Political Strategy (al-Ra'y)*

In spite of his pious preoccupation and his disinterest in the material world, 'Umar is represented in the sources as having an appreciation for sound judgment. This quality of "*al-ra'y*" (sound rational opinion) was applied, mostly in Ṭabarī's chronicle, to political and military matters. There are numerous instances when 'Umar consulted his commanders about the soundest course of action by asking, "*aḥdirū al-ra'y*" or "*ashīrū 'alayy*." The most notable of these instances comes when 'Umar discussed whether he should lead the Islamic armies to Qādisiyya in person.[51] After much deliberation, the caliph opted to stay behind, but only after wise counsel showed that the enemy might be emboldened if they knew of his presence. In a similar vein, 'Umar later advised Sa'd b. Abī Waqqāṣ to send a delegation from the people of "*al-ra'y*" to debate Rustam.[52] The caliph encouraged the selection of a team from "*ahl al-najda wa'l-ra'y wa'l-quwwa wa'l-'idda*"[53] to help Sa'd make decisions.

As the record shows, most of those who offered 'Umar the seasoned opinions he needed to extend the conquests, safeguard the community, and stamp out opposition were primarily political figures: al-Mughīra b. Shu'ba, 'Amr b. al-'Āṣ, Mu'āwiya b. Abī Sufyān, and Ziyād b. Abīhi. These individuals all had a reputation for being crafty leaders—long before Islam, in the case of some—who knew not only the right decisions at difficult junctures, but also what to say to 'Umar and when to say it. 'Umar's reliance on such religiously dubious figures stressed a theme that underlay Sunnī political philosophy in the ninth century, namely that political office (whether military, gubernatorial, or caliphal) required not the most pious person, but the one most experienced in strategy and politics. 'Umar asked al-Mughīra b. Shu'ba who he thought should hold the governorship of Kufa after the dismissal of 'Ammār b. Yāsir, "Do you think a weak Muslim or a strong man is suitable? [*mā taqūlūn fī tawliyat rajulin ḍa'īfin Muslimin aw rajulin qawiyyin mushaddad*?]." Al-Mughīra answered, "A weak Muslim will have his faith for himself [*islāmuhu li-nafsihi*] and his weakness shall fall upon you, but the strong man, his strength is for himself and the Muslims." "Then we shall send you, O Mughīra," 'Umar replied.[54]

Never again would 'Umar commit the blunder he did in A.H. 14/A.D. 636, when he removed the competent chief of the Bakr b. Wā'il, al-Muthannā b. Ḥāritha, a veteran of years of fighting the Sasanids in southern Iraq, from the Islamic command to which Abū Bakr had assigned him, and replaced him with the obscure Abū 'Ubayd al-Thaqafī, an untested soldier who came from the town of Ṭā'if, hundreds of miles away. Abū 'Ubayd may have impressed the caliph with his zeal, being the first to volunteer for an unpopular and slow-going campaign of mobilization in Medina against the Sasanids. However, the many elaborate accounts that follow about the Battle of the Bridge and the defeat that ensued under Abū 'Ubayd's command describe less history than an incident of folly, showing the poor judgment of that commander. Against all advice from al-Muthannā that the Arab army should wait for the Persians to cross to the southern side of the Euphrates river, Abū 'Ubayd refused, saying, "We shall not let them be more daring to fight than we are!" Soon after, these words proved to be the new commander's last, as the Arab army crossed the river piecemeal to face the Persian army in its perfect defensive position. Abū 'Ubayd would enter history as someone who abandoned the use of "*al-ra'y*" (sound strategy) and brought about a defeat as embarrassing as the Battle of Uḥud during the Sīra. With considerable effort, al-Muthannā was able to save the remnants of the troops, but he would later comment about Abū 'Ubayd, as would other commanders, "We told him so," and 'Umar would shed tears for the loss of so many of his troops as the result of his decision. He became careful not to seek out brash zealots over experienced men as commanders, and he would defer to the wisdom of the first caliph, who had relied on al-Muthannā, when he said, "May God's mercy be upon Abū Bakr, he knew men better than I do." This lesson, however, would never register fully with 'Alī.

The theme of *ra'y* appeared widely in the narratives of early Islam in spheres of morality and politics. In the biography of 'Umar, this theme was used to stress a main difference between this caliph and 'Alī. 'Alī, as we shall see in chapter 6, refused to appoint the aforementioned officials of 'Umar, even if that meant the disintegration of his rule in the provinces. To 'Alī, political war was a crusade of virtue, and he stigmatized any attempt at compromise (in other words, sound strategy) as something bordering on hypocrisy (*idhān*). Thus, 'Alī would be haunted by political setbacks.

All these themes converged in shaping the key structure of 'Umar's biography in the chronicles. We shall examine next how widely different narratives set in 'Umar's reign indirectly revolved around these aforementioned themes. While admired for structuring the Islamic state and enforcing religious law, 'Umar would also be viewed as being indirectly responsible for generating the Hāshimite tragedy by thwarting 'Alī's chances for succession and appointing Mu'āwiya to the governorship of Syria, where future tragedies against the Hāshimites would be born. Discerning this perspective in the early texts—is at once submissive and subversive of 'Umar, and looks on Persia's conversion to Islam as a stepping stone for reviving the Hāshimite cause is an elusive task in the midst of different voices that advocate Jamā'ī-Sunnī, 'Alid, and Sasanid views within the same narrative. In the next section we shall examine how these themes unfold in the story of the conquests and the legends about 'Umar.

## MORALITY AS THE GROUNDS OF THE ARAB-SASANID CONTEST

The religious coloring of the early Islamic conquests often leads readers into conceiving of these campaigns as a crusade anchored in a conflict over religion. Their representation in the chronicles, however, can point to a different understanding. True, the Islamic message is constantly repeated in the Arab embassies to the Sasanid officials prior to war, and the memory of the Prophet Muḥammad is glorified. A close look, however, shows that the dispute is based not on religious doctrine so much as on certain facets of morality that were seen to have died in the Sasanid lands (although these moral codes are portrayed as having once flourished there) and come to life again in Arabia with Islam. The clash is between two systems of values rather than a dispute over the prophecy of Muḥammad, and the rivalry is between camps with opposite social characters and ethical views of historical change. The Sasanid leaders are portrayed as a class of landed elite, overconfident in their power and condescending toward lower classes and outsiders, while the Arabs are represented as unified and willing to follow leaders of different affiliations.

Intensely frustrated with the arrogance of his subordinate commanders, Rustam, the supreme Sasanid commander at Qādisiyya, confirms this message when he rebukes his lieutenants after the visit of an Arab envoy, telling them that their own behavior created the conditions that made them the target of conquest:

> By God, O people of Persia, the Arab [ambassador] was right. It was our evil deeds that brought this to us. . . . There was certainly a time when God made you victorious over your enemies and gave you firm control of the land because of your proper behavior, opposition to oppression, fulfillment of covenants, and generosity to others. But now that you have abandoned this conduct and turned yourselves to such [evil] deeds, I can just see how God will turn you over, and I fear he will discharge you of authority.[55]

The problem, therefore, lies in a leadership turned vain and abusive toward its subjects. Understanding Rustam's character and role in the story of the conquests is pivotal to gauging the medieval view of the Islamic conquests and their historical significance. Although some accounts make Rustam a skilled astrologer and depict him as having feared ominous astral changes,[56] more often his anxiety is depicted as deriving from wisdom and deference to the Islamic principles. In various other statements, such as the one quoted above, he appears frustrated with his commanders more because of their vanity and arrogance than because of their military failure. Rustam is a lone voice of Persian wisdom, acting out the role of victim and historical commentator. Combining an understanding of signs with a sense of coming social change, Rustam recognizes, for instance, that when Yazdajird ordered the leader of the Arab delegation, 'Āṣim b. 'Amr, to carry a sack of Persian soil on his back and ride back to Arabia, this did more than level a humiliation on a delegation member who claimed to be "*ashraf al-qawm*" (the most noble of the delegation members): it also served as an omen of the loss of Persian land.[57] If foreign heads of states or social elite were kinsmen in destiny ("*ashrāfu al-nās ṭabaqa ka-mā anna awḍā'āhum ṭabaqa*"), as the caliph al-Ma'mūn used to say, then Yazdajird had just symbolically yielded his inheritance to another counterpart in this class of leaders. Later we are told that Rustam had premonitions of the conquests when, on the eve of the battle with the Arabs, he saw in a dream an angel descend from the heavens, seal the weapon of Persia, and hand it over to the caliph 'Umar.[58]

The contrast on the Persian side is most stark between the portraits of Rustam and of Yazdajird. The Persian emperor is depicted consistently as conceited, vain, temperamental, and hasty to the extent that he accelerates the coming of defeat. His negative reaction to the Arab embassies, diversely portrayed by various narrators before Qādisiyya and Nihāwand, becomes a favorite theme in the stories leading up to battle. When a certain al-Mughīra b. Zurāra leads an Arab embassy to Yazdajird just before the Battle of Qādisiyya, the emperor strongly chides him for coming to him with a message, telling him that his race had long been viewed by Persians as "the weakest, most wretched, and most miserable of people." Here al-Mughīra is shown first as agreeing that this is "indeed the way we were," but then he sets out to describe how things have changed since the appearance of Muḥammad, who introduced the Arabs to the worship of the One God and eliminated injustice, internal rivalries, and social inequities.[59]

This entire scene is built up as a parallel to the Qur'ānic standoff between Moses and Pharaoh, Muḥammad and Abū Jahl, reflecting the contrast between the humility of the faithful and the hubris of the powerful and concluding with the emperor's yielding a sign of the promised land with the aforementioned loss of Persian soil.[60] The attitude of Yazdajird toward these embassies is negative, without exception (unlike the case of Heraclius, who on more than one occasion is shown as having been inclined sympathetically to Islam); in this way the narrators carefully intended to rob him of any flattering behavior, strengthen the juxtaposition with Rustam, and explain the total conquest of Persia prophesied by Muḥammad. Yazdajird's pride is also built up to make his eventual tragic death in Marw redemptive for his political life-cycle.[61]

Throughout the war with the Arabs, Rustam stands out as the only leader with a chance of saving the Persian nation. The fact that he was the defender of the "*thaghr*" of Khurāsān (being the son of the Ispahbadh of Khurāsān)[62] prior to being summoned by Būrān, who was briefly a caretaker of the crown before Yazdajird's accession, was something that no doubt resonated with symbolic importance to a medieval Muslim audience that saw Khurāsān eventually rising to become the gateway to revolution and Islamic revival under the 'Abbāsids. In the end, however, whatever advantages Rustam had gained as strategist and wise counselor, first to Būrān and later to Yazdajird, were taken from him by the very situation in which he found himself trapped. His predicament lies in the fact that he is called on to lead a campaign that he knows is doomed to failure, and so he finds himself caught between his loyalty toward his suzerain and his sense that it is his duty to reform the Sasanid realm and return it to its founding moral principles.[63]

## *'Umar and Hurmuzān*

Yazdajird and Rustam represent polar opposites in Ṭabarī's representation of their view of the Arabs. However, it is really Rustam whose opinion is meant to be seen as representing the true soul of the Persian state. As long as he is not defeated in battle, Rustam tells Yazdajird, "the people of Persia will keep their hopes on me." Then he asks that another commander, perhaps Jalinus, be sent instead, until it becomes absolutely necessary that he join the war.[64] Rustam's trepidation here mirrors 'Umar's reluctance to lead the Arab armies in person in the mobilization for Qādisiyya, and the argument cited by Rustam (that the enemy will fight more boldly in order to capture the enemy leader) is the same argument used by the *ṣaḥāba* to dissuade the caliph from leading the campaign in person.[65] The elements of *ra'y* and *makīda* that Rustam fails to attain because of Yazdajird's overruling him become aspects that lead to the success of the Islamic strategy when 'Umar stays behind in Medina. 'Umar and Rustam are therefore the true counterparts in opposition, despite Yazdajird's nominal leadership. Still, the two opponents never come face to face and are only related in a surreal outcry of frustration that Rustam utters just before the armies clash at Qādisiyya: "'Umar has eaten my liver!"[66]

The task of a real personal standoff with the caliph is shifted instead to Hurmuzān, another member of the Persian political leadership, who engages the caliph in dialogue about the historical significance of their confrontation. This occurs in a debate that provides a symbolic portrait of the rivalry between the two powers, set in the context of the story of Hurmuzān's surrender to 'Umar in Medina. Hurmuzān, the uncle of the former monarch Qubadh II (known as Shiruy) and governor of the region of Ahwāz,[67] played a pivotal role in regrouping the Persian defenses after the Battle of Qādisiyya, scoring some significant success in holding back the conquests. With the gradual fall of Khuzistān, however, we are told that Hurmuzān fortified himself in Tustar and put up a tenacious fight there. The account of the siege of Tustar, led by Abū Mūsā al-Ash'arī, includes some very vivid descriptions of individual heroism, especially that of al-Barā' b. Mālik, who is credited with breaching the defenses of the city in a brave manner not unlike the one he displayed when he took the lead in breaking through the fortified enclosure of Musaylima at Yamāma in the Ridda war. Al-Barā''s military achievement was critical in pushing Hurmuzān to consider surrender. Still, Hurmuzān reportedly showed that he had the ability to resist. Having fortified himself in the town's citadel, he engaged in combat at a leisurely pace, coming out occasionally to engage in individual duels, two of which brought about the deaths of a pair of well-known companions, al-Barā' b. Mālik and Majza'a b. Thawr. The Persian governor declared that he would stop fighting only if he were allowed to surrender to the caliph in Medina. Otherwise, he said, "My quiver holds a hundred arrows, and I would not leave before I kill as many of you as these arrows can take." So in his first brush with political compromise, Abū Mūsā accepted the terms, and Hurmuzān, accompanied by Anas b. Mālik and al-Aḥnaf b. Qays (and twelve Iranian chiefs, according to one version),[68] was sent to Medina, where the crucial story begins.

The narrative of Hurmuzān's arrival in Medina and meeting with 'Umar is described in great detail by Ṭabarī. A reader can virtually sense the pulse of daily life in Medina in that account. Ṭabarī describes how, when the conquest embassy arrived with Hurmuzān (who was dressed in his official regalia and crown to impress the caliph), they initially had trouble finding the caliph. Having not found him at his residence, the group reportedly started wandering about the area of the mosque, looking for him, until they were spotted by a group of children playing in that area. When the children saw the new arrivals, they asked who they were looking for and directed the group to the caliph, said to have been sleeping in the right wing of the mosque with his cloak folded under his head for a pillow ("*mutawassidun burnusahu*").[69] All the details in this account, minor and unnecessary by the standards of a conventional chronicle, are indispensable here in casting the image of a utopian world thriving under 'Umar in Medina at the time. The children are a metaphor for the subjects of the caliph, and their precocious inquisitiveness represents the vigilance of the community as a whole. In one sense, the children in this story may be seen to provide a parallel to or evolution of another group of children that 'Umar famously protects by saving them from the brink of starvation on one of his night journeys in Medina.[70] 'Umar himself is shown to be withdrawn from active political life by virtue of the success of a new system of values and the victory of belief.

The Islamic historical commentary about the scene so far is then given to Hurmuzān, who is described as incredulous at how the Arab ruler could live so ascetically, without any guards or associates, after the

Islamic victories. "He must be a prophet," Hurmuzān tells his guards, but those in Hurmuzān's company tell him, "He is not a prophet, but he lives up to the prophetic model." Amid the commotion of a growing crowd, 'Umar is shown awakening from his sleep. He then reportedly looked at the prisoner at length and said, as if in anticipation, "Are you Hurmuzān?" "Yes," the latter replied. 'Umar then declared, "Praise be to God, who has humbled this man and his followers through Islam." He then stated that he would have nothing to say to him until the latter was stripped of his ornaments and dressed in simple garb.[71] When this was duly done, Hurmuzān sat down before the caliph, and a remarkable conversation then took place. 'Umar began by saying, "Hey, Hurmuzān, how do you look now upon the evil consequences of your perfidy and the outcome of God's command [*kayfa ra'yta wabāl al-ghadr wa 'āqibata amri allāh*]?" Hurmuzān replied, "In the days before Islam, 'Umar, God left things between us and you as they were, so we had the upper hand over you, since He was neither with us nor with you. But when he took your side, you gained the upper hand over us." To this 'Umar replied, "You only succeeded in defeating us in the days before Islam because you were united, whereas we were divided. But [what now] is your excuse . . . for going to war against us time after time?" Hurmuzān here said, "I fear that you will kill me before I have told you." "No, do not be afraid," 'Umar assured him. Then, when Hurmuzān asked for something to drink and was brought water in a primitive cup, he said, "Even if I were to die of thirst, I could not possibly drink from a cup like this." So he was brought some water in a vessel he approved of. But then his hand began to tremble and he said, "I am afraid that I will be killed while I am drinking." 'Umar then said, "No harm will come to you until you have drunk it." Hereupon Hurmuzān spilled the water by turning the vessel upside down. "Give him some more," 'Umar ordered, "[and don't push on him thirst and death at once.]"

Then Hurmuzān spoke, "I do not need water; what I wanted was that you grant me immunity." 'Umar then said, "I shall certainly kill you," but Hurmuzān interrupted and said, "But you have already granted me immunity." "I shall certainly kill you," shouted 'Umar, but Hurmuzān again asserted, "But you have already granted me immunity." "You lie," roared 'Umar. Anas (b. Mālik) here intervened and said, "He is right, Commander of the Faithful, you have indeed granted him safety." "Woe unto you, Anas," said 'Umar to him. "Should I grant immunity to the killer of

Majza'a and al-Barā'? By God, think of a subterfuge or I shall surely chastise you!"

Anas then explained, "You did tell him that no harm would come to him before he had told you what you asked him, and you also told him that no harm would come to him until he had drunk the water." Then all those who were standing around 'Umar joined in, telling him the same thing. 'Umar approached Hurmuzān and said, "You have [deceived] me [*laqad khada'tanī*] and, by God, I shall not be hoodwinked by anyone who is not a Muslim." So Hurmuzān embraced Islam.[72]

The description of Hurmuzān's surrender in this account does more than describe a limited event of personal surrender or a defiant exchange. This narrative was essentially symbolic of the standoff between two worlds, the Perso-Sasanid and the Arab-Islamic, and was meant to raise key moral questions concerning the historical meaning of the Islamic conquest and the character and role of the Persian nation before and after Islam. Hurmuzān speaks on behalf of a fallen kingdom, articulating the voice of its vanquished elite.[73] He is shown appreciating the turn in Persia's fortunes and explaining defeat in light of revelation. Curiously, 'Umar does not confirm Hurmuzān's invocation of a religious argument but rather casts the explanation of change in strictly moral terms. To 'Umar, the Persian state was successful when it acted in unity while the Arabs were divided, and on the whole the caliph shows a greater interest in the ideal functioning of politics—why the Sasanid state worked as a political system—than in how that empire reacted toward Islam. Unity, loyalty, and conviction in one's beliefs represent for 'Umar the key reasons governing the rise and fall of states.

Still, one should be aware that Hurmuzān is not entirely a broken figure. Rather, he acts more like an adopted political ally. A major intention of this story was basically to elucidate the terms on which the Persian state established its entry into the political fold of Islam, and Hurmuzān's surrender personified this accommodation. It was this act of debate and conversion by Hurmuzān at the hands of 'Umar, more than Qādisiyya and Nihāwand, that narrators probably saw as establishing the submission of Persia. Hurmuzān's refusal to surrender to anyone but the caliph gives a sign from the outset of the Tustar agreement that Persian political loyalty and official submission can be enacted only at the highest level of the political hierarchy. Religious conversion and political allegiance were closely interconnected acts in the event of surrender; and hence Hurmuzān could not give in to any commander in the field (as, for instance, the Byzantine Jarja did at the Battle of Yarmūk). When, where, and to whom he submitted/converted were crucial factors because they determined his new identity under the caliphate—as a partner or follower in the new state—and highlighted the voluntary nature of Persia's recognition of Prophetic truth.[74] The whole digression over the act of drinking water and the game to entrap 'Umar into uttering the grant of safety were devised by Hurmuzān to drive home the unique terms of his surrender. The request for water represented a request for political life. Appropriately enough, Hurmuzān still wanted to drink in his classical Sasanid style, a clear signal of his intent to retain cultural and social continuity within the world of Islam. When 'Umar granted Hurmuzān the right to drink water, he was essentially sanctioning the future political rebirth of Persia.

Once the symbolic conversion happens, Hurmuzān is incorporated into the circle of 'Umar as a companion who offers him advice on how to better plan further Persian conquests. When, at a later point, 'Umar reportedly consults Hurmuzān on how to proceed with the conquest campaign in Iran, Hurmuzān advises him, "Iṣbahān is the head, while Fars and Azerbayjān are like the wings. If you cut off one of the wings, then the head will sway with the other. Therefore begin with Iṣbahān."[75] Hurmuzān's advice rings with echoes of Salmān al-Fārisī's advice to the Prophet just before the Battle of al-Khandaq.

Stylistically, the story of Hurmuzān's conversion exhibits certain features that can be positioned against an older, diverse background of images. In the way in which Hurmuzān is brought to the caliph flanked by al-Aḥnaf and Anas, one sees a replay of the story of 'Umar's own conversion to Islam, when he was brought into the Prophet's presence with Ḥamza standing guard alongside other companions. 'Umar speaks to Hurmuzān in the same forceful way the Prophet spoke to 'Umar earlier (and to Abū Sufyān at a similar moment of surrender),[76] which creates a continuity between the two stories that makes Hurmuzān's conversion, indirectly, a conversion at the hands of Muḥammad. Another literary formula reapplied in Hurmuzān's story can be seen in the section in which 'Umar appears incredulous that he could have given Hurmuzān a grant of amnesty. When 'Umar asks Anas b. Mālik, "Woe to you, Anas, should I grant immunity to the killer of Majza'a and Barā'?" we see a parallelism with a statement 'Umar directed toward Ṭulayḥa b. Khuwaylid after his surrender at the end of the Ridda wars. When asked if he would pardon Ṭulayḥa, the caliph, furious at the battle deeds of the latter, said, "You are the one who killed 'Ukāsha and Thābit? By God, I shall never develop a liking for you."[77] The double naming of victims in 'Umar's statements points to parallels in style and identical origins in the historical composition at that juncture.

## Khid'a *and Succession*

A far more important feature that operates both stylistically and thematically in the story is the method by which Hurmuzān obtained his immunity—through the process of "*khid'a*" (guile). When the caliph granted Hurmuzān the right to drink water, as mentioned above, he was in effect recognizing the political survival of Persia in Islamic history. The technique by which Hurmuzān gained this right was not meant to be merely playful or witty, but also to reflect political strategy. Craftiness and calculation were features that 'Umar was known to have admired in his lieutenants, particularly in 'Amr, Mu'āwiya, and al-Mughīra. As tools for achieving conquest and effective government, these techniques were viewed as critical to safeguarding the community. Yet while these methods were recognized as necessary in wars with non-Muslims,[78] the degree to which a Muslim ruler could apply them in governing the community was a controversial religious issue, one indirectly debated throughout the history of the first century of Islam, most notably in the narratives about the conflict between 'Alī and Mu'āwiya.

Throughout his reign, 'Umar is never directly portrayed as applying *khid'a* to achieve his goals. His charisma and strict moral example are shown to be sufficient deterrents in all political affairs.[79] This said, the image of 'Umar's forthrightness depends largely on how strictly one interprets his actions. A significant case in point is the episode of the Saqīfa of Banū Sā'ida, which brought about the election of Abū Bakr for the caliphate. We have seen how 'Umar played a critical role on that occasion in cajoling different groups to accept Abū Bakr as the first caliph, while 'Alī, who was said to be absent due to his preoccupation with preparing the Prophet's body for burial, was effectively pushed aside. The victory of the Muhājirūn over the Anṣār (and 'Alī) in securing Abū Bakr's caliphate can hardly be viewed as the result of mere force, but rather of shrewd diplomacy (or *khid'a*). And although Ṭabarī throws a blackout on any negative assessment of that decision and, more importantly, denies 'Alī any direct criticism of these events, it seems clear that those who do express their anger (mainly Sa'd b. 'Ubāda and al-Ḥubāb b. al-Mundhir, leaders of the Anṣār) speak as if on behalf of 'Alī and view the event as a deception engineered by 'Umar.[80]

While the events of the Saqīfa are tightly controlled in description and the reaction of 'Alī is minimized, in later times 'Alī could not be kept silent any longer. The first of these occasions came at the *shūrā* for the succession to 'Umar's position. When 'Abd al-Raḥmān b. 'Awf screened the candidates suggested by 'Umar in a way that ultimately favored 'Uthmān over 'Alī, the latter, although conceding again to the other *ṣaḥāba*, was quick to comment as he rose to give the *bay'a* to 'Uthmān, "Verily this has been a deception. What a deception! [*khid'atun wa ayyu khid'a*!]."[81] To maintain a logical chain between the characters and statements, it should here be remembered that 'Abd al-Raḥmān b. 'Awf did not act as he did at the *shūrā* because of his own thinking, but only in light of procedures and priorities that 'Umar had established among the six members of the *shūrā* council just before he died. For it was 'Umar who had restricted the slate of candidates, fixed their number, empowered Ibn 'Awf as arbiter, and deprived 'Alī of any primacy for succession.

'Alī's reaction about the "*khid'a*", therefore, no matter how strongly he is portrayed as being cooperative with 'Umar from a Jamā'ī-Sunnī perspective, was ultimately an outburst against 'Umar as much as against 'Uthmān and Ibn 'Awf. Similarly, the deceptions that 'Alī was to suffer later at the Taḥkīm (the Arbitration) at the hands of 'Amr and Mu'āwiya were not the fault just of these two men, but also of the caliph who had once empowered them by appointing them to posts of administrative leadership in Syria and Egypt respectively. It is well known that, in his vehement arguments with 'Alī just before Ṣiffīn, Mu'āwiya repeatedly invoked the fact that his own legitimacy derived from the fact that 'Umar had appointed him for the Syrian command and had never dismissed him (see debates in chapter 5). If such memories were relevant forward in time, looking backward may have also contained a foreshadowing relevance. One wonders, for example, whether 'Umar's cheering of 'Amr's famous deception of the Byzantine governor "Arṭabūn" at Ajnādayn targeted simply the machinations of that conquest or disclosed an ironic comment foreshadowing—and endorsing—'Amr's later deception at Ṣiffīn.[82]

'Umar's involvement in shaping the conditions that led to 'Alī's political loss over time provides a central theme in the story that demands a remedy, and this answer emerges very slowly under the cover of a theme we mentioned above, namely Persia's accommodation of Islam and political reemergence. Simultaneously, while 'Umar's relations with the *ṣaḥāba* were contributing to 'Alī's disadvantage, 'Umar's relation to Persian personalities were cast as seeding the ground for a Perso-Hāshimite affinity and revenge. For his part, therefore, Hurmuzān speaks in his dialogue with 'Umar not only on behalf of a fallen Persian empire, but also on behalf of 'Alī. The Persian leader is oblivious to the role that he indirectly plays by deceiving 'Umar and addressing what seems to be the separate issue of succession to rule. Hurmuzān's behavior and speech in that meeting are meant to show the latter reworking the earlier skills of 'Umar and settling an old score on behalf of 'Alī and the Anṣār. The irony of his role is strengthened by the fact that the interpreter at his meeting with 'Umar is said to be none other than al-Mughīra b. Shu'ba, whose slave Abū Lu'lu'a later assassinated 'Umar. Al-Mughīra, we should recall, was the Arab ambassador to the Sasanids before Qādisiyya and was known for even greater political guile than 'Amr. During the conflict between 'Alī and Mu'āwiya, al-Mughīra took a key part in subverting 'Alī's political strategy and thus is shown as having acted throughout on the 'Umar-Mu'āwiya side of the political fence.

A further confirmation of the fact that Hurmuzān's role shows the birth of a Perso-'Alid affinity in the form of a new Anṣār camp supporting the 'Alid cause can be seen later, at the Battle of Ṣiffīn, when 'Alī zealously pursues and attempts to punish 'Ubaydallāh b. 'Umar for killing Hurmuzān soon after the murder of 'Umar. 'Ubaydallāh's attack, it will be remembered here, grew out of suspicion that Hurmuzān was involved in a premeditated assassination plot against the second caliph. This suspicion was based on statements from 'Abd al-Raḥmān b. Abī Bakr that he had seen a dubious gathering on the night before the murder between Hurmuzān, Abū Lu'lu'a, and Jufayna (a Christian of Medina). Ibn Abī Bakr reported that Hurmuzān was examining the double-edged dagger that later was used in the attack on 'Umar and that he dropped the weapon clumsily when he realized he was being observed.[83] Ultimately, these rumors fostered suspicions of a wider Persian-led conspiracy in Medina and created a rift between the old Meccan elite and later Arab and non-Arab converts.

Like 'Umar's, Hurmuzān's role in the story is allusive and shaped in a way that pronounces a historian's commentary on events. Hurmuzān weaves together different issues of political and moral commentary through the exercise of irony. He accomplishes his goal of surrendering to a leader, thus confirming the primacy of hierarchy while indirectly affirming 'Alī's succession rights. Still working within the framework of the *jamā'a*, Hurmuzān recognizes 'Umar's unique religious importance and concedes to the primacy of *jamā'ī* cohesion emphasized by Sunnīs. However, this is also the moment when 'Alī's lost leadership becomes the new religious cause of a new phase in history, to be realized with the community of eastern (mainly Persian) converts to Islam. Outsiders to the traditional community of Medinan rule from then on will fight on behalf of a political issue with a similar situation of exclusion: 'Alī's loss of the caliphal role. The issue pertaining to leadership and the one relating to the community of believers interact to shape a new phase in a cyclical history.

## THE ASSASSINATION OF 'UMAR

Hurmuzān's debate with 'Umar evokes the twin themes of the Iranian defeat and the 'Alid loss of the caliphate. It honors 'Umar simultaneously as a guide of the *jamā'a* and as a moral-religious exemplar, but it subverts him on the succession front. All the characters we have examined so far in various scenes from the chronicles—Rustam, Hurmuzān, and al-Mughīra—finally converge and clash in an allusive climax in the scene of 'Umar's assassination. This is mediated through the construction of the image of Abū Lu'lu'a, who carries out the murder in Medina. And now, just as we saw Hurmuzān acting unwittingly on behalf of the 'Alids, we will see Abū Lu'lu'a acting on behalf of Rustam and the 'Alids in another elliptical and suggestive way. To appreciate this, we must first digress to examine briefly what the sources tell us about this assassin's unusual profile and associations with the above-mentioned figures.

Prior to coming to Medina, Abū Lu'lu'a was said to have been either a former captive from Qādisiyya or Nihāwand[84] or a former slave of Hurmuzān.[85] He reportedly later became the slave of al-Mughīra b. Shu'ba, who settled down after the conquests as governor of Basra. Some sources call Abū Lu'lu'a a Christian,[86] while others leave his beliefs vague, calling him "*majūsī*" (Magian).[87] The story is famous in the sources, where Abū Lu'lu'a one day had his only chance encounter with the caliph a few days before the murder. 'Umar, on one of his typical tours of the city, was reportedly stopped by Abū Lu'lu'a, who complained to the caliph about his tax burden and asked for a reduction. When 'Umar inquired about Abū Lu'lu'a's vocation, the latter said that he was a stone mason, blacksmith, and carpenter.[88] Upon learning of this, 'Umar refused to adjust Abū Lu'lu'a's taxes because, we are told, 'Umar found him too skilled to be taxed lightly. The caliph then asked Abū Lu'lu'a, "I have heard that you claim you can make a mill that grinds by wind power if you wish. [Is this true?]"[89] to which Abū Lu'lu'a replied in the affirmative, saying, "If you survive, I shall certainly make you a mill that will be the talk of everyone in both East and West!" We are told that the caliph quickly recognized a veiled threat in the statement and departed, perturbed.[90]

The next meeting between 'Umar and Abū Lu'lu'a was to be the fateful one when Abū Lu'lu'a, three days after this marketplace encounter, came to the mosque of Medina and attacked 'Umar while he was leading the congregation in the dawn prayer. There are two versions of the event, which differ only on the number of times 'Umar was stabbed and how many people were killed. Wielding a unique dagger that had two pointed sharp edges, with a handle in the middle, Abū Lu'lu'a set on the caliph, stabbing him six times along with attacking another man (according to Ṭabarī). Balādhurī and Ibn Sa'd rely on another version that says Abū Lu'lu'a stabbed the caliph three times, and that in a frenzy the assassin then attacked those who came to restrain him, wounding thirteen people, before he finally killed himself. The account is greatly sensitive to details of fact and drama. Ṭabarī's version states that of the six stabs one hit the caliph beneath his navel—and that this was the lethal wound. Balādhurī's and Ibn Sa'd's versions record the caliph's shout when he was attacked, "The dog has bitten me!" Then the accounts converge to show the caliph falling and, somewhat uncertain about who was close to him of the companions, calling out, "Is 'Abd al-Raḥmān b. 'Awf amongst you?" "Yes," the answer came, "there he is." 'Umar then said: "Come forward then and lead the prayer." While the wounded caliph still lay there, 'Abd al-Raḥmān led the congregation and completed the prayer. Then

'Umar was carried home. Soon after he set about discussing the issue of succession, indicating that he wanted to "make a covenant to ['Abd al-Raḥmān b. 'Awf] [*urīdu an a'hada ilayka*]," but before he could clarify what this covenant was, 'Abd al-Raḥmān refused any attempt to make him a successor. "Then hold your peace until I make the pact with those whom the Prophet died pleased with," 'Umar said, referring to the six members he had designated for the *shūrā*: 'Alī, 'Uthmān, 'Abd al-Raḥmān, Sa'd, al-Zubayr, and Ṭalḥa.

Ṭabarī's scene of 'Umar's assassination in Medina seems to have been handed down from storytellers with little variation, unlike the accounts of the death of the Prophet, and it does not seem to lack a credible context, as in Abū Bakr's death. For the first time, Islamic history is firm that this death resulted from assassination, identifies the assassin, and gives the caliph some interesting few hours in which to discuss the succession issue. Death in the mosque, for 'Umar, was like death befalling Julius Caesar on the steps of the Roman forum, and in almost a similar dramatic enactment, the caliph falls uncertain who of the companions was around, as if he beheld his companions with a measure of uncertainty or astonishment—astonishment highlighted further by the silence, and no doubt unlikely absence, of 'Alī b. Abī Ṭālib, the caliph's Brutus. Finally, the caliph had to yield his forceful persona and give up the fight for the law and for an obedient community. His only plea, according to several versions, was that the community finish performing the prayer before the sun rose, even at such an hour of distress (*lā ḥaẓẓa li-man taraka al-ṣalāt*). The narrative of 'Umar's death and beginning moves toward charting the succession wove together the Prophet's designation of a leader for prayer with Abū Bakr's sparse discussion of succession at the hour of death. Ibn 'Awf, in the hour of 'Umar's death, now assumed the role that Abū Bakr had assumed in Muḥammad's last days, along with the authority (however ambiguous) that Sunnī belief derived from that action. All the while, pro-'Alid sympathies were once again concealed in silent reaction to the scene of assassination.

The only additional detail we know about Abū Lu'lu'a's plot to assassinate 'Umar comes via a story already described about a so-called conspiracy in Medina among three characters, Abū Lu'lu'a, Hurmuzān, and Jufayna (a Christian), when 'Abd al-Raḥmān b. Abī Bakr spotted Hurmuzān wielding the dagger. In one account, an additional detail is given of how Hurmuzān explained that the dagger was a tool for eating meat, since according to Persian custom meat was impure and needed to be handled with a utensil. As unconvincing a character as al-Afshīn later would be when he defended himself during the treason trial at the court of the caliph al-Muʿtaṣim, Hurmuzān is somehow accommodated to a greater degree by the Islamic tradition, which ultimately does not dwell much on his possible complicity in a murder conspiracy.[91] ʿUbaydallāh b. ʿUmar, however, bought none of these excuses and set out to avenge his father, killing Abū Lu'lu'a, Hurmuzān, and Abū Lu'lu'a's daughter. From then on, another train of events was set in motion against the new assassin, ʿUbaydallāh, to which we will return later as a new crisis of justice is hurled upon the accession of the third caliph.

In spite of the murder scene's importance in the story of ʿUmar's assassination, it is really the marketplace encounter between caliph and assassin that deserves closer scrutiny. For here the role Abū Lu'lu'a appears to play draws important ironic connections to the topic of the Arab conquest of the Sasanid empire, the controversy over caliphal succession, and another rarely discussed issue. On its surface, the story of the marketplace encounter seems straightforward. Abū Lu'lu'a's response is usually read as an ominous sign of his coming plot against the caliph's life. The moment is meant to show the lingering hostility of the subjected Sasanid unbeliever and to demonstrate a contrast with the unsuspecting, pious behavior of ʿUmar. In the end, ʿUmar gains the death of a martyr, and the story seems to end there. Yet by closely reading the details of Abū Lu'lu'a's character and role in the story as well as the motifs and language used, we can uncover various strata of implication intended in the text. We can begin by raising some puzzling questions, such as: why did narrators attribute the above-listed professions (mason, carpenter, and blacksmith) and not others to Abū Lu'lu'a? What was this man doing in Medina, if his master was governor in Basra? And why did a caliph exceedingly famous for having the last word and parsing words and gestures to their punishing ends take Abū Lu'lu'a's comment in stride?

To appreciate these and other questions, we need to discern at least two tracks of associations that generate the significations of the story. The first centers on a triangle involving ʿUmar–Rustam–Abū Lu'lu'a. Rustam's role, as we saw, had ended with his defeat and death at Qādisiyya. On the surface, Rustam may seem irrelevant to the story of Abū Lu'lu'a's confrontation with ʿUmar, unless we believe that the two Persian men shared certain feelings that crossed the barriers of geography and social rank. And there is evidence for this. The cry that we heard Rustam utter just before Qādisiyya, for example, is later repeated by Abū Lu'lu'a: When the Persian captive children (of the Nihāwand campaign) were brought to Medina, Abū Lu'lu'a was reportedly so distressed by the scene of Persian humiliation that he was seen filing past the captives, stroking them on the head and saying, weeping, "'Umar has eaten my liver."[92] This direct parallel in the speech of actors of different social, political, and moral profiles was meant to link them in a way that served the theme of sympathy with the fallen Iranian state. By depicting Abū Lu'lu'a and Rustam as equidistant from 'Umar in their expressions of national frustration, narrators intended to show a vindication of Sasanid political pride and Rustam's final failure. Thus, while Rustam was unable to overcome his dilemma of reconciling his conflicting obligations to Yazdajird and to the Persian state, not to mention his tacit awareness of the righteousness of the Islamic mission, Abū Lu'lu'a emerged as a character unencumbered by historical and moral restraints. A man of unknown origins, Abū Lu'lu'a fit the archetypal mold of the monarchs' assassin who could ultimately be expendable on both Sasanid and Islamic grounds. His identity as blacksmith also adhered to a universal folkloric perception of such an artisan playing a pseudo-magical role in bringing about pivotal historical change.[93]

The second layer of connections in the assassination scene centers on the triangle of 'Umar–Mughīra–Abū Lu'lu'a, and this relates more closely to the 'Alid issue. In exploring this layer we can hypothesize that the attribution of Abū Lu'lu'a to al-Mughīra was meant to be read less as historical fact than as ironic touch. This interpretation builds on other subtle references about the interactions of al-Mughīra and 'Umar and relates in particular to what can be termed the "Mughīra problem." Here yet a further digression on al-Mughīra and what he represented to a medieval audience is necessary. Al-Mughīra, the sources agree, had the personality of a rogue trickster before Islam,[94] one who, after conversion, became a loyal follower, first of the Prophet and then of 'Umar. Later, as we saw, he headed the key Arab embassy that debated Rustam/Yazdajird before the Battle of Qādisiyya and was generally remembered for his foxy political acumen and an instinct for outmaneuvering opponents that could be unscrupulous. 'Umar, narrators indirectly imply, knew this about this man, who was a kindred spirit to 'Amr b. al-'Āṣ and Mu'āwiya, and knew how to ignore his peccadilloes to keep the services of a capable military command. But toward the end of his reign, ʻUmar's patience was tested when rumors flew to Medina of an adulterous affair involving Mughīra. ʻUmar, ever the champion of draconian judgments, especially on such extremities of the law, summoned his governor to Medina and held a small investigation. Three witnesses condemned Mughīra, but a fourth (Ziyād b. Abīhi, the well-known alleged half-brother of Muʻāwiya) equivocated.[95] In the end, and with such division, the charge could not be proven, and the caliph found himself forced to bring punishment on the man who originally put forward the accusation, a companion of good repute named Abū Bakra. Al-Mughīra survived the day but was dismissed as governor of Basra to allay further public doubts. And thus the case was closed.

This romantic scandal may strike the reader as odd for the considerable attention it receives in the sources, as well as for how narrators place it amid other, more important narratives that deal with the topics of conquest, succession, and government in general. Perhaps the legal aspects of the case were important in that they tested the procedures of the law, especially on issues of *ḥudūd* (penalties). However, the more far-reaching nuances of the tale lay in its conflicting moralizing messages, which narrators seem to have admired and considered as the key, perhaps only, link between narratives on totally different topics. Here narrators could discuss freely through anecdotes what no later legal or *ḥadīth* mind could dare to broach: a rare moment of a miscarriage of justice under ʻUmar, the very architect of a penalty for adultery. Irony now descended on this caliph who had once ceaselessly pestered Abū Bakr about the latter's letting Khālid b. al-Walīd get away with big and small offenses without punishment, only to find himself (i.e., ʻUmar) now showing leniency under similar vulnerable circumstances.[96] The sources leave no doubt that the caliph knew where the real truth of this case lay and that reputation mattered more than numbers of witnesses, but a tradeoff of priorities was unavoidable.[97]

Why the caliph let al-Mughīra off the hook that day is left ambiguous. He may have wanted to preserve a key statesman of the *jamāʻa*, or perhaps he wanted to preserve confidence in the companions of the Prophet or simply to maintain the procedure of the law by stressing the dimension of evidence demanded by the Sharīʻa. But, like a biblical tale or the Arthurian legend involving Lancelot and Guinevere, this Islamic legend was meant to illustrate the sour vignette that still demanded poetic justice, even if religious justice had been satisfied. Thereafter it would set in motion a train of events that pushed the episode's key actors toward a redemptive close, but not before bringing about tragedy and affecting the fortunes of the community and the state. Tragedy here lay on more than one level. The punishment of Abū Bakra was clearly the obvious error, but in more political and perhaps futuristic terms, the bigger tragedy lay in 'Umar's letting al-Mughīra survive to fight another day. For when the day of conflict between 'Alī and Mu'āwiya came, al-Mughīra would incline heavily toward supporting Mu'āwiya and through this he undermined 'Alī's chances for consolidating power.

All of this may seem far removed from our story about 'Umar's interaction with Abū Lu'lu'a, unless we appreciate the unity of action at play here, along with the affinity we spoke of between 'Alī and the Hāshimite cause in general and a Perso-Khurāsānī role in history in particular. Viewed within this frame, Sasanid figures were operating unwittingly in word and deed in support of the 'Alid position. Abū Lu'lu'a acted here not only on behalf of Rustam, but on behalf of the 'Alid cause as well, a cause that, we must remember, rested not only on family merit but also on the symbolic loyalty of non-Arab converts to the Hāshimite family as a messianic symbol that links them to the Prophet Muḥammad.

In broad historical terms therefore the story of 'Umar's assassination not only vindicated Persian political pride and signaled Persia's comeback as the future focus of the Islamic state after the success of the 'Abbāsid revolution but also offered a subtle rebuttal from 'Alī to 'Umar. The theme of silent rivalry between the two figures is carefully preserved till the moment of 'Umar's death. And just as 'Umar vented his anger indirectly at 'Alī by admonishing Sa'd b. 'Ubāda for challenging Abū Bakr's succession, 'Alī speaks up after 'Umar's death by zealously leading the cause of having 'Ubaydallāh b. 'Umar punished for his cathartic revenge against Hurmuzān and Abū Lu'lu'a's daughter. 'Alī would continue talking about this issue and seek to punish 'Ubaydallāh b. 'Umar even twelve years later at the Battle of Ṣiffīn.[98]

The Persian emphasis in the story of 'Umar's assassination may make it seem connected only to a tradition of Persian historical lore, were it not for a key element that shows that it is ultimately rooted in a biblical frame as well. This relates to the role that Ka'b al-Aḥbār, the controversial Jewish convert, occupies in the story, which reveals a process of bending in representation from one fiction to another. To examine Ka'b's biographical information would be a significant digression in the present context, but it is worth remembering that he was present with 'Umar during the conquest of Jerusalem in A.H. 17/A.D. 638 when the caliph sought the companions' advice on how to direct the *qibla* of a mosque he sought to build in that area. Ka'b's advice on that occasion, as is well known, was to direct the new mosque toward the former Jewish Temple; this prompted the caliph's chiding comment that Ka'b has still not abandoned his faith in Judaism after converting to Islam. The incident was meant to set the standard of rivalry between the Islamic leader and the leading representative of another culture.[99]

A similar incident of claim and rebuttal that is more relevant to the present story happened a few days before 'Umar's death. Three days before the event, Ka'b suddenly makes an unexpected appearance at the caliph's residence, telling him in ominous terms, "Appoint your successor [*i'had*], Commander of the Faithful, for you are going to die in three days!" When 'Umar asked how Ka'b knew this, the latter replied, "I find it in the Torah." Then a brief comical expression from 'Umar follows, as he declares, "*ā-llāh*"—lengthening the phrase—perhaps to express a satire (in the sense of the more popular expression of marvel, "*mā shā' allāh*") against the spiritual bravado of a Jew. "Can you actually find 'Umar b. al-Khaṭṭāb in the Torah?" 'Umar asked. "Indeed no, but I do find a complete description of you and also that your allotted time span has come to an end,"[100] Ka'b said. A day later, Ka'b stops by and tells the incredulous 'Umar that two days are left, then does the same the day after, warning that now only one day is left, through the next morning. Ibn Sa'd's version of the events adds a crucial elaboration in the dialogue, which prefaces Ka'b's comment to 'Umar that he is destined to die within three days by saying, "There is a king of Israelites who reminds us (i.e., the Jews) of 'Umar, and whenever we mentioned 'Umar we thought of that king. He used to have a prophet beside him who was inspired by God. God inspired that prophet to tell [that king], 'Make your succession covenant, and write and entrust to me your testament of succession [*i'had 'ahdak wa uktub ilayya waṣiyyataka*], for you shall die within three days.' When the third day came, he [i.e., the king] collapsed between the wall and the throne [*bayna al-jadri wa'l-sarīr*]. [The king] then pleaded with his Lord, 'God, if you judge me to have been a just arbiter in rulings, and that when matters became confusing I sought your purpose, then extend my life until my offspring grows up and my community becomes more numerous.' God inspired the prophet to tell [the king] that he was truthful in saying this, and that I have extended his life by fifteen years until his child grows up, and his community grow in number." The narrator concludes, "When 'Umar was stabbed, Ka'b declared, 'If he asks his Lord, God will certainly preserve him.' When 'Umar was told of this, he said, 'O God, whenever your will be done [i.e., death], do it without my being in a position of weakness or blame.'"[101]

Ka'b's remarks can be read at face value as literary tools used by narrators to anticipate 'Umar's assassination with foreboding and tragic fulfillment. However, both the content and the manner of the statement warrant some commentary. Islamic sources may have attributed the comment to Ka'b to show an example of extra Jewish knowledge that was being used with some gloating (especially if the caliph was to heed the warning). But 'Umar's reaction was to dismiss the warning in a sign that he places his trust in God and that he would not give in to unorthodox prophecies, which required no response. These layers of polemic that surround the warning and 'Umar's response may distract the reader from the real foundation frame of the anecdote, which was in essence none other than the biblical frame of casting the relation between a prophet and a king. Ka'b to 'Umar was in essence being represented in the manner that Nathan was to Solomon, but with the latter relation (indeed the existence of Nathan) rejected in Islam, the Islamic historical narrative applied the issue in a mostly political context to the second caliph and gave the latter the chance to dismiss any lingering attachment to that Israelite frame of religious-historical composition.

Were it not for Ibn Sa'd's inclusion of the story of Ka'b and the king, Ṭabarī's version of the narrative would have never by itself revealed how biblical narration interacted with a moralizing Persian political narrative. This is as close a proof as Islamic sources afford that the frame of the stories of the prophets was adapted to the lives of the caliphs.

## 'UMAR AND YAZDAJIRD: THE LINK OF FATE

We have thus far examined the theme of Iran's transformation by looking at 'Umar's association with different Iranian actors (Hurmuzān, Abū Lu'lu'a, and Rustam). Yazdajird has been marginalized as the character who brought on defeat with his poor strategy and lack of wisdom. However, we cannot understand the closing segments of 'Umar's life until we account for what Ṭabarī and others also say about Yazdajird's end. In the story of the Islamic conquest of Iran there is no trace of any direct contact between Yazdajird and 'Umar. They do not officially write to one another, nor do they refer to one another through envoys or commanders. This distance between the two is not accidental but calculated; it detaches them from the particularities of their places of rule, allowing them to connect on a higher plane as symbolic heads of state caught in a turning universal struggle. Still, the extant stories about Yazdajird connect him far more heavily with narratives about 'Umar than anything that has to do with 'Uthmān, in whose reign Yazdajird's final fall from power and death actually occurred.

One report even forces a reference to Yazdajird's end into a speech made by 'Umar. We are told that after 'Umar received news of al-Aḥnaf b. Qays' conquest of Khurāsān in the year A.H. 22/A.D. 643, he assembled the community, then showed gratitude to God for fulfilling His promise and declared,

> [Know that] the king of the Magians has perished [*qad halak*], and they [the Magians] do not own one foot of land [*shibran*] that can bring danger to a Muslim. [Know that] God has bestowed their land onto you and their wealth, domiciles, and progeny [*qad awrathakum arḍahum wa diyārahum wa amwālahum wa abnā'ahum*] to see how you will conduct yourselves. . . . Do not change your ways lest God replace you with another people [*lā tubaddilū wa lā tughayyirū fa-yastabdil allāhu bi-kum ghayrakum*]. I fear nothing for this *umma* except that it may become vulnerable because of you [*fa-innī lā akhāfu 'alā hādhihi al-umma illā an tu'tā min qibalikum*].[102]

Although historically impossible, given that Yazdajird's fall happened after 'Umar's death, this speech highlights the fact that narrators cared less about accurate chronology than compatibility of themes and completion of a dramatic storyline, which in this case centered on the growing fight between the emperor and the pivotal second caliph. In this context, it was 'Umar who was viewed as having everything to do with bringing about the accommodation with Persia. 'Umar's speech is placed by Ṭabarī after an extensive account of a last-minute exchange of embassies between the Persian monarch and the Chinese emperor in which the latter was asked to help roll back the Arab conquerors. In a story that reiterates the predestined fall of Persia, this time through the voice of a leader with a more neutral opinion, the Chinese emperor echoes Rustam's earlier reaction after the Arab embassies at the outset of the conflict. The emperor recognizes the moral superiority of the new challenge, which is again not cast as a function of a divine message but rather as a set of virtues that govern the Arab camp, namely a loyalty to covenants, deprecation of greed, and an austere outlook on life. The Chinese emperor asks the Persian emissary who came seeking help,

> "I know that in truth rulers must give aid to [other] rulers against those who overcome them. So describe these people who drove you out of your land to me. I notice that you mention they are few and you are many. Such a small number will not affect you in this way with your great numbers. They can do this only if they are good and you are evil." [The messenger] suggested that he ask him whatever he wanted. So he asked him if they kept to their agreement and he replied that they did. [The ruler] asked what they said to them before they made war on them. [The messenger] replied, "They called upon us to choose one of three things: [to accept] their faith—and if we do they treat us as themselves—or [to pay] tribute and [enter] their protection or to be subjected to open warfare." [The ruler] asked about how obedient they were to their leaders. [The messenger] replied that no one was more obedient to him leading them. [The ruler] asked what they permitted and what they forbade, and [the messenger] told him. He asked if they ever forbade what was permitted to them or permitted what was forbidden them. [When] [the messenger] replied that they did not, [the ruler] remarked that they would never perish until they permitted what was forbidden and forbade what was permitted to them. He then asked about their clothes, and [the messenger] told him. [He asked] about their riding animals, and [the messenger] mentioned their pure Arabian horses and described them [to him]. "What fine horses they are!" exclaimed [the ruler]. [The messenger then] described camels to him, how they kneel down and go forth to carry [loads]. The ruler's response was that this was the description of long-necked beasts!
>
> [The ruler of China] sent a letter to Yazdajird with (the messenger) as follows: "I am not prevented from dispatching an army to you

stretching from Marw to China by my not knowing what is proper for me. But if these people described to me by your messenger were to try, they could demolish mountains; if nothing were to stand in their way, they would wipe me out, as long as they are as described! Make your peace with them therefore and accept some modus vivendi with them. Do not stir them up, as long as they do not stir you up."

Yazdajird and the royal family remained in Ferghana in [formal] agreement with the ruler of the Turks.[103]

As a secular leader, the Chinese emperor serves to confirm or appreciate all the themes we discussed at the outset—sound political judgment, the coming turn in Persia's fortune, and even the romanticized attention to the rustic lifestyle of the Arab nomad. It probably did not escape a medieval reader's notice in the greater picture of things that China was left undisturbed by the conquerors because it was being ruled by such a wise infidel. Secular wisdom was clearly as much of a religion to Ṭabarī and the moralizing storytellers of the ninth century as the biblical or *ḥadīth* traditions. And foreign monarchs, having risen to the height of the social hierarchy by some measure of divine selection, were viewed as worthy men capable of recognizing divine intervention when it occurred. Such was the role assigned to al-Najāshī of Abyssinia when he received the mission of the Prophet, and similar was the reaction of Heraclius, who is portrayed as having verged on accepting the new faith but then being dissuaded by the influence of the Christian clergy. Even Yazdajird is carefully portrayed at times as someone who was susceptible to divine awakenings, albeit only in the realm of the unconscious.[104]

Yazdajird's situation after the defeat at Nihāwand is quite hazy in the sources. The story of his end does not follow quickly after the famous defeats of the Sasanian armies at Qādisiyya and Nihāwand; it takes some years. After the defeats, narrators describe an emperor on a slow retreat, moving around the country from town to town—Rayy, Iṣfahān, Iṣṭakhr, Kirmān, and Sistān—trying in vain to drum up support among the provincial governors for another counterattack, with the sacred fire all the while carried before him. Failing to gain support, he gradually fled toward Khurāsān and sought out the marzubān of Marw, Māhawayh, who promised to help reconquer the lost kingdom but in reality began plotting simultaneously with his neighboring Turkic monarch to finish off Yazdajird.

Alerted to the new menace, the Turks soon invaded the Iranian border region to capture Yazdajird, and the latter attempted to fight them, leading a force with Māhawayh that engaged in a confrontation on the river Murghab. But all this was doomed to fail because of the treachery of Māhawayh, who switched to the side of the Turks during the course of battle. This finally made Yazdajird lose all hope and led him to flee the scene of battle in search of personal safety. Hence we get the famous scene of how he crossed the river and entered the countryside in search of safety while his enemies came after him. From the chronicles we get the impression of a disillusioned monarch, exhausted and traumatized, aimlessly escaping from his people and his enemies alike. When finally he thought he had found shelter in a miller's cabin it was to prove his undoing.

Arabic and Persian sources agree on the closing anecdote to Yazdajird's life, where they describe the emperor pleading with the peasant miller for shelter. The latter, not knowing Yazdajird's identity, reportedly asked him to pay the daily fee of 4 dirhams for food and shelter. Yazdajird had no money but offered to give up a sache, or cape, he was wearing, which he said was worth fifty thousand dirhams. Incredulous at this and suspicious about the identity of Yazdajird, the peasant then left him behind in the cabin to sleep while he went into town to spread the word about his unusual guest. It was then only a matter of time before Yazdajird's opponents came to the mill, put him to death, and threw his corpse into the river.[105] A significant detail in Ṭabarī adds that after this happened, the bishop of Marw salvaged the body out of the river and held a funeral mass for the deceased king because he was reputed to have treated Christians well and was descended from a Christian mother.[106]

The story of this final standoff between the emperor and the peasant in the mill cabin is heavily imbued with folkloric motifs and thereby historically doubtful. The tale of an emperor reduced to nothing but his clothes and put at the mercy of an average member of his former subjects no doubt touched on a universal theme about the ephemeral nature of power and its turning fortunes. The scene of the king choosing to hide in a mill cabin (*ṭāḥūna*) was meant to evoke the staple foods (grain and barley) generally associated with royal control over subjects,[107] and the Sasanid king's interaction with the peasant underscored the traditional bond between the monarchy and the peasantry, who sustain the prosperity of the state.[108] However, this time, instead of ruling over the granary of his subjects, Yazdajird is placed at the mercy of the peasant. The 4 dirhams the miller demanded as a fee may have been chosen because four is the numerical symbol of justice (thereby referring to the main task of the ruler), or it may have symbolized the cardinal points in the universal empire he used to rule over and which was now collapsing on him.[109] Finally, that all of these events were set in Marw—a town that in later Islamic times would come to be viewed as playing a role parallel to Medina's during the Prophet's time—no doubt triggered awareness of the irony of Yazdajird's death in Khurāsān, given the subsequent rebirth of the Iranian state in that province during the 'Abbāsid revolution.

But what made this anecdote central, probably more than any other factor, was its connection with the story of 'Umar's assassination. This can be established through the motif of the mill, which connotes the turning wheel of fortune. This motif, as we saw, also occurred in the narrative that describes Abū Lu'lu'a's threat to 'Umar. And Abū Lu'lu'a's statement, "If you survive, I shall make you a mill that will be the talk of people East and West," was heavily allusive to the context of Yazdajird's story. Just as we saw Abū Lu'lu'a uttering words that connected with Rustam's discourse without the two ever having met, Abū Lu'lu'a is shown as being unwittingly privy to what will later happen to the Persian emperor, with Yazdajird's death context as a metaphor for the coming assassination of 'Umar.[110] The motif of the mill in the two stories tied the fates of the two leaders as actors caught in the turning cycle of Persia's fortune. This motif, it should also be noted, is repeatedly used in Ṭabarī's narratives to connote the life cycle of an event or person,[111] or to describe the motion of battle.[112]

The mill as a motif of the tragic turns of life on earth was connected to a wider cosmological perception among medieval authors, who compared the astrological turn of the zodiac to the image of a mill. Astronomical observations on how the world (*al-falak*) rotates on an axis, like a mill rotates on its millstone (*ka-ḥajar al-raḥā*),[113] were expressions closely tied to the figurative language that historical narrators and authors such as Ṭabarī used to describe events on the ground, denoting the rotating fortunes of states (*duwal*), communities and leaders.[114] Tragedy was woven with morality in the metaphor of the mill, with its motion that could be viewed both as a source of life, in grinding grain and providing sustenance, and as an instrument that, at times of war, separated those who won from those who lost.[115]

CHAPTER FOUR

# 'Uthmān

## *The Challenge of Innovation*

The foundations that 'Umar b. al-Khaṭṭāb laid for the nascent Islamic state rested on a complex balance of networks among Meccan and Medinan elites, western Arabian and eastern tribes, Islamic beliefs, and tribal custom. His renowned charisma and ascetic example probably played a key role in holding together an early Islamic coalition of divergent interests. However, religious factors aside, the second caliph seems to have also recognized the pragmatic limits that tribal politics placed on his political power. 'Umar came from a minor branch of the clan of Quraysh, and this forced him as a leader to rely heavily on more established Meccan merchant and military families, such as the Sufyanids, Yazīd b. Abī Sufyān, and his brother Mu'āwiya, who played a key role in integrating Syria into the orbit of the caliphate.

In central Arabia and on its northeastern front, 'Umar had to make a different compromise by reaccepting fighters who had been involved in the Ridda wars to join the Muslim campaign against the Sasanids. This policy represented a break with the first caliph, who had doubted the loyalty of former Ridda tribes, such as Tamīm, Bāhila, and Kinda, and barred them from joining the Islamic army. In Iraq, the newly founded garrison towns of Kufa and Basra quickly became magnets for Arabian tribes from the central and eastern parts of the peninsula as well as the former apostate groups. There was constant grumbling among these new settlers about their Ḥijāzī governors and probably a strong desire for equality with the first generations of Muslim converts in pay and authority.

During his reign the caliph showed tact in forestalling Iraqi dissent by granting the settlers of Basra and Kufa greater control over the revenues of the conquered lands, and gave symbolic concession to their demands by changing their governors frequently. The latter were no doubt often misjudged and being slandered by provincial tribesmen. Charges of haughtiness or privilege, or against the religious puritanism of the governors, were known to find a listening ear in Medina. Whether 'Umar saw through the cynical use of religion and austere ideals by the Iraqis is never explicitly stated, but Ṭabarī's Sunnī worldview and tendentious welding of history and epic myth guarantees that the reader will appreciate the issue more for what it says about 'Umar than what it really tells us about the Iraqi garrison towns. The spotlight on Kufa and Basra as breeding grounds of irresponsible religiosity and pretentious demands will be a vivid theme in his narratives of the early caliphate.

However, although 'Umar's policies were based on a two-tiered attention to Meccan and central Arabian tribes, the third caliph, 'Uthmān b. 'Affān, would emerge as far more unabashedly pro-Meccan than either of his predecessors. 'Umar had been more the self-made leader, which explained his compromises and cautions. By contrast, 'Uthmān came from one of Mecca's wealthiest families and had close kin ties to the clan of Abū Sufyān and the Umayyads, who had fought Muḥammad tenaciously until they found that the new Prophet's reach was unstoppable and gaining wide hold in Arabia.[1]

Tradition reports few things about the early life of 'Uthmān. He is said to have converted early to Islam, before the Hijra and the Battle of Badr, and so is shown as having stood with the new faith even in its early, uncertain days. But there are no stories about his being a daring defender of Islam or using his social clout (as Abū Ṭālib and Abū Bakr did) to defend the first Muslims from persecution.[2] Thus, there seem to be some gaps of logic in his companionship career that entice the historian to presume that much of 'Uthmān's prestige in appearing to accompany Abū Bakr and 'Umar during the days of the Sīra represents a back-projection of Sunnī praise on account of his having become third caliph.

Perhaps the most famous fact given in the tradition about 'Uthmān's companionship is that he funded the Prophet's final battle aimed at Syria (*ghazwat Tabūk*) at such a great level of generosity that the Prophet famously declared 'Uthmān forgiven of all his sins, both present and future.[3] This statement was clearly meant to serve as a Sunnī apologetic for 'Uthmān's controversial policies when he became caliph. But in less direct terms, the Prophet's statement was crafted by narrators for a wider context of political intention that sought to depict the Umayyad rulers as generous patrons of the community's welfare even if their rule was authoritarian and their religiosity was not sufficient. In such a situation, praise for 'Uthmān reflected a later Sunnī bias in favor of Syria and the Umayyads against Shī'īsm (see chapter 7).

In terms of personality profile, we are less informed about 'Uthmān than the first two caliphs. Tradition attributes little to him by way of religious erudition (dream interpretation, legislative insight, or wisdom sayings, as in the cases of the other Rāshidūn). Instead, the only quality attributed to him besides giving away generous charity is shyness in character (*ḥayā'*),[4] an attribute that, although praised as a mark of piety, may have been used by narrators to signal the danger of weakness in his personality.[5] The third caliph's tendency toward indecision and frequent shifts of opinion under the influence of counselors was probably woven ambiguously in this context to cast doubt on his leadership capabilities. A seemingly private tendency to be withdrawn suddenly became a public and crucial matter when it presented a problem in the way the caliph was to use the procedure of *shūrā* in government. For while Sunnī theory generally praised the procedure of consultation, it also always assumed that the leader was powerful enough to arbitrate decisions when a crisis arose. This was the example that 'Umar provided at the Saqīfa and that Ibn 'Awf supplied on the eve of 'Uthmān's succession, when in the end they delivered a binding opinion on succession. The third caliph, however, was far from being this decisive. Caught between ambitious advisors, such as 'Amr b. al-'Āṣ and Marwān b. al-Ḥakam, on the one hand and 'Alī and the more pious companions on the other, 'Uthmān never seemed to know who to believe and trust, much less how to articulate a consistent political position to all sides.[6] This made him detrimental to community unity and eroded the image of the caliphal office.

## THE ACHIEVEMENTS OF 'UTHMĀN'S REIGN

Historians generally agree that on the whole 'Uthmān did not depart much from 'Umar's policies upon assuming power.[7] For several years the third caliph kept the governors appointed by 'Umar, maintained the same systems of taxation and stipends in the conquered territories, and continued the expansionist policy. Over the course of a twelve-year reign, 'Uthmān's conquests probably even overshadowed 'Umar's in significance, and on different regional fronts. In Egypt, 'Uthmān's new governor, 'Abdallāh b. Abī al-Sarḥ, was given permission to march on North Africa and venture into Nubia. On the sea, Ibn Abī al-Sarḥ confronted the Byzantines at the famous Battle of Dhāt al-Ṣawārī in A.H. 31/A.D. 651 off the Lycian coast, which opened the way for the conquest of Cyprus by Mu'āwiya,[8] who also led incursions into the Byzantine domain on land at Malāṭya and on sea toward the straits of Constantinople. From Kufa, a campaign was initiated in A.H. 24/A.D. 644 by al-Walīd b. 'Uqba, heading north toward Armenia and Azerbayjan. The army, which was led by Salmān b. Rabī'a al-Bāhilī, was later followed by reinforcements led by 'Abdallāh b. Shubayl b. 'Awf al-Aḥmasī, and strengthened by another army sent from Syria led by Ḥabīb b. Maslama al-Fihrī. The accounts describe cursory truces and submissions achieved but consistently report the success of Ibn Maslama's campaign, which reached as far as Tiflīs in the middle of the Caucasus. On the eastern front, Islamic armies fanned out on different routes to conquer the major Iranian cities, including Iṣṭakhr (Persepolis), Isfahan, Herat, and Nīshapūr, and reached the Oxus River valley, where the Arab commander al-Aḥnaf b. Qays reportedly drank from the river as if in a gesture of defiance. Another commander, 'Ubaydallāh b. Ma'mar al-Taymī, is said to have conquered Makrān and reached the Indus River, while another commander, 'Abdallāh b. 'Umayr, moved from Sijistān to the boundaries of Ferghāna.[9] The greatest success, however, accompanied a column led by 'Abdallāh b. 'Āmir, who pursued the fleeing Sasanid emperor from southern Iran into Khurāsān and toward the capital of that province, Marw, where Yazdajird ultimately died in unclear circumstances, just before the arrival of the Arab army in A.H. 31/A.D. 652. Throughout the reports on these campaigns, there are no signs of disgruntlement among the troops.

These stories of conquest, however, receive none of the fanfare that surrounds the conquests in 'Umar's time. The detailed, day-to-day accounts that Ṭabarī so vividly gives of the battles of Yarmūk, Qādisiyya, and Nihāwand are virtually nonexistent for similar pivotal battles in 'Uthmān's time. There are no images of religious fulfillment, no portraits of miracle victories, just a plain progression of conquest campaigns noted in brief listing. More critically, perhaps, we lack the record of correspondence between the caliph and his governors and commanders that could describe how this expansion was directed. For 'Umar's time, Ṭabarī and others provide a mountain of documents that show the caliph managing, or at least made aware of, every decision made in the field, whether the issue was deciding where to begin the conquest of Syria (Damascus or Pella), where to build the first garrison towns, whether to invade by sea, or how the governors were faring in general. None of this exists for 'Uthmān's reign. Some letters describe a few rearrangements that 'Uthmān made regarding the revenues of Iraq, but these are positioned only to foreshadow the sources of grievance and trouble later in his reign, and on the whole the caliph always appears to have been reacting belatedly when he dismissed a governor or made a decision. 'Umar's deep probing of affairs everywhere, his network of spying on commanders, and his supervising letters to Abū Ubayda, Sa'd, 'Amr, Mu'ādh, Ḥudhayfa, and others are simply not matched in 'Uthmān's reign.

Instead, what receives the attention of the chroniclers of 'Uthmān's reign are the endless problems that preoccupied his last years: stories about the disgruntlement of marginal settler tribesmen in Kufa and Basra, the march of the opposition on Medina, and the murder of the caliph. Since these events, generally characterized as having provoked the first civil war in Islam, were followed by an even more tumultuous civil war between 'Alī and Mu'āwiya, which fed the great rivalry over succession between the Umayyads and Hāshimites afterward, retrospective views on these events took a tendentious and prophesying form. This complex and divisive climate that haunted the last years of 'Uthmān's reign has thus imbued his biography with a disproportionate emphasis on conflict, which was described in various ways that mix forms of reserved criticism and regret. The length of 'Uthmān's biography in the compendia of Ibn Sa'd's *Ṭabāqat* pales in comparison with that of 'Umar ('Uthmān's spanning forty pages as compared with 'Umar's hundred plus), and shows many signs of orthodox guardedness. The author sums up his view best when he declares the following:

> 'Uthmān reigned for twelve years as emir. In the first six of these, no one criticized anything in him, and indeed he became more popular with Quraysh than 'Umar b. al-Khaṭṭāb because 'Umar used to treat them harshly [*kāna shadīdan 'alayhim*], but when 'Uthmān acceded he treated them gently and extended bounty to them. Then he became lax in affairs [*tawānā fī amrihim*] and began appointing his kinfolk and members of his household [for rule] in the last six years. He bequeathed to Marwān b. [al-Ḥakam] one-fifth of the revenues of Egypt, he gave financial wealth to his relatives—justifying this as a type of filial support demanded by God [*ta'wwala fī dhalika al-ṣila allatī amara allāhu bihā*], appropriated wealth [*ittakhadha al-māl*], borrowed money from the state treasury, and used to say, "Abū Bakr and 'Umar cast away [their share of] wealth that was theirs, whereas I have chosen to take it and divide it among my kinfolk [*aqrubā'ī*]." People resented this greatly."[10]

Ibn Sa'd's statement can only be described as vaguely historical. The moralizing, religious thrust of writing here clearly goes beyond the mere recounting of factual history, and makes the reader wonder about some biblical influences that went into shaping stories about 'Uthmān's reign. The division created between six "good" years and six "bad," for example, echoes the biblical image of even division between seven prosperous years and seven lean years that Joseph predicted for Pharaoh in interpreting the latter's dream. The parallel between the positions of political authority of Joseph and 'Uthmān no doubt encouraged the writer's choice for making such a broad chronological frame for comparing a process of rise and decline in each reign.[11]

In addition, the model of even division of years is untenable because 'Uthmān's political and provincial policies in fact did not undergo a radical break after six years. Al-Walīd b. 'Uqba, for example, the most maligned of governors in 'Uthmān's reign, accused of drunkenness and misgovernment and on the whole resented for being the son of 'Uqba b. Abī Mu'īṭ, a staunch enemy of the Prophet in former times, had been appointed governor from the outset of 'Uthmān's reign and did not simply appear later on the scene. Ṭabarī complicates matters by saying that

Kufans thought al-Walīd was the best and kindest governor they had ever had during his first five years of rule.[12] Other allegedly flagrant appointments of 'Uthmān's relatives had already been laid out by 'Umar. Mu'āwiya had been in the governorship of Syria long before 'Uthmān's time, while Ibn Abī al-Sarḥ was made governor of southern Egypt by 'Umar just before he died.[13] These patterns indicate that 'Uthmān's later appointments of relatives only extended a policy, laid down already by 'Umar, that favored the old Meccan aristocracy.

If 'Uthmān's provincial appointments were not radically new, one wonders what else may have happened toward the middle of his reign that led to such widespread resentment against him. A more realistic explanation for a turning point in 'Uthmān's reign that provoked a public reaction would probably have to focus on certain measures that reflected the caliph's new centralizing program, where he sought to garner a larger share from the revenues of the conquered territories to be sent to the capital.[14] These policies helped rally a reaction in Kufa and Basra by tribesmen from Tamīm, Asad, and Bājila—tribes that had shown a similar resistance to Abū Bakr before, during the Ridda.

On the whole, the chronicles do not give much detailed information on how this movement of social and political reaction to 'Uthmān's rule was formed. However, there is a particular policy they describe that merits some attention. This relates to the caliph's distribution, starting in A.H. 30/A.D. 650, of conquered lands in Iraq (particularly the vast estates in the area of Kufa and Basra formerly owned by the Sasanid royal family and aristocracy but abandoned after their defeat and escape) to elite members of the Quraysh who were living in Medina. The background to this action is that the caliph had responded to complaints of the Kufans about their governor, al-Walīd b. 'Uqba, by replacing him with Sa'īd b. al-'Āṣ, a distant kinsmen but also a close protégé of his as well, who had been supported earlier and recommended for public service by 'Umar b. al-Khaṭṭāb.[15] Apparently, Sa'īd had accepted his appointment to Kufa only reluctantly, and he publicly declared this to the Kufans upon his arrival—a step that may have been politically unwise because it emboldened them against him later. Furthermore, striving to be cooperative with them and being malleable in personality, he reportedly brought with him from Medina a group of Kufan opposition leaders who had earlier gone to complain about al-Walīd b. 'Uqba (the group included al-Ashtar, Abū Khushsha al-Ghifārī, Jundub b. 'Abdallāh, and Abū Muṣ'ab b. Jaththama). Once at Kufa, Sa'īd encouraged the local leaders to bring to his attention public grievances and to publicize his desire to address people's concerns. This was the beginning of a new environment of trouble, as it opened the way for a new climate of rumor, intransigence, and chaos. Sa'īd thus wrote to 'Uthmān about these developments, saying:

> "The affairs of the Kufans are in turmoil. The nobles among them, the men of distinguished family [*buyūtāt*], and the veterans of the early campaigns [*ahl al-sābiqa wa'l-qudma*] have been overwhelmed, and the dominant element in these lands are recent immigrants and bedouin [*rawādif radafat wa a'rāb*] who have attached themselves [to the regular forces. It has gotten] to the point that one does not see a man of noble lineage or experience among the settlers or youth [of this place]." And 'Uthmān wrote back, "Among those to whom God granted the conquest of these lands, give preference to the veterans of the early campaigns [*faḍḍil ahl al-sābiqa wa'l-qudma mimman fataḥa allāh 'alayhi tilka al-bilād*]. Then let those who settled here because of (those veterans) be subordinate to them [*wa li-yakun man nazalahā bi-sabibihim taba'an lahum*], unless the latter regard [their obligations] as a burden and fail to perform them, while [the newcomers] do strive to carry out their duties. Keep everyone in his proper rank [*iḥfaẓ li-kullin manzilatahu*], and give them all their due measure (*wa a'ṭihim jamī'an bi-qisṭihim min al-ḥaqq*]. For through knowledge about the people is justice attained [*fa-inna al-ma'rifa bi'l-nās bihā yuṣāb al-'adl*]."[16]

'Uthmān's new policy suggestion only exacerbated the situation, and forced Sa'īd to write again asking for help. This is when 'Uthmān began to explore a new restructuring policy. After summoning the congregation in Medina for a meeting, he described to them the situation in Iraq, and proposed to "restore" to them (more accurately, "grant" them) some of the conquered lands in Iraq as their own feudalistic estates (*iqṭā'*). When asked how he would do this, he proposed selling to the Qurashī elite in Medina plots of the conquered (*fay'*) lands in exchange for their estates or other assets in the Ḥijāz. Aside from demonstrating a blatant caliphal seizure of land and an arbitrary dispensing with what belonged to other members of the community, this step would have allowed the creation of a Qurashī economic and political control in both the Ḥijāz and Iraq. The idea quickly proved popular and several individuals took advantage of this offer soon after.[17]

The narrators do not record the economic benefits of such a land swap. They mainly seem interested in showing through this account the philosophical value of granting land and authority to individuals who are more deserving of it or capable of using influence wisely. As the public's statement to 'Uthmān in response to his complaints and speech put it: "Do not humor [the Kufans] in this, and do not let them aspire after something for which they are not fit. For if someone undertakes matters in which he is incompetent, he cannot manage them and [instead] corrupts them [*innahu idhā nahaḍa fi'l-umūr man laysa lahā bi-ahl lam yaḥtamilhā wa afsadahā*]"[18]—a moralizing swipe that was undoubtedly intended against 'Alī as much as it responded to the immediate situation in Kufa. Nor do the narrators record the immediate reaction among the Kufan commune to the new policy. The revolt against the governor will be described later in light of the crisis of the year A.H. 33/A.D. 654. It seems certain, however, that this policy was sure to invite massive resentment against both governor and caliph.[19] The Kufan settlers resented this feudalistic consolidation of power in Medina as preferential and arrogant and began to rally against it.[20]

Although more historically plausible than the religious myths cited above, this story also served a purpose as a political exemplum, and would have interested Ṭabarī because of its emphasis on the relation of political order and sound government to social hierarchy and the various qualities of social groups. 'Uthmān was here setting in place an authority system based not simply on his direct rule, but on restoring privilege to pre-Islamic Arab tribal elite (specifically the Quraysh), and this was a theme that would get further developed and advocated in the speeches of Mu'āwiya when the crisis gives way to conflict.[21] Thus, there is even in such plain contexts as the historical description of a matter like the land swap incident a possibility that narrators crafted and expanded narratives to serve moralizing and polemical purposes, in this case on behalf of the monarchal (Umayyad) interest and the goal of guarding the collectivity of the community of Medina.

Another likely reason for the growth in opposition to the caliph must have been his attempt to codify an official text of the Qur'ān. Orthodox tradition is reticent about both the history of the codification of the Qur'ān, and attempts to portray variations in the texts of the Qur'ān in the provinces as variations of tribal dialects for reading the text rather than variations of substance—the comparison here usually made with the case of scriptural differences between Jews and Christians.[22] The difference between at least one owner of a *muṣḥaf* (Qur'ān codex), 'Abdallāh b. Mas'ūd, who was settled in Kufa but does not seem to have made common cause with the opposition there, and 'Uthmān led to a famous story of bitter confrontation and suppression of Ibn Mas'ūd (nothing similar is attributed to another owner of a *muṣḥaf*, Ubayy b. Ka'b, whose copy was also sequestered by the caliph). Historians do not possess a firm picture of what these disagreements in content were, and what is even more puzzling is that in the long list of transgressions by 'Uthmān, there is no mention of a dispute over accepting a particular *sūra* (chapter) or *āya* (verse), even though there are other disputes revolving around details of ritual or *sunna*.[23] Whatever the differences were, it seems clear that 'Uthmān tried to do something daring for religious scripture that had not been done before—perhaps the mere turning of an oral religious discourse into a written and codified text.[24] The attempt to disseminate an official text of the Qur'ān from the capital to the provinces represented another layer of provocation that would have created a controversy in the provinces.

The story about the first appearances of the dispute regarding Qur'ānic readings can also help shed some light on the interrelation between the religious and literary elements that go into the shaping of a historical text. The first disagreement over Qur'ānic reading reportedly began between Syrian and Iraqi tribesmen during the Islamic campaign in Armenia in 'Uthmān's time. Noting this, Ḥudhayfa [b. 'Usayd al-Ghifārī][25] reportedly traveled to Medina, and described how the two factions had nearly came to blows over whose recitation was the correct one, and urged the caliph to protect the *umma* from further discord. This instance is usually reported as the main impetus for the caliph's plan to codify the text of the Qur'ān.[26] The story is probably apocryphal, but is significant in a number ways. Aside from providing an orthodox apologetic for the caliph's motivation, it is interesting in that its narrators placed the first dispute on the Armenian frontier, where the Islamic armies had reached their peak of conquest during the last years of 'Umar's reign in A.H. 22/A.D. 642, during the campaign of 'Abd al-Raḥmān b. Rabī'a, dubbed "Dhū al-Nūr," who was then accompanied by Ḥudhayfa.

The campaign, then, is said to have targeted the farthest corner of al-Bāb on the northern frontier, which was ruled by Shahrbarāz, a man described as a descendant of the king who marched on Syria and ended the Israelite state in an earlier period.[27]

We shall examine below other aspects of that Muslim-Christian encounter between the Arab commander and the enemy leader. What is relevant to the Qur'ān issue here, however, are two aspects in particular: first, that discord appears by chance among the troops at the peak of their conquests; and second, that the enemy leader is given an association with the biblical narrative, as another Bukhtnaṣar. These aspects are noteworthy because they may hint of yet another segment of biblical influence on Islamic parabolic writing. The story of discord among troops over proper Qur'ānic recitation could well have been inspired by the biblical story of the tower of Babel and the beginning of discord in language among the builders as they reached the peak. In this context, the limits of Islamic territoriality provided the counterpart to the biblical monument, and the variation in Qur'ānic recitation provided the parallel to the discord over language. The contours in the fortune of the Israelite community, its rise and fall, are represented as repeating in the Muslim community centered in Medina. And this process is accentuated by a numerical resemblance whereby just as the discord at the tower of Babel led to the rise of seventy-three languages,[28] so would the Islamic community divide, as per the prophecy of the famous *ḥadīth*, into seventy-three sects. The eventually destructive conquest of Medina in A.H. 63/A.D. 683 by the armies of the Umayyads in Yazīd's reign would later be viewed as a moment of redemptive closure that paralleled the conquest of the Israelite state by leaders such as Bukhtnaṣar and Sharbarāz.

Even the focus on Kufa as the beginning place of opposition to 'Uthmān is historically questionable. An element of myth has always surrounded the culture of Kufa, to a greater extent than many other Islamic cities. That it was a frontier town with a socially diverse populace, especially with the first arrival of Arabian tribal military contingents, was no doubt a source for political instability.[29] However, Kufa's restless political nature is exaggerated by the Islamic narrators in light of the town's future support for various 'Alid and Khārijite rebellions against the Umayyads and 'Abbāsids. Kufa's frequent espousal of a rebellious cause, and equal treachery toward the leaders of these movements in the seventh and eighth centuries, came down as an enduring moralizing and negative lesson in Islamic history, inviting a sociocultural view of the Kufans as unfaithful; hence the rhyming adage "*al-Kūfiyy lā yūfiyy*" ("a Kufan is never loyal").[30] This may seem unusual, given that originally Kufa had received high praise from 'Umar[31] and is connected in some accounts to the ancient prophets with a rich lore.[32] However, such traditions have to be placed within a cyclical view of history that was parabolic in intention and served a polemical purpose. In giving the city some praise but later describing its challenges to caliphs and betrayal of the 'Alid *imāms*, narrators were describing a treacherous locale that underwent transitions. It was in some sense intended in representation as the counterpart to Jerusalem and that city's mixed reception for prophets, but in a wider sense it also served to illustrate the Qur'ānic parable about a universal city or village that loses divine favor and becomes the playing field for cataclysm and parable after initially being the culminating point of success.[33]

Ṭabarī seems to have had a low regard for the tribes that settled in Kufa, whom he viewed as uncouth tribesmen (*a'rāb*) or irregular auxiliaries (*rawādifun radafat*), and implicitly contrasts them with Meccan and other sedentary tribes, labeled as "purebred tribes" (*dhawī al-aḥsāb wa'l-uṣūl*). Kufans are viewed as the source of decline, as in the account that describes the campaigns of 'Abd al-Raḥmān b. Rabī'a on the Khazar front. There Ṭabarī relates: "He ['Abd al-Raḥmān] launched a number of incursions in the time of 'Uthmān. 'Abd al-Raḥmān was then struck down when the people of Kufa changed in the emirate of 'Uthmān after he accepted the Ridda folk in his service in an effort to set them on the right path [*ḥīna tabaddala ahl al-Kūfa fī imārati 'Uthmān li-isti'mālihi man kāna irtadda istiṣlāḥan lahum*]."[34] Whatever good the governors (*umarā'*) would try to accord the Kufans, the latter would little heed any authority and championed various oppositions, first against Medina, then against Damascus, in the hope of selfish gain. The first signs of their discord would appear in 'Uthmān's reign, as we shall see later, when they would take on a range of pious causes, whether Hāshimite or Khārijite, only to betray these when the hour of real fighting came.[35]

## THE MYTHOLOGY OF 'UTHMĀN'S SEDITIOUS REIGN

Where history ends and pious or didactic memory begins is an issue that confronts the reader in various stories about this caliph, and each reader may discern different problems in 'Uthmān's reign. From the perspective of the established caliphate of the ninth century, where the concept of divine right had long been internalized into 'Abbāsid political ideology, 'Uthmān's refusal to abdicate would have been considered a righteous and sound political move, but this view would have overlooked other dimensions of 'Uthmān's problem. From the juristic view, which preoccupied itself with implementation of the law and the security of the principles of *sunna* and *jamā'a*, political criticisms (concerning the charge of nepotism and the caliph's lack of willingness to compromise) fell outside the question of *ḥudūd*: what sins deserved the death penalty in Islam? And, since the latter were said to be a specific set of three (apostasy, murder, and adultery of the married person), the political discussion was hard to accommodate, especially when it was seen brandishing slogans that were dear to the Khārijites, such as "*al-amr bi'l-ma'rūf wa'l-nahy 'an al-munkar*."[36]

The religious apologetic on behalf of the caliph best represented 'Uthmān's dilemma as a form of tribulation (*balā'*), a concept generally applied in religious narratives to the biographies of prophets to show the divine testing of their faith. The hagiography of this representation is strengthened because the trouble facing the caliph was said to have been foretold to him by the Prophet, who reportedly urged 'Uthmān not to renounce the caliphate (*qamīs al-khilāfa*) and predicts his coming death as a martyr (*shahīd*).[37] When 'Uthmān later does face such a crisis and the opposition demands his abdication, the caliph then makes his famous comment in which he refuses to give up the caliphate.[38] After his death comes the famous story about how Mu'āwiya used the bloodied shirt of the caliph to rouse public support in the war he led against the fourth caliph.[39]

Within this frame of reading, the orthodox religious position is totally on the side of 'Uthmān, since the caliph's errors are not perceived as something against the fundamentals of the law, and the caliph uses the language of *ḥadīth* to defend his rule. Ibn Sa'd displays the pro-'Uthmān orthodox viewpoint by redacting accounts in a way that downplays 'Uthmān's missteps, and by commenting with a careful choice of words. When describing the controversy over the third caliph's financial subsidies to his relatives, for instance, Ibn Sa'd makes the issue one of religious interpretation, using the term "*ta'awwala*" (to interpret or reckon), rather than "*ibtada'a*" (to innovate deliberately)—a term with negative connotations—to explain the action. Since the term "*ta'awwala*" is closely related to the concept of scholarly "*ijtihād*" and to an openness of this exercise to an acceptable range of right and wrong, the implication is that whatever error resulted from this action could be termed as "*khaṭī'a*" (error) and thus safely distanced from the more damning territory of "*dhanb*" (sin), which demands atonement, chastisement, and possibly abdication.

Qur'ānic evocations that imply a similarity between the tragedy of 'Uthmān and the deaths of previous prophets are also favored by Ibn Sa'd, although the wider parabolic context from which he drew these accounts is lost. In a key passage we read of how 'Uthmān cautioned of imminent divine punishment toward those planning an attack on him, using a tone closer to that of the prophets and martyrs than to that typical of the caliphs. 'Uthmān reportedly addressed those who besieged his house before the attack, saying: "O People, do not inflict harm on me for I am [your] ruler and Muslim brother. By God, I have sought only to be constructive [*in aradtu illā al-iṣlāḥ*] to the best of my ability, whether I acted correctly or erred at times. [Know] that if you kill me, you will never pray in unity again, nor carry out the *ghazw* [military campaigns] united or receive your rightful booty. You will all become enemies of one another like this" (clasping his hands in way that the fingers cross one another). 'Uthmān then said (quoting the Qur'ān): "O my people, let not the breach with me move you, so that there smite you the like of what smote the people of Noah, or the people of Hūd, or the people of Ṣāliḥ; 'and the people of Lot are not far away from you.'[40]"[41]

When they refused, he said: "Do you claim that I seized this authority by the sword and conquest, and not by the *shūrā* of the Muslims? Or do you claim that God did not know something about me when I first acceded that became known at the end?" With the opponents still refusing to listen, 'Uthmān declared a prayer, saying: "O Lord, take account of all this multitude, kill them to the last man, and do not let any of them remain." Mujāhid (the narrator) said: "God killed of them whom he killed during the *fitna*, and then Yazīd later sent an army of twenty thousand who made Medina open for conquest for three days because of the people's complicity [in the murder] [*li-mudāhanatihim*]."[42]

This account successfully builds up the range of Sunnī defenses against sedition in general and against questioning 'Uthmān in particular. Opposition is cast as a threat to community unity, as well as to its prospects for *jihād*, the equitable division of booty, and proper assembly for prayer. 'Uthmān himself is made to articulate this orthodox view as a doctrine and a question. Furthermore, the accounts generally portrayed (at least on the surface) 'Uthmān as legitimately elected by the *shūrā* council, and therefore a representative of the community's political consensus. No believer in the idyllic background of the companions could therefore conceive of a sour transformation in their lot. This would have implied either that God was misleading the community or that this chosen community was subject to unpredictable turns of fate.[43]

An indirect discussion of the topic of *qaḍā'* and *qadar* (fate and predestination) figures prominently in this contentious historical representation as the narrators tried to defend or criticize 'Uthmān and decide on his role as a righteous caliph. When the debate breaks down between the caliph and his opponents in the end, 'Uthmān's posture ceases to be that of a temporal ruler and becomes closer to that of a message-bearing prophet. Faced with a stubborn and hostile community of followers, 'Uthmān resembles prophets, like Nūh, Hūd, or Ṣāliḥ, who completely fail to convince their communities of their divine message and ultimately abandon their locale to let divine punishment fall on their towns. The lack of willingness among 'Uthmān's enemies to reason and debate further and their shrugging attitude is exaggerated by the narrator to draw a symmetry with Qur'ānic stories of divine judgment.

Yet in spite of predictions and the merit of a martyr's death, the orthodox perspective faced the problem of explaining not just the tragic death of 'Uthmān, but also the discord among the companions and how to characterize the group who attacked the caliph. Ibn Sa'd's explanation here tried to mitigate the fallout on the companions by isolating the final outburst of violent action against 'Uthmān as perpetrated by a band of outside brigands from Kufa, Basra, and Egypt. This position helped to distance the companions of the Prophet living in Medina from responsibility for the assassination, and it also seemed to fit within the frame of a quietist strand of juristic political thinking that favored obedience to authority (although here this gets lost in a mood of apathy and tacit hostility) and avoidance of political activity in times of *fitna*.

Ibn Sa'd best presents this view, when he quotes a report that says, "The Egyptians who surrounded 'Uthmān were six hundred;[44] at their head were 'Abd al-Raḥmān b. 'Adīs al-Balawī, Kināna b. Bishr b. 'Attāb al-Kindī, and 'Amr b. al-Ḥamiq. Those who came from Kufa were two hundred, headed by Mālik al-Ashtar al-Nakh'ī, and those who came from Baṣra were one hundred, headed by Ḥukaym b. Jabala al-'Abdī. They all acted as with one hand in the evil deed. And they were joined by a group of lowly people whose oaths and sincerity were dubious and misguided (*maftūnūn*). The companions of the Prophet, peace be upon him, who failed to support him (*alladhīna khadhalūh*) had disinclined to be part of a seditious event (*karihū al-fitna*) and thought that matters would not reach killing him. They [the companions] regretted what they did in this matter, and by God, had they or some of them only so much as spoken up and hurled some soil in the face of these [the opponents], the latter would have departed with shame."[45]

This statement downplays any complicity in Medina in the assassination by painting the companions' lack of involvement as being the result of a virtuous desire to avoid sedition (*fitna*). Although this account is attributed to Wāqidī, the extra commentary on history that it includes toward the end may well have been Ibn Sa'd's, since it is not characteristic of the rest of the narration style. In this commentary, Ibn Sa'd does not deny the fact that, whatever the motive, the caliph was let down by the companions (*khadhalūh*), and they were negligent. Ibn Sa'd's closing line rebukes the companions to an unusual degree, and stresses how important it would have been for them to interfere, and shows how much leverage the companions wielded in Medina irrespective of the size of the opposition. Ibn Sa'd's main thrust, therefore, epitomizes the pro-'Uthmān drift of the Sunnī texts, which tend to isolate the companions' scene from a real historical context and reduce history to a mere frame for the religious viewpoint of the *sunna* and *jamā'a*.[46]

## ṬABARĪ'S VIEW: THE EARLY DATING OF TROUBLED TIMES

The controversy surrounding 'Uthmān that is included in summary form by Ibn Sa'd and discussed within largely a Sunnī religious frame in his text is elaborated in extensive tales in the chronicle of Ṭabarī, who, unlike other writers, withholds judgment and does not allow his own intrusions to defend or detract from the caliph. Ṭabarī's account of the reign of 'Uthmān contains the usual directions of his interests: attention to conquests in the east, a focus on companion interaction in Medina, and the scene of Arab tribal politics in Arabia and the provinces.

Compared to his previous accounts of the Ridda wars and conquests in 'Umar's reign, his coverage of campaigns in 'Uthmān's reign is again, like Ibn Sa'd's, relatively short. But unlike Ibn Sa'd and Balādhurī, who transmit accounts outside any chronological frame, Ṭabarī's history has a sequential and causal frame. This allows the reader to explore cause and effect among anecdotes more accurately in Ṭabarī's work, even though his work frequently contains inexplicable gaps. These puzzling gaps, however, can often be completed by anecdotes recounted by the even less bashful Balādhurī and sometimes Ibn Sa'd, who occasionally transmitted brief accounts to foster a biographical text, ignoring the broader historical context from which these statements came (as in Hurmuzān's biography). Despite the lacunae, Ṭabarī's work remains the working benchmark for the original master narrative of that early period, and his text is the key reflection of that lost genre of historiographical literature that communicated allusive meanings while recounting a seemingly feasible historical outline. Like other ninth-century writers, Ṭabarī judges 'Uthmān's last years as ones of sedition and failure, and highlights the symbolic turn of fortune from the six good years to the six bad ones that occurred upon the loss of the caliphal ring. However, Ṭabarī's version of 'Uthmān's reign, unlike other chroniclers, hints that the trouble began from the start.

## *Precursor Events*

The litany of trivial innovations (*bida'*) that surrounds 'Uthmān in his early years in power can make the reader unable to perceive any one factor as more important than others in tarnishing the caliph's image. However, it is likely that, in the original narrative of the Rāshidūn caliphs, the most important of these transgressions was seen to have occurred at the start of 'Uthmān's rule, when the caliph issued a controversial judgment on a case connected to the story of 'Umar's assassination, namely the case of 'Ubaydallāh b. 'Umar's murder of Hurmuzān.

This was the famous retribution affair in which 'Ubaydallāh b. 'Umar set out to avenge his father's death by killing Hurmuzān and Abū Lu'lu'a's daughter, and voicing the threat that he was going to kill all Persians resident in Medina after he had heard rumors of Hurmuzān's complicity in a conspiracy to assassinate 'Umar. The narratives make it clear that

'Ubaydallāh's actions were wrong and deserved punishment, since his opinion was based on no more than an uncorroborated word from 'Abd al-Raḥmān b. Abī Bakr.[47] This case is treated in the sources as a first signal test of how scrupulous the new caliph was going to be in applying religious law. Things were not so simple as the zealous advocates of the law conceived, however, since 'Uthmān faced a potential storm from a public that refused to see 'Ubaydallāh punished with death. A counterassessment of the evidence probably shaped this position, but it was mainly based on a strong nostalgia for the memory of the assassinated caliph. "'Umar is killed yesterday, and his son gets put to death today!"[48] the crowds yelled. 'Uthmān thus had to weigh his options: face a civil war in Medina after executing 'Ubaydallāh or turn over a new leaf by paying Hurmuzān's blood money (after the tribal custom of *lex talionis*) and therefore risk appearing somewhat lax in applying religious law. With some maneuvering advice from 'Amr b. al-'Āṣ, who said that the caliph was availed of responsibility for this issue since it happened before his accession and jurisdiction began, 'Uthmān chose to pay the blood money for Hurmuzān, claiming to be his patron, and he let 'Ubaydallāh go.

This was a major legal debacle from a variety of angles. The caliph was assuming the right of *lex talionis* in the place of the close kin who normally assumed this role (one narrative pushes forward an alleged son of Hurmuzān, al-Qumādhbān, who in another story gives up his right for revenge).[49] The caliph was viewed as compromising a matter of religious law for political considerations,[50] and 'Alī would voice his anger here not by criticizing 'Uthmān but by vowing to punish 'Ubaydallāh if he ('Alī) ever got the chance, thus anticipating not only his own accession but future events at Ṣiffīn, where 'Ubaydallāh died fighting on the side of Mu'āwiya. The explicit clash of the 'Alid opinion and 'Uthmān's verdict once again, as in the case of the affair of al-Mughīra in 'Umar's reign, does not surface in a direct confrontation between 'Alī and the ruling caliph, but rather between a pro-'Alid speaker, al-Miqdad b. 'Amr, and 'Uthmān. When the caliph declared at the mosque, "I am guardian of Hurmuzān's blood, and I have chosen to grant it to God and 'Umar, and leave it for [the blood of] 'Umar," al-Miqdad stood up and declared, "Hurmuzān is the servant of God and His Prophet [*mawlā allāh wa rasūlihi*]. It is not for you to grant what is for God and His Prophet!"[51]

However, the caliph may not necessarily have been lax in applying the law. The case of 'Ubaydallāh was challenging because it depended not only on those identified as victims of 'Ubaydallāh's attack (Hurmuzān, Abū Lu'lu'a's daughter, and/or Jufayna), but also on what evidence was used to substantiate the conspiracy case. If 'Ubaydallāh's only victim was Hurmuzān (since Abū Lu'lu'a's daughter doesn't figure in all accounts),[52] then 'Uthmān had much ambiguous evidence to digest. The conspiracy-to-murder charge, unlike adultery, did not require four witnesses, and if 'Umar had been around, a question or two might well have been raised about why Hurmuzān was examining the dagger and consorting with the enemies of Islam. The two conflicting questions that 'Uthmān was caught between were these: Was the testimony of 'Abd al-Raḥmān b. Abī Bakr enough to go by? And, was ignoring it permissible if the judgment was to execute 'Ubaydallāh? Further arguments that the caliph was the only rightful authority to exact revenge or punishment would have activated a broader debate about the final authority of a ruler's opinion.

These questions about the legitimacy of 'Uthmān's action therefore form a classic example of the famous ninth-century debates as to whether a caliph's political legitimacy is defined by religious excellence or political skill. The debate over whether *al-afḍal* (the most excellent) or *al-mafḍūl* (the less excellent in religious terms but competent in political terms) should be allowed to be caliph occupied much of the theoretical attention of both Sunnī and Shī'ī thinkers, who looked upon the Rāshidūn, Umayyad, and 'Abbāsid dynasties, and even 'Alid pretenders, through this lens of religious versus secular assessment. In the present case, 'Uthmān had shown his political skill of keeping the community united, but he had done so at the enormous price, Shī'īs especially might argue, of suspending a clear religious ruling. A Sunnī argument would have countered that 'Uthmān's act of safeguarding peace in the community by using the license of *lex talionis* was a religiously valid means to deliver justice. Implicitly, this opened the door to, and seemed to condone, there being much freedom accorded by Sunnīs to caliphs in exercising (or arbitrating) authority at such pivotal moments of decision.

Ṭabarī was conscious of how these early narratives factored into a complex debate that would grow in time. However marginal an issue the pardon of 'Ubaydallāh may have seemed in its time, and whatever merits there were to either angle in the debate, Ṭabarī and the narrators were implying that the age of righteous justice and of synchrony between a secular and a religious order had come to an end with the death of 'Umar. The age of Muslim consensus had effectively ended.

Modern historians have traditionally ignored viewing the episode of 'Ubaydallāh b. 'Umar as a source of discontent against 'Uthmān. However, the sources strongly suggest that the rift between 'Alī and 'Uthmān began precisely over this issue, which reflected their divergent philosophies of rule. 'Alī had pushed for punishing 'Ubaydallāh, while 'Amr b. al-'Āṣ swayed the caliph's opinion, as he would Mu'āwiya's later on. This was a case of Ṣiffīn without the swords being drawn or arbitration reached, and it hinted of things to come. Suddenly the death of an average Persian believer, Hurmuzān, became the defining event in the life of the community, and the skies darkened, hinting at divine displeasure with 'Uthmān's verdict.[53] The episode was undoubtedly connected in the original narrative to the pro-Persian and pro-'Alid themes discussed earlier, as al-Hurmuzān came to be portrayed as an example of the devoted Muslim.[54]

From the moment of that crisis of justice onward, Ṭabarī's accounts condition the reader to be wary of any new unusual action, by either 'Uthmān or his lieutenants, as a new signal of sinister innovation. In this context, it becomes a source of surprise that he used to have his bread made out of sifted flour or that he laid out a significant tent (*fusṭāṭ*) in the field of Mina while on pilgrimage,[55] and even stories about insignificant events in the provinces became indicators of potential trouble ahead. When a commander, Muḥammad b. Abī Ḥudhayfa, was heard announcing *takbīr* at the end of the Battle of Dhāt al-Ṣawārī, he was summoned by Ibn Abī al-Sarḥ and rebuked for being out of line and making this *bid'a*.[56] And when Mu'āwiya was said to have declared that the wealth of the state is "*māl allāh*" (the wealth or treasury of God), he was criticized by Abū Dharr al-Ghifārī as making a *bid'a* (religiously inventive statement).[57] All manner of major and minor developments were taken as signs that an unrighteous rule was underway and drifting almost mystically in the wrong direction. Between the center and provinces, between caliph and governors, there was, Ṭabarī's narratives imply, a pattern being set for discord. This pattern is the reverse of the virtuous harmony between caliph and governors that prevailed in 'Umar's reign. Thus 'Uthmān and al-Walīd b. 'Uqba provide the degenerative antithesis to the famous purported miracle of harmony between 'Umar and Sāriya.[58]

In his narration of military events in the year A.H. 32/A.D. 653, Ṭabarī's religious message about the loss of divine grace for the community and imminent trouble is voiced vividly. One year before the slide into civil war, a small battle occurs on the northern front involving Muslims and Khazars (and Turks) that foreshadows ill fate for the community. After years of victorious raids by 'Abd al-Raḥmān b. Rabī'a al-Bāhilī in which no Muslim died and the Turks saw constant defeat, Muslims finally witnessed their first defeat. Evidently, the Turks had prepared for that confrontation at the city of Balanjar with much introspection. "We were a nation to whom there was no match until this small nation came along against which we have been unable to stand," one of the Khazars is quoted as saying. Another reportedly responded that Muslims do not die, and this myth circulated until one day the arrows of some Khazars finally found their mark in an ambush against a group of passing Muslim soldiers. When news of the soldiers' death spread, the Khazars became emboldened and mounted an attack on the commander 'Abd al-Raḥmān b. Rabī'a. The Muslims fell in retreat, and 'Abd al-Raḥmān was killed. His body was afterward taken by the Khazars, and included in their other battles as a good omen.[59]

To what extent this picture of defeat on the Khazar front is real is difficult to say. The superstition it relates about carrying a commander's body in battle may be historic or may reflect some custom in that region or beyond in Ṭabarī's time. The constructed nature of this vivid description and the switch from a tide of victory to a sudden fall of the conquerors becomes clearer when we view it in conjunction with other events in 'Umar's reign, especially in the year A.H. 22/A.D. 642, where it finds an opposite antecedent. In that year, which saw the submission of just about every significant Iranian region (Hamadan, Rayy, Qūmis, Jurjān, Ṭabaristān, and Azerbayjan), Arab armies finally reached the northern extremity of the Persian domain on the Caucasus at the passage of Balanjar, an area described as "al-Bāb." The local Persian governor, a man said to be of the family of Shahrbarāz, reportedly admired the noble pedigree of the ruling Arabs, describing them as "*dhawī aḥsāb*," and contrasted them to the social groups across the frontier he was entrusted with fighting, whom he identified as al-Qibj (possibly a Turkic group) and Armenians. Those people, he explained, "did not have a noble pedigree, nor did it befit noble men [i.e., the Arabs] to help them [*lā yunsabūna ilā aḥsāb wa lā yanbaghī li-dhī al-ḥasab an yu'īna hā'ulā'*]," and therefore he earnestly asked that the Arabs drop the requirement of al-Jizya (poll tax) so as not to humiliate him in the enemies' eyes (*fa-lā tudhillūnā bi'l jizya fa-tūhinūna li-'aduwwikum*). The Arab commander raised this with Surāqa b. 'Amr, who in turn wrote to 'Umar, asking for permission to grant the governor this indulgence. 'Umar, in keeping with his sympathy to a Khusraw-like worldview of order and rank, reportedly agreed [*fa-ajāzahu wa ḥassanahu*].[60]

The whole episode of this conquest in the Caucasus then becomes symbolic, as the Arabs emerge as the clear successors to the Persian state and as the ones now defending civilization against barbarism on the northernmost *thughūr*. Surāqa died and was succeeded by 'Abd al-Raḥmān b. Rabī'a, who entertained Shahrbarāz as a part of his entourage. On one occasion, the latter showed the Arab governor a treasure he had acquired on one of his exploits into a mythic-sounding cave. 'Abd al-Raḥmān took a jewel in his hand, turned it about, and then gave it back to Shahrbarāz, who then commented: "This [jewel] is more precious than this entire region [i.e., al-Bāb], and you are, by God, closer to my liking as suzerains than the family of Khusraw, for had they been here, they would have confiscated this [jewel] from me. By God, nothing shall stand in your way, so long as you keep the faith, and your high chief remains faithful [*wa aymu allāh lā yaqūmu lakum shay'un mā wafaytum wa wafā malikukum al-akbar*]!"[61]

This situation of an infidel ruler admiring the Arabs for the general virtue of order and faithfulness (to treaties, covenants, and established laws) and predicting their providential guidance and success is a device that Ṭabarī used on several occasions to indirectly praise the righteousness of the Islamic conquest. In this particular case, however, the story was meant to compare the reigns of 'Umar and 'Uthmān and the fortune of the Arab community under both leaders. The defeat of the Arab army in 'Uthmān's reign was indirectly connected with this leader's departure from established principles of proper government, just as victory in 'Umar's reign was attributed to adherence to ideals propounded by the Islamic mission.[62] In the way Ṭabarī positions the story of defeat in 'Uthmān's reign as a turning point from an age of victory to one of incipient discord, we see how he wove together threads of history and fiction to signal the end of the utopian age. The spilling of a commander's blood became an omen of what was to come later at the center of government.

## *Precursor Speech*

Along with the foreshadowing description of discord through events, Ṭabarī organizes 'Uthmān's speeches from the beginning of his reign to show anxiety about impending trouble. At the outset of 'Uthmān's reign,

Ṭabarī describes how the new caliph laid out a virtuous program and exhorted the people in a speech about their religious and moral duties. 'Uthmān's behavior here is reminiscent of Abū Bakr and 'Umar, who delivered accession speeches that exhorted the populace to obey the caliph if he obeys God and to criticize him if he did not. Interestingly, 'Uthmān holds back from encouraging the people to criticize him if they find fault, as if to foreshadow the clashes of his later years. However, the speeches of 'Uthmān serve a unique purpose here, in that they contain a thread of self-criticism adapted for this caliph's unique tragedy. 'Uthmān here lays out the religious ideals of rule, then lets the reader judge whether the caliph lived up to these words or contradicted them. Ṭabarī's narrator describes 'Uthmān's first public appearance as follows: After the men of the *shūrā* had rendered the oath of allegiance to 'Uthmān, he went out, more distressed than any of them. He came to the pulpit of the Messenger of God and preached to the people, praising and extolling God and asking His blessing upon the Prophet. He said: "Verily you are in a transitory abode and in the flower of life, so set forth until the time appointed for your death and aim for the best you can attain, for you may be met [by your end] morning or evening. Surely this world harbors deceit [*inna al-dunyā ṭuwiyat 'alā al-ghurūr*], 'so let not the present life delude you,' and 'let not the deceitful one delude you concerning God.'[63] Consider those who have gone before you, then be in earnest and do not be neglectful, for you will surely not be overlooked. Where are the sons and brothers of this world who tilled it, dwelt in it, and were long granted enjoyment therein? [*ayna abnā' al-dunyā wa ikhwānuhā alladhīna athārūhā wa 'amarūhā wa mutti'ū bihā ṭawīlan*] Did it not spit them out? Cast aside this world as God has cast it aside and seek the hereafter, for verily God has coined a parable for it and for that which is better. The Almighty has said: 'And strike for them the similitude of the present life [*mathal al-ḥayāt al-dunyā*]: it is as water that We send down out of heaven, [and the plants of the earth mingle with it; and in the morning it is straw the winds scatter; and God is omnipotent over everything. Wealth and sons are the adornment of the present world; but the abiding things, the deeds of righteousness, are better with God in reward, and better in] hope.'"[64] Then the people came forward to render the oath of allegiance to him.[65]

The ascetic coloring of 'Uthmān's words here is unmistakable and shows little sign of an ambitious caliph who in future years would become an absolutist tyrant. On the surface, this speech confirms what is said about 'Uthmān as starting out similarly to Abū Bakr and 'Umar, with a renunciatory lifestyle and warnings of the divine wrath and historical ill fortune to come if the community were to stray. However, the same speech contains much irony, as it anticipates 'Uthmān's future departure from these principles. 'Uthmān's statement, "*alā inna al-dunyā ṭuwiyat 'alā al-ghurūr*," sounds like general religious advice, but it can also be viewed as an elliptical commentary on his political situation in later years, when he became very jealous of sharing authority and refused to abdicate. The reflexive nature of this advice even hints that 'Uthmān knew who his audience was (himself), when the narrator declares from the outset that 'Uthmān appeared before the public more distressed than any of them (*kharaja 'alayhim wa huwa ashadduhum ka'āba*). His sadness here perhaps reflects the caliph's undisclosed premonition of his coming change of character and eventual collapse. The speech provides a heralding summary of concepts and beliefs that 'Uthmān would abandon and helps the reader contextualize all of the turns taken in the years of 'Uthmān's reign.

The same message of idealism and exhortation is repeated in a letter that the caliph sends to provincial governors, in which he again outlines a set of key virtues that define political stability and community success: *ḥayā'*, *amāna*, and *wafā'*. Ṭabarī relates that in this letter, 'Uthmān declared:

> "To proceed: God has commanded the *imāms* to be shepherds [*ru'āt*]; He did not command them to be tax collectors [*jubāt*]. Indeed, at the inception of this community, they were made shepherds and not tax collectors [*inna ṣadra hādhihi al-umma khuliqū ru'āt, lam yukhlaqū jubāt*]. But your *imāms* are surely on the verge of becoming tax collectors rather than shepherds. If they turn out thus, then modest manners, integrity, and good faith will come to an end [*fa-in 'ādū kadhalika inqaṭa'a al-ḥayā' wa'l-amāna wa'l-wafā'*]. Verily, the most just conduct is for you to examine the affairs and obligations of the Muslims, so that you can give them what is properly theirs and take from them what they owe. Do likewise as regards the Pact of Protection; Give them what is theirs and take from them what they owe. As to the enemy whom you encounter, faithfully seek God's aid against them."[66]

This declaration can be viewed as moralistic rather than specifically Islamic. The virtues of *ḥayā'*, *amāna*, and *wafā'* are secular social and political concepts that overlap with religious principles, but the aim of the exhortation is ultimately ethical. 'Uthmān, as in 'Umar's earlier debate with Hurmuzān, does not invoke the miracle of Islamic belief per se (as a ritualistic or legalistic source of power) as the source of Islamic success, but rather casts the success of the Islamic community (still viewed as exclusively Arab in this phase) as tied to the revival of universal moralistic principles: the strict division of right and wrong, loyalty, unity, and devotion to justice, whether delivered to Muslims or non-Muslims. The miracle of religious success, according to this speech, is tied to these virtues—qualities that although are of religious value and are attested in the Qur'ān, are ultimately treated in nonconfessional terms as key operating parameters in history. In describing the conditions of triumph, the caliph's declaration also describes the conditions of ideal times and the beginnings of the Islamic state. Life was at its ideal when rulers were shepherds, as at the time of 'Umar, or the prophets, or even of Abel at the dawn of history. Pastoralism created the idyllic society, the community of Muḥammad and 'Umar in the desert, where egalitarianism and a simple lifestyle reigned. The spread of conquests and the invasion of urban life, with its temptations, competitive pace, and materialism, transformed the community of first believers. The ruler had ceased to be a shepherd (*ru'āt*, pl.) or *imām*, becoming instead a scrutinous tax collector (*jubāt*, pl.) who is keen on imperial interests more than those of the average community. The theme at work here is universal, spanning Islamic as well as Christian history, and it resonates in vernacular forms in various cultures and societies.

Complementing his speech to the companions and his speech to the governors are a speech that 'Uthmān makes to the military commanders (*umarā' al-ajnād*), a letter addressed to the tax officials (*'ummāl al-kharāj*),[67] and a letter to the public or common people (*al-'āmma*).[68] The clear stratification of messages and audiences in these letters reflected a philosopher/historian's view of a hierarchical world with segmented classes of political and social power. Ṭabarī's Persian worldview, and the continuity he envisaged between Sasanid and Islamic times, allowed the Rāshidūn caliphs (especially the most monarchical among them, 'Uthmān) to speak as both caliphs and kings. In his speech to the commanders, 'Uthmān warns of dangers that they in fact bring on his rule later on,[69] and in the speech to the common people, 'Uthmān warns of certain inevitable problems that will come about when the Islamic state reaches its limits of growth. 'Uthmān declares: "To proceed: You have attained so much only by strict adherence to sound models [of conduct]. Let not this world turn you away from your proper concerns [*amrikum*], for this community will become involved in innovation after three things occur together among you: complete prosperity [*takāmul al-ni'am*], the attainment of adulthood by the children of the captive women, and the recitation of the Qur'ān by both Arabs and non-Arabs [*qirā'at al-a'rāb wa'l-a'ājim al-Qur'ān*]. The Messenger of God has said, 'Unbelief stems from speaking Arabic badly [*al-kufru fi'l-'ujma*]; if something seems foreign to them, they will do it awkwardly and [thereby] bring about innovation [*fa-in ista'jama 'alayhim amr takallafū wa ibtada'ū*].' "[70]

In this letter 'Uthmān appears apprehensive of what the transition from an Arabian to a Perso-Arab society might bring. The idea that decline begins after the attainment of perfection (*takāmul al-ni'am*) is a religious theme anchored in many Qur'ānic verses describing divine judgment coming at the hour of full prosperity. However, the way Ṭabarī positioned this religious transition within a historical process that included the growing assertiveness of *a'rāb* (i.e., central and northeast Arabian tribes), class mobility, and the intrusion into religious interpretation by foreigners is unique to his version of history. It spans symbolically the problems that 'Uthmān and 'Alī faced in Iraq, first with the Saba'iyya and then with the Khārijites, and contains a prophetic note on the growing power of the *mawālī* in 'Abbāsid times.

These letters addressed concerns of the present. 'Uthmān's words accurately project the later medieval opinion that saw the Rāshidūn golden age begin to wane at the beginning or in the middle of 'Uthmān's reign. Various aspects that defined the religious and political peak of 'Umar's reign had come to an end. The simple faith based on *sunna*, a cohesive culture undiluted by foreign influence, and a political authority that deterred ambitious instincts and was just in its dealings are all elements that come to a grinding halt with 'Uthmān's reign. History shifts from a celebration of biography and *futūḥ* to a recounting of tribulation and an attempt to make sense of *fitna*. Ṭabarī's focus shifts to an exhaustively detailed account of the crisis at the end of 'Uthmān's reign and into 'Alī's reign, which becomes the dominant theme in his chronicle.

## THE AUTHORITARIAN CALIPH

An evaluation of 'Uthmān's rule, policies, and behavior must constantly be mindful of the spectrum of representations applied to him. We have seen Wāqidī's and Sayf b. 'Umar's apologetic statements about 'Uthmān and the companions, the myth that surrounds this history, and his speeches, which offer meanings that range between the hagiographic and the ironic. Abū Mikhnaf's account, which is also detailed in its reporting but clearly derivative from Wāqidī's and Sayf b. 'Umar's accounts, tends to accentuate the discord between the caliph and companions such as Abū Dharr, 'Ammār b. Yāsir, and 'Abdallāh b. Mas'ūd, and paints an image of the caliph as an arrogant and despotic ruler.[71] The exaggerated representation in this build-up, however, while helpful to the Shī'ī position, makes the assassination of the caliph at the end a highly illogical development, because it is left unclear why the caliph did not use military force to defend against the attackers.

Whatever the variances among these accounts, they all share a crucial common denominator that relates to the question of political authority, the legitimation of caliphal control, and the latitude that the caliph may have in governing. This issue was of major concern for Sunnī political theory in the ninth century, and in part catered to the defense of the 'Abbāsid caliphate in the ninth century—the 'Abbāsid authority not so much as a government but as the focal point of Sunnī religious ideology and a political symbol against Shī'īsm and other sects. There was the crucial question of whether a caliph can take liberty in setting rules and taking innovative measures beyond following the *sunna* of the Prophet and the first two caliphs, and the degree to which his authority is binding on the community and deserves continued obedience. On the latter issue, Sunnī doctrinaires in the ninth century gave free rein to the concept of *al-sulṭān* (the hegemone) and its importance to the stability of the faith, and cited numerous general *ḥadīth*s that exhorted Muslims to be obedient to rulers, whether or not the ruler was just.[72]

The centrality of 'Uthmān's historical dilemma to the shaping of Islamic political theory deserves some extra scrutiny. The debate over whether a Sunnī caliph holds both religious and political authority in ruling the community or simply has an honorary leadership status in religious terms has long been controversial, especially in light of the ambiguous terminology used to characterize the caliph as *imām*, *sulṭān*, successor, or symbolic representative (*khalīfat allāh* or *khalīfat rasūl allāh*). Many statements codified in chapters on political theory in classical literary compilations, such as Ibn Qutayba's *'Uyūn al-Akhbār*, Ibn 'Abd Rabbihi's *al-'Iqd al-Farīd*, as well as later political treatises by al-Ṭurṭūshī and Sibṭ Ibn al-Jawzī, often represent mere excerpts from the wider texts of historical narrative. For example, Ḥudhayfa's statement, "Those who strive to humiliate the ruler will be humiliated," is taken from the escalating story of conflict in 'Uthmān's reign and the conclusion about what happened to his attackers. Another statement, often given without attribution (*ma yaza' allāh bi al-sulṭān akthar mimmā yaza' bi al-qur'ān*), is originally Ḥudhayfa's statement as well.[73] That a comparison was being made to the Qur'ān probably serves as a rebuttal to the Khārijites, who had insisted on establishing a firm interpretation of the judgment of the Qur'ān at the arbitration after the Battle of Siffīn before they would allow the caliphate of 'Alī to continue.[74]

Although the narrative of 'Uthmān's reign, especially in its occasionally apologetic version by Sayf b. 'Umar, is often read as a defense of the companions, it seems also to offer a strong statement of political exhortation that defends caliphal authority as "*sulṭān allāh*." Ṭabarī seems to have omitted many of the narratives of Sayf b. 'Umar that dwell on this metaphor during the controversy between the caliph, the opposition, and religious advisors on the sidelines (Sa'd, Ḥudhayfa, Ka'b, 'Abdallāh b. Sallām). This appears to have been the historian's main method of condemning the wrongdoings of 'Uthmān, but these statements, which were made mainly by the religious advisors, and generally led to a defense of the ruling institution of "*al-sulṭān*" outside any religious connotation, are crucial not only for clarifying the meaning of the historiography of 'Uthmān's reign but also for discerning the parabolic foundation of these political statements. Although, for example, the orthodox Islamic narration tends to favor commentaries made by Sa'd b. Abī Waqqāṣ and Ḥudhayfa b. al-Yamān, due to their orthodox image in *ḥadīth*, there is an equally crucial role for the religio-political commentaries of Jewish converts such as Ka'b al-Aḥbār and 'Abdallāh b. Sallām.

As the pressure grows on 'Uthmān to abdicate rule after the arrival of the opposition in Medina, various commentators urge 'Uthmān to remain steadfast, and they give him religious advice. 'Abdallāh b. 'Umar said, "I do not recommend that you remove a shirt that God has girded you with, and make a precedent whereby every time a people disliked their caliph or *imām* they overthrew him, thus endangering the foundations of religion and the order of the community [*lā arā an takhla' . . . fatakūn sunna kullamā karih qawmun khalīfatahum aw imāmahum khala'ūh . . . ḥattā lā yaqūm li-allāh dīnun wa lā li'l-muslimīn sulṭān*]."[75] Another, al-Nu'mān b. Bashīr, advised him, saying, "Be patient and do not give in to weakness, and do not undermine the dominion of God [*iṣbr wa lā tu'ṭī al-daniyya wa lā tahdim sulṭān allāh*]."[76] In arguing with 'Ammār for challenging the caliph, Sa'd b. Abī Waqqāṣ goes as far as equating opposition to the caliph (or to authority generally, *al-sulṭān*) with apostasy (*ridda*).[77] Abū Mūsā al-Ash'arī also exhorted people to defend 'Uthmān, declaring, "God the Almighty has commanded you to aid His religion, the mainstay of this religion is its political authority [*inna qawāma hādhā al-dīn al-sulṭān*]; go forth to defend the dominion of God [*bādirū ilā sulṭān allāh lā yustadhall*]."[78] Mu'āwiya would advise in similar terms as well, however through reference to *sulṭān allāh*.[79] As for Ka'b al-Aḥbār, he established a simile for political authority that would become famous when he stated, "The situation of Islam, political authority, and the public [*mathal al-Islām wa al-sulṭān wa al-nās*] is like that of a tent with its pillars, ropes, and pegs. The tent itself is similar to Islam, the pillar is the authority, and the ropes and pegs are the subjects. The tent is not complete except when all is together [*lā yaṣluḥu ba'ḍuhu illā bi-ba'ḍ*]."[80]

That individuals such as Sa'd and Mu'āwiya would heighten their rhetoric in defending the authority of 'Uthmān is not perhaps unusual, but it is the convergence of their political language with that of Ka'b and Ḥudhayfa that underscores an interesting historiographical phenomenon, namely the transformation of a biblical storyline into an Islamic political polemic. What would have remained in the biblical context a story about religious dissent in the community becomes in the Islamic one a political story as well, one concerning the fragmentation of the Islamic community into religio-political sects (*shiya'*), and various contending concepts of the imamate, its legitimacy, and its range of authority.[81]

For readers who sought a more nuanced answer to the justification of caliphal authority, however, a more specialized array of *ḥadīths* was offered that dealt with matters of economic and administrative practice in the early Islamic period; these addressed various questions: whether a ruler can declare control over conquered territory, bequeath it in a feudalistic fashion as an *iqṭā'*, establish a central treasury in monetary and other terms (*ḥimā*), and dispense with state wealth as he saw fit. These were all things that 'Uthmān did, and they find answers in precedents cited from the times of the Prophet, Abū Bakr, and 'Umar.[82] The polemical constructions of Sunnī *ḥadīths* in the ninth century ran parallel to the standard narrative of the Rāshidūn caliphate with all its controversies, and consistently legitimized what the Rāshidūn caliphs did (with minor dissenting occasions representing 'Uthmān as having departed from the practices of his predecessors). Treatises such as Abū Yūsuf's *kitāb al-kharāj* and Ibn Zanjawayh's *kitāb al-amwāl* are filled with traditions of a legalistic and doctrinal nature that establish this crucial link between history and religious *sunna*. Examples of this include topics such as the Prophet's bequeathing the former land of the Jewish communities of Khaybar and Banū al-Naḍīr to his supporters (not coincidently to the Muhājirūn)[83] and 'Umar's establishment of *ḥimā* reserves but refusal to divide the conquered lands.[84]

And the correlation comes across as well in Ṭabarī's chronicle in the way the Islamic legal voice hawkishly defends a particular reading of how the Sawād region was conquered, describes the system as *sunna*, and attributes a similar precedent of organization to the Prophet that he applied after Khālid b. al-Walīd's conquest of the land at Dūmat al-Jandal.[85] The system of Iraq's agricultural organization and tax revenue rules in 'Umar's time, it seems assumed, had implications about the status of the land, its availability for purchase and settlement, and the status of its people in the religious legal sense (whether or not they are *ahl dhimma*),[86] and would thus have set a precedent for other examples of conquered Islamic lands elsewhere, and have similar implications about laws and social regulations in these lands, not to mention their relation to the ruling dynasty in Baghdad.[87]

But perhaps the most interesting aspect of these discussions is that although there is no precedent to justify the caliph's assertion of authority, here the Sunnī voice comes on the side of the caliph regardless. Discussing the case of a parcel of land that has been neglected by its owners for three years, traditions legitimize the caliph's dispensing with the land and bequeathing it to others who could plant it.[88] The caliph in these traditions is consistently referred to as "*al-imām*" in a clear attempt to strengthen his political authority with a religious symbolism. And a followup statement on this example, attributed to Abū Yūsuf, goes farther by stating that this possibility of a land transfer is "equivalent to the case of monetary wealth which does not belong to anyone and is not claimed as inheritance by anyone, then it is the privilege of the just *imām* to dispense with it and give it to those whom he finds competent to furthering the cause of Islam [*fa-li'l-imām al-'ādil an yujīza minhu wa yu'ṭī man kāna lahu ghanā' fī al-islām . . . fa-kadhalika al-arḍ . . . fa-hādhā sabīl al-qaṭā'i' 'indī fī arḍ al-'Irāq*]."[89] The reference to "*al-imām al-'ādil*" in this tradition also shows the idealizing context of this religious discourse, one which viewed the caliph as a utopian kind of leader, perhaps represented by 'Umar in Islamic history. The Sunnī "caliph-*imām*" therefore stood as a counter-focal point for the Islamic community to the Shī'ī *imām*, and was being helped in strengthening the legitimacy of his powers by the "*ulama*." This said, however, it was always a short distance in Sunnī politics between emir and caliph when polemicists were discussing the issue of the just ruler, and it is not unlikely that such *ḥadīth* discussions could have thrived in the caliphal environment of Iraq as they would in the courts of the Tahirids in Nīshāpūr or the Samanids in Bukhārā.

The defense of 'Uthmān's authority, however, not only answered to Sunnī ideological imperatives that related to matters of community cohesion, the stability of the leadership, and application of the law, but was also a matter of equal centrality to the Persian social and political culture in 'Abbasīd times.[90] The organization of the early Islamic caliphate's government, with the establishment of the *diwan*, a calendar, and taxation rules, relates more to 'Umar's than 'Uthmān's reign, but these are all topics that are back-projected from the ninth century to the Rāshidūn period in order to idealize Persian governmental foundations as having been revived in Arab and Islamic forms at such an early date. 'Uthmān is perhaps adapted to the same path, in the way that he sought to establish a system of *iqṭā'* for the Arab conquering elite, and even more critically in the way he sought to devise a hierarchy of social classes that adapted a Sasanid system of privilege and aristocracy to new criteria of Arab tribal and Islamic merit.

'Uthmān's appointment of his kin relations to positions of authority would have been viewed as a throwback not only to the Jāhiliyya and its tribal elites, but, from a Persian perspective, to the monarch's right to appoint his family members to positions of political importance. 'Umar did not fit in this framework because he did not promote the Qurashī elite in the same way, and he placed more emphasis on evidence of religious precedence among people than on a rigid system of social hierarchy and rank.[91] That he believed there existed a system of hierarchy, such as 'Uthmān and Mu'āwiya spoke of, is also mildly attested to in other statements attributed to 'Umar,[92] and in his exasperation with tribesmen who challenged his establishment of state land (*ḥimā*) out of conquered land in Arabia.[93] But 'Umar ultimately considered religion, pious behavior and zeal on behalf of the faith to be matters that deserved more merit than did social lineage. To accept established customs of social hierarchy would have redefined the caliph's office as that of a king, which he rejected.[94]

The time for the establishment of an Islamic kingship was yet to come officially with Mu'āwiya, and Sunnism will keep its distance from the direct expression of the Umayyad monarchy. However, this did not prevent Sunnī writers from discussing the political challenges that faced 'Uthmān and defending him in the context of the Islamic imamate. 'Uthmān's imamate, however, was more that of the 'Abbāsid caliphs than of the Rāshidūn companions—authoritarian, monopolistic, and highly structured, and religion (in the example of the codification of the Qur'ān) was but a tool being used to strengthen the centralizing policy of the state.[95]

The facade of modesty, political consultation, and abidance by the traditions of predecessor caliphs, however, will gradually be lifted in Mu'āwiya's reign. The Umayyad leadership, although battered for having radically departed from the political traditions of 'Umar, and having made the transition to kingship, would nevertheless be accepted as a credible authority system for the *jamā'a*. The Umayyads, as much as 'Uthmān, relied on the same lineage of 'Abbāsid and Sunnī political legitimation to put up a successful challenge to 'Alī's caliphate and the Shī'ī polemic. We will see in the next chapter how the interactions and discussions that 'Uthmān and Mu'āwiya carry out with the opposition in Medina and Damascus will build up the Sunnī philosophy of the competent leadership in a way that legitimizes Umayyad authority before it arrives to power.

CHAPTER FIVE

# The Road to Civil War

## *Issues and Boundaries*

### PRELUDES TO CONFLICT: THE ARGUMENT FOR AUTHORITY

Ṭabarī begins to lay the groundwork for describing the causes and conditions that eventually led to the challenges to 'Uthmān under the year A.H. 33/A.D. 653. Although these events, which will take place in Iraq and Syria and will involve the governors of 'Uthmān (Sa'īd b. al-'Āṣ and Mu'āwiya b. Abī Sufyān), do not yet involve 'Uthmān or 'Alī, they do introduce some of the controversial political and moral themes that will be magnified in subsequent years. The absence of 'Alī and 'Uthmān from the beginning scenes of conflict probably had a double purpose. On one level this allowed the Sunnī reader to maintain his view of the leaders as well-intentioned individuals caught in a situation that others were shaping in an ignorant or selfish fashion. On another, deeper, level, the narratives kept the two figures in the background while their supporters articulated the two leaders' positions vividly and revived the standoff over succession rights and divergent perspectives of government.

The initial setting for this sideshow of sedition is the residence of 'Uthmān's governor in Kufa, Sa'īd b. al-'Āṣ, during the course of a social gathering. We are told that Sa'īd's guests on these occasions generally tended to be "those who settled Kufa, witnessed al-Qādisiyya, and joined in previous raids of the Jāhiliyya [*ahl al-ayyām*], the *qurrā'* of al-Baṣra and the stubborn folk [*nāzilat ahl al-Kūfa wa wujūh ahl al-ayyām wa ahl al-Qādisiyya, wa qurrā' ahl al-Baṣra wa'l-mutasammitūn*]."[1] These were his guests during private sessions (*majlis al-khāṣṣa*). However, in public sessions, a diverse group of guests would join in. It was on one of these occasions, when Sa'īd was hosting the above-mentioned Qādisiyya veterans (later "Kufan extremists" or *ahl al-'Irāq*), that a minor protégé of the governor, Khunays b. Ḥubaysh (possibly without official role), made the random observation that Ṭalḥa b. 'Ubaydallāh was a truly generous figure. Sa'īd responded to this cynically, saying that it is not extraordinary for one who owns so much property to be a generous giver.[2] "If only I owned as much as he did, by God, I would have made you live in luxury,"[3] he remarked, to which Khunays' son, 'Abd al-Raḥmān, responded by saying, "Would that you owned this stretch of land *al-milṭāṭ*" [referring to the farm domains on the western bank of the river, adjoining Kufa, that were owned by the Sasanid family before the conquest]. Hearing this, the Qādisiyya crowd grew angry and said, "Shut up, you moron, before we deal you a beating." Sa'īd here tried to explain that Khunays' son was just a simple-minded youth to whom they should not pay attention, but the Kufan guests were not convinced. "How dare he wish you owned this property of our own Sawād [i.e., which we conquered] personally," they added. Sa'īd responded, "He probably just as well wishes that you yourselves owned this domain." "Let him not wish it either for you or for us," they said.[4] Sa'īd here grew impatient with them, and said, "This is none of your business anyway [*mā hādhā bi-kum*]," which caused the Kufans to become suspicious that the conversation was a setup at the behest of the governor to introduce the idea of a possible takeover of the Sawād land. So they said, "It seems you ordered him to say this."[5] Then this group of Kufans, which included Mālik b. al-Ḥārith al-Ashtar, Ka'b b. 'Abda b. Sa'd al-Nahdī (the so-called Ibn dhī'l-Ḥabaka), Jundub b. Zuhayr al-Azdī, Ṣa'ṣa'a b. Ṣūḥān al-'Abdī, Ibn al-Kawwā', Kumayl b. Ziyād, and 'Umayr b. Ḍābi', joined to attack 'Abd al-Raḥmān b. Khunays and started beating him. Sa'īd pleaded with them to stop but they would not, and when Khunays tried to intervene, they beat him, too.[6]

By now word of what was going on at the governor's residence had spread in the streets of Kufa, and a whole bunch of tribes, including Banū Asad, led by Ṭulayḥa, came to the governor's residence and surrounded it. Sa'īd was now anxious to defuse the situation from deteriorating further, so he asked all parties to be quiet about what had happened. The two beaten men, however, complained to Sa'īd about the uncouth elements he continued to entertain in his sessions, so Sa'īd promised not to let them visit him again. "Do not entice people to rise against me with your rumors and talk [*iḥfaẓā 'alayya lisānikumā wa lā tujarri'ā 'alayya al-nās*]," he told the two men.[7]

As events showed, however, it was the seditious "Qādisiyya extremists" who set about fomenting rumors against the governor. The people of Kufa advised the governor that it would be better if he did something about them. Sa'īd, trying to be as noncontroversial as possible, since he had taken over the governorship after the controversial al-Walīd b. 'Uqba was dismissed for his drinking bouts, told the Kufans that he had orders not to stir things up. If they chose to write the caliph, however, on the matter, he told them, they were free to do so. Thus the "*ashrāf ahl al-Kūfa wa ṣulaḥā'uhum*" reportedly wrote to 'Uthmān, asking him to deport this rowdy bunch of Qādisiyya veterans.[8] 'Uthmān then wrote back to them, ordering this group to go to Mu'āwiya; he simultaneously wrote to Mu'āwiya, warning him about the imminent arrival of a "seditious group" ("The Kufans have expelled and sent to you certain innately rebellious individuals. Deal with them caringly when they arrive. If you observe right conduct in them, then reconcile with them. But if they are burdensome to you, then send them back (to the Kufans) [*inna ahl al-Kūfa qad akhrajū ilayka nafaran khuliqū li-fitna fa-ru'hum wa qum 'alayhim fa-in ānasta minhum rashadan fa-iqbal minhum wa in a'yūka fa-irdudhum 'alayhim*]").[9]

Although seemingly marginal to the affairs of 'Uthmān, this episode involving Sa'īd and his guests is significant because it provides a miniature of the type of political challenge that 'Uthmān would later face on a greater level in Medina. The guests of Sa'īd question the governor's liberty in using, or even contemplating using, the booty of the Persian conquests (frequently called in the sources "*mā afā' allāh 'alaynā*") for his own political purposes, irrespective of how noble his dispensation of wealth might turn out to be.

The story encapsulates on a local level some of the well-known questions that surround the legitimacy of 'Uthmān's dispensation of wealth among his kinsmen and their appointment to key political posts. Also, like 'Uthmān's, Sa'īd's personality appears malleable during these sessions. His openness and hospitality toward different elements made it impossible to have a cooperative assembly. And Sa'īd, like 'Uthmān later, did not have the charismatic strength to keep conflicting leaders at bay. During arguments in his assembly, he quickly is ignored, and contenders argue over his head in a manner a reader would have found unthinkable earlier under ‘Umar’s rule. Meanwhile, rumors start flying across the land, and the tribes and political elite begin to question the efficacy of the system of government.

In this initial scene of debate and discord in Kufa, we examine some of the long-term questions around which the *fitna* would develop: Can the status of the conquered lands change down the generations? How do different tribal and social groups (Quraysh, non-Quraysh, settled elite/non-elite) relate to one another in light of Islamic equality versus the discrepancy in their military achievements? How much freedom does a ruler/governor have in deciding these questions, and whose opinion (among these groups) should official policy follow?[10] And, the final question: Is the caliphate an institution built on kin-ties and elite status (‘Uthmān and the Banū Umayya), or is it based on religious criteria and tribal precedence according to contributions for Islam (conquests, settlement, etc.)? Although nowhere in this session do the different speakers address the question of caliphal succession and right to rule, it is clear that such a question lies at the dead end of these lines of inquiry, since the controversy leads to a total discrediting of caliphal rule.

This propensity to quick dismissal of the right to political leadership gets even more accentuated in light of the way different contenders refer to the reigns of Abū Bakr and ‘Umar as measures for judging the circumstances of their own times.[11] ‘Alī is nowhere mentioned as a favorite by the contenders, but the controversy in Kufa creates a vacuum in which later, with further developments, they will try to seek an alternative. Ṭabarī leaves it to the reader to connect the dots between the memory of ‘Alī’s loss of succession to the caliphate before, the grievances of the Kufans at present, and Sa‘īd’s (‘Uthmān’s) mismanagement of an evolving political program, and the imminent religious calls from other corners (Abū Dharr, ‘Abdallāh b. Mas‘ūd, ‘Abd al-Raḥmān b. ‘Awf).

It is also worth noting that, although the narratives make it clear why the Qādisiyya veterans became angry when someone suggested the transfer of conquered lands to the governorship’s ownership, the text forces the reader to look with disdain on this opposition crowd and view its motives suspiciously. The group may have had a justifiable cause for a moment but they exaggerated the threat and transgressed on the prerogative of the governor—not to mention abused his hospitality—when they attacked his guests and spread rumors to undermine his government. Thus the "group of ten"—symmetrically opposed to the ten most righteous companions in Sunnī Islam—is portrayed as a mostly seditious faction that was prone to challenge any sort of organized government. To what extent this would have happened anyway, even if ʿUthmān or his kinsmen were not ruling Kufa is probably made clear in the characterization of this group as "members of *ahl al-ayyām*" who were still accustomed to a lifestyle of raids, tribal negotiation, and resistance to singular leadership from the days before Islam. The Islamic conquests originally gave this group a further advantage by offering them a more official equality with Quraysh and a sharing of conquests, but they themselves kept operating within a particular framework of the Jāhiliyya.[12]

## THE VISIT TO MUʿĀWIYA

When the Kufan group arrived in Syria, Muʿāwiya reportedly showed them great kindness. He kept them in comfortable quarters at a monastery, continued to pay their stipends, and kept a schedule of having both lunch and dinner with them, until one day he initiated a debate with them.

"You are a community among the Arabs who have both strength and argument [*lakum asnān wa alsina*]," he said. "And Islam has further allowed you honor and made you victors over nations whose inheritance you have coveted. I have been told, however, that you are angry with Quraysh. But were it not for Quraysh, you would have returned to being lowly, like you were before. [The community leaders] are a shield for you [*al-aʾimma junna*], so don't break with your *aʾimma*, for they bear burden of providing for you. By God, you must end [your dissidence] or God will most assuredly put you to the test with [rulers] who impose heavy demands on you and then do not praise you for enduring [them]. Then you will be their accomplices in (the evils) that you have brought upon the subjects [*raʿiyya*] both during your lifetime and after your death [*thumma takūnuna shurkāʾ lahum fīmā jarartum ʿalā al-raʿiyya fī ḥayātikum wa baʿda mamātikum*]."[13]

Muʿāwiya's statement was elaborate and contemplative, but the response of one unidentified speaker, who appears to have spoken on behalf of the group, came fast and rude: "Quraysh was never the strongest among the Arabs during the Jāhiliyya so that they can frighten us [now], and as for what you say about the shield, it can be penetrated, which puts us in danger."[14]

With this reply Mu'āwiya's mood and tone changed drastically, as he declared:

> "Now I know you! I now recognize that what has encouraged you to do this is lack of reason [*qillat al-'uqūl*]. You speak as the orator of your people, and yet you have no reason. I remind you of the grand role of Islam, and you remind me of the Jāhiliyya. . . . Don't you understand that Quraysh was grand before and after Islam because God willed it to be so? Quraysh was not the greatest in number among the Arabs, nor the strongest among them, but it was the most noble among them, and the most perfect in chivalry [*murū'a*]. . . . Quraysh was protected by God when nations all around it were preying on each other and becoming victims to loss [pestilence] [*yutakhaṭṭafu al-nās min ḥawlihim*].
>
> "Have you ever heard of a nation among the Arabs, 'Ajam, Black, or Red, that has endured in time without loss [*illā qad aṣābahu al-dahr fī baladihi wa ḥurmatihi bi-dawla*] except for the situation of Quraysh? For whenever anyone laid a plot against [Quraysh] God abased him. Until finally God sought to redeem those who would follow his religion, to save them from the hardship of life and the punishment of the hereafter; thus he chose for them the best of mankind [i.e., Muḥammad]. Quraysh were thus his select people. He invested them with dominion [*thumma banā hādhā al-mulka 'alayhim*] and gave them the caliphate . . . God had already protected them in the Jāhiliyya. Do you not think he will protect them under Islam? Truly, how ignorant you are."

This second phase of encounter between the Kufan opposition and Mu'āwiya shows the heightened level of confrontation with a more senior member of 'Uthmān's government. The occasion provides that flattering direction for representing Mu'āwiya's personality. From the very outset, Mu'āwiya is shown extending great hospitality to this group, despite the warnings he receives from 'Uthmān about them. Mu'āwiya is portrayed as showing his natural, graceful style of rule, fulfilling his duty of providing a tribal welcome, and engaging his guests in debate, and he only changes his tone when they fail to act within the limits of class and reason. This section of their encounter is significant in the narratives for the way it allows Mu'āwiya to express his views on politics and history. Interestingly, Mu'āwiya is shown emphasizing the divine selection of Quraysh before Islam as well as after, and he is shown as placing the most emphasis on Quraysh's virtues, their honorable social rank, and their virility. His statement sets the parameters for how the *fitna* would be portrayed partly as a moral/class conflict.

This whole section is essentially an occasion for a speech by Mu'āwiya and barely is interrupted by a brief response from his anonymous interlocutor. The style and tone of Mu'āwiya's statements closely resemble the countless similar speeches and declarations that 'Alī will eventually make during the *fitnas* to his rivals and followers. Mu'āwiya weaves ethical concerns with Sunnī defenses of authority, and in another version he includes references to Qur'ānic verses in a style highly unlike the way he would later be represented as speaking during his confrontation with 'Alī. Ṭabarī and his narrators clearly wanted to lend a dimension of respectability to Mu'āwiya here by allowing him to weave together strands of (Sunnī) religious and secular wisdom in his discourse. It is equally important that this is the only time Mu'āwiya speaks with such religious wisdom. Later, when 'Alī's role in the story becomes central and he assumes the position of religious wisdom, Mu'āwiya's moral profile greatly deteriorates, and his discourse becomes bereft of any religious elements.

Then Mu'āwiya's speech turns to an attack on the background of the Kufan group. Mu'āwiya here describes them as an evil group drawn from a marginal region of the Persian lands who engage in lowly professions. He doles out individual insults to the various tribesmen present that reflect on their whole tribes and regions. In one such representative attack, Mu'āwiya tells a man named Ṣa'ṣa'a:

> "As for you, Ṣa'ṣa'a, your town [*qarya*] is surely the worst of Arab towns—the one whose vegetation is the most malodorous, whose riverbed is deepest, whose evildoing is most notorious, and whose protégés [*jīrān*] are the vilest. No one of noble or humble birth has ever dwelt there without being insulted on that account and without [that fact] being a defect in him. Moreover, they had the ugliest nicknames among the Arabs, the basest marriage ties, and were the outcasts of the nations. You [yourselves] were protégés in al-Khaṭṭ and lackeys of Persia until the Prophet's call befell you. His summons touched you [*sing.*]

while you were an outcast isolated in 'Umān rather than a resident of Baḥrayn, so that you might share with them in the Prophet's call. You are the worst of your people, to such a degree that when Islam brought you out [of isolation], mingled you with the people, and lifted you up over the nations that heretofore had dominated you, you begin desiring crookedness in God's religion and inclining towards wickedness and baseness. But that does not derogate from Quraysh, it will neither harm them nor prevent them from fulfilling their obligations. Verily, Satan is not heedless of you [*pl.*]. He has recognized you by the evildoing within your community. Thus, he has aroused the people against you while he casts you down. He knows that he cannot oppose through you any judgment that God has decreed nor any command that God has willed [*lā yastaṭī'u an yarudda bi-kum qaḍā' qaḍāhu allāh*]. [He knows also] that you never cause evil in any affair unless God has disgraced [you] by imbuing you with evil from him."[15]

The narrator then reports that Mu'āwiya continued, "I give you leave to go where you want. No one shall benefit or be harmed by your presence . . . If you want to be saved, you should stick to the *jamā'a* and not grow vain [*lā yubṭirannakum al-in'ām*]." As they were about to leave, Mu'āwiya reportedly called them back and told them, "I am repeating to you and I want you to remember that I was first employed by the Messenger of God—and remember that he was infallible. Then Abū Bakr became caliph and he appointed me, and so did 'Umar and 'Uthmān. All of them were satisfied with me. The Messenger of God sought for office only men fully capable of acting on behalf of the Muslims, and did not appoint those who were ignorant, weak, or who improvised according to circumstances [*ṭalaba li'l-a'māl ahl al-jazā' 'an al-muslimīn, wa lam yaṭlub lahā ahl al-ijtihād wa'l-jahl bihā wa'l-ḍa'f 'anhā*]. Verily God holds the power and exacts retribution, deceiving those who have deceived him. Do not champion a cause about which you know you are not sincere [*fa lā ta'ruḍū li-amrin wa antum ta'lamūn min anfusikum ghayra mā tuẓhirūn*], for God will not leave you without examining you and revealing your secrets to the people. Almighty God has said: 'Alif, Lām, Mīm, Do the people reckon that they will be left to say, "We believe" and will not be tried?'[16]"[17]

After the session concluded, Mu'āwiya reportedly wrote to 'Uthmān, telling him that he had found this group to be a mindless one, prone to *fitna* and *shaghab*. "They have neither reason nor faith [*aqwāmun laysa la-*

*hum 'uqūlun wa lā adyān*]," he wrote. "Islam to them is a burden, and justice is annoying to them. In nothing do they seek God, nor do they speak with proof. Their only aim is dissidence and the wealth of the non-Muslim subjects. God will be the One to test and examine them, then reveal and humiliate them. They are not men who can injure anyone unless they are allied with others. Therefore, keep Sa'īd [b. al-'Āṣ] and his followers away from them, for they are no more than trouble-makers and slanderous gossipers."[18]

In this second session, we notice that the narratives merely continue the earlier speech of Mu'āwiya with little interruption. The Kufan group is given little chance to state a substantial answer before Mu'āwiya escalates his attack on them. Having asserted the primacy of Quraysh, Mu'āwiya turns his attention to describing the opposition's background and denigrating their motives and goals on the basis of their social standing. The Kufan group is thus portrayed as ungrateful and seditious by nature. And this attack is resumed in the letter that Mu'āwiya wrote to 'Uthmān assessing the Kufan opposition. One should note here that on the whole, Mu'āwiya's statements were crafted to address the reader of later times and to flatter the Umayyad clan for its skill at governance rather than to help 'Uthmān sort things out in the debacle at hand.

The third and final segment of Mu'āwiya's speech, in which Mu'āwiya defends his governorship, may seem odd and out of place, since up until now the argument has had nothing to do with Mu'āwiya's credentials or how he came to office. However, given that the Kufan group will eventually go on to become a key opponent at Ṣiffīn and will lead the opposition to the Umayyads later on, this early debate becomes a platform for Mu'āwiya to describe the grounds of his political legitimacy (to the caliphate more than the governorate) as something rooted both in the precedent of his designation to office since early times and in his merits, talents, and skills. Between his implicit claim to inheriting the authority of 'Uthmān and his glorification of the Quraysh, particularly the memory of its leadership in the example of Abū Sufyān, Mu'āwiya succeeds in turning the occasion of Kufan grievances into an advertisement for his unique political qualities. What Sa'īd b. al-'Āṣ originally complained about and wrote 'Uthmān about had become entirely marginalized in the sweep of narratives that focus increasingly on the chief protagonists in the coming *fitna*.

In another version in Ṭabarī, recounted on the authority of Muḥammad b. ʿUmar (al-Wāqidī), the same events that led to a conference between Saʿīd b. al-ʿĀṣ and the Kufans are recounted in a more pointed way. This time we are told that the Kufans became angry when Saʿīd, during the course of a session, declared (without context) that the Sawād belonged to Quraysh (*innamā hādhā al-Sawād bustān Quraysh*). Al-Ashtar here angrily retorted, "Are you now claiming that the Sawād, which God has bestowed on us as *fay'* by our swords to be the personal property of your family [*a-tazʿamu anna al-sawād alladhī afā'hu allāhu alaynā bi-asyāfinā bustānun laka wa li-qawmika*]?! By God, your share in it should be no greater than the share of any of us."[19] Here a certain associate of Saʿīd, ʿAbd al-Raḥmān (who was head of *al-shurṭa*), intervened and zealously told al-Ashtar, "Do you dare answer back when the prince says something?" and added some rough words. Al-Ashtar, we are told, called on the other Kufans to attack this man (*lā yafūtannakum al-rajul*),[20] which they did until he fainted. Saʿīd had proven too weak to hold back the crowd, and after the Kufans departed, he promised not to entertain them again and wrote to ʿUthmān about this group of "ten," saying these men were active in inciting against the caliph (*yu'allibūna wa yajtamiʿūna ʿalā ʿaybika wa ʿaybī wa'l-ṭaʿni fī dīninā*).[21]

This second version, by Wāqidī, not only is briefer than Sayf b. ʿUmar's account, but it also addresses the thematic aspects of the story directly and with little theatrical flourish. Whereas, in the earlier version, it was left unclear whether Saʿīd encouraged his associate to insinuate that the governor could claim the former crown lands of the Sasanids, here Saʿīd himself declares all the Sawād as the property of Quraysh. Al-Ashtar, in response, directly explains his position on this issue: that the governor and Quraysh have no greater rights with respect to the Sawād, a conquered land, than the others. In the end, Saʿīd is shown, as in the previous version, too weak to hold back the attackers, in a manner that echoes the famous representation of ʿUthmān as a weak caliph.

The continuation of the Kufan debate with Muʿāwiya in the version based on the authority of Wāqidī also differs from Sayf b. ʿUmar's version in important details.[22] Here Muʿāwiya talks about the merits of his family in more open terms, and the Kufans challenge his religious qualifications and right to "rule" in terms that become the official argument against the Umayyads. Muʿāwiya declares, "By God, I do not order you to do anything unless I, my household, and my personal retinue [*khāṣṣatī*] have started [doing] it. The Quraysh recognized that Abū Sufyān was the noblest among them and the son of the noblest, save for what God did for His prophet, the prophet of mercy. For indeed, God elected him and showed him honor. God did not create upright qualities in anyone without singling out [the prophet] for the noblest and finest of them. Nor did He create evil qualities in anyone without ennobling him beyond [such things] and keeping him utterly free of them. I believe that if the people were sons of Abū Sufyān, they would all be prudent and resolute men [*wa innī la-aẓunnu ana abā Sufyāna law walada al-nāsa lam yalid illā ḥāziman*]."[23]

Ṭabarī's description of the assembly then continues:

> Ṣaʿṣaʿa replied, "You lie! They are sons of a better man than Abū Sufyān—one whom God created by His own hand, 'into whom he breathed His spirit,'[24] before whom He commanded the angels to bow down. Among [the people] are the pious and the sinner, the stupid and the clever."
>
> That night [Muʿāwiya] departed from them. Then he came to them the following night and spoke at length among them. He said: "O band of men [*qawm*], answer me properly or be still. Reflect and consider what will bring benefit to you, your households, your tribes, and the whole community [*jamāʿa*] of Muslims. If you seek this, you will prosper and we shall prosper with you." Ṣaʿṣaʿa replied, "You are not worthy of that, nor is your noble rank such that you should be obeyed in defiance of God." [Muʿāwiya] said, "Did I not begin by commanding you to fear God and obey Him and His prophet, 'to hold fast to his bond, together, and do not scatter?'"[25] "On the contrary," they answered, "you have commanded schism and opposition to what the Prophet has brought."
>
> [Muʿāwiya] said, "Well, then, I command you now. If I have done [what you say], I turn to God and His prophet, and I command you to fear Him and obey Him and His Prophet, to adhere to the community and to abhor schism, to revere your *imāms* and to direct them so far as you are able to every good thing, and to admonish them gently and graciously concerning anything that comes from them."
>
> Ṣaʿṣaʿa replied, "And we then command you to resign your office [*ʿamal*], for among the Muslims there is one who has a better right to it than you." [Muʿāwiya] asked, "Who is that?" [Ṣaʿṣaʿa] answered, "Someone whose father had a higher standing in Islam than did yours,

and who himself has a higher standing than you." [Mu'āwiya] said, "By God, I have some standing in Islam. There were others whose standing surpassed mine, but in my time, there is no one better able to do my job than I. 'Umar b. al-Khaṭṭāb was of this opinion, and had there been a man more capable than I, 'Umar would not have been indulgent with regard to me or anyone else. Nor have I instituted any innovation that would require me to resign my office. Had the Commander of the Faithful and of the Community of Muslims thought so, he would have written to me by his own hand, and I would have stepped down from office. Should God decree that He do this, I hope that he would not decide on someone for this [position] unless [that person] were better. Go easy, or Satan will find what he hopes for and commands in this [situation] and others like it. By my life, if affairs were decided according to your opinion and wishes, things would not go well for the people of Islam by day or by night. But affairs are determined and directed by God, and 'He attains His purpose.'[26] So come back to what is good and speak of that."

They responded, "You are not fit for that." He said, "By God, in truth it is God's right to attack and take vengeance. I fear for you, lest you become so entangled in submission to Satan and rebellion against the Merciful one that God's vengeance will cause you to reside in the abode of humiliation in the present and [in the abode of] everlasting abasement in the future."

Then they jumped on him and seized his head and beard. He said, "Hey, this is not the province of Kufa! By God, if the Syrians saw what you have done to me, their *imām*, I could not restrain them from killing you. By my life, you always act the same way." Then he arose from among them and said, "By God, I shall never enter your presence again as long as I live." Then he wrote to 'Uthmān [as follows]: "In the name of God, the Merciful, the Compassionate. To the servant of God, 'Uthmān, Commander of the Faithful, from Mu'āwiya b. Abī Sufyān. To proceed: O Commander of the Faithful, you sent to me certain bands of men speaking with the tongue of devils, saying things which [the latter] were dictating to them. They come to the people, so they allege, for the sake of the Qur'ān, but they render [it] obscure and ambiguous. Not all the people understand what they mean to do, for they only desire schism, and they bring discord [*fitna*] nearer. Islam has been a burden to them and has vexed them. The spells of Satan have become

> fixed in their hearts, and they corrupted many of the Kufans around them. If they remain in the midst of the Syrians, I worry that they may delude them with their sorcery and depravity. Send them back to their garrison town [Kufa] and let them reside there, where their dissembling first appeared. Peace."[27]

This second version of the debate differs in the way most of the arguments center on issues of legitimacy and involve Mu'āwiya more than the earlier dispute with the governor did. Here Mu'āwiya does not appeal to reason or diplomacy, nor does he attack the Kufans on the grounds of class. His flattery of Quraysh is meant more as a way to flatter the Umayyad family and its political leadership in the past. Mu'āwiya pays lip service to the primacy of the Prophet but is interested more in announcing the Jahilī virtues of Abū Sufyān. When Mu'āwiya reminds the Kufans of how he rose to office, it is significant that he omits the mention preserved in the early version that the Prophet had first set the precedent by employing him. He only refers to the patronage that 'Umar extended to him and appeals to the argument of power and political skill over the argument for precedence in conversion. Pointing to 'Umar's judgment served also as an aside against 'Alī's readiness for caliphal leadership, since 'Umar did not designate him for succession.

The emphasis of the Kufans on precedence in conversion in this second version is also different from Sayf b. 'Umar's version, since they seem to imply their desire to see 'Alī assume political leadership. The issue of whether 'Alī should rule, and who is more qualified between the two, 'Alī or Mu'āwiya, clearly takes this narrative far from its original goal, namely reprimanding the Kufans for their bickering with Sa'īd over the Sawād. Mu'āwiya's statement (*law kānat al-umūr tuqḍā 'alā ra'yikum wa amānīkum mā istaqāmat yawman wa lā laylatan*) is meant to justify the grounds for his future rivalry with 'Alī. Mu'āwiya here articulates his own merits to rule the community effectively and casts a preview of his challenge to 'Alī at Ṣiffīn. The debate has wider polemical uses that reach into future events and relate to a wide range of personalities, and so does not merely address Sa'īd's day-to-day troubles with the Kufans.

Although Mu'āwiya does not attack the Kufans' class background as he overarchingly does in the first version, he does reiterate in various ways throughout the narrative that the Kufans are a threat to the cohesion and harmony of the community, not just to the possibility of establishing effective government. The Kufans are still represented as a seditious element that seeks to divide (*yurīdūna al-firqa wa yuqarribūna al-fitna; qad athqalahum al-Islām wa aḍjarahum*).[28] In a way, they are portrayed as a group harkening to the Ridda. This association is highlighted in a side-story to the first version of the narrative about the debate between the Kufans and Muʿāwiya (recounted by Sayf b. ʿUmar). In this digression, we are told that, after the failure of the meeting between Muʿāwiya and the Kufans, a member of the dissident party said to his companions that they should go to Jazīra. "Let's not return to Kufa at once," this man said, "for they shall mock us. Let's instead make a detour to the Jazīra [province]." This random decision provides the occasion for a follow-up to Muʿāwiya's earlier attack on the Kufans. The story says that when the Kufans arrived in Jazīra, ʿAbd al-Raḥmān b. Khālid, governor of Ḥimṣ, heard of them and summoned them over. He had prepared a few harsh words. "O instruments of Satan, you are not welcome here," he said. "Satan has come back exhausted, while you are still full of energy. I do not know whether you people are Arabs or non-Arabs. But may God ruin ʿAbd al-Raḥmān if he does not chastise you until he wears you out, lest you speak to me as I heard you have spoken to Muʿāwiya. I am the son of Khālid b. al-Walīd—the son of a man tested by long experience, a man who gouged out the eye of the Secession [*al-ridda*]. By God, O Ṣaʿṣaʿa, son of shame, if I learn that anyone among my followers has smashed your nose and then called you a filthy sucker, I will send you off on a very long flight."[29]

The decision by the Kufans to set out to Jazīra seems completely random at first glance, and intended by a narrator no more than as another opportunity for a speech. The very strong tone of ʿAbd al-Raḥmān's speech, however, suggests that narrators intended here something special, namely to add another voice to those expressed so far and to mark the transition from a mild governor to a harsh one. While Saʿīd b. al-ʿĀṣ represented the pacifist governor and Muʿāwiya the more reasoned yet firm governor, ʿAbd al-Raḥmān represented the voice of violence. This was meant to foreshadow the future transition from the mild and sober government of someone such as al-Mughīra b. Shuʿba in Muʿāwiya's reign to more ruthless governors such as Ziyād b. Abīhi and al-Ḥajjāj b. Yūsuf. ʿAbd al-Raḥmān's evocation of the name of his father, Khālid b. al-Walīd, and that commander's critical role in fighting the armies of the Ridda, was meant to align the stars of coercive commanders and evoke those individuals as final arbiters for such situations of chaos. It is here worth stressing not only the way Muʿāwiya is elevated in depiction (through his mannerism of speech and action) to the rank of caliphal behavior long before he becomes caliph, but that narrators also meant to establish a pairing of interactions of leaders and governors: ʿUthmān and Saʿīd b. al-ʿĀṣ, and Muʿāwiya and ʿAbd al-Raḥmān b. Khālid. The text's transition in describing debates from one pair to another represented the gradual transition from Rāshidūn style of politics to that of the Umayyads.[30]

The Kufan threat is portrayed here as small but having the possibility of growing to reach the caliph himself. When the argument between Muʿāwiya and the Kufans escalates, we are told that they became so bold as to attack Muʿāwiya physically, seizing his head and beard. Muʿāwiya's rebuking statement to them, "*inna hādhihi laysat bi-arḍi al-Kūfa; inna la-ṣanīʿikum yushbihu baʿḍahu baʿḍan*," is a clear allusion to how the attackers of ʿUthmān will later behave in Medina, with Muḥammad b. Abī Bakr grabbing ʿUthmān's beard before the assassination. Events on the margin of the caliphate are therefore shown as foreshadowing a similar tendency in the center against the caliph later on, and Muʿāwiya alludes to this recurrent tendency by saying, "You always act the same way [*inna ṣanīʿikum la-yushbihu baʿḍahu baʿḍan*]." Muʿāwiya thus steps out of his role as an actor to become a critical narrator of events both past and current.

## ʿUTHMĀN'S PREDICAMENT: THE THEME OF IRRECONCILABLE MORAL DEMANDS

Under the year A.H. 34/A.D. 654 Ṭabarī recounts how the opponents of ʿUthmān began to increase their demands against the caliph. After detailing what seemed like a local dispute between Saʿīd and the Kufan personalities, suddenly the accounts turn to describing how Saʿīd had to abandon Kufa, which became a field for conspiracies and disorder (*khalat al-Kūfa min al-ruʾasāʾ illā manzūʿan aw maftūnan*),[31] and sallied forth to Medina to confer with the caliph about the "demands" of the opposition. In Medina, ʿUthmān inquired about what was going on in the province, and Saʿīd described how the Kufans were now exploiting the vacuum to spread rumors and inciting the people against the caliph "*aẓharū annahum yurīdūna al-badl*."[32] When asked about whom they want as governor instead, Saʿīd said, "Abū Mūsā [al-Ashʿarī]." So ʿUthmān concluded, "Let them have him then. By God, we shall not give them an excuse or leave them an option they would claim they have not tried. And let's be patient with them."[33] Soon afterward the caliph reportedly convened a council of his governors from the provinces to discuss his next move with them.

In this account, the way that events deteriorate so quickly and severely to the disadvantage of the caliph seems very unrealistic. How did such a small band of marginal dissidents—who were presumably brought to thorough submission after they met with Mu'āwiya and 'Abd al-Raḥmān b. Khālid b. al-Walīd—come to be such a serious threat to the caliph? This is never convincingly explained. Suddenly we find the caliph summoning his key governors (including Mu'āwiya, 'Amr b. al-'Āṣ, Ibn Abī al-Sarḥ, and 'Abdallāh b. 'Āmir) to consult them about the political threat.[34]

It seems unlikely that events actually happened this way. Instead of being historically accurate, the narratives in this year had two primary purposes. The first was to give the reader the opportunity to see how unruly and fickle the Kufan opposition was, especially when they chose Abū Mūsā, thereby foreshadowing the same type of ignorant and stubborn demand they would force 'Alī to accept at the Taḥkīm. Throughout these events, 'Uthmān is shown giving the Kufans the benefit of the doubt and caving in to their demands to avoid conflict. This lends some ambiguity to the image of 'Uthmān, since it seems unclear whether his conciliatory gesture reflected weakness, as the quality generally ascribed to him, or a willingness to find a compromise that would avert a conflict in the community. The latter interpretation would also run counter to other standard voices in the tradition that represent 'Uthmān as stubborn and willing to concede neither his personal authority nor that of his kinsmen in the provinces. We may detect faint signals here of a type of behavior that 'Alī would later be forced to adopt in the face of similar types of sedition. 'Alī, like 'Uthmān, will also be forced to compromise with seditious groups, all the while knowing that his decision is not the ideal one, but will be a step to avert the fragmentation of the community. In both cases, 'Uthmān and 'Alī prove wrong, although the price they pay for their compromise differs.

The second purpose of the narratives of this year was to allow the reader to sample the different portraits of 'Uthmān's senior advisors at that juncture. Each governor's statement was meant to shed light on his personality and to show how he was exploiting 'Uthmān's predicament to his advantage. This is especially so in the part pertaining to 'Amr, where he takes a position and makes a declaration that shows his foresight about how the public will react to news about their conference. Indeed, it may not be an exaggeration to say that the whole narrative of the assembly debating the situation was crafted solely to show 'Amr's motives and political style within the context of that problem and among that group of leaders.[35]

After that debate is concluded, 'Alī makes an individual appearance to counsel 'Uthmān. 'Alī's appearance here is totally unexpected and lacks even a proper introduction or context. Throughout the previous events, he was absent from the picture, and the story of 'Uthmān's conflict with the provincial opposition seemed unrelated to the question of 'Uthmān's original legitimacy in respect to the succession. However, in the simultaneous timing of 'Alī's appearance at that particular moment, and the Kufan opposition's ongoing clash with the caliph, one reads an implication that draws a connection between legitimacy to succession, the 'Alid right to rule, and the question of righteous governance. For his part, 'Alī does not declare any affinity to the Kufan opposition's claims, and maintains a neutral voice of criticism throughout. This representation of events kept 'Alī's portrayal consistent with the Jamā'ī-Sunnī reading of history, which extricated the companions from responsibility for initiating discord. Within this frame of belief, the reader is led to see how difficult it was to remain neutral during the *fitna*, and how even without taking sides, 'Alī's words (weightier than other people's talk), like any speech made in that environment of tension, were likely to be misinterpreted or exaggerated by the Kufans or a sub-branch of them (the Saba'iyya), leading to a worsening of the situation.

The interview of 'Alī with 'Uthmān is the first time that the narrators cast the two talking directly to one another. On previous occasions, such as the *shūrā* for 'Umar's succession and the trial of 'Ubaydallāh b. 'Umar, they had expressed opposite views but without addressing one another directly. This now changes as they set out to settle some old scores. Probing deeper into their encounter, one sees how 'Alī uses the occasion of Kufan troubles to imply that things would never have deteriorated to this point of chaos had he been caliph, thereby alluding to his higher religious grounds to rule (as a Hāshimite, an *imām*, and the one directly favored by the Prophet). And, for his part, 'Uthmān uses his own legitimacy of succession and the religious exhortation for obeying authority to cover his own style of promoting his clan to power.

'Alī's speech to 'Uthmān starts out in a conciliatory tone, with a nod to the caliph's religious knowledge and merit as a companion. 'Alī appears magnanimous, ignoring his passing over for succession in the past, although he refers to this by using 'Uthmān's case in comparison with the first two caliphs. Trying to make 'Uthmān a parallel victim to the first two caliphs, as he is, 'Alī states, "You were one of his [i.e., the Prophet's] companions and became a son-in-law to him. [Abū Bakr] b. Abī Quḥāfa was not better suited than you to act rightly, nor did ['Umar] b. al-Khaṭṭāb enjoy greater merit in any way, and indeed you had a closer blood relationship to the messenger of God [than either of them]. You obtained a marriage tie to the Messenger of God such as they never did, nor did they have any precedence over you" (full text below). The Arabic of these words is indeed strong (*innaka aqrab . . . wa qad nilta mā lam yanālā . . . wa lā sabaqākq ilā shay'*), especially when we consider them in light of the fact that Abū Bakr was not only the first convert but the man who introduced 'Uthmān—along with the five other key companions at the *shūrā*—to the Prophet. Clearly, however, 'Alī's words were being used to allude to his own situation rather than to 'Uthmān, albeit for the present context they served the purpose of deferential respect for 'Uthmān and praise for the companions as a whole. Be that as it may, these were events of the past, 'Alī is made to imply, and bygones were forgiven.

The debate of 'Uthmān and 'Alī now had a new beginning—the people's grievances and proper governance. 'Alī's advice to 'Uthmān in a lengthy declaration takes the form of general religious wisdom and does not suggest a specific solution to the challenge in the provinces. Unlike 'Uthmān's governors, 'Alī's parameters of cautioning advice for the caliph are religious, using words such as "*ḍalāl*" (ignorance), "*bida'*" (innovation), and "*jūr*" (oppression). 'Alī ominously warns about the spectre of war and the prediction of a certain "*imām*" who, it is said, will be assassinated. Alī's full declaration goes as follows:

> "[The people are in the background (i.e., to this opposition)], and they have spoken to me about you. By God, I do not know what to say to you. . . . We have not perceived something before you have, so that we must inform you of it. Nor have we gained sole knowledge of anything

so that we must bring it to your attention. In no affair have we been assigned greater distinction than you. You have seen and heard the Messenger of God; you were one of his Companions and became a son-in-law to him. [Abū Bakr] b. Abī Quḥāfa was not better suited than you to act rightly, nor did ['Umar] b. al-Khaṭṭāb enjoy greater merit in any way, and indeed you have a closer blood relation to the Messenger of God than they ever did, nor did they have any precedence over you [*wa innaka aqrabu ilā rasūl allāh raḥiman wa laqad nilta min ṣihri rasūl allāh mā lam yanālā wa lā sabaqāka ilā shay'in*] . . . Verily the path is manifest and clear, and the signposts of true religion are standing up right. Know, 'Uthmān, that the best of God's servants in His eyes is a just *imām* [*imām 'ādil*], one who has been guided aright and who himself gives right guidance, for he upholds accepted prescriptions and destroys rejected innovations [*fa-aqāma sunnatan ma'lūma wa amāta bid'atan matrūka*]. By God, everything is clear. Sound prescriptions stand clearly marked, as do blameworthy innovations. The worst of men in God's sight is a tyrannical *imām*, one who has gone astray himself and who leads others astray, for he destroys an accepted prescription and revives a rejected innovation. Verily, I heard the Messenger of God say, 'The tyrannical *imām* will be brought on the Day of Resurrection; he will have no helper and no advocate; he will be cast into Hell, turning about in Hell, as the mill turns; and then he will be plunged into the fiery flood of Hell.'[36] I tell you to beware of God and His sudden assault and His vengeance, for His punishment is harsh and painful indeed. I tell you to beware lest you be the murdered *imām* of this Community [*uḥadhdhiruka an takūna imām al-ummati al-maqtūl*]. For it is said that an *imām* will be killed in this Community, and that bloody strife will be loosed upon it until the Day of Resurrection, and its affairs will become hopelessly entangled. [God] will leave them as sects [*shiya'*], and they will not see the truth due to the great height of falsehood. They will toss about like waves and wander in confusion."[37]

'Alī's words of gloom and doom were not the reviving words 'Uthmān was looking for. The quick movement of 'Alī from discussing a repair of an incidental situation of public dispute to talking about a caliph's/*imām*'s imminent assassination left the caliph more despondent and defensive. Although the companions, as Wāqidī states earlier in the narrative, had given signs of animosity to the third caliph by letting the public vent their anger on 'Uthmān and shunning him, it was 'Alī's words here that now played the decisive role. 'Alī may have been an exception to the other companions in coming over to the caliph's house to have a frank discussion with him—and frankness is no doubt shown to be the bane of 'Alī in putting himself in the crossfire—but 'Uthmān had now come to know what the scene in Medina really looked liked and who his friends and enemies were. Scrambling for defense, 'Uthmān told 'Alī, "By God, if you were in my place, I would not have berated you nor left you in the lurch nor shamed you nor behaved foully [*law kunta makānī mā 'annaftuka wa lā aslamtuka wa lā 'ibtu 'alayka*]."[38] Implicit in these words, which ironically hint of 'Uthmān's blaming 'Alī for the coming assassination, is what will be emphasized more later, namely that 'Alī commands huge leverage in the community at large and especially with the opposition, and that he could have averted the tragedy about to befall 'Uthmān. 'Uthmān's statement reflects the greater Sunnī affinity to him as compared with 'Alī, and provides an indirect Sunnī rebuke for 'Alī as well.

Like 'Alī, 'Uthmān here gives a lengthy rebuttal that stands as a cogent speech and anticipates events soon to happen, especially his loss of 'Alī's support. In a key juncture in his conversation with 'Alī, 'Uthmān draws the latter to specifics by asking why there is such particular disapproval when he (i.e., 'Uthmān) is doing no more than what his predecessor 'Umar had done (as in appointing al-Mughīra b. Shu'ba and Mu'āwiya to political offices).[39] 'Alī's response to this is essentially that 'Uthmān is simply no match for 'Umar. 'Uthmān lacks the charismatic strength that 'Umar commanded and made governors work within the bounds of integrity and impartiality. 'Umar, 'Alī elaborates, used to punish his governors for the slightest criticism he heard about, "but you," 'Alī says, "do not do [that]. You have been weak and easygoing with your relatives [*wa anta lā taf'al, ḍa'ifta wa rafiqta 'alā aqribā'ika*]."[40] 'Uthmān moves on to defend his actions toward his relatives/governors (such as his dispensation of wealth among them) by saying that some were worthy of it and others in need of it, but most importantly that this decision was the caliph's alone to make, not something to be shaped by divergent public whims.[41] 'Uthmān felt that he also had a moral obligation to his kinsmen (on the basis of *qarāba* or *ṣilat al-raḥim*) that coincided here with his role as caliph. The harmony between his role as caliph and as patriarch of his family in his giving of wealth to his governors should have been easily understood as far as he was concerned, but the conversation between

'Alī and 'Uthmān puts the reader in direct contact with the crux of the matter: How can a caliph separate his moral duty toward kin, family, and tribe (an individual's religious duty) from his political obligation (collective religious duty) to the community as a neutral religious leader? From another, more practical angle, 'Uthmān was essentially asking, How can caliphal authority be effective and act as a magnet for the *jamā'a* if minor criticisms[42] are elevated to become challenges to caliphal legitimacy?

One must wonder whether 'Alī's comments to 'Uthmān about 'Umar's strength (and how governors dared not say anything to challenge him) have an ironic tinge, since 'Alī's open criticism of 'Uthmān, in a style unevident during the time of 'Umar, is itself evidence of the leniency with which 'Uthmān indulged his subjects. On the whole, however, the narrative gives 'Uthmān some key moments in which he provides a response to 'Alī that rises well above the stereotype of this third caliph as submissive, carefree, unreasoned, and passive. 'Uthmān explains all his actions and concludes with a tragic reflective reaction to what everyone is saying:

> "For everything there is some bane and in every situation there is some defect. The bane of this Community [*umma*] and the defect in this [divinely bestowed] beneficence are the maligners and slanderers who let you see what is pleasing to you and conceal what is hateful to you. They talk and talk to you. Men who resemble ostriches follow the first one to make a noise. Their favorite watering place is the one far away; they fail to quench their thirst, and they get only the sediment. No leader arises, affairs have worn them out, and they possess no means of gain. By God, you have surely blamed me for things like those you accepted from Ibn al-Khaṭṭāb. But he trampled you underfoot, smote you with his hand, and subdued you by his tongue, and so you submitted to him, whether you liked it or not. I have been lenient with you. I let you tread on my shoulders while I restrained my hand and tongue, and therefore you have been insolent toward me [*ammā ba'd fa-inna li-kulli shay'in āfa wa inna āfata hādhihi al-umma 'ayyābūn ṭa''ānūn . . . 'ibtum 'alayya bi-mā athartu li-ibn al-khaṭṭāb bi-mithlihi wa lakkinahu waṭa'akum bi-rijlihi wa lintu lakum bi-yadī wa lisanī 'ankum fa-ijtra'tum 'alayy*]."[43]

'Alī's vision—"By God, the best of the servants of God is one who is an '*imām 'ādil*' " (where "'*ādil*" is understood as balancing the moral and political obligations between family and state considerations)—is a lofty, even messianic dream.[44] But one wonders whether anyone but a prophet at that hour could have possessed the direction and binding authority to save the community.

Ṭabarī essentially leads the reader to the final question, which will endure and cause even more turbulence in 'Alī's reign, namely, Where does one find this "just *imām*," and how does he make decisions in the gray area that 'Uthmān was facing? The answers to this question would vary according to the split in the Islamic community. To the Shī'a, the *imām* (legatee of the Prophet) was the answer, while to Sunnīs, the search for the ideal *imām* was viewed as unattainable after 'Umar, and the whole question needed to be dropped or at least made secondary to the collective welfare of the *jamā'a*. Ṭabarī's answer to this dilemma meanders between the two sides as his narratives engage the rich polemical dialogue between the two camps. At that particular juncture after 'Alī's debate with 'Uthmān, the story gives its own answer in a new set of narratives.

## THE CONFLICT IN MEDINA

The aforementioned encounter between 'Alī and 'Uthmān represented the official moment of polarization between the two, and a staking of war positions that will be repeated and fine-tuned but not radically altered. The next phase of narration in Ṭabarī is a long one. It covers the slow progress toward the overthrow of 'Uthmān in an extensive set of narratives, which sometimes overlap but more often vary on important secondary details. It was clearly not an easy story for Ṭabarī to tell—about the companions abandoning 'Uthmān to certain death while he was in their midst—and so in an effort to dilute the effect of what would otherwise have been a scandalous biblical tale, he deployed a variety of stories that gave a wide range of viewpoints and explanations. There were those that exculpated 'Alī from responsibility for the attack on 'Uthmān, those that defended 'Uthmān as repentant caliph or contrite companion, and still others that placed on him the responsibility for political failure through his relying on mischievous advisors, resorting to guile or treachery, or simply acting stubbornly. All manner of nuance and variation are assigned to the motives of the caliph, his circle of supporters, and the opposition and the critics of the caliph, so that the complete story addresses a range of viewpoints but defies a single interpretation. This plethora of accounts about the interactions between ʿUthmān and the various actors, and the numerous dialogues at every stage along the way to conflict, is far richer than anything else for the Rāshidūn period. This was not, for example, the style of the second caliph's biography, which, although connected by a set of underlying themes, was ultimately cohesive and progressed in a linear manner and unequivocally. In ʿUthmān's case, while the focus of issues is narrow, the range of descriptions offered is varied and extensive, and the pace of progress toward the end seems glacial.

The complete picture of the original accounts of ʿUthmān's story has not survived in full in Ṭabarī's, Balādhurī's, or Ibn Saʿd's works. Ṭabarī frequently points out that he omitted portions of the original texts that sounded offensive or unsuitable, but he does not elaborate on this criterion. Nevertheless a lot survived in Ṭabarī's chronicle that can inform us not only about the original texts, but about the preferences of ninth-century redactors in selecting material that could coexist with Jamāʿī-Sunnī views. The main sources of these accounts are Sayf b. ʿUmar and Muḥammad b. ʿUmar al-Wāqidī as well as a substantial few from Jaʿfar b. ʿAbdallāh al-Muḥammadī, with some occasional inserts from Abū Mikhnaf, Yaʿqūb b. Ibrāhīm, and Muḥammad b. al-Sāʾib al-Kalbī. These texts share a similar style of narration and connect in a flowing sequence in the chronicle. They also do not exclusively side with one party or another. However, a close reading of these texts shows that al-Wāqidī's version includes dimensions apologetic for ʿUthmān that are not found elsewhere (hagiography, companion closeness), while Sayf b. ʿUmar's version has fewer of these features; and Abū Mikhnaf's version shows a more politically minded caliph, unwilling to compromise and eager to hold on to power.

In the end, the divergences among the narratives are less significant in and of themselves than they are for the way they mesh together to build a complete tragic portrait of the caliph and the companion society at the time. The ability of the chronicler to combine a vast body of accounts indirectly shows his criteria for selecting narratives, which had their own crucial, self-contained meanings or took on a different sense when read in relation to other texts in pre-Islamic and Islamic history. In the next section, we will examine the steps that made up the final obstacles for ʿUthmān, and how he and the opposition reacted to developments.

## *'Abdallāh b. Saba' as a Catalyst to Civil War*

This phase of background to the conflict represents in Ṭabarī's sequenced narratives a kind of new point of departure to be added to the disputes in Kufa, and the arguments between 'Alī and 'Uthmān. There is no variation in the narratives here, and so the story provides what seems be a key polemical and religious tool for apologetic innuendo regarding the conflict.

Right about the time that these arguments over government were brewing, Ṭabarī tells us, a certain 'Abdallāh ibn Saba', a Yemenite convert from Judaism,[45] began to disseminate the idea of prophetic return, preaching that the Prophet Muḥammad would one day return, just as the Qur'ān promised that Jesus would. This notion of "*al-raj'a*" was reportedly being spread along with another idea of Ibn Saba''s, namely that historically every prophet had a legatee (*waṣiyy*), and that Muḥammad's legatee was 'Alī.[46] Whether it is here implied that Ibn Saba' meant that 'Alī represented a prophetic continuum or else a representative for Muḥammad is not explicitly stated by Ṭabarī. However, it seems obvious from the overarching religious profile that we get of 'Alī as a spiritual master with a great cache of wisdom sayings, somber assessments of history and human behavior, and from the timing of Ibn Saba''s preachings that the narratives are describing a growing social current that finds 'Alī more than worthy of the caliphate because he was both competent and unfairly passed over before. The call of Ibn Saba' reportedly declared that Muḥammad was the seal of the prophets and 'Alī the seal of the legatees, and asserted that 'Uthmān had wrongfully seized the caliphate.

Ibn Saba' then reportedly sent out his propagandists (*baththa du'ātihi*) and wrote to the corrupted elements in different locales (*kātaba man istafsada min al-amṣār*), instructing his followers to begin a campaign of feigning piety (*wa aẓhirū al-amr bi'l-ma'rūf*) and criticism of the caliph all the while they worked for a different purpose (*ibda'ū bi'l-ṭa'ni 'alā umarā'ikum wa aẓhirū al-amr bi'l-ma'rūf wa'l-nahy 'an al-munkar*).[47] Ibn Saba' himself traveled to Ḥijāz, Basra, Kufa, and Syria to disseminate his ideas—or, as Ṭabarī puts it, "seeking to misguide people [*yurīdu iḍlāla al-nās*]"—but found little welcome. Most notably, in Syria he seemed to face his biggest obstacle when the population rebuffed him more strongly than elsewhere (*fa-lam yaqdir 'alā mā yurīdu 'inda aḥadin min ahli al-shām*).[48] This detail may easily slip by in the thick of the narrative, but it seems crucial in that it signals empathy in Ṭabarī's narratives to the Jamāʿī-Sunnī current of Syria, as well as to how the community in that region rebuffed the messianic (Hāshimite) *daʿwas*. However fleeting and ordinary the description of the reaction of ahl al-Shām in this narrative may seem, in all likelihood it accommodates the positive image assigned to this community, particularly in the days of *fitan*, in *ḥadīth* literature.[49]

The insertion of the Ibn Saba' story at this tense juncture of disagreement in 'Uthmān's reign was meant to discredit the position that emphasized the superiority of 'Alī on religious grounds and to show that the emerging threat to the unity of the *jamāʿa* was both political and religious.[50] While 'Alī's historic religious prestige on grounds of *ṣābiqa* and kinship as well as his individual wisdom is widely attested by Ṭabarī, this allusion to a sectarian movement championing a religious cause on behalf of 'Alī shows Ṭabarī detracting from 'Alī's cause in another way. Whereas Muʿāwiya could draw on the memory of Abū Sufyān's leadership in the Jāhiliyya to prop up his political legitimacy, 'Alī is cast as the candidate of the former enemies of Islam (the Jews), sectarians, and anarchists in general. The line "*ibda'ū bi'l-ṭaʿni ʿalā umarā'ikum*" is as close as Ṭabarī gets to giving his own historical commentary. The turn of phrase itself, put in direct speech, mocks the very essence of the egalitarian-pietistic platform of 'Alī's supporters in general.[51]

The Kufan demand for equality in booty revenues and their contention with Muʿāwiya was discredited even earlier, as we saw, on grounds of class and morality. And it would have remained an empty and minor threat, as Ṭabarī implies, were it not for the religious threat that Ibn Saba' developed. Ibn Saba', according to Ṭabarī, had initiated a false call for "instituting the good" into a political ploy for undermining the government (*hādhā al-amr*) (*fa-inhaḍū fī hādhā al-amr fa-ḥarrikūh wa ibda'ū bi'l-ṭaʿni ʿalā umrā'ikum wa aẓhirū al-amra bi'l-maʿrūf*).[52] Next he sent out *duʿāt* to the various provinces and wrote to the "rotting elements" (*kātaba man kāna istafsada min al-amṣār*) (*wa jaʿalū yaktubūna ilā al-amṣār bi-kutubin yaḍaʿūnahā fī ʿuyūbi wulātihim*). One gets the impression of a concerted underground conspiracy that targeted the provinces, with different activists reaching various locales and purporting a religious veneer different from what they claimed to believe. Because they are effective in their preaching to the point of having a hypnotizing effect on the community, the *daʿwa* of Ibn Saba' takes on a plague-like quality, making different communities fear that they will soon be affected and pray that they will not have to come to hear it (*yaqūl ahl kull miṣr: innā lafī ʿāfiya mimmā ibtuliya fīhi hāʾulāʾ*). Individual cases of temptation by the spreading rumors are cited. ʿAmmār, who was initially sent to Egypt to investigate the situation, is said to have lingered longer than he should have there and become tempted by the propaganda (*inna ʿAmmār qad istamālahu qawmun bi-miṣr*).[53]

## *ʿUthmān's Consultations with Governors*

ʿUthmān's first reaction to the emerging crisis is represented in the narratives in pious terms reminiscent of Abū Bakr and ʿUmar. Sayf reports that the caliph summoned his governors to Medina to evaluate the situation, and that he was eager to provide justice for all who had grievances and to abide by the call for "*al-amr bi'l-maʿrūf wa'l-nahy ʿan al-munkar*." The caliph appears personally without a genuine fault, and his declaration to the public at times sums up the image of a self-deprecating caliph that will reappear frequently in the evolving story of crisis. "Neither I, nor my household," ʿUthmān declared, "claim any priority in rights over the subjects [*raʿiyya*], save the rights bequeathed to them [*laysa lī wa li-ʿiyālī ḥaqqun qabla al-raʿiyyati illā matrūkun lahum*]."[54] This position was reportedly deeply appreciated in the provinces.

Contrary to perspectives that depict him as passive or complicit in the authoritarianism of governors (Muʿāwiya), ʿUthmān is portrayed as alert to possible gubernatorial abuses and ready to correct them. When he first heard of these rumors, he reportedly convened a council of his governors and told them, "Woe to you! What is this complaining and protest? By God, I fear that you are rightly accused and that I alone will be reproached for [your misdeeds][55] [*innī la-khāʾif an takūnū maṣdūqan ʿankum*]." This image of ʿUthmān chiding his governors is typical of Ṭabarī's balance of narratives, where support for authority is always upheld but rebuke is also assigned to those in office. In contrast to ʿUthmān, the governors suggested that wise strategy (*al-raʾy*) recommended some sternness (*ḥusn al-adab*, according to Muʿāwiya), and even more stringent policies (*al-shidda*, according to ʿAmr b. al-ʿĀṣ). In reply to these views, ʿUthmān shows some understanding, but he is portrayed as more anxious about the spread of sedition and the need for coaxing and careful treatment of the public (*al-līn wa'l-muʾātāt wa'l-mutābaʿa*) except in matters that touched the law (*ḥudūd allāh*). So, as if to show that he learned from his conversation with ʿAlī, ʿUthmān declares, "By God, the mill of revolt [*al-fitna*] is turning; blessed will ʿUthmān be if he dies without having set it in motion. Restrain the people, bestow their rights upon them, and forgive them."[56] Thus ʿUthmān indirectly here shows understanding of potential abuses, but it is left ambiguous whether he is too weak to control his headstrong governors or unwilling to do something that would embolden the *raʿiyya* (community of subjects) to become more presumptuous in its challenge.

In another independent account (according to Sayf), Ṭabarī describes an individual conversation between Muʿāwiya and ʿUthmān that evaluates the situation. Here Muʿāwiya suggests to the caliph that he quit Medina and come to Damascus. The people in Syria, Muʿāwiya points out, are still loyal to the caliph and, implicitly, to the *jamāʿa* (*inna ahl al-shām ʿalā al-amr lam yazālū*). ʿUthmān rejected this invitation on the grounds of his pious feelings of affinity to the sanctuary of the Prophet's mosque. But when Muʿāwiya offered to send the caliph additional troops to help him in the event of a crisis, ʿUthmān also refused on the ground that such an influx of troops would make the newcomers compete with the local townspeople for scarce resources.[57] With these two options closed, Muʿāwiya predicted that the caliph would then become vulnerable to attack and assassination. Through their brief dialogue, the two Umayyad personalities are made to appear complementing one another, albeit in different roles, within the paradigm of Sunnī politics: ʿUthmān represents the legitimate caliph with attentiveness to the concerns of the Medinan population (*ahl dār al-hijra wa'l-nuṣra*) and the memory of the Prophet, and Muʿāwiya the skilled politician willing to serve a member of the Rāshidūn caliphate.

A particularly unique message that emerges from this dialogue is the representation of Syria as the stronghold of traditional Islam. The Syrians are portrayed as continuing loyalists to the government of Medina (*inna ahl al-shām ʿalā al-amr lam yazālū*), and will be contrasted later with the seditious schismatics of southern Iraq, and Syria is thus presented to the caliph as a worthy haven for the caliphate of Medina.[58] In typical Ṭabarī style, the emphasis in Muʿāwiya's remark is on simplifying religious orthodoxy (*ʿalā amr lam yazālū*), which is centered on Syria and the *jamāʿa* and is to be contrasted with the environment of fuzzy religious tendencies that flourished in southern Iraq and were later to be viewed as having brought about 'Alī's undoing. Whether his motives were religiously simplistic or politically misconceived, 'Uthmān's refusal of Mu'āwiya's advice, in a manner unlike what 'Umar would have done in a similar context, will lead to the difficulties he later faces. Viewed within this frame, 'Uthmān's upcoming tragedy was in a sense self-inflicted, like the 'Alid tragedies, and the lesson of Ṭabarī's progressing story points to how the Umayyads will depart in behavior from 'Uthmān in the future, using force instead of discussion to deal with rebels and preempting—rather than reacting to—events.

### *Tolerance*

'Uthmān's tolerance of the rising voices of opposition in the provinces continues after Mu'āwiya's departure. When two scouts (one from the tribe of Makhzūm, another of Zuhra) whom 'Uthmān sent out to the provinces came back with more alarming news about a group of people intent on coming to Medina to overthrow the caliph, 'Uthmān still displayed a combination of misplaced religiosity and easygoing politics. In response to advice that he preempt the situation by quashing the rebels, following the *ḥadīth* (*man da'ā ilā nafsihi aw ilā aḥadin wa 'alā al-nās imām fa-'alayhi la'natu allāh*),[59] 'Uthmān replied, "Let us forgive and accept them and guide them in our utmost. We will not coerce anyone until he transgresses a boundary of the law or displays infidelity [*bal na'fū wa naqbal wa nubaṣṣiruhum bi-jahdin wa lā nuḥādī aḥadan ḥattā yarkab ḥaddan aw yubdī kufra*]."[60] Instead of writing to request reinforcements, 'Uthmān wrote letters to the provinces, inviting anyone with a grievance to come to Medina and complain.[61] When this letter was read, we are told, the provincial populace felt great sympathy for the caliph.

### *The Grievances* (ḥuqūq)

What was meant by *ḥuqūq* in the evolving crisis of 'Uthmān has only the faintest historical root. For although the original spark for conflict in Kufa had to do with the governor's seeming ambition to dominate the revenues of the conquered lands, the list of grievances as the situation progressed became long and diverse, and more polemical than real:

why did the caliph create private grazing reserves?, why did he appoint youths as governors?, why did he give Ibn Abī Sarḥ a huge stipend?, why did he show greater closeness to his family and bestow on them gifts?, why did he allow al-Ḥakam b. al-ʿĀṣ to return to Medina?, why did he collect the Qur'ān?, why didn't he pray like a traveler in Ṭā'if?, etc. It seems clear that the topic of grievances became a favorite polemical theme for religious dialogues and was revisited periodically with more drama and embellishment as the dilemma of ʿUthmān advanced. Sometimes these grievances did no more than try to defame ʿUthmān's past (such as in the questions as to why he was absent at Badr, why he retreated at Uḥud, and why he was absent at *bayʿat al-riḍwān* during al-Ḥudaybiyya).[62]

On the whole, these questions and arguments appear to have aimed more at testing ʿUthmān's religious purity and knowledge than at judging his political wisdom and integrity. The caliph consistently offered complete answers to the questions put to him, in a clear sign that narrators wanted to depict the caliph as having the advantage of religious response, and to show that through the whole exercise he was as a ruler living up to the model of ʿUmar, who indulged the public's curiosity about all public and private matters relating to his household and rule. A preview of these grievances is given early on by Ṭabarī (according to Sayf b. ʿUmar's version),[63] but other narrators introduce these discussions later.

ʿUthmān's responses to several of these questions illuminate the methods of religious argumentation used to address differences with the opposition. When asked, for example, why his kinsman Ibn Abī Sarḥ had received a high stipend, ʿUthmān pointed out that this was indeed the governor's due fifth of the booty of conquest, and that Abū Bakr and ʿUmar had done this before. To the question about gifts and handouts to his family relations ʿUthmān defended himself by arguing that such gifts fostered filial closeness, and that he had done this (given away even bigger sums) during the Prophet's time, and never got criticized for it then, so why were questions being raised now. ʿUmar had chosen to express his piety through frugal asceticism, ʿUthmān argued, while he (ʿUthmān) was doing the same through charitable support of his family. Both are valid means of getting close to God, ʿUthmān argued. While such answers may not have always convinced the opposition movement, which viewed the entire Umayyad clan with suspicion, they do offer religious arguments that defended the action from a traditional viewpoint.

*The Opposition's Departure to Medina*

Sayf then moves on to describe how three camps of opposition (from Basra, Kufa, and Egypt) began to gather for a march on Medina. The names of these rebels partly overlap with the circle of critics who earlier had arguments with Sa'īd b. al-'Āṣ and Mu'āwiya. They include famous names such as Ibn al-Sawdā' (Ibn Saba'), al-Ashtar al-Nakha'ī, Abū 'Amr b. Budayl b. Warqā', Ḥukaym b. Jabla al-'Abdī, Ṣa'ṣa'a, and Zayd b. Ṣūḥān, and those later implicated in the murder of 'Uthmān, such as Ḥurqūṣ b. Zuhayr, Sawdān b. Ḥumrān, and al-Ghāfiqī b. Ḥarb al-'Akkī.[64] These individuals were leaders of a much larger grouping of three factions, each variably estimated between five hundred and a thousand that set out to Medina. The names mentioned by Ṭabarī, and more fully by Balādhurī, betray consistent markings of tribes that were generally looked down upon (and disliked by both the Prophet and 'Umar), such as the Sakūn, the Banū 'Āmir b. Ṣa'ṣa'a, the Nakha', Tamīm, and the 'Abd al-Qays.[65] This makes it difficult to ascertain whether this pattern of inferiority was historically real or partly contrived to fit in with Ṭabarī's general philosophy of how caliphal (monarchal) rule was being subverted. Furthermore, some names listed are suspicious for being either incomplete (Qutayra b. fulān [so and so] al-Sakūnī) or suggestive of their role in fomenting troubles (Ibn al-Muḥarrish).[66]

In all, Sayf carefully distances this group from the companions ('Alī, al-Zubayr, and Ṭalḥa), who are represented as condemning the rebels when these first arrived in Medina. Each of the factions approached the person whom they sought to make leader—the Egyptians came to 'Alī, the Basrans to Ṭalḥa, and the Kufans to al-Zubayr—and yet they heard the same condemning refrain from all of them. 'Alī's situation is perhaps the more significant. When the Egyptians approached him, he reportedly was at a place called Aḥjār al-Zayt (the oil stones), and was wearing a white-stripped cloak and a turban wrapped from a strip of red Yemeni cloth. He was girt with a sword but did not have on a shirt, and had dispatched al-Ḥasan to 'Uthmān among those who had gathered (presumably the other sons of the companions who gathered at 'Uthmān's house). The Egyptians then greeted 'Alī, and as they presented their aims to him, he reportedly shouted at them and drove them away, saying, "The upright [*al-ṣāliḥūn*] know that the armies at Dhū al-Marwa and Dhū Khushub have been cursed by the tongue of Muḥammad, peace and blessings be upon him. Go back, and may God be no friend to you!"[67] The same reaction was reported from Ṭalḥa and al-Zubayr.

Sayf b. 'Umar's portrayal of 'Alī's and the companions' reaction in this segment falls squarely within Sunnī expectations of companion harmony and their aversion to attacking 'Uthmān. Additional details—about the children of the companions having already gone to defend 'Uthmān—further enhance this image. The specific mention of al-Ḥasan was clearly calculated to connect with the Jamā'ī-Sunnī paradigm, since he was the member of the 'Alid family most favored by Sunnīs for his attitudes of political compromise and acquiescence. The account therefore presents a clear Islamic apologia for the companions, but it does not concur with many of the other descriptions and dialogues given by Sayf and the various narrators for these years. The same narrative, however, may contain a layer of subtle commentary in the text that subverts the overt meaning just given.

After the rebels found no support in Medina, they reportedly decided to return to their home provinces, but then suddenly they showed up again in Medina. This episode of return is the famous scene, described in more detail by Wāqidī, where the rebels reportedly intercepted a messenger of 'Uthmān sent to the governor of Egypt with orders to have the rebels rounded up and beaten or murdered. Sayf does not here touch on the key themes of 'Uthmān's initial repentance and promises, which are followed by the treacherous message (essentially the core subject in this story about caliphal duplicity). However, the narrator communicates something else here. Upon the return of the Kufans, Basrans, and Egyptians, all the companions reportedly expressed surprise at the timing that brought the rebels together again. 'Alī's statement can be read as open to double interpretation when he says, "How, O men of Kufa and Basra, did you know what had befallen the Egyptians, for you traveled a certain number of days and then turned back toward us? By God, this is a conspiracy [*amr*] woven in Medina."[68] For while 'Alī may have been pointing to collaborators with the rebels in Medina who brought them back simultaneously, his words could also be read as referring to himself as he weaves this matter against 'Uthmān in Medina. Ṭabarī's narratives occasionally made specific characters pronounce judgments about themselves (e.g., the statement that the 'Abbāsid minister al-Faḍl b. al-Rabī' later made in Khurāsān just before heading back to Baghdad after Hārūn al-Rashīd's death),[69] and this may well be one of his famous hidden declarations (confessions).

### *'Uthmān's Final Plea to the Provinces*

'Uthmān's reaction to the invading rebels was to finally write to his governors for help. The delay of this step was no doubt folly, and the story is meant to illustrate 'Uthmān's political ineptitude compared with more alert governors and caliphs in the future who would seize the initiative long before dissent turned into general chaos. Still, there is another side to crafting 'Uthmān's image of political delay—it was meant to show him as disinterested in power and perhaps ascetic in inclination like the previous companion caliphs. The letter that 'Uthmān finally wrote to the governors offered an opportunity for expressing exactly such pious sentiments even as it underscored the contradiction of the religious impulse with political savvy.

'Uthmān describes in this letter, sent to the provinces, how he was brought into the *shūrā* for the third succession without his request, and how he was selected to be caliph without his demand for office. He then followed the path of his predecessors, imitating precedents (*muttabi'an ghayru mubtadi', muqtadiyyan ghayru mutakallif*) until certain unnamed folk began to reveal their hatred (*ḍaghā'in wa ahwā'*) and showed outward pretenses different from their true intentions (*fa-ṭalabū amran wa a'lanū ghayrahu*).[70] The lack of a specific reference here to the rebels, and 'Uthmān's reference to grudges and hidden agendas, probably hinted at none other than 'Alī. This reading is further strengthened in his next statement, "Lacking any valid proof or excuse, they have in reality sought one goal while publicly claiming another. They have blamed me for things that were previously acceptable to them, and for clearly upright conduct [*ashyā'*] consonant with the considered opinion of the Medinese. For years I have forced myself to be patient with them, and have restrained myself while seeing and hearing [all this] . . . Now they have attacked us in the very precincts of the Messenger of God . . . and they have been joined by the Bedouin. Verily, they are like the hostile confederates at the Battle of the Trench [*ayyām al-aḥzāb*] or those who attacked us at Uḥud."[71]

'Uthmān's statement here clearly relates to the lengthy conversation he had had earlier with 'Alī. 'Uthmān's emphasis on the fact that he was following precedents set by previous caliphs revives his question earlier to 'Alī as to why people were now criticizing him for policies that others had done before, while 'Uthmān's reference to his patience for years (*mundhu sinīn*) in dealing with those who hid their feelings of animosity seems clearly to point at 'Alī's grudge for being passed over for succession. No better irony could have capped the caliph's letter in the end than the way he appropriated an 'Alid and Hāshimite metaphor by referring to the enemy as successors to those who fought "us" at Uḥud and the Trench. Considering the fact that those enemies of old were Umayyad-led, 'Uthmān hardly qualified to label his enemies with such similitude to images from the Sīra. 'Alī, as this study will show later, used this exercise of analogy to a great extent as he set out to motivate his supporters and find parallels between events during his reign and earlier during the Sīra. In crafting 'Uthmān's letter, Sayf's narrator was therefore reversing the roles of 'Alī and 'Uthmān in a witty but effective style.[72]

### *The Siege Against 'Uthmān*

After describing 'Uthmān's failed plea to the provinces, and the caliph's declarations in the mosque in Medina, Ṭabarī's narrative shifts from Sayf b. 'Umar to other narrators. This break will last nearly till the scene of murder. Despite the shift, however, the new narratives smoothly complement the story of Sayf and address the topic of companion disagreement in the same multilayered way.

The new narratives begin by describing how an embassy of the Egyptians debated 'Uthmān on various issues, and how he gave justifying answers to all their questions or agreed to repent any mistakes he may have committed (no specific admissions are made).[73] The crux of this description of interaction between 'Uthmān and the opposition was to show how the caliph would later betray this delegation of rebels. After the rebels gained 'Uthmān's agreement to change his policies and then set out on their return journey, the famous incident occurred wherein they intercepted a messenger who was carrying orders from 'Uthmān to the governor of Egypt to punish them upon their arrival. This contradiction of earlier promises has long stood as a shocking example of treachery.[74] Feeling justified in overthrowing the caliph upon learning this, the Egyptians headed back to Medina. Before they reached ʿUthmān, they reportedly encountered ʿAlī and told him of what happened, and they asked him to join them in the final attack to kill the caliph. ʿAlī refused, saying, "By God, I would not head along with you." Here the Egyptians gave the unusual answer, "Why did you write to us then?" and ʿAlī said, "I did not write anything to you." The rebels then reportedly looked at each other, puzzled at what was going on.[75]

Next the rebels headed to attack ʿUthmān, and they questioned him about the letter they had intercepted. ʿUthmān denied that he had written anything, and took an oath that he neither wrote, dictated, or had knowledge of the letter (*mā katabtu wa lā amlaytu wa ʿalimtu*), in a tripartite denial similar to ʿAlī's denials elsewhere. Explaining his alibi further, ʿUthmān added that these letters could have been forged using his name, and that the seal could have been duplicated as well. Unconvinced by all of this, the rebels declared, "By God, God has made your blood lawful, and you have violated the pact and covenant [which you made with us]." And so they laid siege to him.[76]

This story dovetails with Sayf b. ʿUmar's account in two ways. On the one hand it can overtly confirm the Sunnī view that both ʿAlī and ʿUthmān were victims to unknown zealous supporters seeking to exploit the situation to throw the companions into civil war and divide the community. On the other hand, the stories show linkages on a subtle level where ʿAlī's earlier unwitting comment about himself—"*hādhā amrun ubrima bi'l-madīna* (this is a conspiracy woven in Medina)"—finds confirmation now when the rebels ask him why he wrote inviting them if he was going to stay on the sidelines. Interestingly, the narrative also positions ʿAlī's denial in a way that runs symmetrical to ʿUthmān's denial of having written commands to punish the rebels. The extended reading of these subtexts in these two cases can either make the reader believe that either ʿAlī or ʿUthmān—or both—had actually performed the missteps that were being denied or leave the reader with the more basic reading that exonerates both. Nevertheless, this narrative does not put ʿUthmān on the spot as much as al-Wāqidī does later.

The next juncture described is the rebels' arrival at Dhū Khushub and al-Marwa. The scene here becomes unusually different from before. ʿAlī no longer appears distant from the rebels, but is more familiar with their impending plan and is the only leader capable of turning them back. For his part, 'Uthmān seems more frightened and seems to look upon 'Alī as the only man who can deflect the impending danger. The following report by Wāqidī is crucial for its details and the way it interacts with the warning conversation that 'Alī and 'Uthmān had at the outset of the conflict. Here Wāqidī relates:

> When the dissidents established their camp at Dhū Khushub, the news spread that they intended to kill 'Uthmān if he did not abdicate. At night their envoy came to 'Alī, Ṭalḥa, and 'Ammār b. Yāsir successively. Muḥammad b. Abī Ḥudhayfa had joined them in writing a letter to 'Alī; they brought this to 'Alī, but he did not examine its contents [*fa-lam yaẓhar 'alā mā fīhi*]. When 'Uthmān perceived all this [*fa-lammā ra'ā 'Uthmān mā ra'ā*], he came to 'Alī. He entered his house and said, "O cousin, all ways out have been blocked [*innahu laysa lī muttarak*]; and verily my kinship [with you] is close, and I have a strong claim upon your support [*wa lī ḥaqqun 'aẓīmun 'alayka*]. You see the trouble caused by this band of dissidents when they came to me today. I know that you enjoy prestige among the people and that they will listen to you. I want you to ride out to them and send them away from me. I do not wish them to come before me [*lā uḥibbu an yadkhulū 'alayy*], for that would be an insolent act toward me on their part [*fa-inna dhalika jur'atun minhum 'alayy*]. Let others hear of this as well."
>
> 'Alī said, "On what grounds shall I send them away [*'alāma aruddhum*]?" ['Uthmān] replied, "On the grounds that I shall carry out what you have counseled me to do and thought right [*'alā an aṣīra ilā mā asharta bihi 'alayy*], and that I will not deviate from your direction." Then 'Alī said, "In fact I have spoken to you time after time, and you and I have discussed such matters at length. All this is the doing of Marwān b. al-Ḥakam, Sa'īd b. al-'Āṣ, Ibn 'Āmir, and Mu'āwiya. You have heeded them and defied me." 'Uthmān said, "Then I shall defy them and heed you." ['Alī] thus issued orders to the people, and both Emigrants and Helpers rode forth with him [to meet with the dissidents].[77]

This narrative is remarkable for the way it shows 'Alī deeply involved in the crisis and possessing the singular ability to shape it. The account's description of how news spread that the rebels intended to kill 'Uthmān if he did not abdicate is more directly communicated to 'Alī in the Arabic (*jā'a anna al-qawm yurīdūna . . .*), and the arrival of a messenger with a letter to 'Alī at night, in addition to showing adherence to the classic formula that favored conspiracies hatched at night (*amrun ubrima bi-layl*, as the saying goes), showed 'Alī clearly controlling the traffic of the rebellion. Depicting 'Alī as refusing to open the letter he received muffles his complicity in the conspiring, but this was no doubt transparent to the reader and even to 'Uthmān, who—as if watching from a balcony (or in some other stealth way) 'Alī's action at a different part of the stage (*falammā ra'ā 'Uthmān mā ra'ā*)[78]—now immediately held 'Alī responsible for the developments and came to him to resolve the crisis. The conversation seems to assume a number of previous interactions between 'Uthmān and 'Alī, which Ṭabarī seems to have omitted, since 'Alī expresses exasperation that he had been down that road of compromise with 'Uthmān before and it had proved futile (*innī qad kuntu kallamtuka marratan ba'da marra*) (either because 'Uthmān delayed action on dismissing his governors or simply reneged on the agreement). Nevertheless, the dialogue's crucial link is ultimately with the beginning scene, since 'Uthmān hastily concedes what he had contested before.

The importance of Wāqidī's story here lies in what will follow next, since 'Uthmān and 'Alī put each other to the test. 'Uthmān proves 'Alī's crucial role by gaining his acceptance that he would talk to the Egyptians,[79] while 'Alī is represented waiting for 'Uthmān to undertake a change of policy (change his governors and make a public declaration of renouncing past abuses). Keeping to their bargains, 'Alī convinced the Egyptians to depart (*wa rakiba 'Alī 'alayhi al-salām ilā ahli miṣr fa-inṣrafū rāji'īn*), and 'Uthmān set about to do his part. As events showed, however, the problem with 'Uthmān was the same it had been all along, namely, maintaining the status quo. There never appears any concrete sign of political change (such as changing governors) in the caliph's government in spite of the caliph's exaggerated language of self-deprecation, expressions of contrition for any misdeeds, and rich religious vocabulary of keeping to the right path. Things tended to remain the same on 'Uthmān's side, Ṭabarī's narrators imply, because of a recurrent dynamic in his household, which was that every time 'Uthmān concluded a meeting and an agreement with 'Alī, it happened that soon after Marwān b. al-Ḥakam would visit 'Uthmān and influence him to keep things as they were. To no avail would 'Uthmān's wife, Nā'ila, try to convince the caliph that 'Alī meant well for him, and that it was Marwān who gave flawed advice. The caliph would momentarily listen to this advice but soon afterwards shift his opinion again.

Wāqidī describes two different ways in which ʿUthmān abandoned the promises he had made to ʿAlī.[80] In one case, Marwān reportedly urged ʿUthmān to address the public in person. "Speak and inform the people that the Egyptians have gone back, and that what they had heard about their *imām* is false," Marwān told ʿUthmān. "Your sermon [*khuṭba*] will spread throughout the lands before the people can gather against you from their garrison towns [in such numbers] that you are unable to fend them off."[81] Wāqidī then describes how ʿUthmān refused to go out but that Marwān kept after him until he went forth, took his seat upon the pulpit, and made a declaration that diluted and even revoked previous agreements. ʿUthmān there declared, "[This band of Egyptians] had heard certain matters about their *imām* [ʿUthmān], but when they came to realize that this news was false, they returned to their homes [*kāna qad balaghahum ʿan imāmihim amr, fa-lammā tayaqqanū annahu bāṭil mā balaghahum ʿanhu rajiʿū ilā bilādihim*]." The implication of this statement was then that the withdrawal of the Egyptians happened not because of ʿAlī's intercession on behalf of ʿUthmān after the latter pledged change, but because the rebels themselves, having acted on hearsay, had come to recognize their error.[82]

According to another report, Marwān's guile in this matter took a different form. Playing on the caliph's fears (which were the polemical argument made on behalf of monarchal and Jamāʿī-Sunnī authority) that negotiation and concession compromised the image of the ruling authority, Marwān said, "By God, I wish that you had made this statement [before the people] while you were still strong and invincible, and fulfilling it. However, you have said these things when the girth has reached its limit and the torrent has overflowed the hilltops and when a humiliated man has submitted to humiliation. By God, to persist in an error for which you must seek God's forgiveness is better than to repent because you are afraid. If you so will, you may seek repentance without acknowledging error. The people have piled up at the gate against you like a mountain." Thus ʿUthmān was influenced by another point of view, but aware of the contradiction this represented in respect to his earlier stance, ʿUthmān told Marwān, "Go out and speak to them, for I am ashamed to do so."[83] Marwān finally had his chance to position his own power. With the people crowded outside ʿUthmān's house, waiting to hear the caliph's speech, Marwān came out instead and yelled at them, saying, "What's the matter [*mā sha'nukum*]! Why have you gathered here like looters! Your faces are deformed, and every man is holding the ear of his confederate! Whom are you after? You have come here to snatch our power [kingship] from us [*ji'tum turīdūna an tanzi'ū mulkanā min aydīnā*]! Go! By God, if you mean us [any harm], you will encounter something distasteful . . ."[84]

This gives a preview of what a future Ziyād b. Abīhi or al-Ḥajjāj b. Yūsuf would do in a similar context, but it was too much for the people of Medina to see at that hour Marwān, the son of the Prophet's famous enemy, suddenly in a position of political precedence, and claiming that the caliphate was the exclusive right of his clan (his phrase: "our kingship"). When 'Alī heard what had happened, he flew into a rage and came to 'Uthmān with final scolding words. "Do you and Marwān stop at nothing, even if it strays away from religion?" 'Alī declared, "Where is your mind, you have become like a camel carrying a litter that is led around at will. By God, Marwān is devoid of sense in regard to his religion and his soul. I swear by God, I think he will bring you in and then not send you out again [*la-arāhu sa-yūriduka thumma lā yuṣdiruka*] [the reference is probably to the final judgment]. I am never returning to you again to chide you. You have destroyed your own honor and let yourself be dominated [*adhhabta sharafaka wa ghulibta 'alā amrika*]."[85]

'Uthmān reaches his weakest point with this embarrassing mix of events. He no doubt did not expect Marwān to make that statement, nor did he probably intend to repudiate his agreement with 'Alī. Preserving a semblance of dignity for the caliphal office was what he sought, but now he had come to lose it completely with this final development. For his part, 'Alī was furious, not merely for religion's sake, but for considerations of honor as well. He had used his influence with an angry public, and put his prestige on the line by guaranteeing that 'Uthmān was going to make amends, only to find himself coarsely brushed aside and ignored after Marwān's intervention. How many times could this pattern happen, 'Alī kept asking. When he received a last plea from 'Uthmān (again upon Nā'ila's advice) to come back to him so that they can repair their ties, 'Alī refused. "I have told him I am not returning!"[86] 'Alī reportedly shouted loudly, in a manner clearly intended to be heard by 'Uthmān.[87] Reaching the limits of his patience, 'Alī now added, "I seek refuge with God . . . were I to stay at home, he ['Uthmān] would say, 'You have abandoned me and ignored my kinship and rights.' But if I were to counsel him, Marwān would then come and turn him every which way he pleases . . . [what fate is this!] After his companionship to the Messenger of God, Peace be Upon Him, and his reaching that age."[88]

How much of 'Uthmān's offense in these vacillations was a religious transgression and how much of it was just "dishonorable" in individual terms toward 'Alī is left ambiguous in order to show the tension between offenses to religious/moral principles and personal offenses to individuals' pride. If there is a juncture that underscores the dilemma of 'Uthmān's leadership, it lies in this context of tension between moral and political measures on the one hand, and the pious demands of religious perseverance on the other. The story of 'Uthmān's caliphate becomes the parable of a ruler borne down by age and no longer able to face challengers with the resolve and strength necessary for state affairs that 'Umar had commanded.[89] 'Uthmān is represented as weakened by shyness and indecisiveness, and as someone torn between a domineering advisor, Marwān (who personified the devious image of the court vizir), and a devoted wife whose advice is unheeded. With every breach of his previous commitment to 'Alī, we are told, 'Uthmān's sense of personal guilt and recognition of his political inadequacy grew worse, leaving him in the end turning helplessly to Sa'd b. Abī Waqqāṣ and urging him to convince 'Alī to change his mind and come over to his home for a final negotiation.[90]

Political aloofness in such a climate, the narratives make clear, could hardly be read as neutrality, and it is not coincidental that the murder scene is positioned after the total breakdown of relations between 'Alī and 'Uthmān. For a brief moment, Sa'd seemed about to revive the contacts between 'Alī and 'Uthmān, when Sa'd states that at last he had heard 'Uthmān say things to him that were truly compunctious and that unfortunately nobody else had heard. Now it was at the behest of Marwān b. al-Ḥakam that Sa'd had even come to 'Alī to ask him to give 'Uthmān one last chance, and declare his satisfaction with 'Uthmān publicly. "You would be fulfilling your filial duty, saving his ['Uthmān's] blood from being shed, and life would return to the way we knew it before,"[91] said Sa'd. It was not to be. "May God hear him, O Abū Isḥāq," 'Alī said. "By God, I have persisted in defending him until I am filled with shame. But Marwān, Mu'āwiya, 'Abdallāh b. 'Āmir, and Sa'īd b. al-'Āṣ have dealt with him as you see. When I gave him sincere counsel and directed him to send them away, he became suspicious of me, until what you now see has happened."[92] 'Alī's summary of the personalities who shaped the story from beginning to end and his heartfelt frustration signaled the imminent conclusion of the story. As the two men were reviewing the past and the odds now seemed evenly divided over going back to negotiation, Muḥammad b. Abī Bakr reportedly came to 'Alī and whispered something in his ear. 'Alī then reportedly took Sa'd's hand, got up, and, walking away at the time of sunset, said to him, "And what good is his repentance now?" The narrator Abū Ḥabība then concludes, "By God, no sooner had I reached my house than I heard 'Uthmān had been killed. And by God, we have remained in an evil state down to this day."[93]

This narrative brings a conclusion to the scene within the opposition in Medina at the moment just before 'Uthmān's death happened. The hurried pace of Sa'd's initiative and the acceleration of the news of 'Uthmān's death were no doubt intended to stress the missed moment of reconciliation among the companions. 'Alī is shown in the end as slow to act because of a variety of possible motives. It may be that he was now working by the ethic of individual honor rather than by that of religious duty and filial cooperation. Or his motives may be entirely religious, but represented the position of ultra-righteousness and puritanism (*al-ghuluww fī'l-dīn*), which closed all doors to forgiveness, thus foreshadowing the beliefs of some of his stubborn followers later (the Khārijites).

But perhaps the most important aim of this account was to describe a moment of perfect enigma that the reader/observer was called on to decipher, all relating to the question: What did Muḥammad b. Abī Bakr whisper in 'Alī's ear? Did Ibn Abī Bakr warn that 'Uthmān was about to be killed, announce that he had been killed, or merely that he was awaiting orders on what to do? Like the scene of al-Muntaṣir's getting up and leaving al-Mutawakkil's assembly just before the scene of al-Mutawakkil's assassination, 'Alī's action is followed by the caliph's death. Being more problematic for narrators than the case of the 'Abbāsid caliphs, the issue of responsibility for the third caliph's death had to be shrouded with much innuendo, subtle actions, and ambiguity.

## POLITICAL QUESTIONING OF 'UTHMĀN

In general, the accounts of the various stages leading to 'Uthmān's downfall are organized by Ṭabarī in a manner that preserves an apologetic voice on behalf of ʿUthmān (although this was not the only criterion for selecting narratives). The third caliph is distanced by Ṭabarī from the more intransigent postures and vicious deeds (the mistreatment of Ibn Masʿūd, the treacherous letter, the stubborn dismissal of public opinion) attributed to him in accounts preserved by Balādhurī and Yaʿqūbī. This particular structuring of accounts allowed ʿUthmān's tragedy to fit better within the broader parabolic mythology with which Ṭabarī sought to shroud the entire history of the Rāshidūn (the decline after ʿUmar, the cessation of the conquests, and the occultic signs about transition). ʿUthmān's frequent admonitions to the opposition—"If you kill me, you will never again have love for one another, nor will you ever pray together again, nor will you ever be united in fighting an enemy"[94]—are meant to confirm the wider trends that we examined above about the Arab failure against the Khazars, and the emergence of religious dissent within the community.

For Ṭabarī and other narrators of the ninth century, ʿUthmān's story was important not only for its hagiography about a companion but also for his position as caliph and how to define (or back-project) a consensus-centered faith. Taking as their focus the ʿAbbāsid caliphs in the post–civil war and post-miḥna period, who were presented as the worthy successors to the Sasanid monarchy and the guardians of *sunna*, these narrators saw in ʿUthmān a forerunner to the ʿAbbāsids and their religious orthodoxy. His confrontation with dissenters, while shrouded in artful polemic with conflicting points of view, represented on a basic political and religious level the case of a caliph challenged along an ideological continuum between the examples of ʿUmar b. al-Khaṭṭāb and Hārūn al-Rashīd. The elaborate letter of religious explanation attributed to ʿUthmān, which was read and reported by none other than ʿAbdallāh b. ʿAbbās in Mecca at the height of the siege against ʿUthmān, summarizes the position of Jamāʿī-Sunnī ideology that Ṭabarī favored and disseminated intermittently across narratives from the Sasanid to the ʿAbbāsid periods.[95] The leader as the political authority who must be obeyed even if he was unjust was a tenet that existed in Sasanid political philosophy long before it was put in Qur'ānic and *ḥadīth* forms. Similarly, the image of a mainstream religious culture defined by the law and a circle of scholars who uphold the law resonated as a paradigm of social organization in parallel manners for the Sasanid and Islamic periods. And dissent against the established caliphate (in ʿUthmān's and ʿAlī's times) was viewed as anathema much as religious dissent was to the Zoroasterian kingship of the Sasanids.

If the voice of orthodoxy and loyalty to the caliph is widespread in Ṭabarī's chronicle, this does not mean that Ṭabarī was intent on censoring all criticism of the caliph. The religious criticisms made against 'Uthmān are certainly suppressed as zealous, misconceived, or exploitative. However, the political criticisms retain some credible hold even though they are pushed to the margin. We see this done in two representative cases. The first is the story of the treacherous letter sent by 'Uthmān to the governor of Egypt ordering the punishment of the opposition. When confronted by the Egyptian opposition, questioning him about how he could write a letter in such direct contradiction to his negotiation and agreement with them earlier, 'Uthmān, as well known, claimed that his signature must have been forged and that the seal was used without his knowledge. As for his camel, which the messenger took, it also, 'Uthmān claimed, was used for the journey without his knowledge. 'Uthmān's answers defy credibility, as does the notion that a messenger would need to ride the caliph's camel to Egypt to deliver commands or that he would loiter along the way among the Egyptian group so that they would recognize him and foil the plot! The story is a clear fiction, probably intended in origin to show the shortcomings of guile.

But not withstanding the fact that on this perfunctory anecdote rests the entire story of why 'Uthmān got killed and who killed him, we see that narrators gave voice to some powerful political arguments in the way this episode put 'Uthmān to questioning. As the Egyptian returnees now declared, "You are either truthful or a liar. If you are lying, you deserve to be deposed because you have unjustly ordered our blood to be shed. If you are telling the truth you deserve to be deposed because of your weakness and neglect [*ghafla*], as well as the wickedness of your entourage. It is not right that we allow someone whose commands are ignored due to his weakness and neglect to have authority over us."[96]

The exchange over this incident is repeated in various accounts, and it generally opens up the issue as to whether 'Uthmān was living up to the promises he had made to 'Alī and the provincial delegations, which entailed his dismissing disliked governors and redressing other (unidentified) grievances. In all the accounts, 'Uthmān is shown as unable to give any better answer to the above "checkmate" comment of the opposition than to merely warn about the dire consequences of deposing (*al-khal'*) or killing him and how this would break up the community. But while in light of the preceding debate deposition was established as a credible option, caliphal murder was not. Indeed, according to one account, the opposition is shown accepting 'Uthmān's apology that the letters were forged, and they declare, "We will not act precipitously even though we suspect you. Remove from us your sinful governors and appoint others over us who are not accused [of taking] our lives and property."[97] To this comment, 'Uthmān arrogantly replied, "How do I look if I name officials whom you desire and remove those hateful to you? Authority would then belong to you [*al-amru idhan amrukum*]."[98] This summed up the argument for monarchal authority but it failed to address the problems of duplicity and lack of responsiveness to the public. The second caliph had no doubt offered a different model when he dismissed governors in response to public pressure, but 'Umar often did not wait for events to get out of hand, and he dismissed governors even before discontent grew significantly against them.

From this discussion, we see how by allowing conversations to flow, Ṭabarī enabled criticisms to surface as well, and did not bar depictions of 'Uthmān's inadequacy and incompetence. That the caliph was very generous with religious repentance and that his death was a gratuitous act did not mean that 'Uthmān's political crisis was all the fabrication of heretics and that it did not need a solution. An even more powerful condemnation of 'Uthmān, on the authority of al-Wāqidī, is related by Ṭabarī in an isolated context after the story of murder had had its effect. There, when 'Uthmān repeats his refrain to the opposition, "Do not kill me, for a man may be put to death only in three cases: when he commits adultery, when he disbelieves after accepting Islam, or when he takes another's life except in legitimate retaliation," the comment does not seem to command the position of a final word of a religious verdict, for the opposition then vigorously replies:

> "You say that after 'Umar, the people asked Almighty God for guidance in choosing someone to rule over them, and having sought God's guidance, they chose you. Truly all God's acts are the best acts [*fa-inna kulla mā ṣana'a allāhu al-khīra*] but God—glory be to Him!—has made your case a test for his servants [*ja'ala amraka baliyyatan ibtalā bihā 'ibādihi*]! You refer to your longstanding ties and priority with the Messenger of God. You did indeed possess ties of long standing and precedence, and

> you were worthy of authority [*wilāya*], but since then you have changed and brought about innovations that you are well aware of [*wa lakin baddalta baʿda dhalika wa aḥdathta mā qad ʿalimta*]. You mention the trials that will afflict us if we kill you. But it is not right to fail to uphold the truth [*iqāmat al-ḥaqq*] against you out of fear of discord [*fitna*] sometime in the future. You say that it is lawful to kill a man only in three cases. But in the Book of God, we find that other men are put to death besides the three named by you. [We find that] the man who spreads corruption in the land is put to death and likewise the oppressor who fights to continue his oppression and the man who prevents justice [*al-ḥaqq*] in any way and resists it, then scornfully battles against it. You have committed oppression. You have scorned justice, resisting it and preventing it from being carried out. You refuse to exact punishment against yourself for those whom you willfully wronged [*ta'bā an tuqīda min nafsika man ẓalamta ʿamdan*]. You have clung tenaciously to the caliphate over us, and you have been tyrannical in your legal judgments and in the allocation of booty [*wa qad jurta fī ḥukmika wa qasmika*]. If you allege that you were not arrogant toward us, and that those who have risen up to defend you from us are fighting without orders from you, [we say that] they fight only because you maintain your grip on the caliphate. Were you to abdicate, they would depart without fighting on your behalf."[99]

This narrative is remarkable on a number of levels: personal, political, and religious. Amid the numerous anecdotes sympathetic or apologetic to ʿUthmān, this narrative provides the only cogent voice of the opposition that is couched in religious and political argumentation untainted by association with past succession grudges of ʿAlī or the vested interests of provincial dissenters. Here ʿUthmān's definition of when a caliph or a believer deserves punishment is overturned by evidence that is both Qur'ānic and moral. The three cases given in reply to ʿUthmān (the oppressor, the man who spreads corruption, and he who resists justice) can be viewed as drawing on an evolving textual base that fostered the rich polemics used in these narratives. However, the core of the argument remains that oppression and injustice are moral defects in need of correction. The opposition clearly speaks from within the *jamāʿī* perspective (rather than the ʿAlid or otherwise zealous groups) when they agree about the danger of *fitna*, agree that ʿUthmān had merit and qualification for the caliphate in earlier times, but find that he had changed his ways. This not only was a real dilemma in need of remedy, but also was viewed as a providential trial (*balā'*) that the community recognizes to be something beyond their control in having happened. The notion of predestination (*qaḍā'* and *qadar*) seems clearly to be the common denominator for both 'Uthmān and the opposition, but whereas 'Uthmān considers his rule to be permanently legitimate once he came to power, the opposition disagrees and argues a type of Sunnī view on conditions that warrant replacing the leader. Their comment, "It is not right to fail to uphold the truth against you out of fear of discord sometime in the future," is the type of wisdom argument that will be repeated by various court ministers in Ṭabarī's history, most notably when al-Ma'mūn consulted his advisors on whether he should allow al-Amīn to continue transgressing and placing demands on Khurāsān. While some advisors suggested that al-Ma'mūn absorb his pride since his side was weak, al-Ma'mūn rejected this view on identical grounds to what the opposition to 'Uthmān was saying, namely that breaches should not be allowed to happen out of weakness or a fatalistic attitude to life.[100]

But perhaps the most scathing juncture in this extended exchange that caps the story of 'Uthmān's downfall is the opposition's comment that irrespective of their differing views with the caliph on various matters, the reality of the situation was that those who were fighting on behalf of the caliph were fighting only because he was stubbornly holding on to the office of leadership. Were he to choose to abdicate, they added, 'Uthmān's defenders would give up combat on his behalf. This meant that both the opposition and the followers of 'Uthmān were in agreement on issues of justice, fairness, and caliphal qualification (*sābiqa*, *salaf*, *'adl*, etc.) and that it was 'Uthmān's attachment to power that was causing the division of the community. Viewed within this frame, the opposition was not an alien group of people set against the people of Medina, but were a part of the community itself.

Such criticism of 'Uthmān—formulated in dispassionate, reasoned terms and directed at him not by leading companions but by average members of the community—was rare in Ṭabarī's chronicle, and as we have seen Ṭabarī throws this account far away from the main stages of the narrative of downfall, which we examined earlier, as if hoping to minimize its effect. But that point of view, namely the appreciation of the opposition's frustration, was not without prominent supporters. One such example can be found in a blunt statement attributed to ʿAbd al-Raḥmān b. ʿAwf, who reportedly declared, "Make haste in moving against him [ʿUthmān] before he transgresses further in his rule [*ʿājilūh qabla an yatmādā fī mulkihi*]."[101] This statement, given on the authority of al-Wāqidī, is preserved by Balādhurī but not by Ṭabarī, who clearly saw the religious problem such a comment posed. Elsewhere, however—and this is much earlier in the narratives about ʿUmar—Ṭabarī allowed room for comments from ʿUmar that, although they do not mention ʿUthmān by name, seem to address a hypothetical situation that fits the third caliph's condition. In one of these statements, ʿUmar reportedly declared to the public one day, "O subjects, you have an obligation to us to give advice on what is unknown and to cooperate in doing good.[102] There is no forebearance [*ḥilm*] dearer to God and more generally advantageous than that of a gentle leader [*ḥilmu imām wa rifquhu*]. O subjects, there is no ignorance more hateful to God and more generally evil than that of a harsh leader [*jahlu imām wa khurquhu*]. O subjects, he who enjoins well-being for someone in his midst, God will bring him well-being from above."[103]

Here ʿUmar's words were no doubt intended to be read as judging the future, since ʿUmar insinuates that he is giving advice about the future (*al-naṣīḥatu bi'l-ghayb*), and his speech was clearly meant to draw a comparison between the merits of Muʿāwiya and ʿUthmān, with the former noted for his forebearance, even though left unnamed, while the latter is judged by ʿUmar to be clearly incompetent in light of the treacherous letter affair. Both leaders are labeled as *imāms*, although one is favored by God, while the other is not. The comment highlights Sunnī attention to political talent as something that is different from religious merit, and how God judges a leader according to action and not merely piety. ʿUthmān's defense to the opposition about the three conditions needed for overthrow are therefore undermined here by ʿUmar's stress on just and wise rule.

However, if here ʿUmar merely deplored the case of the unwise ruler, in another speech he commanded that this man be finished off to forestall an even worse future. In an anecdotal report that describes how a group of people came to ʿUmar asking that he increase their stipends, the caliph reportedly immediately saw through their excess in lifestyle, and commented, "You are responsible [for your own problems]! From God's wealth you have married fellow wives and have taken servants. Yes, indeed, I would like to be on a ship with you out at sea, traveling east and west. It would not then be difficult for those [on board] to appoint one of them as their leader. If he went straight, they would follow him. If he deviated from the right cause, they would kill him." Ṭalḥa said, "Why did you not say, 'If he deviated, they would dismiss him [*in ta'awwaj 'azalūh*]?'" ('Umar) replied, "No, killing is a better deterrent to those coming after him. Beware of the young man of Quraysh and the son of their nobleman who always sleeps content and who laughs when angry, dealing with those above him and those below him [in the same way]."[104]

This passage draws the hypothetical situation of a group of believers on a ship and their interaction with the ship's leader. The scene is reminiscent of the discord between Muḥammad b. Abī Ḥudhayfa and Ibn Abī al-Sarḥ in the expedition of Dhāt al-Ṣawārī in A.H. 31/A.D. 652,[105] but the main target of the account here is 'Uthmān himself, whom 'Umar does not name but merely alludes to through the metaphor of the ship captain (cleverly chosen, since 'Uthmān was the first to dispatch Arab naval campaigns, which 'Umar had strongly resisted doing in his own reign). Ṭalḥa, the companion with the highest level of complicity in 'Uthmān's death, is carefully positioned as the man wondering whether deposition of a ruler would not be enough, and 'Umar bluntly says no. The story is a strongly worded one, and runs directly counter to the acquiescent *ḥadīths* frequently recounted about the need to obey authority even if the *imām* is unjust. 'Umar's argument, as in al-Ma'mūn's case later, rests on an ethical view of history rather than on a religious interpretation, and thus underscores the literary logic that permeates the unfolding plot of early Islamic history. The opposing viewpoint, which rested on a traditionalist praise of 'Uthmān, would have thus grown in response to the ethical suggestiveness the historical narrators were weaving into their stories.

## THE MURDER OF 'UTHMĀN

By the time the story of opposition to the caliph builds up toward a final confrontation in Medina, the list of 'Uthmān's weaknesses and offenses has become extensive: bad advisors, nepotism, stubbornness, a weak will, and duplicity are but a few. However, all these shortcomings are in the end overshadowed by the scene of the caliph's murder, which sways the sympathy decisively toward the caliph in Islamic historical memory. As

H. A. R. Gibb once remarked, "No event in Islamic history has gotten so deeply under the skin of the Muslim world, or has continued so long to be a running sore."[106] The murder of the aged companion of the Prophet in the full light of Medina while the community stood by was viewed, against the backdrop of criticisms raised against him, as far too disproportionate a punishment and the main cause for the phases of political chaos and civil war that ensued.

Despite their divergence in describing the political contests leading up to 'Uthmān's downfall, the narratives of the various chronicles concur in providing a pitiful and sometimes hagiographic account of 'Uthmān's death. And the agenda shifts from blaming 'Uthmān to investigating the culpability of different segments of the opposition (more specifically the companions) for 'Uthmān's assassination. Various chroniclers, most notably Ṭabarī, do not portray the attitudes of the opposition in monolithic terms toward the end, nor do they describe the caliph's death as a foregone conclusion. There was a range of groups among the aggressors, from hard-line opponents of the caliph, such as al-Ashtar, to those who were somewhat malleable, such as Muḥammad b. Abī Bakr, and still others who were involved in the conspiracy for mere robbery.[107]

Furthermore, Ṭabarī describes an atmosphere of considerable hesitance among the attackers against 'Uthmān. With every attempt among the group of attackers to muster the courage to break into 'Uthmān's house, someone would voice a wise or religious piece of advice (*maw'iẓa, tadhkira*) about the magnitude of the wrong about to be committed, and reportedly this would temporarily change their minds. Layla b. 'Umays voiced a key exhortation to Muḥammad b. Abī Bakr and Muḥammad b. Ja'far, saying, "Verily the lamp consumes itself as it gives light to people. Do not sin in a matter that you may bring on to someone who has not sinned against you. This matter that you are pursuing today will affect someone else tomorrow. Beware lest your deeds today should become a source of grief to you."[108]

'Uthmān himself would assume the posture of a preacher, warning those besieging his house about the magnitude of their error, and reminding them of his deeds in support of Islam from its early beginnings.[109] Such admonishments were temporarily successful in awakening restraint among the mainstream and encouraged them to stop the siege (*fa-fashā al-nahy*), and Ṭabarī seems to indicate a potential turn of opinion in favor of the caliph at the final moments of the siege, when exhortation and reminders nearly turned the tide of support. Hardliners, however, often soon revived the animosity to a lethal level (as al-Ashtar would comment to the moderates, cautioning them that they were being tricked, "Perhaps ['Uthmān] has deceived you [*la'allahu qad makara bihi wa bi-kum*]").[110]

Finally, when word reportedly reached the Egyptian besiegers that people in the provinces had begun to turn away from hostility to the caliph and that those coming on hajj from the provinces were going to add support for the caliph to their actions, the besiegers said among themselves, "The only way to extricate ourselves from the dire situation we are in is to kill this man. This way, people will be busy with this and won't come after us."[111] Then they tried to break down the door (of 'Uthmān's house), but they were prevented by al-Ḥasan, Ibn al-Zubayr, Muḥammad b. Ṭalḥa, Marwān b. al-Ḥakam, Sa'īd b. al-'Āṣ, and sons of the companions, who held steady. But then 'Uthmān called out to these guards, "You are all free to go and don't have to protect me." Initially the guards refused, but gradually they began to vacate the scene. The spatial context of these actions is somewhat confusing, since the withdrawal of the guards seems initially to have been to outside the precincts of the caliph's estate, but they later trickled back in to take part in some skirmishes in the grounds outside his home. The sources then describe how the Egyptians began attacking the door of 'Uthmān's home and then set both the door and "*al-saqīfa*" (probably the courtyard of a house) on fire. As the door and *al-saqīfa* began to burn, the roof (*saqīfa*) collapsed on the door. Those inside the house rose to prepare for defense, while 'Uthmān was praying. It seems that it was again on the caliph's orders that these guards finally agreed to withdraw entirely, possibly as a symbol of obedience to the caliph, and left him to face his fate. In reporting these developments, the sources do not seem to be implying that the caliph was becoming weak against the aggression, since he reportedly had numerous troops to fend the attackers off, but rather that he was being lenient and avoiding an armed confrontation.

The story here was probably crafted in light of biblical and early Islamic narrative types. When 'Uthmān ordered his troops to leave the grounds of his house, he was being represented in a manner similar to Jesus, who also refused to fight his attackers and rebuked one of his apostles for drawing a sword and striking off the ear of a Roman sentry.[112] The imagery about the attack on the door of his house, however, conveyed a symbolism that was particular to Islamic political dramaturgy, regarding the opening of the gate of the *fitna*. The detailed description that follows of how the roof caught fire and collapsed on the door confirmed the evocation of an interrelation between the beginnings of the civil war and and the original controversy over succession from the reign of the first caliph. The collapsing roof (*al-saqīfa*) was supposed to symbolize the collapse of the original pact of succession at the Saqīfa of Banū Sā'ida, which paved the way for Abū Bakr's and 'Umar's succession. The overthrow of 'Uthmān finally not only served as the subversion of this original setting for a Sunnī covenant, but signaled the coming collapse of the early Islamic state.[113]

'Uthmān was left alone with his wife and servants to confront the attackers. He would soon be overwhelmed and killed as the community of companions remained away, reportedly not believing that such a blatant attack could happen. 'Uthmān's murder occurred just before sunset,[114] unlike 'Umar's, which occurred just before dawn. When news of the assassination spread in the city and on the roads leading to Medina, there was contrition and regret among the populace. Al-Zubayr, having set out to Mecca so that he would not witness 'Uthmān's murder, said upon receiving the news, "Verily we belong to God and to Him we shall return. May God have mercy on 'Uthmān and avenge him."[115] When told that the rebels regretted their deeds, he replied, "They planned this and brought it about. 'And a barrier is set up between them and what they desire.' "[116] When the news reached Ṭalḥa, he said, "May God have mercy on 'Uthmān, and may He avenge both him and Islam." He was told, "The rebels regret their deeds." "May they perish!" he replied, and he recited the verse, "They will not be able to make any testament, nor will they return to their people!"[117]

Then the reaction of 'Alī is gauged. When told of 'Uthmān's murder, he said, "May God have mercy on 'Uthmān, and replace [the evil we have suffered] with good." When he was told, "The rebels regret their deeds," he recited the verse, "Like Satan, when he said to man, 'Disbelieve.' "[118] Finally, the reaction of Sa'd b. Abī Waqqāṣ is surveyed. He had taken refuge in a garden, having said, "I will not witness his murder." When the news reached him, he said, "We have taken refuge in something contemptible and have become contemptible thereby." Then he recited,

"Those whose striving goes astray in the present life, while they think they are working good deeds,"[119] and said, "O God, make them regret this, and seize them."[120]

The reactions of all these companions were essentially predicting the coming civil war. The companions' abandonment of 'Uthmān evoked in no small measure the reaction of the twelve apostles to Jesus. The ambiguous support and duplicity that the companions showed toward 'Uthmān just before his death were not unlike the doubt and denial that the apostles showed toward Jesus after his arrest. The Qur'ānic recitations the companions uttered after 'Uthmān's death provided what was effectively the guilt-ridden analogy to the apostles' compunction after their abandonment of Jesus.

But the final word in this drama is given to none other than 'Uthmān himself, whose quoting of the Qur'ān provided the divine verdict about the fate of the aggressors. This happens during the final scene of 'Uthmān's situation in his household, where he is described as sitting and reciting the Qur'ān. His recitation moved about different chapters of the Qur'ān, reportedly because he was a fast reader, but since the reading is not consecutive, it may well have been intended to suggest that his choice of readings was unpredictable but ultimately apt for his situation. Examples of this include the verse, "Ṭa Ha, We have not sent down the Qur'ān upon thee for thee to be unprosperous,"[121] and "Those to whom people said, 'The people have gathered against you, therefore fear them'; but it increased them in faith, and they said, 'God is sufficient for us; an excellent Guardian is He.' "[122] As 'Uthmān then moved on to read another verse, he was stabbed by one of the assassins. The force of the thrust against the caliph caused him or the attacker[123] inadvertently to kick the rotating base of the *muṣḥaf*, which now scattered before him in loose leafs as his blood began to spill on it (*fa-istadāra al-muṣḥaf wa intashar wa istaqarra bayna yaday 'Uthmān wa sālat 'alayhi al-dimā'*).[124] And while this account does not mention 'Uthmān speaking, other accounts state that as 'Uthmān came under attack, he said, "In the name of God, I seek refuge in God [*tawakkaltu 'alā allāh*], and glory be to God," and then leaned on his left side.[125] He was still reciting from the Qur'ān as blood from his wounds covered the lines until it stopped at the verse that reads "*fa-sayakfikahumu allāh* [God shall suffice you],"[126] in a clear prophesy of divine revenge for 'Uthmān's murder.

CHAPTER SIX

# ʻAlī

## *In the Image of the Prophets*

### THE BACKGROUND OF ʻALĪ'S CALIPHATE

The death of ʻUthmān marks a key turning point in the narrative of the Rāshidūn caliphate. For the last six years of ʻUthmān's reign there are conflicting arguments in the texts, as we saw, about how to judge the third caliph: whether he had provoked the opposition with his innovations and bias to his family or if it was the opposition that exaggerated the case against him and was ultimately to blame for the breakdown of negotiations and the beginning of the attack. All these divergences, however, come to a halt once ʻUthmān is killed. Suddenly the various narrative voices coalesce to reflect a singular position of pity for the fallen caliph, and the event of his death takes on the character of the martyrdom of a religious saint. Gone are all the doubts about ʻUthmān the politician—about his competence, sincerity, and authoritarianism—as all blame is leveled on those who abandoned him: ʻAlī and the companions but, interestingly, neither the Sufyanids nor the Marwanids.

The scheme used to represent the significance of the caliph's overthrow draws on a Christian notion of atonement that is filtered through the words of converted Jews, such as Kaʻb al-Aḥbār and ʻAbdallāh b. Sallām. In this context, the latter's comment before ʻUthmān's death becomes more meaningful, when he is said to have exhorted the attackers, saying: "Do not do this! God has shielded you from the sword of discord ever since He brought out our Prophet, Muḥammad, and you will remain so until you kill your *imām*. If this happens, God will unleash the sword of the *fitna* on you, and not hold it back until the reemergence of Jesus. . . . Your town has been guarded by the angels, ever since the Messenger of God settled in it. But if you kill ['Uthmān], they shall abandon you until the Day of Judgment."[1] In another remark, Ibn Sallām warns that the death of a caliph leads to a divine punishment like what follows the murder of a prophet.[2] The cycle of 'Uthmān's death and the events that followed were clearly made to resemble the story of John the Baptist and the destruction of Jerusalem in A.D. 70, which in Ṭabarī's accounts is attributed to an Eastern ruler, Bukhtnaṣar, rather than to the Romans.[3] Also emphasizing the inevitable nature of the subsequent conflict is a comment attributed to Ibn 'Abbās in which he reportedly says, "If the people had not sought vengeance for 'Uthmān, they would have been smitten with stones from the heavens."[4]

The hagiographic lamentations about 'Uthmān's overthrow now give way to a cycle of salvationist atonement that is represented by the onset of the first civil war, known as the first *fitna*, among the leading companions. It is not only through the description of the military conflict that narrators convey the process of atonement, but also through the depiction of confusion and of the sudden shifts in companion positions after 'Uthmān's death. If the narratives leave it unclear why 'Āisha suddenly switched sides to avenge 'Uthmān, or why companions with conflicting interests would join in fighting 'Alī, this is in part because the various traditions wanted to show the illogical drift of the community in this phase of atonement.

## POSITIONING UMAYYAD LEGITIMACY

Only Mu'āwiya's personality is kept stable during the interim of the Battle of the Camel, as the story completely neglects to record his view of the contenders in the first *fitna*. This omission was calculated not only to keep the focus on 'Āisha's incoherent political role, but also to preserve Mu'āwiya's political role for a later kingship and to shield him from the chaotic scene of the religious community (the companions), which was enduring the lesson of political setback after its abandonment of 'Uthmān. The depiction of Mu'āwiya's diplomacy and political skill is consistently favorable during 'Uthmān's reign and will be resumed with consistency in various stories about his speeches, behavior, and temperament after he accedes to the caliphate. The depiction of Mu'awiya's role in the emergence of the early Islamic state and the general positioning of Umayyad political legitimacy will be examined later in more detail, but it is important here to examine an early speech, which was meant not only to project confidence in his ability to rule, but also to represent a prophesy about the *fitna* that would come if 'Uthmān were overthrown. In an incident that gives Mu'āwiya the high ground and foreshadows his rise, Ṭabarī recounts a long declaration that Mu'āwiya made to the companions just before Medina descended into the chaos that brought about the murder of 'Uthmān. The account says:

> When Mu'āwiya bade farewell to 'Uthmān, he left [the latter's] residence attired for the journey, girded with a sword and with his bow on his shoulder. Then [Mu'āwiya] happened to meet a few of the Emigrants, among them Ṭalḥa, al-Zubayr, and 'Alī. He rose and greeted them; then he leaned on his bow and said, "You know that this situation has come about because the people are struggling among themselves to achieve supremacy for certain men. There is not one among you but that some member of his clan used to claim leadership over him, dominate him, and decide matters without him, seeking neither testimony nor advice from him. Then at last Almighty God sent His Prophet, through him ennobling those who heeded him. When the Muslims turned the leadership over to his successors, they did so through consultation among themselves, assigning superiority on the basis of priority [of conversion], precedence [in religion], and legal judgment [*ijtihād*]. If [the community's leaders] act on that basis, then they will keep control of matters and the people will submit to them. But if they pay heed to the things of this world and seek them in a struggle for supremacy with one another, they will be deprived of [power] and God will give it back to those who used to lead them. Otherwise, let them beware of the vicissitudes of fortune, for God has the power to alter [His decree], and He can dispose as He wishes of the kingship and authority that are His. I have left among you an old man, so display goodwill toward him and protect him. Thereby you will be more fortunate than he." Then [Mu'āwiya] bade them farewell and went on his way. 'Alī said, "I see no good in this [man]." Al-Zubayr said,

"No, by God, there was never anything more distressing to you than he was this morning."[5]

This episode conveys implications in both the descriptive postures taken and the speech delivered. Mu'āwiya's encounter with a trio of companions suspected of complicity or at least gross negligence as regards 'Uthmān's murder was meant to evoke the scene of the night conspiracy between Abū Lu'lu'a, Hurmuzān, and Jufayna. The event is set just before 'Uthmān's murder, as is the conspiracy relating to 'Umar's assassination, but this time the narrative is developed by making Mu'āwiya issue a warning about what would happen if the caliph were killed. In both look and tone, Mu'āwiya is cast as the symbolic heir of 'Umar, with the sword replacing the *darra* (the whip) of 'Umar, and with Mu'āwiya's menacing words echoing the preachings of 'Umar.[6]

Here there is none of the pragmatic and opportunistic character that one finds in portrayals of Mu'āwiya at the Battle of Ṣiffīn and afterward. Mu'āwiya's words are carefully shielded from religious criticism, and they throw 'Alī on the defensive instead of giving him the final word of noble judgment, as he later tended to be represented. It is almost as if Mu'āwiya gives fair warning about the kind of Jāhilī politics that might once again come to prevail—and the kind of person he will become—if the fabric of the *jamā'a* is torn. Mu'āwiya's role provides a range of reflections all summed in one. He is used to reflect qualities of 'Umar, his own political style, and the narrators' philosophy of history, which saw an imminent turn about to occur and cause the community to fall from its peak.

'Alī was unanimously elected as caliph soon after 'Uthmān's death. The community, reportedly distraught over 'Uthmān's assassination, turned to 'Alī as the most senior surviving member of the Muhājirūn community. Ṭalḥa and al-Zubayr, by encouraging 'Alī to accept the caliphate, almost reenact the roles that 'Umar and Abū 'Ubayda took at the Saqīfa in nominating Abū Bakr. Language similar to what Abū Bakr once used is enunciated by 'Alī when he declares to those present, "I would serve you better as *wazīr* than I would as *amīr*."[7] 'Alī also offered to abide by the choice of another individual as caliph, promising full obedience to whoever this might be ("*da'ūnī wa iltamisū ghayrī . . . in taraktumūnī fa-innamā anā ka-aḥadikum . . . wa aṭwa'ukum li-man wallaytumūh amrakum*"),[8] but the community refused. His time had finally come, after three successions that had overlooked him. He used the moment to stress the imperative of obeying authority, and he put himself forward as an example of a loyal subject willing to obey another leader. He had consented to rule only after no one else seemed to be a possible candidate.

'Alī's first step, after his initial hesitation at assuming power, was to insist that the oath of allegiance to his rule (*bay'a*) be taken in public at the mosque. Here one senses his oblique rebuke of the narrow way the *bay'a* of Abū Bakr was accomplished, within a narrow group of Qurashīs at the Saqīfa of Banū Sā'ida. The message of this gesture is that a true *bay'a* should include the *jamā'a* as a whole, involving both the Muhājirūn and the Anṣār; only such a *bay'a*, he said, would satisfy all Muslims ("*riḍā al-muslimīn*").[9] Furthermore, such a step was meant to discredit future dissent from the opposition, especially from Ṭalḥa and Zubayr, who broke their *bay'a* soon after swearing allegiance and rallied with the opposition, and as such were portrayed as breaking with the *jamā'a*. Dīnawarī includes this sense of popular consent as characterizing 'Alī's *bay'a* when he quotes the new caliph as saying, "O you people, you have now given me *bay'a* as you have those before me. Changes in opinion [*al-khayār*] happen before the *bay'a*, but once the oath is taken there is no more choice. It is for the *imām* to lead in an upright fashion, and for the people to give in to him. And know that this a public declaration of loyalty [*bay'atan 'āmmatan*]. Whoever repudiates it repudiates his faith in Islam. It was not an accident [*lam takun falta*]!"[10]

Very quickly after 'Alī's accession, allegiance to his rule began to crumble, as 'Āisha mysteriously made her way to the outskirts of Medina at Rabdha and started defaming 'Alī and preaching the righteous call to seek out 'Uthmān's assassins for punishment. She was followed by Ṭalḥa and al-Zubayr, who claimed that they had been coerced into giving the *bay'a* to 'Alī and were now ready to throw off his rule. Plans were laid in place for the three to go to Basra, where they would organize their opposition, try to coopt sympathizers in Kufa, and wage war against 'Alī. This dissent among three leading companions of the Prophet would form the backdrop for the conflict of the first *fitna*, which would culminate with the Battle of the Camel, an event that receives great attention in the sources as the first of three major wars that 'Alī would be forced to wage (the wars against Mu'āwiya and the Khārijites were the two others). Why the people of Basra and Kufa would join the opposition against 'Alī if their grievances against 'Uthmān were presumably solved with his overthrow is not clear; nor is it clear how a town like Kufa could champion two leaders at once, ʿAlī and Ṭalḥa.

The accounts leading up to the Battle of the Camel should not be read for political and military details. The extant references to troop mobilization and movements, battle locations, and the actual war are all quite hazy and seem generally secondary to the bigger story that Ṭabarī was trying to tell about the interaction of key personalities (at that juncture, these were ʿAlī, ʿĀisha, Ṭalḥa, and al-Zubayr). Portraying the vehement disagreement among these companions and the religious justification for their actions preoccupied narrators the most. At the center of the debate was the question of religious responsibility for seeking out and punishing the assassins of ʿUthmān. After a long hiatus of inaction by some companions (such as ʿĀisha and al-Zubayr) as well as the complicity of others (such as Ṭalḥa) in his downfall, the zealous posturing of this group seems strange.

Alī is generally represented as both convincing and decisively successful during this first phase of civil war. Each of his opponents suffered from a tainted motive in challenging him, and this comes across clearly in the chronicle accounts. ʿĀisha is represented as a fickle personality who used an old grudge against ʿAlī—dating back to the issue of *ḥadīth al-ifk* (the affair of the slander)—to cover her personal hostility to ʿAlī. Her incoherent and ultimately harmful planning of a challenge to ʿAlī is further used to convey a fairly direct message about the detrimental role of women in politics. A major aim from the descriptions of her political activities at that juncture was to show how she exacerbated the problem. While her followers among the opposition were originally motivated to dissent because of the death of ʿUthmān, their anger had grown at the Battle of the Camel over a matter of honor, namely the presence of ʿĀisha in the war zone. Her camp fought desperately to protect her while her enemies sought to capture her. Al-Zubayr's role during the conflict is represented as flawed by his primary motives of pride and a heroic impulse to prove himself a chivalrous warrior. And Ṭalḥa is shown as the one tainted the most in the way he showed a consistent trend of ambition for leadership. Conspicuously absent from this depiction of the opposition to ʿAlī is Muʿāwiya, who seems deliberately distanced from the scene in order to let the discussion focus more on ʿĀisha. ʿĀisha is thus put in the ironic position of arguing against ʿAlī in a manner that facilitates the later rise of the Umayyad political claim, gives some momentum to the Sunnī opposition to 'Alī, and even facilitates the emergence of Shī'īsm generally.

## THE IMAGE OF 'ALĪ AND THE PROPHETS

The image of 'Alī in the sources rests on a complex web of intersection with imagery drawn from the lives of the prophets. His successive losses and his steadfast resolve in dealing with them, as caliph and spiritual leader, echo the tribulations faced by previous prophets. Whether in limited segments of experience or snapshots of expression and profile, one sees diverse similarities and variations on situations and features from the lives of Saul, David, Moses, John the Baptist, and Muḥammad. Indeed, when juxtaposed with the Sīra of the Prophet, the story of 'Alī provides on many occasions what appears to be the exact antithesis of the various successful and religiously triumphant contours of Muḥammad's experience. Just as some moments come to repeat closely, they suddenly break off into failure. 'Alī fails to co-opt public support as Muḥammad did, fails to have his religious authority recognized, and leads a fragmented community in a failed struggle against the very Sufyanid camp that Muḥammad had earlier vanquished.

A beginning for reading the kernel of linkage between the two figures, 'Alī and Muḥammad, can be found in the Prophet's famous assertion to 'Alī, "You are to me like Aaron was to Moses, except that there is no prophet after me."[11] This declaration—which appears to have more depth of representation in the sources than the comparisons we saw the Prophet establish earlier between Abū Bakr and 'Umar and the personalities of Abraham and Noah, respectively—takes 'Alī to a social level higher than that of being just a companion.[12] Muḥammad's comment starts to take on a different light when placed within the full picture of 'Alī's life and experience. Recalling the incident of "*mu'ākhāt*" already cited, along with the story of how 'Alī occupied the Prophet's bed when the latter had set out on the hijra to Medina, impels the reader to see a story that casts 'Alī as acting out a role that is not just that of a second in command but that of a historical "double" for Muḥammad in various contexts.

The existence of a parallel structure between the Sīra and the biography of 'Alī has been overlooked by modern historians, yet this issue permeates the entirety of the narrative of 'Alī's reign. A sampling of such analogies can set the stage for a thematic linking of the two story cycles. Ṭabarī tells us, for example, that when the lines were drawn for battle between 'Alī and Mu'āwiya at Ṣiffīn, 'Abdallāh b. Budayl, a key commander in 'Alī's camp, characterized 'Alī's war with Mu'āwiya as a repeat of the picture of the Battle of Badr. Ibn Budayl exhorted his troops, saying: "We have fought against them with the Prophet, and now we do so again [*wa qad qātalnāhum ma' al-nabiyyi marra wa hādhihi thāniya*],"[13] while 'Alī himself gave a spirited plea to God before Ṣiffīn in a manner reminiscent of Muḥammad's supplications for victory before Badr.[14] 'Alī's camp, made up predominantly of a mix of non-elite Meccan families and non-Meccan emigrants to Kufa, was viewed in parallel terms to Muḥammad's early Medinan community—as the camp of the marginalized and unjustly treated. In addition, strategies from Badr are repeated in 'Alī's time, with significant moral overtones. When 'Alī's opponents tried to control the water wells and to prevent 'Alī's troops from drinking, as the Prophet had done to the Meccans earlier, they failed. But although 'Alī's followers did succeed in seizing the wells, they did not bar the enemy from the water as the Prophet had done. This story was meant to show the recurrence of the Umayyad grudge at Ṣiffīn just as it reworked the Prophet's posture by empowering 'Alī to once again use that strategy to Hāshimite advantage as Muḥammad had before. And one could argue that Mu'āwiya's success in evading a military confrontation at Ṣiffīn reworked the success of Abū Sufyān when he escaped safely with the trading caravan before the Muslims and the Meccans engaged in the first battle.

These similarities between Muḥammad's and 'Alī's lives are distinctly marked at the Taḥkīm, when a truce was negotiated between the famous representatives of the warring parties, 'Amr b. al-'Āṣ and Abū Mūsā al-Ash'arī. We are told that in the preliminary stages of the negotiations, when Abū Mūsā began drafting the truce document, he started by writing: "This is what 'Alī, Commander of the Faithful agreed to . . . [*hādhā mā taqāḍā 'alayhi 'Alī amīr al-mu'minīn . . .*]." 'Amr objected to referring to 'Alī as Commander of the Faithful and said: "Just write his name and that of his father. He is your commander but not ours." Hearing this, 'Alī said: "God is the Greatest! Verily this event has happened before, and is again like a parable [*sunnatun bi-sunna wa mathalun bi-mathal*]. I now remember how, when I was a scribe serving the Messenger of God during the day of al-Ḥudaybiyya, they [the unbelievers] said: 'You are not the Messenger of God, nor do we hold witness that you are that, so just write your name and the name of your father.'" Hearing that 'Alī had compared him to Suhayl b. 'Amr, the representative of the unbelievers at al-Ḥudaybiyya, 'Amr b. al-'Āṣ now said: "Praise be to God! Are you saying that the lesson of this is that we are now similar to the unbelievers, even though we are believers? [*subḥān allāh, wa mathalu hādhā an nushabbahu bi'l-kuffār wa nahnu mu'minūn?*]."[15] The statement underlines 'Amr's resentment of being characterized in a way that puts him on par with non-Muslims, and thus from a polemical angle engages the complex debates that later developed in Jamā'ī-Sunnī Islam about whether one can side with one party over another in that conflict. But the more central point, which provides the mirror image to 'Alī's comparison but was intentionally left to be inferred, is that 'Alī was essentially comparing himself and Muḥammad.[16] The omission of the outright comparison between 'Alī and the Prophet (unlike the comparison between communities on which 'Amr comments) is not absent from the text because of redaction but was crafted in origin in such a brief and artistically uneven way to evoke a debate on several levels.

Taking into account such innuendo casts into a new perspective other seemingly factual points about 'Alī's life. The anti-Hāshimite boycott that 'Alī experienced after the death of the Prophet because of 'Alī's refusal to recognize the *bay'a* of Abū Bakr was probably meant to echo the earlier, more well-known occasion when the Meccans boycotted Muḥammad and the Hāshimite family in an attempt to stop him from preaching Islam.[17] 'Alī, like Muḥammad, was being represented in those critical years as the new head of the Prophetic/Hāshimite family, suffering an equal measure of social rejection and pressure.

Parallels in the life of 'Alī, as stated earlier, reach out farther than the Sīra, however, and touch on symmetries with the lives of the pre-Islamic prophets, especially Moses and his relation to the Israelites. Viewing the early Islamic victory as a cyclical renewal of the success of the ancient Israelites led to the connection of the motifs of victory and redemption. Just as Moses and David (taking over from Saul) were viewed as leading across the threshold of salvation (both territorial and moral), Islamic narratives showed Muḥammad's victory as inaugurating a similar religious success.

A vivid example of these linkages between the biography of 'Alī and images from the pre-Islamic past is provided in a self-contained anecdote recounted by Ṭabarī about an event 'Alī once took part in. 'Alī, we are told, happened to be leaving his residence when a man called out screaming for help: "By God, help me." The narrator continues: "Two men were fighting with one another [*fa-idhā rajulān yaqtatilān*]. 'Alī then poked the chest of this man and that [*fa-lakaz ṣadra hādhā wa-ṣadra hādhā*], and said to them, 'Get out of the way.' One of the men then said: 'O Commander of the Faithful, this man bought a lamb from me, and I had set the condition that he would not give me punctured coin in return [*maghmūzan wa lā muḥazzafan*], yet he gave a dirham that is damaged [(*maghmūzan*]. When I tried to return it to him, he punched me.' 'Alī then turned to the other man and said: 'What do you say?' 'He is telling the truth, O Commander of the Faithful.' 'Alī then said: 'Then give him what he set as condition,' and followed by ordering both men to sit down before him, and said to the man who was struck: 'Exact your punishment on this man [*iqtaṣ*].' The man, however, said: 'May I pardon him, Commander of the Faithful?' 'That's your right, too,' 'Alī said. When the man [who was slapped] got up and left, 'Alī ordered that the offender be carried on the back of another man, and then struck him fifteen punches using the *darra*. 'Alī then said: 'This is in return for what you violated from the man's right [*ḥurma*].' "[18]

This story applies a literary rearrangement of the themes and phrasing from two different Qur'ānic stories about Moses and David. The opening of the scene of the two men fighting one another resembles the Qur'ānic scene in which Moses witnesses an Israelite fighting an Egyptian. The phrasing applied to describe 'Alī's initial intervention echoes the Qur'ānic phrasing in that account. Ṭabarī's words, "*fa idhā rajulān yaqtatilān, fa-lakaz ṣadra hādhā wa ṣadra hādhā*," evoke the Qur'ānic description of the two men "fighting" (*yaqtatilān*), as well as the element of surprise relating to the fact that Moses did not expect to see this. The Qur'ānic verse states: "*wa dakhala al-madīnata 'alā ḥīni ghaflatin min ahlihā wa wajadā fīhā rajulayn yaqtatilān, hādhā min shī'atihi wa hādhā min 'aduwwih, fa-istaghāthahu alladhī min shī'atihi 'alā alladhī min 'aduwwihi, fa-wakazahu Mūsā fa-qaḍā 'alayhi* (And he [Moses] entered the city, at a time when its people were unheeding,[19] and found there two men fighting; the one was of his own party, and the other was of his enemies. Then the one that was of his party cried to him to aid him against the other that was of his enemies; so Moses struck him, [and the man fell dead])."[20]

The two stories of 'Alī and of Moses intersect in the most tangible way when the word "*fa-wakazahu*" from the Qur'ān is reworked with minor variation to apply to 'Alī, "*fa-lakaza ṣadra hādhā wa ṣadra hādhā*." However, whereas in the Qur'ānic account the story describes a tragic trial of Moses, in 'Alī's situation the incident takes on the character of a legal test and evokes yet another Qur'ānic comparison, namely with the story that describes the two men in dispute who come to David and ask him to resolve their conflict. In 'Alī's story, the plaintiff describes the aggression of his business partner, and the dispute over money payment, which points to the fact that the transaction involved a lamb, thereby hinting at a stylistic connection with the story of David, in which one man accuses the other of having stolen his lamb and adding it to his flock of ninety-nine.[21] Unlike in David's case, in which the Qur'ān points to that prophet's mishap of rushing to judgment in favor of one party without listening to both, in the story of 'Alī the caliph shows a repair of David's lapse. 'Alī carefully examines the statements of both sides before he decides to rule in favor of one party against the other. The anecdote thus illustrates how both stylistic and thematic points were reworked to show the ways in which 'Alī's behavior was reminiscent of prophetic experiences and to illustrate an occasion with a similar challenge of moral temperance and legal knowledge. Caliphs—or more accurately Hāshimite caliphs, it is also implied—were especially vulnerable to the types of divine tests that the biblical prophets faced.

The analogy that this anecdote creates between the profiles of 'Alī, Moses, and David illustrates the reshaping of older images and wordings in the stories about the caliphs. But it is here worth stressing that the parallelism between 'Alī and Moses goes beyond self-contained images, and is in fact an exercise that permeates the accounts of the two histories. We can see evidence of this in the drift of the central historical narratives as well as in the marginal anecdotal material if we consider the symmetry between the two constituencies. 'Alī's supporters can seem—and indeed a group of them are shown—to be entirely devoted to his cause and loyal to his leadership. They can speak with a firm loyalty resembling that of the followers of Muḥammad at Badr, such as when one commander is quoted telling 'Alī: "Commander of the Faithful, lead us wherever you wish," while another, Ṣayfī b. Faṣīl al-Shaybānī, declares: "Commander of the Faithful, we are your party [*ḥizb*] and your supporters. We oppose those whom you oppose and join together with those who are obedient to you. Lead us against your enemies, whoever they are, wherever they are. God willing, you will not lack followers great in number and firm in intention [*sir binā. . . . fa innaka lan tu'tā min qillati 'adadin wa lā ḍa'fi niyyati atbāʿin*]."[22] Even 'Alī at the beginning sounds entirely impressed with the unity and loyalty of his camp when he tells them: "I have chosen you specially out of all the garrison cities, in preference to others [*innī qad ikhtartukum 'alā al-amṣār wa innī bi'l-athra*]."[23] And elsewhere he lauds them, saying: "Men of Kufa, it was you who repelled the power of the Sasanids and their kings. You scattered their troops, and their inheritances fell to you [*yā ahla al-Kūfa wullītum shawkata al-'ajam wa mulūkahum wa faḍaḍtum jumūʿahum ḥattā ṣārat ilaykum mawārithuhum . . .*]."[24] *Ahl al-Kūfa* are here meant to personify the Islamic victory over the Sasanids and inheritance of the land in a way that echoes the ancient Israelite conquest of Pharaoh. *Ahl al-Kūfa* are shown victorious, in the words of 'Alī, because they were the abused party (*naṣarakum allāh 'alayhim bi-baghyihim wa ẓulmihim*).[25]

However, not too long a time would pass before 'Alī himself would become so frustrated with the fractious nature of his community and its seditious leaders, such as al-Ashʿath, that he would tell them: "Would that I had in exchange for every eight of you one of ahl al-Shām."[26] The problem 'Alī had with his community was not one of outright treachery but, as was the case with the followers of Moses, a problem of inconsistent abidance by the word of the religious leader and by the established rules in general. The Kufans are shown as fickle, overzealous in their claims of piety and adherence to the 'Alid cause, and often totally unreliable, such as when they ask 'Alī, as he exhorts them to march quickly against Muʿāwiya after they defeated the Khārijites, to give them a break before resuming the war on another front. Their claim "*kallat suyūfunā wa nafadhat nibālunā* (our arrows are exhausted and our swords have become blunt)"[27] is a statement that has the ring of ancient Israelite discourse in the post-exodus years. The words of the Kufans, like those of the ancient Israelites, illustrate the impossible nature of human desires and the folly of individual temperaments even among the followers of a prophet.

## THE CRISIS OF DECISION MAKING

How 'Alī came to be disillusioned with his community of followers, and perhaps with the use of political action altogether, is a process that unfolded over time in response to various political developments. This experience left its mark on 'Alī's outlook on political life and human behavior. Yet what comes across in the detailed accounts of 'Alī's encounters, debates, and wars with various enemies is the constancy of his spirit amid the very unconstant camp he was leading.

'Alī's character is the most mature when it engages questions of religious correctness, and this has been the main impetus behind the Sunnī view, following an 'Abbāsid propagandistic current, that saw 'Alī as an individual more erudite than politically astute.[28] However, in the case of 'Alī, unlike that of Abū Mūsā al-Ash'arī, it was idealism rather than naivete that led the way to failure. Sometimes it was also a sense of religious *tawakkul* (religious trust in fate)—similar to that of the Prophet when he agreed to set out for Uḥud even though he recognized it would be a mistake from the beginning. Hence too the similarity of 'Alī's acquiescence to having Abū Mūsā represent his camp at the Taḥkīm. Those around who could second-guess the past were many, starting with his own son al-Ḥasan. "I advised you but you disobeyed me," al-Ḥasan said. "I urged you to leave Medina [when 'Uthmān was besieged] so that when he was killed you would not be present. Then the day he got killed I commanded you not to take on the allegiance until the delegations from the garrison cities and the Arab tribesmen and every area's allegiance had come to you. Then when these two men [Ṭalḥa and al-Zubayr] did what they did, I commanded you to stay at home until they had got their settlement . . . you disobeyed me in all this." 'Alī responded, "My son, [listen]! As for your saying, 'If only you had left Medina when 'Uthmān was besieged,' by God! We were under siege no less than he! Then, as for your words 'Do not take on the allegiance until allegiance from the garrison cities comes,' the choice of ruler belonged to the people of Medina and we didn't want to destroy that tradition. Then, as for your words 'when Ṭalḥa and al-Zubayr left,' the whole Muslim community was facing weakness. By God! Since I became caliph, things have continually gone against me and diminished me, and I never attain anything I should. Then as for your words 'Sit at home,' how then could I fulfill my responsibilities? What do you want me to be? Do you want me to be like the hyena that gets surrounded and calls '*dabābī dabābī*' until its hocks are untied and it is forced to come out? This is no situation for me to be in. If I don't look after my responsibilities and concerns in this question, then who will? So that's enough, dear boy."[29]

This conversation, reported by Sayf b. 'Umar, purportedly happened back in A.H. 36/A.D. 656, before the Battle of the Camel, when 'Alī was setting out from Medina to Basra. However, 'Alī repeated a similar defense of his position just before the Battle of Ṣiffīn, in an account relayed by Abū Mikhnaf.[30] And he continued this line of conversing with his son, al-Ḥasan, during the Battle of Ṣiffīn, when 'Alī concluded with the words: "My son, there is a day coming for your father that he will inevitably face, and going fast will not postpone it for him, and walking normally will not hurry it up. By God, it does not matter for your father whether he comes upon death or death comes upon him."[31] In all these situations, 'Alī explained to his son, he was taking the best option that the situation presented him with. All alternative actions, whether refusing the *bay'a* or leaving matters in the hands of his opponents, would have meant abandoning the situation to an even worse war, or sacrificing the moral stature that the Hāshimite family held in the community. The problem of 'Alī was not only that ideal behavior for him rested in making strict religious evaluations, but also that a leader must conduct himself according to honorable, even chivalrous criteria, which in his dictionary even meant going against sound strategy, as at Ṣiffīn, when he allowed the camp of Mu'āwiya to drink from the wells (these happened to be under 'Alī's control) even though a better move would have been to prevent them access.[32]

The nobility of 'Alī's approach to war is also evident from the detailed scenes that describe the combat, where it is often overlooked that at Ṣiffīn 'Alī fought alongside his troops in the thick of battle, unlike Mu'āwiya, who was sheltered behind layers of guards (as the scene of Ibn Budayl's attack will later show). While his action underscores his sincerity and his solidarity with his community, it was politically questionable. When 'Umar had proposed earlier to lead the Qādisiyya campaign in person, he was advised by his companions (including 'Alī) against doing this, because it would embolden the enemy to fight more, and because if the war resulted in his death, the community would be thrown into disarray. At Ṣiffīn, therefore, 'Alī was going against his own advice in order to stress the righteousness of his war against Mu'āwiya. Narrators may not have appreciated Mu'āwiya's excessive cowardice any more than they did 'Alī's extra daring in battle, but they undoubtedly meant to juxtapose two extreme images and to show that a middle ground should be found. The lesson of 'Alī's military mistakes was that a successful political leadership acts with prudence and pragmatism rather than in puritanical or heroic ways.

The tragedy of 'Alī is unique among the caliphs, since he arrives late to the succession in spite of all his merits. But his plight is exacerbated by the difficult times that emerged after 'Uthmān's death, which brought in an era of moral ambiguity. When Muḥammad fought against the Quraysh, the division between believers and infidels was clear, as was the singularity of leadership. But 'Alī's enemies were not infidels, and they had their own set of demands, which the caliph was expected to deliver. For 'Alī to lead in such a climate required prodigious explanations, argued with such fineness of religious interpretation that the situation almost required of others a religious belief in his credibility as *imām* that went beyond his role as political leader. 'Alī spent the entirety of his reign trying to achieve this, yet with every new stage of explanation, his quest only seemed to provoke a new battle. *Ḥadīth* preserves the irony of his condition in the statement predicting 'Alī's dilemma, when the Prophet declares, "Verily, there shall be among [the community] one who will fight over the interpretation of the Book as I fought for its revelation."[33]

## THE ROAD TO ṢIFFĪN: THE QUESTION OF RESPONSIBILITY FOR 'UTHMĀN'S MURDER

Unlike his victory at the Battle of the Camel and his successful arguments there against 'Āisha's coalition, 'Alī's conflict with Mu'āwiya, which led to the Battle of Ṣiffīn, is represented in the sources as a genuine trial for the caliph. At the Battle of the Camel, 'Alī's fight was against a group of leaders who had once pledged their *bay'a* to him, and so the caliph's moral right was clearer in the fight against a *ridda* of sorts. The coalition of 'Āisha had few coherent arguments against 'Alī, since its leaders were themselves once vocal opponents of 'Uthmān and were confused about the real reason for their march against 'Alī. The fact that a war had taken place among the companions was still severely jarring, and the various hyperbolic descriptions about the fighting that took place around 'Āisha's camel are meant to express this later sense of disbelief within the *jamā'a* that such a conflict could happen. Nevertheless, the conflict was brought under control, with different sides regretting their roles in mobilizing for conflict, or meeting deaths that carried a redemptive quality for the *ṣaḥāba*. 'Alī equally regretted that this conflict had to happen, and the superiority of his political leadership as caliph and against the seditious voices is vindicated in a way that 'Uthmān never managed to enjoy.

With Ṣiffīn, however, the challenges to 'Alī are more diverse in both their nature and their places of origin, and the story does not end with healing but with greater social dissent within the community; it eventually culminates in the caliph's assassination. At Ṣiffīn, 'Alī's challenge lay in making cohesive arguments to those who refused to give him allegiance unless he showed a willingness to punish 'Uthmān's assassins. From this confrontation, war erupts, and new religious issues are raised within his camp, ostensibly over the possibility of compromise. In the process, 'Alī's camp fragments, and as every new camp raises new arguments to the caliph, the level of polemics becomes more intertwined and frustrating. The original issue of 'Uthmān stood from the beginning as the central problem. Mu'āwiya embraced the cause of seeking justice for 'Uthmān in the name of religion and kinship right, and as cover for retaining control of his own governorship in Syria.

There is no doubt for anyone who reads the narratives, even at a cursory level, that Mu'āwiya, in the events leading up to Ṣiffīn, comes off very badly from a religious point of view. His image is that of a pragmatic power organizer who stops at nothing to win, although it is to be noted that the historical accounts on the whole still place a greater blame on 'Amr b. al-'Āṣ than on Mu'āwiya.[34] Mu'āwiya knows that his credentials are no match for 'Alī, and he realizes that 'Alī's statements about him are true—that he has no *sābiqa* in Islam (or "*salafu ṣidqin*") and that he is a "*ṭalīq*" and son of a "*ṭalīq*" who converted to Islam only as a last resort.[35] Throughout the contentions with Mu'āwiya—through emissaries and in discussions with his own followers—'Alī appears more sincere and in command of the Qur'ānic discourse, which he uses to confirm his arguments.

The big questions at Ṣiffīn, however, do not concern Mu'āwiya as much as they do 'Alī himself and whether he had convincing arguments against Mu'āwiya. The reader is given the opportunity to observe the complications that keep mounting in 'Alī's government. The story is not about exploring the sincerity of Mu'āwiya in seeking justice for 'Uthmān's death, but rather concerns the legitimate questions that can be asked of 'Alī, such as why 'Uthmān had been murdered in the full light of Medina and why he had been left insufficiently protected by the *ṣaḥāba*, and, more importantly, what 'Alī was doing to bring the assassins to justice. Mu'āwiya's role as contender on grounds of kin and even the flimsy memory of his role as a *ṣaḥabī* become irrelevant, since his voice, aside from being the voice of an ambitious politician, represents the questions that an ordinary subject of the caliphate would raise. The importance of Mu'āwiya's questioning process lies in the way it puts 'Alī in the spotlight, while 'Alī's answers, although seemingly neutral, are frequently argued with loopholes and digressions to other topics that show an apologetic sentiment hanging over his declarations. One key declaration by 'Alī in which this style is evident is made as he engages the first embassy sent by Mu'āwiya to negotiate the conflict.

'Alī's answer directed to this group (consisting of Ḥabīb b. Maslama al-Fihrī, Shuraḥbīl b. al-Simṭ, and Ma'n b. Yazīd b. al-Akhnas) starts out with a description of the historical background and then addresses his view of the *ṣaḥāba* as well as the question of caliphal succession, but it avoids giving an opinion on 'Uthmān's murder.[36] 'Alī begins by recounting how Abū Bakr and 'Umar succeeded to the caliphate and comments that they did govern rightly ("*aḥsanā al-sīra wa 'adalā fī al-umma*") even though they had ignored the right of the family of the Prophet to succession.[37] However, when he gets to 'Uthmān, 'Alī does not say that *he* had had misgivings about the caliph, but rather that the people did, and that the murder occurred when the public decided against having 'Uthmān continue to rule. After the murder, it was also the public that came to 'Alī and asked him to be caliph. 'Alī not only emphasizes here that his candidacy was unsolicited but hints that his acceptance was a religious duty, for had he refused, he said, the community would fragment. 'Alī's tone then turns more specifically sour against his opponents. Although he may be stating a fact by noting that Ṭalḥa and al-Zubayr reneged on their *bay'a*, his digression into a defamation of Mu'āwiya is clearly out of place in the context of the argument at hand, and it implies that Mu'āwiya does not deserve to debate the politics of the caliphate because his family converted late and had a history of opposing Islam from the very beginning, and thus that his motives are suspicious.

Then, when asked by Mu'āwiya's delegation to declare that 'Uthmān was unjustly killed, 'Alī's ambiguity is put on the spot and he replies with an elliptical answer: "I will not say either that he was killed unjustly or that his killing was justified, because he was unjust himself [*lā aqūl innahu qutila mazlūman wa lā innahu qutila ẓāliman*]."[38] The delegation members then said: "Whoever does not assert that 'Uthmān was killed unjustly, we disassociate ourselves from him," and they got up and left. 'Alī then said, quoting a Qur'ānic verse: "You will not make the dead hear, you will not make the deaf harken to the call when they turn away, going back, and you will not guide the blind from going astray. You will only make those who believe in our signs give ear, for they are Muslims."[39, 40]

On the surface, the citing of the Qur'ānic verse at this juncture seems straightforward, showing 'Alī's religious erudition. However, the context is not entirely flattering to him, as the verse here caps the dubious reply, "I will not say either that he was killed unjustly or that his killing was justified, because he was unjust himself." Had this evasive answer been uttered by Abū Mūsā al-Ash'arī, narrators would have poured their satirical wrath on him, as they did during a debate recounted for the Battle of the Camel. At the time, when 'Abd Khayr al-Khaywanī had asked Abū Mūsā: "Do you not admit that those two men [Ṭalḥa and al-Zubayr] had offered their *bay'a* to 'Alī?" Abū Mūsā agreed, but when then asked, "And do you know if ['Alī] did anything to warrant the breaking of his *bay'a*?" Abū Mūsā replied, "I don't know." 'Abd Khayr then said: "We shall then abandon you until you make up your mind [*fa-innā tārikūka ḥattā tadrī*]."[41] An equivalence of evasion and erudite naivete therefore does exist here between the two reactions of Abū Mūsā and 'Alī on the issue of 'Uthmān. However, when 'Alī concludes by stating a Qur'ānic verse, the text here warrants closer scrutiny, since it includes dual implications. While on one level the narrator was implying that Qur'ānic verses were punctuating events in 'Alī's life as they did during the Prophet's life earlier, on another level the comparison breaks down, since the historical circumstances of the two figures were not similar. Unfortunately for 'Alī, his opponents were not clear infidels, individuals opposing a religious message, but merely political opponents, however suspect their piety and problematic their religious arguments. Thus, the citing of an apt verse becomes mainly a boastful line, serving a rhetorical purpose rather than offering true religious vindication.[42]

The broader questions the narratives were addressing in this and other debates were the following: When is abandonment of political action ("*i'tizāl*") right ("*wa anā mu'tazil*")? If the people first chose 'Uthmān and then killed him, what worth is there to the judgment of the people? 'Uthmān may have been right that his rule would amount to nothing if he appointed whomever people had a whim for ("*mā arānī idhan fī shay'in in kuntu asta'milu man hawaytum*").[43] And finally, the hypothetical question: what would 'Alī's reaction be if Mu'āwiya, whose background 'Alī described correctly, were sincere about seeking justice for 'Uthmān? Would it then not be that 'Alī, who was championing the cause of the marginal Arab tribes and the non-Arab converts of Iraq, was declaring an opinion that subverted the very grounds of his support?

'Alī's comment that Mu'āwiya and his allies were only fighting to gain dominion ("*in yuqātilūna illā 'alā hādhihi al-dunyā li-yakūnū jabābiratan fīhā mulūkan*"),[44] and 'Ammār's comment during the battle that Mu'āwiya's demand for vengeance for 'Uthmān was only a ploy to gain more ground ("*wallāhi mā ṭilbatuhum bi-damihi* [i.e., *'Uthmān*] *wa lākinna al-qawma dhāqū al-dunyā fa-istaḥabbūhā wa istamra'ūhā . . . wa tilka makīdatun balaghū bihā mā tarawn*")[45] are true, but the question 'Alī then fails to answer is what he would have done if the demands put forward by Mu'āwiya had come from someone else—that, is if the demand was not a "*makīda*" and reflected no "*idhān*," and if the alternative opposition was not fighting to gain glory in the world. These hypothetical possibilities are opened not just by the circumstance of 'Uthmān's murder but by the very nature of 'Alī's strategy of defending his argument.

The ambiguity in 'Alī's role is heightened further when he seems to show an inconsistent attitude in dealing with the assassins. Why, for instance, did 'Alī take a scrupulous stand, exacting punishment against 'Ubaydallāh b. 'Umar for his assassination of al-Hurmuzān following 'Umar's death,[46] but not show the same type of vigorous scrutiny with regard to 'Uthmān's death?

All this evidence and direction of argumentation represents the case that could be made against 'Alī and his defenses. Ṭabarī would have imagined the companion foes of 'Alī (*jumhūr al-ṣaḥāba*) and Sunnīs more generally arguing this view. However, the same pool of narratives also includes potential for counterarguments that showed 'Alī not so much an apologist for the assassination but a helpless leader in the midst of a political storm. Dīnawarī here preserves this other image of 'Alī's reaction to the demands of Mu'āwiya. The author describes how a certain ascetic from Syria ("*min 'ubbād ahl al-shām*"), Abū Muslim al-Khawlānī, visited Mu'āwiya, hoping to defuse the conflict. When Mu'āwiya informed him that he would quickly drop the challenge to 'Alī if only he brought the assassins to justice, the ascetic resolved to mediate between the two and took this demand to 'Alī. Carrying a letter from Mu'āwiya about this basic demand, Abū Muslim traveled to see 'Alī and when they met, began by saying:

> "O Abū'l-Ḥasan, You have assumed political leadership [*innaka qad qumta bi-amrin wa wullītahu*], and by God we would not like anybody else to assume the caliphate in your place so long as you follow the righteous path [*mā nuḥibbu annahu li-ghayrika in a'ṭayta al-ḥaqqa min nafsika*]. 'Uthmān was killed unjustly. If only you would hand over to us his assassins, you will be recognized as our leader, and then truly you shall find us supportive of you if someone dares to challenge you afterwards . . ."

'Alī was not able to discuss the situation at the time and told Abū Muslim to come by the next day, when he would give him an answer. Meanwhile, 'Alī ordered that the guest be treated generously and with great hospitality. However, when Abū Muslim came to 'Alī in the mosque the next day, Dīnawarī says, he found the caliph seated in the mosque with some ten thousand people, all wearing armor and shouting: "We are all the murderers of 'Uthmān."[47] 'Alī's point here was clear. Although he was caliph, he stood helpless, knowing that if he extracted the assassins from the crowd, he would plunge the community into a bigger civil war than would be solved at first impression. The murder of 'Uthmān, in this context, was not the work of a few but reflected the will of a substantial segment of the community. As caliph, 'Alī could not ignore the pressure of his followers. The circumstances were in some sense very similar to those that faced 'Uthmān after 'Umar's death, when the new caliph had to resolve the crisis of punishing 'Ubaydallāh b. 'Umar without splitting the community. How to uphold religious justice while preserving the political unity of the state was becoming a worse dilemma over time.[48] Other accounts also contradict reports about 'Alī's ambiguity on the murder of 'Uthmān and show him greatly saddened by it.

Dīnawarī's account has a significant continuation that merits consideration. After 'Alī wrote a letter to Mu'āwiya, he also wrote to 'Amr, warning him about the evil distraction that worldly interest can bring about: "The world is a distraction from other pursuits. He who gains a portion of it becomes so eager to preserve his share that he becomes even more attached to it, nor does he stop at what he gained but keeps hoping for what lies ahead, which he can't reach. Alas, in the end he shall be parted from all that he gathered. Verily the joyful one is he who learns a lesson from the example of others. Do not destroy your merits by going along with Mu'āwiya and his *bāṭil* (fraud or blasphemy), for he is ignorant of the righteous and has chosen the *bāṭil*."[49]

'Amr, we are told, wrote back to 'Alī, inviting him to agree to what they (Mu'āwiya and 'Amr) called for. 'Alī, of course, rejected this and began preparing to march against the Syrians (ahl al-Shām) when an important development occurred. Just as he was exhorting his followers to mobilize, and to march against the enemies of "the *sunan* and the Qur'ān," and against "the killers of the muhājirūn and the Anṣār," a man from Fizāra called "Arbad" reportedly stood up and challenged 'Alī, saying: "Do you want us to kill the people of al-Sham, just as you had us kill the people of Basra before? By God, this shall not happen." Here al-Ashtar reportedly shouted: "Would someone shut this man up?" The Fazārī man then decided to make a run for his life, but a small throng pursued him and beat him up until he fell dead. When 'Alī was informed of this man's death, he reportedly said: "A man killed by an uncertain hand [*qatīlu 'amiyya, lā yudrā man qatalahu*]" and decided to pay his blood money from the treasury.[50]

This sideshow of confrontation between 'Alī and the Fazārī echoes in part the famous Qur'ānic story that describes Moses facing a situation in which an Israelite and an Egyptian engaged in a fight. The first time this happened, Moses aided the Israelite and killed the Egyptian without knowing what was happening. Moses' sympathy was based only on blood solidarity, and in ignorance of the moral dispute at stake. However, when a similar situation later confronted Moses, the Egyptian confronted Moses with the words: "Moses, do you want to slay me just as you slew a living soul yesterday? Do you just desire to be a strongman [*jabbāran*] in the land, never attempting to be a peacemaker? [*qāla yā Mūsā a-turīdu an taqtulanī kamā qatalta nafsan bi'l-ams? in turīdu illā an takūna jabbāran fī'l-arḍ wa mā turīdu an takūna min al-muṣliḥīn*]."[51] Hearing these words, we are told, Moses stopped aiding the Israelite without inquiring further. The Egyptian's cautioning words: "Do you seek to be a '*jabbār*' in your acts," parallels the Fazārī's words: "Do you want us to kill the ahl al-Shām as we killed the ahl al-Basra yesterday?" The stylistic resemblance between the two leaves little room to doubt the symmetry between Moses and 'Alī. Both men appear in a situation of moral crisis, meting out punishment in ways that do not follow religious law or common morality.

The fact that 'Alī's followers kill the Fazārī dissident does not ease the burden on 'Alī, but rather complicates matters more for him, since soon after, instead of punishing the assassins, he pays the victim's blood money and declares that the murderer is unknown. The resemblance between 'Alī's attitude toward the assassins of 'Uthmān and the assassins of the Fazārī man is too striking to overlook. So what can the reader do here but find a double standard in 'Alī's behavior: calling for justice for the death of Hurmuzān, but overlooking the aggression of his followers. This followup segment to the meeting between Abū Muslim and 'Alī shows how a narrative's moral implications could entirely change with the slightest digression or embellishment on an original account. When 'Alī first invited Abū Muslim to the mosque and we saw the ten thousand shouting anti-'Uthmān slogans, we saw 'Alī remain silent, and even Abū Muslim said nothing after 'Alī mentioned that he will give him a letter to Mu'āwiya. The silence of these key actors in the debate is meant to leave much ambiguity about what happened, and, just as importantly, about whether the ascetic thought that 'Alī was in a genuine bind with his followers or that the scene was staged. 'Alī's pious letters to Mu'āwiya and 'Amr do little to elucidate his real position on punishing 'Uthmān's assassins. It is then not until the dissension of the Fazārī man that we are led to examine the commentary of the narrators on 'Alī's position by exploring the vicissititudes of the moral crisis Moses faced before.

What exactly 'Alī's true feelings about the past were is an open topic that allows for much speculation. Various narrators knew the religious, moral, and political significance of his sayings and actions, and in response they set out to tinge various anecdotes with shades of argument and innuendo that evoked questions relating to justice, as well as to political legitimacy and polemics about religious interpretation. Throughout the story of Ṣiffīn, and based on the evidence presented about the various personalities, the sympathy of the reader is intended to gravitate to 'Alī, and the reasons for this are many: he was overlooked for succession in the early days, he was pushed to accept the caliphate by the community after 'Uthmān's death, and he was forced to go to war by opposing seditious groups. Throughout the conflict he tries to take the high ground of religious principles, to place the welfare of the community above particular concerns, and to behave nobly in war, even at the direst of times. At Ṣiffīn, for instance, 'Alī's troops did not prevent those in Mu'āwiya's camp from access to the water wells even though the latter had initially implemented a strategy that prevented Ali's camp from access to the water wells.[52] Numerous similar gestures of forgiveness are attributed to 'Alī, and these incidents color, in retrospect, the fact that 'Alī in essence allowed Mu'āwiya the chance to debate him later.

However, despite his great efforts to save lives, ultimately 'Alī was trapped in a war in which he had to fight to preserve his leadership, and so the question that must inevitably follow his trail of battle was whether it was worth it. How to explain the loss of life and the bloodshed was an onerous task, even with his thorough religious arguments about the inferiority of Mu'āwiya and his camp. Over the years, 'Alī had developed a string of epithets to describe his opponents—*al-nākithūn*, *al-qāsiṭūn*, *al-fāsiqūn*, and *al-māriqūn* (those who break their oaths, are unjust in their dealings, resemble in behavior the infidels, and the transgressors)—drawn from Qur'ānic language. However, if on occasion meaningful, such as when he characterized those who broke their *bay'a* ('Āisha's camp, *al-nākithūn*), this exercise of labeling became—in the rhetorical scheme of Ṭabarī—ambitious and trifling at the same time. It was ambitious for the way it made 'Alī act like a prophet casting religious judgments on people, and trifling for the way it made him appear showing off his knowledge of the Qur'ān on appropriate occasions. Qur'ānic recitation had turned into an art for reading events on the ground and competing artfully in placing frames around events and people. And as such it was no surprise that 'Alī was king of the Qurrā'. With the conflict now reaching to include average believers, who were forced to choose sides, 'Alī's claims of *faḍl* (merit) and *ṣābiqa* (religious seniority for precedence in conversion) were subverted by an enterprise increasingly vain and florid rather than substantial. The sharp demarcation that the community had known in Muḥammad's time between believers and unbelievers and the clear definition of a righteous war was now replaced with the interminable ambiguity of material and political goals masquerading in religious terms.

Individual scenes of erroneous destruction at the Battle of Ṣiffīn were also used to sharpen the critique of 'Alī, to show the limits of his control (even of his supporters), and to raise questions about the margins of caliphal responsibility for acts of violence. When 'Alī's followers torched the house of Jarīr b. 'Abdallāh, an emissary of 'Alī who tried to be duplicitous in his negotiation with 'Uthmān, we are told that a son of Jarīr came out and told 'Alī: "If one man in this house committed a crime, there are others in there who have done you no offense." 'Alī was gripped by guilt over the incident, and said: "We ask forgiveness of God," and abandoned the place.[53] 'Alī could do his best to avoid innocent bloodshed, but narrators found it still complex to see how the rules of conquest could be applied to a Muslim opponent. At the Battle of the Camel, for instance, after 'Alī achieved victory, we are told that he forbade his troops from claiming the booty of the opposing camp (except for the weapons and beasts of burden used in the war), but here a foot soldier told 'Alī: "Commander of the Faithful, how is it that it was legitimate that we fight them but not legitimate to claim their belongings? [*kayfa ḥalla lanā qitāluhum wa lam yaḥill lanā sabyuhum wa amwāluhum*]."[54] Although this comment occurred before Ṣiffīn, it was clearly written to convey a wide-ranging, ironic critique of 'Alī's attempt to maintain a purity of arms. Even from an average soldier's view, it is implied, the idea that one could justify fighting with the possibility of killing but could not justify claiming the booty because that would amount to theft seemed surreal. 'Alī's only reply was that one cannot claim booty from monotheist enemies and told his followers that they should refrain from asking about things they don't know and just do as they are told.

## THE AMBIGUITY OF MOTIVES: HONOR AND PIETY

Mu'āwiya and 'Alī, as we have seen so far, received widely different levels of representation from the medieval narrators. Whereas narrators could directly portray Mu'āwiya's ambitious pursuit of power and place his motives beneath a very transparent moral lens, their approach to analyzing 'Alī was more complex and rarely so direct. The ways they examined 'Alī's view of 'Uthmān and the opponents of 'Uthmān, as we saw, leave their messages highly elusive and lead the reader to doubt the moral direction of the community under 'Alī's leadership. Another area in which ambiguity played an important role was their portrayal of the moral dimension of the war, specifically in how they represented the motives and goals of 'Alī's followers as the two parties prepared for war.

At the outset of the preparation, and from the perspective of 'Alī, the war was an inevitable choice. In a speech at the beginning of mobilization, 'Alī ordered his followers not to begin combat until they were first attacked by the enemy, and he advised them to avoid excessive or gratuitous violence, and not to take any booty that had not been used in the enemy camp for the purpose of the war. And no matter what provocation came, 'Alī commanded them, they must not direct their aggression against the women and the elderly among the enemy.[55] Later, when the conflict began, 'Alī followed up with additional advice, exhorting the troops to maintain a steadfast belief in God and to fight shoulder to shoulder in one formation ("*ṣaffān*") in a manner that adhered to the Qur'ānic description of the united camp of believers. He urged them to hold their ground and to fight without speaking or making grandiose gestures. Only their bravest, he said, must carry their banners, and they should all purify their intentions and keep patient until the end, for only with patience does God grant victory.[56]

These two speeches complete the picture of 'Alī's hope that his troops will live up to their role as defenders of religious righteousness. As the battle erupts, 'Alī's troops fulfill the reader's anticipation of their commitment to 'Alī's leadership and to their religious cause. However, as narrators focus their description on vignettes of combat, exhortation, and individual heroism, and as the war begins to take on a life of its own, it starts to seem as though 'Alī's followers are fighting more for individual honor and tribal glory than for achieving the religious objective that 'Alī described. Soldiers begin making sensational declarations as they are galvanized by the zeal of combat, and they exhort one another to leave a mark on the collective memory of the camp.

Two chief lieutenants of 'Alī, Mālik ibn al-Ḥārith al-Ashtar and 'Abdallāh b. Budayl, come under the spotlight in this context and stand out as epitomes of the hero with complex motives. Al-Ashtar, who led the left wing of 'Alī's army, is quoted at times as exhorting his troops with religious language that mirrors earlier advice by 'Alī, telling them: "These people [i.e., the enemy] are only fighting you for your religion, to stamp out the *sunna* and give rise to *bid'a*, and return you to the days of ignorance from which God had extracted you."[57] However, he then follows up with a zealous secular statement, telling the troops: "Verily, retreat from battle will rob you of dignity and the *fay'*, and will bring you shame both in this life and the next."[58] Al-Ashtar's words are timed just before his battallion makes an assault to relieve the besieged right flank of the army, led by 'Abdallāh b. Budayl. When they rescued this flank, we are told, they found them (numbered between two and three hundred) holding their ground in a block formation. Ibn Budayl's troops, we are told, thought that 'Alī had died in battle and immediately asked about him. When they heard that he was safe ("*ḥayyun ṣāliḥun fī'l-maysira*"), the troops expressed thanks to God.

Al-Ashtar's words were no doubt situated at that juncture to show his strategic role in preserving the army. However, just when it seemed that both commanders were ready to retreat and regroup, we are told that Ibn Budayl told his troops to follow him in launching an assault on Mu'āwiya's headquarters. Al-Ashtar, portrayed as the wiser strategist, told Ibn Budayl: "Don't do this! Hold your ground with the others," but Ibn Budayl refused. Then a Homeric portrait is cast: wielding two swords, Ibn Budayl charges in the direction of Mu'awiya, a place defended by so many troops that "they looked like the mountains." Ibn Budayl went ahead of his followers, killing anyone who came within his path, until he got to Mu'āwiya. There was still some distance between the two, and Mu'āwiya, seated in the shade of a man ('Abd al-Raḥmān b. Khālid, according to some) who carried a golden shield to protect Mu'āwiya from the sunlight, now said, "*atarawnahu kibsh al-qawm*?" wondering how the struggle would end. But as Ibn Budayl came closer to Mu'āwiya, enemy soldiers came at him from all directions and surrounded him ("*nahaḍa ilayhi al-nās min kulli jānib*"). He fought there until he was killed, together with many of his followers. When a surviving party of his troops returned, al-Ashtar told them: "Wouldn't my judgment have been better than yours? Didn't I advise to stay with the camp?"[59]

The portrait of Ibn Budayl's reckless mission against Mu'āwiya is as operatic in display as it is epic in style, and it conveys an ethical lesson about the folly of reckless heroism and its detrimental effect on central army strategy. The portrait, together with al-Ashtar's words exhorting his troops to war, shows us the extent to which heroic motives had come to prevail once the war had started. When al-Ashtar, in another context, sees the corpse of Yazīd b. Qays al-Arḥabī being carried back to his camp, he reportedly says reflectively: "By God, this is how bravery and sincerity should be. Doesn't a man feel shame going to battle, then coming back, not having killed or gotten killed?!"[60] In this we hear confirmation that the goals of the war had gradually altered into a quest for individual honor in the style of "*ayyām*" chivalry and warfare of the Jāhiliyya. Al-Ashtar's performance in battle impresses viewers in 'Alī's camp, but some wonder about his individual hopes. When someone named Munqidh in 'Alī's camp saw al-Ashtar mounted on his horse, in full armor and brandishing a broad shining sword that glittered under the sun, he reportedly commented with mixed feelings: "This man's combat makes him truly the noblest among the Arabs, if what he is doing is sincere [*in kāna mā arā 'alā niyyatihi*]." When a companion told him: "And what could his intention be other than what we see?" Munqidh said: "I only fear that he is doing this to gain authority [*innī akhāfu an yakūna yuḥāwilu mulkan*]."[61]

The same types of temptations for achieving honor are seen affecting large military groupings as they do individuals. One key example of this involves the tribe of Rabī'a, a tribe that was famous for its heroic stand during Qādisiyya and was dubbed at the time as the "lion." As the tribe of Muḍar faltered during the Battle of Ṣiffīn, we are told, Rabī'a held its ground and showed great endurance ("*ṣabarū ṣabran ḥasanan*"), fighting bravely, while one Khālid b. al-Maḥraz began exhorting them, saying: "O the party of Rabī'a, God has assembled you all in this battle in a way that you have not been together since you were created. . . . Do not let anyone, young or old, later say 'Rabī'a has brought shame on us and escaped from battle, and brought about the defeat of the Arabs.' Beware lest you become a bad omen today in the eyes of the Arabs and Muslims. Keep marching and be patient, for surely the forward march has long been your habit, and endurance is second nature to you [*fa-inna al-iqdāma lakum 'āda wa'l-ṣabru minkum sajiyya*]. Be steadfast and keep your intention sincere for reward, for the reward of one who seeks God is honor in this world [*sharaf al-dunyā*] and rank in the hereafter [*karāmat al-ākhira*]. Verily, God does not withhold reward from one who acts sincerely."[62]

This blending of honor and religious reward as incentives was intended by narrators to show how the motives for war underwent a gradual transmutation as the pressure of combat forced some tribes to compensate for the defeat of others in 'Alī's camp and impelled them to demonstrate their prowess. This pressure for tribes to do their best as fighting got worse becomes even more tragically pronounced when 'Alī on one occasion reportedly happened to ride by the wing of Rabī'a during his inspection of the camp formation. As 'Alī came into their midst, Rabī'a, it is said, became more zealous than ever about defending him ("*tabārat Rabī'a baynahā*"), while a certain Shaqīq b. Thawr shouted among them: "O the people of Rabī'a. The Arabs will never forgive you, nor do you deserve to live, if anyone reaches 'Alī while he is in your midst and there is a soul among you still alive. But if you defend him, then you garner the glory of the world [*wa in mana'tumūh fa-majdu al-ḥayati iktasabtumūh*]."[63] In one sense, this declaration shows a type of wholehearted support reminiscent of the support that the early Muslims gave to the Prophet, and this connection was indeed meant to be read through the imagery of passionate support showed by followers of 'Alī during battle. However, given that 'Alī's mission from the Sunnī perspective was not a prophetic one, with its setting of intra-Muslim fighting, such zealous exhortations for battle among Rabī'a could only be read as a type of tribal "*ḥamiyya*" (zeal) that was exacerbating the war.[64] 'Alī's passing through an individual tribal camp thus becomes a moral liability rather than a blessing, since the combat will then worsen as different warriors compete to show their skill and elevate their tribe's name. The tragic irony in the episode lies in the fact that while 'Alī appeared to be doing his political duty of joining in with his troops, the event took on a dubious religious meaning in the context of a worsening war among Muslims.[65]

Military heroism occupied a complex role in the narratives of Ṣiffīn. As a manifestation of dignity and commitment, this quality tended to be viewed as a branch of religious morality. The famous accounts of Mu'āwiya's cowardice whenever he was challenged to engage in individual combat by 'Alī and the stories about 'Amr's shying away from fighting 'Alī are widely held to be illustrative of an overall defect in Mu'āwiya's personality, just as 'Alī's bravery completes his image of religious righteousness. Yet outside the circle of these well-known leaders, the virtues of bravery and the stress on individual dignity had to be assessed in harmony with the effect on community agreement and stability. The war at Ṣiffīn, from the perspective of the *jamā'a* of later times, suffered from imperfect grounds of contention among the leaders and from imperfect commanders advising the two parties. In this context, therefore, warfare lacked the compelling moral necessity that it had carried at the time of the Prophet, for example, when the boundaries between the protagonists were sharply drawn, and incentives of personal prowess and religious obligation reinforced one another. With Ṣiffīn, in contrast, the spectre of Muslims fighting each other raised doubts about the legitimacy of the conflict, even if a few factors—such as defending the caliph, combating Mu'āwiya, and self-defense—carried some weight as justifications.

This doubt about the conflict's legitimacy is alluded to in remarks of grumbling among the troops and in pitiful descriptions. Ṭabarī describes, for example, how at the outset of battle one man in 'Alī's camp marched out to duel with his opponent and was surprised to find out that the opponent who came to challenge him was his brother. When they recognized each other, we are told, each retreated without engaging in a fight.[66] In another corner of the battlefield we hear of a member of the tribe of Azd who declared that "it is one of the gravest errors and biggest trials that we have to fight our kinsmen [of the Azd]."[67] These images calling for a rapprochement and peace stand in contrast with the images of heroic conflict and vindication and appear to have been constructed in tragic dialogue with one another. Some fighters were made to appear as zealous as their forerunners at Badr, but without having the same moralizing parameters that defined their zeal, and this underscored the depiction of misfortune for those who found themselves fighting their kin-relations—an image that was somehow avoided, or at least downplayed, in the battles of the Sīra.

## THE LINKAGES OF ṢIFFĪN

### *Linkages of Leadership*

The spirit of moral doubt and mood of religious frustration that accompanied the behavior of some participants in the Battle of Ṣiffīn, as we just saw, was for some motivated by their agony over the internal civil war. The obligation to fight to defend the caliphate of 'Alī when community opinion was divided was too great of a sacrifice and cast a shadow of disillusionment upon 'Alī's political drive that was similar to the disgruntlement directed against 'Āisha at the Battle of the Camel. Expressions of isolated frustration among ordinary soldiers therefore reflect a key layer of communication between narrator and reader about the religious legitimacy of the war. Still, such instances of subtle commentary were embedded in a wider, artful depiction of Ṣiffīn that lent it similarities to some of the expeditions of the Prophet. Within this frame, the diverse set of allusions in these narratives therefore deserve some attention.

'Alī is frequently cast in situations that replay events from Muḥammad's life and moments from the stories of the prophets. We see one example of this in the way 'Alī addressed the victims of the battle. Ṭabarī recounts that 'Alī somberly spoke in the area of the cemetery of the Ṣiffīn victims, saying: "Peace be upon you, you of the desolate abodes and forsaken places, of the believing men and women, and of the Muslim men and women. You are they who have gone ahead before us, while we come after you and will shortly join you. Oh God, pardon us and them and forgive us and them. . . . He will make you arise from it again and gather you together upon it. Blessings upon he who remembers the return, acts for the final reckoning, is content with a sufficiency, and is satisfied with the reward that God will bestow upon him."[68] In another version, also recounted by Abū Mikhnaf, 'Alī states upon passing by the so-called Thawriyyūn weeping for the slain of Ṣiffīn: "I bear witness for those of them who were killed patiently holding fast and expecting the rewards of martyrdom."[69] 'Alī's behavior here would have reminded a classical reader of what Muḥammad did after the Battle of Badr, when he stood at the cemetery (al-Qalīb) of the Meccan pagans who fell in battle and chided them, saying: "O the People of al-Qalīb, have you found what God had promised to be a reality? For I have." When the companions expressed surprise at this address to the dead, Muḥammad replied: "Verily, they hear what I say, but they just can't answer."[70] 'Alī, like Muḥammad, is here portrayed as being capable of penetrating the veil between the seen and the unseen, and of carrying out a dialogue that confirms his prophetic powers.[71]

## *Linkages of Community*

Thus far we have mainly examined narrative intersections with the past as they relate to 'Alī himself. However, the caliph's saga is laden with allusions that relate to his followers. In this context, a comparison between the community of 'Alī's followers and those of the prophets before is crucial to illuminate the sources of tragedy in 'Alī's life.

We have already noted the potential parallel that narrators sought to establish between 'Alī's community of supporters, the "neo-Anṣār" of Iraq, and the Anṣār of the Prophet. The declaration that Qaysī b. Faṣīl al-Shaybānī made at the Battle of al-Nahrawān—when he told 'Alī: "O Commander of the Faithful, we are your party and helpers. We befriend whomsoever you are allied with and are enemies to your enemies. . . . Take us with you against any enemy that you choose, wherever they may be. . . . By God, you will not find yourself failing because we are few or lack a firm intention to follow"[72]—reminds the reader of a key moment just before the Battle of Badr, when al-Miqdād b. 'Amr pledged to the Prophet on behalf of the Anṣār that they would support him wherever he went. Al-Miqdād's statement in this context was: "O Messenger of God, march to whatever God has commanded you, we are with you. By God, we shall not say to you like the Israelites said to Moses, 'Go forth, thou and thy Lord, and do battle; we will be sitting here.'[73] But we say, 'Go forth, thou and thy Lord, and do battle; we will fight with you.' I swear by the One who sent you with Truth, were you to march into the land of Bark al-Ghimād [i.e., Abyssinia], we would endure with you until we reached our goal."[74] Thus, just as al-Miqdād sought to demonstrate that the Anṣār were not going to abandon the Prophet as the Israelites had abandoned Moses, the supporter of 'Alī, narrators implied, emulated the commitment of the first Muslims. How true and unified this support for 'Alī would remain, and how it compared with the ancient Israelites, then becomes a question for comparison.

From a traditional reading of Islamic history a comparison of the Anṣār of the Prophet to the supporters of 'Alī may not seem an area with much potential for analysis. One may concede an incident of analogy such as the one recounted above, but on the whole the impression may be that while the Anṣār were remembered as steadfast supporters of their leader, 'Alī's supporters quickly fragmented into a range of factions: the Saba'iyya, the Qurrā', the Khārijites, and the remaining Shī'a group. This traditional view, however, fails to recognize the intimate bond that original narrators saw existing between the Sīra and the Rāshidūn narratives, and the fact that to some extent the Anṣār were not so different in religious profile or behavior from the supporters of 'Alī. Both were non-Qurashī, anxious for their privilege, and overzealous in supporting their leader's mission.[75] To probe this comparison a little more, one can examine antecedents for 'Alī's group's behavior in Muḥammad's time, as well as the tendentious turn of the Anṣār into religious militants in 'Alī's time.

Far from being the constantly abiding supporters of the Prophet, the Anṣār on occasion behaved in a selfish or insubordinate way. Their famous abandonment of their designated positions on the battlefield of Uḥud (in the case of the archers) was in origin intended to signal their potential fear of losing out on personal gain, while the grumbling of some members of the Anṣār (Sa'd b. 'Ubāda) after the Battle of Ḥunayn about the inequitable division of booty, as we saw, was overlooked by the Prophet, although he then sounded the alarming note to 'Umar by saying that the day might come when a group of these would turn into overzealous practitioners of the faith, much to their detriment. This was in reference to Hurqūṣ b. Zuhayr, who bore a large part of the responsibility for the attack on 'Uthmān, and to another man, al-Mukhaddaj, who became a leader of the Khārijites. When the Prophet made these predictions, the Anṣār appeared devoid of any social or tribal affiliation, much as the followers of 'Alī appear without a clear social identity and merely as symbolic factions. The Qurrā' are mentioned in a report about a raid (*sariyya*) made by al-Mundhir b. 'Amr to bi'r Ma'ūna, when a narrator says, "The Messenger of God sent with him seventy men of the Anṣār, who were youthful and called al-Qurrā' [*shabībatan yusammawn al-qurrā'*]."[76]

Going well beyond their famous support for the early prophetic *da'wa* before the Hijra and their pivotal support at the Battle of Badr, the Anṣār themselves are frequently portrayed in exceptional terms as the crack troops of the Prophet in times of crisis. At the Battle of Ḥunayn, when the tide of battle began turning against the Muslims, the Prophet reportedly commanded his uncle al-'Abbās to call out, "O Anṣār, the people who were at the tree, you who are the [keepers of, or those] intended in sūrat al-baqara [*yā ma'shara al-anṣār . . . ya aṣḥāba al-samura, ya aṣḥāba sūrat al-baqara*]!"[77] The word "*al-samura*" is explained by the narrator in the same context as "*shajarat al-riḍwān*" (i.e., referring to the tree where the companions offered their *bay'a* during the episode of al-Ḥudaybiyya).[78] These references make the Anṣār seem quite akin to the passionate followers of 'Alī.

Although the Prophet himself did not face a religious or a serious political challenge from the Anṣār, the narratives represent him as fearful that discord could one day come from them. In his farewell speech, Muḥammad bids the Anṣār to be patient with the Muhājirūn and to remain content with their share of influence, even if it seems to fall short of their aspirations (*sa-talqawna ba'dī athratan wa 'alaykum bi'l-ṣabr*).[79] He tells them as well to avoid religious zealousness (*al-guluww fī'l-dīn*).[80] The community at large, especially the Muhājirūn, he exhorts to look after the Anṣār, and he confesses that his story with the Anṣār—i.e., his reliance on their support—reflected a moment of weakness in his career that forced him to seek outside support.[81] Between the fear that the Anṣār might one day use their zealotry to serve the wrong cause and the likelihood that their situation would be mishandled politically, the Prophet is shown as anticipating the danger that, with a revived sense of beleaguerment, the Anṣār could one day turn into a bunch of wild factions.

The rough combatives, the messianists, the Qurrā', and the zealots were all combined as one group in the Sīra, but they had become fragmented in 'Alī's time, and narrators portrayed these fragments in a sprawling exercise of representation that characterized the new socioreligious mosaic of 'Alī's camp, including both his partisans and his enemies (the dissidents).

Continuing in this reading of subtexts in the Prophet's statements and the narrators' representation of the group, one may also hypothesize the inference that the Anṣār were either an extraction of the Jewish community or their representational counterpart.[82] As the Islamic parabolic novel, best represented in Ṭabarī's chronicle, continued the tradition of biblical narration, it described the growth of Muslim zealots and messianists in a way that makes them comparable to Jewish factions in the Roman and early Christian periods. The collectivity of the Anṣār and its breakup in 'Alī's time therefore provided the key parallel to this earlier diversity. If the story were simplified, the narrators appear to be saying that the Anṣār were the Jewish community of Muḥammad, waiting to be fragmented.[83] That the Anṣār themselves were Jewish would no doubt be difficult to establish, but what matters more here in this context of historical representation is that the narrators' descriptions of the attitudes of the Anṣār during the Sīra and 'Alī's time are framed in a manner consistent with earlier stories of the role of the Jews in supporting and then dissenting from the leadership of Moses. In a similar pattern of behavior, the Anṣār varied their support for 'Alī while they simultaneously clung to narrow interpretations of the scripture (in the case of the Qurrā').[84] It is within this frame that some observations preserved in the traditional sources make sense, such as 'Umar's statement that "the Banū Isrā'īl entered their phase of downfall when their Qurrā' became numerous"[85] and "began to apply their own reasoning [*al-ra'y*] to interpret religion." And it is within this frame that we must understand the Prophet's summons to the Anṣār at the Battle of Ḥunayn that referred to them as "*aṣḥāb sūrat al-baqara*"; in essence, he was saying that the parable of *sūrat al-baqara* was none other than a parable about them.[86]

All this evidence may not give an exact accounting for the Anṣār, the Shī'a, or the Israelites, and their correspondence in real historical terms, but the story preserved in the early Islamic narratives was neither real in its details nor intended to be factual. Rather, it played with classical biblical imagery to communicate a parable on the folly of religious zealotry (the Qurrā', the Khārijites),[87] the folly of political puritanism ('Alī's style of government), and the detrimental role that pride and heroism play in shaping certain religious conflicts. These are timeless moral lessons that span Ṭabarī's chronicle from beginning to end, but the reader constantly finds these problems answered in a certain synthesis, either with religious compromise or political wisdom. It is for this reason that all fringe calls for "*al-amr bi'l-ma'rūf*" are diminished in favor of the caliphs, and that Mu'āwiya's system of political toleration and avoidance of direct conflict are implicitly favored by the narratives of the early period.

### *'Alī and His Supporters—Moses and the Israelites*

With the analogies established between the followers of 'Alī, the Anṣār, Ṣiffīn, and the Sīra, it is worth taking a closer look at 'Alī's dilemma with his followers and the Islamic version of its biblical antecedents. The specific problems with 'Alī's camp range across a wide spectrum of newly developed character flaws: its members are unreliable, they question the decisions of their leader, they offer excuses to avoid doing their duty, and on the whole they try to impose their own will, on the basis of motives favoring the here and now, over considerations of strategy and faith.

From the outset of the troubles at Ṣiffīn, we see that 'Alī was forced to accept a truce because a sizeable faction in his camp refused to keep fighting, claiming that in doing so they were respecting the "call for the book" and showing their piety. No amount of explanation by 'Alī that this was a ploy from the weakened pro-Umayyad party could change their minds, and 'Alī was forced to stop. Later, as 'Alī tried to regroup his forces and march against Mu'āwiya in Syria, at the time when the Khārijites were becoming a threat in Iraq, we find 'Alī's supporters refusing to obey his order to march against Mu'āwiya, and forcing him to fight the Khārijites first. It is never explained why 'Alī's supporters insisted on fighting the Khārijites first, but one can surmise that the Iraqis feared for their immediate property and livelihoods in Iraq.[88] Once again, 'Alī was here forced to concede and begin by fighting the Khārijites first. However, even as this conflict came under his control, 'Alī was still unsuccessful at persuading a key faction in his army to now march against Syria. When 'Alī ordered his troops to do so, the reaction that he now heard from them was: "O Commander of the Faithful, our arrows are exhausted, our swords have become blunt, and our spear tips have fallen off . . . Let us go back [*fa-irji' ilā miṣrinā*] and let us get ready with better equipment, and maybe the Commander of the Faithful would even give us the arms of those who have fallen, for that would give us more strength against the enemy [. . . *fa-li-nasta'idda bi-aḥsani 'uddatinā wa la'alla amīr al-mu'minīn yazīdu fī 'uddatinā 'uddata man halaka minnā*]."[89] Then Ṭabarī's narrator singles out al-Ash'ath b. Qays as having been the one who took charge of making these statements to 'Alī.

These excuses about "empty quivers and weakened swords" that are raised after the Battle of al-Nahrawān are meant to highlight the continuing transformation of this community of supporters. They are also emblematic of 'Alī's immediate and practical problem with his troops: their insubordination ("*ma'ṣiya*"). His speeches were to repeatedly juxtapose the difference between the loyalty of the Syrians and the insubordination of the Iraqis. "What is the matter with you?! Don't you feel the tie of religion or chivalry [*ḥamiyya*]? . . . Is it not astonishing that Mu'āwiya summons the uncouth [*jufāt*] and the lowly and they follow him without stipend ['*aṭā*'] or support [*ma'ūna*)], and they respond to him twice or thrice in one year for whatever purpose he desires? But I call on you, you who are possessed of understanding, some of whom have a stipend and the rest receive support, but you remain apart from me, disobey me, and oppose me!"[90]

Later, in the famous "*khuṭbat al-jihād*," 'Alī catalogues the entire range of flaws that his supporters show and reveals his frustration in full. This speech, which marks the climax of the problem of insubordination in 'Alī's camp, provides a vivid portrait of 'Alī's degree of anger and disillusionment with his followers and underlines the absurd nature of their excuses. It is at such peak moments of frustration that we can sense that 'Alī's career stands on a parallel footing with that of Moses. Two speeches set his frustration in relief. The first occurs after he receives pleas from Muḥammad b. Abī Bakr to help him defend Egypt, although the account is set after the death of Ibn Abī Bakr. After rallying the people to mobilize and receiving no support, Alī calls on the headmen of his constituency (*ashrāf al-nās*) and says in a distressed, somber voice:

> "Praise be to God for what He has decreed concerning my affairs and ordained regarding what I do, and for my being put to the test through you, your party [*firqa*] of those who do not obey when I com-

mand or respond when I call. You are not worthy to be called sons! What do you expect for your steadfastness [*mā tantaẓirūn bi-ṣabrikum*] and *jihād* for your rightful cause [*wa'l-jihādu 'alā ḥaqqikum*]? Death and humiliation are for you in this world for anything but what is right. By God, if death comes—and it will indeed come—it will certainly separate you and me, for I detest your companionship and I care nothing for you. I am amazed at you. No religion unites you and no zeal inflames you [*lā dīna yajma'ukum wa lā ḥamiyyata taḥmīkum*] when you have heard that your enemy is coming to your country and launching an attack against you. Is it not astonishing that Mu'āwiya summons the uncouth and the lowly and they follow him without stipend ['*aṭā'*] or support [*ma'ūna*], and they respond to him twice or thrice in one year for whatever purpose he desires? But I call you, you who are possessed of understanding, some of whom have a stipend and the rest receive support, but you remain apart from me, disobey me, and oppose me!"[91]

The second speech occurs after 'Alī receives news of Muḥammad b. Abī Bakr's death within the same report. Here 'Alī gives a eulogy of Ibn Abī Bakr and then expresses his agony with his followers. He declares:

"Muḥammad b. Abī Bakr has been martyred—may God have mercy on him—and we seek for his recompense with God. By God, he was, as I know, indeed one of those who await the [divine] decrees [*mimman yantaẓir al-qaḍā'*], act [to attain] the [eternal] reward, loathe the way of the wicked [*fājir*], and desire the right path of the Believer. By God, I do not blame myself for failing, for I am fully experienced in enduring in war; I set about the matter boldly and resolutely, and I stand expressing my views effectively [*innī la-uqdimu 'alā al-amr wa a'rifu wajha al-ḥazm wa aqūmu fīkum bi'l-ra'yi al-muṣīb*]. I publicly call upon you for help and openly cry to you for assistance, but you do not heed what I say or obey what I command, so that things could not become worse for me. You are a people for whom vengeance will not be attained and revenge not taken. I have called you to the aid of your brethren for some fifty days, but you have gurgled as do slack-jawed camels slurping their water, and you were sluggardly, like people with no intention of waging *jihād* against the enemy or acquiring eternal reward . . . Shame on you!"[92]

All the difficulties that 'Alī faced were meant to be seen as emanating from a central moral defect, namely the lack of patience (*ṣabr*) on the part of his supporters, and their concomitant lack of willingness to persevere in the path of God. These problems were ultimately responsible for bringing about the failure of the caliph to unify his camp and suppress dissidents. Here the cyclical parallel with the story of the Israelites after the exodus comes into better focus. The nature and magnitude of 'Alī's failure to have his community cohere fully and follow his command faithfully was undoubtedly intended to trigger a memory of the Qur'ānic account of Moses and the Israelites.

The Qur'ānic account, which must be reconstructed from various verses, provides a cohesive picture of Moses' years after the exodus and highlights particular moral flaws that undermined his mission. The story starts out with a declaration about the victory of the Israelites and how they were rescued and selected, in verses such as the following:

> —"We delivered the Children of Israel from the humbling chastisement, from Pharaoh; surely he was a high one, of the prodigals; and We chose them out of a knowledge, above all beings."[93]
>
> —"and We bequeathed upon the people that were abased all the east and the west of the land We had blessed; and perfectly was fulfilled the most fair word of thy Lord upon the Children of Israel, for that they endured patiently; and We destroyed utterly the works of Pharaoh and his people, and what they had been building."[94]

As the community of Moses makes the transition to safety, the Qur'ān highlights the various ways in which they start to transform. Interaction with the comforts of life and with other communities impels new desires and sows among Israelites the seeds of doubt in their mission and in the binding leadership of Moses. Hence we are shown how they begin to put forward a set of new demands, ranging from material desires regarding food[95] to religiously intransigent requests, asking to have deities as other communities do[96] or even to witness God directly.[97] In the area of military perseverance this sense of doubt and desire for self-preservation brings together these divergent voices of disgruntlement. When Moses called upon the Israelites to challenge the Canaanites and invade their land, the Qur'ānic account describes how the Israelites refused to obey, telling Moses to go on and fight by himself and God.[98]

Throughout these verses, the language of the Israelites is cast in the imperative form—"*lan naṣbira*" (we will not endure), "*ud'u lanā rabbaka*" (pray to thy Lord), "*ij'al lanā ilāhan*" (make for us a god), "*idhhab anta wa rabbuka*" (go forth, thou and thy Lord)—reflecting a combination of religious blasphemy and political insubordination. This refusal to abide by commands is shown in the end driving Moses to great heights of anger, frustration, and personal reflection on his mission. A comparison can here be established between the representations of 'Alī and Moses. The frustration of Moses rises from the social to the political level in 'Alī's story, and the two leaders often become similar not just in the stages of escalating dissent they have to deal with, but also in their resulting moods and tones of speech as well.

## THE LINKAGE WITH 'UTHMĀN'S FATE

The Taḥkīm marked the key moment in the beginning of that fateful transition in the character and belief of 'Alī's community. Whereas before the reader viewed Mu'āwiya's party as the greatest threat to 'Alī, after the Taḥkīm, it quickly becomes clear that 'Alī's own party had become the greater threat. Bored with the conflict and showing signs of fickleness and unpredictability, 'Alī's supporters, as shown so far, refused to abide by his command and insisted that he stop the fighting and agree to arbitration. Although the theatrical nature of the debate between 'Amr and Abū Mūsā invites skepticism, one must mainly focus on the structure of the account and how it relates to earlier episodes in Islamic history. The exclusion of 'Alī from the discussion and the evocation of 'Umar b. al-Khaṭṭāb's legacy as the perfect model of the caliphate evoke memories of the Saqīfa of Banū Sā'ida, at which 'Alī was excluded from the caliphate and which showed 'Umar playing a decisive role in steering the caliphate away from the Hashīmites. However, the Taḥkīm episode probably also evoked in the minds of readers a variation on the treachery that happened with the Ridda, and here one would note that it was al-Ash'ath b. Qays, who once was a key leader among the Ridda folk, who led the call for the Taḥkīm and pressured 'Alī to yield.

Insisting on a halt to the war, al-Ash'ath demanded that 'Alī send an order to all the army units, and specifically to al-Ashtar, to stop fighting. Hesitant at first, 'Alī sent a messenger who, we are told, reached al-Ashtar at a spot where he was fighting and closing in on victory. When he received 'Alī's order, al-Ashtar told the messenger, "Tell him this is not the hour to call for a withdrawal. I am very hopeful of an imminent conquest, so don't hold me back."[99] As al-Ashtar kept on fighting, the dissenters in 'Alī's camp claimed that 'Alī had forfeited his agreement and in fact ordered al-Ashtar to do the opposite and keep fighting. Exasperated, 'Alī responded: "How could this be . . . didn't you hear me command him in front of you?" The character of al-Ash'ath's party was now becoming clearer. They were not only moody and poor in judgment, but stubborn as well.[100] They showed further signs of treachery when they told 'Alī, "Either you call back al-Ashtar or we will kill you as we killed ['Uthmān] ibn 'Affān."[101]

To no avail could 'Alī convince his followers[102] that the raising of the Qur'āns on spears was nothing but a ploy, and that he knew the ill intentions of enemy leaders from days long past. Al-Ashtar leads the way in this medley of discord, scolding these followers after he quits the fight on the front and goes back to the camp to examine the situation. Ṭabarī gives al-Ashtar a major spotlight as he debates and attacks the dissenting followers. He begins with a cry of outrage and frustration that mirrors 'Alī's tone and anger later on. Al-Ashtar declares: "Men of Iraq [*ya ahl al-'Irāq*], men of baseness and feebleness! [Will you abandon the battle] when you have won the upper hand over the enemy and they think that you are defeating them? They have raised the *maṣaḥif* [sing. *muṣḥaf*; Qur'ān codex or leaves], calling you to what is in them, but, by God, they have abandoned what God commanded in them and the example [*sunna*] of him to whom they were sent down. Do not respond to those people . . . Just grant me the respite of a time of the running of a horse, for I am sure of victory." They replied, "In that case we would be partaking in your sin [*khaṭī'a*]." Al-Ashtar said: "Tell me, now that the best of you have been killed and only the base ones remain, when were you in the right? Was it when you were fighting and the best of you were killed? In that case, since you have now withdrawn from the fighting, you are in the wrong. Or are you now in the right? In that case, those of you who have been killed, whose merits you do not deny and were better than you are in hell. . . . Oh you of the dark foreheads, we used to think your prayers were a renunciation of this world and a longing to join God. But now I see that you merely flee to this world from death. Shame on you . . . After this you will never see glory again. May you perish just as those people perished."[103]

In these narratives al-Ashtar generally confirms the statements of 'Alī and goes beyond him in taking more daring and controversial positions. Al-Ashtar's speech engages questions relating to moral and religious debate that made halting the war not only a poor strategy but a betrayal of religious principle as well. Why did the idea of raising the Qur'āns occur now and not before, al-Ashtar asks. And what is the real meaning of *jihād* if it can be manipulated for different purposes? Not only were these questions aimed at 'Alī's immediate crisis, but they opened wider issues of dissent within the community. The dispute highlighted the absence of a binding religious opinion of the sort that had existed in the days of the Prophet, and its absence now illustrated what he had prophesied about the trouble that 'Alī would face over the interpretation (*ta'wīl*) of the Qur'ān.[104]

The exchanges that 'Alī and al-Ashtar had with the dissenting party clearly show that 'Alī's strategy to continue the war was the sound political choice, and that his plans as caliph were being subverted by the whims of some of his followers. At that moment 'Alī's biography suddenly intersects with episodes in the final year of 'Uthmān's reign, when 'Uthmān tried to engage the Kufans and Egyptians in argument. 'Alī was about to suffer the same pressure that 'Uthmān's government had faced and tried unsuccessfully to resist. 'Uthmān had insisted that caliphal authority should not be questioned on the whim of individual and factional loyalties: "I would be no ruler if I did what your whims desire me to do [*mā arānī idhan fī-shay'in in kuntu asta'milu man hawaytum wa a'zilu man karihtum; al-amru idhan amrukum*],"[105] 'Uthmān once said. And as if to emphasize that they were using identical lenses in portraying the plights of 'Alī and 'Uthmān at that moment, narrators here make the dissidents in 'Alī's camp declare that if he refused to act upon their opinion, they would kill him as they had 'Uthmān.

The irony in 'Alī's fate at that juncture lies in the fact that while he had earlier urged 'Uthmān to negotiate with the dissidents even as 'Uthmān insisted on the primacy of caliphal authority over all objections, 'Alī now found himself in a situation almost identical to 'Uthmān's. The thematic connection between the two events is further strengthened by the fact that 'Alī identifies the group as "*ahl al-'Irāq*" in a clear reference to the fact that the same feisty group who challenged 'Uthmān was now posing the threat to 'Alī. Narrators here intended not only to show a continuity of group behavior from one reign to the next, but also to reveal similarity in the failures that brought down both caliphs.[106]

'Alī's plight with the dissidents did not stop with his agreement to halt the fighting. Matters became even worse when this group insisted that 'Alī designate Abū Mūsā al-Ash'arī, a man lacking in political skill and characterized as "*mughaffal*" or "*mudhin*" (naive or duplicitous)[107], as his representative in the Taḥkīm. 'Alī tried to resist his followers' choice of Abū Mūsā, suggesting instead a more capable man such as Ibn 'Abbās or al-Aḥnaf, yet he was again pressured to accept this designation.[108] One can see no clear reason behind the dissenters' insistence on Abū Mūsā, except to allow narrators to illustrate once again the poor judgment and detrimental behavior of the Iraqi folk (*ahl-Kūfa*).[109] 'Alī was again put in a position similar that of 'Uthmān, when the latter was pressured by the Kufans to replace the governor of Kufa, Sa'īd b. al-'Āṣ, with Abū Mūsā al-Ash'arī. Events from long ago, in the reign of 'Uthmān, were shown here coming back to haunt 'Alī's political career, and showing the damage that earlier concessions were leading to.

There was similarity in the pattern of circumstances that 'Alī and 'Uthmān confronted but also, and more importantly, a trend of accentuation. Aside from their grievances and their pressure on 'Uthmān to appoint a governor of their choice, the Iraqis, for example, also demanded that he publicly acknowledge his error and offer penance or engage in atonement (*iqtiṣāṣ* or *iqāda*). While on some level we are shown that 'Uthmān was ready to negotiate some issues, as he frequently declared in his talks with 'Alī, it is repeatedly hinted at in the sources that 'Uthmān was hesitant to make a public declamation of his rule, and even more reluctant to offer physical penance. Pietistic and self-deprecating speeches he certainly made, but these are treated as religious, not political, declarations. As a caliph conscious of his authority, 'Uthmān viewed making a declaration (*shahāda*) of atonement a sign of political defeat.

As we move into the story of 'Alī and the Khārijites, we notice that the earlier demand that the opposition had placed on 'Uthmān had grown in the hands of the Khārijites to become a religious cause, as they now stated that they would no longer obey 'Alī unless he declared publicly that he had apostasized by accepting the Taḥkīm. For their part, the Khārijites said, they had sinned when they once accepted the Taḥkīm and had atoned for that act ("*fa-lammā ḥakkamnā athimnā wa kunnā bi-dhalika kāfirīn wa qad tubnā fa-in tubta kamā tubnā fa-naḥnu minka wa maʿaka*"), and now they expected ʿAlī to follow. Shocked at such a request, ʿAlī declared: "May a whirlwind strike you and not one of you survive! After my believing in the Messenger of God, should I [now] testify to unbelief against myself? 'Then I would have gone astray and would not be of the rightly guided.'[110]"[111] Thus the ambiguous accusation that ʿUthmān had violated the law ("*khālafa ḥukm al-kitāb*") and acted selfishly had now reached a new extreme, becoming an accusation of apostasy against the new caliph. The stories of ʿUthmān and ʿAlī were clearly crafted in synchrony to show the extremes to which a perverted piety can go, thereby destroying the community and all measures of right and wrong.

The conjunction of setback for ʿUthmān and ʿAlī, however, did not grow out of entirely identical responses by these two caliphs. ʿUthmān had rejected compromise, while ʿAlī, who agreed to the arbitration, still found himself rejected. ʿUthmān had once stubbornly refused to abandon Medina, claiming his preference to be in the sanctuary of the Prophet, as if implying that his successor intentionally wanted to break with this link, while ʿAlī left Medina for the more strategic location of Kufa, but this did not help him either. Ṭabarī's work surely recognized the irony of how these divergent responses nevertheless produced identical results. In both cases, the caliphs had done what they saw would save the caliphate (absolutism or compromise) but still found themselves defeated.

All this was now leading toward the fulfillment of a sad prophecy made by Muḥammad about the emergence of a militant breed of schismatics. These were not outsiders to the community, but individuals who had actually fought in some later *ghazwa*s during the Sīra and essentially overlapped with the Anṣār. Their career transformation was cast as a parable for the individual believer about the danger of overconfidence among the pious and as a warning that served later Sunnī political consciousness about the limits of challenging authority. The occasion *ḥadīth* literature gives for this prophecy was the time ʿAlī sent to the Prophet a piece of raw gold from Yemen. When the Prophet divided it among four individuals (ʿUyayna b. Badr [al-Fazārī], al-Aqraʿ b. Ḥābis [al-Ḥanẓalī], and a fourth, said to be either ʿAlqama [b. ʿUlātha al-ʿĀmirī] or ʿĀmir b. al-Ṭufayl),[112] a man stood up and challenged him, saying, "Be equitable," or "Fear God, O Messenger of God!"[113] "Woe to you," said the Prophet. "Who would be more fearful of God than I am?" Khālid b. al-Walīd (or ʿUmar, according to other versions) volunteered to kill the dissident (*munāfiq*), but the Prophet prevented him, saying that the man was a believer. "But there are many who say on their tongues what is not really in their hearts," Khālid said. "Even so," the Prophet said, "I was not ordered [by God] to dig through the hearts of people." Then he looked at this man, who is described as having a protruding forehead, deep-set eyes, a thick beard, and a shaven head, and said: "There will come from the same origin as this man [*min ḍi'ḍi' hādhā*] a people who recite the Book of God, but Its word will not mean anything to them. They will pass through faith like an arrow pierces through a hunt clean of blood. If you catch up with their time, destroy them the way Thamūd was destroyed."[114]

This emergent group was none other than the Qurrā' and Khārijite opponents of 'Alī, as mentioned earlier. The circumstances of their original disgruntlement, charging the Prophet with unfairness and exhorting him to be more strict in religion, foreshadow their similar challenge to 'Alī. Later *ḥadīth* categorizations of this group are murky (easterners, Anṣār, Qur'ān reciters), and Ṭabarī's usage of these terms is equally loose, but from the similarities in the accusations and tone of the man who told the prophet to "be equitable" and the disgruntlement of Sa'd b. 'Ubāda over the division of booty after the Battle of Ḥunayn, it becomes readily apparent that the future members of the Saba'iyya, the Qurrā', and the Khārijites grew out of the Anṣār faction (possibly more specifically the Khazraj group).

Muḥammad, as shown on the occasion of al-Ḥudaybiyya and Ḥunayn, was consistently represented as lucky or successful in averting conflict. But 'Alī would in time face the full burden of similar challenges. The radicalized offshoots of the Anṣār would wage a brutal campaign against those who did not join them. The story of the Khārijite attack on and murder of 'Abdallāh b. Khabbāb, when he declared, contrary to their demands, that the *ḥadīth* "*al-qā'id fī'l-fitna khayrun min al-qā'im bihā*" (he who is sitting during a time of sedition is better than the one who is standing) is an authentic saying of the Prophet, is greatly emphasized by Ṭabarī as a tragic example of the revival of the same zealousness that the Anṣār had displayed during the Sīra.[115] At the same time, when a Khārijite saw a companion of his pick up a date that had fallen from a tree and eat it, he was severely reprimanded by another Khārijite on the grounds that "this was money taken without permission."[116] Ṭabarī juxtaposed the two incidents to illustrate the warped piety of extremists in general, and the

Khārijites in particular. The incident of Ibn Khabbāb's murder happened before the Battle of al-Nahrawān and was a key factor that forced 'Alī to postpone his march on Syria in order to deal with the Khārijites.[117]

## THE SECULAR POLITICAL THEMES

We have thus far examined the religious representation of 'Alī's interaction with his followers as an exercise anchored in several approaches: the reworking of the Qur'ānic saga of the Israelites, the deprecation of extremist piety, and the cathartic and ironic suffering of 'Alī for his own history of overpious stances in 'Uthmān's time. Ṭabarī's narratives rework various angles of action from 'Uthmān's time to show how they come back to haunt 'Alī through more extreme offspring examples, such as 'Ammār b. Yāsir, the Khārijites, and the Qurrā' and the way these actors use language that 'Alī had used before.

The ever-cascading irony in the migration of actions and statements from 'Uthmān's reign to 'Alī's provides key proof that narrators were subjecting 'Alī to the same judgment he had cast before. A glaring case of this happens in one incident when 'Alī was reportedly giving a sermon in the mosque, and he was interrupted by a Khārijite man named Yazīd b. 'Āṣim, who repeated the rejectionist refrain against the Taḥkīm, saying, "Giving in to compromise is a form of hypocrisy [*inna i'ṭā'a al-daniyyati fī al-dīni idhānun fī amri allāh*]."[118] Like all such confrontations between 'Alī and the Khārijites, this one led to nothing except a bitter parting between the two sides, but the key allusion in the story lies in the Khārijite's borrowing of 'Alī's own earlier usage of the term when he refused to reappoint Mu'āwiya as governor after 'Uthmān died. 'Alī's explanation at the time included the point that doing this appeasement would be tantamount to dissembling (*idhān*). 'Alī's words were: "*lā udhinu fī dīnī wa lā u'ṭī al-daniyya fī amrī, lā asta'milu Mu'āwiya yawmayn abadan.*"[119]

Another case of similar derivation occurred when 'Alī later confronted the Khārijites before the Battle of al-Nahrawān, demanding that they surrender the murderers of 'Abdallāh b. Khabbāb, and they refused. 'Alī ordered them: "Hand us those who killed our brethren so that we kill them in punishment. Then I will let you go and turn my attention to the people of Syria [*ahl al-shām*]. Perhaps God will in the meantime reform your hearts and turn you to better conduct." In response, the Khārijites sent back to 'Alī the declaration: "We are all involved in the killing of them and we all consider the shedding of their blood legitimate."[120] The relation here is to the episode recounted by al-Dīnawarī in which a Syrian emissary asked 'Alī to surrender the murderers of 'Uthmān. 'Alī, as we saw earlier, was at a loss as to how to respond to this request, and when the Syrian emissary came face to face with the followers of 'Alī in the mosque the next day, he heard them make a declaration similar to the statement the Khārijites made above. 'Alī was thus putting forward the same limited demand that Mu'āwiya had earlier put forward, but he received a similar rejection from the opposition.

In addition to serving as a parabolic religious saga, the story of 'Alī addressed a set of secular political themes that ultimately made it sound both realistic and historical. An efficient summary of the secular dimension of 'Alī's story can be found in a comment that Mu'āwiya made about 'Alī, reportedly after the end of the war. There Mu'āwiya declared: "I was aided in the war against 'Alī with four things. I used to guard my secrets while he divulged his; my troops were the best in order and obedience, while his were the most vile and insubordinate; at the time of the Battle of the Camel, I left him to deal with his enemies. If they won, I would have found them easier to handle, and if he won, I realized, this would embolden him into thinking that he commanded the righteous cause [*wa in ẓafira bihim ightarra bihā fī dīnihi*]; and I was more beloved to the Quraysh than he was."[121] In this statement, narrators sum up all the key political issues around which these religious narratives were woven. The failings in 'Alī's political style dated back to his first days in power, when he refused to compromise with Mu'āwiya or to listen to advisors who urged that he work in this direction. But 'Alī's failure to hold his military camp together was to become more pronounced as the years passed, especially toward the end of his reign. On the whole, the years after the Taḥkīm were some of the grayest in the life of 'Alī. Although successful in suppressing the Khārijites at Nahrawān, with a divided power base he never seemed able to advance on Syria. Mu'āwiya's armies carried out raids on Egypt while 'Alī's followers undermined his authority in a variety of ways. Defections and insubordination were two of the most common flaws that challenged 'Alī's ability to wage a sustained war against Mu'āwiya. The sources, as noted earlier, emphasize the problem of insubordination by juxtaposing the behavior of 'Alī's followers with Mu'āwiya's. Whereas in Mu'āwiya's camp much of the discussion of strategy was carried out in secret and then applied by the pro-Umayyad camp with no objections or interference, in 'Alī's camp the opposite was far more the norm. Whether through raising objections to 'Alī's decisions or reneging on their pledges, the 'Alid camp was exasperatingly fractious and obstructed the crafting of an efficient and guarded plan to undermine Mu'āwiya's political challenge. Every suggestion 'Alī would put forward elicited a questioning challenge and an alternative opinion.[122]

Set against the background of his early political and moral statements, this situation in his camp may have an explanation. One can trace a root for this indulgent behavior of the pro-'Alid party perhaps to 'Alī's original desire to make the caliphal office accountable to the public. His insistence that the *bay'a* to his caliphate be taken publicly when he was first nominated to succeed 'Uthmān and his belief that private planning was synonymous with exclusive family rule had begun this trend. Now, with complicated circumstances on hand, and with his followers having grown audacious and divided, 'Alī was unable to draw any boundary between spheres of authority. One narrator offers a vivid illustration of this problem. In the course of describing how each side of the conflict planned for arbitration while negotiations were still going on at Dūmat al-Jandal, we are told that Mu'āwiya's messenger to 'Amr during those days used to come and go with messages from 'Amr's camp without anyone knowing what information was exchanged. On 'Alī's side, in contrast, every time messengers traveled back and forth, the pro-'Alids would come to Ibn 'Abbās—who was in charge of leading the prayers in Abū Mūsā's camp—and ask him: "What did the Commander of the Faithful send?" Ibn 'Abbās reportedly grew frustrated with this situation and told his camp on one occasion: "Do you not have any reason, men! Can't you see how the messenger of Mu'āwiya comes and goes and no one knows what information he came with or sent back, and no one in their camp raises his voice or makes an utterance, while you are every day doubting and having suspicions *taẓunnūn al-ẓunūn*]!"[123]

'Alī was without doubt unlucky in having the supporters that he did, but the political failure that he endured was also in part a result of flawed strategy. The lack of discipline in his camp, for example, was worsened by the way he allowed himself to be misled by rumors told by his associates about competent governors. Hoping to maintain an emphasis on religious values and to stress the accountability of governors (in a style reminiscent of 'Umar b. al-Khaṭṭāb, whom he cited as an example during the controversies with 'Uthmān), 'Alī proved hasty when he dismissed Qays b. Sa'd b. 'Ubāda, the competent governor of Egypt, and replaced him with the inexperienced Muḥammad b. Abī Bakr. Only after the latter failed to govern Egypt and brought about its loss to Mu'āwiya did 'Alī realize that Qays was truly the more worthy of the two and that the information he had received about him was slander.[124] Another victim of the caliph's ill-considred judgment was 'Abdallāh b. 'Abbās, who was accused by an anonymous source (sometimes named as Abū'l-Aswad al-Du'alī) of having used government funds for his own purposes. This time, however, the story does not give 'Alī the chance to recognize Ibn 'Abbās' competence.[125] Ibn 'Abbās is portrayed as having finally become angry with the caliph and resigned his governorship without giving any further chance for debate.

This issue of the divergence between Mu'āwiya's and 'Alī's approaches to planning was an area of historical description that served important political lessons in the ninth century, as writers began to craft treatises on statecraft and government. The theoretical issue of ideal government was intertwined with religious considerations when the subject, as in this case, focused on the contentions among the *ṣaḥāba* over the caliphate and particularly on the relative merits (religious and historical) of 'Alī and Mu'āwiya. That 'Alī's religious character was superior (*al-afḍal*) was well recognized. However, whether a man who was reasonably acceptable in religious terms (*al-mafḍūl*) and who possessed the political qualities that suited the time (Mu'āwiya) was a credible political choice would have been the subject of controversy. In this particular case, examining how government ought to handle the issue of public versus private planning of strategy, narrators used the historically real conflict between 'Alī and Mu'āwiya to discuss a theoretical ethical, political, and religious debate of the ninth century.

## *ḤILM* VERSUS *IDHĀN*

Just as he failed both to preserve the secrecy of private discussions and to keep himself from being misled by rumors, 'Alī lost the battle of image politics. Mu'āwiya, although less regarded under the Islamic system, had proved able to revive the image of the Sufyanids as heirs to a tradition of tribal politics and its modes of compromise. With his famed qualities of forbearance (*ḥilm*) and endurance and his discretionary system of pardons to wrongdoers and former foes, Mu'āwiya gradually reconstituted a base of tribal support focused on his new center in Damascus. 'Alī proved to be at a diplomatic disadvantage in this regard. Hampered by strict legal and religious codes that sacrificed all political and social considerations, 'Alī was unable to compromise for political expediency. Even if he wanted to, his image as a religious guide devoted to repurifying the faith prevented him from showing diplomatic skill.

A key test for him on this level came soon after al-Khirrīt b. Rāshid's defeat. The story in question relates to the case of the defection of the commander Maṣqala b. Hubayra al-Shaybānī, which invites attention because it had nothing to do with Mu'āwiya, sympathy for the Khārijites, or anger against the Taḥkīm. Maṣqala, who reportedly was the governor of Ardashīr Khurra, had been sent by 'Alī to back up Ma'qil b. Qays al-Riyāḥī in his final campaign against al-Khirrīt b. Rāshid. When the war against al-Khirrīt's coalition of pro-'Uthmānids, Khārijites, and Christians has finally finished, the narrator describes a very poignant scene: the masses of prisoners of war, desperate men and women, crying out and anxious to reconcile before being separated from their families in exile. Ma'qil himself reportedly admitted that he was greatly moved by the scene.[126] As commander of the punitive campaign, however, he could not do much to change the judgment of war without violating his loyalty to 'Alī. As the prisoners were led off through the territory of al-Ahwāz, however, they reportedly crossed paths at one point with Maṣqala b. Hubayra al-Shaybānī, a leader among the Bakr b. Wā'il, a tribe that had always had a mind of its own, and they pleaded with him to help them, "O Abū'l-Fadl, protector of the men and liberator of the captives, be good to us—buy us and free us [*yā abā'l-faḍli, yā ḥāmiya al-rijāl wa fakkāk al-'unāt umnun 'alaynā fa-ishtarinā wa a'tiqnā*]."[127] No tribal chief, especially a leader in the Banū Shaybān, could ignore the duty of responding to such a plea, no matter what other considerations were involved. Ma'qil b. Qays was a member of Tamīm, and he was about to see how Bakr b. Wā'il acts in such situations. Maṣqala now instantly wrote to Ma'qil, offering to ransom the Banū Nājiya prisoners. Ma'qil at first disliked having to make a deal on this issue just to appease an important chief of the Bakr b. Wā'il. "Had I known he [i.e., Maṣqala] was asking me this out of [political] sympathy for them," he said, "I would have ordered his head struck off, even if this were to lead to a war of annihilation between Tamīm and Bakr b.

Wā'il."[128] Under the circumstances, however, Ma'qil saw the virtue involved and agreed to the request but set the huge sum of a million dirhams for ransom. Maṣqala could not pay the whole sum at once, so he offered to pay part of it (two hundred thousand) immediately and promised to deliver the remainder soon afterward to 'Alī. The issue seemed settled for the time being. Maṣqala had acted honorably, and the pain of the *fitna* prisoners was lifted unexpectedly.

It soon became clear, however, that Maṣqala's chivalrous instinct vastly outstripped his economic means, since he was unable to come up with the rest of the money. 'Alī's repeated reminders to Maṣqala brought back no answers, and Maṣqala, now in a bind, turned to a companion of his and asked him if he thought 'Alī could forgive him the remainder of the money. Was it possible that 'Alī could emulate 'Uthmān's example with Ibn al-Ash'ath when the latter was allowed to hold a 100,000 dirham concession annually from the tax revenue (*kharāj*) of Azerbayjān? "By God, if it was the son of Hind who held me in this debt or the son of 'Affān, he would have forgiven me," Maṣqala said. "[You know] this man [i.e., 'Alī] does not do things this way," Dhuhal b. al-Ḥārith reminded Maṣqala.[129] Unable to keep his promise, Maṣqala thus panicked and felt that his only way to safety lay in escape to Mu'āwiya. And so one day, without giving notice to anyone, Maṣqala packed his belongings and went over to Mu'āwiya's camp. When he heard of the news, 'Alī is said to have shown great surprise at the contradiction in Maṣqala's behavior and commented: "He first acted like a nobleman, then fled like a slave . . . If only he let us know [of his predicament]," 'Alī said, "we would have done no more than investigate him and detain him. We would then have taken what he could pay and then released him."[130] This solution may have been lenient in 'Alī's view, but it is unlikely that Maṣqala would have accepted even this limited rebuke. The whole incident came to illustrate a key example of contradiction between moral and religious duties.

Maṣqala had acted at the outset in a gracious manner fitting with his rank and credibility within his tribe and region. Whether his motives reflected a genuine nobility of character or merely his sense of pride in his tribal affiliation and rank is difficult to determine and beside the point. The important fact is that his action, wisely gracious, fell more within the system of the pragmatic politics of Mu'āwiya than within 'Alī's style of functioning. It was an action based on political considerations and not religious ones, and he would have been saved, as he indeed imagined, had he been living in a state ruled by Mu'āwiya, since the two thought along similar lines of social behavior. From 'Alī's perspective, or at least from what his followers perceived his thinking to be, Maṣqala's action was a form of *idhān* (a behavior of concession tantamount to dissembling) that deserved punishment. From the commander's perspective, however, the situation he confronted demanded a change in policy, and so when narrators elaborated the details of this story that culminated with the defection of Maṣqala, they were in essence justifying the need for a regime like that of Mu'āwiya.[131] Precedents for pardon were already set by the Prophet after his victory at Badr and at the conquest of Mecca, and with such a background, 'Alī was perceived as overzealous in suggesting a reprimand for Maṣqala. One could argue that 'Alī's uncompromising measure had a precedent in 'Umar's exacting policies, but the logic of the Islamic historical narrative would have distinguished between the times of 'Umar and those of 'Alī, with the former being characterized by a more pious generation presided over by a more astute ruler and the latter times depicted as a generation influenced by the experience outside Arabia and in a climate of conflict. There was no reason for Maṣqala to be exacting for a state treasury whose government had all but collapsed.

## FRUSTRATION AND FAREWELL

The fall of Muḥammad b. Abī Bakr, 'Alī's governor in Egypt, and the loss of that province to Mu'āwiya in A.H. 38 was a major strategic loss for 'Alī and created an opening for Mu'āwiya's attacks on Iraq. The defeat of Muḥammad b. Abī Ḥudhayfa—another loyal commander of 'Alī in Egypt—and the news of his murder dealt another major setback to 'Alī. The fallout of these events materialized in the subsequent year, A.H. 39, when Mu'āwiya's commanders and frontier tribal affiliates were able to harass 'Alī's domain in Iraq and Arabia at will.

These political and military changes, however, are obscured by a narrative scheme that favors showing the pattern of an endemic crisis on 'Alī's side. Ṭabarī does not give an evenly detailed picture of how this came about, but Ya'qūbī's history gives a succinct overview of the twilight of 'Alī's rule. Typically, the chain of events runs as follows: Mu'āwiya's followers initiate a raid (*ghāra*) on a town under 'Alī's rule; then, frustrated with the negligence of his followers to defend his lands,

'Alī makes a spirited summons to battle (*da'wa*) that is heeded only by an exceptionally loyal commander, such as Jāriya b. Qudāma al-Sa'dī. By the time 'Alī's troops eventually respond to the distress call in a particular town, however, Mu'āwiya's troops would have fled, and the failure in 'Alī's camp leads to further demoralization. 'Alī then concludes the cycle by making a lamentation speech (*khuṭba*) that batters his followers for their delayed response and general lethargy and expresses his hope for divine help.[132]

What resonates most in the tussle of these events is neither the actual military successes nor the failures on either side, but the spectacular speeches that 'Alī makes to his followers. These exhortations to the 'Alid followers intensify, particularly after the loss of Egypt, and provide us with some of the most eloquent speeches in Arabic literature.[133] With the exception of occasional shouts of support, however, 'Alī's exhortations fell on deaf ears and highlighted to him the sad reality that his worst enemies were not just Mu'āwiya's camp and the Khārijites but also his own followers. In addition to lecturing his followers, 'Alī is described as writing various letters to his governors, advising them on proper political action. These letters, which provide a more flattering image of 'Alī's attentive governing, invent various scenarios of governors' shortcomings, and show how 'Alī sometimes advised a correcting path that would have confirmed a set of familiar maxims such as was known from the mirrors-for-princes genre. Ziyād b. Abīhi was advised not to tamper with the delivery of the tax revenue of Fars after word had reached the caliph about this; Qurẓa b. Ka'b al-Anṣārī was advised to repair the canal system for the benefit of the community and its livelihood in his region; and Qays b. Sa'd b. 'Ubāda was advised to treat his troops with equity.[134] History clearly yields to plain belles lettres (*adab*) in these documents, and these letters and covenants eventually give birth to an extensive list of wisdom sayings by 'Alī.[135] Chronology is clearly of no importance after a certain point in this context, for these sayings become important for the way they stand outside historical narrative and provide the language and tools necessary for appreciating other narratives set in 'Alī's reign and elsewhere.

Although it is very difficult to draw boundaries around 'Alī's actual territorial sphere of control, much less to determine his exact whereabouts when such incidents as those concerning al-Khirrīt and the fall of Ibn Abī Bakr happened, one can get from the speeches and letters attributed to 'Alī a very accurate profile of his personality and how it was shaped by political changes over the years. By A.H. 38/A.D. 658, as his reign approached its close, 'Alī had grown disillusioned with any effort, political or religious, to rally public support. Soon after making his eulogy speech after the death of Muḥammad b. Abī Bakr, 'Alī wrote to Ibn 'Abbās, describing his frustration with his supporters:

> "In the name of God the Merciful and Compassionate, from the servant of God, 'Alī, the Commander of the Faithful, to 'Abdallāh b. 'Abbās, peace be to you. Praise be to God, for there is no other than He. Now Egypt has been conquered and Muḥammad b. Abī Bakr has been martyred. We look for his reward with God and we treasure him [in our hearts]. At the very start I stood among the people and commanded them to help him before the calamity should occur. I summoned them in secret and in public, over and over again. Some of them came unwillingly, some made lying excuses, and some stayed where they were. I ask God that He give me a way out and an escape from them and that He deliver me from them before long. By God, if I were not desirous of dying in God's cause [*shahāda*], then I would not want to remain with these people for one day. May God strive to bring about for us and for you right guidance, rightful fear of Him and His right way. 'He has power over everything.' Salutations."[136]

Ever the understanding and loyal follower of 'Alī, Ibn 'Abbās wrote back encouraging 'Alī to be patient and gave him prayers for imminent victory, saying:

> "In the name of God, the Merciful and Compassionate. To the servant of God, 'Alī b. Abī Ṭālib, the Commander of the Faithful, from 'Abdallāh b. 'Abbās. Peace be upon you, Commander of the Faithful, and God's mercy and blessings. I have received your letter in which you mention the conquest of Egypt and the killing of Muḥammad b. Abī Bakr. God's help is to be implored in every eventuality. May God have mercy upon Muḥammad b. Abī Bakr and may He reward you, Commander of the Faithful. I have asked God to give you a way out and an escape from the flock with which you have been afflicted and that before long He strengthen you with the support of angels [*wa qad sa'altu allāha an yaj'ala laka min ra'iyyataka allatī ibtulīta bihā farajan wa makhrajan wa an*

*yu'izzaka bi'l-malā'ikati 'ājilan bi'l-nuṣrati*].[137] God will do that for you and He will strengthen you and answer your call, and He will crush your enemy [*fa inna allāha ṣāni'un laka dhalika wa mujību da'watika wa kābitun 'aduwwika*]. I tell you, Commander of the Faithful, that the people sometimes drag their feet and then become eager. Treat them well, O Commander of the Faithful, flatter them and give them something to hope for [*fa-irfiq bihim yā amīr al-mu'minīn wa dājinhum wa mannihim*]. Ask God for help regarding them. May God suffice to comfort you for the trouble they cause you. Salutations."[138]

This exchange between 'Alī and Ibn 'Abbās is unlikely to have happened and instead was mainly a pro-'Abbāsid digression positioned after the story of 'Alī's speech to his camp in order to serve an important legitimizing purpose. That 'Alī would write such a revealing letter to Ibn 'Abbās was intended to show how close the two were. The pro-'Abbāsid tangent in this narrative therefore carefully strengthened the alliance between 'Alī and Ibn 'Abbās in order to legitimize the 'Abbāsid claim to inheriting the 'Alid right for the caliphate in the future. 'Alī writes to Ibn 'Abbās almost like a governor would write to a caliph, seeking counsel and awaiting orders, and Ibn 'Abbās, fitting the role, writes back with some words of wisdom on social behavior and effective government. Ibn 'Abbās comes across as a pragmatic and shrewd judge of human nature, resembling Mu'āwiya more than he does 'Alī. This exchange of letters therefore had more to do with historical argumentation over caliphal qualifications than it did with addressing a realistic event. Through Ibn 'Abbās, the 'Abbāsids can appear sympathetic to 'Alī's sense of frustration, but they seem also to argue for less idealism on the part of the caliph and greater sensitivity to social and personal motives. Political followers may be mundane and materialistic, according to Ibn 'Abbās, but a competent ruler must work around these motives and co-opt them with short-term gains in order to realize the true and final goal.[139]

The correspondence purportedly exchanged between 'Alī and Ibn 'Abbās provides a concluding occasion wherein the caliph sums up his political frustrations to one of his key officials. Another context that the narrators used to evoke a summary of 'Alī's beliefs was in his final testament to his children, al-Ḥasan and al-Ḥusayn. There the emphasis is twofold, on ethics and on the affirmation of proper religious rituals. The ostensible occasion for this testament is the question put forward to 'Alī about whom he was going to name as successor. 'Alī avoided naming a successor, however, perhaps in a manner meant to emulate the Prophet's final situation. He then addressed his children as follows:

> "I commend to you both the fear of God and that you do not seek this world even if it seeks you. Do not weep for anything that is taken away from you, speak the truth, show compassion for the orphan, succor those who are anxious, act on behalf of the foolish, be enemies to the wrongdoer and helpers to the wronged, act according to the Book, and let no man's censure affect you while you work for God."

More specific advice on the ideal manner of applying the ritual was then addressed to al-Ḥasan, as 'Alī told him:

> "I commend to you, my son, the fear of God, the holding of prayer at its appointed times, the payment of the *zakāt* on its due date, and a scrupulousness in performing ritual ablution, for there is no prayer without purification, and the prayer of the one who holds back the *zakāt* is not accepted. And I commend to you the pardoning of sin, the suppression of anger, observance of the ties of relationship, maturity in the face of coarseness [*al-ḥilm 'inda al-jahl*], acquiring knowledge of religion [*al-tafaqquh fī al-dīn*], firmness in authority, frequent mindfulness of the Qur'ān, fulfillment of the duties of hospitality [*jiwār*], commanding the good and forbidding the evil, and keeping clear of immorality [*al-fawāḥish*]."

In the final testament 'Alī gives to his children, he states:

> "In the name of God, the Merciful, the Compassionate, this is the testament of 'Alī b. Abī Ṭālib. He testifies that there is no god but God alone without partner and that Muḥammad is His servant and messenger 'whom He sent with right guidance and the religion of truth to make it triumphant over every other even though the polytheists abhor it.'[140] 'My prayer and my ritual [*nusukī*], my life and my death, belong to God, the Lord of the worlds, Who has no partner. Thus I was commanded and I am one of those who submit [*al-muslimīn*].'[141] I commend to you, Ḥasan, and all of my offspring and family, the fear of God your Lord. 'Die only as Muslims and hold fast together to the rope of God, not

separating.'[142] I heard Abū'l-Qāsim [i.e., the Prophet] saying, 'The restoration of unity is better than all prayer and fasting.'

Look to your relatives and unite them, that God may make the reckoning easy for you. Fear God, fear God with regard to the orphans, and neither restrain their entreaties, nor let them be lost while in your care, . . . with regard to those who have a right to your protection and hospitality [*jīrānukum*], for they are the commendation of your Prophet, who never ceased to commend them so that we thought he would include them as heirs.

Fear God with regard to the Qur'ān and do not allow anyone to do more than you in acting in accordance with it, . . . with regard to the prayer, for it is the pillar of your religion, . . . with regard to the house of your Lord, and do not leave it as long as you live, for if it is abandoned, there will never be another to be compared with it, . . . with regard to the *jihād* in the path of God with your property and your lives, . . . with regard to the *zakāt*, for it quenches the anger of the Lord, . . . with regard to the protection [*dhimma*] granted by your Prophet and do not allow the *dhimmī* to be oppressed among you, . . . with regard to the Companions of your Prophet, for the Messenger of God commended them to us, . . . with regard to the poor and the destitute, with regard to what your right hands possess. Observe the prayer always!

Do not fear before God the blame of any man—He is sufficient protector for you against anyone who has designs upon you and oppresses you. 'Speak good to the people'[143] as God has commanded you and do not abandon the commanding of the good and the forbidding of the evil, so that the worst ones among you obtain power: then you will call but no answer will be given to you. You must pursue mutual harmony and generosity, avoiding mutual opposition, separation, and fragmentation. 'Help one another in piety and fear of God but not in sin and enmity to Him. Fear God, for His retribution is mighty.'[144] May God preserve you as members of a family and your Prophet as one of you. I entrust you to God and I bid you farewell, and the mercy of God be upon you."[145]

These two testaments by 'Alī stand out for their comprehensive provision of religious advice. In the first testament, the focus is mostly on summarizing the ritual, while in the second it centers on inculcating social and ethical views derived from Qur'ānic verses that stress themes of cooperation and communal unity. The emphasis on filial cooperation, avoiding conflict, and equitable treatment of all humanity point to goals that 'Alī strove for in the disputes of the *fitna* but found elusive because of political factors. His advice to al-Ḥasan on the need to forgive wrongdoing and suppress his anger (*ghafr al-dhanb wa kaẓm al-ghayẓ wa ṣilat al-raḥim*) spells out important qualities that characterized 'Alī's behavior, although they pushed his endurance to the limit (whether in dealing with 'Uthmān, 'Āisha, Ṭalḥa, the Khārijites, or his own followers).

Speeches and wisdom sayings at the closing sections of important biographies are a common feature in early Islamic historiography. 'Alī's testaments, however, are different in the way they resemble the tone and some of the content of the Prophet's famous farewell speech. On a basic level, 'Alī's testaments offer well-known religious advice, albeit his advice generally represents an efficient summary of religious issues. However, with the emphasis given to religious and ethical issues, it seems clear that narrators wanted 'Alī to play the role of a religious preacher at the end rather than simply being a political leader. The fact that he was addressing his words to his children rather than to the public makes this whole scene appear more like a Shī'ī *waṣiyya* from one *imām* to the next.

In enumerating the rituals or in describing the proper manner of ablution, how one should keep the prayer times, or be mindful of the duty of *zakāt*, 'Alī's statements would have been acceptable to Sunnī Islam. This is perhaps one reason Ṭabarī included them. However, Ṭabarī's history also contained meanings that did not always square with Sunnī interpretations. When 'Alī was given the opportunity to describe various religious tasks and principles, he was in essence being represented as the legatee of the Prophet, to whom he refers with a degree of overfamiliarity or daring as "Abū'l-Qāsim."

When 'Alī advised his children to abide by the Book, he was in one sense expressing an obvious Islamic position, yet he was also expressing in another sense a partisan (Shī'ī) opinion, one which dismisses the *sunna* of the first two caliphs as an additional resource for establishing the law and political practice. In this he was acting within the boundaries of what he had promised he would do at the *shūrā* scene: rule not according to the precedents set by Abū Bakr and 'Umar, but according to his own "*sunna*" ("*bi-mablagh 'ilmī wa ṭāqatī*," as 'Alī put it). A Sunnī aspect to the narrative was here stressing the independent thinking of 'Alī by showing that he has to repeat the obvious, and it depicts him giving this advice to his sons, rather than to the public at large. The narrative thus shows that 'Alī acted till the end as if he was a second point of reference for the faith. Whether wittingly (and here the narrative would be satirizing the fourth caliph) or unwittingly (and here the text would be stressing how 'Alī was thus allowing Shī'īsm to read more into these events than necessary), 'Alī's words inevitably were making his stature in the early period a source of increasing partisanship.

CHAPTER SEVEN

# From Caliphate to Kingship

## *'Umar's Reign and Future Changes*

A reader who seeks to establish a firm sequence of causality for the political turmoil that spanned 'Alī's reign and the civil wars can easily concentrate on the reign of 'Uthmān for having provided the background and various radical changes that affected the government of the early Islamic state. However, when the history of this period is read from the perspective of the inferences of the Islamic historiographical scheme, it becomes evident that in fact it is the reign of 'Umar that holds the real answers, not only about the reigns of 'Uthmān and 'Alī but also about the emergence of the Umayyads and the transformation of the Islamic state from a caliphate to a kingship.

We have already seen that information about the reign of 'Umar was often intended to stand in deliberate dialogue with events and actions from 'Uthmān's time. Stories of the conquest, of revived tribal solidarity, and of proper manners of government control that occured in 'Umar's reign are twisted or overturned in 'Uthmān's time. This type of historical construction is particularly obvious when analyzing speeches attributed to 'Umar that often establish the ideal against which the reader is expected to read later change, both in 'Uthmān's reign and beyond. Perhaps the most significant of these speeches are those given at the end of 'Umar's reign, when the second caliph seems to capture a key historical moment of power and equilibrium in both the civil and the religious life of the community. In one such speech, 'Umar declares,

"God has imposed on you gratitude and instituted the pilgrimage for you as part of the bounty of the hereafter and this world that He has provided for you, without your asking Him or wishing it from Him. He created you, after you were nothing [*inna allāh khalqakum wa lam takūnū shay'an*], for Himself and for you to worship Him. He had the power to make you subservient to the weakest of His creation, but rather He made subservient to you the general mass of His creation. He did not make you subservient to anything other than He. And He 'subjected to you what is in the heavens and on earth and made His favors abound upon you, both open and hidden.'[1] 'He carried you by land and sea.'[2] 'And He gave you of good things, perchance you might be grateful.'[3] Then He made for you hearing and sight. Of God's favors to you are those that He granted to mankind in general and others that He granted exclusively to the people of your faith. These general and special favors are continued during your turn of fortune, your time, and your generation [*thumma ṣārat tilka al-ni'am fī dawlatikum wa zamānikum wa ṭabaqatikum*]. None of these favors has come to anyone in particular without, if he were to share out what he received among all the people, their gratitude for it being difficult for them and their right to have it overburdening them, except with God's help along with faith in God and His Messenger. You are appointed successors on earth and conquerors of its people [*fa-antum mustakhlafūn fī al-arḍ qāhirūn li-ahlihā qad naṣara allāh dīnakum*]. God has given your faith victory. No other community who differs from you in faith is left except two: one rendered submissive to Islam and to those who follow it, they paying you tribute, while the Muslims take the best of their livelihood . . . and a [second] community waiting for God's battles and attacks every day and night. God has filled their hearts with terror. They have no refuge to which they can flee or an escape by means of which they can guard against attack. God's armies came upon them suddenly and right into their own territory. [All this you have been granted] along with an abundance of food, a pouring out of wealth, the repeated dispatch of [victorious] troops and the [successful] defense of the frontier areas with God's permission, together excellent general security better than which this community had not experienced since Islam came into existence . . .[4]

This speech reiterates a sentiment frequently evident in the exchanges between the Arabs and the Sasanids before the battles of conquest in Iraq and Persia. The reminders about the hardships that the Arabs knew prior to Islam, their ignorance of religion, and the change in their way of life draw on familiar themes. What sets this speech apart, however, is that its composition is similar to that of the Prophet's farewell speech. Whereas in the earlier speech the Prophet outlined certain ritualistic points and legal customs, 'Umar's speech mainly discusses the subject of historical change and the community's role among the nations. As he captures the moment of Islamic victory over other nations, 'Umar provides what amounts in essence to a sketch of a new Genesis story, however this time it is a story of the creation of empire and a new community rather than a story of the creation of man. The *ni'ma* (bounty) of mankind's creation is transposed into a *ni'ma* of statebuilding and dominance over other nations. What God had enjoined into a covenant with Abraham and a minority community in ancient time had come to maturity with an enterprise of expansive conquest. And, the Qur'ān's characterization of Adam's primordial creation as the symbolic representative of God on earth is extended by 'Umar into a vision of the entire community of believers as such *khalīfas*.

However, no sooner does 'Umar summarize this ebullient theme in moral and religious terms than he begins to give caution, in other speeches, against transformation and downfall. The two pillars of Islamic triumph, according to 'Umar, are the law-abiding behavior of rulers and the faithfulness of their subjects. He summarizes this partly when he declares, "O subjects, you have an obligation to us to give advice on what is unknown and to cooperate in doing good. There is no forbearance [*ḥilm*] dearer to God and more generally advantageous than that of a gentle leader [*ḥilmu imām wa rifquhu*]. O subjects, there is no ignorance more hateful to God and more generally evil than that of a harsh leader [*jahlu imām wa khurquhu*]. O subjects, he who enjoins well-being for someone in his midst, God will bring him well-being from above."[5]

The words here were undoubtedly meant to allude to 'Uthmān and to offer a reminder of how 'Umar differed in his style of rule. But 'Umar's words of wisdom and reflections on potential change do not exist in isolation in Ṭabarī's chronicle. They simply bring to culmination myriad exhortations made earlier, in various speeches, by Abū Bakr and various Arab commanders on both the Iraqi and Syrian fronts. Abū Bakr's famous instructions (*waṣāya*) to his leading commanders (first to Usāma, but also to Yazīd b. Abī Sufyān[6]), Khālid's *jihād* speech before the Battle of Yarmūk, al-Muthanna's speech before the Battle of the Bridge, and Sa'd's victory speech after Qādisiyya all revolve around a set of closely related themes. The idea that man should conduct himself toward God with piety (*taqwā*) and conduct himself in life with the qualities of endurance and economy (*al-jidd wa'l-qaṣd*), patience (*ṣabr*), and trust in God (*tawakkul*); and the recognition of *jihād* (*īthār al-jihād*) as a noble form of '*amal* are matters that are linked to divine satisfaction (*riḍā*), favor (*ajr*) and support (*ma'ūna*). Together, these ideas and modes of action converge to describe the epic transformation of the Arab nation from a state of servility and ignorance to one of concordance and triumph.

Before the Battle of Qādisiyya, 'Umar gives Sa'd advice consistent with later speeches. "Renew your commitment!" 'Umar commands. "Admonish your soldiers, and speak to them about [the necessity to have the right] intention and about seeking God's reward . . . Stand firm! Help will come from God according to the [purity] of intention, and reward will come according to what you sought. Be cautious with those who are under your command and with the mission entrusted to you. Ask God to grant you well-being, and say frequently, 'There is no power and no strength except in God!' . . . Fear God, hope for Him, and do not be haughty! Know that God has made a promise to you, has taken this matter upon Himself, and will not break His promise. Be careful not to turn Him away from you, lest He put someone else in your place."[7] In another letter to 'Utba b. Ghazwān in A.H. 17/A.D. 638, 'Umar advises him as follows: "Keep the people far from injustice, fear God, and take care lest fortune turn against you [*iḥdharū an yudāla 'alaykum*] because of an act of treachery or concupiscence [*li-ghadr aw baghy*] committed by one of you. For through God you have attained what you have, on the basis of a covenant that He has concluded with you [*'alā 'ahdin 'āhadakum 'alayhi*], and He has shown you His grace in matters He reproached you for. So fulfill the covenant with God and carry out His commands; then He will give you help and victory [*yakun lakum 'awnan wa nāṣiran*]."[8]

From various angles, 'Umar's speeches warn about the danger of lapsing over time (*dawāl*), and the possibility of the transmission of divine favor to another nation.[9] This process of change is not tied to a particular religious dogma or to a chosen group of people as much as it is linked to a profane routine of human conduct. 'Umar delivers this message clearly when he declares, "The Arabs are noble through the Messenger of God. Some of them may share many ancestors with him. We ourselves meet his line of descent after [going back] only a few generations, then do not diverge from it as far back as Adam. [Even so], if non-Arabs carry out [good] deeds and we do not, then they are nearer to Muḥammad than we [*fa-hum awlā bi-Muḥammad*] on the Day of Resurrection. Let no one rely on close relationship; rather, let him act for God's reward. For he whose effort falls short cannot get ahead by means of his ancestry [*fa-man qaṣṣar bihi ʿamaluhu lam yusriʿ bihi nasabuhu*]."[10] ʿUmar's reputation for egalitarian rule made him an appropriate person to give warning on this score, but the invocation of the image of lineage dating back to Adam and the changing of the present situation that ʿUmar fears are tied to a role for the Creation story in the overall casting of the community's turn toward *fitna* in Ṭabarī's chronicle. In this speech, ʿUmar's words not only allude to the parable of Cain's genealogical pride, which cost him divine favor, but also link the fate of Islamic history at that juncture with the whole parable of Adam and Eve.

Although this broader reference cannot be inferred from this speech alone, it does seem to be intended in other declarations made by ʿUmar and from reported events that are scattered through the last years of the caliph's reign. ʿUmar's invocation of the Creation parable occurs in a prologue to his instructions where he outlines the *shūrā* plan. There one can find the caliph bringing that ancient religious theme to closure in political terms. ʿUmar describes to the community how he had debated whether to appoint a successor, but then found it impossible to find a perfect successor. He then relates in a manner resigned to fate, and more in keeping with the dreamy style of Abū Bakr at his moment of death, how he had come to that decision. He says,

> "I had decided after talking to you that I would look [into the matter] and appoint someone over you, the most suitable of you to bear you along the true path [*aḥrākum an yaḥmilakum ʿalā al-ḥaqq*]"—and he pointed to ʿAlī—"but I fell into a swoon [*wa rahiqatnī ghashya*] and saw a man who had entered a garden that he had planted [*fa-raʾaytu rajulan dakhala janna qad gharasahā*]. He began to pick everything, both the young tender plants and the mature ones, clutching them to him and putting them beneath him. I knew that God was in control and was taking ʿUmar into His mercy. I do not want to take on the burden [of the caliphate], dead as well as alive. You should [approach] that group of men who the Messenger of God said are 'among the people of paradise.'"[11]

This statement is unusual not only for its clear admission that 'Alī was the most suitable candidate, but also for its establishment of an unusual metaphor, of a man entering a garden and making judgment on its harvest. The imagery used here bears some resemblance to the description in the Book of Genesis of how God entered the garden after Adam's sin and found out what had happened with the affair of the tree. 'Umar's parable uses the garden as a metaphor on life and the abode of the Islamic state, while the act of Adam's temptation (*fitna*) is shifted to become the act of the community's political trial (*fitna*) with various civil wars about to ensue. The parable is interesting not only for how it links the coming death of 'Umar with the ensuing trial—a notion consistent with various accounts that portray 'Umar as the gateway guarding the community from civil war—but also for its transposition of a biblical religious tale into a political and historical one. To the narrator of the story, the Garden of Eden of the Bible had reached its earthly counterimage in Islamic history with the garden of state, a kind of virtuous society presided over by an ideal caliph. There is here the messianic vision of a just ruler (God's caliph), symbolized by 'Umar, who presided over an idealized setting that existed in both concept and physical setting, a desert Arcadia, perhaps, that 'Umar had guarded day and night through vigilant scrutiny of its public and political life. This kingdom was now about to pass, while 'Umar would thereafter be viewed as the last to rule over it until the time of redemption should come with the *mahdī* or Jesus.

Therefore, far from being the joyous act of political pluralism and consultation that a modern reader might find it to be, the episode of the *shūrā* council's debate over the succession was thus in origin a cataclysmic narrative about the end of the Islamic state and the end of history. The temptation of Adam in the garden is translated into the political temptation of the Islamic community after Muḥammad's (or 'Umar's) death. Since Adam was viewed not only as the father of humanity (*Abū'l-bashar*) but also in his Persian capacity as Jayumart (*Abū'l-furs*)—the father of all successive kings whose line came to extinction with the fall of Yazdajird (a fact tellingly mentioned early in Ṭabarī's chronicle soon after the Creation/Fall narrative)—it would have been immediately discernable to the literate medieval reader that universal history was finally coming full circle in 'Uthmān's reign, with divine judgment falling after the twin peaks of revelation and conquest of Persia in the Prophet's and 'Umar's reigns respectively. This theme of anxiety about what is to come is then referred to more extensively in 'Umar's final words to the community about the need for agreement on the matter of succession. 'Umar warns of the specific reasons he believes conflict may come about. The threat to the community, he warns in a manner akin to that of the Prophet in his final sermon (*ḥijjat al-wadāʿ*), comes from within rather than from without.

"I have no fear for you with the people if you remain on the straight path," 'Umar declares in his outline of the *shūrā* procedure. "However, I do fear for you if there is a difference of opinion among you and the people then differ among themselves. Off you go to 'Āisha's room, with her permission, and deliberate. Choose one of you." Then he added, "Do not go to 'Āisha's room; rather stay near at hand." The narrator then reports, "He [i.e., 'Umar] put down his head, exhausted by the loss of blood."

Soon afterward, almost simultaneously with the event of his death, as in the Prophet's succession, the companions confirm the late caliph's fear when they quickly enter into a rivalry that seems to be a resumption of the dispute first begun at the Saqīfa of Banū Sāʿida. The first sign of this comes as 'Abd al-Raḥmān b. 'Awf opened the *shūrā* proceedings by asking, "Who among you would be willing to withdraw from [the race for the caliphate]?" No one answered his call.[12] Then, when the community assembled for the funeral prayer over 'Umar, 'Alī and 'Uthmān reportedly competed as to who should lead the congregation in the prayer (presumably with the precedent formerly set for Abū Bakr's political legitimacy when he led the community in prayer during the Prophet's illness). Here Ibn 'Awf had to reprimand them both, saying, "Each of you likes to be a leader, but this matter is not for either of you. It is for Ṣuhayb, who was designated by 'Umar to lead the community in prayer for three days, until they agree on an *imām* [*kilākuma yuḥibb al-imra, lastumā min hādhā fī shay', hādhā ilā Ṣuhayb . . .*]*,"*[13] thereby casting the orthodox praise for Ṣuhyab as the model believer who is disinterested in politics. These images of companion competition and eagerness for leadership were meant partly to illustrate that future rivalries in the civil war had had such early signs written all over them. 'Uthmān's future statement against his critics—when he refused the urgings of the opponents to his rule that he resign, claiming that the caliphate had come to him as a bestowal from others rather than as a result of his eager seeking of it—is clearly subverted here by such depiction.

The scene of the *shūrā* perfectly illustrates 'Umar's forebodings ("I do fear if there is a difference of opinion . . ."). Although here 'Umar's comment is general, assigning blame to all of the companions, occasionally the caliph gets more specific. He implies some concern, for example, that Ṭalḥa could prove stubborn and refuse to give his *bay'a* (*wa man lī bi-ṭalḥa . . . arjū an lā yukhālif, in shā' allāh*),[14] and he urges 'Uthmān not to lord it over the community by appointing his relatives to positions of power.[15] 'Umar even suspects that 'Āisha will one day use her prestige as Mother of the Faithful to wage war. His criticism of her is indirect, however, and needs to be inferred from the way he modifies his instructions. When 'Umar declared, "Off you go to 'Āisha's room," then hesitated and said, "Rather stay near at hand ['*inhaḍū ilā ḥujrat 'Āisha bi-idhnin minhā fa-tashāwarū wa ikhtārū rajulan minkum', thumma qal, 'lā tadkhulū ḥujrat 'Āisha wa lakin kūnū qarīban'*]", it seems clear that he was offering some knowledge of 'Āisha's ability to stir trouble. After thinking that he had honored 'Āisha for her stature as purveyor of *ḥadīth* by inviting the *shūrā* members to her house, 'Umar quickly holds back on his command, clearly fearful—or tendentiously critical—that the religious expertise of a woman would be used for political gain. Given that 'Umar's voice in the *ḥadīth* sources defines many religious laws pertaining to women, his voice in this historical narrative was clearly meant to be consistent with his religious voice, which often controlled or curtailed their rights (a later Sharī'a development, as discussed above). His quick change of opinion thus shows the incorporation of a Jamā'ī-Sunnī political commentary that later repudiated 'Āisha's political activism and limited her role to that of a *ḥadīth* transmitter only.[16]

## DISCORD IN THE GARDEN: THE DISPUTE OF THE *SHŪRĀ*

We have thus far examined the *shūrā* scene in its preliminary phase as the declaration of 'Umar's instructions and the expression of forebodings.[17] However, the full density of the *shūrā* scene's range of allusions only comes to the reader's attention when 'Abd al-Raḥmān b. 'Awf sets out to implement it. Here the story weaves together a subtle web of statements and actions that foreshadow diverse moments of future tragedy. In this second phase of the *shūrā* narrative, the reader should note the cascading style that narrators employed to show a character—here ʿAbd al-Raḥmān—inheriting roles (in words, gestures, or dramatic temperament) that others (himself or ʿUmar) played in previous narratives. ʿAbd al-Raḥmān continues the role that ʿUmar played in Abū Bakr's succession and foreshadows the role that ʿAmr b. al-ʿĀṣ will play at the Taḥkīm. ʿAbd al-Raḥmān had played a role in advising Abū Bakr on ʿUmar's succession, but at the *shūrā* the two characters of ʿUmar and ʿAbd al-Raḥman seem at times to merge. ʿAbd al-Raḥman, for example, begins his opening speech to the crowd of the *shūrā* by telling them about an epiphany he had, which he describes in terms highly reminiscent of the language ʿUmar used to preface his succession plans. When Saʿd sought to quickly arrange the succession by inviting ʿAbd al-Raḥman to appoint himself as caliph with the statement "Have yourself accepted [as caliph], give us some respite and raise up our heads [*ayyuhā al-rajul bāyiʿ li-nafsika wa ariḥnā wa irfaʿ ruʾūsanā*]"[18]—ʿAbd al-Raḥmān brushed this aside, saying that he had withdrawn his name from the candidacy. He then described a vision that had motivated him to come to this decision:

> "[I saw myself in a dream][19] as if in a green meadow rich in fresh herbage. A stallion camel came in—I have never seen such a noble stallion—and passed through like an arrow, without paying attention to anything in the meadow, right to the other side without stopping. A stallion followed him in immediately after and left the meadow. Then a fine thoroughbred stallion entered, dragging his halter, turning right and left, going where the other two went and leaving. Then a fourth stallion camel entered, and pastured in the meadow. No, indeed, I shall not be the fourth. No one can take the place of Abū Bakr and ʿUmar after their death and [then] be approved of by the people."[20]

There is no doubt a similarity between ʿAbd al-Raḥmān's dream and what ʿUmar described at the outset of the *shūrā* story. ʿAbd al-Raḥmān reuses the metaphors of garden (earth) and passage (life) to convey his own disinterest in a political adventure, and this link between the two stories suggests that the narrators were offering a link between these two architects of Jamāʿī-Sunnī politics and doctrine from a later perspective. ʿAbd al-Raḥmān, like ʿUmar, is portrayed as a man disinterested in holding the caliphal office, as if in an aside of religious advice about the ultimate wrongfulness of the ambition for political power, whether it be crafted by *shūrā* or other means.

The link with 'Umar also takes the reader farther back, to the scene of the Saqīfa of Banū Sā'ida, a story not coincidentally recounted on the authority of Ibn 'Abbās. There Ibn 'Abbās quotes 'Abd al-Raḥmān, who describes 'Umar resisting nomination to the caliphate in the strongest terms.[21] The usually roaring 'Umar is portrayed as modest and calm when Abū Bakr offers to give him the *bay'a*, and in this we see a clear attempt to harmonize the voices and temperaments of 'Umar and 'Abd al-Raḥmān between the Saqīfa and the *shūrā*. Both men on these occasions act like masters of ceremony and sources of pressure rather than as real candidates for the caliphal office. And just as 'Umar gives advice about the proper relation of the Anṣār to Quraysh, so does 'Abd al-Raḥmān advise at the end of the *shūrā* that the results of companion "agreement" should not be challenged. The connections between the two scenes were clearly intended to be examined in detail.

A more subtle and potentially more controversial line of allusion in the narrative of the *shūrā*, however, would have tied 'Abd al-Raḥmān's actions to those of 'Amr b. al-'Āṣ and the Taḥkīm later on. As in the events leading up to the Taḥkīm, 'Abd al-Raḥmān consults key candidates for the caliphal office in private. 'Amr and 'Abd al-Raḥmān's actions are not identical, since the treachery of the former is not so blatantly evident in the *shūrā* scene. However, there is plenty of overlap in the two episodes, with subplots of caucusing day and night and even a Satan-like intrusion when 'Amr exhorts 'Alī to show disinterest in holding the office because this would be more likely, according to 'Amr, to win him 'Abd al-Raḥmān's admiration and the group's support.[22] Even without 'Amr's role, however, the story of the *shūrā* shows a process of consultation that is apprehensive of 'Alī and appears designed to seek his isolation from the group.

Whereas the Taḥkīm provides an embarrassing case of blatant political deception, the *shūrā* story was meant to illustrate the need for firmness in political decisions and the crucial role that a statesman plays, even though the principle of *shūrā* itself showed the religious merit of community consultation and of the companions interacting as equals. The secular messages were equally critical: that consultation can be distorted by kin ties (Sa'd and 'Abd al-Raḥmān), that guile can take lesser forms than open deception, as 'Amr did (the quality of *idhān*), and that political resolve in the end is necessary for the survival of the state. The word of 'Abd al-Raḥmān is backed by the sword of Abū Ṭalḥa al-Anṣārī, and it is shown that the community must emerge with a single voice in order to avoid *fitna* and division. Viewed from this vantage point, the Taḥkīm was undoubtedly a deteriorated form of something that started out more civil—albeit morally ambiguous. But the thrust of Ṭabarī's political narration probably views the rise of the Umayyads as the natural drift of such secular, political matters of state toward kingship. The bitter edge of 'Amr's treachery is removed in 'Abd al-Raḥmān's seemingly fair consultation, but it is clear that narrators across these various texts and personalities ('Umar, 'Abd al-Raḥmān, and 'Amr) were celebrating the role of the skillful politician, whether or not he acted with guile.

A reader can gain a firmer grasp of the linkage intended in all these episodes by examining 'Alī's victimization as the consultation progresses. On the whole, the story of the *shūrā* is not sympathetic to 'Alī's political assertiveness, and one sees that some companions are in a rush to wrap up matters, just as in the Saqīfa scene. Sa'd—who seems to control a running back-and-forth dialogue with 'Abd al-Raḥmān at the *shūrā* that is reminiscent of the interactions of 'Umar and Abū Bakr at the Saqīfa, and had started out the whole deliberation by suggesting that Ibn 'Awf accept the *bay'a* himself—becomes panicked when voices of dissent start rising between 'Ammār and Ibn Abī al-Sarḥ at the *shūrā*, and he (i.e., Sa'd) anxiously prompts, "Get it over with, 'Abd al-Raḥmān, before our people fall into civil war! [*ifragh qabla an yaftatin al-nās*]." Unlike at the Saqīfa, however, where 'Alī's presence is diminished and his victimization is applied by proxy through Sa'd b. 'Ubāda, at the *shūrā* 'Alī's anxieties and expressions are more passionate and target specific individuals. In the preliminary backstage discussions that the companions reportedly had before 'Abd al-Raḥmān assembled everyone for a public hearing, the narrator describes how 'Alī came to Sa'd b. Abī Waqqāṣ, a cousin of 'Abd al-Raḥmān, and pleaded with him not to collude in any unfair lobbies. 'Alī's words were "I am asking you, in the name of the kinship of this son of mine with the Messenger of God and that of my paternal uncle, Ḥamza, with you, not to stand with 'Abd al-Raḥmān and assist 'Uthmān against me. I have connections 'Uthmān does not."[23] That Sa'd, a companion who reportedly stood neutral in the future wars of the Battles of the Camel and Ṣiffīn, was selected to be the object of 'Alī's anxiety may seem puzzling, especially in the absence of a recorded reply from Sa'd to

'Alī's plea. However, the narrator's intent in this case was not so much to illustrate Sa'd's role as a participant in the *shūrā*, but to show Sa'd as the father of 'Umar who would commit the atrocity against the 'Alid family at Karbalā later on. Through his pleadings, 'Alī was trying to forestall not merely Sa'd's bias at the *shūrā*, but also Sa'd's family's future collusion in an anti-Hāshimite war that would lead to tragedy.

This particular exchange between 'Alī and Sa'd may form an exception, with its pointed reference to an event so distant in the future. However, in the main body of the *shūrā* narrative, 'Alī's grievances and anxiety relate directly to the threat being posed against his candidacy. After it seemed that 'Alī was the sure candidate for the office and everyone present tacitly recognized this (with 'Uthmān showing that he had no chance of getting elected by sitting at the back of the mosque), 'Abd al-Raḥmān came forward and, after a brief questioning, proclaimed 'Uthmān as the designated third caliph. Then an interesting development happens, when 'Alī begins to voice his displeasure with the outcome of the *shūrā*, something he had not done openly on previous occasions such as the Saqīfa, and 'Abd al-Raḥmān sternly tries to silence him by warning him not to challenge the outcome of what he claimed to be the *jamā'a*'s agreement. "Do not make yourself open to criticism, 'Alī," 'Abd al-Raḥmān replies. "I have looked into the matter and consulted the people. They regard no one as the equal of 'Uthmān [*yā 'Alī lā taj'al 'alā nafsika sabīlan fa innī qad naẓartu wa shāwartu al-nās fa-idhā hum lā ya'dilūna bi-'Uthmān*]."[24] The words of both actors here are worthy of notice, as 'Alī replies, "You have always been partial in his favor [*ḥabawtahu ḥabw al-dahr*].[25] This is not the first time you have banded together against us. But '[my course is] comely patience and God's help is to be asked against what you describe [*fa-ṣabrun jamīlun wa allāhu al-musta'ān 'alā mā taṣifūn*].'[26] You have appointed 'Uthmān only so that the rule will come back to you. 'Every day God exercises power.'[27]"[28]

'Ali's disgruntlement finally sounds the opening shot of Hāshimite war with Quraysh, as he gives free expression to the Hāshimites' frustration that they are being deliberately discriminated against. Evoking the image of Jacob's victimization by his children (and of 'Āisha's ironic use of the same expression in the ordeal of *ḥadīth al-ifk*),[29] 'Alī says, "My course is comely patience and God's help is to be asked against what you describe," thereby connecting the fortunes of the Hāshimite family with that of biblical patriarchs. In contrast, 'Abd al-Rahman's comment is that of the established political power, which sternly warns 'Alī. 'Abd al-Raḥmān not only misrepresents the election of 'Uthmān as the result of a judgment of excellence ("I have looked into the matter and consulted the people [*fa-innī qad naẓartu wa shāwartu . . . wa al-nās . . . lā ya'dilūna bi-'Uthmān*]"), since what in fact what had tipped the balance was 'Uthmān's answer that he would abide by the practices of his predecessors, but he also threatens 'Alī by saying that the new authority would be justified in acting against him if he continued to grumble (*lā taj'al 'alā nafsika sabīla*). The exchange ends as 'Alī departs upset, saying, "[God's] decree will come in its time! [*sa yablughu al-kitābu ajalahu*]."

Amid this shocking outcome of the third succession, which still ignored the merits of the Hāshimites, and with the image of 'Alī's angry departure putting an end to a premature open conflict with the companions, the narrators leave it to a supporter of 'Alī to voice amazement at the outcome of the *shūrā* and express sympathy for him. Standing aside as 'Alī departs and in full view of what had just taken place, this man, al-Miqdād b. al-Aswad, comments in dazed grief, "I have never seen such things as have been visited upon the people of this house after the death of their Prophet. I am amazed at Quraysh [*innī la-a'jabu min Quraysh*] that they have abandoned someone who cannot be matched, in my opinion, in knowledge and the ability to act justly. What, indeed, if I were to find supporters against 'Uthmān."[30] Although himself a member of the Anṣār, al-Miqdād is used here by narrators as the symbolic stranger-in-town who recognizes the simple truth that the Prophet's closest kin deserve to succeed him first, and is incredulous at the attitude of the natives, who, like the Israelites before, turned against their prophets and *imāms*. Al-Miqdād in this context continues a theme captured best in the words of Jesus, when he lamented that a prophet is rejected by his people and accepted by foreigners ("A prophet is not without honor, except in his own country, and among his own kin, and in his own house" [Mark 6:4]).[31] 'Abd al-Raḥmān offers a warning to al-Miqdād as he did to 'Alī, saying, "Fear God, Miqdād, I am afraid you might fall into temptation [*ittaqī allāh fa-innī khā'ifun 'alayka al-fitna*]."[32] But al-Miqdād appears to take a more active stand on behalf of 'Alī. And, just as 'Alī had effectively declared war on the *shūrā* members with his comment and his sudden departure, al-Miqdād was used here by narrators as the paradigm of all successive supporters of the 'Alid revolts, namely foreign support in foreign lands.

## 'ALĪ'S DISPOSSESSION: THE SIN OF ISLAMIC HISTORY

'Alī's dispossession from the succession on the third round could no longer be viewed as a passing political event or the result of accident. The rich art and crafty attitude with which narrators shroud the *shūrā* highlight how significant they conceived this event to be. Viewed in the broader sweep of early Islamic history, 'Alī's dispossession was an epoch-defining event that would usher in future conflicts and nurture hopes of a messianic figure from the family of the Prophet who would set right the 'Alid claim to succession.

And yet in spite of the wrong done to 'Alī, narrators conceived a contradictory perspective of Islamic history, whereby even though 'Alī was pitied for his loss of the caliphate, his political distancing was still considered a necessity. A number of layers of ideological motives converged in the text to ensure 'Alī's loss. Perhaps the most obvious among these is the layer of 'Abbāsid political interest, which constantly tried to steer Hāshimite leadership away from the 'Alids and toward the 'Abbāsid line. Through the depiction of 'Alī as an unwise strategist, the 'Abbāsids generally sought to position their competing claim to political leadership from early times.

The 'Abbāsid political motive overlapped greatly with the Jamā'ī-Sunnī religious motive, which rested on a different—albeit related—ideological thrust. With the close interrelation among religious textual clusters (*ḥadīth*, *tafsīr*, lore) and the reporting role of Ibn 'Abbās in each of these areas, the subordination of 'Alī's historical quest was not considered an unrelated political issue but an integral and necessary part of the religious lore. Ibn 'Abbās, the ancestral symbol of the 'Abbāsid dynasty and the anchor of a sprawling legal and exegetical discourse, stood as the key political and religious beneficiary of the narrative trend of the *shūrā* scene. But in this maze of Hāshimite rivalry and historical-religious links, the man who protected the roles of the 'Abbāsids and of Ibn 'Abbās—and, more comprehensively, the Sunnī ideological imperative—was ultimately 'Umar, which leads us back to the beginning portions of the *shūrā* narrative and impels the reader to re-explore the unique behavior that 'Umar displayed when he set out to draft the puzzling arrangement of a limited *shūrā*.

A prelude to exploring 'Umar's role in shaping 'Alī's political loss ought to begin with appreciating the drama of his words and actions as he laid out the plan for succession. From the outset, it is worth noting the surprising nature of 'Umar's indecisiveness on the issue of the third succession. Whereas in earlier years 'Umar was famous for stressing the importance of quick, firm steps toward political action, with the benchmark remaining the episode of Abū Bakr's succession—which 'Umar never tired of praising as the high point of religious faith and consolidation of power—at the *shūrā* 'Umar becomes soft and ambiguous. He appears to distance himself from the community of companions, treating them as equals, and displays a resignation to fate, as if leaving the community to fend for itself in the coming phase of discord and tribulation.

The few words he gave before launching the detailed description of the *shūrā* offer a nice disclaimer that he has not abandoned his preference for a sure candidate. "If Abū 'Ubayda b. al-Jarrāḥ were alive," 'Umar said, "I would appoint him, and if my Lord questioned me, I would say, 'I heard Your prophet say that [Abū 'Ubayda] was the guardian of this community.' If Sālim, client of Abū Ḥudhayfa, were alive, I would appoint him, and if my Lord questioned me, I would say, 'I heard your prophet say that Sālim loves God vehemently.' "[33] But both men that 'Umar mentioned were conveniently not around to spoil the flood of allusive tale-telling Ṭabarī was going to amass. Abū 'Ubayda had died a few years earlier in a plague in Syria, while Sālim (*mawlā* of Abū Ḥudhayfa) was most likely either a fictitious character—whose name related to the root of the word "Islam" and thus served as a generic icon of the ideal Muslim believer or ruler, disinterested in politics and greatly devoted to God—or a prophetic praise from the caliph for the future *ḥadīth* scholar Sālim b. 'Abdallāh b. 'Umar.[34]

With these possibilities unlikely, however, 'Umar could then be used by narrators to interact with the companions who were around, and not with those who were absent. Thus he turns to announcing in clear knowledge of what is to come how the *shūrā* will evolve and that it will come down to a choice between 'Alī and 'Uthmān. "I think one of these two, 'Alī or 'Uthmān, will become leader," 'Umar declares. "If it is 'Uthmān, he is a gentle person; if it is 'Alī, he has a sense of humor. How suitable he is to carry them along the true road!"[35] 'Umar's recognition that 'Alī was a leading candidate and his even stronger endorsement of 'Alī in other conversations with Ibn 'Abbās leads the reader to wonder why 'Umar did not choose 'Alī.

This was the core dilemma that the *shūrā* narrative artfully dodges, and the fatal error that brought about the fall of the community. 'Umar could not choose 'Alī because, in the entwined political and religious spheres of Islamic valuation, such a political endorsement of 'Alī at the expense of the companions implicitly meant accepting the Shī'ī claim of the Hāshimite *imām*'s infallible leadership. As such, 'Umar's choice of 'Alī would have undermined basic doctrinal and legalistic Sunnī views of the ninth century that challenged Shī'ī premises of *qarāba*, *waṣiyya*, and *'ilm* (the principles of religious authority based on prophetic kinship, designated testament, and gnosis), all of which were considered the assets of 'Alī. The religious and the historical problems ran parallel. While ninth-century *ḥadīth* scholars tried to ignore history, however, narrators of these tales set about crafting a story of contested succession, setting two key viewpoints, the Hāshimite and the Sunnī, in conflict and in dialogue on many levels and in various manners, both soberly argumentative and irreverent; but they ultimately always made sure that the voice confirming the *jamā'ī* and *ḥadīth*-oriented views stood out more prominently.

'Umar's whole effort from the contingency procedures of the *shūrā* was essentially crafted to try to put 'Alī at a disadvantage by equating him with others, involving Ibn 'Awf as an arbiter (even involving Ibn 'Umar if need be), and hurrying through the entire process in three days. Religious factors were not alone in shaping 'Umar's push of the caliphate away from 'Alī. Narrators implicitly suggest that 'Umar (or perhaps the later Sunnī view) saw in 'Alī a lack of political skill and a certain quality of naive puritanism. In many instances from the time of the Prophet's death onward, 'Alī is shown as having lacked the necessary political initiative, and Ibn 'Abbās as never losing the chance to remind him of that. At the *shūrā*, too, 'Alī's conduct is meant to confirm this impression. Had he shown a little more craft, he could have turned the path of deliberation in his favor and thus forestalled Sunnī gravitation to Mu'āwiya in later times.[36] But this did not happen. And, so from his vantage point, 'Umar set out to craft a procedure that would lead to a choice of a caliph who would fit Sunnism's doctrinal and political interests. 'Uthmān, a man with a reputation for extra ease (*līn*) and a preference for his clansmen, became here the link with the ideological Sunnī emphasis on the collectivity of the companions, *sunna* (*ḥadīth*), and the legitimation of the concentrated political authority about to be vested in the third caliphate.

Sunnī Islam (or 'Umar's tendentious view of the new caliph) was certainly not enamored with 'Uthmān, but if the latter's qualifications and reign were to be scrutinized, this risked a problematic discussion of the civil war, and the changing worth of the companion community after the war. And although the literature of *ḥadīth* itself did not rest primarily on the authority of these companions, a lot in Sunnī ideology depended on accepting the companion community as a model of the *jamā'a* and as the individuals who abided by the Prophet's covenants, both in his lifetime and afterward, unlike predecessor communities of the Israelites. Under those circumstances, a defense of 'Uthmān was ultimately a defense of a complex web of Islamic dogma that rested on the attributed authority of 'Āisha, Ibn 'Abbās, Ibn 'Umar, and 'Umar. An inquiry into the succession controversy, in turn, essentially amounted to a questioning of the paradigm of Jamā'ī-Sunnism. When faced with a choice between 'Uthmān and 'Alī, Ṭabarī's narrators could not but choose 'Uthmān. In spite of the latter's political mishaps recounted above (his poor advice to 'Umar on the Persian campaign, his indulgence of governors, and his stubborn ways of rule), 'Uthmān was made to appear as the loyal follower of precedent, not just of the Prophet but more significantly of Abū Bakr and 'Umar.[37] In light of this, there was no question that 'Uthmān would receive the coalescing opinion of the *shūrā* and indeed be recognized as an expected heir apparent for 'Umar long before the *shūrā* even happened.[38] As far back as the year A.H. 14/A.D. 635, when 'Umar first set out on a ruse expedition that preceded the Arab campaign at Qādisiyya, Sayf b. 'Umar refers to 'Uthmān as having been called "*radīf*" for the caliph, a term the narrator explains as meaning "the individual whom the Arabs hope will succeed their leader [*ba'da ra'īsihim*]."[39]

## THE RETURN OF THE UMAYYADS

With the community plunged into civil war and the rule of the Prophet, Abū Bakr, and 'Umar ended, the reader may well imagine that the cycle of Islamic historical narration would conclude with chaos, awaiting perhaps a singular moment of final redemption with the 'Abbāsid revolution in A.D. 750. Far from being the end of the story, however, the civil war brings about the emergence of the Umayyad dynasty as the credible, newly emerged Arab/Islamic power.

The Umayyad emergence was by no means an anomaly in the logic of narrators who welded the master narrative of Islamic history from ancient times to the ninth century. While narrators conceived of the early Rāshidūn period as an era of ideal rule aided by the grace of providence, they appreciated the Umayyads within a more secular frame of valuation that conceived of the rise of the Umayyads as a return of history to its pre-Islamic stream of secular struggle, where political authority is defined by a moralistic dialectic and by the search for leaders who are competent, charismatic, and of elite social lineage. The gradual shift of the caliphate to Mu'āwiya was read as emblematic of this transition back to the Jāhiliyya, where the Banū Abd Shams were politically prominent.

Warnings of a potential historical turn in the life of the community have already been noted in the speeches of 'Umar (*iḥdharū an yudāla 'alaykum—innamā balaghtum mā balaghtum bi 'ahdin*, etc.). The second caliph's words, however, did not say how history would shape up during this transition or who would inherit political authority. It seems to have been left to Mu'āwiya to pick up this theme and elucidate it further, to the advantage of the Umayyad family. This Mu'āwiya does in two crucial narratives that appear to complement one another. The first is his lengthy debate with the Kufan opposition. The second is his blunt address to the companions after he bade farewell to 'Uthmān and set out on the return journey to Syria. On both occasions, Mu'āwiya is used by the narrators not only to confirm the views of 'Umar, but also to articulate a philosophy of history that Ṭabarī and/or his narrators espoused. Of particular importance in Mu'āwiya's words is the juxtaposition of two worlds, those of the Jāhiliyya and of Islam, where Islam represents a utopian-heavenly synthesis, which was once realized in 'Umar's reign but will henceforth become otherworldly and unattainable. He notes that the *umma* was blessed in that utopian phase (from Muḥammad to 'Umar) when it observed its covenants, forsook ambitions, obeyed its rulers, and remained egalitarian.

The danger of historical turn is best summarized in Mu'āwiya's declaration to the companions. There, as we saw, he began by praising them as the ones who once presided over this ideal ("You are the companions of the Messenger of God, the best [of his followers] on earth, and those charged with the affairs of this community. No one other than you can hope for that [*antum aṣḥāb rasūl allāh wa khīratuhu fi'l-arḍ wa wulātu amri hādhihi al-umma lā yaṭma'u fī dhalika aḥadun ghayrukum*]").[40] But he then gives them strongly cautionary words of how this could change if they were to seek to dominate and compete in power. If this happened, he warned, then the traditional, pre-Islamic rhythm of history would return ("But if they pay heed to the things of this world and seek them in a struggle for supremacy with one another, they will be deprived of [power] and God will give it back to those who used to lead them [*wa in aṣghū ilā al-dunyā wa ṭalabūhā bi'l-taghālub sulibū dhalika wa raddahu allāh ilā man kāna yar'isuhum*]").[41]

His words of rebuke to the companions contain a religious admonition as well as a reminder that, on secular terms, his family was more suited to rule before Islam and would become so afterward if the community were to abandon the ethic of equality and mutual support that had lent it divine grace since the time of the Prophet. His words also seem to echo what Hurmuzān said to 'Umar when the two argued as to why the Sasanids were victorious against the Arabs in pre-Islamic times ("In the days before Islam, 'Umar, God left things between us and you as they were, so we had the upper hand over you, since He was neither with us nor with you. But when He took your side, you gained the upper hand over us [*innā wa iyyākum fī al-jāhiliyya kāna allāh qad khallā baynanā wa baynakum fa-ghalabnākum idh lam yakun ma'anā wa lā ma'akum fa-lammā kāna ma'akum ghalabtumūnā*].")[42] Jāhiliyya, in this context, does not refer merely to a state of religious ignorance, but to a secular balance of political society (of Arabs and non-Arabs) in an environment shaped only by secular mores and coercive power. In this environment, leadership is invested in those competent to hold it and of elite lineage (*akramahum aḥsāban wa amḥaḍahum ansāban*), and who have the virtues associated with their noble rank (*wa akmalahum murū'atan*).[43]

In his other speech to the Kufans, Mu'āwiya extols the merits of the tribe of Quraysh as a divinely selected and preserved tribe that had existed since pre-Islamic times, and he becomes more specific in praising his father, Abū Sufyān, as the most noble of the Quraysh. He digresses only briefly to pay respects to the Prophet's excellence as a case of divine exception (*intikhāb*) connected to the religious mission and gift of prophecy. Mu'āwiya defines authority in terms of class, honor, and moral responsibility, attributes the Kufan challengers lack, then caps his pro-Umayyad speech by rationalizing a religious endorsement of his rule.[44]

As he argues with the Kufans, Mu'āwiya uses the term "*imāma*" to refer to political authority, and characterizes his rule, and that of the Sufyanids more generally, as taking charge of the role of the *imāms*. But what Mu'āwiya means in this usage goes beyond the Sunnī religious sense of "*imām*" as a prayer leader to encompass a more secular and universalist meaning that perhaps stood closer in meaning to the ancient Persian conception of the monarch as a divinely blessed ruler.[45] Mu'āwiya was speaking more of the hierarchical order when he spoke of the "*a'imma*," even as his words may have intersected with the polemical *ḥadīth* conceptions of the *imām*'s importance.[46] This deliberate double use of the term *imām* was not the only example of a term in Mu'āwiya's polemic harboring a double meaning, one that is generic and linguistic, and another that is politically authoritarian.[47]

The emphasis on class in Mu'āwiya's political definitions surfaces in another way when he denounces the social background of his opponents, particularly that of Ṣa'ṣa'a b. Ṣuḥān, and their lack of purpose in challenging the governor of Kufa. This attack was perhaps meant to run parallel to his other criticisms of the companions, such as when he warned them before his return to Damascus of what might happen if they overthrew 'Uthmān. Although Mu'āwiya's words there are not as scathing as those he gives to Ṣa'ṣa'a (that his village was the most wretched, etc.), he makes his point clearly enough when he tells the companions that none of them were leaders before Islam (*fa-lam yakun minkum aḥadun illā wa fī faṣīlatihi man yar'isuhu wa yastabiddu 'alayhi wa yaqṭa' al-amr dūnahu wa lā yushhiduhu wa lā yu'āmirahu ḥattā ba'tha allāh jalla wa 'az nabiyyahu*).[48] The notions that various tribes are headed by natural leaders and that the Islamic community inherited the same pattern of leadership seems clear from Mu'āwiya's language. His speeches to the Kufans and to the Medinans were meant to intersect at several points and eventually to allow the reader to take a conclusion from one, apply it to the other, and then build on it with the words of 'Uthmān.[49] In the declarations of both Mu'āwiya and 'Uthmān there is an emphasis on the need for leadership, which is juxtaposed with the alternative of chaos (*fitna*). Challenging leadership as thoroughly as the opponents of 'Uthmān did is viewed by Ṭabarī's narrators as leading to the downfall of nations. As 'Uthmān commented in his warnings to the opposition, "You will never find a community [*umma*] that has been destroyed except after it has fallen into discord. [Such a community can be saved] only if it has a head who can unite it. If ever you do that, you will not perform the prayer together, your enemy will be given power over you, and you will disagree as to what is lawful or forbidden [*fa-innakum lam tajidū ummatan halakat illā min ba'di an takhtalifa illā an yakūna lahā ra'sun yajma'uhā wa matā taf'alū dhalika lā tuqīmū al-ṣalāta jamī'an wa sulliṭa 'alaykum 'aduwwukum wa yastaḥillu ba'ḍukum ḥurama ba'ḍin . . . wa takūnū shiya'an*]."[50]

What differentiated 'Uthmān and Mu'āwiya was not the adamant stress on preserving central rule, but the methods they used in dealing with the opposition. Unlike Mu'āwiya, 'Uthmān was willing to debate with the opposition at greater length and with more patience, and he was hesitant to use force even when it was recommended by his advisors. At the famous general gathering in Medina of 'Uthmān's governors on the heels of complaints cast by the Kufans against their governor, 'Uthmān listened patiently to all the proposed views, in the sober manner characteristic of al-Ma'mūn at a similar later assembly before the outbreak of war with his brother in A.D. 194/A.D. 810.[51] After 'Uthmān's governors advised strong action against the dissidents, Mu'āwiya recommended to the caliph that he listen to their advice, since they knew the situation in their provinces best. He then boasted that Syria was a model of a stable community, and said that this was a result of his capable rule and/or the virtue of the people of that province (this is left ambiguous). "You have made me a governor over a people," Mu'āwiya said, "about whom you hear nothing but good [*qad wallaytanī fa-wullītu qawman lā ya'tīka 'anhum illā al-khayr*]."[52] He then added, "These two men [Sa'īd b. al-'Āṣ of Kufa and 'Abdallāh b. Sa'd of Egypt] know best about their own districts [*wa al-rajulān a'lam bi-nāḥiyatihimā*]."[53] When asked what he thought was the wise strategy or sound opinion in handling the situation (*fa-mā al-ra'y?*), Mu'āwiya said the caliph should use some toughness in dealing with opponents: "stern discipline" (*ḥusn al-adab*), his code for repression.[54] This 'Uthmān refused to do. His refusal in this context was not grounded in weakness (although this is certainly a layer of reading for the text that puts it in a continuous line with his pattern of interaction with 'Alī and Marwān later on), but rather was a choice made in light of his pious apprehension of causing bloodshed. The significance of the text then turns from being an analytic political counsel to a description of a predestined issue when 'Uthmān declares in resignation, "What we fear might happen to the umma shall indeed come to pass, but the way to hold things back is through leniency, generous treatment, and the gratification [of desires], except if the matter relates to the commandments of God [*al-līn wa'l-mu'ātāt wa'l-mutāba'a illā fī ḥudūd allāh*]. . . . Restrain the people, bestow their rights upon them, and forgive them [*kafkifū al-nās wa ightafirū lahum*]."[55] He had opted to become a Jesus-like victim of an irreconcilable opposition.

In a comparison of Mu'āwiya's and 'Uthmān's viewpoints on the crisis and the consequences of 'Uthmān's pious stance, Ṭabarī's accounts of subsequent events seem clearly intended to show the series of dilemmas that were bound to face the community as a result of the opposition 'Uthmān confronted, the kind of ruler he was, and the clash between secular and religious methods being discussed by the caliph and his governors. In an important sense, it was 'Uthmān's lenient policies that led to the caliph's victimization and the spread of chaos, which thus raised the question of whether 'Uthmān's conciliatory religious approach ought to be replaced by a more authoritarian government that would be more effective in establishing public order and stability. On this political level, Ṭabarī's accounts succeed one another with a clear secularist escalation. The religious 'Uthmān gives way to the more savvy Mu'āwiya, and the lenient government of al-Mughīra in Mu'āwiya's time will in turn give way to the tougher policies of Ziyād b. Abīhi. Everything is strung together in Ṭabarī's narratives to favor the priority of political order as the crucial condition for the religious well-being of the *jamā'a*.

During the *fitna* Mu'āwiya's discourse is closely tied in with 'Uthmān's on this level, but they both find a political ancestor in the discourse of 'Umar and his exhortations for obedience to authority. That 'Umar also held the caliphs accountable for their own actions was crucial—as was the recognition that 'Uthmān's varied innovations provoked much of the resentment against him—but such counterarguments were something that the narratives suspended when other lines of meaning were held as more prominent. It was now not the egalitarian quality of 'Umar's government that the later narratives sought to evoke, but the second caliph's *hayba* (charisma), his all-encompassing definition of the caliphate (*sulṭān allāh*, the hegemone of God) as a binding moral institution, and his emphasis on the subjects' duty for obedience.[56] The stern language of 'Umar's speeches, which was meant to herald the religious triumph over the Sasanids and provide warnings about changes to the lifestyle of faith, gradually provides a model of pure political control as similar phrases, exhortations, and commanding language are used by Umayyad leaders to establish their rule.

Such parallels of borrowing in Umayyad times sometimes appear in Mu'āwiya's wise and somber sayings, in speeches that seem to echo the wisdom of 'Umar. But the most uncanny resemblance occurs in offspring speeches by commanders such as al-Mughīra b. Shu'ba and Ziyād b. Abīhi. Without attribution, some declarations of these commanders could easily be mistaken for the assertions of 'Umar.[57] The texts show a similarity in their charismatic presence, firm and quick assertions, and varied tones of reflection on past experience and what methods of government work best with the public. Different styles of governing and toughness are meant to be a response to threats to caliphal rule, but indirectly they are also justified as ways of managing the security of the community. The chain of Sasanid political logic is Arabized by the Umayyads, although their rule is never quite Islamized, except in the broadest respect to broad principles and the claim of continuity with the early Medinan caliphate. Al-Mughīra, the more lenient of the two commanders, showed his skill in forestalling a Khārijite revolt in A.H. 42/A.D. 662. Despite his assertiveness, however, al-Mughīra remained a patient governor, made wiser by years of interaction with different leaders and the shifting tide of Qurashī rivalry.

But as times changed—and the chronicles portray Kufa and Basra as having become zones of chaos and depredation, not just because of zealots but also brigands and gangs—the narratives seem to prepare the way for the arrival of greater authority with Ziyād b. Abīhi. With various threats meant to intimidate the established government and openly contentious issues about the previous *fitnas*, Ziyād would take his approach of emulating 'Umar to a very menacing extent in the thundering speech he gave upon his assumption of the governorship of Basra in A.H. 45/A.D. 665. The irony of this transition toward a path of authority lies not only in the way narrators crafted later speeches that evoked parallels with the past, but also in how they sometimes showed 'Umar himself as having expected the transition to happen, making him anticipate the trend toward despotism, albeit in purely parabolic terms.[58] The same issues of how to establish public order and community loyalty concerned personalities as varied as 'Umar, 'Uthmān, Mu'āwiya, al-Mughīra, and Ziyād, yet the response constantly brought an increase, not a lessening, in political authoritarianism in the transition from Rāshidūn to Umayyad rule.[59]

## MU'ĀWIYA B. ABĪ SUFYĀN: THE FIFTH OF THE RĀSHIDŪN?

That the Umayyads were praised by the Sunnī narrators can indeed seem odd, given that their rule is recognized in traditional histories as that of "kings" and given the Umayyad clashes with various religious oppositions over the years. Mu'āwiya in particular could be faulted the most, since he challenged 'Alī's caliphate, used all manners of conspiracy to further his control, and left the community with his designated successor, Yazīd, who ruined any chances for reconciliation after the civil war. The image of the Umayyad dynasty, however, rests on various considerations in the texts, many of which were not meant to be negative. Although the Umayyads did act in a clan-centered manner, introduced the principle of a double succession, and levied excessive taxes on occasion, they were also viewed as possessing tribal virtues that made them worthy to rule even if they were secular. The qualities of *muruwwa*, *najda*, *ḥilm*, and *'aql* (chivalry, bravery, patience, and common sense) that they brought to the caliphate offered the best that pre-Islamic Arabian society could offer, and these attributes would be represented so often as the forte of the Sufyanids that in a way they handed them down in their family as a *waṣiyya* (testament of advice), in a way strong enough to rival the gnostic testaments that the 'Abbāsid *imāms* handed down in their own family.[60] And in spite of the Umayyad disinterest in collaborating with *ḥadīth* and other religious scholars, their rule was generally viewed in later times as more beneficial in material terms than even that of their successors, the 'Abbāsids.[61] Mu'āwiya represented the epitome of the munificent Umayyad whose generosity and tolerance toward allies and rivals made him seem to be the last of the tribal shaykhs.

That Mu'āwiya represented an admirable example of an Arabian "king" can easily be appreciated from these qualities. However, it may be possible even to argue that in the way they depicted Mu'āwiya, Ṭabarī's narrators also intended to portray him as the last of the Rāshidūn caliphs. Admittedly, the term "Rāshidūn" has a strong polemical Sunnī sense, which religious scholars devised to suggest a harmony among the first four caliphs as individuals of equal virtue. The term was also intended to refer, however tenuously, to the existence during this time of a cohesive *jamā'a*—a community with a consensus—which the caliphs were eager to preserve. It is in the context of this latter feature particularly that the historian can actually link Mu'āwiya's approach to political action during the civil war with the Rāshidūn. For, much as 'Alī asserted his authority on the basis of community support, Mu'āwiya also laid a similar claim to leadership on the basis of *jamā'ī* support,[62] and spent much of his political career adapting his authoritarian claim to the frame of the community's interest, negotiating this on the basis of a set of secular virtues.

These merits were of course enhanced by the fact that Mu'āwiya was a companion of the Prophet. It was well known that the Sufyānids had converted late, and that Mu'āwiya did not have as illustrious a religious past as Abū Bakr or 'Umar, but Mu'āwiya was viewed as having other attributes that made his family close to that of the Prophet. Mu'āwiya's sister was married to the Prophet, which put him on a footing to rival Abū Bakr and 'Umar,[63] and *ḥadīth* literature would later exaggerate Mu'āwiya's role as a companion to the Prophet, calling him "*kātib al-waḥy*" (scribe of revelation), and in fact claimed that the Prophet had predicted his rule. (Much of this dates to ninth-century Ḥanbalī propaganda.[64]) Also strengthening his early Sunnī credentials for later generations was the fact that he had served the second caliph as governor of Syria, where he succeeded his brother Yazīd after the latter died in A.H. 17/A.D. 638; Mu'āwiya was allowed to remain in that office even as the caliph shuffled and dismissed governors in the southern Iraqi towns.[65]

It was the association of his name with the caliphate of 'Umar that greatly enhanced Mu'āwiya's political image in the *jamā'ī* view. This is evident from the very beginning, in arguments with the Kufan opposition in A.H. 33/A.D. 653, when Mu'āwiya prepared the public for his leadership. Al-Wāqidī's version of the context of Mu'āwiya's declaration begins with a brief exchange in which a member of the opposition delegation asserts, "We command you to resign your office ['*amal*], for among the Muslims there is one who has better right to it than you." When Mu'āwiya asked, "Who is that?" Ṣa'ṣa'a b. Ṣūḥān replied, "Someone whose father had a higher standing in Islam than yours, and who himself has a higher standing than you." Here the delegation was clearly referring to the office of the caliphate, rather than mere provincial administration, when they were asking Mu'āwiya to step aside. Ṭabarī's narrator was reifying the rivalry and debate between ‘Alī and Mu‘āwiya four years before its time, turning it into a subplot of this debate between a governor and his opposition. Mu‘āwiya’s assertion of political self-legitimation then comes across strongly in the next part of the exchange, when he declares,

> “By God, I have some standing in Islam. There were others whose standing surpassed mine, *but in my time* there is no one better able to do my job than I [*laysa fī zamānī aḥadun aqwā ‘alā mā anā fīhi minnī*].[66] ‘Umar b. al-Khaṭṭāb was of this opinion, and had there been a man more capable than I, ‘Umar would not have been indulgent in regard to me or anyone else [*fa-law kāna ghayrī aqwā minnī lam yakun lī ‘inda ‘Umar hawāda wa lā li-ghayrī*]. Nor have I instituted any innovation that would require me to resign my office. Had the Commander of the Faithful and of the Community of Muslims thought so,[67] he would have written to me.”[68]

The language Mu‘āwiya uses throughout is one of loyalty to the caliph and service to the *jamā‘a*. ‘Umar’s appointment of Mu‘āwiya to Syria’s governorship had an almost irrevocable quality in the absence of a flagrant transgression. So for ‘Alī to have sought to dismiss Mu‘āwiya from office, even before the latter opposed him on the grounds of avenging ‘Uthmān, appeared in Sunnī valuation as a symbolically impertinent action, however altruistic it may have been in motive. By the same token, Mu‘āwiya’s resistance to ‘Alī seemed in this context more understandable, since he was appointed by ‘Umar and was posing legitimate questions (about bringing ‘Uthmān’s assassins to justice) to a caliph whose involvement in the event was dubious and whose political wisdom was questionable. With such a networking of past and present discourses, narrators could negotiate a greater level of authority for Mu‘āwiya’s rule in Syria, framing it as a remnant unit of Rāshidūn rule capable of ruling the entire caliphate.[69] As such, Mu‘āwiya was not the first of the Umayyads, but the last restorer of political order in the early Islamic state.

From this perspective, Mu‘āwiya’s election is judged not in light of the freak result of the Taḥkīm, but as an effort to repatch the community, which is reflected in the way chroniclers generally referred to Mu‘āwiya’s final accession to the caliphate in A.H. 41 as “the year of the consensus” (*‘ām al-jamā‘a*). Through this action, and due to his association with the times of the Prophet and the first two caliphs, Mu‘āwiya’s reputation gains merit.[70] Ṭabarī's chronicle confirms this impression when he devotes more attention to praiseful anecdotes about Mu'āwiya's qualities and capability to rule than to 'Alī, who gets but a slim two pages.[71] And here, as in the aforementioned speech by Mu'āwiya, the reader can note the high proportion of anecdotes attributed to 'Umar in which he makes favorable comments about Mu'āwiya. In all of these 'Umar admires Mu'āwiya on political and moral grounds, not religious ones. One such anecdote, describing an encounter between Mu'āwiya and 'Umar when the caliph came to examine the province, deserves a full description for its allusive implications.

Ṭabarī relates that when the caliph arrived with his advisor, 'Abd al-Raḥmān b. 'Awf, both were riding donkeys. Mu'āwiya, who had set out in a lavish parade of cavalrymen to meet them, seems to have passed them on the road, not knowing who they were, until he was alerted that these were probably the visitors. When he returned to them, Mu'āwiya dismounted and walked beside 'Umar for some distance as the caliph ignored him. 'Abd al-Raḥmān b. 'Awf then said to 'Umar, "You have tired the man!" 'Umar turned to Mu'āwiya and declared, "O Mu'āwiya, you head such retinues, while petitioners, I heard, are standing at your door." Mu'āwiya replied, "Yes, O Commander of the Faithful." "Why is that?" 'Umar asked. Mu'āwiya replied, "Because we are in a land which is infiltrated by the spies of the enemy, and there is a need that they be awed by the majesty of Islamic rule [*fa-lā budda lahum min haybat al-sulṭān*]. If you command me to remain in this manner, I will do so, and if you command me to change ways, I will also do it." 'Umar then answered, "If this is true, then yours is the wise judgment of an intelligent man [*ra'yu labīb*], and if it is untrue, then it is the savvy deception of the sophisticated man [*khid'atu adīb*]. [I never debated you in anything and found myself anything but puzzled.] I shall neither command you, nor forbid you to do this."[72]

At first the dialogue between the caliph and his governor seems to form the primary point of the anecdote, as it shows the wit and political tact of Mu'āwiya in handling both the affairs of his province and the criticism of his suzerain. While it achieves a literary purpose, however, the anecdote also opens a broader dialogue regarding political methods between a ruler from one era (the Rāshidūn) and a ruler from another (the Umayyad). Mu'āwiya is not here disparaged as an arbitrary autocrat, as the stereotype of the Umayyads generally goes, but as a ruler adjusting to the conditions of a province adjoining the Byzantine empire that required a different style of rule. Still, even as he is allowed such an exception for political behavior, Mu'āwiya is portrayed as the loyal official willing to bend to the commands of the arch symbol of Sunnism. Taking all of this into account, 'Umar in the end opts to let Mu'āwiya remain in his established condition, it is implied, because he either admires his skillful answers, believes that there is a danger in the continuing rivalry with the Byzantines, or simply finds in Mu'āwiya the new way of the future and its needed rulers. A greater political legitimacy is thus bestowed on Mu'āwiya as someone who is semi-autonomous in forming judgments, and he is allowed this new status less on the basis of his lineage or companionship than on his discernable qualities of statecraft. Mu'āwiya in essence becomes a successful Arab counterpart for Khusraw or Caesar, in the words of 'Umar, much as circumstances once demanded that the Arabs put forward 'Amr b. al-'Āṣ to match the military guile of al-Arṭabūn.[73]

Narrators clearly saw in Mu'āwiya a worthy successor of 'Umar and commander of the *jamā'a*. The unusual praise that 'Umar bestowed on Mu'āwiya finds no parallel in the evaluations of any of the other governors or even the senior companions, whom 'Umar directly considered for caliphal succession (as is evident in the discussion between 'Umar and Ibn 'Abbās on this topic).[74] However more practical was 'Umar's leadership than that of 'Alī, it was clear that narrators saw Mu'āwiya's political style as even more realistic. Narrators who compared 'Umar and Mu'āwiya found the latter to have better political skills for the *jamā'a*, and showed their distance from the ultra-asceticism of 'Umar.[75]

The medieval narrators recognized that leaderships need to adjust differently as people change with changing times.[76] This undoubtedly created a deficit of piety for later caliphs, who compared themselves with the earlier times of the Rāshidūn but could do little to make the religious and political welfare of the community remain in harmony. Mu'āwiya was the first caliph to note this, when he compared himself with the Rāshidūn and found himself falling short. This happened on one occasion when he was examining conditions in Syria. As he journeyed back to Damascus, and just before he entered the city, he ordered a stop for rest. The narrator then describes:

> Carpets were laid out for the caliph on a summit location overlooking the road, and he sat down and gave me permission to sit with him.

> [Soon] the caravans were passing by, as were the loaded baggage trains, camels of transport, and the horses. He then reflected and said to me, "O Ibn Mas'ada, may God have mercy on Abū Bakr. He did not seek this world, nor did it want him. As for 'Umar," or he may have said "Ibn Ḥantama" [the Sufyanid pejorative nickname of 'Umar], "the world sought him but he turned away from it. And then came 'Uthmān, who chose to take things from this world, and it took its share from him. And then we wallowed in this world [*wa ammā naḥnu fa-tamarraghnā fīhā*]." But as if he then felt regret [*thumma ka'annahu nadim*], the narrator says, he added, "[By God], it is only kingship that God seems to have bestowed on us [*innahu la-mulkun ātānā allāh iyyāh*]."[77]

Ṭabarī's account of Mu'āwiya's context for this statement is a classic Sunnī political anecdote of the ninth century, which looked back on certain periods of political stability before the onset of conflict as exemplary times for the *jamā'a*, the most prominent of these being the reigns of 'Umar b. al-Khaṭṭāb, Mu'āwiya b. Abī Sufyān, and Hārūn al-Rashīd. Since the latter caliph was contemporaneous with and may have interacted with the famous ascetic 'Abdallāh b. al-Mubārak, Ibn al-Mubārak was chosen in these anecdotes to recount such edifying stories about the caliphs.[78] In descriptive terms, the story bears two aspects of linkage. The first is with the Sīra, specifically the scene of the conquest of Mecca when Abū Sufyān is described as sitting with al-'Abbās, also at a vantage point, surveying the marching troops of the Prophet as they passed on a road symbolizing the establishment of the Islamic state. What Abū Sufyān had once admired as the rise of the prophet's "kingship" in his famous observation to al-'Abbās—"The dominion of your nephew has indeed become great [*laqad aṣbaḥa mulku ibni akhīka 'aẓīman*]"—now becomes the dominion of Mu'āwiya as the latter surveys the riches of the world passing by his throne in Damascus. The second probable link relates to the above-described scene of 'Umar's encounter with Mu'āwiya in Syria. Mu'āwiya expresses his reflective sentiments as he is about to reenter Damascus, just where 'Umar did the same; and in contrast to his sure comments to the second caliph at the time, Mu'āwiya speaks with some regret, as if this time finally accepting the caliph's criticisms.

The message of religious reflection is woven via artful displacement and restoration in the main actors' positions ('Umar and Mu'āwiya). In the latter story, however, Mu'āwiya's reflection goes beyond commenting on the differences in the ways of the early caliphs, to encompass some doubt about how the succession had ended and was yet to go. The narrator seems to imply that after the tumultuous events leading to Mu‘āwiya’s accession—circumstances that were undoubtedly acknowledged to be an error (a final *falta*, perhaps)—there needed to come a phase of stability when authority would not be questioned again. Mu‘āwiya gets the advantage from this, with the narrator implying that he was predestined to rule (*innahu la-mulkun ātānā allāh iyyāh*), and the community is implicitly exhorted to accept a stable political regime to serve as a foundation to its more important pursuits: maintaining the unity of the *jamā‘a* and observing religious rituals. Any nostalgia for the times of the Rāshidūn, especially for the open government of the second caliph, is rejected as no longer suitable.[79]

‘Abd al-Malik b. Marwān would go farther than Mu‘āwiya, who did no more than acknowledge the difference in his rule from that of the Rāshidūn, by banning the pious publicizing of stories about the Rāshidūn, especially about the caliph ‘Umar. The continued recounting of such historical lore (*al-maghāzī wa’l-siyar*), he asserted, was often meant to be insulting to current rulers, and emboldened subjects to challenge those in authority.[80] In another famous remark (sometimes included in a speech he reportedly gave after the pilgrimage in A.H. 75/A.D. 694), ‘Abd al-Malik confirmed this theme when he addressed the people of Medina, saying, “A lot of unrecognizable lore has been coming to us from the east [*wa qad sālat ‘alaynā aḥādīth min qibal al-mashriq lā na‘rifuhā*], but I command you to adhere to what is in the Qur’ān that ‘Uthmān [referred to as “*al-imām al-maẓlūm*”] compiled for you, and to your religious obligations [*‘alaykum bi’l-farā’iḍ*].”[81] He also declared, “We shall tolerate anything from you except leading an insurrection or starting a religious war [*‘aqdu rāya aw wuthūb ‘alā minbar*].”[82]

The Islamic state makes a decisive turn toward kingship in Mu‘āwiya’s reign, and Islamic tradition seems to accommodate this within a new conception of predestiny. The concept of the divine selection of rulers is disconnected from any pious competition among traditional contenders for the caliphate among the Quraysh; the caliphate is viewed by later thinkers as simply the gift of inscrutable providence. This was the message enshrined in the Qur’ānic verse that reads: “Say: ‘O God, Master of the Kingdom, Thou givest the Kingdom to whom Thou wilt, and seizest the Kingdom from whom Thou wilt, Thou exaltest whom Thou wilt, and

Thou abasest whom Thou wilt; in Thy hand is the good; Thou art powerful over everything.' "[83] This verse raises the question of dynastic transitions above the national or tribal levels, placing it more within a cosmology that includes a broader and parallel pattern of astronomical transition, and this is confirmed in the sequentiality of the next statement, which dwells on the cycles of the day and the night: " 'Thou makest the night to enter into the day and Thou makest the day to enter into the night. . . . Thou providest whomsoever Thou wilt without reckoning.' "

The medieval chroniclers never invoke this verse in the historiography of the civil war as a means for legitimizing the rise of the Umayyads, relying instead on *ḥadīth* and on sayings from the companions. The reader was expected to accept the Umayyad state as the fulfillment of a *ḥadīth* attributed to the Prophet in which he states, "[The Islamic state] shall start with prophecy, then turn into a caliphate, and then become a kingship."[84] And although this was not a flattering assessment of the kind of government that was emerging at the third stage, *ḥadīth* and legal texts discourage Muslims from challenging this authority, since such questioning was construed as a challenge to the unfolding will of God. Thus, when someone expresses a mere exasperation to 'Āisha that Mu'āwiya had become caliph, she voices a rebuke clearly meant as a corrective to her previous rebellious actions during her war with 'Alī: "It is the kingdom [or rule] of God [*sulṭān allāh*]. He grants it to whomsoever He wills."[85] Islamic political tradition would also frequently cite the Qur'ānic verse that exhorted believers to obey rulers ("obey God, obey the Messenger, and those in authority among you"),[86] to discourage them from rebelling against a Muslim ruler.[87]

The understanding of the Qur'ānic reference to "*sulṭān allāh*" now took on a different sense of political rule from the more humble category of "*imāra*" (command), although the two terms converged in their basic reference to the idea of political leadership. The term *imāra* seems to have preserved the idyllic image of early caliphal rule, with both all its openness to consultation and its demonstrations of the limitations of puritanical religious practice.[88] However, the concept of *sulṭān* (authority) became something nebulous and was allowed to slide in connotation to encompass a government based on coercive power that was less accountable to the dictates of religion. Mu'āwiya remained cautious about the introduction of this new system of rule, but a later caliph such as 'Abd al-Malik is represented in the sources as nothing but a dictator who honored no religious advice.

The Rāshidūn caliphate and the time of 'Abd al-Malik can easily be seen as belonging to different periods and thus as having no connection, but this was not how Ṭabarī's narrators perceived matters. The emergence of the despotic regime of 'Abd al-Malik was viewed as the final phase in the cycle of seditious wars that had plagued the community since the times of 'Uthmān. The catharsis for 'Uthmān's overthrow comes when 'Abd al-Malik's governor in Kufa, al-Ḥajjāj b. Yūsuf, questions the companions in A.H. 74/A.D. 694 about why they neglected 'Uthmān during his time of need,[89] and it is also evident in his punishing those who allegedly took part in the abuse of the caliph.[90] 'Abd al-Malik is represented in this context as having compared his method of rule to those of his predecessors, particularly 'Uthmān, Mu'āwiya, and Yazīd, and stressing the difference—or corrective, from his perspective—of his policy in relation to the methods of predecessors.[91]

Piety and politics were clearly very different matters in the early Umayyad period. Contrary to the orthodox portrayals of Mu'āwiya, the Umayyads were not actively seeking to rally the *jamā'a* to their side, although they eventually acquired this image through an 'Abbāsid back-projection on history.[92] Indeed, what is remarkable in this context about the emergence of Islam in Arabia is not that it overthrew the traditional social elite of Mecca, which may have happened temporarily during the lifetime of the Prophet, but that it brought them together against it. This is reflected in the way the first caliphs, Abū Bakr and 'Umar, found themselves obliged to rely on Sufyanid commanders in Syria, but it is even more evident in the coalescence of disparate branches of the wider clan of the Banū 'Abd Shams during the caliphate of 'Uthmān and afterward. When they in turn acceded to power, the Umayyads became a magnet for Arab tribesmen (Muslim and Christian) who found the Hāshimite or Medinan-led religion to be too messianic. The dynasty itself kept its distance from the full picture of the religion of the Ḥijāz, with all its details of ritual and its redefinitions of the ethical and social worldview.

Islam for the Umayyads was an important tool for imperial development, but they used it only on the level of symbolism—such as in the building of the great mosque of Damascus, the mosque of the Prophet in Medina, and the Dome of the Rock—or as a grand gesture of conquest (against Constantinople and on other frontiers). The reality of their interest in the faith seems to have been superficial—as superficial, perhaps, as was Constantine's adoption of Christianity as the official faith of the Roman empire in the fourth century A.D. This is reflected not only in the absence of a clear involvement by the dynasty in the shaping of the texts of Islamic lore and doctrine (as is strongly the case for the 'Abbāsids), but also in their caution about venturing much beyond Syria to nurture Islam in the Ḥijāz, something that later caliphs such as al-Manṣūr, al-Mahdī, and al-Rashīd did. In spite of their roots in the Ḥijāz, the Umayyads conducted all their propaganda locally, in Syria. Mu'āwiya chose to receive his *bay'a* in Jerusalem after the abdication of al-Ḥasan in A.H. 41/A.D. 661, and 'Abd al-Malik set out to build the Dome of the Rock as the dynasty's own symbol of connection to the new faith and temporarily as an alternative site for pilgrimage during the time 'Abdallāh b. al-Zubayr was in control of the Ḥijāz.[93] When he finally added the profession of faith to the first fully Arabic type of the Islamic dinar, 'Abd al-Malik was not starting something new with this religious message, but rather showing a final Umayyad recognition of the need to harness the force of religious propaganda in the war against pietistic and messianic opposition within the caliphate, and in preparation to raise the threshhold of challenge to the Byzantine empire in subsequent years.[94]

The transition from the Rāshidūn to the Umayyads changed not only the caliphal institution but also the methods of political control and centralization. With the Umayyads, a host of issues that had been religiously contested throughout the Rāshidūn caliphate were established as integral to their rule. The caliph's controversial reliance on his kin in government service and its corollary of introducing hereditary rule were continued from 'Uthmān's time by the Umayyads. The assertion of caliphal privilege in taking a share of land revenues, which was contested when 'Uthmān established agrarian reserves and made some feudalistic bequests, was an economic practice continued by Mu'āwiya.[95] And finally, the brute assertion of political power, which previous contenders were hesitant to make and debated extensively in polemics (such as in the Khārijite challenge to 'Alī as to why he would not take the booty of those whom he fought), becomes a central feature of Umayyad political hegemony.

## SYRIA: THE BASE OF THE ISLAMIC EMPIRE

Just as the cycle of Rāshidūn history culminates in Islamic historiography with the establishment of Umayyad rule, Syria comes to be viewed as the seat of the caliphate in territorial terms. Statements of praise for Syria abound in the sources, and can reflect in certain contexts a central theme for the Islamic chronicles. Goldziher once argued that this current of praise was promoted by partisans of the Umayyad family during the time of the dynasty or was simply an expression of local patriotism.[96] This view, however, must be revised to consider the possibility that this praise came from 'Abbāsid narrators during the ninth century when an ascendant Sunnism was asserting itself. The favorable current toward the province was in the first instance an assertion against a Hāshimite sympathy that was increasingly shifting its loyalty from the 'Abbāsid family to the more sectarian devotion of Shī'īsm and to the 'Alid family.

But on a second and equally crucial level, this Sunnī assertiveness reflected a ferment of dispute within the methods of Sunnī doctrine itself, where the faction that favored reliance on *ḥadīth* (*ahl al-ḥadīth*) was contesting the use of *ra'y* (reasoned speculation) as a credible method of orthodox juridical practice. This traditionist approach to *ḥadīth* had been on the rise since the late eighth century. It represented in part the followers of the Medinan school of Mālik b. Anas, but it also embodied an 'Abbāsid caliphal interest that constructed a master narrative about early Islam that reconciled the privilege of the 'Abbāsid name in Islam's early history with other traditionalist formulations of *ḥadīth* and lore that centered on such figures as 'Āisha and 'Abdallāh b. 'Umar. It was in part within this process of synthesis and back-projection that the 'Abbāsids also allowed the invention or embellishment of stories about the formation of an early Syrian *ḥadīth*, current during the reign of 'Abd al-Malik, that centered on such figures as Ibn Shihāb al-Zuhrī, Sa'īd b. al-Musayyib, Ibn Jurayj, and al-Sha'bī.[97] In the ferment of competition in Iraq during this time between the followers of Abū Ḥanīfa and those of Mālik b. Anas, there was probably a Shu'ūbī dimension to the growing rivalry as well. Thus, the *ra'y* crowd was taunted by the *ahl al-ḥadīth* for not knowing the Arabic language well enough, which caused them to fail to keep up with the corpus of *ḥadīth*, and the *ahl al-ra'y* took pride in the logical acumen of Abū Ḥanīfa in solving juridical dilemmas.[98] It was in such an environment of juridical polarization, with both currents sponsored by the 'Abbāsids until the time of Hārūn al-Rashīd, that the *ḥadīth* current was imbued with an Arabist identity and became increasingly pro-Ḥijāzī and pro-Syrian in the face of a host of challengers, from the followers of *ra'y* to those of Shī'īsm and the Mu'tazila.

The synchrony of and frequent interaction between religious dicta and the historical narrative of the early Islamic state, as has been examined in this study, thus give a final shaping to the role of Syria in light of religious expectations of the ninth century. In various sundry statements in *ḥadīth*s, Syria is usually referred to as the land of those who are religiously steadfast, the region that harbors the so-called *al-abdāl*, a group of forty sages who are divinely ordained to guide the faithful of their land and shield it from catastrophe.[99] Other *ḥadīth*s count Damascus as one of the heavenly cities,[100] and numerous other *ḥadīth*s dwell on the merits of the mosque of Damascus and the blessedness of the region as the place of the initial nurture of Jesus and his eventual second coming.[101]

The historical narratives of Ṭabarī and other sources for the early caliphate do not invoke these sayings of religious praise. The chroniclers, as usual, focus more on a seemingly feasible political narrative and on nonmythical stories. However, here too one finds an undercurrent of favorable depiction of the Syrian-based community of the faithful. We have already seen how, in describing the first signs of dissent in 'Uthmān's time, Ṭabarī made the propaganda of Ibn Saba' seem successful in various regions, including Egypt, Iraq, and Ḥijāz, although failing to gain any support in Syria. The event showed that Syria, in that context, was the keeper of the Sunnī mission, even as sectarian fragmentation took over in other provinces.

However, it is likely that several other segments of Ṭabarī's chronicle that describe matters relating to Syria were meant in origin to be allusive and to explain, for instance, the attention of the Rāshidūn caliphs to that province. The Prophet's directing the first army of Islamic conquest toward Syria—and the determination of Abū Bakr to keep this campaign on track no matter how badly the troops of Usāma b. Zayd were needed in Medina, for example—probably reflected the narrators' intent to link up Syria with the Medinan state as soon as possible. Usama's campaign, although less significant than the bigger expeditions sent out later in 'Umar's time, is described with great fanfare in Abū Bakr's time as the fulfillment of the Prophet's wish. Important speeches and dialogues are assigned to key personalities during its departure in disproportion to the modest conquest it was expected to accomplish. The reason for this was mainly symbolic, because in hindsight the acquisition of Syria would come to be perceived as an early step toward the formation of a Jamāʿī Islamic state (characterized as well by an inflexibility in dealing with the Ridda factions).

However, even before the Sunnī orthodoxy of the ninth century redirected the interest in Syria to a polemical purpose, this theme had a parabolic role in the original drift of Islamic historical composition as well. We have already seen how Kaʿb al-Aḥbār predicted to Muʿāwiya that he would assume the caliphate during the civil war contestations, and that Kaʿb played a significant role in the mythology of ʿUmar's biography as the paradigm of the just and triumphant king. In tracing the Syrian theme in Islamic historiography, it can be said that ʿUmar's conquest of Jerusalem formed only a part of the overall Syrian direction of the Arab caliphate. Aside from his fame for hailing ʿUmar as the redeemer of Jerusalem, Kaʿb is also famous for traditions in which he hails Muḥammad as an expected prophet who would emerge in Mecca and find his kingdom established in Syria. The full text of this tradition has Kaʿb declare, "I find it written in the Torah: ʿAḥmad [a related name to Muḥammad] is my chosen servant [*ʿabdī al-mukhtār*]. He is neither aggressive, nor rough, nor loud in the marketplace. He does not repay a bad action with a bad action, but forgives. His birthplace is in Mecca, his migration is to Medina [Ṭāba], and his kingdom will be in Syria [*wa mulkuhu biʾl-shām*].ʾ"[102]

Later an abbreviated version of this saying merely states: "Muḥammad's caliphate is in Medina, and his kingdom will be established in Syria."[103] The connection between the fullfillment of prophecy in Mecca and the rise of the Arab caliphate in Syria should therefore not be perceived as direct, but as something mediated by a whole saga about the ideal rule of ʿUmar, who legitimizes the comeback of the Umayyads. This has already been examined in secular and moralistic terms above, but the narrators go farther in the way they have ʿUmar make the culminating speech of his reign while he was in Syria rather than in the Ḥijāz or in Iraq.

Ṭabarī records this highpoint of ʿUmar's caliphate in the year A.H. 17/A.D. 638, when the caliph set out to visit Syria, a year after he had come to the region to gain the surrender of Jerusalem. The year A.H. 17 is packed in Ṭabarī's chronicle with various strands of storytelling that herald important topics that unfold later. However, the most notable episode that the chronicler describes for that year is the caliph's visit of inspection in Syria. For that occasion, the narrators assign to 'Umar a declaration that amounts to a farewell speech, similar in emotion though not in substance to what the Prophet made during the *Hijjat al-Wadāʿ*. Ṭabarī also inserts innuendo about 'Umar's tacit designation of Muʿāwiya on that occasion as a viceroy in Syria and a potential successor to the caliphate.

After completing a tour of inspection of the region, 'Umar reportedly decided to use Syria as a base from which to make important administrative changes and declarations. While there, he announced the replacement of Yazīd b. Abī Sufyān and Shuraḥbīl b. Ḥasna as governors by Muʿāwiya and placed both Abū 'Ubayda and Khālid under Muʿāwiya's command, and settled various inheritance questions in Syria. Then he reportedly "ordained various matters and stood with the people for a moment of goodbye [*thumma qāma fi'l-nās bi'l-wadāʿ*]."[104] In his speech 'Umar declared,

> "I have been put in charge over you and I have carried out what I had to do with respect to those matters concerning you, which God has entrusted to me. If He wills, we will justly distribute among you the revenues of your *fay'* lands, your living quarters, and your raiding assignments. We have given you your due. We have mobilized armed forces for you; we have put your access routes in order. We have indicated places for you to settle. We have extended the revenues of your *fay'* lands for you and of that part of Syria you fought for [*wa mā qātaltum 'alayhi min sha'mikum*]. We have ordained your foodstuffs for you, and we have given orders that you be given your stipends, allowances, and supplementary allocations. He who possesses information on a certain issue should act upon it. Let anyone inform me [about something special he knows]; then I myself shall put that into practice, God willing. There is no power except with God."[105]

What immediately seems unusual in this speech is the way 'Umar speaks to his audience in Syria, as if they were his central community of followers in Medina. For an experienced reader, such a speech and such intimacy with the audience could be recognized as traditionally more the habit of 'Umar in Medina, where he frequently would summon a congregational prayer gathering when something important happened, such as the arrival of news related to the conquests; then he would outline his policy and ask for public counsel. Here, however, he takes this posture in Syria. He speaks about organizational steps he has taken for the military and the people of that province as if these actions were for the good of the entire empire. And, just as significantly, one finds in the scene an aspect of foreshadowing, at that critical juncture where the leading members of the community were assembled and the moment was one of celebrating triumph and the coming tenure of a "strong governor"—presaging Mu'āwiya's future political importance. Syria, in the vaguest of ways, is made to seem the successor to the Medinan caliphate, which ended in idealist terms with 'Umar's reign.

Whereas the Prophet had legislated about individual rights and ritualistic matters in his farewell speech, 'Umar legislated about governmental organization in this speech in Syria and established what he considered to be the equilibrium of the Islamic state. Unlike the sacred occasion of the Prophet's pilgrimage in Mecca, 'Umar's assembly was civil and perhaps leisurely. It was through the moral example of 'Umar that the decrees on that occasion gained religious weight as *sunna*, but it was also because of a willing community of followers, the *jamā'a*. The sacrality of 'Umar's speech is only finally established when the satisfied crowd now subconsciously remembers the Prophet, and asks 'Umar to have Bilāl make the call for prayer. Not everyone in that assembly had known the Prophet, but Ṭabarī implies a coalescence in the public spirit when Bilāl made the call to prayer. Those who did know the Prophet were moved to tears by the occasion, with 'Umar being the one who wept the most copiously, but those too young to have seen the Prophet wept as well, moved by the emotions of the others.[106] Bilāl's call to prayer thus provided not just a religious conclusion for the story, but a link of political legitimation with the Sīra as the base of the Islamic state, now shifted from Medina to Damascus.

CHAPTER EIGHT

# Conclusion

The religion of Islam strongly contrasts with predecessor Near Eastern religions, especially Judaism and Christianity, in the way the political history of the early Islamic caliphate greatly defines sectarian differences as well as political controversies in later times. Certain central questions, such as whether the Prophet's family should have succeeded to the caliphate first, whether the ʿAlids or ʿAbbāsids should have inherited the caliphate, and what the nature of the authority of the caliph was as *imām* (whether political, religious, or symbolic), produced political conflicts in the period between the seventh and the ninth centuries.

In a reading of the turbulent record of this history in the chronicle of Ṭabarī and other medieval sources, it is easy to contrast the main points of view during the civil wars as those of Sunnism and Shīʿīsm, the former being supportive of the legitimacy of the first three caliphs and the collectivity of the companions in general, while the latter being supportive only of ʿAlī. In light of the preceding reexamination of the texts, however, it should be evident that the narratives of Ṭabarī and others ought not to be categorized as being in favor of one sect or another. In its wider scope of parabolic narration, early Islamic historiography contained both the Sunnī and the Shīʿī points of view. What Shīʿīsm emphasizes in the tribulations of ʿAlī forms a part of the Sunnī narrative, while much of the behavior and political language of ʿAlī, as admired in Shīʿīsm, is dependent on the depictions (often favorable) of other companions. ʿAlī's biography forms simply one component in a structured narrative about religious figures and caliphs with specific qualities, patterns of interaction, and changing interests during the course of rivalry over the succession.

This diversity in companion imagery, especially relating to their different favorable qualities, has been well known from an early period and was characterized by the later medieval scholar al-Juwaynī as a phenomenon of contradiction.[1] Remarkably, however, and in spite of its clear political and moral complexity, the narrative about the Rāshidūn caliphate was tenuously accommodated in the orthodox version of Islamic traditions. This was done by focusing attention on the continuing religious highlights that served a legalistic or traditionist purpose, such as the episode of the Ridda War, which confirmed the requirement of *zakāt*; the conquests in ʿUmar's time, which presented a continuation of the Maghāzī of the Prophet; and the story of ʿUthmān's collation of the Qur'ān, which set an example of political and religious centralization. ʿUthmān's action effectively set a precedent for future caliphal attempts to codify Islamic law and religious sciences (as in the example of ʿUmar II, who gave official backing to the writing down of *ḥadīth*, and al-Manṣūr, who sought to make Mālik's *al-Muwaṭṭa'* the exclusive legal code of the empire). And to these one should add the often-neglected contribution attributed to ʿAlī, who commanded the establishment of the rules for Arabic grammar.

All of these stories can be read on the didactic, legal level as simple religious affirmations. The historical context can seem to be no more than an occasion for narrative composition. As the preceding chapters have shown, however, when these stories are read within the wider context of the chronicles, it becomes clear that the history of the companions did not constitute a secondary issue but was part of the wider legalistic-historical structure of narration. The moral dilemma over the crisis of caliphal succession and over the process of political interaction among the companions was a central issue that was addressed on a variety of levels.

And while it is true that the first two caliphs are represented as having, on balance, saved the path of Islamic history, they are nevertheless chastened in oblique and artful ways for the dilemma over the succession, and especially for having distanced ʿAlī from the caliphate, and thus for having inadvertently shaped the beginnings of a history of political conflict and religious dissent. Abū Bakr and ʿUmar are represented, on balance, as central religious figures whose sheer ascetic example and charismatic way of leading kept the unity and progress of the community intact. Troubles began, officially, when 'Uthmān proved incapable of providing a religious example and/or the leadership style of his predecessors. 'Uthmān's reign provided the moment of division between effective leadership and a restless community, and the occasion impelled the narrators to shift attention from placing the emphasis on ideal leaders to stressing the importance of the community's unity, along with its welfare and religious security.

Still, whatever the variations among the caliphs, and whatever the controversies that were being debated, in the end the narrators always stress through various dialogues, speeches, and official documents that the most important objective was the establishment of a rule that was equitable, honorable, and pious.[2] The concept is not so much particularly religious or dogmatic as it is ethical, and it is not just Arab but also Persian. It is from within these domains of interest in the concepts of just rule and community stability that Ṭabarī's concern with Sunnism primarily arises—and it is as an offshoot of this concern with communal consensus that the collectivity of the companions becomes a central issue. And from there it quickly becomes a political issue about the establishment of proper rule (monarchal and then caliphal) and the suppression of threatening dissidence. Shī'ism is undermined not only because of the 'Alid claim to exclusive knowledge (*'ilm*), but even more because of its ultra-idealism and the susceptibility of its puritanical concept to infiltration by messianic groups and sectarians.

The preceding chapters have shown the extents to which Ṭabarī's historical narration would go in defending the interests of the *jamā'a*, even if it meant the return to the Umayyad (Sufyanid) leadership from the times of the Jāhiliyya. The transition from the caliphate of 'Umar to those of Mu'āwiya and 'Abd al-Malik is cast as a need for the establishment of public order and security for the community and its faith. And it is as a result of this achievement (and not merely due to apocalyptic affectations for Jerusalem) that later Islamic narrators projected the province of Syria as the bastion of Sunnism in the caliphate. It was the *ḥadīth* group that advocated the merits of Syria, and these praises often came from Khurāsānīs such as Ibn Ḥanbal and many other *ḥadīth* scholars who challenged the Miḥna program of al-Ma'mūn. The fact that Syria, unlike Iraq, was devoid of sectarian pretensions made it all the more possible for *ḥadīth* scholars to call it home, just as Shī'ism, the 'Abbāsid Mu'tazila, and other syncretistic sects and theological trends laid claim to the intellectual centers of Iraq and Iran.

And yet while Sunnism was represented as redeemed in the steadfastness of Syria against the Saba'iyya movement and other off-shoots of Shīʿīsm, the question of ideal caliphal rule remained inadequately answered with Umayyad rule. Muʿāwiya was an exception who could be praised for being a companion, 'Abd al-Malik was an authoritarian leader who pulled the state together at a fractured political juncture, and 'Umar II offered an interesting interlude as a ruler who became an ascetic. However, the rest of the Umayyads provided what often was a gratuitous monarchal rule, and the chroniclers punished them for it by robbing them of any flattering speeches that could answer to either religious or ethical purposes.

It is within this context that the reader was expected to appreciate the advent of the 'Abbāsids. That the 'Abbāsids hold a privileged position across the breadth of Islamic religious tradition is very familiar from the use of the name of 'Abdallāh b. 'Abbās in *ḥadīth* and *tafsīr*. In history, as well, as noted from the controversies at the Saqīfa and at the Shūrā, Ibn 'Abbās was consistently portrayed as the wiser assessor of the political situation, and as having advised 'Alī with sound counsel about the need for patience and neutrality. The 'Abbāsid advantage, or more accurately the pro-caliphal perspective, however, does not fully crystallize except with the reign of the caliph al-Manṣūr. It was to al-Manṣūr that the narrators attributed the best political speeches, wisdom sayings, and declarations of counsel to his son. While the biographies of other caliphs often received strong sections of miscellaneous accounts and speeches, these were often specialized in nature, such as in the inheritance testimony of Abū Bakr, the preachings of 'Umar, and the various stories about Muʿāwiya's patience and forbearance. Al-Manṣūr's biography after the conclusion of the narratives of his reign is different: particularly rich and multifaceted in its flattering content, and showing a superlative literary quality. This was not accidental in the wider scope of the narratives, but rather a carefully calculated decision of historical composition. Al-Manṣūr's speeches synthesize a wide range of predecessor secular and religious literature of political wisdom.

The fragmented and disparate background of Islamic political history reaches a moment of resolution and climax with the concluding biographical information for al-Manṣūr. Everything that the medieval reader would have wanted to hear earlier in the speeches of the Prophet and the first three caliphs—such as a firm testament about succession, a policy statement about how the land was being ruled, and a clear statement that balanced the role of secular and religious principles in government and politics in general—is fully outlined in elaborate speeches and testaments by al-Manṣūr. Previous gaps are filled in and vital correctives on the experiences of previous caliphs and earlier Muslim communities are offered at this concluding moment of early 'Abbāsid history. And the result seems at once a historical account and a type of official political treatise that combines the secular and strategizing wisdom of Ibn al-Muqaffa' with the pious advice of the Rāshidūn caliphs and the sage counsel of a father toward his son. The latter image is complete with the wistful cynicism of the father about the likelihood of the son following his advice; in another version, the task of outlining all duties is so complete that the narrators put in at the end a word of congratulation from the father to the son for the succession.[3]

In the most telling version of al-Manṣūr's commands to his son, the chroniclers have the caliph describe the ideal ways of proper government and how to secure the state. The monarchal counsel, however, is also combined with extensive religious advice that previously would have been delivered by religious scholars to the caliphs, and is now instead directed from the caliph to his son.[4] Al-Manṣūr advised al-Mahdī as follows:

> "Fear God in what I have turned over to you, the rule of the Muslims after me, and He will give you a way out of what distresses you and grieves you. . . . Mind Muḥammad in his Community, and God will watch over your affairs. . . . Stick to what is lawful; it will be your credit in the hereafter, and your welfare in this hasty world. . . . Sovereignty is God's strong halter, and binding tie, and upright service of God, so guard it, protect it, and fortify it. . . . Judge with equity, and do not wrong anyone, for this cuts off rancor, cauterizes your enemy, and is most wholesome in the treatment. Keep your hands off the booty [*fay'*] of the Muslims, for you have no need of it, with all that I have caused you to inherit. Begin your Caliphate with favors to kinsmen and with kindness to relatives. Beware partiality, and squandering the wealth of the subjects. Garrison the frontiers and police the provinces, favor the prominent, and see to it that state salaries are adequate. Settle the

> commoners, give free entry to what benefits them, and drive away noxious things from them. . . . Reckon your men and transport animals and the troops, insofar as you can, and beware of putting the work of today off until tomorrow so that matters crowd together against you and go amiss. Try to deal with matters and misfortunes when they occur, one by one, and exert yourself and be in readiness for them. Oversee matters yourself, and do not grow annoyed, or be lazy or remiss. Expect good of your Lord, but expect ill of your governors and secretaries . . . and look after those who sleep at your door. Let your ear be accessible to the people, and look into the matter of whoever has recourse to you. Appoint as your agent for them an eye which never sleeps and a soul which is never diverted. . . . This is my testimony to you, and God will be my successor over you."[5]

In other accounts of al-Manṣūr's will (according to al-Haytham b. 'Adī), the caliph is shown to be in command of a book of esoteric knowledge (akin perhaps to *kitāb al-Jifr* of the 'Alid *imāms*), and advises his son to seek answers from that precious book in times of crisis. However, in the above testament, al-Manṣūr's advice does not rest on any miraculous claim to religious knowledge. The declaration puts the ruler within a moralistic frame of action, subjecting him to the same secular and religious rules that apply to other Muslims. That the ruler is entrusted with more duties by God is obvious, but it is important to stress that this depiction of the caliph as a fallible being derived its inspiration from the example of David among the biblical prophets, rather than from that of Solomon, who was famous for his access to secret religious knowledge.

This pattern of reference to the past was not used only to offer a comparative exemplum; for the 'Abbāsids, it also served to justify their political legitimacy in more complete terms as well. Al-Manṣūr did not dwell much on this topic toward the end of his reign because he had already covered it extensively in earlier speeches. And here as well the foundations of 'Abbāsid caliphal claims and how they came to power were meant to be read in synthetic and teleological terms that take into account the community's knowledge of its political history and various stories about failed reigns and oppositions.

In one such speech, al-Manṣūr establishes the grounds for his own legitimacy by describing the 'Abbāsid rise to power in terms that offer a tendentious and pious vindication of the Sunnī view of history. Al-

Manṣūr makes it clear that the ʿAbbāsids were never interested in politics, much less in gaining power, and that it was the ʿAlid war with the Umayyads that drew the ʿAbbāsid branch of the Hāshimite family into the conflict. Al-Manṣūr revisits the tactical missteps of the ʿAlids, starting with ʿAlī himself, and shows that these were sometimes not simply flaws in personal judgment but also a result of the treachery of the Kufans. What to make of Kufa, as friend or foe, is still not clear for al-Manṣūr, but the question is rendered irrelevant with the foundation of Baghdad as the new capital and city of ʿAbbāsid loyalists, as well as with the emergence of the Khurāsānīs as a corrective on the past in the way they reliably championed the cause of the ʿAbbāsid revolution.[6] In this speech, al-Manṣūr does not go so far as to demonstrate a willingness to give up the throne to a more worthy or pious person, as some more hagiographic anecdotes report—but clearly a Sunnī hagiography about politics is at work in his declaration. The Shīʿī notion regarding the divine election of *imāms* (in the way the ʿAbbāsids came to inherit the Hāshimite leadership) is combined with the Sunnī exhortations in *ḥadīth* that an individual's distance from the pursuit of authority can lead to a serendipitous process of divine favor that allows him to gain authority or to be aided in exercising power afterward. This was known to be the case with the first two Rāshidūn caliphs, and it was here appropriated to justify the ʿAbbāsid leadership in a new way.

In terms of legitimation, therefore, as much as in setting out religious or secular exempla, ʿAbbāsid history was intended by narrators to be read in relation to the history of the Rāshidūn and other previous rulerships. Al-Manṣūr's speeches and various declarations combine a Sunnī and Hāshimite apologetic with an idealization crafted from previous images of the patriarchs, prophets, and caliphs; and these in turn are infused with a tradition of secular wisdom advice from the Persian monarchal heritage. Caliphal history was intended to be read not as an idealization of individuals, but as a language of resolution for cycles of political and moral tribulation that spanned the histories of peoples who dwelt in the shadow of kingship and prophecy.

APPENDIX ONE

# Abū Mikhnaf's Account of the Saqīfa of Banū Sā'ida

In addition to the four versions given by Ṭabarī of the account of the first succession to the Prophet,[1] a fifth version, narrated by Abū Mikhnaf, is added after the concluding descriptions of the Prophet's time of death. This fifth version comprises the most detailed story of the Saqīfa incident and, typical of Abū Mikhnaf's richest accounts, unveils the full drama of the dispute, which is either only partially given or glossed over in other reports. The account does not combine elements from the various currents examined in chapter 2, but rather gives the story as an unflinching dispute between the Muhājirūn and the Anṣār.

Ṭabarī reports:

> According to Hishām b. Muḥammad←Abū Mikhnaf←'Abdallāh b. 'Abd al-Raḥmān b. Abī 'Amrah al-Anṣārī: When the Prophet passed away, the Anṣār gathered on the portico of the Banū Sā'ida and said, "Let us appoint Sa'd b. 'Ubāda to be in charge of our affairs after Muḥammad." They made Sa'd come out to them; but he was sick, and after they had gathered he said to his son or to one of his cousins, "Because of my illness I cannot make my word heard by all the people. Take my speech from me and make them hear it." So he spoke, and the man memorized what he said and said [it] in a loud voice so that his companions would hear it. After praising and extolling God, he said:

"Company of the Anṣār! You have precedence in religion and merit [*lakum sābiqa fi'l-dīn wa faḍīla*] in Islam that no [other] tribe of the Arabs can claim. Muḥammad remained ten-odd years in his tribe, calling them to worship the Merciful and to cast off idols and graven images, but only a few men of his tribe believed in Him, and they were able neither to protect the Apostle of God, nor to render His religion strong, nor to divert from themselves the oppression that befell them all; until, when He intended excellence for you, He sent nobility to you and distinguished you with grace [*sāqa ilaykum al-karāma wa khaṣṣakum bi'l-ni'ma*]. Thus God bestowed upon you faith in Him and in His Apostle, and protection for him and his companions, and strength for him and his faith, and battle [*jihād*] for his enemies. You were the most severe people against his enemies who were among you, and the most troublesome to his enemies who were not from among you, so that the Arabs became upright in God's cause, willingly or unwillingly, and the distant one submitted in abject humiliation, until through you God made great slaughter in the earth for His Apostle [*athkhan . . . li-rasūlihi bikum al-arḍ*], and by your swords the Arabs were abased for him. When God took [the Prophet] to Himself, he was pleased with you and consoled by you. [So] keep [control of] this matter to yourselves, to the exclusion of others, for it is yours and yours alone."

They answered him all together, "Your opinion is right, and you have spoken correctly. We will not diverge from your opinion, and we shall put you in charge of this business. For indeed, you are sufficient for us and satisfactory to whoever is righteous among the believers." But then they began to debate among themselves, and [some] said, "What if the Muhājirūn and the first companions of the Apostle of God say, 'We are his kinsmen and his friends. So why do you dispute this matter with us after him?'" [Another] group of [the Anṣār] said, "Then we should say, 'Let us have a leader from among ourselves, and you a leader from among yourselves,' for we should never be satisfied with less than this leadership." When Sa'd b. 'Ubāda heard this, he said, "This is the beginning of weakness."

'Umar learned of this and went to the Prophet's house and sent Abū Bakr, who was in the building. Now 'Alī b. Abī Ṭālib was working busily preparing the Apostle [for burial], so ['Umar] sent a message to Abū Bakr to come out to him. Abū Bakr sent back that he was occupied, but ['Umar] sent him another message, saying, "Something has happened that you must attend to in person." So he came out to him, and ['Umar] said to him, "Didn't you know that the Anṣār have gathered at the portico of the Banū Sā'ida intending to put Sa'd b. 'Ubāda in charge of this affair? [Even] the best of them is saying, 'A leader for us and a leader for Quraysh.'" So the two of them hurried toward them; they met Abū 'Ubayda b. al-Jarrāḥ, and the three of them marched toward them. [On their way] they were met by 'Āṣim b. 'Adī and 'Uwaym b. Sā'ida, who said, "Go back, for it will not be as you wish." But they refused [to turn back] and arrived while [the Anṣār] were gathered.

According to 'Umar b. al-Khaṭṭāb: We came to them, and I had pieced together a speech that I wanted to deliver to them but when I had pushed in among them and was to begin my address, Abū Bakr said to me, "Easy does it, 'Umar, until I have spoken; then afterward say whatever you wish." So he spoke [first], and there was nothing that I had wanted to say that he did not come to, or amplify.

According to 'Abdallāh b. 'Abd al-Raḥmān: Abū Bakr began by praising and extolling God. Then he said, "Verily God sent Muḥammad as an Apostle to His creatures and as a witness to his community, that they should worship God and affirm his oneness. For they had worshiped various deities other than Him, alleging that [those deities] were intercessors before Him on their behalf and were beneficial for them. [Those gods] were of carved stone and hewn wood." Then he recited, "And they serve beside God that which can neither harm nor help them, saying: 'These are our intercessors before God.'" And they said, "We worship them only that they make us nearer to God." [Abū Bakr continued,] "Now the Arabs found it most distressing that they should leave the religion of their forefathers; so from among his tribe God singled out the first Muhājirūn, by having them affirm that he spoke the truth and by their belief in him, and consoling him and enduring patiently with him the harsh insults their tribe [directed] against them and [their tribe], calling them liars. All the people were opposed to [the Muhājirūn] and rebuked them; but they were not distressed by their small numbers or by the hatred of their people for them or by [the people's] single-minded opposition to them, for they were the first who worshiped God on earth and who believed in God and the Apostle. They are his friends and kinsmen and the most deserving people in this matter after him; only a wrongdoer would dispute that. O company of the Anṣār, your superiority in religion and great precedence in

Islam are undeniable. May God be satisfied with you as helpers [*anṣār*] for His religion and His Apostle. He made his *hijra* to you, and the majority of his wives and his companions are among you; so—after the first Muhājirūn—there is no one among us who is in your station. We are the leaders, and you the helpers; matters shall not be settled without consultation, nor shall we decide on them without you."

Then al-Ḥubāb b. al-Mundhir b. al-Jamūḥ stood up and said, "O company of the Anṣār, take command of yourselves, for you overshadow [other] people."[2] No one will dare oppose you [if you do], nor will the people proceed, except in accordance with your opinion. You are the people of power and wealth, numerous and strong in resistance and experience, having boldness and courage. The people look only to what you do; so do not differ among yourselves, lest your judgment [*ra'y*] be spoiled and your cause [*amr*] collapse. This one [i.e., Abū Bakr] insisted on what you have heard. So [let us have] a leader from among us, and [they] a leader from among them." At this 'Umar said, "Absolutely not; two cannot come to an agreement in a joining. By God, the Arabs will not be content to give you the leadership when their Prophet was not one of you; but they would not prevent their affairs from being led by one of those among whom prophethood [had appeared] and from whom the guardian of their affairs [was chosen]. In that [fact] is manifest argument and clear proof for us against those Arabs who deny [it]. Who would attempt to wrest from us the sovereignty [*sulṭān*] of Muḥammad and his authority [*imāra*], seeing that we are his friends and kinsmen, except someone advancing falsehood, inclining to sin, or hurtling into destruction?" [But] al-Ḥubāb b. al-Mundhir stood up [again] and said, "O company of the Anṣār, take charge of your own affairs and do not listen to what this one and his companions say, for they would do away with your share in this matter. If they refuse to give you what you ask for, then drive them out of this country, and seize control of these matters despite them. For you are more deserving of this country than they are, as it was by your swords that those who were not yet converted came to obey this religion. I am their much-rubbed little rubbing post, and their propped little palm tree loaded with fruit. By God, if you wish to return it as a stump [then do so!][3] 'Umar said, "Then may God kill you!" and al-Ḥubāb replied, "Rather may He kill you!" At this Abū 'Ubayda said, "O company of the Anṣār, you were the first who helped and strengthened, so do not be the first to substitute and change for the worse."

Then Bashīr b. Sa'd, father of al-Nu'mān b. Bashīr, stood up and said, "O company of the Anṣār, if indeed by God we were the first in merit and battling the polytheists and in precedence in this religion, we would want by [these deeds] only [to gain] our Lord's pleasure, and obedience to our Prophet, and sustenance for ourselves; it is not appropriate for us to exalt ourselves over [other] people. Let us not seek by it some transitory thing of the world, for indeed God is the One Who provides [such things] for us out of His grace. In truth Muḥammad was from Quraysh, and his people are more entitled to [hold] [authority] and more suitable. I swear by God that He shall never see me contesting this matter [*amr*] with them. So fear God and do not oppose them or dispute with them."

At this Abū Bakr said, "This is 'Umar, and this is Abū 'Ubayda; render the oath of allegiance to whichever of them you wish." But they both said, "No, by God, we shall not undertake [to hold] this authority over you, for you are the best of the Muhājirūn, the second of two when they were in the cave, and the Apostle of God's deputy [*khalīfa*] over the prayer; and prayer is the most meritorious obedience [*dīn*] of the Muslims. So who would precede you or undertake this authority over you? Extend your hand so we may render the oath of allegiance to you!"

When the two of them went forth to render the oath of allegiance to him, Bashīr b. Sa'd went to him ahead of them and swore allegiance to him [first]. At this al-Ḥubāb b. al-Mundhir shouted to him, "Oh Bashīr b. Sa'd, you are in opposition [to your kinsmen]; what drove you to do what you have done? Did you envy your cousin the sovereignty?" He replied, "By God, no! But I abhorred contending with a group for a right that God had given them." Now when the Aws saw what Bashīr b. Sa'd had done and what Quraysh had called for and what the Khazraj were demanding by way of giving sovereignty to Sa'd b. 'Ubāda, they said to one another [and among them was Usayd b. Ḥuḍayr, one of the *naqībs*]: "By God, if once you appoint the Khazraj over you, they will always have the advantage over you on that account, and will never give you any share in it with them. So stand up and render the oath of allegiance to Abū Bakr." So they came forth to him and rendered the oath of allegiance to him. Thus that which Sa'd b. 'Ubāda and the Khazraj had agreed to do was defeated.

Hishām←Abū Mikhnaf←Abū Bakr b. Muḥammad al-Khuzā'ī: [The tribe of] Aslam approached en masse until the streets were packed with them, and they rendered the oath of allegiance to Abū Bakr. 'Umar used to say, "It was not until I saw Aslam that I was certain we had won the day."

Hishām←Abū Mikhnaf←'Abdallāh b. 'Abd al-Raḥmān: People approached from all sides swearing allegiance to Abū Bakr, and they almost stepped on Sa'd b. 'Ubāda. Some of Sa'd's associates said, "Be careful not to step on Sa'd!" At this 'Umar said, "Kill him; may God slay him!" Then he [i.e., 'Umar] [stood up facing him][4] and said: "I was about to tread upon you until your arm is dislocated." At this Sa'd took hold of 'Umar's beard and said, "By God, if you remove a single hair from it you'll return with no front teeth in your mouth." Then Abū Bakr said, "Take it easy, 'Umar; compassion would be more effective at this point." So 'Umar turned away from him. Sa'd said, "By God, if I had the strength to get up, you would have heard from me in the regions and streets [of Medina], roaring in a way that would make you and your companions take cover; by God, I shall join to you a group among whom you would be a follower, not a leader. [Now] carry me from this place." So they carried him and took him into his house. He was left for several days; then he was sent to [and told] that he should come to render the oath of allegiance, for the people [generally] had done so and his tribe as well. But he said, "By God, I shall not do it, before I have shot at you with whatever arrows are in my quiver, and have reddened the head of my spear, and struck you with my sword, as long as my hand controls it. I will fight you with my family and those who obey me of my tribe. I swear by God, [even] if the jinn gathered to you with the people, I would not render the oath of allegiance to you, until I am brought forth before my God and know what my reckoning is."

When Abū Bakr was informed of this, 'Umar said to him, "Pester him until he renders the oath of allegiance." But Bashīr b. Sa'd said, "He has refused; he has made up his mind, and wouldn't render the oath of allegiance to you even if he were killed; and he would not be killed without his children and family and a party of his kinsmen being killed with him. So leave him alone; leaving him won't harm you, he is only one man." So they left him alone. They came to accept the advice of Bashīr b. Saʿd, consulting him whenever it seemed right to them to do so.

Saʿd [b. ʿUbāda] used not to pray in their [daily] prayer or congregate with them [for Friday prayer]; he performed the pilgrimage [to Mecca] but did not press on with them in the multitudes. He continued thus until Abū Bakr died, may God have mercy on him.

APPENDIX TWO

# The Succession to ‘Umar

Ṭabarī’s extended version of the narrative of ‘Umar’s succession (*qiṣṣat al-shūrā*) is the following:

> According to ‘Umar b. Shabba←‘Alī b. Muḥammad [al-Madā’inī]← Wakī‘ [b. al-Jarrāḥ]←al-A‘mash←Ibrāhīm and Muḥammad b. ‘Abdallāh al-Anṣārī←Ibn Abī ‘Arūba←Qatāda←Shahr b. Ḥawshab and Abū Mikhnaf←Yūsuf b. Yazīd←Abū al-‘Abbās Sahl and Mubārak b. Faḍāla←‘Ubaydallāh b. ‘Umar and Yūnus b. Abī Isḥāq—‘Amr b. Maymūn al-Awdī:
>
> When ‘Umar b. al-Khaṭṭāb was stabbed, it was suggested to him that he should appoint a successor. “Whom shall I appoint caliph?” was his reply. “If Abū ‘Ubayda b. al-Jarrāḥ were alive, I would appoint him, and if my Lord questioned me, I would say, ‘I heard Your prophet say that [Abū ‘Ubayda] was the guardian of this community.’ If Sālim, client of Abū Ḥudhayfa, were alive, I would appoint him, and if my Lord questioned me, I would say, ‘I heard your prophet say that Sālim loves God vehemently.’ ” Someone said to ‘Umar, “I can point to someone: ‘Abdallāh b. ‘Umar.” But [‘Umar] replied, “God curse you! You were not saying this for God’s sake! You wretch! How can I appoint caliph someone who has been unable to divorce his wife! We have no desire [to get involved] in your affairs. I have not found [the caliphate] so praiseworthy that I should covet it for my own family. If things turn out

well, we shall have gained our reward from them; but if they turn out badly, then it is enough for the family of 'Umar that [only] one of them should be called to account and held responsible for what happened to Muḥammad's community. I have striven and have kept my family out. If I succeed in coming out [of all this] even, and no recompense [being given to me], I shall indeed be happy. I shall look [into the matter]: if I do appoint a caliph, then someone better than I has made the appointment; but if I abandon [the idea], someone better than I has done this. God will never neglect his faith."

So [those with him] left and returned in the evening, suggesting to the Commander of the Faithful that he draw up a succession agreement. He replied, "I had decided after talking to you that I would look [into the matter] and appoint someone over you, the most suitable of you to bear you along the true path." And he indicated 'Alī. [He continued], "But I fell into a swoon and saw a man who had entered a garden that he had planted. He began to pick everything, both the young tender plants and the mature ones, clutching them to him and putting them beneath him. I knew that God was in control and was taking 'Umar into his mercy. I do not want to take on the burden [of the caliphate] dead as well as alive. You should [approach] that group of men who the Messenger of God said are 'among the people of paradise.' Sa'īd b. Zayd b. 'Amr b. Nufayl is one of them. I am not bringing him into the matter, but rather the following six: 'Alī and 'Uthmān, son of 'Abd Manāf, 'Abd al-Raḥmān [b. 'Awf] and Sa'd [b. Abī Waqqāṣ], maternal uncles of the messenger of God, al-Zubayr b. al-'Awwām, the true friend and cousin of the Messenger of God, and Ṭalḥat al-Khayr b. 'Ubaydallāh. Let them select one of themselves. When they appoint a leader, [you all] should give him good help and support. If he entrusts any one of you with authority, he should convey to him what is committed to his care."

They left and al-'Abbās said to 'Alī, "Do not get involved with them." He replied, "I do not like dissension [in our family]." [Al-'Abbās] said, "Then you will see something you do not like!" When morning came, 'Umar summoned 'Alī, 'Uthmān, Sa'd, 'Abd al-Raḥmān b. 'Awf, and al-Zubayr b. al-'Awwām and said, "I have looked into the matter and consider you to be the chiefs and leaders of the people. This matter will remain among you alone. When the Messenger of God died, he was well pleased with you. I have no fears for you with the people if you remain on the straight path. However, I do fear for you if there is a difference of opinion among you and the people differ among themselves. Off you go to 'Āisha's room, with her permission, and deliberate. Choose one of yourselves." Then he added, "Do not go to 'Āisha's room; rather stay near at hand." He put down his head, exhausted by the loss of blood.

So they went in and held secret discussions. But then their voices became raised and 'Ābdallah b. 'Umar exclaimed, "Good heavens, the Commander of the Faithful is not yet dead!" 'Umar overheard this and awakened, then said: "All of you, stop this![1] When I am dead, hold your consultations for three days. Let Ṣuhayb lead the people in prayer. Before the fourth day comes you should have your commander from among you. 'Abdallāh b. 'Umar will be there as adviser, but he shall have nothing to do with the matter [of the actual appointment]. Ṭalḥa shall share with you in the decision. If he comes within the three days, include him in your decision. If the three days go by and he does not come, make the decision nevertheless. Who will deal with Ṭalḥa for me?" "I shall," responded Sa'd b. Abī Waqqās, "and he will not give a differing view, God willing." 'Umar said, "I hope he will not give a differing view, God willing. I think one of these two, 'Alī or 'Uthmān, will become a leader. If it is 'Uthmān, he is a gentle person [*fīhi līn*]; if it is 'Alī, he has a sense of humor [*fa-fīhi du'āba*].[2] How suitable he is to carry them along the true road [*wa aḥri bihi an yaḥmilahum 'alā al-ṭarīq*]! If you appoint Sa'd, he is worthy of the office, but if not, the one appointed should seek his assistance. I have never dismissed him for disloyalty or weakness. How perceptive 'Abd al-Raḥmān b. 'Awf is! He is disposed to what is right. [He is] rightly guided and has a protector in God. Listen to what he has to say."

['Umar] said to Abū Talḥa al-Anṣārī, "For a long time had God strengthened Islam through your Helpers, Abū Talḥa. Select fifty helpers and urge them to choose one of them." To al-Miqdād b. al-Aswad he said, "When you put me into my grave, assemble these people in one room to choose one of their number." To Ṣuhayb he said, "Lead the people in prayer for three days. Let into [the deliberations] 'Alī, 'Uthmān, al-Zubayr, Sa'd, 'Abd al-Raḥmān b. 'Awf, and Ṭalḥa, if he arrives. Have 'Abdallāh b. 'Umar present, but he shall have nothing to do with the matter [of the actual appointment]. Stay with them and if five agree to approve of one man, but one refuses, smash in his head, or strike it with a sword. If four agree to approve of one man, but two refuse, cut off the [latters'] heads. If three approve of one of them, and three approve of another, get ʻAbdallāh b. ʻUmar to make a decision. Let whichever party in favor of which he makes his judgment select one of themselves. If they do accept ʻAbdallāh b. ʻUmar's judgment, be on the same side as ʻAbd al-Raḥmān b. ʻAwf. Kill the rest if they do not go along with the general consensus."

So they left. ʻAlī said to some Banū Hāshim who were with him, "If your people are obeyed [only] among themselves, you will never be appointed to positions of leadership." Al-ʻAbbās came to him, and [ʻAlī] said, "[The caliphate] has slipped from us!" [Al-ʻAbbās] asked him how he knew. He continued, "[ʻUmar] paired me with ʻUthmān and told us [all] to fall in with the majority. If two approve of one, and two another, [he said], we should be on the same side as ʻAbd al-Raḥmān b. ʻAwf. Saʻd will not go against his cousin, ʻAbd al-Raḥmān, who is related by marriage to ʻUthmān. They will all [three] agree in their opinion. ʻAbd al-Raḥmān will appoint ʻUthmān to the caliphate, or ʻUthmān will appoint ʻAbd al-Raḥmān. If the other two were with me, they would be of no benefit to me, to say nothing of the fact that I have hope of one of them." Al-ʻAbbās said to him, "I have never urged you to do anything without your later responding to me by holding back in a way I do not like. When the Messenger of God died, I ordered you to ask him [on his deathbed] who should have the rule, but you refused. After [Muḥammad's] death I ordered you to bring the matter to a speedy conclusion, but you refused. When ʻUmar nominated you a member of the electoral council, I advised you to have nothing to do with them, but you refused. Just learn one thing from me: whenever people make you a proposal, say no, unless they are appointing you [caliph]. Watch out for these people; they will continue to push us out of this matter [of the caliphate] until someone takes our [rightful] place [*ḥattā yaqūm bihi lanā ghayrunā*]. I swear in God's name, no such person will get [the caliphate] without the help of some evil together with which no good will be of benefit!"[3] ʻAlī replied, "If ʻUthmān survives, I shall certainly remind him of what has happened. If he dies, they will certainly take [the caliphate] by turns among themselves. If they do, they will certainly find me in a position they do not like." Then he quoted the following verses, applying them to his own situation:

I swore by the lord of the mares prancing one evening—
 but in the morning they came, nimble hastening to al-Muḥaṣṣab
"The family of Ibn Ya'mar will certainly stand apart, facing
 a bloody place, difficult to drink from, they being the sons of
 al-Shuddakh.

And he turned and saw Abū Ṭalḥa, but did not like his being there. Abū Ṭalḥa said, "Nothing to be afraid of, Abū al-Ḥasan!"[4]

When 'Umar died and his bier was brought out, both 'Alī and 'Uthmān pretended not to mind which of them would pray over him. But 'Abd al-Raḥmān said, "Both of you are candidates for the caliphate. This matter has nothing to do with you. It is for Ṣuhayb, whom 'Umar appointed to lead the people in prayer for three [nights] until they can agree on a leader." So Ṣuhayb prayed over ['Umar]. When he had been buried, al-Miqdād assembled the members of the electoral council in the house of al-Miswar b. Makhrama—another version is that it was in the treasury and yet another that it was in 'Āisha's room with her permission—five in all, accompanied by Ibn 'Umar and with Ṭalḥa still absent. They ordered Abū Ṭalḥa to prevent anyone from disturbing them. 'Amr b. al-'Āṣ and al-Mughīra b. Shu'ba arrived and sat at the door, but Sa'd threw pebbles at them and made them get up, saying, "You want to say, 'We were there; we were members of the electoral council.'" The electoral council argued about the affair and a great deal of talking went on among them. Abū Ṭalḥa said, "I was more afraid that you would reject [the caliphate] than I was that you would compete for it. No, by Him who has taken away 'Umar's soul, I shall give you no more than the three days that you were ordered. Then I shall sit down in my own house and see what you are up to!"

'Abd al-Raḥmān said, "Which one of you will withdraw from the [race for the caliphate], and undertake to appoint the best of you?" No one answered. So he continued, "I withdraw." 'Uthmān said, "I am the first to accept [this]. I heard the Messenger of God say, '['Abd al-Raḥmān] is trustworthy on earth and will be in heaven [*amīnun fī al-arḍ, amīnun fī al-samā'*].'" All the members, with the exception of 'Alī, who remained silent, expressed their approval. So ['Abd al-Raḥmān] said, "What do you say, Abū al-Ḥasan?" ['Alī] replied, "Give me your word you will consider truth paramount, you will not follow your whim, you will not show any preference for a relative, and you will not let the community down." ['Abd al-Raḥmān] said [to the others], "Give me your solemn promises you will stand with me against anyone who reneges [on your final decision] and you will approve of anyone I choose for you. I impose a pact with God upon myself that I shall show no preference for a relative, because he is a relative, nor shall I let down the Muslims." He took a promise from them and similarly gave them his word. ['Abd al-Raḥmān] said to 'Alī, "You say you have the most right of those present to the office because of your close relationship [to the Prophet] and your long standing [in Islam] and the good deeds you have done in the cause of Islam, and you have not, [in saying so], said anything remote [from the truth]. But if you were not involved in the matter and were not here at all, whom would you think of them all has most right to [the office]?" He replied, "'Uthmān." ['Abd al-Raḥmān] took 'Uthmān on one side and said, "You say you are a *shaykh* of Banū 'Abd Manāf and related to the Messenger of God by marriage and his cousin, an excellent man of long standing [in Islam]—and you have not said anything remote from the truth and that [the caliphate] cannot therefore be taken from you. But if you were not here, which of the members do you think has most right to [the office]?" He replied, "'Alī."

Then ['Abd al-Raḥmān] took al-Zubayr on one side and addressed him in the same way as he had 'Alī and 'Uthmān. He replied, "'Uthmān." Then ['Abd al-Raḥmān] took Sa'd on one side and spoke to him. He answered, "'Uthmān." 'Alī met Sa'd and quoted, " 'Fear God, by whom you make demands one of another, and the wombs [which bore you]. God is ever watching you.' I am asking you in the name of the relationship [*raḥim*] of this son of mine with the Messenger of God and that of my paternal uncle, Ḥamza, with you, not to stand with 'Abd al-Raḥmān, assisting 'Uthmān against me. I have connections 'Uthmān does not." 'Abd al-Raḥmān went round at night meeting the Companions of the Messenger of God and those army commanders and nobles who arrived in Medina and consulting with them. Everyone he took to one side gave instructions to opt for 'Uthmān. Then on the eve of the morning of the deadline, he came to the house of al-Miswar b. Makhrama well into the night and woke him up, saying, "You're asleep, when I have had very little tonight? Off you go and summon al-Zubayr and Sa'd!"

So [al-Miswar] summoned them and ['Abd al-Raḥmān] began with al-Zubayr at the back of the mosque under the covering that adjoins the house of Marwān, saying, "Let the rule go to the sons of 'Abd Manāf!" [Al-Zubayr] said, "I throw in my lot with 'Alī." ['Abd al-Raḥmān] said to Sa'd, "We are cousins. Throw in your lot with me so that I can choose." He replied, "If you choose yourself, that is fine! But if you choose 'Uthmān, then I prefer to support 'Alī. Have yourself accepted [as caliph], give us some respite and raise our heads." ['Abd al-Raḥmān] said, "Abū Isḥāq, I have withdrawn from [the caliphate] on condition that I make the choice. [Even] had I not done so and the choice had come back on me, I would not have [the caliphate]. I saw myself in a dream as if in a green meadow rich in fresh herbage. A stallion camel came in—I have never seen such a noble stallion—and passed through like an arrow without paying attention to anything in the meadow, right to the other side without stopping. A stallion followed him in immediately after and left the meadow. Then a fine thoroughbred stallion entered, dragging his halter, turning right and left, going where the other two went and leaving. Then a fourth, a stallion camel, entered and pastured in the meadow. No indeed, I shall not be the fourth. No one can take the place of Abū Bakr and 'Umar after their deaths and [then] be approved of by the people." Sa'd replied, "I am afraid that weakness has overcome you. Do as you think best. You know what 'Umar's deathbed instructions were."

Al-Zubayr and Sa'd left. ['Abd al-Raḥmān] sent al-Miswar b. Makhrama for 'Alī and talked with him in private for a long time, [the latter] not doubting that he was to be selected for the office [of caliph]. Then ['Alī] left, and ['Abd al-Raḥmān] sent al-Miswar for 'Uthmān, but the call to the morning prayer interrupted their private conversation.

According to 'Amr b. Maymūn: 'Abdallāh b. 'Umar told me, "'Amr, anyone who tells you that he knows what 'Abd al-Raḥmān discussed with 'Alī and 'Uthmān does not know what he is talking about! Your Lord's decision fell on 'Uthmān."

When they had said the morning prayers, ['Abd al-Raḥmān] convened the members [of the electoral council] and sent for all the Emigrants and the Helpers of long standing [in Islam] and of excellence and the military commanders who were [in Medina]. They all assembled and there was confusion among the people in the mosque. ['Abd al-Raḥmān] said, "People, everyone wants those of the garrison towns to return to them having learned who their supreme commander is." Saʿīd b. Zayd said, "We think you are worthy of [the caliphate]." He replied, "Give me some different advice!" ʿAmmār [b. Yāsir] said, "If you want the Muslims to be in full agreement, give ʿAlī the oath of allegiance." Al-Miqdād b. al-Aswad said, "ʿAmmār is right; if you give ʿAlī the oath of allegiance, we shall say that we are in full agreement with what you are doing." Ibn Abī al-Sarḥ said, "If you want Quraysh to be in full agreement, give ʿUthmān the oath of allegiance." ʿAbdallāh b. Abī Rabīʿa said, "He is right; if you give ʿUthmān the oath of allegiance, we shall say that we are in full agreement with what you are doing." ʿAmmār upbraided Ibn Abī al-Sarḥ, saying, "When did you ever give the Muslims any good advice?!"

Banū Hāshim and Banū Umayya held talks. ʿAmmār said, "O people, God has ennobled us through His Prophet and strengthened us through His religion. How can you take this appointment away from those of the house of your Prophet?" A member of Banū Makhzūm said, "You have gone too far, Ibn Sumayya! Why should you have anything to do with Quraysh taking the leadership for themselves?" Saʿd b. Abī Waqqāṣ said, "Get it over with, ʿAbd al-Raḥmān, before our people fall into civil war." ʿAbd al-Raḥmān said, "I have looked into [the matter] and consulted. Do not, members of the electoral council, lay yourselves open to criticism." He summoned ʿAlī and said, "God's agreement and covenant is binding on you. Will you indeed act in accordance with God's Book, the practice of His Messenger and the example of the two caliphs after him?" [ʿAlī] replied, "I hope to do this and act to the best of my knowledge and ability."[5] [ʿAbd al-Raḥmān] summoned ʿUthmān and said to him the same as what he had said to ʿAlī. [ʿUthmān] replied, "Yes." So [ʿAbd al-Raḥmān] gave him the oath of allegiance. ʿAlī said, "You have always been partial in his favor! This is not the first time you have banded together against us. But '[my course is] comely patience and God's help is to be asked against what you describe.' You have appointed ʿUthmān only so that the rule will come back to you. 'Every day God exercises power.' " ʿAbd al-Raḥmān retorted, "Do not lay yourself open to criticism, ʿAlī. I have looked into the matter and consulted the people. They regard no one as the equal of ʿUthmān." ʿAlī left, saying, "God's decree will come in its time!" Al-Miqdād said, "You have indeed, ʿAbd al-Raḥmān, passed up the one who makes decisions based 'on the truth and thereby acts justly.' " [ʿAbd al-Raḥmān] replied,

"I have indeed exerted all my efforts for the Muslims, Miqdād." [The former] said, "If you sincerely did what you did for God's sake, may He reward you as He does those who do good." [But] al-Miqdād said, "I have never seen such things as have been visited upon the people of this house after the death of their Prophet. I am amazed at Quraysh that they have abandoned someone who cannot be matched in my opinion in knowledge and the ability to act justly. What indeed if I were to find supporters against 'Uthmān!" 'Abd al-Raḥmān replied, "Fear God, Miqdād, I am afraid you will cause dissension." Someone questioned al-Miqdād, "God have mercy upon you, who are the people of this house and who is this man?" He replied, "The people of this house are Banū 'Abd al-Muṭṭalib and the man is 'Alī b. Abī Ṭālib." 'Alī said, "The people are looking to Quraysh, while Quraysh are [also] looking to their own house. [Quraysh] say that, if Banū Hāshim are put in authority over you, [the caliphate] will never leave them; but so long as it is in the hands of [clans] other than [Banū Hāshim] of Quraysh, you will pass it around among yourselves."

Ṭalḥa arrived on the day on which the oath of allegiance was given to 'Uthmān. He was asked to give his own oath to 'Uthmān, but asked, "Do all Quraysh approve of him?" and was told they did. He came to 'Uthmān and the latter said, "You still have your opinions open; if you refuse [to give me the oath of allegiance], I shall reject [the caliphate]." Ṭalḥa said, "Will you really reject it?" 'Uthmān replied that he would. Ṭalḥa asked, "Have all the people given you the oath of allegiance?" 'Uthmān replied that they had. [Ṭalḥa] said, "Then I approve; I shall not go against the general consensus." He gave ['Uthmān] the oath of allegiance.

Al-Mughīra b. Shu'ba said to 'Abd al-Raḥmān, "You were right to give 'Uthmān the oath of allegiance, Abū Muḥammad." He also said to 'Uthmān, "If 'Abd al-Raḥmān had given the oath of allegiance to anyone other than you, we would not have agreed." But 'Abd al-Raḥmān retorted, "You one-eyed liar! If I had given anyone else the oath of allegiance, you would have done so also and would have said what you say now."[6]

## APPENDIX THREE

# Manūshihr's Declaration

Ṭabarī includes a letter attributed to the Kayanid king Manūshihr that comprises advice that figures in later Islamic historiography in both concept and phrasing.[1] The language of the speech, as will be noted, not only bears a strong connection to Islamic religious and ethical discourse of later times but also addresses in theory problematics that occurred during the Rāshidūn caliphate (among others). Some of the exhortations in the declaration greatly resemble the advice that 'Umar b. al-Khaṭṭāb gave to the Arab troops during and after their great military campaigns against the Sasanid empire, while other statements of advice serve other purposes of governmental advice that either foreshadow or correct certain policies. Manūshihr's advice to the leader or governor to apply moderation in pursuing an official delinquent in delivering tax revenues or other financial obligations, for example, contrasts with 'Alī's ill-advised persecution of Maṣqala b. Hubayra al-Shaybānī and 'Abdallāh b. 'Abbās over financial disputes.

The backdrop of the declaration is the beginning of depredations against the Persian kingdom by the Turks, which prompted Manūshihr to counsel the elite of the state and its military commanders about the need to harken back to the time-honored values of the Sasanid state and the original legal principles of its society. In the statement that precedes this declaration, Manūshihr reportedly rebuked his people (*wabbakha qawmahu*)—in the manner of prophets, perhaps—and said: "O People!

Not all those you have sired are people [*innakum lam talidū al-nās kulla-hum*]; for people are only truly people so long as they defend themselves and repel the enemy from them [*innamā al-nās nās mā ʿaqilū min anfusihim wa dafaʿū al-ʿaduwwa ʿanhum*], but the Turks have seized a part of your outlying districts. That is only because you abandoned warfare against your enemy and you lacked concern [*laysa dhalika illā min tarkikum jihāda ʿaduwwikum wa qillat al-mubālāt*]. But God has granted us dominion as a test [*li-yabluwanā*] of whether we will be grateful, and He will increase us, or He will disbelieve and punish us, though we belong to a family of renown, for the source of rule belongs to God. When tomorrow comes be present!" They said they would and sought forgiveness.

When the next day came, he sent for those possessing royalty and the noblest commanders (*ahl al-mimlaka wa ashrāf al-asāwira*). He invited them and made the leaders (*al-ruʾasāʾ*) of people enter: he invited the Chief Magus, who was seated on a chair opposite his throne. Then Manūshihr rose on his throne, with the nobles of the royal family and the noblest commanders rising to their feet. He said: "Be seated! I stood up only to let you hear my words." They sat down.

The following is an excerpt of his declaration.

> O people! All creatures belong to the Creator; gratitude belongs to the One Who grants favors, as does submission to the All-Powerful. What exists is inescapable, for there is none weaker than a creature, whether he seeks or is sought; there is no one more powerful than a creator. . . . Verily, contemplation is light, while forgetfulness [*al-ghafla*] is darkness; ignorance is misguidance [*al-jahāla ḍalāla*]. The first has come, and the last must join the first. Before us there came principles of which we are derivative [*qad maḍat qablanā uṣūl naḥnu furūʿahā*]—and what kind of continued existence can a derivative have after its purpose disappears [*fa-mā baqāʾu farʿin baʿda dhahābi aṣlihi*]?
>
> Verily God has given us this dominion, and to him belongs praise. We ask Him to inspire us with integrity, truth, and certainty [*al-rushd wa'l-ṣidq wa'l-yaqīn*]. For the king has a claim on his subjects, and his subjects have a claim on him, whereas their obligation to the ruler is that they obey him, give him good counsel, and fight his enemy; the king's obligation is to provide them with their sustenance in its proper times, for they cannot rely on anything else, and that is their commerce. The king's obligation to his subjects is that he take care of

them, treat them kindly, and not impose on them what they cannot do. If a calamity befalls them and diminishes their gains because a heavenly or earthly evil comes upon them, he should deduct from the land tax that which was diminished. If a calamity ruins them altogether, he should give them what they need to strengthen their rebuilding. Afterward he may take from them to the extent that he does not harm them, for a year or two years.

The king must possess three qualities: first, that he be truthful and not lie, that he be bountiful and not be miserly, and that he be in control of himself in anger, for he is given power with his hand outstretched and the land tax coming to him. He must not appropriate to himself what belongs to his troops, and his subjects. He must be liberal in pardon, for there is no king more long lasting than a king who pardons or one more doomed to perish than one who punishes. Moreover, a man who errs regarding pardon and pardons is better than one who errs in punishing. . . . If a matter requiring punishment is brought to him [i.e., the king] regarding one of his officials, he must not show him favor. Let him bring him together with the complainant, and if the claim of the wronged one is proved right against him, the sum is transferred from the official to him. But if [the official] is unable to [pay], then the king should pay the sum for him and then return the official to his position, requiring that he make restitution for what he extorted.

The Turks have coveted you, so protect us and you will only protect yourselves. I have commanded arms and provision for you. I am your partner in this matter [*wa anā sharīkukum fī al-ra'y*], for I can only call myself a king as long as I have obedience from you. Indeed, a king is a king only if he is obeyed. For if he is contradicted, he is ruled and is not a ruler. Whenever we are informed of disobedience, we will not accept it from the informer until we have verified it [*mahmā balaghanā min al-khilāf fa-innā lā naqbaluhu min al-mubligh ḥattā natayaqqanahu*]. If the report is true, so be it, if not, we will treat the informer as a disobedient one.

Is not the finest act in the face of misfortune the acceptance of patience and rejoicing in the comfort of certainty? Whoever is slain in battle with the enemy [*mujāhadat al-'aduww*], I hope for him the attainment of God's pleasure. The best of things is the submission to God's command, a rejoicing and satisfaction in His judgment [*al-riḍā bi-qaḍā'ihi*]. This world is only a journey for its inhabitants, they cannot loosen the knots of the saddle except in the other [world], and their self-sufficiency is in borrowed things.

How good is gratitude toward the Benefactor and submission to the One to Whom judgment belongs! Who owes submission more to the One above him than he who has no refuge except in Him, or any reliance except on Him! So trust in victory if your determination is that succor is from God. Be confident of achieving the goal if your intent is sincere [*thiqū bi'l-ghalaba idhā kānat niyyātukum anna al-naṣr min allāh*]. Know that this dominion will not stand except through uprightness [*inna hādhā al-mulk lā yaqūm illā bi'l-istiqāma*] and good obedience, suppression of the enemy, blocking the frontiers, justice to the subjects, and just treatment to the oppressed. Your healing is within you; the remedy in which there is no illness is uprightness, commanding good and forbidding evil [*al-amr bi'l-khayr wa'l-nahy 'an al-sharr*]. For there is no power except in God [*lā quwwata illā bi-allāh*]. Look to the subjects, for they are your food and drink. Whenever you deal justly with them, they desire prosperity [*al-'imāra*], which will increase your land-tax revenues and will be made evident in the growth of your wealth. But if you wrong the subjects, they will abandon cultivation and leave most of the land idle. This will decrease your land-tax revenues, and it will be made evident in the decrease of your wealth. Pledge yourselves to deal justly with your subjects [*ta'āhadū al-ra'iyyata bi'l-inṣāf*]. Whatever rivers or overflows there are, of which the cost [of repair] is the ruler's, hurry to take care of it before it increases. But whatever is owed by the subjects which they are unable to take care of, lend it to them from the treasury of the land taxes. When the times of their taxes come due, take it back with their produce tax to the extent that it will not harm them: a quarter [of it] each year, or a third, or a half, so that it will not cause them distress.

This is my speech and my command, O Chief Magus! Adhere to these words, and hold onto what you have heard this day. Have you heard, O people?

They said, "Yes! You have spoken well, and we will act, God willing."

# Notes

## 1. INTRODUCTION

1. J. Wansbrough, *Quranic Studies* (Oxford, 1977), 1–20. A. Rippin, "Interpreting the Bible Through the Qur'an," *Approaches to the Qur'an*, ed. G. R. Hawting and Abdul-Kader A. Shareef (London: Routledge, 1993), 250–251.

2. Qur'ān 16:74: "So strike not any similitudes for God" (trans. A. J. Arberry, *The Koran Interpreted*, 2 vols. [London, 1955], I, 294); Qur'ān 17:48: "Behold how they strike similitudes for thee, and go astray, and cannot find a way" (Arberry, I, 307). Qur'ān 25:9: "Behold, how they strike similitudes for thee, and go astray, and are unable to find a way" (Arberry, II, 57). Qur'ān 43:58: "And when the son of Mary is cited as an example, behold thy people turn away from it and say, 'What, are our gods better, or he?' They cite not him to thee, save to dispute; nay but they are a people contentious" (Arberry, II, 204). Numerous other verses describe the divine creation of a parable in reference to historical figures (Qur'ān 43:57, 66:10–11, 25:39, 30:58).

3. Qur'ān 12:3: "We relate to thee the fairest of stories in that We have revealed to thee this Qur'ān, though before it thou wast one of the heedless" (Arberry, I, 254).

4. This Qur'ānic exhortation to curtail storytelling may find a precedent in the biblical discouragement on adding further books to the scripture. D. S. Margoliouth, *The Early Development of Mohammedanism* (London, 1913), 24, 43.

5. F. Rosenthal, "The Influence of Biblical Tradition on Muslim Historiography," in *Historians of the Middle East*, ed. B. Lewis and P. Holt (Oxford, 1962), 35–45; N. Abbott, *Studies in Arabic Literary Papyri II: Qur'ānic Commentary and Tradition* (Chicago, 1976), 15.

6. The fact that the detailed accounts about the Islamic *fitan* (sing. *fitna*) were not flattering to religious interests does not mean that they are factual (as per G. Schoeler's comments about the affair of the slander: "Characteristics and anecdotes of this sort should be seen as being reliable, since they have resisted the tendency towards idealization" [G. Schoeler, "Character and Authenticity of the Muslim Tradition on the Life of the Prophet," *Arabica* 48 (2002): 362]). The opposite of *ḥadīth* was not factual history, but another type of *ḥadīth*.

7. It is within this frame of parabolic history, which anticipates the coming discord among the companions, that some of 'Umar's prophesying words to the companions make sense as he attempts to forestall further discord. This happens most notably in a report appended at the end of 'Uthmān's reign when the second caliph is seen discouraging the companions who had fought in the early battles of Islam on the side of the Prophet from seeking to join the conquest campaigns against the Persians and the Byzantines. "You have obtained your reward by your campaign with the Messenger of God," ['Umar would tell the companions]. "It is better for you to avoid entanglement in worldly affairs than to go on campaigns now [*wa khayrun laka min al-ghazw al-yawm allā tarā al-dunyā wa lā tarāka*]." The narrators then continues, "When 'Uthmān took power, however, he freed them from such restrictions. They betook themselves to the conquered territories, where the people attached themselves to them. Therefore (the Quraysh) preferred ('Uthmān) to 'Umar." Ṭabarī, *Tā'rīkh al-Rusul wa'l-Mulūk*, ed. M. J. De Goeje, III series (Leiden, 1879–1901), I, 3026. Trans. R. S. Humphreys, *The History of al-Ṭabarī*, XIV: *The Crisis of the Early Caliphate* (Albany, 1990), 224 (with minor modification). 'Alā' al-Dīn al-Muttaqī al-Hindī, *Kanz al-'Ummāl fī Sunan al-Aqwāl wa'l-Af'āl*, ed. Ṣafwat al-Saqqā and Bakrī al-Ḥayyānī (Beirut, 1985), XVI, 47 (no. 37978).

8. Although political achievement is viewed as a key outcome of the religious triumph, it is heavily downplayed. In this context one thus understands the bleak remarks of 'Umar upon receiving news of the conquest of Jalulā'. As the caliph began to weep, 'Abd al-Raḥman b. 'Awf reportedly asked: "Why do you lament, O Commander of the Faithful, this is indeed a time for gratitude [*inna hādhā la-mawṭina shukr*]." 'Umar then replied: "By God, this is not why I weep but God never gave this kind of wealth to a people who found themselves spared jealousy, rivalry, and eventual conflict among themselves." Ṭabarī, I, 2466–2467.

9. Hence the religious saying (sometimes attributed to 'Umar), "The community renders [its duty] to the *imām* so long as the *imām* renders his duty toward God. If the *imām* becomes lax, his followers will become so as well [*idhā rata'a al-imām rata'ū*]." Abū 'Abdallāh Muḥammad b. Sa'd, *al-Ṭabaqāt al-Kubrā* (Beirut, 1957–1968), III, 292. Aḥmad b. Yaḥyā al-Balādhurī, *Ansāb al-Ashrāf, Sā'ir Furū' Quraysh*, ed. I. 'Abbas (Wiesbaden, 1996), V, 405. Furthermore, this system in fact included keeping the faith not only within the community, but equally with the non-Muslim populations being conquered. There are numerous examples from

the reigns of Abū Bakr and 'Umar where the caliph cautions his troops that a transgression against fair dealing with the enemy is still a transgression of the covenant.

10. Ya'qūbī, Aḥmad b. Abī Ya'qūb b. Wāḍiḥ, *Mushākalat al-Nās li-Zamānihim* (Beirut, 1962), 13–15. The translation partly draws on that by W. Millward, "The Adaptation of Men to Their Time: An Historical Essay," *Journal of the American Oriental Society* 84 (1964): 329–344. Similar stories about the fortunes some companions made are also attested in other sources, where they are linked to the good fortune of the companions in making commerce. In one sense, such success is usually described to legitimize the practice of commerce by showing the companions active in it, as well as to show divine favor upon them in their prosperity. However, the same descriptions, especially when set in 'Uthmān's reign, are meant to show some licentiousness in the companions' imitations of the practices of the caliph. The idea that a political leader usually set the norms of the time in practical and mystical terms was a widely accepted tenet in the social and political philosophy of medieval Islam. Hence al-Aḥnaf reportedly tells Mu'āwiya, "You represent the times to your people. If you act well, they will act righteously as well." Abū'l-Faraj 'Abd al-Raḥmān b. al-Jawzī, *al-Miṣbāḥ al-Muḍī' fī Khilāfat al-Mustaḍī'*, ed. Nājiya 'Abdallāh Ibrāhim (Baghdad, 1976) I, 183, 244.

11. Ṭabarī, I, 358.

12. G. H. A. Juynboll, *Muslim Tradition* (Cambridge, 1983), 200–202.

13. About this controversy, al-Juwaynī for example states: "It is incumbent on the believer that he interpret all controversies that he relates [about these matters] in a positive way [*yanbaghī [li'l-mutadayyin] an lā ya'lū jahdan fī ḥaml kull mā yanqul 'alā wajh al-khayr*]." The last phrase is misread by the editor as "'*alā wajh al-khabar*." Abū'l-Ma'ālī 'Abd al-Malik b. 'Abdallāh al-Juwaynī, *Kitāb al-Irshād*, ed. Muḥammad Yūsuf Mūsā and 'Alī 'Abd al-Mun'im 'Abd al-Ḥamīd (Cairo, 2002), 433. Ibn al-'Arabī concludes his defenses on this topic by quoting 'Umar b. 'Abd al-'Azīz, who reportedly responded when asked about the companion controversies by saying (quoting a Qur'ānic verse): "That is a nation that has passed away; there awaits them that they have earned, and there awaits you that you have earned; you shall not be questioned concerning the things they did" (Qur'ān 2:134 [Arberry, I, 46]). Abū Bakr Muḥammad b. al-'Arabī, *al-'Awāṣim min al-Qawāṣim fī Taḥqīq Mawāqif al-Ṣaḥāba ba'd Wafāt al-Nabī*, ed. Muḥibb al-Dīn al-Khaṭīb (Cairo, 1968), 202.

14. Humphreys, *HT*, XVI, xvi.

15. When one companion, for example, asks the Prophet: "Will there be trouble after this phase of good?," the answer comes in the affirmative. Abū 'Abdallāh Muḥammad b. Ismā'īl al-Bukhārī, *Ṣaḥīḥ*, ed. Muḥammad Muḥsin Khān, 9 vols. (Riyad, 1997) (*kitāb al-fitan*), IX, 160 (no. 206).

16. "*mā akhāfu 'alaykum an tushrikū ba'dī wa lakin akhāfu 'alaykum an tatanāfasū fīhā*." Muslim b. al-Ḥajjāj al-Qurashī al-Nīsābūrī, *Ṣaḥīḥ*, ed. M. M. 'Abd al-Laṭīf,

18 vols. in 9 (reprinted, Beirut), V (pt. 15) (no. 2296), 57. Bukhārī (*kitāb farḍ al-khums*), IV, 254 (no. 385); V, 257 (no. 374).

17. Other *ḥadīths* confirm the aforementioned fear. In one, the Prophet declares, "Do not turn against one another after my death, striking each other with swords [*lā tartaddū ba'dī kuffāran yaḍribu ba'ḍukum riqāba ba'ḍ*]." Bukhārī (*kitāb al-fitan*), IX, 156 (no. 200); (*kitāb al-maghāzī*), V, 485 (no. 687). Another version replaces "*la tartaddū*" with "*lā tarji'ū bad'ī ḍullālan . . .*" and the context of the statement is placed in the Prophet's farewell speech (Ḥijjat al-Wadā'). (*kitāb al-tawḥīd*), IX, 406 (no. 539). Abū 'Īsā Muḥammad b. 'Īsā al-Tirmidhī, *al-Jāmi' al-Ṣaḥīḥ wa huwa al-Sunan*, ed. Aḥmad Muḥammad Shākir, 5 vols. (Beirut, 1987), *kitāb al-fitan*, IV, 421 (no. 2193). Ibn Māja, *Sunan*, II, 1300 (no. 3943). Ibn Sa'd's version includes "*lā tarji'unna ba'dī kuffāran yaḍribu ba'ḍukum riqāba ba'ḍ.*" Ibn Sa'd, II, 184. Muḥammad b. 'Umar al-Wāqidī, *Kitāb al-Maghāzī*, ed. Marsden Jones, 3 vols. (Oxford, 1966), III, 1113 (Wāqidī's account is narrated on the authority of 'Ikrima and Ibn 'Abbās). Also, in excerpt, Aḥmad b. Ḥanbal, *Musnad*, ed. Shu'ayb al-Arna'ūṭ, 50 vols. (Beirut, 1993–2001), IX, 411. Ṭabarī's version of the farewell speech, reliant on Ibn Isḥāq, omits the aforementioned line (*fa-lā tarji'ū ba'dī kuffāran . . .*), but it seems clear from the context of that speech, with its emphasis on the promise of the believers and the inviolability of blood and property, that the line is original to the main version but was omitted because it sounded a very jarring note in a convivial context. Isolating the comment in *ḥadīth*, however, made it less damaging to the upward drift of the Islamic historical narrative. For a more likely version of the speech, see Abū 'Umar Aḥmad b. Muḥammad b. 'Abd Rabbihi, *Kitāb al-'Iqd al-Farīd*, ed. A. Amīn et al., 8 vols. (Cairo 1940–53), IV, 58. *Al-'Iqd*'s texts are generally among the closest to Ṭabarī's history. Also, 'Amr b. Baḥr al-Jāḥiẓ, *al-Bayān wa'l-Tabyīn*, ed. Abd al-Salām Muḥammad Hārūn, 4 vols. (Cairo, 1948), II, 33. Aḥmad, *Musnad*, XXXIV, 299–301.

18. In a followup meant to deflect the ominous meaning of the statement, Abū Bakr is portrayed as weeping, and asking the Prophet, "Are we going to live after you? [*wa innā la-kā'inūna ba'daka*]." Mālik b. Anas, *Kitāb al-Muwaṭṭa*, ed. M. F. 'Abd al-Bāqī, 2 vols. (Beirut, 1988), *kitāb al-jihād* (*faḍl al-shuhadā' fī sabīl allāh*), II, 462. This *ḥadīth* is recounted as a statement in praise of martyrs in general, and is capped with a conclusion that is meant to soften the earlier prophetic warning by making the main focus of the conversation Abū Bakr's awareness that the Prophet would one day pass away.

19. Aḥmad, *Musnad*, XXXIV, 133. This *ḥadīth*, which has elements resembling *ḥadīth al-shafā'a*, has the Prophet ask God why the companions are barred from entry to the *ḥawḍ*, and the answer given is: "You do not know what they did after you, they retreated backwards [*innaka lā tadrī mā aḥdathū ba'daka, innahum irtaddū 'alā a'qābihim al-qahqarā*]." Bukhārī, *Saḥīḥ* (*kitāb al-qadar*), VIII, 382 (no. 585). Another version states: "*inna ha'ulā lam yazālū murtaddīn 'alā a'qābihim mundhu fāraqtahum.*" Bukhārī (*kitāb al-tafsīr*), VI, 236. A similar version in Muslim,

V, pt. 15, 55–57 (nos. 2294–2297). In another version, when the Prophet inquires why the companions are kept away, the answer states: "You do not know what they changed after you [*innaka lā tadrī mā baddalū ba'daka*]." And whereas in the previous version the Prophet expresses a helpless regret for what happened, in this one the Prophet expresses approval for punishment. Here he adds: "Punishment to those who changed their ways after me! [*suḥqan, suḥqan li-man baddala ba'dī*]." Bukhārī (*kitāb al-fitan*), IX, 144 (no. 174). A similar *ḥadīth* given by Bukhārī (*kitāb al-qadar*), VIII, 383 (no. 587). Abū 'Abdallāh Muḥammad b. Yazīd b. Māja, *Sunan*, ed. Muḥammad Fu'ād 'Abd al-Bāqī, 2 vols. (Beirut, 1980), *kitāb al-zuhd*, II, 1440 (no. 4306).

20. Al-Nasā'ī, *Ṣaḥīḥ Sunan al-Nasā'ī, kitāb al-janā'iz, bāb dhikr awwal man yuksā*, II, 449 (no. 1973).

21. The relevant verses read, "And when God said, 'O Jesus son of Mary, didst thou say unto men, "Take me and my mother as gods, apart from God"?' He said, 'To Thee be glory! It is not mine to say what I have no right to. If I indeed said it, Thou knowest it, knowing what is within my soul, and I know not what is within Thy soul; Thou knowest the things unseen. I only said to them what Thou didst command me: "Serve God, my Lord and your Lord." And I was a witness over them, while I remained among them; but when Thou didst take me to Thyself, Thou wast Thyself the watcher over them; Thou Thyself art witness of everything. If Thou chastisest them, they are Thy servants; if Thou forgivest them, Thou art the All-mighty, the All-wise'" (Qur'ān 5:116–117 [Arberry, I, 147]).

22. Needless to say, Islamic orthodox writings later sought to cleanse the narrative of the early caliphate by discouraging any historical commentary on companion behavior. Hence one reads the frequent exhortation in various biographical dictionaries that the most anathemous activities are three: discussing the subject of *qadar* (fate), the subject of the stars (i.e., astronomy or astrology), and telling stories about the companions. Abū al-Qāsim al-Sahmī, *Ta'rīkh Jurjān* (Beirut, 1987), 295, 429. The two *ḥadīths* are narrated on the authority of Ibn 'Umar and Ibn 'Abbās. A variant version on this *ḥadīth* is given by 'Abd al-Karīm b. Muḥammad al-Rāfi'ī al-Qazwīnī *al-Tadwīn fī Akhbār Qazwīn*, ed. 'Azīz allāh al-'Uṭāridī, 4 vols. (Beirut, 1987), II, 39.

23. The comparison of the day after 'Uthmān's assassination to the episode of the golden calf is attested in a conversation between al-Ashtar and Masrūq (according to Sufyān al-Thawrī). Ibn 'Abd Rabbihi, *al-'Iqd*, IV, 295. It is within this context of comparison that much of the representation of the Kufan dissidence during 'Uthmān's reign was intended to be understood. Sayf b. 'Umar's characterization of the rowdy Kufan opponents to Sa'īd b. al-'Āṣ with the term "*al-sufahā'*" was meant to evoke the Qur'ānic verse in which Moses pleads with God, "Wilt Thou Destroy us for what the foolish ones of us have done? [*a-tuhlikanā bi-mā fa'ala al-sufahā' minnā*]" (Qur'ān 7:155 [Arberry, I, 189]). In reading narratives within this frame of representation, a reader can start to piece together

other fragments in Rāshidūn history so that they begin to make sense. 'Umar's famous denial at the Saqīfa—that the Prophet had died, and that it was not a death that had occurred but that the Prophet had departed (in spirit) to meet with God, as Moses had done, and that he would come back in both body and spirit and punish those who claimed he died—shows a narrative conflation of two different prophetic experiences, those of both Moses and Jesus (the latter being the one departed in spirit). Two different reports given by Ibn Sa'd about the elevation of Jesus and Moses in spirit (the first reported on the authority of al-Wāqidī, and the second on that of 'Ikrima) show the intertextual inspiration for the discourse attributed to 'Umar about Muḥammad's elevation in spirit. Ibn Sa'd, II, 266, 271

24. In a range of *ḥadīths* the Prophet is said to comment that his community is "the most resembling for the Banū Isrā'īl . . ." or that they "shall follow exactly in their footsteps," "be afflicted as the Israelites were," and "divide into 72 sects as the Christians and Jews before them." All these *ḥadīths* originated from a sense of resemblance in historical fate and the transition from triumph to temptation. For such *ḥadīths*, see al-Hindī's *Kanz*, XI, 246 (no. 31396). This can be found in the *ḥadīth* that states, "There shall come upon my nation exactly what has happened to the Banū Isrā'īl [*la-ya'tiyanna 'alā ummatī mā atā 'alā banī isrā'īl mithlan bi-mithl ḥadhwa al-na'li bi'l-na'l*]. The Banū Isrā'īl dispersed into 72 sects and my community will divide into 73 sects." *Kanz*, I, 183 (no. 928).

25. The famous *ḥadīth*: "You shall follow the *sunan* of those who came before you—*shibran bi-shibr*" (the reference is confirmed as being to both Christians and Jews). Aḥmad, *Musnad*, XVIII, 357. Ibn Ḥajar, *Fatḥ al-Bārī* (*kitāb aḥādīth al-anbiyā'*), VI, 613 (no. 3456). Sayf b. 'Umar, *Kitāb al-Ridda wa al-Futūḥ and Kitāb al-Jamal wa Masīr 'Āisha wa 'Alī*, ed. Q. al-Samarrā'ī (Leiden, 1995), I, 131. It should be mentioned here that the Islamic view of the past established a collectivity between Christians and Jews under the term "Israelite" (Banū Isrā'īl). Whenever used in *ḥadīth* literature the term refers to both groups in a historical sense as a national continuum rather than distinguishable religious sects.

26. Here 'Umar's famous statement, "Do you not find [in the tradition] that the Prophet is followed by the caliph, and the latter by the kings?" al-Hindī, *Kanz*, XVI, 686 (no. 14191). The Prophet reportedly states in a *ḥadīth*, "Prophets used to run the affairs of the Banū Isrā'īl [*kānat banū isrā'īl tasūsuhum al-anbiyā'* ]. Every time a prophet died, he was succeeded by a prophet. There shall be no prophet after me, but there will be caliphs who will become many in number." Then when asked by his companions how they should deal with them, he said, "Give them the oath of allegiance and your loyalty. God will question them about how they ran your affairs." Aḥmad, *Musnad*, XIII, 340; al-Hindī, *Kanz*, V, 785 (no. 14380–14381); VI, 51 (14805). Abū Bakr Aḥmad b. 'Alī al-Khaṭīb al-Baghdādī, *Ta'rīkh Baghdād*, 14 vols. (Cairo, 1931), V, 473. Muslim, V (pt. 10), 231 (no. 1842). Another *ḥadīth* declares that the history of the Islamic state would comprise

twelve caliphs in equal number to the twelve disciples (*nuqabā'*) of Moses. Abū al-Faḍl 'Abd al-Raḥmān al-Suyūṭī, *Ta'rīkh al-Khulafā'* (Cairo, 1964), 13 (the *ḥadīth* is quoted from Aḥmad's *Musnad*, and on the authority of Ibn Mas'ūd). U. Rubin has noted the influence on this tradition by the idea of twelve princes projected from the line of Ishmael in Genesis 17:20, and the attestation for disciples in Numbers 7:2. U. Rubin, *Between Bible and Qur'ān* (Princeton: Darwin Press, 1999), 252–256. Also relevant is an 'Abbāsid version of the *ḥadīth* that is provided in the biography of the caliph al-Manṣūr. Ibn 'Abbās there reportedly predicts a line of twelve *amīrs* to be followed by the rule of *ahl al-bayt* (the family of the Prophet), and then the rule is concluded with the reigns of al-Manṣūr, al-Mahdī, and, afterward, Jesus. Abū'l-Qāsim 'Alī b. al-Ḥasan b. 'Asākir, *Ta'rīkh Madīnat Dimashq*, ed. 'Umar b. Gharāma al-'Amrawī, 80 vols. (Beirut, 1995–2000), XXXII, 303. The mention of the twelve rulers is sometimes not specified as caliphs (just as those in charge of authority). However, a followup clarification that all of these will be from the Quraysh provides the main message about the path of Islam's political history (irrespective of whether the Rāshidūn or the Umayyads were being counted within this process). Muslim, VI (pt. 12), 201–203.

27. A report attributed to Ka'b declares, "no nation ever escaped being tried after more than thirty-five years of the passing away of its prophet had elapsed." Nu'aym b. Ḥammād al-Marwazī, *Kitāb al-Fitan*, ed. S. Zakkar (Beirut, 1993), 421, 426. Other *ḥadīths* also highlight the thirty-five-year horizon of the successful community. Aḥmad, *Musnad*, VI, 276, 300–301. Balādhurī, *Ansāb (Sā'ir)*, 572. Ṭabarī seems to use this time horizon consistently for states, such as when he notes that the Turks began their depredations against the Persian kingdom in Kayanid times, after thirty-five years had elapsed from the rule of Manushihr, and then uses the event as the background for Manushihr's famous speech calling on his people to reform their ways. Ṭabarī, I, 436. See appendix III. Other traditionalist texts set the history of the caliphate at thirty years, and categorize what followed as kingship (*mulk*). 'Imād al-Dīn Ismā'īl b. 'Umar b. Kathīr, *al-Nihāya fī'l-Fitan wa'l-Malāḥim*, ed. A. 'Abd al-Shāfī (Beirut, 1988), 6 (also citing Aḥmad, Abū Dāwūd, al-Nisā'ī and al-Tirmidhī).

28. S. Sandmel, *Judaism and Christian Beginnings* (Oxford, 1978), 361.

29. Best strengthening such a linkage here are the numerous warning statements attributed to 'Abdallāh b. Sallām, a former Jew. Whereas Ka'b al-Aḥbār warned about what would happen after 'Umar's death, Ibn Sallām cautioned about the aftermath of 'Uthmān's overthrow. On the eve of 'Uthmān's death, Ibn Sallām warned the attackers, saying, "Do not unleash the sword of God upon you. . . . today your community is governed with the whip [*al-darra*], but if you kill him [i.e., 'Uthmān] it will only be governed with the sword. Woe to you! Your city is today guarded by the angels, but if you kill him, they shall abandon the place." Muḥammad b. Abī Bakr Yaḥyā al-Māliqī, *al-Tamhīd wa'l-Bayān fī Maqtal al-Shahīd 'Uthmān*, ed. Maḥmūd Yūsuf Zāyed (Beirut, 1964), 135. The travails of Ismā'īl's

lineage of prophets thus turn out to run parallel to those faced earlier by Isaac's lineage, and the whole cycle of religious salvation concludes with the divine unleashing of a monarchal power that brings an expiating conquest to the elected nation (the Jews and the Hāshimites). A close reading of the scene of 'Uthmān's downfall also shows direct borrowing from the story of Jesus' surrender.

30. 'Abdallāh b. Sallām is said to have cautioned that the death of a caliph would bring punishment on the community with the death of thirty-five thousand people, much as the murder of a prophet in the past had led to the punishment of fifty thousand people. Ibn Sa'd, *Ṭabaqāt*, III, 83. Balādhurī, *Ansāb al-Ashrāf, Banū 'Abd Shams*, ed. 'Abd al-'Azīz al-Dūrī (Wiesbaden, 1979), I, 565, 582. Abū'l-'Arab Muḥammad b. Aḥmad al-Tamīmī, *Kitāb al-Miḥan*, ed. Y. al-Jubūrī (Beirut, 1983), 82. A report quoting Ibn 'Abbās states, "Had the people not sought vengeance for the death of 'Uthmān, they would have been struck down by stones falling from the sky." Ibn Sa'd, III, 80.

31. Al-Hindī, *Kanz*, XI, 223 (no. 31306). Ibn 'Asākir, XXXIX, 447. Another tradition adds, "When 'Uthmān is killed, the sword is unleashed until Judgment Day." Ibn 'Asākir, XXXIX, 444. The perception of 'Uthmān's death as causing cataclysm is also included in 'Alī's initial warning speech to 'Uthmān at the onset of the Kufan opposition. Ṭabarī, I, 2938. It should be noted here that narrators also expected readers to recognize that the first *dajjāl* (fraudulent leader) was 'Abdallāh b. Saba', who was compared to Paul of Tarsus. Sayf b. 'Umar, *Kitāb al-Ridda wa'l-Futūḥ*, 135.

32. Occasional *ḥadīths* in *fitan* literature can perhaps provide guiding parameters for how to read underlying moralizing themes in the historical narratives. One such *ḥadīth* addressing the *muhājirūn* declares that five traits bring on certain cataclysms. Paraphrased, these are: the spread of sin (*al-fāḥisha*), which leads to the plague; tampering with trading scales (*inqāṣ al-mikyāl*), which leads to inflation and oppression (*shiddat al-ma'ūna wa jūr al-sulṭān*); the holding back of almsgiving (*zakāt*), which leads to droughts; the breaking of covenants, which leads to invasions by the enemy; and the neglect of divine injunctions (*ḥukm al-a'imma bi-kitāb allāh*), which leads to civil war. Ibn Kathīr, *al-Nihāya*, 19.

33. Ṭabarī, I, 1846. Donner, *HT*, X, 12.

34. Ṭabarī, I, 1847. Donner, *HT*, X, 13.

35. In a speech that 'Uthmān reportedly made shortly after being designated caliph, he declares, "Surely this world harbors deceit [*inna al-dunyā ṭuwiyat 'alā al-ghurūr*], 'so let not the present life delude you,' and 'let not the deceitful one delude you concerning God.' Consider those who have gone before you, then be in earnest and do not be neglectful, for you will surely not be overlooked. Where are the sons and brothers of this world who tilled it, dwelt in it, and were long granted enjoyment therein? [*ayna abnā' al-dunyā wa ikhwānuhā alladhīna athārūhā wa 'amarūhā wa mutti'ū bihā ṭawīlan?*] Did it not spit them out? Cast aside this

world as God has cast it aside and seek the hereafter, for verily God has coined a parable for it and for that which is better. The Almighty has said: 'And strike for them the similitude of the present life [*mathal al-ḥayāt al-dunyā*]: it is as water that We send down out of heaven, [and the plants of the earth mingle with it; and in the morning it is straw the winds scatter; and God is omnipotent over everything. Wealth and sons are the adornment of the present world; but the abiding things, the deeds of righteousness, are better with God in reward, and better in hope.'] (Qur'ān 18:42–44)." Ṭabarī, I, 2800–2801. Humphreys, HT, XV, 3–4.

36. Ṭabarī, I, 2802–2803. Humphreys, HT, XV, 6.

37. 'Uthmān here declares: "Verily you are the guardians and protectors of the Muslims and 'Umar laid down for you [instructions] that were not hidden from us; on the contrary, they were in accordance with our counsel. Let me hear of no change or alteration on the part of any one of you, lest God change your situation and replace you with others [*wa lā yablughannī 'an aḥadin minkum taghyīr wa lā tabdīl fa-yughayyir allāhu mā bi-kum wa yastabdil bi-kum ghayrukum*]. So examine your conduct, for I shall examine what God has required me to examine and watch over [*fa-innī anẓur fī-mā alzamanī allāhu al-naẓara fīhi wa'l-qiyāma 'alayhi*]." Ṭabarī, I, 2803. Humphreys, HT, XV, 6. Ṭabarī, I, 2803–2804. Humphreys, HT, XV, 7. In another speech, 'Uthmān also advises, "Beware of the Divine wrath. Adhere to your community; do not divide into hostile sects [*ilzamū jamā'atakum, lā taṣīrū aḥzāban*]. 'Remember God's blessing you when you were enemies, and He brought your hearts together, so that by His blessings you became brothers' (Qur'ān 3:98)." Ṭabarī, I, 3059. Humphreys, HT, XV, 257.

38. 'Uthmān declares: "To proceed: You have attained so much only by strict adherence to sound models [of conduct]. Let not this world turn you away from your proper concerns [*amrikum*], for this community will become involved in innovation after three things occur together among you: complete prosperity [*takāmul al-ni'am*], the attainment of adulthood by the children of the captive women, and the recitation of the Qur'ān by both Arabs and non-Arabs [*qirā'at al-a'rāb wa'l-a'ājim al-Qur'ān*]. The Messenger of God has said, 'Unbelief stems from speaking Arabic badly [*al-kufru fī'l-'ujma*]; if something seems foreign to them, they will do it awkwardly and [thereby] bring about innovation [*fa-in ista'jama 'alayhim amr takallafū wa ibtada'ū*].'" Ṭabarī, I, 2803–2804. Humphreys, HT, XV, 7. The uncanny resemblance of these letters to what 'Umar would say led another source to cap this letter attributed to 'Uthmān with a concluding statement from 'Umar. After the statement "*takallafū wa ibtada'ū*," al-Māliqī's version states: "'Umar b. al-Khaṭṭāb stated: 'The affairs of Banū Isrā'īl remained stable until their offsprings from foreign women [captives of war or slaves] increased among them, and these began to interpret religion in speculative ways. Thus, they went astray and led the Israelites astray [*inna amra banī isrā'īl lam yazal mu'tadilan ḥattā kathura fīhim al-muwalladūn abnā' sabāyā al-umam fa-qālū fīhim bi'l-ra'y fa-ḍallū wa*

*aḍallū banī isrā'īl*].'" Al-Māliqī, *al-Tamhīd wa'l-Bayān*, 31. Yūsuf b. 'Abdallāh b. 'Abd al-Barr, *Jāmi' Bayān al-'Ilm wa Faḍlihi*, II, 138. Later a similarly constructed declaration assigned to Mālik b. Anas would attribute the bane to Abū Ḥanīfa (*lam yazal amru al-Kūfa mu'tadilan ḥattā nasha' fihim Abū Ḥanīfa fa-qāla bi'l-qiyās*). Ibn 'Abd al-Barr, *Jāmi'*, II, 147.

39. Ṭabarī, I, 2409. When 'Umar inquires about this prophecy, Ka'b tells him the story of the Roman destruction of Jerusalem, and the prediction of one prophet, who came to the city after the arrival of the Muslim armies, and declared, "Rejoice O Jerusalem. Al-Fārūq will come to you and cleanse you." This was hence the context through which 'Umar came to be recognized as "al-Fārūq." The title was therefore acquired not on the grounds of the *ḥadīth* that reflects Sunnī hagiography wherein the Prophet gives this title to 'Umar, but through the context of parabolic narration, which wove a different myth around the conquest. See chap. 3.

40. Isaiah 45.1. About the image of Cyrus as a conqueror, see G. Fowden, *Empire to Commonwealth: Consequences to Monotheism in Late Antiquity* (Princeton, 1992), 138.

41. Ṭabarī, I, 673.

42. One contemporary of 'Umar reportedly commented on the significance of 'Umar's death for the fortunes of Islam, saying: "Today Islam has set in retreat. Not even a man running away from an enemy pursuing him on the open plains is faster in flight than Islam is today." Ibn Sa'd, III, 369. Balādhurī, *Ansāb (Sā'ir)*, 501. Another commented in memory of 'Umar later, "He [i.e., 'Umar] was the fortress of Islam, which Muslims entered and did not leave. When 'Umar died the fortress was breached, and the people have been leaving Islam and not rejoining it." Ibn Sa'd, III, 371. Balādhurī, *Ansāb (Sā'ir)*, 502. Another report declares, "The death of 'Umar created a breach in Islam that will not be closed until the Day of Judgment." Ibn Sa'd, III, 372; Balādhurī, *Ansāb (Sā'ir)*, 503. Related to this theme is also the commentary of Salmān after the conquest of Ctesiphon where, impressed by the rapidity of the conquest across the Tigris River, he declared, "Islam is at fresh start, the waters have been made obedient to them as the overland passages. . . . Verily, they shall abandon [the faith] in droves just as they entered it in droves." Ṭabarī, I, 2437.

43. Ka'b al-Aḥbār's prediction to Mu'āwiya, "You are to be the *amīr* after him [i.e., 'Uthmān], but you will not obtain [this office] until you dismiss what I have just related." Ṭabarī, I, 2947. In another account Sayf uses another Jewish sage (*ḥabr*) in Oman to convey the prediction about Mu'āwiya's succession (after the four caliphs, whom he describes) to the caliphate. This prediction was made to 'Amr b. al-'Āṣ when he came as envoy of the Prophet to Oman, and became intrigued reportedly to find out from this credible scholar what events would transpire after the Prophet's death. Ṭabarī, I, 3251–3252. Ka'b also attributes a refer-

ence to 'Uthmān's death in the Torah. Abū Zayd 'Umar b. Shabba, *Kitāb Ta'rīkh al-Madīna al-Munawwara (Akhbār al-Madīna al-Nabawiyya)*, ed. 'Alī Muḥammad Dandal, 2 vols. (Beirut, 1996), II, 192.

44. It is worth noting that Mu'āwiya in turn reportedly praised Ka'b al-Aḥbār after his death for having been a genuine scholar (*aḥad al-'ulamā'*) who did not receive his due recognition. Ibn Sa'd, II, 358.

45. Some traditions also attribute to Ka'b al-Aḥbār a statement about the divine right of rulers.

46. Thus the historian Ya'qūbī quotes Abū Mūsā al-Ash'arī as finding an analogy for the Taḥkīm episode in Israelite history, while a report attributed to Ka'b al-Aḥbār declares a similarity between the first *fitna* war and previous Jewish wars. Stopping once at the locale of Ṣiffīn in Syria, Ka'b reportedly declared, "The Israelites fought one another nine times with these rocks [on the road], and the Arabs will fight one another in the tenth time using the same stones." Ya'qūbī, *Ta'rīkh*, II, 191; Ibn Kathīr, *al-Bidāya wa'l-Nihāya*, 14 parts in 8 vols. (Beirut, 1985), IV (pt. 7), 286. Ibn Shaddād, *al-A'lāq al-Khaṭīra fī A'lām al-Shām wa'l-Jazīra* (Damascus, 1991), I (pt. 2), 30.

47. Others who make a similar reference to "*al-kitāb al-awwal*" include Zayd b. Khārija al-Anṣārī. 'Umar b. Shabba, *Ta'rīkh al-Madīna*, II, 184–185.

48. It is within this frame of meaning that 'Alī's comment at the conclusion of the selection process for a caliph at the Shūrā makes sense: "God's decree will come in its time [*sayablugh al-kitābu ajalahu*]." Ṭabarī, I, 2786.

49. 'Umar b. Shabba, *Ta'rīkh al-Madīna*, II, 225–228.

50. It is worth noting in this context a report that depicts Ka'b al-Aḥbār asking al-'Abbās to grant him his *shafā'a* (intercession for forgiveness) on Judgment Day. Balādhurī, *Ansāb al-Ashrāf, al-'Abbās b. 'Abd al-Muṭṭalib wa waladuhu*, ed. A. al-Dūrī (Wiesbaden, 1987), III, 17. Chain of transmission: 'Umar b. Ḥammād b. Abū Ḥanīfa←Muḥammad b. al-Fuḍayl b. Ghazwān←Zakariyya b. 'Aṭiyya←'Aṭiyya. On one occasion Ibn 'Abbās is described beginning a *ḥadīth* session with Ka'b al-Aḥbār by saying, "I shall ask you about certain matters. Do not narrate to me what has been modified in tradition [*mā ḥurrifa min al-kitāb*] or what has been reported in later time [*wa lā bi-aḥādīth al-rijāl*]. If you do not know, then just say 'I don't know' for this gives a better judgment of you [*fa-innahu a'lam laka*]. *Ansāb (al-'Abbās)*, 38. Aḥmad b. Ibrāhīm al-Dawraqī←Shujā' b. Mukhlad al-Fallās←al-'Awwām b. Ḥawshab←al-Qāsim b. 'Awf al-Shaybānī. Another report depicts a Jew from al-Ḥīra who is knowledgeable about biblical lore deferring to the wider expertise of Ibn 'Abbās. *Ansāb (al-'Abbās)*, 37.

51. One need only survey the concluding chapter of Muir's study of the caliphate to discern the wide-ranging contrasts and challenges that the author draws between the West and the Islamic world during his time period, and to recognize that he perceived the study of the classical Islamic period to be a di-

dactic and relevant exercise for Western interaction with the contemporary Islamic culture. W. Muir, *The Caliphate: Its Rise, Decline, and Fall* (Edinburgh, 1915), 603–609.

52. While this challenge has come mainly from scholars of religious studies, the historical literature on the early Islamic period has remained until recently largely traditional in its approaches of credulity and synthesis. A sampling of studies that sought to analyze in positivist terms political, social, and religious issues for the early Islamic period includes the following: Hichem Djaït, *La Grande Discorde: Religion et politique dans l'Islam des origines* (Paris: Gallimard, 1989); Fred Donner, *The Early Islamic Conquests* (Princeton, 1981); M. Hinds, "Kufan Political Alignments and Their Background in the Mid-Seventh Century A.D.," *International Journal of Middle East Studies* II, 1971; H. Lammens, "Le Tirumvirat Abou Bakr, 'Omar et Abou 'Obaida," *Mélanges de la Faculté Orientale de l'Université St Joseph de Beyrouth* IV (1910): 113–144; M. A. Shaban, *Islamic History, A New Interpretation* (Cambridge, 1976); W. Madelung, *The Succession to Muhammad: A Study of the Early Caliphate* (Cambridge, 1997). A fuller list of relevant titles is given in the bibliography.

53. Only rarely does one encounter a blunt admission of this reality, such as when Stanley Lane-Poole states in the preface to a collection of commentaries by Edward Lane on *The Thousand and One Nights*, "To the records of these medieval writers [referring to Ibn al-Jawzī, al-Maqrīzī, and al-Suyūṭī, among others], Mr. Lane added the results of his personal experience; and in doing so he was guilty of no anachronism: for the Arabian society in which a Saladin, a Beybars, a Barkook, and a Kait-Bey moved, and of which the native historians have preserved so full and graphic a record, survived almost unchanged to the time of Mohammad 'Alee, when Mr. Lane spent many years of intimate acquaintance among the people of Cairo. The Life that he saw was the same as that described by El-Makreezee and Es-Suyootee; and the purely Muslim society in which Mr. Lane preferred to move was in spirit, in custom, and in all essentials the same society that once hailed a Haroon er-Rasheed, a Jaafar el-Barmekee, and an Aboo-Nuwas, among its members. The continuity of Arabian social tradition was practically unbroken from almost the beginning of the Khalifate to the present century, at least in such a metropolis of Islam as Cairo, or as Damascus, or Baghdad" (Edward William Lane, *Arabian Society in the Middle Ages, Studies from the Thousand and One Nights* [London, 1883], xxi). A similar view of a continuity that is monolithic in cultural and textual terms is propounded by R. B. Serjeant, who uses the examples of diplomatic dealings in Arabia, and especially Yemen, in the post-WWI period as evidence for how the early Muslim state might have functioned: R. B. Serjeant, "Early Arabic Prose," in *Arabic Literature to the End of the Umayyad Period*, ed. A. F. L. Beeston et al. (Cambridge, 1983), 150.

54. For a survey of the state of debate between these two camps among historians, see F. Donner, *Narratives of Islamic Origins: The Beginnings of Islamic Histori-*

*cal Writing* (Princeton: Darwin Press, 1998), 1–31; and H. Motzki's survey of the debate in the fields of law and *ḥadīth*, *The Origins of Islamic Jurisprudence: Meccan Fiqh Before the Classical Schools*, trans. Marion Katz (Leiden, 2002), 1–49. Also, H. Berg, "Competing Paradigms in the Study of Islamic Origins: Qur'ān 15:89–91 and the Value of *Isnāds*," in *Method and Theory in the Study of Islamic Origins*, ed. H. Berg (Leiden, 2003), 259–290. Although the skeptical approach was well established among specialists of religious studies (or more typically specialists whose work fell mainly in the sphere of religious studies, such as I. Goldziher, H. Lammens, R. Brunschvig, and J. Schacht), it was not until the publication of M. Cook and P. Crone's *Hagarism* that historians began debating questions about historical authenticity for the early Islamic period anew. Cook and Crone's work was influential in the way it again highlighted the picture of religious interaction among Judaism, Christianity, and Islam as a background and an influential context for reading the process of Islam's crystallization in the period of the seventh–ninth centuries. However, the authors' speculative theses about an alternative historical reality, based on the use of scant non-Muslim texts from the early period and combining these whenever convenient with the traditional Arabic sources, presented problems of methodology and inconsistency that made it difficult to corroborate their work. A crucial problem with *Hagarism* (as well as with the even less compelling work of G. Hawting) is its early dating of the formative period of religious flux (the "sectarian milieu") to the seventh century and, more significantly, its authors' neglect of the phenomenon whereby texts can often be representational and derivative rather than factual—whether written by Muslims or non-Muslims. Be that as it may, the ensuing historical debate has once again rekindled among religion specialists the question of the authenticity of Islamic tradition. Recently, however, a new cluster of opinion has emerged that argues for the credulous point of view, declaring that *ḥadīth* material does in fact seem to preserve within it some authentic record about the past. A key example of this latest trend is the work of H. Motzki, "The *Muṣannaf* of 'Abd al-Razzāq al-Ṣan'ānī as a Source of Authentic *Aḥādīth* of the First Century A.H.," *Journal of Near Eastern Studies* 50 (1991): 1–21. It should be recognized, however, that the endeavors of this latter camp of scholars have primarily focused on *isnād* criticism rather than on analysis of the content of *ḥadīth* or on trying to place these texts in a historical context. For a survey of this literature, see H. Berg, *The Development of Exegesis in Early Islam: The Authenticity of Muslim Literature from the Formative Period* (London, 2000), 69–73.

55. As J. Wellhausen puts it, "The accounts are sifted, edited, and blended together by them [i.e., the later narrators]" (J. Wellhausen, *The Arab Kingdom*, xii). P. Crone puts the process of growth in accounts somewhat differently, stating, "It is obvious that if one storyteller should happen to mention a raid, the next storyteller would know the date of this raid, while the third would know everything that an audience might wish to hear about it " (*Meccan Trade and the Rise of*

*Islam* [Princeton, 1987], 224). And elsewhere Crone characterizes the work of the compilers of accounts as something that is "strikingly devoid of overall unity" (*Slaves on Horses* [Cambridge, 1980], 13). J. Lassner also emphasizes the ways in which the story is changed over time with reference to the 'Abbāsids; *Islamic Revolution and Historical Memory* (New Haven, 1986), 25. And, finally, A. Noth and L. Conrad agree with the previous opinions in stating that the historical documents underwent "a long process of transmission, in the course of which they have been subjected to all sorts of changes" (*The Early Arabic Historical Tradition: A Source-Critical Study* [Princeton: Darwin Press, 1994], 72). The most recent survey of this secondary literature, F. Donner's *Narratives of Islamic Origins: The Beginnings of Islamic Historical Writing*, provides an introductory survey of the debate about the sources, but generally maintains the categories of analysis introduced by Noth and Conrad, without giving additional textual analysis.

56. A. Noth and L. Conrad, *The Early Arabic Historical Tradition*, 4–17. R. S. Humphreys, *Islamic History: A Framework for Inquiry* (Princeton, 1991), 102 (with reference to a discussion of Balādhurī's sources). E. L. Petersen, *'Alī and Mu'āwiya in Early Arabic Tradition: Studies on the Genesis and Growth of Islamic Historical Writing Until the End of the Ninth Century*, trans. P. L. Christensen (Copenhagen, 1964), 73–74, 88.

57. It should be noted that Wansbrough's notion of salvation history in the Islamic context did not take into account an apocalyptic and messianic component in the narrative of the Prophetic dispensation or in the historiography of the early period in general; *The Sectarian Milieu: Content and Composition of Islamic Salvation History* (Oxford, 1978), 88–89, 138, 142, 146–150. Wansbrough's notion of salvation history in the Islamic context remained centered on the idea of a reworked covenant with its more developed concept of law. As noted earlier in regard to the traditions about the transformation of the community during the *fitna*, however, and as can be discerned from the chiliastic Meccan *sūrās* of the Qur'ān, there is considerable evidence that make his restrictive opinion untenable.

58. The Sīra and the Maghāzī, for example, can take on additional methodological meanings—besides the aspects of salvation history and religious triumph—when examined in light of the wider scope of the Islamic historical narrative. The Qur'ānic verse about the Prophet's share of the war booty (Qur'ān 8:41) that Wāqidī includes at the end of the story about the Battle of Badr, for example, was not merely ornamental or superfluous to a story of salvation history, as Wansbrough argued (*Sectarian Milieu*, 29–30), but legitimist and polemical, relating more to the financial controversy of 'Uthmān's reign and contentions in the 'Abbāsid period than to the context of the Sīra. In general, Wansbrough's emphasis on the construct of salvation history reduced the Sīra to being an aetiology of the law, and a story of consistent success where ideal and reality coincide, unlike the case of the Judaic and Christian experiences. *Sectarian Milieu*, 148.

This, however, oversimplified the aims of the Sīra. There are in fact a variety of instances where the Prophet had to manage a situation of uncooperative companions, and theology is not usually the foundation of much of this discourse as much as morality (D. S. Margoliouth had already pointed to this odd representation of the Companions in the Sīra when he stated that "the character which [Ibn Isḥāq] gives the Companions of the Prophet is rarely pleasing, even if it is not actually repulsive" [*The Early Development of Mohammedanism*, 237]). This limited perception of the Sīra, however, leads to a more general misreading of Islamic historiography when Wansbrough asserts that "a dialectic of theology and history is hardly attested in Islamic literature," and speaks of history as simply being "the proving ground for the claims made by revelation" (*Sectarian Milieu*, 137). If indeed this were the case, Ṭabarī's chronicle should not have been about the history of prophets and kings, but only of prophets.

59. This absence of an Islamic historical sense reduced Wansbrough's judgment about textual composition to a contradictory set of opinions. His view that religious texts originated in an environment of inter-confessional polemic (akin to that of Qumran vs. Karaism) can conjure up an earlier, and militantly combative, period of sectarian strife in Islamic history such as between the Khārijites and Sunnīs in the seventh century. *Sectarian Milieu*, 40. However, the author later proposes a more leisurely and pedantic environment for literary composition of religious history that presumes a secure academic environment in the late eighth and early ninth centuries. *Sectarian Milieu*, 59, 138; *Qur'anic Studies*, 47, 70. And even then, Wansbrough could not but accept some texts about the early period as authentic (such as the text that deals with the conversation between the Prophet and Ḥuyayy b. Akhṭab, simply because it is "witty and spicy"); *Sectarian Milieu*, 16 (another example is the author's acceptance of the group of the Qurrā' who figure among Islamic armies as a historical fact reminiscent of biblical parallels; *Sectarian Milieu*, 69). The variety of such opinions meant that questions of historical context and motivations for composition got oversimplified, such as in Wansbrough's observation that the primary aim of Ibn Isḥāq's *Sīra* was to provide (or justify) a Ḥijāzī context for the origin of Islam. *Sectarian Milieu*, 58, 79.

60. P. Crone and M. Cook, *Hagarism: The Making of the Islamic World* (Cambridge, 1977), 18–19. G. Hawting, *The Idea of Idolatry in Early Islam* (Cambridge, 1999), 14. J. Johns, "Archaeology and the History of Early Islam: The First Seventy Years," *Journal of the Economic and Social History of the Orient* 46 (2003): 411–436. Others who have emphasized the Umayyad background for the coalescence of the Islamic historical tradition include U. Rubin, who finds that the story of the Islamic conquest of Syria (Palestine and Jerusalem, more specifically) shows the incorporation of biblical-messianic notions in a way that was "designed to serve the apologetic Umayyad needs and mainly to legitimize the Islamic presence in the Holy Land." Rubin then compares the conquest of Syria to the notion of a "new exodus," marking Jewish deliverance and the emergence of a new community of

believers, and argues that this adaptation of theme was done by Ka'b al-Aḥbār. *Between Bible and Qur'ān*, 5, 17. There are a number of problems with this reading, including the fact that it mistakes a parabolic cycle of narrative for a propagandistic one, and that it shows the author as accepting of the historical reality of Ka'b al-Aḥbār's sayings. An Islamic conquest of Syria (unlike the usurpation of caliphal succession rights such as between the 'Abbāsids and the 'Alids) did not require an apologist enterprise, and the Syrian front in the grand sweep of the early Islamic chronicles was at any rate not the main story that commanded Islamic attention about triumph and tribulation; it was the Iraq–Iran trajectory that commanded the logic of religious and literary composition. Syria figured prominently as a haven for a return to orthodoxy after the closure of the *fitna* narratives. More recent studies have begun doubting and rejecting the notion that Islam underwent its critical formation during 'Abd al-Malik's reign and that this happened in the vicinity of late seventh-century Syria. C. Robinson, *'Abd al-Malik* (Oxford, 2005), 113. And for a more perceptive rebuttal of *Hagarism* and its followers see R. Hoyland, "New Documentary Texts and the Early Islamic State," *BSOAS* 69 (2006): 395–416. Also, F. Donner, *Narratives of Islamic Origin*, 275–290.

61. For Schacht's opinion that *ḥadīth* and *sunna* reflected Umayyad practice in certain spheres of law, see *The Origins of Muhammadan Jurisprudence* (Oxford, 1950), 190–198. Also, Schacht's *An Introduction to Islamic Law* (Oxford, 1964), 23–27; "A Revaluation of Islamic Traditions," *Journal of the Royal Asiatic Society* (1949): 152–153; and "The Law," in *Unity and Variety in Muslim Civilization*, ed. G. Von Grunebaum (Chicago, 1955), 68–70. In this, Schacht built on the conclusions of Goldziher, who placed considerable emphasis on the Umayyad patronage of the *ḥadīth* scholar al-Zuhrī. I. Goldziher, *Muslim Studies*, trans. S. Stern, 2 vols. (London 1967–71), II, 43–47. P. Crone and M. Hinds would follow the same chronological frame for dating the tradition but placed even stronger emphasis on the Umayyads as promulgators of the law. *God's Caliph: Religious Authority in the First Centuries of Islam* (Cambridge, 1986), 45–53.

62. Whatever application Schacht envisaged for his work beyond the scope of law was based on a theory of *isnād*, rather than a theory of historical context, which would have allowed a more critical evaluation of the polemical, political, and even legalistic interests of later times. As he put it with respect to the Sīra, "historical information on the Prophet is only the background for legal doctrines and therefore devoid of independent value" ("A Reevaluation of Islamic Traditions," *Journal of the Royal Asiatic Society* [1949]: 149). If it is not with reference to the Umayyads as the authority that shaped the context for the systematization of *ḥadīth*, Schacht and others have been fixated on using that time period as the earliest possible time for the beginning of *isnād* formation. Historians have tended to adopt Schacht's conclusion for their research as well. E. L. Petersen, *'Alī and Mu'āwiya*, 25. Recently, H. Berg also accepted Schacht's scheme about *isnād* attribution and the back-projection of traditions to the sphere of ex-

egetical narratives. *The Development of Exegesis in Early Islam: The Authenticity of Muslim Literature from the Formative Period* (London, 2000), 209.

63. Others who accepted the historicity of reports about al-Zuhrī include I. Goldziher. J. Horovitz, N. Abbott, A. Duri, G. Juynboll, M. Lecker, and G. Schoeler. The starting point for this flaw among modern scholars is thus twofold: credulity regarding the idea that al-Zuhrī was the pioneer of the writing down of *ḥadīths*, and acceptance of what the primary sources say about the Umayyad use of al-Zuhrī to propagate information (both their own propaganda and *ḥadīth* in general). The starting point in a trail of anecdotes that are strung together to produce the traditional (and revisionist) reading probably begins with al-Zuhrī's purported statement, "We disliked writing until the authorities [the *umarā'*] compelled us to do so; then I decided not to prevent any Muslim from doing likewise." Ibn Sa'd, II, 389 (narrated on the authority of 'Abd al-Razzāq). Who those "*umarā'*" were is a glaring question; they should have been easily identified with one Umayyad ruler, but instead there is a range of evidence referring to 'Abd al-Malik or his much later successor, Hishām (a thirty- or forty-year margin of error). M. Lecker, "Biographical Notes on Ibn Shihab al-Zuhrī," *BSOAS* 61 (1996): 26. The next report in this cluster of information is Ṣāliḥ b. Kaysān's, which describes how al-Zuhrī went about the task of *ḥadīth* collecting. Ṣāliḥ states, "Ibn Shihāb and I were looking for *'ilm* [religious knowledge] and we agreed to record the *sunna*. Thus we wrote down everything we heard about the Prophet. Then al-Zuhrī said, 'Let us write down what we can find attributed to his companions.' But I said, 'No, that is not *sunna*.' Al-Zuhrī, however, insisted that it was and recorded this also." Ṣāliḥ then added with some regret, "I did not record it, so al-Zuhrī became a successful traditionist, whereas I did not." Ibn Sa'd, II, 388 (narrated on the authority of 'Abd al-Razzāq); Ibn 'Abd al-Barr, *Jāmi'*, I, 76. G. Juynboll, *Muslim Tradition*, 35. Once al-Zuhrī's reputation as an avid *ḥadīth* collector was established, he is described as having served the Umayyads in various official tasks, including being a tax collector, a chief of the police, and a tutor of Hishām b. 'Abd al-Malik's children. The most notable *ḥadīth* that al-Zuhrī reportedly narrated in connection with Umayyad interests was the Jerusalem *ḥadīth* when 'Abd al-Malik told the public, after seeking to promote the Dome of the Rock as an alternative pilgrimage site during the revolt of 'Abdallāh b. al-Zubayr, "Here is Ibn Shihāb al-Zuhrī who transmits to you the Prophet's saying: 'The saddles of the camels shall only be fastened for a journey to three mosques, namely the Ka'ba, my own mosque [i.e., in Medina] and the mosque of Jerusalem.'" Ya'qūbī, *Ta'rīkh*, II, 261. Goldziher, *Muslim Studies*, II, 47. Also, Josef Horovitz, *The Earliest Biographies of the Prophet and Their Authors*, ed. L. Conrad (Princeton: Darwin Press, 2002), 53–63. N. Abbott, *Studies in Arabic Literary Papyri*, I, 25–40. A. A. Guillaume, *The Traditions of Islam: An Introduction to the Study of Hadith Literature* (Oxford, 1924), 47–50. A. A. Duri, "Al-Zuhrī: a Study of the Beginnings of History Writing in Islam," *BSOAS* 19 (1957): 1–12. G. Schoeler, *The Oral and the Written in Early Islam*, trans. Uwe

Vagelpohl (London, 2006), 73–83. M. Cook has pointed to the range of contradictory evidence relating to the process of the writing down of tradition: M. Cook, "The Opponents of the Writing of Tradition in Early Islam," *Arabica* 64 (1997): 459–463. G. Juynboll also stresses the Umayyad role in shaping the early *ḥadīth*, but cites the caliph ʿUmar II and his pietistic impulses as the reason behind a crucial Umayyad motive in codifying *ḥadīth*. G. Juynboll stresses that *ḥadīth* underwent its main development in the last decades of the first century (700s–720s), and places emphasis on the founding role in *ḥadīth* formation to al-Zuhrī, al-Shaʿbī, and al-Ḥasan al-Baṣrī (but excludes Saʿīd b. al-Musayyib). G. Juynboll, *Muslim Tradition*, 19, 39, 34–35, 73, 74. While rejecting an Umayyad political or pietistic role in stimulating the development of *ḥadīth*, J. Burton does place credence in the saying of Ṣāliḥ b. Kaysān about the precedence of al-Zuhrī in having initiated the writing down of the sayings of the companions. J. Burton, *An Introduction to Hadith* (Edinburgh, 1994), xxiii, 51. In his later work, Schacht was careful not to associate his theory about Umayyad administrative practice transformed into the religious law of Islam with al-Zuhrī, and conspicuously omitted any mention of al-Zuhrī's name from a relevant chapter on "The Umayyad Administration and the First Specialists" (*A History of Islamic Law*, 23–27). Instead, he used the term "pious specialists" to generalize about those who served Umayyad interests or challenged them, and only conceded mention of the names of Rajāʾ [b. Ḥayawa] and Abū Qilāba as "among the familiars of the Umayyad caliphs" (p. 26). It seems clear, however, that any theory about the Umayyad interaction with Islam in the seventh century could go nowhere without a recognition for the crucial role of al-Zuhrī, and that Schacht was almost unconvinced of the working of his theory (he was also contradicting what he had earlier conceded about al-Zuhrī's contribution, *Origins of Muhammadan Jurisprudence*, 246–247).

64. This process of caliphal patronage had already begun with al-Manṣūr's support for Ibn Isḥāq's writing of the *Sīra*, and would continue during the reign of al-Maʾmūn. The exact functioning of this belles-lettrist exercise is not clear, and it may well have continued outside caliphal control, among traditionist scholars, without further caliphal support after the beginning of the Miḥna. As for al-Wāqidī, one should note some remarkable references about him that show that he had a greater role in the composition of Islamic history than other narrators. Ibn al-Nadīm claims that al-Wāqidī was a pro-Shīʿī (*yatashayyaʿ*) and then adds that he had a proper attitude (or approach) to religion, and that he exercised secrecy (*ḥasan al-madhhab, yalzam al-taqiyya*). These characterizations would not normally invite great scrutiny were it not for the fact that Ibn al-Nadīm begins al-Wāqidī's biography by saying that he used to believe that ʿAlī was one of the signs or miracles of the Prophet Muḥammad, much as Moses and Jesus had their famous miracles. Abūʾl-Faraj Muḥammad b. Abī Yaʿqūb Isḥāq al-Warrāq b. al-Nadīm, *Kitāb al-Fihrist*, ed. G. Flügel, 2 vols. (Leipzig, 1871–1872), 98. In light of the particular frame of Rāshidūn historiography, which heavily centers on the tragic

career path of 'Alī, Ibn al-Nadīm's reference could well be meaningful only as a reference to the parabolic aspect of 'Alī's biography.

65. T. El-Hibri, *Reinterpreting Islamic Historiography: Hārūn al-Rashīd and the Narrative of the 'Abbāsid Caliphate* (Cambridge, 1999).

## 2. ABŪ BAKR: THE MOMENT OF CONFIRMATION

1. Later narrators would use 'Āisha's monopoly over the final hours of the Prophet to stress that the latter did not designate 'Alī as successor. 'Āisha reportedly said, "He [the Prophet] died while I was alone in his company, so when would he have designated a successor?" Abū 'Abdallāh Muḥammad b. Yazīd b. Māja, *Sunan*, ed. Muḥammad Fu'ād 'Abd al-Bāqī, 2 vols. (Beirut, 1980), *kitāb al-janā'iz*, I, 519 (no. 1626). Ibn Sa'd, II, 261. The intended target of this *ḥadīth* was the Shī'a, whose argument regarding *waṣiyya* (official investiture of a religious successor through designation and a testament) implied another setting of closeness between the Prophet and his presumed legatee. In any case, the argument from silence also helped the 'Abbāsids, whose involvement in both discourses of legitimacy (*ḥadīth* vs. *waṣiyya-qarāba*) would strip the 'Alids of claims to inheritance of the Hāshimite leadership at the same time that it placed them as allies of the Sunna. Al-'Abbās is portrayed specifically as asking if anyone from the companions had a will (*'ahd*) from the Prophet. In the absence of an answer, al-'Abbās declares: "Let anyone who claims later he heard the Prophet grant him an exclusive testament be known as a liar." Ibn Sa'd, II, 272.

2. Ibn Sa'd, II, 249.

3. Ibn Sa'd, II, 250; Ṭabarī, I, 1808. The whole account, from the Prophet coming to 'Āisha's house accompanied by 'Alī and al-'Abbās till the final will, is also accepted by Bukhārī. *Ṣaḥīḥ*, *bāb hibat al-mar'a li-zawjihā*, III, 460 (no. 761); *kitāb al-ṭibb*, VII, 411–412 (no. 612).

4. Ṭabarī, I, 1754. Trans. I. K. Poonawala, *The History of al-Ṭabarī: The Last Years of the Prophet* (Albany, 1990), IX, 112. Bukhārī (*kitāb al-tafsīr*), *bāb inna 'iddata al-shuhūri*, VI, 148. (no. 184).

5. Ya'qūbī, *Ta'rīkh*, 2 vols. (Beirut, 1960), II, 114.

6. Ṭabarī, I, 1816, 1828. Hence the disappointment of some tribes at his death, which impelled them to renounce Islam during the Ridda. Ibn al-Ṭiqṭiqā, Muḥammad b. 'Alī b. Ṭabātabā, *Kitāb al-Fakhrī* (Beirut, 1966), 74.

7. Not satisfied with the news, some would wonder: "How could he die before he had conquered the world? By God, he has only been lifted in spirit like Jesus was before, and he shall return." Ibn Sa'd, II, 271.

8. Ibn Sa'd, II, 274.

9. Ṭabarī, I, 1816; Ya'qūbī, II, 114.

10. Ibn Sa'd adds in a similar account that Abū Bakr addressed the Prophet, saying: "Verily you are far honored by God to drink twice [i.e., from the cup of death]." Ibn Sa'd, II, 265, 268, 270. Ṭabarī, I, 1816. Poonawala, *HT*, IX, 184. Bukhārī (*kitāb al-janā'iz*), II, 188 (no. 333); *kitāb al-maghāzī, bāb maraḍ al-nabī*, 5:523 (no. 733). Al-Nisā'ī, *Sunan, kitāb al-janā'iz*, II, 397 (no. 1737).

11. Ṭabarī, I, 1804. Ibn Sa'd, II, 227–228, III, 176. Muslim (*faḍā'il Abī Bakr*), V (pt. 15), 150–153 (no. 2382). Bukhārī (*faḍā'il aṣḥāb al-nabī*), V, 5–6.

12. In a curious account the Prophet appears aware of the coming rivalry over succession between Abū Bakr and 'Alī but refuses to settle it, telling 'Āisha: "I have been inclined to summon your father and your brother to settle the matter and bind the succession [*fa-aqḍī amrī wa a'had 'ahdī*] so that no one will grow ambitious over it and I can put an end to rumor." An added variation claims he then said, "But, no. God does not will it, and the believers will have to cope [*ya'bā allāh wa yadfa' al-mu'minūn* or *yadfa' allāh wa ya'bā al-mu'minūn*]." Ibn Sa'd, II, 226. The last comment is very ambiguous, but the more significant is the aforementioned statement "I have been inclined to summon your father and brother [*hamamtu an ursila ilā abīki wa ilā akhīki fa-aqḍī amrī wa a'had 'ahdī*]." The reference to "your brother" here does not mean 'Āisha's kin brother but rather her symbolic one, namely 'Alī. This symbolism functioned on two levels: first, in reference to the rivalry and eventual war between 'Āisha and 'Alī, which made brotherhood here an epithet of irony or reconciliation; and second, in reference to the Qur'ānic verse that portrays the Jews addressing the Virgin Mary with the interporlated comment "O Sister of Hārūn [*yā ukhta Hārūn*], your father was not an unrighteous man . . ." (Qur'ān 19:28). Some commentators assert that Hārūn was not meant here as her brother but as the man equivalent in situation (Moses' brother Hārūn, who found himself in a similar situation of misunderstanding after Moses' return from the Mount and the beginning of the crisis of al-Sāmirī, the man implicated in the ruse of the Golden Calf). The deployment of signifiers arising from such a comparison of interpretive examples—a not uncommon condition in parabolic narration—would have been combined with the comparison established in the Prophet's famous *ḥadīth* about 'Alī: "You are to me like Hārūn was to Moses." As this *ḥadīth* was well known, it seems obvious that this statement, with its oblique reference to father and "brother," assumed a reader's understanding of previously interpreted narratives anchored in other religious contexts.

13. This exercise of using memories of religious merit to build legitimacy was later to be used in an opposite fashion to detract from 'Uthmān's political legitimacy by his opponents.

14. Ṭabarī, I, 1806. Ibn Sa'd, II, 242–243. Bukhārī, VII, 389 (no. 573). Poonawala, *HT*, IX, 174.

15. Ibn Sa'd, II, 242. A slightly variant version given also by Ṭabarī drives home the biblical connection even further when the Prophet asks for "*al-lawḥ*" (a stele)—"or *al-katif*," a narrator hastens to add—to write on. The concept of "*al-*

*lawḥ*" was closely identified with Moses and the tablet, and so the narrator tried to contain two opposite images in the account. Ibn Sa'd omits the variation of "*al-lawḥ*," clearly because of its Hebraic implications. Ṭabarī, I, 1807. Ibn 'Abbās is named as the narrator of Ṭabarī's account, which sheds light on the 'Abbāsid interest in the *waṣiyya* principle of succession and the Israelite (biblical) imagery that was borrowed to build a continuity between prophecy and imamate and to make its judgment as binding as the law of Moses.

16. Bukhārī (*kitāb al-marḍā*), *bāb qawl al-marīḍ 'qūmū 'annī*,' VII, 389 (no. 573); (*kitāb al-waṣāyā*), *bāb hal yustashfa' ilā ahl al-dhimma wa mu'āmalatihim*, IV, 183 (no. 288); (*kitāb farḍ al-khums*), IV, 260 (no. 393); (*kitāb al-tawḥīd*), IX, 347 (no. 468). Bukhārī (*kitāb al-maghāzī*), V, 512 (no. 717).

17. This account's style where it describes the Prophet's purported three wishes reproduces a standard form of *ḥadīth* technique used elsewhere, as when, for example, the Prophet declares that Abū Bakr and 'Umar will be among the people of paradise in the afterlife, but then the narrator holds back on naming the third figure ('Uthmān or 'Alī), allowing ambiguity.

18. There is great significance in the fact that Ṭabarī's versions of this story generalize this remark, usually attributed to 'Umar in other accounts, to the community of companions. This was clearly an attempt by Ṭabarī to downplay the role of 'Umar in shaping the action that deprived 'Alī of the succession. Other Sunnī sources, including *ḥadīth* texts that cite 'Umar's direct responsibility for turning away the crowd, clearly did not care about the artful aims of historical redaction that Ṭabarī was applying. The 'Umar-specific account (reported on the authority of Ibn 'Abbās) is given by Aḥmad, *Musnad*, V, 135. In spite of the demands of Sunnism, Ibn 'Abbās would hedge the need for regret over the loss of the opportunity to name a specific successor by saying elsewhere, "Truly, it was a day of calamity that the Prophet was prevented"—note here the critical ambiguity as to whether it was a person or a malady that prevented the Prophet from proceeding with a specific political testament—"from writing down a testament of succession [*inna al-raziyya, kull al-raziyya, mā ḥāla bayna rasūl allāh wa bayna an yaktub lahum dhalika al-kitāb*]."

19. Ṭabarī, I, 1807. Ibn Sa'd, II, 245. Ibn Sa'd adds another version in which 'Alī tells al-'Abbās that the caliphate undoubtedly belongs to his family (Ibn Sa'd, II, 246).

20. Ṭabarī, I, 1807. Poonawala, *HT*, IX, 173–174. Bukhārī (*bāb maraḍ al-nabī*), V, 519 (no. 728). Aḥmad, *Musnad*, V, 139. Ibn Hishām, *Sīra*, IV, 305. Ibn Isḥāq←al-Zuhrī←'Abdallāh b. Ka'b b. Mālik←Ibn 'Abbās. Ibn Hishām's version of 'Alī's statement varies slightly in style but includes the essential points in Ṭabarī's account.

21. See chap. 6.

22. The trepidation of 'Alī also has to be read in light of a previous report in the Sīra according to which he asked the Prophet, after the conquest of Mecca,

for the honorific title to guarding *al-ḥijāba wa'l-siqāya* (the religious custodianship of the Ka'ba). At the time his request was declined, since the Prophet wanted to bestow this honor either on 'Uthmān b. Ṭalḥa, according to Ibn Isḥāq, or on al-'Abbās, according to al-Wāqidī. 'Abd al-Malik b. Hishām, *al-Sīra al-Nabawiyya*, ed. 'Umar Tadmurī, 4 vols. (Beirut, 1993), IV, 55; *Maghāzī*, II, 832–833, 837–838.

23. The reference is to the women friends of Potiphar's wife, who exacerbated her pursuit of Joseph with gossip and machinations.

24. Ṭabarī, I, 1811. Muslim, II (pt. 4), 140 (no. 418). A similar version exists in Bukhārī (*kitāb aḥādīth al-anbiyā'*), *bāb qawlihi 'laqad kāna fī yūsuf wa ikhwatihi ayātun li'l-sā'ilīn,'* IV, 391 (no. 598).

25. This account of Abū Bakr leading the prayer until the Prophet's arrival is included by Bukhārī under a different heading, besides the final prayer episode. *Ṣaḥīḥ*, *kitāb al-ṣulḥ* (*mā jā'a fī'l-iṣlāḥ bayna al-nās*), III, 532 (no. 855). There the Prophet was simply late on one occasion and then caught up with Abū Bakr. Bukhārī includes this story under the heading: *abwāb al-'amal fī'l-ṣalāt: 'bāb man raji'a al-qahqarā fī'l-ṣalāt bi-amrin yanzil bihi,'* II, 166 (no. 297). Also, *Ṣaḥīḥ*, *kitāb al-aḥkam*, IX, 227–228 (no. 300). Muslim, II (pt. 4), 144–148 (no. 421).

26. Ibn Sa'd, II, 217, 219, 225. Ibn Hishām, *Sīra*, IV, 302 (reported on the authority of al-Zuhrī).

27. D. Spellberg, *Politics, Gender, and the Islamic Past. The Legacy of 'Aisha b. Abi Bakr* (New York: Columbia University Press, 1994); also, "Niẓām al-Mulk's Manipulation of Tradition: 'Āisha and the Role of Women in the Islamic Government," *Muslim World* 77 (1988): 111–117.

28. Ṭabarī, I, 1811.

29. Ṭabarī, I, 1810–1811. Poonawala, *HT*, IX, 179.

30. Tradition frequently portrays 'Umar as being unaware of the machinations of his daughter in the Prophet's household, and then as becoming angry with her over her actions, unlike Abū Bakr, who never criticizes his daughter for her more well-known whimsy.

31. Ibn Sa'd, II, 221.

32. There is a sudden change here in the address.

33. Ibn Sa'd, II, 221. An abbreviated version with a different *isnād* given by Abū Dāwūd, *Sunan*, *kitāb al-sunna*, IV, 215 (no. 4661). A similar version of this account in Bukhārī has a telling twist. There Ḥafṣa issues the command to have 'Umar lead the prayer not of her own thinking but on 'Āisha's advice. When the whole episode ends in embarrassment for Ḥafṣa, she reportedly turns to 'Āisha and tells her: "I knew I wouldn't get benefit out of you! [*mā kuntu li-uṣība minki khayran*]." Bukhārī, IX, 299–300 (no. 406). Tirmidhī, *Sunan*, *kitāb al-manāqib*, 573 (no. 3672).

34. It is worth noting that later on, at the episode of the Saqīfa, neither Abū Bakr nor the others refer to the prayer leadership as an argument to legitimize his rule.

35. Bukhārī (*kitāb al-ṣulḥ*), III, 532 (no. 855). Muslim, II (pt. 4), 146. For this version, Ṭabarī gives the phrasing: "*fa-lammā danā min Abī Bakr, ta'akhkhara Abū Bakr* [When [the Prophet] approached Abū Bakr, Abū Bakr went backwards]." Ṭabarī, I, 1811.

36. Bukhārī (*abwāb al-'amal fī al-ṣalāt*), *bāb man raji'a al-qahqarā fī al-ṣalāt*, II, 166 (no. 297). In the similar version, Ṭabarī phrases the retreat as: "*nakaṣa [Abū Bakr] 'an muṣallāh* [Abū Bakr retreated from his prayer place]." Ṭabarī, I, 1813.

37. The relevant verses from *sūrat al-anfāl* urging the believers to show devotion during battle state: "O believers, whensoever you encounter a host, then stand firm, and remember God frequently; haply so you will prosper. And obey God, and His Messenger, and do not quarrel together, and so lose heart, and your power depart; and be patient; surely God is with the patient. Be not as those who went forth from their habitations swaggering boastfully to show off to men, and barring from God's way; and God encompasses the things they do. And when Satan decked out their deeds fair to them, and said, 'Today no man shall overcome you, for I shall be your neighbor.' But when the two hosts sighted each other, he withdrew upon his heels [*nakaṣa 'alā 'aqibayhi*], saying, 'I am quit of you; for I see what you do not see. I fear God; and God is terrible in retribution' " (Qur'ān 8:46–48 [Arberry, I, 202–203]).

38. Bukhārī, VIII, 382–383 (nos. 585, 587). The alternate phrasing: "*innahum irtaddū 'alā adbārihim al-qahqarā*" or "*innahum raji'ū 'alā adbārihim al-qahqarā.*" Other *ḥadīths* state the divine warning to the Prophet: "*innaka lā tadrī mā aḥdathū ba'daka.*" In a different *ḥadīth* the Prophet intercedes with God in the manner of Noah for his companions, saying: "O Lord, my companions?" He is then told: "You do not know what they did after you [*innaka lā tadrī mā aḥdathū ba'daka*]." The Prophet then says: "I therefore answer like the saintly servant [*al-'abd al-ṣāliḥ* (i.e., Jesus)]: 'And I was witness over them, while I remained among them; but when Thou didst take me to Thyself, Thou was Thyself the watcher over them; Thou Thyself art witness of everything' (Qur'ān 5:117 [Arberry, I, 147]). I would then be told: They (i.e., these companions) had stepped back since you left them [*inna hā'ulā' lam yazālū murtaddīn 'alā a'qābihim mundhu fāraqtahum*]." Bukhārī (*kitāb al-tafsīr*), VI, 236 (no. 264).

39. Ṭabarī, I, 1816. Bukhārī (*faḍā'il aṣḥāb al-nabī*), V, 13 (no. 19).

40. Qur'ān 3:144.

41. Ibn Sa'd, II, 267. Ṭabarī, I, 1817. Poonawala, *HT*, IX, 185. Bukhārī (*kitāb al-maghāzī*), V, 524 (no. 733); *kitāb al-janā'iz*, II, 189 (no. 333). Bukhārī states: "It is as if people did not know that this was a revealed verse until Abū Bakr recited it at that hour. People afterwards took cognizance of it and everyone began to recite it" (no. 333). The account is recounted by al-Zuhrī on 'Āisha's authority.

42. Ibn Sa'd, II, 270.

43. Aside from the rare occasion when 'Alī advises 'Umar about whether to lead the Arab armies at Qādisiyya in person, 'Alī does not appear an active or-

ganizer for Islamic society, as for example 'Umar is represented in Abū Bakr's reign. The *ḥadīths* that speak of 'Umar's frequent consultation of 'Alī on juristic matters are a pure Sunnī fiction meant to restrict the image of 'Alī to religious erudition as a judge alongside other companions who have equally restricted qualities (Qur'ān recitation, asceticism, military bravery, etc.).

44. The content of Abū Bakr's accession speech after the Saqīfa episode confirms all these implications. His famous words, "Now then: O people, I have been put in charge of you although I am not the best of you. Help me if I do well; rectify me if I do wrong. Truthfulness is loyalty and falsehood is disloyalty. The weak among you shall be strong in my eyes until I ensure his right, God willing; and the strong among you shall be weak in my eyes until I wrest the right from him, God willing. No one from you should refrain from fighting in the cause of God, because if it is forsaken by a people, God will smite them with disgrace. Foul things never become widespread in a people but God brings calamity upon them. Obey me as long as I obey God and His Messenger; if I disobey them, you are not bound to obey me. Perform your prayers. May God have mercy upon you!" Ṭabarī, I, 1829. Poonawala, *HT*, IX, 201. Anas b. Mālik←al-Zuhrī←Muḥammad b. Isḥāq←Salama←Ibn Ḥumayd.

45. Ṭabarī, I, 1823.

46. Ṭabarī describes how, when word reached the Prophet of grumbling among the Anṣār—after he coincidentally had not been warned of this by Sa'd b. 'Ubāda (in a clear sign that it was the Khazraj that caused this disruption as they would later at the Saqīfa)—he asked Sa'd: "Where do you stand in this matter, O Sa'd?," to which the latter responded, "I stand with my kinsfolk." So the Prophet said: "Then gather your people in [this] enclosure." When Sa'd assembled the crowd, the Prophet appeared to them and addressed them saying: "O community of Anṣār, what is this talk I hear about you? [What is] the grudge you have harbored in your hearts [against me]? Did I not come to you when you were erring and God guided you; [were you not] needy and then made rich by God; [were you not] enemies and [did not] God reconcile your hearts?" They answered, "Yes indeed, God and His Messenger are gracious and kind." He said, "Why do you not answer me [directly], O Anṣār?" They said, "What shall we answer you, O Messenger of God? Kindness and graciousness belong to God and His Messenger." He said: "Now then, by God, had you wished you could have said—and you would have spoken the truth and have been accepted as truthfull—'You came to us [when your message] was rejected [by the Quraysh] and we believed in you; [you were] forsaken and we assisted you; [you were] evicted and we sheltered you; [you were] needy and we comforted you.' O Anṣār, that people should take away sheep and camels while you go back to your homes with the Messenger of God. By Him in whose hand is the soul of Muḥammad, were it not for the migration [*hijra*], I would have been one of the Anṣār myself. If all the people went one way and the Anṣār another, I would take the way of the Anṣār. O God, have mercy

on the Anṣār, their sons, and their sons' sons!" The narrator concludes by saying: "The people wept until the tears ran down their beards and said that they were pleased with the Messenger of God as their lot and good fortune." Ṭabarī, I, 1684–1685. Poonawala, *HT,* IX, 36–37. Muslim (*bāb i'ṭā' al-mu'allafa wa man yukhāf 'alā imānihi*), III (pt. 7), 151–157 (nos. 1059, 1061); Bukhārī (*manāqib al-Anṣār*), V, 80 (no. 122); (*kitāb al-maghāzī*), V, 433 (no. 619), V, 435 (no. 621); V, 438 (no. 626). Also, more briefly cited in Ibn Sa'd, II, 154.

47. This will be immediately evident next, when Abū Bakr responds to the Anṣār's demand that they have their caliph by saying: "The rulers shall be from us, and the vizirs from you," in reference to the Persian vizirs who would serve the Arab caliphs.

48. Qur'ān 3:144. Poonawala, *HT,* IX, 185.

49. Ṭabarī, I, 1817. This version is shared by Ya'qūbī. However, he mixes elements from version IV below. Ya'qūbī, II, 123. Ibn Sa'd, II, 269.

50. Poonawala, *HT,* IX, 186. Ibn al-Athīr, 'Izz al-Dīn 'Alī b. Aḥmad b. al-Athīr, *al-Kāmil fī'l-Ta'rīkh*, 13 vols. (Beirut, 1965–1967), II, 325. A hidden irony here is "*illā 'aliyyan*"—meaning "only the lofty or powerful"—thus inadvertently predicting and admiring 'Umar's pressure at that incident.

51. Poonawala, *HT,* IX, 187. Ya'qūbī, II, 126. Ya'qūbī adds a vivid description of Fāṭima's agonized outrage over the attack on her house, in which she threatens to invoke divine wrath on the intruders (*la-a'ujjanna li-llāh*). The event is similar to Nā'ila's anger over the intrusion into the house of 'Uthmān in A.H. 36/A.D. 656, but the particular use of the word "*la-a'ujjanna*" (verbal noun: "'*ajīj*," the sound of a camel) invokes the Qur'ānic reference to the miraculous camel of Thamūd. Ibn 'Abd Rabbihi's version states that when 'Umar came threatening, Fatima confronted him, saying, "Have you come to set our house on fire?," and he answered, "Yes, or you join what the community has agreed on." Ibn 'Abd Rabbihi, *al-'Iqd*, IV, 260. Balādhurī, *Ansāb al-Ashrāf, 'Alī wa Banūh*, ed. W. Madelung (Wiesbaden, 2003), II, 14. Balādhurī's account (based on al-Madā'inī) concludes with 'Alī's stepping out to give the *bay'a*. 'Alī's justification for his delay in coming out to give the *bay'a* is that he had intended not to do so before he had collected the Qur'ānic text.

52. Ṭabarī, I, 1819. The phrasing here borrows the Qur'ānic wording in *surat Yāsīn*, "*wa jā'a min aqṣā al-madīnati rajulun yas'ā* . . . [then came a man from the furthest part of the city, running; he said, 'My people, follow the Envoys! Follow such as ask no wage of you, that are right-guided']." Qur'ān 36:20 (Arberry, II, 145). However, Ṭabarī's narrator reverses the thrust of the phrase from being one of glad tiding to ill omen and *fitna*. The narrator's full meaning here can be gauged only in relation to the *ḥadīth* "*al-qā'im fī'l fitna khayrun min al-sā'ī bihā* . . . [he who is standing (*al-qā'im*) in *fitna* is better than the one riding with it (*al-sā'ī bihā*)]." See below.

53. The two actions, electing the caliph from the Anṣār and calling for a leader for each camp, were undoubtedly contradictory. Narrators, however, always

insisted on adding the remark "A commander from us and a commander from them" to add another layer of presumption to the Anṣār's action, since such language brought the Saqīfa challenge very close to the rhetoric of the Ridda apostates (*minna nabiyy wa min Quraysh nabiyy*, "a prophet from us and a prophet from them"). See below, narrative 3.

54. Ṭabarī, I, 1819–1820. Poonawala, *HT* IX, 188–189.

55. Ya'qūbī, II, 180.

56. Muslim (*kitāb al-fitan*), VI (pt. 18), 9 (no. 2887). Bukhārī, *Ṣaḥīḥ*, *bāb 'alāmāt al-nubuwwa fi'l-islām*, IV, 514 (no. 799). Tirmidhī (*kitāb al-fitan*), IV, 422. (no. 2194). Aḥmad, *Musnad*, XIII, 207.

57. Muslim (*kitāb al-fitan*), VI (pt. 18), 9 (no. 2887).

58. Ṭabarī, I, 1824. Ibn al-Athīr, II, 331.

59. Ṭabarī, I, 1824.

60. Ṭabarī, I, 1940. A. Noth first noted this symmetry in phrasing between these two phrases, but found no "coherent tendency" for the literary resemblance. See A. Noth, *Early Arabic Historical Tradition*, 171. Noth's assessment of this example is typical of his wider view of the narratives as representing compositions out of a common set of stock themes and motifs. This view would later be taken to an extreme with P. Crone's perception of the early Islamic traditions and historical narrative as lacking in overall unity; she considered them mainly to reflect the wreckage of past tradition that was tidied up later in the eighth and ninth centuries, rather than being a back-projection of a coherent tradition from that time period, as the present study argues. P. Crone, *Slaves on Horses*, 6–13; *Meccan Trade and the Rise of Islam*, 225. One account explains the Anṣār's reasoning for seeking to designate two leaders with the assertion of al-Ḥubāb b. al-Mundhir, "This way if the Muhājirūn [leader] does something wrong to the Anṣār, the Anṣār [leader] will correct him," and vice versa. Balādhurī, *Ansāb ('Alids)*, 8. Muḥammad b. Sa'd←al-Wāqidī←Abū Ma'mar←al-Maqburī and Yazīd b. Rumān←al-Zuhrī. There is also the possibility that the Anṣār, in proposing two candidates, were being portrayed as invoking a precedent for the Taḥkīm, and more specifically emulating the Qur'ānic verse that ostensibly set the standard for the Taḥkīm, "If you fear a breach between the two, bring forth an arbiter from his people and from her people, if they desire to set things right; God will compose their differences [*wa in khiftum shiqāqa baynahuma fa-ib'athū ḥakaman min ahlihi wa ḥakaman min ahlihā, in yurīdā iṣlāḥan yuwaffiqu allāh baynahumā*]" (Qur'ān 4:35 [Arberry, I, 106]). This verse will later be much contested by the Khārijites, who asserted that its content does not apply to political and military disputes and therefore that it does not justify the Taḥkīm. Such later developments in their argumentation, however, do not change the fact that they were the ones who accepted the call for the Taḥkīm when it was first proposed. As such, there is therefore a continuity in that group's action and declarations from

the time when they were still called al-Anṣār until some of them became the factions of al-Qurrā' and the Khārijites later on.

61. Ibn Kathīr's version adds: "and you will be in the company of the scholars and the elite [*wa takhluṣ bi-'ulamā' al-nās wa ashrāfihim*]." *Al-Bidāya wa al-Nihāya*, V, 215.

62. The Arabic in Ṭabarī's version is "*lā targhabū 'an ābā'ikum fa-innahu kufrun bi-kum an targhabū 'an ābā'ikum*." Al-Zuhrī's version, however, quotes 'Umar as saying: "We used to recite '*wa lā targhabū 'an ābā'ikum fa-innahu kufrun bi-kum*' or '*fa-inna kufran bikum an targhabū 'an ābā'ikum*.'" Whichever version is used, al-Zuhrī's account makes this statement appear as a lost Qur'ānic text. The phrase is repeated by al-Hindī, who includes it with other *ḥadīths* under the theme of one's claiming a different genealogy or father (*nafy al-nasab*). *Kanz*, VI, 208 (no. 15371), *Kanz*, II, 596 (no. 4818). Al-Zuhrī's account then adds another variation to 'Umar's statement when it quotes him adding that the Prophet said: "Do not flatter me as the Christians flattered the son of Maryam—peace be upon him, for I am merely the servant of God. Just say, 'the servant of God and His messenger.'" Muḥammad b. Muslim b. 'Ubaydallāh b. Shihāb al-Zuhrī, *al-Maghāzī al-Nabawiyya*, ed. Suhayl Zakkār (Damascus, 1980), 140.

63. This line seems to have been edited into anonymity because it challenged the Sunnī conception of cooperation among the companions. According to a brief account given by Balādhurī, however, 'Umar states, "It has reached me that al-Zubayr has said, 'If 'Umar is dead, we shall give the oath of allegiance to 'Alī. The *bay'a* of Abū Bakr was just a *falta*.' By God, he lies! The Messenger of God put him in his place, and chose him to strengthen the faith against others"—('*wa ikhtārahu li-'imād al-dīn*' is an expression that encompasses the notion of leading the prayer as well)—"God and the believers refuse anyone [for the caliphate) besides Abū Bakr." Balādhurī, *Ansāb* ('*Alids*), 8. Bakr b. al-Haytham←Hishām b. Yūsuf←Ma'mar←al-Zuhrī←'Ubaydallāh b. 'Abdallāh←Ibn 'Abbās. This isolated account was no doubt intended to be dispensable for the more mainstream Sunnī audiences, since it names the political contenders for the caliphate and shows them in discord well into 'Umar's reign. The account is also remarkable for showing 'Umar rejecting the occasion of Abū Bakr's election as an accident (*falta*), which is something well known from other accounts as in fact being 'Umar's own characterization of the event. It is not therefore unlikely that the more extensive 'Abbāsid account once accommodated such a characterization (*falta*) and attributed it to 'Umar but kept the names of 'Alī and al-Zubayr omitted. It seems clear that it was the proposition that 'Alī should be nominated as successor that provoked 'Umar into making his speech.

64. Ṭabarī, I, 1821–1824. This version is recounted in detail by Ibn al-Athīr, *Al-Kāmil*, II, 326–328. Also, Bukhārī (*bāb idhā aqarra bi'l-ḥadd*), VIII, 537–543 (no. 817).

65. In one version, the two declarations of the verses by Abū Bakr and ʿUmar are presented one after the other in the same scene. Ibn Saʿd, II, 271.

66. It may be that this joining of a religious injunction with a historical anecdote was the exercise of *iqrāʾ* referred to at the outset of the account.

67. See the situation of Ṭulayḥa b. Khuwaylid (Ṭabarī, I, 1891).

68. Saʿd b. ʿUbāda was reprimanded for this remark by having the banner removed from his command and given to his son, Qays.

69. Bukhārī (*faḍāʾil aṣḥāb al-nabī*), V, 13–14.

70. Ṭabarī, I, 1838.

71. This sense of accident is conveyed in a brief account that portrays ʿAlī's dissatisfaction when he asked Abū Bakr: "Didn't you consider the right we have to this matter [i.e., the succession]?," to which Abū Bakr responded: "Yes, but I was afraid that a *fitna* might happen [i.e., if a nomination was not made quickly for someone who was present]." ʿAlī then reportedly praised Abū Bakr's credentials for his companionship of the Prophet during the Hijra, and for having led the prayers during the Prophet's illness, but then asked God to forgive Abū Bakr for his lapse on the succession issue. Balādhurī, *Ansāb* (*ʿAlī wa Banūh*), II, 10. Ibn Saʿd←Wāqidī←Abū Maʿmar←al-Maqburī and Yazīd b. Rūmān←al-Zuhrī.

72. F. Donner, *Narratives of Islamic Origin*, 211.

73. Ṭabarī, I, 1825. Poonawala, *HT*, IX, 196. Also, Ibn Saʿd, II, 315. Bukhārī, V, 248 (no. 368). Ibn Shabba, *Taʾrīkh al-Madīna*, I, 122.

74. Yaʿqūbī, II, 127.

75. Ṭabarī, I, 1826. Poonawala, *HT*, IX, 197. Another version pushes Sunnī defensiveness regarding the implicit idea of prophetic succession to an extreme when ʿAlī responds to Abū Bakr's refusal to hand over Fadak by saying, "Solomon inherited David [*waritha Sulaymān Dāwūd*] [Qurʾān 27:16] and Zakariyya said: 'One who inherits me and inherits the family of Yaʿqūb after me' [Qurʾān 19:6]." Abū Bakr rebuffs the statement by saying, "Such are things [*huwa hakadhā*], and you know this as well as I do." Ibn Saʿd, II, 315.

76. Ṭabarī, I, 1825. Bukhārī (*kitāb farḍ al-khums*), IV, 208 (no. 325) (*kitāb al-maghāzī*), V, 382 (no. 546); (*kitab al-farāʾiḍ*), VIII, 471–472 (no. 718). Curiously, Bukhārī includes a long account about this bitter exchange, which is to be found in Ṭabarī as well. Tirmidhī mentions that ʿUmar was present with Abū Bakr during this argument and that the two of them said the same thing to Fāṭima. In turn, Fāṭima vowed not to speak with either of them. Tirmidhī (*kitāb al-siyar*), IV, 135 (no. 1609). Ibn Shabba, *Taʾrīkh al-Madīna*, I, 122. Ibn Saʿd briefly mentions the bad relations between Abū Bakr and Fāṭima after this incident. *Ṭabaqāt*, VIII, 28.

77. Tirmidhī (*kitāb al-farāʾiḍ*), IV, 373 (no. 2114). Aḥmad, *Musnad*, I, 292 (no. 147).

78. The whole Fadak story is probably an invention from the early ʿAbbāsid period. In origin it was associated with the Prophet, as his exclusive share of the booty from the Jewish colony of Khaybar, to signal the passing of religious

authority from Jews to Muslims. The full story of the changes in ownership of Fadak is described by Yaqūt al-Ḥamawī in his *Mu'jam al-Buldān*, 5 vols. (Beirut, 1957), IV, 238–240. Also, Balādhurī, *Futūḥ al-Buldān*, ed. Ṣalāḥ al-Dīn al-Munajjid, 2 vols. (Beirut, 1957), 45–47. Ibn Qutayba, *al-Ma'ārif*, 195. L. Veccia Vaglieri, "Fadak," *EI*, II (1965), 726. That Fadak was a well-known pro-Shī'ī trope on the caliphate can be gleaned from an anecdote that describes a discussion between the caliph al-Rashīd and Mūsā b. Ja'far al-Ṣādiq. When the caliph offers to return to him the estate of Fadak, the 'Alid *imām* responds that he would only accept it with its complete boundaries, which he enumerated as the frontiers of Samarqand, Armenia, North Africa, and Aden. Zamakhsharī, *Rabī' al-Abrār*, I, 180. The story of contention over a piece of real estate that is misappropriated by the ruler may well have been influenced by the biblical precedent of Ahab seizing the land of Naboth. 2 Kings 21.

79. I. Goldziher, *Muslim Studies*, II, 101. D. Powers, *Studies in Qur'ān and Ḥadīth: The Formation of the Islamic Law of Inheritance* (Berkeley, 1987), 114. N. Coulson, *Succession in the Muslim Family*, 128. W. Madelung, "Shi'i Attitudes Towards Women as Reflected in Fiqh," in *Society and the Sexes in Medieval Islam*, ed. Afaf Lutfi al-Sayyid-Marsot, Giorgio Levi Della Vida Conferences, 6 (Malibu: Undena, 1979), 75.

80. 'Umar would later continue with his plan for a *shūrā* succession along with this Sunnī-inspired effort to distance 'Alī from the caliphate.

81. To erase any lingering doubt over the legitimacy of his viewpoint, Abū Bakr could also cite the fact that even if Fāṭima's opinion was right, Islamic law (the Qur'ān) required two women for the testimony to be valid.

82. Al-Maqrīzī would later stress the fact that Abū Bakr kept on many officials who were originally appointed by the Prophet, and that the Prophet had in fact used members of the Umayyad clan for political office, but never any Hāshimites. Al-Maqrīzī, *Kitāb al-Nizā' wa'l-Takhāṣum fi-mā bayn Banī Umayya wa Banī Hāshim*, ed. H. Mu'nis (Cairo, 1984), 82, 92.

83. Ibn 'Asākir, XLIV, 235. Abū Bakr Aḥmad b. 'Alī al-Khaṭīb al-Baghdādī, *Ta'rīkh Baghdād*, 14 vols. (Cairo, 1931), XI, 47. Ibn 'Abd Rabbihi, *al-'Iqd*, III, 241 (uses the phrase "*ḍa'īfun fī badanihi*").

84. The Prophet is also described in one *ḥadīth* as "*rajulun raqīq*." Bukhārī, IX, 266 (no. 352).

85. In another reference the Prophet declares the analogy, "God has given me power among the angels with [the support of] Gabriel and Michael, and among the people of the earth, with [the support of] Abū Bakr and 'Umar. He who opposes them opposes me." Balādhurī, *Ansāb (Sā'ir)*, 419.

86. Qur'ān 14:36.

87. Qur'ān 5:118.

88. Qur'ān 71:26.

89. Qur'ān 10:88.

90. Ṭabarī, I, 1356–1357. Trans. M. V. McDonald, *History of al-Ṭabarī: The Foundation of the Community* (Albany, 1987), VII, 82–83.

91. Hence the *ḥadīth* that quotes Muḥammad as saying, "I never summoned someone to Islam who did not show some hesitance of reflection, except for Abū Bakr. He accepted the faith without trepidation."

92. The reference here is to the Qur'ānic verse that reads, "Then said a certain man, a believer of Pharaoh's folk who kept hidden his belief, 'What, will you slay a man because he says, "My Lord is God" [*a-taqtulūna rajulan an yaqūla rabbiya allāh?*], yet he has brought you the clear signs from your Lord? If he is a liar, his lying is upon his head; but if he is truthful, somewhat of that he promises you will smite you. Surely God guides not him who is prodigal and a liar'" (Qur'ān 40:28 [Arberry, II, 178]). This verse, set in the context of Pharaoh's deliberation over killing Moses, is used in the Sīra as the rebuttal of Abū Bakr to the infidels who attacked the Prophet. When on one occasion Muḥammad was praying, Ṭabarī relates, the Meccans came upon him and attacked him. Abū Bakr came to his aid, making the declaration, "*a-taqtulūna rajulan an yaqūla rabiyya allāh.*" Ṭabarī, I, 1186; Bukhārī (*kitāb al-tafsīr*), VI, 321 (no. 339); Muḥibb al-Dīn Aḥmad b. 'Abdallāh al-Ṭabarī, *al-Riyāḍ al-Naḍira fī Manāqib al-'Ashara*, 2 vols. (Cairo, 1953), I, 79.

93. Example stories of Abū Bakr's dream interpretations include the following: Ibn Sa'd, II, 293; Abū Nu'aym, *Dhikr Akhbār Iṣbahān*, I, 2–4; Ibn Sa'd, III, 177; Ṭabarī, I, 1803–1804. Ibn Sa'd, II, 227–228, 231; Bukhārī (*faḍā'il aṣḥāb al-nabī*), V, 5–6 (no. 6); *bāb manāqib al-Anṣār*, V, 157 (no. 244). Muslim (*faḍā'il Abī Bakr*), V (pt. 15), 150 (no. 2392). Aḥmad, *Musnad*, XXV, 266; Ibn al-Jawzī, *Ta'rīkh 'Umar b. al-Khaṭṭāb*, ed. Usāma al-Rifā'ī (Damascus, 1985), 262; Muslim (*kitāb al-ru'yā*), V (pt. 15), 28 (no. 2269). Bukhārī (*kitāb al-ta'bīr*), IX, 137 (no. 170). Tirmidhī (*kitāb al-ru'yā*), IV, 471 (no. 2293); Ibn 'Asākir, XXX, 29–30; al-Muḥibb al-Ṭabarī, *al-Riyāḍ al-Naḍira*, I, 70. For additional references to Abū Bakr's dream-interpreting skill, see al-Muḥibb al-Ṭabarī, *al-Riyāḍ al-Naḍira*, I, 141–142. A report by Wāqidī states that Abū Bakr passed on this dream-interpreting ability to his daughter Asmā', who then passed it on to Sa'īd b. al-Musayyib. Ibn Sa'd, V, 124. Also in this context see Ibn Sīrīn's observation: "There was no one more knowledgeable in dream interpretation after the Prophet than Abū Bakr." al-Dhahabī, Muḥammad b. Aḥmad b. 'Uthmān, *al-Khulafā' al-Rāshidūn*, ed. Ḥusām al-Qudsī (Beirut, 1992), 70. Ibn 'Asākir, XXX, 328. In another statement, the Prophet says: "I was commanded to seek dream interpretation from Abū Bakr [*umirtu an u'awwila al-ru'yā Abā Bakr*]." Ibn 'Asākir, XXX, 218. The narrator is Samura b. Jundub.

94. It is worth remembering here the accounts that stress Abū Bakr's steadfast belief in Muḥammad's story of the nocturnal journey, often considered a dream, even as many in Mecca were incredulous. Balādhurī recounts a story in which the Prophet declares to the angel Gabriel that the people will not believe the *isrā'* story, and Gabriel says, "Abū Bakr will believe it, and he is '*al-Ṣiddīq*.'"

Balādhurī, *Ansāb (Sā'ir)*, 123. Ibn Sa'd, III, 170. It is also important to note, however, that the matter of Abū Bakr's title was probably more complex in the historiography than a simple reference to Abū Bakr's acceptance of the new faith. In Ṭabarī's history, the concept of truth (*ṣidq*) represents a fundamental theme in the lives of both prophets and kings. Truth is treated as a manifestation of nature (*fiṭra*) in the character of these individuals, and it is something that is often beleaguered by the intrusiveness of corruption. And while the signal triumph of truth had occurred during the Prophet's lifetime, the confirming nature of Abū Bakr's career is used to reassert the continuing triumph of truth during the first caliphate. It is not a coincidence that the chief opponent of Abū Bakr is hence labeled "the liar," and that Abū Bakr's reign achieves its primary purpose with Musaylima's overthrow.

95. Although 'Umar is often included in this linkage as well, there is considerable evidence suggesting he died at age fifty-five. Ibn Qutayba, *al-Ma'ārif*, 184. Ibn al-Jawzī, *Talqīḥ Fuhūm Ahl al-Athar fī 'Uyūn al-Ta'rīkh wa'l-Siyar* (Cairo, n.d.), 108.

96. Ṭabarī, I, 2127. Balādhurī, *Ansāb (Sā'ir)*, 156. Ibn al-Athīr, II, 419. Shams al-Dīn Muḥammad b. Aḥmad al-Dhahabī, *al-Khulafā' al-Rāshidūn*, ed. Ḥusām al-Dīn al-Qudsī (Beirut, 1992), 70. The account is narrated on the authority of al-Zuhrī. This story bears close resemblance to one account that says the Prophet's death also resulted from poisoned food, specifically a slaughtered lamb, given to him by a Jewish woman. The reference is to a certain Zaynab b. al-Ḥārith, sister of the Jewish chief of Khaybar, the oasis outside Medina conquered in A.H. 7. Ṭabarī, I, 1583–1584. Ya'qūbī, II, 56. Ibn Sa'd, II, 200. Bukhārī (*bāb qabūl al-hadiyya min al-mushrikīn*), III, 475 (no. 786).

97. Ṭabarī, I, 2128. Ibn Qutayba, *al-Ma'ārif*, 171. Balādhurī, *Ansāb (Sā'ir)*, 159. The account is narrated on the authority of al-Wāqidī. Ibn al-Athīr, II, 419. al-Dhahabī, *al-Khulafā' al-Rāshidūn*, 71.

98. There are few references to the length of the Prophet's mortal illness, but Ya'qūbī does indicate that it lasted fourteen days. Ya'qūbī, II, 113. Ibn al-Jawzī gives various reports claiming that it lasted twelve, fourteen, or seventeen days, but makes it clear that both died on a Monday night. Ibn al-Jawzī, *Talqīḥ Fuhūm ahl al-Athar*, 82.

99. Ibn Sa'd, III, 192–195. There is also a third version that cites agony over the passing of the Prophet as the reason behind Abū Bakr's sudden death. Ibn al-Athīr, *Usd al-Ghāba fī Ma'rifat al-Ṣaḥāba*, ed. 'Alī Muḥammad Mu'awwaḍ and Aḥmad 'Abd al-Mawjūd, 7 vols. (Beirut, 1994), III, 331; 'Abd al-Malik b. Ḥusayn al-'Iṣāmī al-Makkī, *Simṭ al-Nujūm al-'Awalī fī Anbā' al-Awā'il wa'l-Tawālī*, 4 vols. (Cairo, 1961), II, 357.

100. Ṭabarī, I, 2120. Excerpts are translated by Khalid Yahya Blankinship, *The History of al-Ṭabarī: The Challenge to Empires* (Albany, 1993), XI, 121. Ibn al-Athīr, II, 416. This declaration may have once included another command that Abū Bakr gave to 'Umar: "And beware a coterie of the companions of the Messenger of God

[*wa iḥdhar ha'ulā' al-nafar min aṣḥāb rasūl allāh*] who have grown fat, become ambitious, and each of them seeks only his own personal welfare. Verily, they shall find themselves deluded after the lapse of one of them [*wa inna lahum la-ḥayratun ba'da zallati wāḥidin minhum*]."—(probably a reference to 'Uthmān)—"Beware that you turn out to be that person. And know that they shall remain deterred by you so long as you are deterred by the fear of God, and obedient towards you so long as you are obedient to the true path of God [*laka mustaqimīn ma-istaqāmat ṭarīqatuka*]. This is my advice to you [*hādhihi waṣiyyatī*]." Abū Yūsuf, *Kitāb al-Kharāj* (Beirut, 1979), 11–12. The statement is reported on the authority of Mūsā b. 'Uqba←Asmā' b. 'Umays. Ṭabarī may have found this statement too strongly critical of the companions, and thus decided to keep only the more general word of caution to the public about the corrupting influence of worldly luxury. However, the statement is crucial for appreciating the continuity in criticism against the politically ambitious companions, first by the Prophet at his last pilgrimage and later by Mu'āwiya just before he returned to Syria after visiting 'Uthmān (see chapter 7).

101. Ya'qūbī, II, 158.

102. Ṭabarī, I, 2137. Blankinship, *HT*, XI, 146.

103. It is hard to know what was intended by the reference to tattoos, since *ḥadīth* strongly rallies against this practice. Tirmidhī, *Sunan*, (*kitāb al-adab*), 5:97 (no. 2782).

104. Ṭabarī, I, 2138. Blankinship, *HT*, XI, 147.

105. Ṭabarī, II, 1342. *Al-'Uyūn wa'l-Ḥadā'iq fī Akhbār al-Ḥaqā'iq*, ed. M. de Goeje (Leiden, 1869), 38–39. Ibn Sa'd, V, 336–337. The scene is reminiscent of the way 'Umar b. 'Abd al-'Azīz would be presented to the Umayyad family as their next successor by Rajā' b. Ḥayawa, messenger of the dying caliph Sulaymān b. 'Abd al-Malik. In a more extensive version by al-Wāqidī, the beginning secret conversation that Abū Bakr has with 'Abd al-Raḥmān is strung together with the whole succession story. There, 'Uthmān is also the one who asks the people if they agree to the undisclosed name of the successor. Ibn Sa'd, III, 200.

106. Ṭabarī, I, 2138–2139.

107. There is in fact here a wider and continuing exercise of legitimation for the members of the *shūrā*, since, as noted by M. Watt, Abū Bakr is cited in the tradition for leading to the conversion of five out of the six members of the *shūrā* ('Uthmān, Ṭalḥa, al-Zubayr, Sa'd, and Ibn 'Awf). "Abū Bakr," *Encyclopedia of Islam*, I (1960), 110. Also, Ibn al-Jawzī, *Talqīḥ*, 105, citing a report by Ibn Ishaq.

108. Ṭabarī, I, 2793. Trans. G. Rex Smith, *History of al-Ṭabarī: The Conquest of Iran* (Albany, 1994), XIV, 159. This is how the stories explain 'Alī's loss of the succession. Historically we know that 'Abd al-Raḥmān b. 'Awf was the brother-in-law of 'Uthmān (Abū 'Alī Aḥmad b. Muḥammad Miskawayh, *Tajārib al-Umam*, ed. Abū'l-Qāsim Emāmī [Tehran, 1987], I, 264), which must have strengthened their alliance, as did their extensive trade interests and wealth.

109. It is partly for this reason that Ibn 'Awf, rather than 'Uthmān, voices some criticism of 'Umar's heavy-handed style. See 'Uthmān's argument with 'Alī in chap. 5.

110. 'Uthmān, as is well known, would later be accused of appointing his kinsmen to important governorships for reasons of tribal and kindred solidarity rather than merit or piety.

111. Ṭabarī, I, 2139–2140. Blankinship, *HT,* XI, 148. Translation slightly modified. Yūnus b. 'Abd al-'Alā←Yaḥyā b. 'Abdallāh b. Bukayr←al-Layth b. Sa'd←'Ulwān←Ṣāliḥ b. Kaysān←'Umar b. 'Abd al-Raḥmān b. 'Awf←'Abd al-Raḥmān b. 'Awf.

112. Ṭabarī, I, 2140. Blankinship, *HT,* XI, 149.

113. Ṭabarī, I, 2140–2141. Blankinship, *HT,* XI, 149–150. Balādhurī, *Ansāb* (*Sā'ir*), 407.

114. Qur'ān 18:78 (Arberry, I, 327).

115. Although no details about this event exist in Ṭabarī (although they are found in Ya'qūbī), Abū Bakr's regret shows that it must have been redacted by Ṭabarī, but not completely.

## 3. 'UMAR B. AL-KHAṬṬĀB: A SAGA OF LAW AND CONQUEST

1. For a range of *ḥadīth*s admonishing hostility to Abū Bakr and 'Umar, see Ibn 'Asākir, XXX, 195, 144, 201, 392; XLIV, 222–227; Khaṭīb, *Ta'rīkh Baghdād*, VII, 357, 387; al-Hindī, *Kanz*, XIII, 3–26.

2. The term originated from 'Umar's famous remark: "*wāfaqtu rabbī fī thalāth, fī maqām Ibrāhīm wa fī'l-ḥijāb wa fī qawlihi 'asā rabbuhu in ṭallaqakunna*' [Divine scripture concurred with my opinion on three occasions: in establishing a place of worship at Abraham's first building foundations at the Ka'ba, in the matter of the veiling of women, and in the ruling relating to divorce] [Qur'ān 66:5]." Dhahabī, *al-Khulafā' al-Rāshidūn*, 147. A core list of these incidents is included by 'Umar b. Shabba in his *Ta'rīkh al-Madīna*, I, 45–51. Also, Suyūṭī, *Ta'rīkh al-Khulafā'*, 142–146. The main list of these concurrences usually includes 'Umar's pious opinion on different matters, especially those that elicited a Qur'ānic revelation. These issues include: imposing the *ḥijāb* on women (Qur'ān 33:53–54), the principle of seeking permission (Qur'ān 24:58), opposing funeral prayer service for the deceased of the hypocrites (Qur'ān 9:84), the prohibition of wine (Qur'ān 2:219), and the idea of using the commemorative foundation place where Ibrāhim began building the Ka'ba as a special prayer location (Qur'ān 2:119). It should be noted that the second chapter of the Qur'ān (*sūrāt al-baqara*), where the latter verse appears, deals heavily toward its ending with themes of social organization, especially as regards women, and outlines rules of marriage, divorce, and

inheritance (verses 221–241), and business contracts, all of which fall squarely within the range of topics that ʿUmar purportedly spoke about the most before and during his reign. These were topics that would have been integral to broader issues of social, political, and legalistic organization in the early ʿAbbāsid period. Other miscellaneous issues associated with ʿUmar include: the three-time divorce, the end of the *mutʿa*, the penalty of stoning for the married adulterer, abolishing the share of *al-muʾallafatu qulūbuhum* (i.e., the wavering converts to Islam) in war spoils, standardizing the *takbīr* for the funeral prayer, adding the *tarāwīḥ* prayer during Ramaḍān, and the idea to exile non-Muslims from Arabia.

3. There are anecdotes that portray ʿUmar holding leafs of biblical text (generically referred to as "*al-tawrāt*") and that show the Prophet commanding him to discard them. Al-Suyūṭī, *al-Khaṣāʾis al-Kubrā*, ed. Muḥammad Khalīl Harrās, 3 vols. (Cairo, 1967), III, 132. Another account describes how ʿUmar used to go among the Jews on their study days (*yawm madārisihim*), and how he used to marvel at how the Torah confirms the Qurʾān and vice versa. Ibn Shabba, *Taʾrīkh al-Madīna*, II, 49. Such stories clearly served to highlight the meaning of the finality of the Prophet, or how the Qurʾān was confirming primary laws from biblical times. Whatever their origin, these accounts about ʿUmar's learnedness link up with other accounts that show ʿUmar as someone versed in reading and writing ("*wa kāna ʿUmar yaqraʾ al-kutub*"). Ibn Shabba, *Taʾrīkh al-Madīna*, I, 348; Ibn ʿAbd Rabbihi, *al-ʿIqd*, IV, 157; al-Muḥibb al-Ṭabarī, *al-Riyāḍ al-Naḍira*, II, 6.

4. Balādhurī, *Ansāb (Sāʾir)*, 358. Ibn Saʿd, III, 270. Variations on this include a saying attributed to ʿAlī that "an angel speaks through the mouth of ʿUmar." Abū Nuʿaym Aḥmad b. ʿAbdallāh al-Iṣbahānī, *Ḥilyat al-Awliyāʾ*, 10 vols. (Cairo, 1932–1938), I, 42. Aḥmad, *Musnad*, IX, 144.

5. Dhahabī, *al-Khulafāʾ al-Rāshidūn*, 147.

6. Balādhurī, *Ansāb (Sāʾir)*, 355.

7. Another *ḥadīth* states: "If the faith of Abū Bakr was put in one scale, and the faith of all the people of the earth put in the other, Abū Bakr's would be the more weighty." Ibrāhīm b. Muḥammad al-Bayhaqī, *al-Maḥāsin waʾl-Masāwiʾ*, ed. M. Ibrāhīm (Beirut, n.d.), 35. Ibn ʿAsākir, XXX, 126.

8. Balādhurī, *Ansāb (Sāʾir)*, 355–356.

9. Tirmidhī, *Sunan*, V, 578. Aḥmad, *Musnad*, XXVIII, 624. Ibn ʿAbd al-Ḥakam, *Futūḥ Miṣr wa Akhbāruhā*, ed. C. Torrey (New Haven, 1922), 288. Dhahabī, *al-Khulafāʾ al-Rāshidūn*, 147. Another exuberant *ḥadīth* would state: "Had I not been sent among you [as a messenger], ʿUmar would have." Al-ʿIṣāmī, *Simṭ al-Nujūm al-ʿAwālī*, II, 383.

10. Tirmidhī, *Sunan*, V, 581. Muslim, V (pt. 15), 166 (no. 2398). Bukhārī (*kitāb aḥādīth al-anbiyāʾ*), IV, 449 (no. 675). Balādhurī, *Ansāb (Sāʾir)*, 435. Dhahabī, *al-Khulafāʾ al-Rāshidūn*, 146. This most widely known form of the *ḥadīth* appears to be amended from an original that began as such: "The Israelites used to have individuals who were inspired. If any of them were to be counted in my nation,

it would be 'Umar [*kāna fī Banī Isrā'īl muḥaddathūn, fa-in kāna fī ummatī minhum aḥad fa-'Umar b. al-Khaṭṭāb*]." Ibn 'Asākir, XLIV, 91; al-Muḥibb al-Ṭabarī, *al-Riyāḍ al-Naḍira*, I, 261. Bukhārī (*bāb faḍā'il aṣḥāb al-nabī*), 5:27 (no. 38); with some difference (*laqad kāna fī man kāna qablakum min banī isrā'īl rijālun yukallamūna min ghayr an yakūnū anbiyā', fa-in yakun min ummatī aḥad fa-'Umar*).

11. The comparison of 'Umar with Paul is especially rich, and several authors have noted the parallel in the key role that these two figures played as "second champions" in articulating and defending these two faiths. See W. Muir, *Annals of the Early Caliphate* (London, 1883), 283–284. D. S. Margoliouth, *Mohammed and the Rise of Islam* (London, 1905), 162–165, 167, 346. W. R. Smith, "Some Similarities and Differences Between Christianity and Islam," *The World of Islam* (London, 1960), 52. And, most recently, Hava Lazarus-Yafeh, "'Umar b. al-Khaṭṭāb—Paul of Islam?," *Some Religious Aspects of Islam, a Collection of Articles* (Leiden, 1981), 1–16. The "second man" analogy, however, has mostly been drawn in symbolic or historic terms. A close reading of the portrait of 'Umar, his discourse, and issues of concern can show that religious sources (whether *ḥadīth* or historical accounts) drew heavily on the New Testament in this context. 'Umar's social regulations, exhortations for modesty, restrictions on women, and injunction for the authority of men as husbands over wives and fathers over children, derive a lot from Paul's First Letter to Timothy and First Letter to the Corinthians. Along with these influences were other miscellaneous issues, such as Paul's deprecation of material things (money, jewelry, etc.) as the root of all evil, and discouragement of the flock not to preoccupy themselves with "myths . . . which promote speculations" (read: *takalluf*).

12. Ibn Sa'd, III, 287.

13. Balādhurī, *Ansāb* (*Sā'ir*), 351. Another statement declares: "Beware the anger of 'Umar. God is made angry with his anger." Ibn 'Asākir, XLIV, 72.

14. Another *ḥadīth* would declare: "*ashaddu ummatī fī amri allāh, 'Umar*." Ibn Sa'd, III, 291.

15. Ibn Sa'd, III, 283. Ibn al-Jawzī, *Ṣifat al-Ṣafwa*, ed. Ibrāhīm Ramaḍān, 2 vols. (Beirut, 1989), I, 143.

16. For examples of this advice literature given to Hārūn al-Rashīd about practices in 'Umar's time, see, Abū Yūsuf, *Kitāb al-Kharāj*, 36–40.

17. There has been a significant discussion in recent scholarship of 'Umar's image as religious deliverer after the conquest of Jerusalem. This was first propounded by Michael Cook and Patricia Crone in their *Hagarism*. The authors there argued that the title "*fārūq*" constituted an Islamic fossilization of a certain Jewish idea of messianism, and that 'Umar was awaited as messianic redeemer (p. 5). While the Jerusalem context of 'Umar's glorifics is real, I would argue that this web of messianism was woven around a single political achievement (the Jerusalem conquest) and lacked the religious substance that Muḥammad's role occupied (e.g., a religious discourse, an aura of kinship magic, a sectarian following

as the Hāshimite cause received, and other aspects). For a discussion of 'Umar's role as deliverer of Jerusalem, see Suliman Bashear, "The Title 'Fārūq' and Its Association with 'Umar I," *Studia Islamica* 22 (1990): 47–70.

18. Implications to this effect can be inferred from a variety of modern studies, such as B. Lewis, "An Apocalyptic Vision of Islamic History," *BSOAS* 13 (1950): 305–338. On the Jewish affinity to the early Islamic narrative in general, see F. Rosenthal, *A History of Muslim Historiography* (Leiden, 1968), 46–47, 140–141.

19. Balādhurī, *Ansāb* (*Sā'ir*), 356. Ibn Sa'd, III, 270. Ṭabarī, *Dhuyūl Ta'rīkh al-Ṭabarī*, ed. M. Abū'l-Faḍl Ibrāhīm, 504. The account is related on the authority of al-Zuhrī. Other reports simply state that 'Umar was mentioned in the books of the Christians but not by the epithet "*al-fārūq*." Ibn Sa'd, III, 326. Balādhurī, *Ansāb* (*Sā'ir*), 465. Also, Balādhurī, *Ansāb* (*Sā'ir*), 572.

20. As the common view will characterize 'Umar's life: "'Umar's conversion to Islam was a conquest, his hijra was a victory, and his reign was a mercy to the people" (Ibn Sa'd, III, 270).

21. For an overview of these overt categories, see the work of A. Noth and L. Conrad; also, F. Donner, *Narratives of Islamic Origins: The Beginnings of Islamic Historical Writing*.

22. Stories about the caliph advocating the use of the Arabic language are well known. Ibn 'Abd al-Barr, *Jāmi'*, II, 168. "Learning Arabic," 'Umar declared, "enhances one's chivalry [*murū'a*]." Ibn Qutayba, *'Uyūn al-Akhbār*, I, 412. A similar report claims that 'Umar ordered two Persians on pilgrimage to switch to speaking Arabic since Persian speaking leads to unworthy behavior (*man takallama al-fārisiyya khabb*). Al-Sahmī, *Ta'rīkh Jurjān*, 426. 'Umar probably made a similar comment directed to al-Mughīra after the latter's failure as a translator of Persian at the encounter between 'Umar and al-Hurmuzān. 'Umar commented: "It doesn't seem you know it [Persian] that much. [Know that] any of you who masters it goes astray . . . ["*mā arāka bihā ḥādhiqan, mā aḥsanahā minkum aḥadun illā khabb wa mā khabba illā daqqa, iyyākum wa iyyāha fa-innahā tanquḍu al-i'rāb*]." Ṭabarī, I, 2560. 'Umar also commanded his governors to punish scribes who miswrote the language (*al-laḥn*). Al-Ṣūlī, *Adab al-Kuttāb*, 35, 129. These latter examples branch off from the image of the caliph in later times as the organizer of dīwans and administration, a process that in fact happened in the later Umayyad period.

23. Ṭabarī, I, 2725. Ibn Sa'd, III, 346.

24. Balādhurī, *Ansāb* (*Sā'ir*), 474. Ibn Sa'd, III, 338, 349–350, 352.

25. All this discussion was no doubt meant to reflect on the 'Abbāsids and their role in transforming the social basis of the Islamic state, and it was equally intended as a commentary on 'Umar and the Arabs.

26. Ṭabarī, I, 2193.

27. The caliph is also said to have discouraged mixed marriages between Arabs and non-Arabs.

28. Ṭabarī, I, 2483–2485. There are different versions of 'Umar's statement here. These include: "*inna al-'arab lā yuwāfiquhā illā mā wāfaqa ibilihā min al-buldān*" (Ṭabarī I, 2483); "*inna al-'araba lā taṣliḥu bi-arḍin lā taṣliḥu bihā al-ibil*" (Ṭabarī, I, 2484); "*inna al-'arab lā yuṣliḥuhā min al-buldān illā mā aṣlaḥa al-shāt wa'l-ba'īr*" (Ṭabarī, I, 2485; Abū Yūsuf, *Kitāb al-Kharāj*, 30). Some images of 'Umar's behavior are also clearly connected with the camel motif in the sources. One narrator states: "When two men with a dispute used to come to 'Umar for a solution, he would kneel down, and say, 'O Lord, help me against these two, for each of them wants me to compromise my religion.'" Ibn Sa'd, III, 289. The expression used to describe 'Umar's action of kneeling down (*baraka 'alā rukbatayh*)—instead of *jathā* or *qa'ada*—is the image associated with the camel's action, and was pointedly selected to be consistent with other motifs about the camel described above. The intent in these texts was to paint the image of a stern leader with a natural sensibility for fairness that drew on nomadic values and blended with the ecological environment of Arabia.

29. Ṭabarī, I, 2483.

30. Ṭabarī, I, 2144.

31. A plethora of colloquial or nonliterate Arabic expressions are attributed to 'Umar in the sources. In asking Abū Lu'lu'a about his profession, 'Umar's question was "*aysh ṣinā'tuka* [what is your profession?]" (Ṭabarī, I, 2722), and in answering 'Amr b. al-'Āṣ, 'Umar would say "(*ī*) *walladhī nafsu 'Umar bi-yadihi*" (Ṭabarī, I, 2742) rather than "(*ay*) . . ." Such bedouin colloquialisms are not assigned to the other companions, and certainly not to 'Alī.

32. Later, in the times of 'Uthmān, 'Alī, and the *fitna*s, the Khārijites become the realization of 'Umar's warnings about the danger of corrupting the A'rāb. Not coincidentally, in a clear narrative linkage, they are shown as being fond of 'Umar even when there is no clear religious or political reason for them to cherish his memory at a time of conflict with 'Alī.

33. Qur'ān 44:25–28 (Arberry, II, 208). Ṭabarī, I, 2443.

34. Debate on the extent of the Islamic conquests in 'Umar's reign nevertheless continues. Tilman Nagel casts reasonable doubt on the possibility that 'Umar was genuinely interested "in expanding the territory of Islam beyond the borders of Arabia," and surmises that the early conquests were only permitted out of Basra and Kufa to thwart the annual raids the Sasanids waged against southern Iraq. T. Nagel, "Some Considerations Concerning the Pre-Islamic and the Islamic Foundations of the Authority of the Caliphate," in *Studies on the First Century of Islamic Society*, ed. G. H. A. Juynboll (Southern Illinois University Press, 1982), 188.

35. When the booty from the conquest of Persia was sent to 'Umar, he reportedly displayed it in the mosque of Medina, and on that occasion wept. When 'Abd al-Raḥmān b. 'Awf asked, "Why do you weep, Commander of the Faithful, is

this not an occasion to express thanks to God? [*inna hādhā min mawāqif al-shukr*]," 'Umar replied, "Indeed, but that is not the reason why I cry. By God, He never gave such as this to any people without that giving rise to mutual envy and hatred [*mā aʿṭā allāhu hādhā qawman illā taḥāsadū, wa tabāghaḍū, wa lā taḥāsadū illā alqā ba'sahum baynahum*]." Ṭabarī, I, 2466–2467. Trans. G. Juynboll, *History of al-Ṭabarī: The Conquest of Iraq, Southwestern Persia, and Egypt* (Albany, 1989), XIII, 46 (with minor modification). Abū Yūsuf's account phrases the caliph's comment slightly differently (. . . *wa lakinna allāh lam yuʿṭi qawman hādhā illā alqā baynahum al-ʿadāwata wa'l-baghḍā'*). Abū Yūsuf, *Kitāb al-Kharāj*, 47. The statement is reported on the authority of al-Zuhrī. See similarity to 'Alī's comments below.

36. Qur'ān 47:38 (Arberry, II, 224).

37. In the opening of his work, Abū Nuʿaym states, "*fa-bada'tu awwalan bi-dhikri aḥādītha ruwiyat fī faḍīlat l-furs wa'l-ʿajam wa'l-mawālī wa-annahum al-mubashsharūn bi-manāl al-imān wa'l-taḥaqquq bihi wa in kāna ʿinda al-thurayyā* [I begin the narration with stories that have been told about the merits of the Persians and the non-Arabs, and about how they have been promised the true acquisition of faith even if it were as remotely positioned as the Pleiades]." Abū Nuʿaym, *Dhikr Akhbār Iṣbahān*, I, 1. The author then lists numerous other *ḥadīth*s that foretell the coming rise of Persia. For other *ḥadīth*s on the merits of Persia, see, Muslim (*faḍl fāris*), VI (pt. 16), 100 (no. 2546), "If knowledge were even in the Pleiades . . ." Bukhārī's version of this *ḥadīth* makes it implicit that the reference is to Persians. Bukhārī (*bāb qawlihi 'wa ākharīn minhum lammā yalḥaqū bihim'*), VI, 390 (no. 420).

38. And here one can recall a whole slew of *ḥadīth*s in which the Prophet praises Persia as the patron of the Hāshimites and endorses Persian culture and language. These *ḥadīth*s were clearly meant to contradict 'Umar's insistence on Arabic and praise of the Arab element. In one *ḥadīth*, for example, the Prophet is reported to have said: "Persia is our close relation [*fāris ʿusbatunā ahl al-bayt*]." Abū Nuʿaym, *Dhikr Akhbār Iṣbahān*, I, 11. Ibn al-Faqīh al-Hamadhānī, *Mukhtaṣar Kitāb al-Buldān*, ed. M. J. de Goeje (Leiden, 1885), 196. And in another *ḥadīth*: "He who converts among the Persians is considered from Quraysh [*man aslama min fāris fa-huwa quraysh*]." I. Goldziher, *Muslim Studies*, I, 112 (citing al-Suyūṭī, *al-Jāmiʿ al-Ṣaghīr*). And, in another *ḥadīth*, the Prophet is quoted berating his grandson al-Ḥasan in a Persian phrase. Bukhārī, *Ṣaḥīḥ*, *kitāb al-jihād, bāb man takallam bi'l-fārisiyya wa'l-raṭāna*, IV, 195 (no. 306). Other statements show no aversion to reading the Qur'ān in Persian (Khaṭīb, *Ta'rīkh Baghdād*, XI, 164), and intermarriage with Iranians, especially Khurāsānīs, is encouraged. Al-Hamadhānī states that Khurāsānī women are envied because they bear mostly male offspring and that this is attested to by the abundance of male progeny in the line of 'Alī b. Abī Ṭālib. *Kitāb al-Buldān*, 75.

39. Ṭabarī, I, 2741 (*la tajlidū al-ʿarab fa-tudhillūhā wa tujammirūhā fa-taftinūhā wa lā taghfilū ʿanhā fa-taḥrimūhā*). Abū Yūsuf's *Kitāb al-Kharāj* substitutes the word

"*muslimīn*" for "*al-'arab*" in a variant, later tradition that tries to Islamize these historical words of advice. *Kitāb al-Kharāj*, 115. Ibn 'Abd al-Ḥakam, *Futūḥ Miṣr*, 167.

40. Ṭabarī, I, 2684. Smith, *HT*, XIV, 55.

41. Ṭabarī, I, 2613; Abū Ḥanīfa Aḥmad b. Dāwūd al-Dīnawarī, *Kitāb al-Akhbār al-Ṭiwāl*, ed. V. Guirgass (Leiden, 1888), 142.

42. 'Alī, for example, is never cited as having accompanied 'Umar on any of the four trips that he made to Syria, while all the significant men who later joined Mu'āwiya, including Ibn 'Abbās, make an appearance there.

43. The description in Ṭabarī and Ibn Sa'd of the Saqīfa incident is well redacted to avoid an open correlation between the goals of 'Alī and the Anṣār. However, other fragmentary texts preserve a memory of an original bond between the two oppositions. Al-Ma'mūn is quoted by al-Zubayr b. Bakkār as berating the Anṣār for having let down 'Alī and al-'Abbās when these figures were advocating the rights of the Anṣār at the Saqīfa. *Al-Akhbār al-Muwaffaqiyyāt*, ed. S. M. al-'Ānī (Baghdad, 1972), 239.

44. Ṭabarī, I, 3286.

45. Ṭabarī, I, 2677. The accusation of the Kufans to 'Ammār was, "He is inadequate, stingy, and has no political skill [*huwa wallāhi ghayru kāfin wa lā mujzin wa lā 'ālimun bi'l-siyāsa*]." The contrast between the politicians and the pious was clearly a core message in this confrontation as well.

46. Ṭabarī, I, 2608.

47. Ṭabarī, I, 2704.

48. Note for example the tradition that has 'Umar say of 'Amr b. al-'Āṣ: "It is not right that Abū 'Abdallāh should be appointed to a position other than that of being a leader [*amīr*]." Ibn 'Abd al-Ḥakam, *Futūḥ Miṣr*, 180. Dhahabī, *Ta'rīkh al-Islām wa Wafayāt al-Mashāhīr wa'l-A'lām*, 29 vols. in 26, ed. 'Umar Tadmurī (Beirut, 1990), IV, 92. In case the reader missed the intended tension between 'Umar and 'Alī, one narrator describes 'Umar's memory of the episode of the treaty of al-Ḥudaybiyya as follows: "The Messenger of God consented to a peace with the Meccans of the sort that were he [i.e., the Prophet] to appoint a leader who would command [*law ammar 'alayya amīran*] me to do what the Messenger of God had done [at al-Ḥudaybiyya], I would never have listened to him or obeyed him [in that deed]." Ibn Sa'd, II, 101. This account, narrated on the authority of Ibn 'Abbās, repeats 'Umar's usual angst at concessions to nonbelievers, but with a turn of witty pun on the words *'alayya/ 'Alī*, we can find 'Umar making a direct challenge to 'Alī.

49. Balādhurī, *Ansāb* (*Sā'ir*), 360, 363.

50. Ṭabarī, I, 1579. The incident is referred to in *ḥadīth* texts but without the competitive edge toward Abū Bakr and 'Umar. Bukhārī (*kitāb al-jihād*), IV, 122, 156–157 (nos. 192, 253); al-Hindī, *Kanz*, X, 463 (no. 30121)

51. Ṭabarī, I, 2213–2214.

52. 'Umar's letter advised: "Do not be perturbed by the information that you receive about them nor by [the army] that they will muster against you . . . Send [to the Persian king] people of [impressive] appearance, sound judgment and endurance, in order to invite him to embrace Islam [*lā yukribannaka mā ya'tīka 'anhum wa lā mā ya'tūnaka bihi . . . wa ib'ath ilayhi rijālan min ahl al-munāẓara wa'l-ra'y wa'l-jalad yad'ūnahu*]." Ṭabarī, I, 2235. Y. Friedmann, *History of al-Ṭabarī: The Battle of al-Qādisiyya and the Conquest of Syria and Palestine* (Albany, 1992), XII, 29.

53. Ṭabarī, I, 2220.

54. Ṭabarī, I, 2680. Ibn 'Abd Rabbihi, *al-'Iqd*, I, 22. The exchange between the two makes the comparison seem like one that extends to include non-Muslims.

55. Ṭabarī, I, 2255. The Arabic here is "*wa-allāh laqad ṣadaqa al-'arabiyy . . . wa-allāh mā aslamanā illā a'mālunā . . . . inna allāh kāna yanṣurukum 'alā l-'aduww wa yu-makkinu lakum fi'l-bilād bi-ḥusn al-sīra wa kaff al-ẓulm wa'l-wafā' bi'l-'uhūd wa'l-iḥsān fa-ammā idh taḥawwaltum 'an dhalika ilā hādhihi l-a'māl fa-lā 'arā allāh illā mughayy-iran mā bikum wa mā anā bi-āman an yanzi'a allāhu sulṭānahu minkum.*" Friedmann, *HT*, XII, 51 (with variation). These comments were crafted to be read in tandem with a narrative planted in the 'Abbāsid period, where it showed a maturity and final resolution for the words of Rustam. The relevant later text surfaces when the Khurāsānī commander Qaḥṭaba tells his troops on the eve of the 'Abbāsid revolution: "Men of Khurāsān [*yā ahla Khurāsān*], this land belonged to your forefathers [*li-ābā'ikum al-awwalīn*] before you, and they were given victory over their enemies because they were just and behaved rightly [*wa kānū yunṣarūna 'alā 'aduwwihim bi-'adlihim wa ḥusni sīratihim*]. God the Mighty and Glorious was then angered with them. Their authority was taken from them, and the humblest people to share the earth with them was given power over them and took their land and their women and enslaved their children [*ḥattā baddalū wa ẓalamū fa-sakhiṭa allāhu 'alayhim fa-intaza'a sulṭānahum wa sallaṭa 'alayhim adhalla ummatin kānat fi'l-arḍ 'indahum*]. Yet this people ruled justly with all and kept their word and succored the oppressed [*fa-kānū bi-dhālika yaḥkumūna bi'l-'adl wa yūfūna bi'l-'ahd wa yanṣurūna al-maẓlūm*]. Then they changed and altered; they went astray in their governance, and people of probity and piety came to fear from the race of God's Apostle, may God's benediction be on him, and peace [*thumma baddalū wa ghayyarū fa-jārū fi'l-ḥukm . . .*]! Thus God has empowered you against them in order that revenge be enacted through you, that you should be their greatest punishment, for you have sought them out for vengeance. The *Imām* has sworn to me that you would encounter them in numbers great as these, but that God would give you victory over them, and you will rout and slay them." Ṭabarī, II, 2005. Trans. J. A. Williams, *The 'Abbāsid Revolution*, XXVII, 110–111. Upon comparing the two speeches by Rustam and Qaḥṭaba, the reader is led to see how divine favor to people turns in relation to a process of "*tabdīl*," and in both the goal is to show that Iran was the object of these historical cycles of moral change throughout. Both Rustam and Qaḥṭaba invoke in their respective speeches simi-

lar Qur'ānically inspired moral language and maintain a universal focus in their exhortations.

56. Ṭabarī, I, 2266.

57. Ṭabarī, I, 2243–2244. Ibn al-Athīr, II, 458. Ya'qūbī, II, 143–144.

58. Ṭabarī, I, 2266, 2286. In a variant version, the weapon of Persia is handed to the Prophet, who hands it to 'Umar. Ibn al-Athīr, II, 460. Ṭabarī, I, 2352.

59. Ṭabarī, I, 2241–2242; also a similar exchange between al-Mughīra b. Shu'ba and Bundār, the Persian commander, just before the Battle of Nihāwand. Ṭabarī, I, 2602, 2279. Dīnawarī makes the standoff between al-Mughīra b. Shu'ba and Rustam (Dīnawarī, 137). Abū Nu'aym sets the discussion in the context of the conquest of Nihāwand between al-Nu'mān b. Muqarrin and Yazdajird. Abū Nu'aym, *Dhikr Akhbār Iṣbahān*, ed. S. Dedering, 2 vols. (Leiden, 1931–1934), I, 21. Ibn al-Athīr mentions that the debate before Qādisiyya was between al-Nu'mān b. Muqarrin and Yazdajird. *Al-Kāmil*, II, 456. Also see, A. Noth and L. Conrad, *The Early Arabic Historical Tradition*, 158. All these versions contain a similar moralizing essence, and could hardly have been accepted as total fact by a medieval audience. The question narrators wrestled with, as the account varied slightly, was which characters the audience wanted to see involved in this debate rather than what was literally said. On the Persian side, the choice of Yazdajird is the overwhelming one, but on the Arab side, division prevails. It could well be that the original account cast al-Mughīra b. Shu'ba in the role but that he was later replaced. Al-Mughīra's later political tilt to the Umayyads against 'Alī and/or the story of his later sex scandal could have contributed to both Sunnī and Shī'ī replacement of this commander with a more wholesome character. This switch of name, however, ultimately threw the network of ties in the story of the conquest of Persia in 'Umar's reign off balance, since al-Mughīra b. Shu'ba had to be involved in this critical embassy to show the ironic ties among 'Umar, Yazdajird, Hurmuzān, Abū Lu'lu'a, and al-Mughīra. Offshoot narratives about the debate between Mughīra and the Sasanids sometimes put Rustam in the position of the arrogant interlocutor, but these narratives, which tend to be more religiously zealous, are secondary imitations of the original account. Al-Maqdisī, *al-Bad' wa'l-Ta'rīkh*, ed. C. Huart (Paris, 1899), V, 173; Ṭabarī, I, 2352; Abū Yūsuf, *Kitāb al-Kharāj*, 29.

60. Within this frame of biblical coloring, the much-criticized statement of Sayf b. 'Umar describing how the victorious Arab cavalry waded through the Euphrates River and conquered Ctesiphon makes sense as a reshaping of motifs from the Moses story. Ṭabarī, I, 2432–2441.

61. This moral contrast in the depiction of Rustam and Yazdajird was anchored to the early narrators in a systemic class difference between the two men, with Yazdajird being of obscure maternal lineage (known as "*ibn al-ḥajjāma*"). Ya'qūbī, II, 144.

62. Ṭabarī, I, 2164. Ya'qūbī, I, 173.

63. It should be said here that Ṭabarī's account of those closing years of Sasanid rule is based less on an accurate sequencing in chronology than on the author's ordering of characters. According to Ṭabarī, for instance, Būrān follows Āzarmidukht and is portrayed as the one who summons Rustam to organize the Persian state. Other sources on the Arab side (such as Ya'qūbī, I, 173) and the Byzantine side, however, clearly place Āzarmidukht after Būrān. See M. Morony, "Sasanids," *Encyclopaedia of Islam*, new ed., IX (Leiden, 1997), 80. R. Frye, *The Heritage of Persia* (New York, 1962), 240. "Dionysius Reconstituted" (as extracted from Michael the Syrian's *Chronicle of 1234*) in *The Seventh Century in the West-Syrian Chronicles*, trans. A. Palmer, S. Brock, and R. Hoyland (Liverpool University Press, 1993), 143.

64. Ibn al-Athīr, II, 455–456. When Yazdajird called on Rustam to lead the armies, the latter reportedly replied, "It is better that you do not send me, for the Arabs will only keep fearing us so long as I am not the one sent to fight them. And perchance the kingdom will last better if I stay behind, and then God will have sufficed us and we will have followed a sound strategy. Sound opinion is verily more beneficial than warfare [*la'alla al-dawla an tathbita bī idhā lam aḥḍur al-ḥarb fa-yakūn allāh qad kafā wa nakūn qad aṣabnā al-makīda, wa'l-ra'y fī'l-ḥarb anfa' min ba'ḍ al-ẓafr, wa'l-ināt khayrun min al-'ajala*]." This relatively long narrative of debate between Yazdajird and Rustam is only included in Ibn al-Athīr's work, although the terminology used by Rustam (*al-dawla, al-makīda, al-ra'y*) meshes with Ṭabarī's language for describing political debates and conflict among Muslims, especially during the *fitnas*.

65. Dīnawarī, 142. Ṭabarī, I, 2213–2217.

66. Ṭabarī, I, 2290 (Ṭabarī←al-Sarī←Shu'ayb←Sayf←Hallam←Mas'ūd. Also in another report narrated by Ṭabarī←al-Sarī←Shu'ayb←Sayf←al-Naḍar←Ibn al-Rufayl).

67. Dīnawarī, 136.

68. Ibn Sa'd, V, 89. The addition here is a clear reference to the twelve *nuqabā'* of the Anṣār, who first pledged support to the Prophet before he made the *hijra*, and the twelve deputies of Moses.

69. The account follows up with an explanatory detail, "'Umar had sat there to receive a delegation from the inhabitants of al-Kufa dressed in a hooded cloak. When he had finished talking to them and they had risen from the audience and left him alone, he took off his cloak, folded it to make a pillow and went to sleep. So the people from al-Basra, together with the bystanders, went to look for him . . ." Ṭabarī, I, 2557. Juynboll, *HT*, XIII, 137–138. The repeated focus in this account on describing in detail what 'Umar was wearing, a burnous, for meeting the Kufans, and how he took it off afterward and put it underneath him in sleep was meant not just as an ascetic symbol. The reference to the burnous was no doubt an allusion to the Qurrā' and the Khārijites (or more generally extremist dissenters from 'Alī's party—bedouins and Kufans, according to Sunnī valuation) who

would get referred to as "*aṣḥāb al-baranis*" (Ibn 'Abd Rabbihi, *al-'Iqd*, IV, 347, 351). In keeping with the Arab theme described above, 'Umar's wearing of a bornous may depict him as a consistent fan of a particular desert garb that had cultural connotations of religious asceticism and zeal. But it may also be that the account intended to portray 'Umar as a savvy leader who wears the particular garb of his visitors, in this case the Kufans who had just departed.

70. The relevant story represents a classic 'Abbāsid anecdote about the caliph scouting the condition of his community of subjects at night. See Ṭabarī, I, 2743–2745.

71. Ṭabarī, I, 2557–2758.

72. Ṭabarī, I, 2558–2559; Juynboll, *HT,* XIII, 138–140. Ibn Sa'd, V, 89–90.

73. Dīnawarī describes how Yazdajird entrusted Hurmuzān with leading a new defensive strategy against the Arabs from al-Ahwāz, clearly showing that his role succeeded that of Rustam. Dīnawarī, 136.

74. The same desire of an Iranian leader to convert in the presence of a caliph and/or at the well-spring of Islamic prophecy in Medina is later attributed to other important figures. Ṣūl, the ruler of Jurjān, for example, asks Yazīd b. al-Muhallab, commander of the Umayyad campaign to Jurjān, if there is a more important leader in Islam to whom he can offer a more honorable submission. When referred to the caliph Sulaymān b. 'Abd al-Malik in Damascus, Ṣūl asks the caliph the same question, and he is told that the only place left that is more honorable is the tomb of the Prophet in Medina. Ṣūl finally heads to Medina and declares his conversion there, in essence establishing a link with the Hāshimite family. See R. Bulliet, *Islam: The View from the Edge* (New York: Columbia University Press, 1994), 44, citing al-Sahmī, *Ta'rīkh Jurjān* (Hayderabad, 1967), 247. A similar myth is attributed to Barmak, the grandfather of Yaḥyā al-Barmakī, who, being the princely and religious leader of Balkh, travels to Medina to offer direct surrender to the caliph 'Uthmān. Al-Qazwīnī, *Āthār al-Bilād wa Akhbār al-'Ibād* (Beirut, n.d.), 331. Ibn al-Faqīh al-Hamadhānī, *Kitāb al-Buldān*, 323. I. 'Abbās, "Barmakids," *Encyclopaedia Iranica*, ed. E. Yarshater, III (London, 1989), 806. Al-Faḍl b. Sahl is later said to have converted at the hands of al-Ma'mūn, while another story attributes the conversion earlier to his father, Sahl, at the hands of the caliph al-Mahdī. Ibn al-Athīr, VI, 197. Ibn Khallikān, *Wafayāt al-A'yān*, ed. M. 'Abd al-Ḥamīd, 8 vols. (Cairo, 1948), III, 209. Another variant tradition says that al-Faḍl b. Sahl disliked converting at the hands of al-Rashīd or al-Ma'mūn; he thus went to the great mosque after performing a ritual bath and there he embraced Islam. Khaṭīb, *Ta'rīkh Baghdād*, XII, 340. The primary model of all of these stories would have been not just the Hurmuzān story but also that of Salmān al-Fārisī, who, as a representative of the Iranian nation, traveled widely in search of the true religion until he finally embraced Islam in Medina at the Prophet's hands.

75. Ṭabarī, I, 2642. Mas'ūdī, *Murūj al-Dhahab*, ed. Ch. Pellat, 5 vols. (Beirut, 1973), III, 66. Abū Nu'aym, *Dhikr Akhbār Iṣbahān*, I, 21. Ibn Abī al-Shaykh, *Ṭabaqāt*

*al-Muḥaddithīn bi-Iṣbahān*, I, 41. A similar story is in Bukhārī (*kitāb al-khums*), *bāb al-jizya wa'l-muwāda'a*, IV, 254 (no. 386).

76. For the story of 'Umar's conversion, see Ibn Sa'd, III, 267–269. Balādhurī, *Ansāb* (*Sā'ir*), 346–350.

77. Miskawayh, *Tajārib al-Umam*, I, 167. Ṭabarī, I, 1898.

78. Relevant to this issue is a famous *ḥadīth* that states: "*al-ḥarbu khid'a* [warfare is guileful strategy]." Bukhārī (*kitāb al-jihād*), *bāb al-ḥarbu khid'a*, IV, 167 (no. 268). Tirmidhī (*kitāb al-jihād*), IV, 166 (no. 1675). Ṭabarī, I, 1479.

79. As al-Mughīra b. Shu'ba is said to have commented, "['Umar's] virtue was greater than any need he had to make him resort to guile [*kāna lahu faḍlun yamna'uhu min an yakhda'*]." Ibn 'Abd Rabbihi, *al-'Iqd*, IV, 270.

80. In all versions, we should recall, the key fight at the Saqīfa is between 'Umar and Sa'd b. 'Ubāda. A secondary skirmish, however, occurs between al-Zubayr and 'Umar (according to Ṭabarī, I, 1818), but 'Alī instead of al-Zubayr (according to Ya'qūbī, II, 126).

81. Ṭabarī, I, 2795. Miskawayh, *Tajārib*, I, 265. Ṭabarī adds a description of how 'Amr convinced 'Alī and 'Uthmān, separately and duplicitously, before the meeting of the *shūrā*, to react to 'Abd al-Raḥmān's offer of the caliphate in a way that ultimately favored 'Uthmān's chances over 'Alī. The incident explicitly foreshadows 'Amr's deception of Abū Mūsā al-Ash'arī later. Balādhurī's account does not have 'Alī utter the statement about the "*khid'a*" but does depict him exiting angrily from the meeting and being pressured to return and give the *bay'a*. Balādhurī, *Ansāb* (*Banū 'Abd Shams*), 508. Al-Maqdisī describes the conclusion as follows: "'Uthmān exited with a cheerful face, while 'Alī departed ashen faced and gloomy [*wa kharaja 'Uthmān wa wajhuhu yatahallal wa 'Alī kāsif al-lawn arbad*]." *Al-Bad' wa'l-Ta'rīkh*, V, 193.

82. There is a well-known story about how 'Amr b. al-'Āṣ broke a stalemate siege at Ajnādayn when he decided to use the ruse of entering the city as a messenger from the Arab army. Once inside and having observed the outline of fortifications, he reportedly was suspected by the governor Arṭabūn of being a more significant officer and was about to be arrested when, recognizing the threat, 'Amr suggested that he could bring other important officers to meet with Arṭabūn. Lured by the prospect of capturing more senior officers, the Byzantine governor allowed him to leave in expectation of his return, but 'Amr departed for good. This occasioned the well-known remark of Arṭabūn, "I have been deceived by this man, verily he is the most cunning of people." When news of this event reached 'Umar in Medina, 'Umar reportedly cheered and said: "We have sent the Arṭabūn of the Arabs to confront the Arṭabūn of the Byzantines. 'Amr got the better of him. How excellent is 'Amr! [*laqad ramaynā Arṭabuna al-rūm bi-Arṭabūni l-'Arab. . . . ghalabahu 'Amr, li-llāhi 'Amr!*]." Ṭabarī, I, 2398–2400. The presence of 'Amr in the succession story and the way he deceived 'Alī about what

to say at the succession provides a clearly intended link across three accounts (at Ajnādayn, at ʿUthmān's succession, and at Ṣiffīn). For ʿUmar's admiration of Muʿāwiya's political savvy and *khidʿa*, see Miskawayh, *Tajārib*, II, 34.

83. Ṭabarī, I, 2797. Balādhurī, *Ansāb (Sā'ir)*, 490. Ibn Saʿd, III, 350, 355–356. On ʿAlī's anger at ʿUbaydallāh b. ʿUmar, see Balādhurī, *Ansāb (Banū ʿAbd Shams)*, 510. Jufayna was randomly added in the story of the conspiracy to create a trio that stood in dialogue with the trio of the Muhājirūn at the Saqīfa.

84. Ibn Saʿd, III, 347. Balādhurī, *Ansāb (Sā'ir)*, 485.

85. Masʿūdī, *Murūj*, III, 125.

86. Ṭabarī, I, 2722.

87. Ibn Saʿd and Balādhurī do not include a mention of Abū Lu'lu'a's religion as Ṭabarī does in the main story of the encounter between ʿUmar and Abū Lu'lu'a. They also mostly imply that Abū Lu'lu'a was a Magian in the report that describes him as belonging to a people who cannot touch meat except with a knife. *Ṭabaqāt*, III, 350. Balādhurī, *Ansāb (Sā'ir)*, 484. This mention is omitted in Ṭabarī, although he includes the story of the late-night conspiracy among Abū Lu'lu'a, Hurmuzān, and Jufayna. Ṭabarī, I, 2797, 2801.

88. Other accounts make Abū Lu'lu'a a "mill maker." Ibn Saʿd, III, 347.

89. The Arabic here is "*qad balaghanī annaka taqūlu law aradtu an aʿmal raḥan taṭḥanu bi'l-rīḥi faʿaltu.*" Ṭabarī, I, 2723.

90. Ṭabarī, I, 2722; Juynboll, *HT*, XIII, 90. Ibn Saʿd, III, 345–347. A significant variant tradition in Balādhurī has ʿUmar ask ʿAlī, who happened to be in the caliph's company, what Abū Lu'lu'a meant, and ʿAlī answered, "Verily he is threatening you, O Commander of the Faithful." Balādhurī, *Ansāb (Sā'ir)*, 482.

91. In fact, biographies of Hurmuzān highlight not only his companionship of ʿUmar but that he observed religious rites, such as the pilgrimage (hence ʿAmmār's later comment to ʿUthmān that Hurmuzān is "a Muslim who has performed the pilgrimage." Balādhurī, *Ansāb (Sā'ir)*, 492. Ibn Saʿd, V, 16. (For the debacle of ʿUthmān regarding how to deal with ʿUbaydallāh b. ʿUmar, see chap. 4.)

92. Ṭabarī, I, 2632. Ṭabarī←al-Sarī←Shuʿayb←Sayf←ʿAmr b. Muḥammad← al-Shaʿbī. According to Ibn Saʿd, Abū Lu'lu'a's statement was, "The Arabs have eaten my liver." Ibn Saʿd, III, 347.

93. Perhaps a parallel symbolism to this can be traced to the role assigned to Kava, who joined the Iranian ruler Faridun in fighting the mythic figure Zohak. Kava, a blacksmith said to be from the people (*al-ʿāmma*) of Iṣbahān, sought in part to avenge the murder of his sons when he rose against the tyrant ruler Zohak (Puyrāsib). Turning his apron that guarded against the fire of metallurgical work into the famous banner *dirafsh-i Kabiyān*, Kava mobilized the people toward a reestablishment of just rule. The banner would continue to be the highest symbol of the Sasanid royal house until it was captured by the Arabs at the Battle

of Qādisiyya. Ṭabarī, I, 207. Miskawayh, *Tajārib*, I, 8. On Kava and the blacksmith symbolism, see D. Davis, "Rustam-i Dastan," *Journal of Iranian Studies* 32 (1999): 233. O. M. Davidson, *Poet and Hero in the Persian Book of Kings* (Cornell University Press, 1994), 11. D. Pickering, *A Dictionary of Folklore* (New York, 1999), 37.

94. Ṭabarī, I, 1537. Ibn Sa'd, IV, 284–286.

95. When Ziyād's turn for testimony came, 'Umar reportedly declared: "Verily this is not the face of someone whose testimony will bring shame to a companion of the Prophet." The implication here is that Ziyād will not ruin al-Mughīra. Although this brief account is set on its own in the story of al-Mughīra's debacle, it was clearly part of the original frame of accounts. Balādhurī, *Ansāb* (*Sā'ir*), 447–448.

96. The most famous criticism of Khālid related to the story of his hasty execution of Mālik b. Nuwayra al-Yarbū'ī in Bahrain during the Ridda war and his betrothal to the latter's widow.

97. Hence in this context Ya'qūbī's statement is meaningful, in that 'Umar would say whenever he ran into al-Mughīra afterward: "O Mughīra, verily I fear every time I see you that I may be struck down by stones falling from the sky." Ya'qūbī, II, 146. For the detailed account of the Mughīra story, see Balādhurī, *Ansāb* (*Sā'ir*), 446–448. The woman's name is reported as Umm Jamīl but the names in her ancestry seem fictitious (bint Maḥjan b. al-Afqam b. Shu'aytha b. al-Ḥazm b. Ruwayba). Her belonging to Banū Hilāl b. 'Āmir [b. Ṣa'ṣa'a] also alludes to a tribe that was typically associated with controversial actions in the sources. Also, Abū'l-Fidā, *al-Mukhtaṣar*, I, 162.

98. At the first assembly held by the new caliph 'Uthmān, 'Alī's famous words to 'Ubaydallāh b. 'Umar after he killed Hurmuzān were, "You are a sinful aggressor [*yā fāsiq*]; should I have command over you one day, I shall certainly have you killed for your murder of Hurmuzān." Balādhurī, *Ansāb* (*Banū 'Abd Shams*), 510. Dīnawarī, 180. The narrator highlights the fact that Hurmuzān was viewed as someone without a direct heir in the community, and thus the Muslim community as a whole viewed itself as his patron or heir (*walī*).

99. It is worth noting the similarity of the pattern of this story to that of an account reported by Isḥāq b. Ibrāhīm al-Mawṣilī that describes the caliph al-Manṣūr's initial attempt to demolish the arch of Khusraw in order to use its material in the construction of Baghdad. As is well known, the reaction of Khālid al-Barmakī at the time was first to discourage the caliph from taking this step, on the grounds that the monument symbolized the triumph of Islam and because it housed the prayer location (*muṣallā*) of 'Alī b. Abī Ṭālib. Al-Manṣūr, however, dismissed this initial advice as a latent Persian sympathy on the part of the minister, saying, "Indeed, Khalid; you insist on partiality for your fellow-Persians [*abayta illā al-mayl ilā aṣḥābika al-'ajam*]"; he then proceeded with the project but later reconsidered and abandoned the plan when it became clear how costly and difficult it would be. Ṭabarī, III, 320.

100. Ka'b's answer here is clearly constructed with skillful attention to rhyme (*ajidu ṣifataka wa ḥilyataka wa annahu qad faniya ajaluka*) Ṭabarī, I, 2723. Smith, *HT,* XIV, 90. Other accounts have slightly more elaboration as Ka'b tells the caliph that he appears in the Torah as the door guarding the community from falling into hell. On the representation of 'Umar as the door protecting the community from *fitna*, see Nu'aym b. Ḥammād al-Marwazī, *Kitāb al-Fitan*, 22–23. Ibn Sa'd, III, 332–333, 371–373. Balādhurī, *Ansāb* (*Sā'ir*), 469, 502. Bukhārī (*bāb 'alāmāt al-nubuwwa fi'l-islām*), IV, 507 (no. 786) (*kitāb al-fitan*), IX, 168 (no. 216). Ibn Māja (*kitāb al-fitan*), II, 1306 (no. 3955).

101. Ibn Sa'd, III, 354. 'Affān b. Muslim←Ḥammād b. Salama←Yūsuf b. Sa'd←'Abdallāh b. Ḥunayn←Shaddad b. Aws←Ka'b.

102. Ṭabarī, I, 2692–2693. Ibn al-Athīr, III, 37. Ibn al-Athīr follows up by stating that it was also said that the conquest of Khurāsān happened in the time of 'Uthmān. Ṭabarī tries to iron out the discrepancy by claiming that Khurāsān, after this initial submission, rebelled two years into 'Uthmān's reign and that this led to a reconquest that ended with Yazdajird's death. But 'Umar's reference to the death of Yazdajird in the speech is very clear.

103. Ṭabarī, I, 2691–2692. Smith, *HT,* XIV, 61–62.

104. We can see this dimension of Yazdajird's image in an account that Ṭabarī relates about Yazdajird as he set out on his escape journey to the east. Ṭabarī describes Yazdajird's experience of a vision of what lay ahead for Islam as follows: While on his escape to al-Rayy after the defeat at Jalūlā', Yazdajird was traveling on a litter that was placed for him on the back of a camel, so that as the journey progressed, the emperor could sleep. "While [Yazdajird] was asleep in his litter," Ṭabarī relates, "they woke him up so that he might be aware [of what was happening] and not be afraid when the camel forded over, [as he would be] if he were awakened from sleep. But he reproached [his men], saying, 'You were wrong to do this! If you had left me alone, I would have found out how long this [Islamic] community will last. I saw in a dream Muḥammad and myself speaking together alone in the presence of God. [God] told [Muḥammad] that he would give them one hundred years' power. He asked for more and [God] made it 110 years. [Again Muḥammad] asked for more and [God] made it 120 years. [Again Muḥammad) asked for more and [God] granted it, but then you woke me up. If you had left me alone, I would have found out how long this community will last!' " Ṭabarī, I, 2681: al-Sarī←Shu'ayb←Sayf←Muḥammad, Ṭalḥa al-Muhallab and 'Amr. Smith, *HT,* XIV, 51–52.

105. Dīnawarī, 146; Ṭabarī, I, 2872–2883; Tha'ālibī, *Ghurar Akhbār Mulūk al-Furs*, ed. and trans. H. Zotenberg (repr., Tehran 1963), 746–748; Ya'qūbī, I, 174; al-Maqdisī, *al-Bad' wa'l-Ta'rīkh*, V, 197.

106. Also, Miskawayh, *Tajārib*, 270.

107. This symbolic interpretation is built on the explanation that Bayhaqī gives for a similar circumstance that occurs in a dream. Given that medieval Is-

lamic society viewed signs about real life and dream situations as rooted in a unified cultural view of religious and moral meaning, and the degree to which the epic of the Sasanid kings itself rested on heuristic interpretations of life (for another example, see E. G. Browne, "Some Account of the Arabic Work entitled 'Niháyatu'l-irab fī akhbári'l-Furs wa'l-'Arab,' particularly of that part which treats of the Persian Kings," *Journal of the Royal Asiatic Society* (1900): 235–236, on the revolt of Bahrām Chūbīn), it seems the narrator of this story meant this anecdote to be read in the same light. The relevant story in Bayhaqī centers on a dream interpretation set in the 'Abbāsid period. It states that the caliph al-Manṣūr once had a dream in the Umayyad era, long before his accession to power, that he happened to be riding a black donkey that also carried sacks of hay. When he inquired about its meaning, a soothsayer told him that the dream indicated that he would come to rule. After his accession, al-Manṣūr once again reportedly inquired into that dream story, asking the dream interpreter how he had known this dream signified a path to power. In answer, the soothsayer told him: "You said that you were riding a donkey, and a donkey signifies the luck of a person; and you added that donkey was black, and this color [*sawād*] is connected with the concept of good fortune [*su'dud*]; and finally you said that the donkey carried sacks of hay, and I thought to myself that *ḥinṭa* and *sha'īr* are extracted from hay, and whoever came to sit on them would become in control of the sustenance of people. This was hence none other than someone who would come to rule over people." Bayhaqī, *al-Maḥāsin wa'l-Masāwi'*, 320. The significance attributed in this dream story to items such as barley and grain, and the situation of the individual in relation to them, was probably not an isolated or localized interpretation. It functioned as a code that permeated through layers of historical narration and would have been accessible as much to Ṭabarī as to Bayhaqī. Its use in articulating political themes, especially the responsibility of monarchs to subjects, is even further amplified in the story referred to earlier that described how 'Umar once helped a destitute family by personally bringing them sacks of grain and preparing their sustenance meal. Ṭabarī, I, 2744–2745. The details of this story have wide political and cultural significance, but what concerns us here is the way it also evokes the theme of a ruler's political control through dispensing a staple food. Both 'Umar's and Yazdajird's stories here share a common link in an allusive sign of control and political responsibility.

108. For a discussion of the famous chain of power described in Persian treatises of political wisdom, see A. Lambton, *State and Government in Medieval Islam*, London Oriental Series, XXXVI (London: 1981), 137.

109. Another association of the number four is to the first four years of peace (*fī di'a*) that Yazdajird experienced at the outset of his twenty-year reign.

110. Some narratives about Yazdajird's end do in fact specify that the peasant who confronted him was "*nāqir arḥā'*," which coincides with how Abū Lu'lu'a is

sometimes described ("*ṣāni' arḥā*"). Ibn Sa'd, III, 347; V, 46. The four dirhams Abū Lu'lu'a complained about to 'Umar as high taxes from al-Mughīra also bear an uncanny symmetry to the four dirhams demanded from Yazdajird by the miller in Marw (also in Ibn Sa'd and Balādhurī, *Ansāb* (*Sā'ir*), 482). It is useful here to note that those versions that do not cast Abū Lu'lu'a as a maker of mills, referring to him just as an artisan (*naqqāsh, najjār, ḥaddād*), also change the tax fees he grieves about to one hundred dirhams (according to one version in Balādhurī, *Ansāb* (*Sā'ir*), 480–481) or two dirhams (in Ṭabarī, I, 2722). The four-dirham grievance is most likely the original feature of the assassination story. We can be confident of this because of a report in Balādhurī that reconciles key features in the above-described novel about 'Umar but also, and more importantly, because the author specifies that the tax grievance was four dirhams per day, adding up to 120 dirhams per month. The number 120 had already been used by Yazdajird to prophesy from a dream vision the age that the Islamic state would exceed. Ṭabarī, I, 2681. Balādhurī, *Ansāb* (*Sā'ir*), 482. The same version of Yazdajird's fee and calculation is found in Ibn Sa'd, III, 347. To conclude the cycle of the "four" motif, Ibn Sa'd's same account on Yazdajird alerts us that 'Abdallāh b. 'Āmir b. Kurayz, the conqueror of Khurāsān, left al-Aḥnaf b. Qays with a contingent of four thousand troops in Marw. Ibn Sa'd, V, 46.

111. Ṭabarī, I, 1891.

112. There are numerous situations in which Ṭabarī uses this metaphor in narrating events. In his account of the Battle of Qādisiyya, Ṭabarī frequently compares the action of combat to the grinding motion of the mill. Describing how the tribe of Asad in particular withstood the brunt of the Sasanid attack, Ṭabarī's account twice uses the phrase "*wa raḥā al-ḥarb tadūru 'alā Asad*" ("while the mill of war turned around Asad"). Ṭabarī, I, 2300, 2301, 2304. The choice of the tribe of Asad as the one encircled by the mill of the Persian cavalry itself evoked another motif related to its name, "the lion," which was meant as an oblique inversion of the name of the Persian empire, since the Arabs used to refer to the Sasanid empire as "the lion" (Ṭabarī, I, 2223). Narrators therefore were intentionally deploying a paradox in their construction of the battle narrative, as an ambiguous dialogue was set underway between the Sasanid "lion" and the Arab "lion," where both victim and victor carry the same name in a symbolic twist on the irony of the fate of the Sasanid state and the continuity of both contenders within the Islamic fold. Elsewhere Sa'd b. Abī Waqqāṣ himself is referred to by 'Umar as "the lion with his paw nails drawn [*al-asad fī barāthinih*]" (Ṭabarī, I, 2215); and as "the lion charging [*al-asad 'ādiyan*]" (Ṭabarī, I, 2216). Miskawayh, *Tajārib*, I, 198. 'Umar himself received his share of this imagery, if we consider that his *kunya* "Abū Ḥafṣ" (given to him by the Prophet, according to Ibn al-Jawzī) meant "father of the lion." Ibn al-Jawzī, *Ta'rīkh 'Umar b. al-Khaṭṭāb*, ed. U. A. al-Rifā'ī (Cairo, n.d), 20.

113. Ibn Rosteh, *Kitāb al-A'lāk an-Nafīsa*, ed. M. J. De Goeje (Leiden, 1892), 8.

114. As Sa'd b. Abī Waqqās would commemorate the Arab victory at Kutha by reciting the Qur'ānic verse "*wa tilka al-ayyāmu nudāwiluhā bayna al-nās*" (Qur'ān 3:140; Ṭabarī, I, 2424), a choice of words that referred to the cyclical process of history as well as to the transient nature of victorious days.

115. This dualistic image of the mill as a source of life and death is best captured by Ṭabarī in the scene of the Battle of Walja. Ṭabarī, I, 2035. Ṭabarī makes frequent use of the image of "the mill of battle" in other contexts. See, for example, Ṭabarī, I, 2258, 2300, 2304, 2330.

## 4. 'UTHMĀN: THE CHALLENGE OF INNOVATION

1. H. M. T. Nagel, "The Authority of the Caliphate," in *Studies on the First Century of Islamic Society*, 188–189.

2. 'Uthmān was conspicuously absent from the famous campaigns of early Islam. When Badr happened, 'Uthmān was absent in Medina, reportedly looking after his ailing wife, Ruqiyya, the daughter of the Prophet, who died soon after. At the Battle of Uḥud, 'Uthmān was one of those who showed weakness and retreated in a fashion frowned upon by the Qur'ān, although tradition claims that he was later forgiven, along with the others who had behaved in the same way.

3. The famous *ḥadīth*, "*mā 'alā 'Uthmān mā 'amila ba'da hādhā*." Aḥmad, *Musnad*, XXVII, 247. Ibn Sa'd, VII, 78.

4. Balādhurī, *Ansāb* (*Banū 'Abd Shams*), 486, 494; *Ansāb* (*Sā'ir*), 135. Ibn 'Asākir, XXXIX, 92–93.

5. *Ḥadīths* that extol the merit of "*ḥayā'*" as a sign of belief (*imān*) include mention of more ancient wisdom sayings (*al-ḥikma* texts), which warn that "some of the *ḥayā'* is bliss and dignity and some of it weakness [*inna minhu sakīnatan wa waqāran li-llāh wa minhu ḍa'fun*]." Although tradition denounces this spin on *ḥayā'* (Muslim, I [pt. 1], 6–7 [nos. 36–37]), it is unlikely to have been absent from the picture of valuation that narrators undertook for 'Uthmān's personality.

6. It should be noted from the outset that this conciliatory depiction of 'Uthmān (whether crafted by narrators as a pious image or as a secular exemplum regarding caliphal weakness) does confront an opposing portrayal of the caliph as an authoritarian leader (most notably according to Ya'qūbī's version). In addition, there is probably an intermediate domain for reading 'Uthmān's reticence in taking the lead in making strong decisions as a deliberately duplicitous political approach.

7. W. Muir, *The Caliphate*, 207. "'Uthmān b. 'Affān," *EI* (2000), X, 497. The entry by Levi della Vida has been updated by R. G. Khoury. H. Djait, *La Grande Discorde: Religion et politique dans l'Islam des origines* (Paris, 1989), 84.

8. There are two versions dating the conquest of Cyprus either before or after the Battle of Dhāt al-Ṣawārī, in A.H. 28/A.D. 648 (Ṭabarī, I, 2820), or A.H. 33/A.D. 654 (Ṭabarī, I, 2926).

9. Ṭabarī, I, 2829.

10. Ibn Saʿd, III, 64: Ibn Saʿd←Muḥammad b. ʿUmar←Muḥammad b. ʿAbdallāh al-Zuhrī. In a variant but clarifying version, ʿUthmān's reference to Abū Bakr and ʿUmar declares: "Abū Bakr and ʿUmar used to interpret things [i.e., religion] by being frugal on themselves and austere on their kinsmen, and I have opted to interpret matters in the way of building my filial bonds [*innī ta'wwaltu fīhi ṣilata raḥmī*]." Both versions are included in Balādhurī, *Ansāb* (*Banū ʿAbd Shams*), 512.

11. Mention should be made here of the famous incident of the caliph's signet ring, which contained the seal of the Prophet. This event, which happened toward the middle of ʿUthmān's reign, occupies a central place in the chronicles as a symbolic turning point in the career of this caliph. The chronicles describe how ʿUthmān, sitting by the edge of a well one day, was reportedly fiddling with this ring when it accidentally slipped from his finger and fell into the well. He then reportedly invested great effort and funds into trying to retrieve it, but it seems to have gone beyond reach, thus causing him much grief. This event too was grounded in mythical biblical antecedents. It may well have been an adaptation of a similar story about Solomon, who also reportedly happened to be fiddling with his ring one day by the seashore when it fell in the sea and disappeared for a period of forty days, during which Solomon lost his throne to a demon and underwent an atoning phase of tribulation before he retrieved the ring by a turn of fortune from a fish he had caught. Solomon's loss of his ring is explained in the Qur'ān commentaries and *qiṣaṣ al-anbiyā'* as an act of divine punishment for religious transgressions that went on in secret at his court (specifically the continuing idolatry of one of Solomon's concubines). In comparison, the religious innovations of ʿUthmān's reign were minor, but there is room to speculate that narrators of the similar episodes of the rings saw a parallel, albeit milder, context of religious disarray in ʿUthmān's reign that led to a similar divine punishment. The story of the ring and its coincidence with a turning point in ʿUthmān's reign was probably mainly valued by medieval readers for its symbolism and as an aside about the continuum between historical events and religious myth, prophetic sagas and caliphal history. It is worth noting in the content of these stories the resemblance in some of the phrasing between the story of how Solomon lost the ring and the story about ʿUthmān. One account recounted on the authority of ʿAlī b. Abī Ṭālib states: "Solomon happened to be by the sea coast one day, and was playing with his ring [*wa huwa yaʿbathu bi-khātamihi*] when it slipped from his hand and fell in the sea." Abū ʿAbdallāh Muḥammad b. Aḥmad al-Qurṭubī, *al-Jāmiʿ li- Aḥkām al-Qur'ān* (Beirut, 1993), VIII (pt. 15), 131. A followup statement declares that the inscription on Solomon's ring was the proclamation, "There is no god but God and Muḥammad is His messenger."

12. Ṭabarī, I, 2813: al-Sarī←Shu'ayb←Sayf←Muḥammad and Ṭalḥa. It is here worth noting that 'Uthmān's other gubernatorial appointee to Basra, 'Abdallāh b. 'Āmir b. Kurayz, was an even more competent and popular leader. The sources concur in praising Ibn 'Āmir for his generosity, bravery, and magnanimity, and seem to accord him a princely image that sometimes outshines the rank of Mu'āwiya. Dhahabī refers to him as an Arabian prince (*min kibār mulūk al-'arab*), while various *ḥadīths* describe the Prophet blessing him even though Ibn 'Āmir's father was a bitter enemy to Islam, as was 'Uqba b. Abī Mu'īṭ. Dhahabī, *Siyar A'lām al-Nubalā'*, ed. S. al-Arna'ūṭ et al., 24 vols. (Beirut, 1994–1998), IV, 21. Ibn Sa'd, V, 45. Ṭabarī, II, 67–68.

13. Muḥammad b. Yūsuf al-Kindī, *Wulāt Miṣr*, ed. Ḥusayn Naṣṣar (Beirut, n.d.), 33. Ibn Abī al-Sarḥ also received praise as governor of Egypt. Ibn Taghrībirdī states that the governor was virtuous in conduct and generous ("*wa lammā wulliya miṣr aḥsana al-sīra fī al-ra'iyya wa kāna jawādan karīman*"). Abū'l-Maḥāsin Yūsuf b. Taghrībirdī, *al-Nujūm al-Zāhira fī Mulūk Miṣr wa'l-Qāhira*, 16 vols. (Cairo, 1963–1972), I, 79.

14. H. Kennedy, *The Prophet and the Age of the Caliphates*, 73.

15. Ṭabarī adds more information about Sa'īd's family, "His uncles were men of long experience and early precedence, and had standing with the Messenger of God (*dhawī balā' wa sābiqa wa qudma ma' rasūl allāh*)." Ṭabarī, I, 2851. Humphreys, *HT*, XV, 57 (with some modification).

16. Ṭabarī, I, 2852. Humphreys, *HT*, XV, p. 58.

17. Ṭabarī, I, 2854–2855. Those who took advantage of the caliph's offer of exchanging lands were Ṭalḥa b. 'Ubaydallāh and Marwān b. al-Ḥakam, but others are also mentioned as having received an *iqṭā'* under this plan—although it is not clear that they exchanged it for assets in Ḥijāz. The individuals mentioned as having received such a benefit included 'Abdallāh b. Mas'ūd, Sa'd b. Abī Waqqāṣ, al-Zubayr b. al-'Awwām, Khabbāb b. al-Arat, and Usāma b. Zayd, Wā'il b. Ḥujr al-Ḥaḍramī, 'Adiyy b. Ḥātim al-Ṭā'ī, Khālid b. 'Urfuṭa, al-Ash'ath b. Qays, and Jarīr b. 'Abdallāh al-Bajalī. Balādhurī, *Futūḥ*, II, 335–336. Ibn Qutayba mentions that 'Uthmān gave Fadak to Marwān b. al-Ḥakam as an *iqṭā'*, although it was classified as the charitable inheritance (*ṣadaqa*) of the Prophet. This was, however, a statement of metaphor implying that 'Uthmān was endorsing the handing over of the caliphate to the Marwanids in the future. Ibn Qutayba, *Kitāb al-Ma'ārif*, ed. T. 'Ukāsha (Cairo 1969), 195.

18. Ṭabarī, I, 2853. Humphreys, *HT*, XV, 59.

19. As early as 'Umar's reign, there are signs in Ṭabarī's narrative that this caliphal seizure of land might happen if the Sawād territory remained vaguely labeled as the collective *fay'* land of the conquerors. In A.H. 16/A.D. 636, 'Umar had advised in generic terms, "Take possession of your *fay'* lands [i.e., as private property]; if you don't [the normal course of] affairs will grind to a halt because

[too] much time has elapsed [*in lam taf'alū fa-taqādama al-amr yulḥaj*]." Ṭabarī, I, 2469. Juynboll, *HT*, XIV, 49.

20. In a crucial passage, Ṭabarī describes how the settlers who lacked the merits of *ṣābiqa* and *qudma* resented those with such advantage and hence precedence in the assemblies of Sa'īd, and reportedly used to characterize such distinctions as hostility (*kanū yu'ībūna al-tafḍīl wa yaj'alūnahu jafwa*). Ṭabarī, I, 2855–2856. 'Uthmān's policy of allocating land according to such social distinctions would have only enhanced the Kufan settlers' feeling that they were becoming the object of prejudice.

21. Mu'āwiya himself had reportedly asked for permission from 'Uthmān to be able to dispense with the abandoned conquered territory according to the needs of his governorship (to establish *ḥimā* and/or *iqṭā'* that would sustain newly arrived troops). 'Uthmān reportedly approved his request. Ibn 'Asākir, II, 206. Ibn 'Asākir gives some accounts about the abandoned conquered territory in Syria in terms that are parallel to the situation in Iraq and Iran. Whereas the elite who abandoned the land in Iraq are referred to as "*asāwira*," in Syria they are labeled "*baṭārika*" (bishops or commanders).

22. Ibn 'Asākir, XXXIX, 241–243.

23. Although Ibn Mas'ūd's *muṣḥaf* is said to have excluded the two *sūrās* known as "*al-mu'wwadhatayn*" and the *fātiḥa*, the drama of this companion's conflict with the caliph is not stressed for these issues. Rather, the episode of Ibn Mas'ūd's punishment is meant to show 'Uthmān's tyrannical behavior in general.

24. 'Uthmān's name was so strongly associated with the codification of the text that one account even states that he undertook the collection of the Qur'ān during 'Umar's reign. Ibn Sa'd, II, 356. Balādhurī, *Ansāb* (*Banū 'Abd Shams*), 489.

25. In 'Uthmān's time the third commander of the campaign, alongside Salmān b. Rabī'a and Ḥabīb b. Maslama, is said to have been Ḥudhayfa b. al-Yamān, who led the ahl al-Kufa. In 'Umar's time the name of the commander is Ḥudhayfa b. Usayd. It is more likely that the latter was the commander all along, but the name was readjusted to Ḥudhayfa b. al-Yamān for 'Uthmān's time.

26. Qurṭubī, *al-Jāmi'* (editor's introduction), 38–41.

27. Ṭabarī, I, 2663. Ibn Kathīr, IV (pt. 7), 126.

28. Ṭabarī, I, 322.

29. M. Hinds, "Kufan Political Alignments and Their Background in the Mid-Seventh Century A.D." *International Journal of Middle East Studies* 2 (1971): 351, 346–367.

30. Tha'ālibī, *Laṭā'if al-Ma'ārif*, ed. P. de Jong (Leiden, 1867), 104. Abū 'Abdallāh Zakariyya b. Muḥammad al-Qazwīnī, *Āthār al-Bilād wa Akhbār al-'Ibād* (Beirut, 1960), 251.

31. A range of statements are attributed to ʿUmar in which he describes ahl al-Kūfa as "*ra's al-ʿArab*" or "*ra's al-Islām*," "*rumḥ allāh*" (the spear of God), and "*kanz al-imān*" (the treasury of religion). Ibn Saʿd, VI, 5. Ṭabarī, I, 2515.

32. Kufa's initial foundation, for example, is attributed to Abraham, and it is later the place where the sign for Noah's flood first appeared, and from which Noah's ark set out. Ibn al-Jawzī, *al-Muntaẓam fī Ta'rīkh al-Mulūk wa'l-Umam*, ed. M. A. ʿAṭā (Beirut, 1992), IV, 219–220. Other sources add still other prophetic connections about Kufa: as the place that holds the staff of Moses and the ring of Solomon, andthat has the tree that shaded Jonah after his rescue. Ibn al-Faqīh al-Hamadānī, *Kitāb al-Buldān*, 174–175. Yāqūt al-Ḥamawī, *Muʿjam al-Buldān*, IV, 492.

33. In the time of Muʿāwiya one observer commented: "O People of Kufa! You were the best of people when you started out in the time of ʿUmar but then you changed, and four bad qualities spread among you: miserliness, deception, treachery and narrowness [in mind]. None of these qualities were in you, but when I looked into it I found it all coming from your mixing with others. Thus, deception came from gypsies [*al-Nibṭ*], stinginess came from Persia, treachery came from Khurāsān, and narrowmindedness came from al-Ahwāz." Ṭabarī, I, 2631–2632. Miskawayh, *Tajārib*, I, 248. ʿUmar himself would change his tune on the Kufans and later say, "The Kufans are impossible people. No *amīr* pleases them, and no *amīr* is pleased by them." al-Hindī, *Kanz*, XIV, 171 (no. 38269).

34. Ṭabarī, I, 2668.

35. The suspect authenticity of some political narratives associated with Kufa can be inferred from the contrast that narrators sometimes sought to establish between Basra and Kufa. The advantage of Basra's image over Kufa's seems to have been a broad-ranging topic of discussion in the early ʿAbbāsid period, and something that was common knowledge. A rare account narrated on this subject by al-Zubayr b. Bakkār describes a debate between two individuals recounting the merits of each town. Among the virtues listed on behalf of Basra is that it was a virtuous land that does not let evil settle on its soil, and that it was the garrison city that fielded the armies that conquered Khurāsān, Sijistān, al-Sind, al-Hind, Kirmān, Mikrān, Fars, al-Ahwāz, and al-ʿIrāq. Notwithstanding the conflation of chronology in these conquests, what is significant here is the particular use of the events of the initial conquests in Persia. It will be recalled that the first wave of Arab conquests in Iran happened under the leadership of ʿAbdallāh b. ʿĀmir b. Kurayz, who was appointed by ʿUthmān as governor of Basra in A.H. 29/A.D. 650 after the dismissal of Abū Mūsā al-Ashʿarī. By contrast, the expeditions that were reportedly dispatched from Kufa targeted Armenia and Azerbayjān, and these conquests eventually stalled. The debate is described in *al-Akhbār al-Muwafaqiyyāt*, 139–143.

36. Ibn Saʿd, III, 67, 69. Balādhurī, *Ansāb* (*Banū ʿAbd Shams*), 566. The very *ḥadīth* that specifies which crimes deserve the death penalty is ʿUthmān's declaration to his besiegers on "*yawm al-dār*." Tirmidhī (*kitāb al-fitān*), IV, 400 (no. 2158).

37. One *ḥadīth* quotes the Prophet telling ʿUthmān directly: "It may come that God may gird you with a shirt one day [*laʿalla allāh yaqmuṣuka qamīṣan*]. If this happens, and people try to make you renounce it, do not let them have their way." Tirmidhī, V, 587 (no. 3705); 589 (no. 3710). Aḥmad, *Musnad*, XLI, 113. Ibn Saʿd's version attributes the saying to ʿAbdallāh b. ʿUmar as a conclusion to a statement of political advice on how to handle the opposition ("do not renounce a shirt that God has girded you with"). *Ibn Saʿd*, III, 66. Ibn ʿAsākir, XXXIX, 43, 182.

38. Hence ʿUthmān's response to the opposition, "I will not renounce a shirt that God has girded me with, but I will make changes in the matters that you criticize" (*wa lakin anzaʿ ʿammā takrahūn*). Ibn Saʿd, III, 66.

39. All the references to ʿUthmān's shirt and the shirt of the caliphate, however, are fictitious adaptations of a biblical motif—namely, the shirt of Joseph—that underwent a careful process of religious transition and was instrumental in the salvation of the patriarchs. In Islamic Qur'ānic commentaries, Abraham was first clothed during his ordeal with this shirt by the angel Gabriel, and the shirt later reappeared in a moment of divine consolation for Joseph when he was cast away by his brothers. Joseph's shirt later stood at the center of the story of the fight with Potiphar's wife and concluded the story of reconciliation of Joseph's family when it was given to—or cast over—Jacob, thus enabling him to regain his sight. Qurṭubī, *Jāmiʿ*, V (pt. 9), 95. While the shirt represented a symbol of familial succession and divine miracle in the biblical story, it was entirely adapted to the political context of the caliphate in Islam. The religious authority of the patriarchs was transformed into the divine right of ʿUthmān to rule. The idea of divine investiture for Islamic caliphal authority was not an actual historical one in these cases (as in most literary attestations), but a polemical back-projection by Sunnī society in the ninth century onto the Rāshidūn caliphate. The construction of the concept of divine right to rule and of the caliphs as "God's caliphs" is even more transparent and ʿAbbāsid-inspired in the case of ʿUmar.

40. Qur'ān 9:89 (Arberry, I, 250).

41. Ibn Saʿd, III, 71. Balādhurī, *Ansāb* (*Banū ʿAbd Shams*), 566. The account concludes by saying that ʿUthmān then asked Ibn Sallām what to do, and that the latter urged him to hold back from fighting the crowd. "Holding back gives you more strength [*al-kaffu fa-innahu ablaghu fīʾl-ḥujja*]."

42. Ibn Saʿd, III, 67: Ibn Saʿd←ʿAmr b. ʿĀṣim al-Kilābī←Ḥafṣ b. Abī Bakr←Hayyāj b. Sarīʿ←Mujāhid.

43. This polemical line was used by ʿUthmān in challenging the argument of the opposition that his rule was unrighteous and that his overthrow would be religiously legitimate. Ṭabarī, I, 3023–3024. Ibn Saʿd, III, 68.

44. The story about a clique of Egyptian culprits leading the way in the attack on ʿUthmān is probably a mythical extension within the reworked use of biblical stories. The choice of the number six hundred for the faction that came from

Egypt is most likely inspired by the biblical account about the departure of six hundred thousand Israelites with Moses when he left Egypt. Exodus 12:37.

45. Ibn Sa'd, III, 71. The Arabic of the latter portion of this statement is significant: "*wa kāna aṣḥāb al-nabiyy . . . alladhīna khadhalūh karihū al-fitna wa ẓannū anna al-amra lā yablugha qatlahu, fa-nadimū 'alā mā ṣana'ū fī amrihi wa la-'amrī law qāmū aw qāma ba'ḍuhum fa-ḥathā fī wujūhihim al-turāb la-inṣarafū khāsirīn.*" The account is narrated by Muḥammad b. 'Umar←'Abd al-Raḥmān b. Abī al-zanād←Abū Ja'far al-qāri' (*mawlā* of Ibn 'Abbās al-Makhzūmī). This is a crucial passage that represents a digest of what another author, Ibn 'Abd Rabbihi, reported in a unique account that explains in more detail what Ibn Sa'd says. Ibn 'Abd Rabbihi's account is based on a response that Sa'īd b. al-Musayyib gave when al-Zuhrī reportedly asked him about the circumstances of 'Uthmān's death, what people's attitudes to the event were, and why the companions neglected to come to his aid ("*li-ma khadhalahu aṣḥābu Muḥammad*"). Sa'īd then set forward in a summary statement the assertions that 'Uthmān was killed unjustly (*maẓlūman*), that his attackers were aggressors (*ẓāliman*), and that those who neglected aiding him were to be excused (*wa man khadhalahu kāna ma'dhūran*). When al-Zuhrī asked what this meant, Sa'īd explained how events had unfolded in different arenas of opposition to 'Uthmān leading up to the conflict. Sa'īd's elaborate account does not shy away from blaming 'Uthmān for errors, and has the important feature of setting the people's anger against 'Uthmān for dealing severely with Ibn Mas'ūd, Abū Dharr, and 'Ammār as a background to the additional matters that inflamed more opposition against the caliph (appointing family members to government positions, tapping into state funds, ignoring complaints about his governors, etc.). However, this account essentially describes the companions as working in a cooperative environment, albeit eventually unable to control (or unwitting to the existence of) a widespread climate of anger among some tribes and individuals who rushed to change the situation with violence. 'Uthmān, according to this account, remained negligent to criticisms leveled against his government (he did not, for example, dismiss Ibn Abī al-Sarḥ from the governorship of Egypt except after repeated pressure from the companions—although it is never explained what the specific grievances against Ibn Abī al-Sarḥ were), and was either negligent or duplicitous in the story of the covert order to have the leaders of the opposition assassinated upon their return to Egypt ('Uthmān's response to the discovery of the letter commanding the assassination is a crucial line; after swearing by God, 'Uthmān declared, "I did not write this letter, nor commanded this, nor sent the servant to Egypt [*mā katabtu al-kitāb wa lā amartu bihi wa lā wajjahtu al-ghulāma ilā miṣr*]"). What is perhaps most important about Sa'īd b. al-Musayyib's account is that it sets the role of Marwān b. al-Ḥakam as the spark for the assassination. After it became clear that Marwān was 'Uthmān's main advisor (or minister), and that he was responsible for the misrepresentation of the situation to the caliph, and for the botched conspiracy against the

Egyptian opposition, the companions all agreed that 'Uthmān should surrender Marwān to them for judgment. This 'Uthmān refused, and his refusal now provoked a siege and an attack on his house. Ibn al-Musayyib's account is nuanced in the way he clearly emphasizes (through the voice of 'Alī) that the aim of the siege was to pressure 'Uthmān to surrender Marwān, and was not intended to harm the caliph. This is where a division of interests then surfaces between the more politically conservative opposition of the older companions (led by 'Alī), and a camp that included younger, more brash Qurashīs, such as Muḥammad b. Abī Bakr, and less respected opposition figures who were eager to overthrow the caliph for immediate material interests (such as robbery). When the attack happened, Ibn al-Musayyib's account could reasonably argue, the leading companions were unaware that 'Uthmān's life was in jeopardy, which explains why they should be excused. In sum, therefore, this account blames 'Uthmān for the political mistakes of his reign, shows the companions disapproving of his policies but trying to sort out matters through negotiation—and hopeful of extracting the caliph from the corrupt situation that Marwān b. al-Ḥakam had created for him—and finally shows that the assassination happened suddenly and without the knowledge of the companions. Ibn 'Abd Rabbihi, *al-'Iqd*, IV, 287–292. Ya'qūb b. 'Abd al-Raḥmān←Muḥammad b. 'Īsā al-Dimashqī←Muḥammad b. 'Abd al-Raḥmān b. Abī Dhi'b←Muḥammad b. Shihāb al-Zuhrī←Sa'īd b. al-Musayyib. Also, 'Umar b. Shabba, *Ta'rīkh al-Madīna*, II, 213–216. The same account is given by Balādhurī but without the initial dialogue between al-Zuhrī and Sa'īd b. al-Musayyib. Balādhurī's initial reporter is Hishām b. 'Ammār al-Dimashqī. *Ansāb (Banū 'Abd Shams)*, 556–560.

46. The focus on the early sources here does not allow discussion of this, but the later medieval period produced lengthy apologetics on behalf of 'Uthmān. Writers such as al-Muḥibb al-Ṭabarī produced an exhaustive list of about nineteen points that they marked as alleged offenses of 'Uthmān and set about rebutting them. See al-Muḥibb al-Ṭabarī, *al-Riyāḍ al-Naḍira*, II, 181–201; Ibn al-'Arabī, *al-'Awāṣim min al-Qawāṣim fī Taḥqīq Mawāqif al-Ṣaḥāba*, ed. Muḥibb al-Dīn al-Khaṭīb (Cairo, 1968), 61–111; al-'Iṣāmī al-Makkī, *Simṭ al-Nujūm*, II, 400–403. It should also be mentioned that in spite of Ibn Sa'd's effort to distance some of the lesser-known attackers of 'Uthmān from the companions, several of them are in fact said to have been former companions who gave a *bay'a* at the gathering of al-Hudaybiyya. These include 'Abd al-Raḥmān b. 'Adīs al-Balawī and Jahjāh b. Sa'īd al-Ghifārī. Balādhurī, *Ansāb (Banū 'Abd Shams)*, 486, 537. Another, Rifā'a b. Rāfi' al-Anṣārī, is reported to have participated in the Battle of Badr, while al-Ḥajjāj b. Ghaziyya is said to have been a companion. Balādhurī, *Ansāb (Banū 'Abd Shams)*, 549. Others who were companions include Ḥurqūṣ b. Zuhayr and Farwa b. Nawfal-Ashja'ī. Al-Jāḥiẓ, *al-'Uthmāniyya*, ed. A. M. Hārūn (Cairo, 1955), 174.

47. A key account in Ibn Sa'd agrees with this where it states: "It was both the opinion of 'Alī and the prominent companions of the Messenger of God that

['Ubaydallāh] be killed. However, 'Amr [b. al-'As] spoke with 'Uthmān regarding this and changed his mind." Ibn Sa'd, V, 17.

48. Ṭabarī, I, 2796. This reaction is indirectly reported by Ibn Sa'd, citing al-Wāqidī. Ibn Sa'd, V, 17. Balādhurī, *Ansāb* (*Sā'ir*), 490

49. Ṭabarī, I, 2801.

50. The gravity of such religious dilution falls within the scope of some religious discussions. See Bukhārī (*bāb karāhiyyat al-shafā'a fi'l-ḥadd idhā rufi'a ilā al-sulṭān*), VIII, 512. Also on this principle, Ibn Sa'd, IV, 69–70.

51. 'Uthmān's words were: "*alā innī waliyyu dam al-Hurmuzān wa qad wahabtuhu li-allāh wa li-'Umar wa taraktuhu li-dami 'Umar.*" Ya'qūbī, II, 164. In the immediately preceding account, Ya'qūbī describes al-Miqdād's great sorrow that the community had chosen 'Uthmān over 'Alī as caliph. This is included by Ṭabarī, I, 2786. Balādhurī includes a version by al-Madā'inī that quotes 'Uthmān as saying: "O you people, We are not orators, and if I live you shall get the correct speech"—also in Ibn Sa'd on the authority of al-Wāqidī (Ibn Sa'd, III, 62)—"It was among the decrees of God that 'Ubaydallāh attacked al-Hurmuzān, a man from among the Muslims who has no heir except the Muslims at large [*wa lā wāritha lahu illā al-muslimūn 'āmatan*]. As your *imām* I have granted ['Ubaydallāh] my pardon, do you grant him your pardon too?" The crowd then said, "Yes." However, 'Alī declared: "Punish the transgressor. He has committed a great sin, killing a Muslim without a reason," then 'Alī turned to 'Ubaydallāh and said: "You transgressor! If I gain control over you one day, I shall kill you for what you have done to al-Hurmuzān." Balādhurī, *Ansāb* (*Banū 'Abd Shams*), 510.

52. Some narrators try to mitigate the unjust actions of 'Ubaydallāh by describing the victim as "a little girl who claimed to be a Muslim [*ibnatan ṣaghīra tadd'ī al-Islām*]." Balādhurī, *Ansāb* (*Sā'ir*), 490. Ibn Sa'd, III, 356. Ṭabarī does not add the apologetic commentary on Abū Lu'lu'a's daughter, but it is clear that an embarrassing problem lay there. Ṭabarī, I, 2795.

53. The original text here states: "The world darkened that day and people became fearful that this was in punishment to them for 'Ubaydallāh's murder of Jufayna, al-Hurmuzān and Abū Lu'lu'a's daughter [*wa aẓlamat al-arḍu yawma'idhin 'alā al-nās fa-'aẓuma dhalika fī ṣudūr al-nās wa ashfaqū an takūna 'uqūbatan ḥina qatala 'Ubaydullāh Jufayna wa al-Hurmuzān wa ibnata Abī Lu'lu'a*]." Ibn Sa'd, V, 15–16.

54. There are various reports in Ibn Sa'd's work that attempt to rush the inclusion of Islamic credentials for Hurmuzān, such as when 'Ammār tells 'Uthmān, "Fear God, and apply the death sentence [on 'Ubaydallāh b. 'Umar], for he [i.e., Hurmuzān] is a Muslim who made pilgrimage." Ibn Sa'd, V, 16; Balādhurī, *Ansāb* (*Sā'ir*), 492. The report on Hurmuzān's hajj forms a separate one-liner in a report that has the narrator al-Miswar b. Makhruma declare that he saw al-Hurmuzān performing the *tahlīl* with 'Umar during the ḥajj and wearing a *ḥibara* garment even. Ibn Sa'd, V, 90.

55. Ṭabarī, I, 3032.

56. Ṭabarī, I, 2869.

57. 'Umar had used this expression earlier. Abū Ubayd al-Qāsim b. Sallām, *Kitāb al-Amwāl* (Beirut, 1981), 125.

58. The antithesis in 'Uthmān's case involves an incident of analogy between the loss of his signet ring and al-Walīd b. 'Uqba's loss of his gubernatorial ring. In the latter case, a group of Kufan religious zealots reportedly stole the ring from al-Walīd's hand while he was sleeping, and brought it to the caliph to show the governor's complete lack of alertness (either for being drunk or simple slumber). The fact that al-Walīd did not guard his residence with firm gates (as per the stringent demands of the second caliph from his governors for accessibility to the public) is implicitly used against the governor this time as a means of judging his competence. 'Uthmān would face a complex issue on that occasion as he tried to balance the image and strength of political authority with the loose credibility of religious evidence and the demands of the law. For details and variations on the background of accusations that led to the loss of al-Walīd's ring, see Ṭabarī, I, 2845–2848; Ya'qūbī, I, 165; and Balādhurī, *Ansāb* (Banū 'Abd Shams), 521, 523.

59. Ṭabarī, I, 2890–2891. The same account with some variation is recounted earlier under the year A.H. 22 and with an *isnād* that diverges on Sayf's authority. Ṭabarī, I, 2668–2669.

60. Ṭabarī, I, 2664.

61. Ṭabarī, I, 2670–2671.

62. It is significant that in Ṭabarī's description of Shahrbarāz's encounter with 'Abd al-Raḥmān the narrator adds a reference to Shahrbarāz as a man "whose origins were from the family of Shahrbarāz, the ruler who had routed the Israelites and driven them out of al-Shām [Syria, including Palestine]." Ṭabarī, I, 2664. Smith, *HT*, XIV, 35. The intent here was clearly to underline the image of communities in succession (Hebrew and Arab) and the approval by a king who was a symbol of divine wrath and the shaping of historical judgment.

63. Qur'ān 31:33; 35:5.

64. Qur'ān 18:42–44.

65. Ṭabarī, I, 2800–2801: al-Sarī←Shu'ayb←Sayf←Badr b. 'Uthmān←his paternal uncle. Humphreys, *HT*, XV, 3–4.

66. Ṭabarī, I, 2802–2803. There is no *isnād* here, simply the reference "they say" (*qālū*). Humphreys, *HT*, XV, 6.

67. Here 'Uthmān declares: "Verily God created mankind in truth, and he accepts naught but the truth. Take what is right and give it what is right. Strive for integrity! Uphold it and be not the first to violate it, so that you may share what you have acquired with those who come after you. Keep faith, keep faith [*al-wafā'*, *al-wafā'*]! Do not wrong the orphan nor one with whom you have made a pact, for God is the opponent of him who wrongs them." Ṭabarī, I, 2803. Humphreys, *HT*, XV, 6–7. Note the strong similarity of this letter to the style and

content of a statement that ʿUmar earlier issued during the Battle of Qādisiyya. ʿUmar's exhorting words to Saʿd then were: "I have been given the feeling that you will defeat the enemy when you encounter him. Therefore cast your doubts away and choose firm faith instead. . . . Beware of frivolity. Be faithful, be faithful [*al-wafā'*, *al-wafā'*], because mistaken faithfulness is a virtue, but mistaken betrayal [entails] perdition; it will be a source of your weakness and of your enemies strength. You will lose your predominance, and they will gain ascendance. I am warning you not to be a disgrace to the Muslims and a cause of their humiliation." Ṭabarī, I, 2230–2231. Friedmann, *HT,* XII, 25.

68. This division perhaps meant that the letter to the governors was viewed as directed to "*al-khāṣṣa*" (the state elite) by the narrators and by Ṭabarī.

69. ʿUthmān here declares: "Verily you are the guardians and protectors of the Muslims and ʿUmar laid down for you [instructions] that were not hidden from us; on the contrary, they were in accordance with our counsel. Let me hear of no change or alteration on the part of any one of you, lest God change your situation and replace you with others [*wa lā yablughannī ʿan aḥadin minkum taghyīr wa lā tabdīl fa-yughayyir allāhu mā bi-kum wa yastabdil bi-kum ghayrukum*]. So examine your conduct, for I shall examine what God has required me to examine and watch over [*fa-innī andhur fī-mā alzamanī allāhu al-naẓara fīhi wa'l-qiyāma ʿalayhi*]." Ṭabarī, I, 2803. Humphreys, *HT,* XV, 6.

70. Ṭabarī, I, 2803–2804. There is no *isnād* here, simply the phrase "It is said [*qālū*]." Humphreys, *HT,* XV, 7. The uncanny resemblance of these letters to what ʿUmar would say led another source to cap this letter of ʿUthmān with a conclusion declared before by ʿUmar. After the statement "*takallafū wa ibtadaʿū,*" al-Māliqī's version tells us: "ʿUmar b. al-Khaṭṭāb stated: 'The situation of Banū Isrā'īl was stable until their offsprings from foreign women began to multiply. These then began to speak about rational opinion and thus went astray and led the Israelites astray' [*inna amra banī isrā'īl lam yazal muʿtadilan ḥattā kathura fīhim al-muwalladūn abnā' sabāyā al-umam fa-qālū fīhim bi'l-ra'yy fa-ḍallū wa aḍallū banī isrā'īl*]." Al-Māliqī, *al-Tamhīd wa'l-Bayān*, 31.

71. Balādhurī, *Ansāb* (*Banū ʿAbd Shams*), 524–525, 538–539, 543.

72. Sample *ḥadīth*s that represent this ideology can be found in the reported advice of the Prophet to Muʿādh, "Obey every ruler, and pray behind every *imām*, and do not defame any of my companions." Another *ḥadīth* has the Prophet declare, "He who obeys the *imām* is obeying me." Abū Yūsuf, *Kitāb al-Kharāj*, 10. That these *ḥadīth*s are included at the outset of a treatise that deals with administrative practice illustrates not only an attempt to strengthen obedience to the state but also the ideologically driven context for the invention of these very practices in the ninth century. A similar message and pattern are evident in the organization of Ibn Zanjawayh's treatise, *Kitāb al-Amwāl*, 3 vols., ed. Shākir Dīb Fayyāḍ (Riyad, 1986), 71–86.

73. Ibn 'Abd Rabbihi, *al-'Iqd*, I, 7; Ibn 'Abd Rabbihi attributes the statement merely by saying, "the wise men say [*qālat al-ḥukamā'*]." al-Ṭurṭūshī, *Sirāj al-Mulūk*, ed. Ja'far al-Bayyātī (London, 1990), 196. Al-Ṭurṭūshī categorizes the statement as a *ḥadīth*, while Ibn al-Ṭiqṭiqā attributes it to 'Umar b. al-Khaṭṭāb and changes its intention to something sedate, suggesting that the statement means that in general people are more anxious about the punishment that a ruler would mete out in the immediate present rather than what will come in the hereafter ("*al-nās yakhāfūn min 'awājil al-'uqūba akthar mimmā yakhāfūn ājilahā*"). *Al-Fakhrī*, 57.

74. It should be said here that Ḥudhayfa played a key role in encouraging 'Uthmān to codify the Qur'ān after he (i.e., Ḥudhayfa) returned from Azerbayjān and reported to the caliph the disputes in the Muslim army over the proper way of reciting the Qur'ān. Sayf b. 'Umar, *Kitāb al-Ridda wa'l-Futūḥ*, I, 48–50.

75. Sayf b. 'Umar, *Kitāb al-Ridda wa'l-Futūḥ and Kitāb al-Jamal wa Masīr 'Āisha wa 'Alī*, ed. Qāsim al-Sāmarrā'ī (Leiden, 1995), I, 171.

76. Ibid., I, 170.

77. Ibid., I, 139.

78. Ibid., I, 167.

79. Ibid., I, 166. Mu'āwiya concludes with a statement confirming the exhortations of the Rāshidūn caliph, "Do not endanger the dominion of God, so that He does not replace you with another people and let you lapse in history [*wa lā takhdhilūh* (i.e., *sulṭān allāh*) *fa-yastabdil bi-kum ghayrukum wa yudālu 'alaykum*]."

80. Ibn Qutayba, *Kitāb 'Uyūn al-Akhbār*, ed. Mufīd Muḥammad Qumayḥa (Beirut, n.d), I, 54 (Muḥammad←Abū Salama←Ḥammād b. Salama←Ayyūb←Abū Qilāba←Ka'b); Ibn 'Abd Rabbihi, *al-'Iqd*, I, 8–9; al-Ṭurṭūshī, *Sirāj al-Mulūk*, 196. Sibṭ Ibn al-Jawzī, *al-Jalīs al-Ṣāliḥ wa'l-Anīs al-Nāṣiḥ*, ed. Fawwāz Fawwāz (London, 1989), 68.

81. Hence 'Uthmān's comparison of the opposition to the coalition of enemies who fought the Prophet at the Battle of the Trench (*fa-hum ka al-aḥzāb yawm al-aḥzāb*). Sayf b. 'Umar, *Kitāb al-Ridda wa'l-Futūḥ*, I, 162.

82. A confirmation of the caliphal authority's right to dispense in a centralized way with the resources of the treasury is eventually capped in a speech of the caliph al-Manṣūr where he famously declares (not coincidentally on an occasion of pilgrimage, to relate the matter to the Prophet's final pilgrimage speech and complete the picture of Islamic law in political terms; on this point see conclusion): "O you people, I am only the authority of God in His earth, and I govern you according to His guidance and His direction. I am His treasurer in charge of the *fay'*, and I work according to His will and divide it according to His wish and give it with His permission [*ayyuhā al-nās innamā anā sulṭān allāh fī arḍihi asūsukum bi-tawfīqihi wa rushdihi wa khāzihunu 'alā fay'ihi bi-mashī'atihi, uqsimuhu bi-irādatihi wa u'ṭīhi bi-idhnihi*]." Ibn 'Asākir, XXXII, 311. Ibn 'Abd Rabbihi, *al-'Iqd*, IV, 99. Ṭabarī,

III, 426–427. Already in Ibn ʻAbd Rabbihi's time, however, al-Manṣūr's speech had been diluted from its original phrasing (the expression "*khāzinhu ʻalā fay'ihi*" is replaced with "*ḥārisuhu ʻalā mālihi.*"). The removal of the term "*fay'*" from the speech distanced the caliph's pretension from any direct religious controversy regarding the question of how the booty of conquests ("*fay'*" and "*ghanīma*") is to be classified and distributed.

83. Abū Yūsuf, *Kitāb al-Kharāj*, 38.

84. Ibn Zanjawayh, *Kitāb al-Amwāl*, I, 196. It is interesting to examine the attitude of ʻUmar on this matter. He had reportedly refused to divide the conquered lands on the basis, according to Ibn Zanjawayh, of a reading of the Qur'ānic verse, "Whatsoever spoils of war God has given to His Messenger from the people of the cities belongs to God, and His Messenger, and the near kinsman, orphans, the needy, and the traveler, so that it be not a thing taken in turns among the rich of you. Whatever the Messenger gives you, take; whatever he forbids you, give over" (Qur'ān 59:7–10 [Arberry, II, 268]) (the verse continues in a way relevant to the legal discussion). Ibn Zanjawayh adds that this reading and interpretation were also the advice of ʻAlī and Muʻādh to ʻUmar. ʻUmar's refusal was also based on the view that a division of the conquered lands would leave little or nothing to subsequent generations of Muslim migrants and settlers. The opposition between the practices of ʻUmar and the Prophet on this matter is very clear, and the Prophet's practice was considered closer to that of ʻUthmān and Muʻāwiya later on. As if to show ʻUmar leaning more in the direction of legitimizing ʻUthmān's and Muʻāwiya's establishment of *iqṭāʻ*, some traditions add that ʻUmar had vowed in his last year to begin taking the Prophet's precedent of dividing territory (as was the case at Khaybar) as a new model for granting rights to conquered or abandoned territory. Ibn ʻAsākir, II, 188. In spite of his purported plan to introduce a policy of *iqṭāʻ*, some traditions strongly rallied against considering *fay'* (immovable booty, especially territory) as *ghanīma* (transferable spoils of war), and at least one *ḥadīth* stated, "My community shall remain on the straight path so long as they don't view the *fay'* as *ghanīma* [*mā lam tarā al-fay'a maghnaman*]." Al-Mubarrad, *al-Kāmil*, I, 303. The positions of ʻUthmān, Muʻāwiya, and even the Prophet earlier were thus considered to be the projection of the *ra'y* school of jurisprudence, but not that of the *sunna* and *ḥadīth*. Ibn ʻAsākir mentions that those who gave the caliph (*imām*) permission to dispense with conquered territory include Abū Ḥanīfa, Sufyān al-Thawrī, and al-Shāfiʻī (the latter, however, making the decision contingent on the community's consent). Only Mālik b. Anas refused the practice of allocating conquered domains as *iqṭāʻ*. Ibn ʻAsākir, II, 186.

85. Several reports describing the situation of the Sawād after the conquest reflect a strongly defended legalistic interest. One such account states: "The Sawād was conquered by force. The inhabitants were invited to return and they became *ahl al-dhimma*, but the property of the royal family and of their followers became booty of those who were entitled to it [*fay' li-ahlihi*]. This was what the people

of al-Kufa were confused about until the matter lapsed into ignorance [*wa huwa alladhī yataḥajjā ahl al-Kūfa ilā an juhila dhalika*], and their view [i.e., that of the Kufans] became that [the term] referred to the entire *sawād*. But the status of their *sawād* is like this." Sayf←'Abd al-Malik b. Abī Sulaymān←Sa'īd b. Jubayr. Ṭabarī, I, 2375. Another report states: "It was not feasible to divide the booty that had belonged to the Persian king and to those who had gone with him because it was scattered all over the entire Sawād. It was administered for those who were entitled to it [*ahl al-fay'*] by people whom they trusted and agreed upon. This is what was debated between the *ahl al-fay'*, not the greater part of the Sawād. When the *ahl al-fay'* were in dispute among themselves, the administrators deemed its division between them easy. This is what made the ignorant people confused about the affair of the Sawād." Ṭabarī, I, 2371–2372. Friedmann, *HT*, XII, 155. In another, more detailed account, which draws a comparison to what the Prophet did with the conquered land at Dūmat al-Jandal, concludes by saying: "The things which are customarily done are not according to the traditions transmitted by the few. Whoever relates things other than those done by the just *imāms* and the Muslims is lying about them and staining their honor." Al-Sarī←Shu'ayb←Sayf←Abū Ḍamra←'Abdallāh b. al-Mustawrid←Muḥammad b. Sīrīn. Ṭabarī, I, 2374. Friedmann, *HT*, XII, 158. The entire survey of the status of the *sawād* is prefaced by a declaration from 'Umar in which he states: "Those who work according to their passions and are disobedient, their fortune will collapse and they will harm only themselves. Those who follow the *sunna*, abide by the laws of religion, and adhere to the manifest way [*wa man yattabi' al-sunna wa yantahī ilā al-sharā'i' wa al-sabīl al-nahj*]—out of desire to obtain what God has in store for people who obey Him—will do the right thing and will be fortunate." Ṭabarī, I, 2369. Friedmann, *HT*, XII, 152. 'Umar's speech reflects not only an orthodox opinion of the ninth century but also a moralizing language about custom (*sunna* and *sharā'i'*) that is equally applied in the chronicles to the righteous path in the Sasanid and Islamic periods. It is also worth noting, beyond the case of Dūmat al-Jandal, that a medieval audience probably recognized a link between the story of what was done with the royal estates in Iraq and the conquests of the Jewish oases of Banū al-Naḍīr, Khaybar, and Fadak. The terms applied to describe the nature of the conquered lands are similar (the royal estates are described as "*ṣawāfī al-mulk*" while the colony of Fadak is described as "*khāliṣa*"). Ṭabarī, I, 1583. The Prophet also gave *iqṭā'* of the lands of Banū al-Naḍīr to Abū Bakr, 'Abd al-Raḥmān b. 'Awf, and Abū Dajjana. Balādhurī, *Futūḥ*, I, 18–21. Ibn Zanjawayh places more emphasis on justifying the division of Khaybar into *iqṭā'* because the Prophet considered that land a *ghanīma* (rather than *fay'*), and because the Prophet was applying the principle stated in the Qur'ānic verse, "Know that, whatever booty you take, the fifth of it is God's, and the Messenger's, and the near kinsman's, and the orphans', and for the needy, and the traveler . . . [*wa i'lamū annamā ghanimtum min shay'*]" (Qur'ān 8:41 [Arberry, I, 201]). Ibn Zanjawayh, *Kitāb al-Amwāl*, I, 196.

86. F. Donner, *The Early Islamic Conquests* (Princeton, 1981), 240. By contrast, Dennet considered reports about 'Umar's policies to be historical facts shaped against the background of interpreting relevant Qur'ānic verses. D. Dennet, *Conversion and the Poll-Tax in Early Islam* (Cambridge, MA, 1950), 37.

87. One report, for example, states that the Sawād was conquered by force ('*anwa*), and so was the land between the Sawād and the river Balkh, except for the fortresses, and adds that the inhabitants of this region were invited to make peace (*ṣulḥ*) and became *ahl-dhimma*, and that their land remained in their possession. Al-Sarī←Shu'ayb←Sayf←Ṭalḥa and Sufyān←Māhān. Ṭabarī, I, 2372.

88. Abū Yūsuf, *Kitāb al-Kharāj*, 58, 60, 64. This principle later also guides the juristic opinion of al-Mawardī. *Al-Aḥkām al-Sulṭāniyya* (Beirut, 1985), 242.

89. Abū Yūsuf, *Kitāb al-Kharāj*, 58. Another tradition defending 'Uthmān's granting of land estates also refers to the Prophet and states, "And thus the Prophet saw a virtue in this practice of achieving harmony with the frame of religion and a development for the land. Similarly, the caliphs granted land to those who they saw as furthering the cause of Islam and would be a thorn against the enemy [*ka-dhalika al-khulafā' innamā aqṭa'ū man ra'ū anna lahu ghinā' fī al-islām wa nikāya fī al-'aduww*]." Abū Yūsuf, *Kitāb al-Kharāj*, 62.

90. In the opening volume of *Ta'rīkh Baghdād*, al-Khaṭīb surveys the legal controversy surrounding the nature of the conquered territory of Iraq (*ṣulḥ* or '*anwa*, by treaty or force) and the divergent practices of 'Umar and 'Uthmān. He cites Abū 'Ubayd as stating that a number of people found arguments for the *iqṭā'* (*wa qad ta'wwal qawmun min ahl al-rukhṣa*) in the allotments that 'Uthmān gave to the companions in the Sawād land. Al-Khaṭīb then builds on this precedent by legitimizing the sale and inheritance of such allotted land. Whatever controversy remained, he cites Abū 'Ubayd as saying, had to do with agricultural land that was producing a yield (*al-arḍ al-mughilla allatī yalzamahā al-kharāj*) and not land that contained homes and presumably was not being exploited agriculturally. Otherwise, the author then concludes, some companions ought not to have established their residences in the Sawād region, particularly in the *khiṭaṭ* of Kufa, as they did and 'Umar should have disapproved of their practices, which he did not. *Ta'rīkh Baghdād*, I, 19–20.

91. 'Umar described his organization of stipends by saying, "I have given you according to your seniority in Islam, not according to your ancestral nobility." Ṭabarī, I, 2412.

92. In one of the miscellaneous speeches attributed to him, 'Umar reportedly states: "Everyone has a right to some of this [community's wealth], whether he has been granted it or not. No one has more right to it than another, except a slave. I am exactly like other people in [this matter of wealth]. But we [are eligible] according to our ranks [as derived] from God's book and our allotments from the Messenger of God [*wa lakinnā 'alā manāzilinā min kitāb allāh wa qisminā min rasūl allāh*]. [It is] a man's achievement in Islam [*wa'l rajul wa balā'uhu fī al-Islām*],

his precedence [*qidmuhu* or *qadamuhu*] in Islam, his usefulness (*ghanā'uhu*) in Islam, and his need [that count]. If indeed I remain alive, the shepherd where he is on the mountain of San'a shall certainly receive the share of this wealth." Al-Ḥārith←Ibn Sa'd←Muḥammad b. 'Umar←'Abdallāh b. Ja'far al-Zuhrī, and 'Abd al-Malik b. Sulaymān←Ismā'īl b. Muḥammad b. Sa'd←al-Sā'ib b. Yazīd. Ṭabarī, I, 2752. Smith, *HT*, XIV, 118. Ibn Zanjawayh, *Kitāb al-Amwāl*, II, 569. Although set among other declarations wherein 'Umar makes his standard affirmations about the equality of Muslims and their success in light of piety, this speech is somewhat different in that it reflects a more royalist (Sasanid) view of hierarchy and social status, which 'Umar implicitly considers a reason for the wealth differential in society. It is consistent with his utopian vision of eventual equality in society that he not only balances this system of rank with the Islamic system of merit but considers the Islamic goal the reason for the equality he aims to establish in society.

93. The incident seems isolated in Balādhurī's biography of 'Umar, but it is clearly included to foreshadow the controversy about a caliph's right to incorporate some conquered land under the central authority. This is related to the issue of establishing extra reserve land (*ḥimā*), whether as an agricultural resource of revenue or as a grazing ground for herds of camels and horses needed for the military. Balādhurī, *Ansāb (Sā'ir)*, 464. Ibn Sa'd, III, 326. 'Umar's justification of this action was that the revenues of such lands were needed to defray the expenses of military campaigns and other state-guided projects with a religious purpose. Ibn Zanjawayh, *Kitāb al-Amwāl*, II, 668–669.

94. As he set about organizing the allocation of the land after the Battle of Qādisiyya, 'Umar declares: "I am not a king so that I shall enslave you [*mā anā bi-malikin fa-asta'bidukum*]." Ṭabarī, I, 2368.

95. 'Uthmān is cited as the first caliph to have introduced the practice of the feudalistic allotment of land (*iqṭā'*). Suyūṭī, *Ta'rīkh al-Khulafā'* (Cairo, 1964), 196.

## 5. THE ROAD TO CIVIL WAR: ISSUES AND BOUNDARIES

1. Ṭabarī, I, 2907.

2. Sa'īd's words here were: "*inna man lahu mithla al-Nashāstāj, la-ḥaqīqun an yakūna jawādan*," referring to the estate "al-Nashāstāj," which Ṭalḥa gained in 'Uthmān's time in a swap for land in Ḥijāz and at Khaybar.

3. Ṭabarī, I, 2908.

4. Balādhurī's version of these events is presented in summary form, and at times seems to conflate Ṭabarī's accounts of the same events. In Balādhurī's version, for example, the remark attributed to 'Abd al-Raḥman b. Khunays, which

caused the dispute, shows him marveling at the territory of the Sawād and saying: "Would that the commander [i.e., Sa'īd b. al-'Āṣ] owned it and that you (*to the guests*) owned even better" (Balādhurī, *Ansāb* (*Banū 'Abd Shams*), I, 529); this seems to assume the initial answer given by Sa'īd to the guests that Ibn Khunays was misunderstood and probably would wish those present had even better. Balādhurī also shows little accuracy in categorizing these opponents of Sa'īd, calling them "*al-sufahā'*" (rabble).

5. By now the reader would have recognized that this conflict was chiefly a misunderstanding, bred by vanity, bravado, and a good measure of the evil eye—all ingredients that shaped a more central image in Iranian memory, namely the way by which the celebrated governor of Khurāsān in the time of Hurmuzd, Bahrām Chubīn, was subverted at an idle moment at court in Ctesiphon. During one banquet held by the emperor to celebrate the conquests of Bahrām in the east, a jealous minister (Yazdān Jushnas) reportedly commented on how really magnificent the bounty must be from which Bahrām sent those few gifts to the Persian emperor's court. Instilled to suspicion by slanderers (*wushāt*), Hurmuzd, it is said, began to question the faithfulness (*amāna*) of his governor and began to turn against him. Dīnawarī, 84–85. This episode would set the Iranian state on a path of tension, eventual civil war, and weakening in the times of Hurmuzd and his successor, Khusraw Parvīz. Mindful of the story's centrality, Dīnawarī interjects the following comment to drive home the lesson: "Behold here how many a calamity, wars and tribulations such words drove [*fa-nẓur kam dāhiyatan dahyā' wa ḥurūb wa balā' jarrat hādhihi al-kalima*]." Dīnawarī, 85.

6. Balādhurī gives a much longer list of names of the guests of Sa'īd. It is unclear, however, whether the author means that his list includes all those who generally visited him or those who were present on that fateful day of argument. Balādhurī's list includes in addition to those mentioned by Ṭabarī: Zayd b. Ṣūḥān (Ṣa'ṣa''s brother), Ḥurqūṣ b. Zuhayr al-Sa'dī, Shurayḥ b. Awfā b. Yazīd b. Zāhir al-'Absī, 'Adiyy b. Ḥātim al-Jawād b. 'Abdallāh b. Sa'd b. al-Ḥashraj al-Ṭā'ī (called Abū Ṭārīf), Kidām b. Ḥaḍramiyy b. 'Āmir, Mālik b. Ḥabīb b. Khirrāsh (from Banū Tha'laba b. Yarbū'), Qays b. 'Uṭāriḍ b. Ḥājib b. Zurāra b. 'Uds, Ziyād b. Khaṣfa, Yazīd b. Qays al-Arḥabī. *Balādhurī, Ansāb (Banū 'Abd Shams)*, I, 529. All these events, including the subsequent visit and debate with Mu'āwiya is recounted by Ibn al-Athīr. *Al-Kāmil*, III, 137–144.

7. Ṭabarī, I, 2909.

8. The question of who wrote to the caliph from Kufa here diverges. Ṭabarī's version (through reports by Sayf b. 'Umar and Wāqidī) states that the *ashrāf* wrote complaining about this small group of the agitators. Balādhurī's version, however, based on a report by Abū Mikhnaf, has Sa'īd b. al-'Āṣ first write to the caliph, identifying the group of dissidents as *al-qurrā'* (also referred to as "*al-sufahā'*"), and then states that the *qurrā'* wrote on their own to the caliph to describe their complaints more generally regarding the caliph's style of rule.

The letter is interesting for setting a boundary between loyalty and opposition. The dissidents state: "Sa'īd has gone overboard in the way he has been treating people who are known for their piety, excellence, and honesty [*ahl al-wara' wa'l-faḍl wa'l-'afāf*] and has led you to do things that are justified by neither religion or morality. We remind you of your duty toward God in ruling the community of Muḥammad, for we are fearful that the corruption of the community will come because of you. You have made your kinsmen dominate affairs [i.e., posts of governorship]. Know that you will find people divided towards you between helpers who are oppressors and those who hold a grudge against you and are oppressed [*laka nāṣiran maẓlūman wa nāqiman 'alayka maẓlūman*]. If the helpers shall come to aid you and the oppressed become vengeful, then the word of the community will fall in disarray. We hold God as witness against you, and He is the best witness. You are our leader so long as you obey God, and follow the straight path." Balādhurī states that the group of the Qurrā' who wrote the letter but did not sign their names on it were: Ma'qil b. Qays al-Riyāḥī, 'Abdallāh b. al-Ṭufayl al-'Āmirī, Mālik b. Ḥabīb al-Tamīmī, Yazīd b. Qays al-Arḥabī, Ḥujr b. 'Adī al-Kindī, 'Amr b. Ḥamiq al-Khuzā'ī, Sulaymān b. Ṣurd al-Khuzā'ī, al-Musayyib b. Najba al-Fazārī, Zayd b. Ḥiṣn al-Ṭā'ī, Ka'b b. 'Abda al-Nahdī, Ziyād b. al-Naḍir b. Bishr b. Mālik b. al-Dayyān al-Ḥārithī, Maslama b. 'Abd al-Qarī. This list was probably meant to foreshadow the supporters of 'Alī.

9. Ṭabarī, I, 2909.

10. On these tensions as a reflection of Kufan hostility to Medinan authority, see M. Hinds, "Kufan Political Alignments and Their Background in the Mid-Seventh Century A.D.," *IJMES* 2 (1971): 346–367.

11. This parallels the praise the Khārijites would later give to the memory of 'Umar at Ṣiffīn. The reader would note that this Kufan skirmish at Sa'īd's residence foreshadows the mentality and attitude of the social group that would later break with 'Alī at Ṣiffīn.

12. The political controversy in Kufa in this period is generally used not only as a doorway for understanding the conflict between provincial and central authority but also for shedding light on the motives and social identity of groups such as the Khārijites and the Qurrā'. J. Wellhausen attempted to define the Khārijites' origins by portraying them as "prodigal sons" of Arab tribes who chose to operate in non-Arab territories to avoid capture and repatriation to their home tribes. He considered Islam, and particularly 'Umar's policy of instating them in the *diwān*, as having given them a legitimate sociopolitical stake in the state. The issue has evoked questions about the social origins of the Khārijites: Were they just marginalized because they were not from Quraysh, Thaqīf, or the Anṣār, or because they were a politically underprivileged group in origin (like the bedouins and *a'rāb*). J. Wellhausen, *The Religio-Political Factions in Early Islam*, trans. R. C. Ostle et al. (Amsterdam, 1974), 11–12. Given the way Ṭabarī's narratives cast the Kufan precursors of the Khārijites as an archetype

of the social group that zealously overinterprets the concept of justice and militantly assaults the state to achieve its goals, it seems difficult to use these narratives when they point to social and provincial origins without running the risk of a circular reasoning. That they were marginalized because they were non-Qurashī, late in conversion, and veterans of the Ridda war and among the rank and file in the Muslim-Persian wars in 'Umar's reign is probably sufficiently suggestive of Ṭabarī's condescension regarding their motives.

13. Ṭabarī, I, 2909–2910. The translation here draws in part on Humphreys, *HT*, XV, 115. The statement "*al-a'imma junna*" is a *ḥadīth*. Muslim, II (pt. 4), 134 (no. 416); IV (pt. 12), 230 (no. 1841). Aḥmad, *Musnad*, XVI, 453. Ibn Qutayba explains that the *ḥadīth* is interpreted as meaning that the *imāms* shield the congregation from going astray during the prayer (*al-sahw wa al-zalal*). Ibn Qutayba, *al-Masā'il wa'l-Ajwiba fī'l-Ḥadīth wa'l-Lugha* (Cairo, AH 1349), 19. Another *ḥadīth* speaks of "*al-ṣiyāmu junna*." Muslim, III (pt. 8), 31 (no. 1151).

14. Ṭabarī, I, 2910.

15. Ṭabarī, I, 2912. Humphreys, *HT*, XV, 116–117.

16. Qur'ān 29:1.

17. Ṭabarī, I, 2913. Translation in brackets is partly based on Humphreys, *HT*, XV, 118.

18. Ṭabarī, I, 2913. Humphreys, *HT*, XV, 118.

19. The use of the term "*bustān Quraysh*" to represent the caliph's hold on Iraq later finds similar analogies in Ṭabarī. In A.H. 102/A.D. 721 the Umayyad governor of Khurāsān, Sa'īd Khudhayna, a descendant of al-Ḥakam b. Abī al-'Āṣ who was appointed by 'Abd al-Malik as governor of Khurāsān, would refer to the Ṣughd as "*bustān amīr al-mu'minīn*." The Ṣughd had challenged caliphal rule, and Sa'īd, after restoring control, showed a mild-mannered amnesty to the defeated reminiscent of Sa'īd b. al-'Āṣ. The story of rebellion in Khurāsān and the response of the central government was probably meant to show the continuity of a paradigm in representing the challenge from the margin of the traditional Arab tribal base, whether at Medina or Damascus. Alluding to the reader's knowledge of what happened in Sa'īd b. al-'Āṣ' time in Kufa, Sa'īd Khudhayna told his Iraqi troops: "Do not pursue them [i.e., al-Ṣughd] anymore. The Ṣughd are the subjects of the Commander of the Faithful [*innamā al-Ṣughd bustān amīr al-mu'minīn*]. You have defeated them and that is enough, what are you trying to do, finish them off?! Look at yourselves, O people of Iraq, you rebelled against the Commander of the Faithful time after time, and yet he pardoned you and let you go." Ṭabarī, II, 1431.

20. Ṭabarī, I, 2916.

21. Ṭabarī, I, 2917.

22. Balādhurī does not include either of Ṭabarī's lengthy narratives on the visit to Mu'āwiya, and only vaguely speaks of a heated argument between Mu'āwiya and al-Ashtar, which is clearly formulaic due to al-Ashtar's later his-

torical prominence. Balādhurī, *Ansāb* (*Banū 'Abd Shams*), I, 532. Balādhurī's summary version is also only based on the statement "*wa qālū* [it is said]."

23. Ṭabarī, I, 2917–2918. Humphreys, *HT,* XV, 122.

24. Qur'ān 32:8.

25. Qur'ān 3:98.

26. Qur'ān 65:3.

27. Ṭabarī, I, 2919–2920. Humphreys, *HT,* XV, 123–124.

28. Ṭabarī, I, 2920.

29. Ṭabarī, I, 2914. Humphreys, *HT,* XV, 119. Despite this attack on Ṣa'ṣa'a and his tribe, other narratives (continuing from accounts of Abū Mikhnaf) show Mu'āwiya having a positive attitude toward Ṣa'ṣa'a's brother, Zayd. The latter was reportedly permitted to return to Kufa with some favorable recommendation to Sa'īd b. al-'Āṣ. Balādhurī, *Ansāb* (*Banū 'Abd Shams*), 532. This exception may be due to Zayd's greater association with 'Alī at the Battle of the Camel.

30. If 'Umar's profile of rough justice and blunt tone is the role model for Kufans, many of whom were former Ridda folk, and if these episodes are made to appear as reviving past vendettas, then it is also not unlikely that 'Abd al-Raḥmān b. Khālid's harsh remarks are meant to clear the memory of his father, who was often accused by 'Umar of having treated rebels harshly. From a different angle, it can also be noted that this group of Kufan opposition was probably viewed as some of the troops who once fought under the leadership of Khālid b. al-Walīd in the toughest initial battles on the Iraqi front during the reign of Abū Bakr in A.H. 12/A.D. 634. As far back as then, a report recounted on the authority of Sayf describes how this group of *ahl al-ayyām* (warriors of old, typically of the Jahiliyya but here applied to a group that caught up with the early Islamic conquests as well) used to scoff when the name of Mu'āwiya was mentioned and comment that the battles that came after their initial raids with Khālid were less significant than what they had experienced before (presumably in reference to Mu'āwiya's participation in the campaigns after Khālid had established control in southern Iraq; Ṭabarī, I, 2085). Ṭabarī, I, 2077, 2110.

31. Ṭabarī, I, 2929.

32. Ṭabarī, I, 2930.

33. Ṭabarī, I, 2931.

34. This account describes how 'Uthmān discussed the crisis. 'Uthmān began by telling those governors assembled: "Every man has ministers [*wuzarā'*] and counselors. Now you are my ministers, my counselors, and my trusted men. The people have acted as you see, demanding that I depose my governors . . . so decide what you think is right and advise me." 'Abdallāh b. 'Āmir said to him, "My advice to you, Commander of the Faithful, is that you command them to undertake a *jihād* that will divert their attention from you. In this way every one of them will be concerned only about himself . . ."—(This call for busying the dissidents with war is understood by M. Hinds as a sign that the stoppage of

the conquests created this unrest; M. Hinds, "Kufan Alignments," *IJMES* 2 (1971): 356. Hind's approach to reading the sources, however, was quite a credulous one, which makes its categories of social and political analysis today as dated as its method of historicization.)—"Then 'Uthmān came to Sa'īd b. al-'Āṣ [*thumma aqbala 'Uthmān 'alā Sa'īd b. al-'Āṣ*] and asked him for his opinion. He said, 'O Commander of the Faithful, . . . every group has leaders. When these are eliminated, they will disperse and will be unable to agree on anything.' Then when 'Uthmān asked Mu'āwiya's opinion, the latter said: 'O Commander of the Faithful, I think it is best for you to send your governors back, on condition that they administer their provinces with care, and I will be the guarantor for you of my province.' Then 'Uthmān asked 'Abdallāh b. Sa'd his opinion and the latter said: 'O Commander of the Faithful, in my opinion the people are greedy. Bestow on them some of this wealth and their hearts will incline to you.' Finally, 'Uthmān asked 'Amr b. al-'Āṣ his opinion, and 'Amr said: 'I think you have perpetrated things against the people that they detest, so resolve to do justice. If you reject [this course], then make up your mind to abdicate. If you reject [that], then be firm in your resolve and continue straight ahead.' The narrator then says: 'Uthmān replied: 'What is wrong with you? May your scalp crawl with lice! Are you serious about this?' 'Amr refused to answer him for some time, until [the rest of] the assembly [*qawm*] had dispersed. Then 'Amr said, 'No, O Commander of the Faithful, you are dearer to me than that, but I knew that the people would hear about the statements of every man among us. I wanted them to learn what I said, so they would trust me, and thereby I would bring you good and ward off evil.'" Ṭabarī, I, 2932–2933. The translated excerpts are from Humphreys, *HT*, XV, 136–137. The account is narrated on the authority of Ja'far b. 'Abdallāh al-Muḥammadī←'Amr b. Ḥammād b. Ṭalḥa and 'Alī b. Ḥusayn b. 'Īsā←Ḥusayn b. 'Īsā←Ḥusayn's father ('Īsā)←Hārūn b. Sa'd←al-'Alā' b. 'Abdallāh b. Zayd al-Anbārī. Ṭabarī recounts another very similar version of this account on the authority of another chain of transmitters: Ja'far←'Amr b. Ḥammād and 'Alī b. Ḥusayn←Ḥusayn←Ḥusayn's father←'Amr b. Abī'l-Miqdām←'Abd al-Malik b. 'Umayr al-Zuhrī.

35. The arguments between 'Uthmān and 'Amr formed a favorite topic with narrators who sought to show that 'Amr had been betraying the caliph ever since the latter removed him as governor of Egypt and placed Ibn Abī Sarḥ in his stead. Wāqidī's version of this disagreement is extensive and portrays 'Uthmān as deeply shaken by 'Amr's treachery; he implicates 'Amr unequivocally in an effort to bring down the caliph. This was not a dispute like the one between 'Alī and 'Uthmān, where a maze of ambiguity, indirect responsibility, and moments of naive negligence could exonerate one party or another at various points in the dispute. In a strong rebuke to 'Amr, when the latter claimed that he had been appointed by 'Umar b. al-Khaṭṭāb, 'Uthmān declared, "If I had controlled you as stringently as 'Umar did, by God, you would act rightly. But I have been lenient

with you and so you have been insolent with me." Ṭabarī, I, 2966. Humphreys, *HT*, XV, 170.

36. In these words the narrator was drawing on a *ḥadīth* that describes the punishment for one, in general, who while calling for commanding the good (*al-amr bi'l-ma'rūf*), in real life does the opposite. The *ḥadīth* even includes the simile of the millstone. Muslim, VI, 117–118 (no. 2889). This *ḥadīth* in fact describes a setting where Usāma b. Zayd (rather than 'Alī) is being exhorted to enter upon 'Uthmān and advise him to change his ways. The *ḥadīth* was probably modified in due time by including Usāma rather than 'Alī in order to distance it from the 'Alī–'Uthmān debate. Also, Bukhārī (*kitāb al-fitan*), IX, 170 (no. 218).

37. Ṭabarī, I, 2937–2938. Humphreys, *HT*, XV, 141–142. This exchange between 'Alī and 'Uthmān is recounted on the authority of al-Wāqidī. Balādhurī, *Ansāb* (*Banū 'Abd Shams*), 549–550. Ibn 'Abd Rabbihi, *al-'Iqd*, IV, 308 (quoting Ibn Da'ab).

38. Ṭabarī, I, 2938. Humphreys, *HT*, XV, 142.

39. This will become a standard assertion, that 'Uthmān did not part ways with 'Umar except in being lenient. Ibn Sa'd, V, 233.

40. Ṭabarī, I, 2939. Humphreys, *HT*, XV, 143.

41. Interestingly, here too 'Uthmān would be anticipating 'Alī's insistence that the authority of the caliph is no longer subject to questioning once the *bay'a* is completed. Later 'Alī would comment after he gained the *bay'a* as fourth caliph that loyalty to the caliph is mandatory once the oath of allegiance has been rendered to him; as he put it: "*innamā al-khayār qabla an taqa'a al-bay'a fa-idhā waqa'at fa-lā khayār; wa innamā 'alā al-imām al-istiqāma wa 'alā al-ra'iyya al-taslīm* [the possibility for debate and choices is one that is available before the *bay'a* is obtained. But once it is rendered then the issue of choice or alternatives is closed. It is only a matter of the caliph remaining on the straight path, and the community accepting his rule]." Dīnawarī, 149. 'Uthmān's argument for the unquestionable nature of caliphal authority here reflects ninth-century Sunnī political theory.

42. These criticisms include all manner of religious, social, and political claims. To the disputes over small scholastic differences in reading the texts, 'Uthmān will use the word "*al-muḥaqqarāt*" (trifles) to describe the argumentation of one reciter (*qāri'*). Ṭabarī, I, 2931.

43. Ṭabarī, I, 2937. Humphreys, *HT*, XV, 143. Balādhurī, *Ansāb* (*Banū 'Abd Shams*), 550. The account in both Ṭabarī and Balādhurī is attributed to Wāqidī, however, whereas Balādhurī merely opens by saying: "*qāla al-Wāqidī fī isnādihi*," Ṭabarī says: "*wa ammā al-Wāqidī fa-innahu za'ama anna 'Abdallāh b. Muḥammad ḥaddathahu 'an abīhi . . .*" Balādhurī's version of this encounter is briefer and clearly based on Ṭabarī. Ibn al-Athīr follows Ṭabarī's accounts of the debate throughout this section. Ibn al-Athīr, 151–152.

44. According to a pro-'Uthmān voice, obedience to the *imām* is necessary even if he is not just. One narrator quotes someone reporting a *ḥadīth* in a version that says: "He who breaks with the community to cause sedition when it has

an *imām*—by God, he [i.e., the Prophet] did not say 'a just *imām*'—deserves to be killed." Ṭabarī, I, 2935.

45. Ṭabarī states only that Ibn Saba''s conversion happened in 'Uthmān's time, but according to a more detailed report by the same narrator (Yazīd al-Faq'asī), one of the sources of Sayf, the conversion of Ibn Saba' happened in the latter six years of 'Uthmān's rule, thereby confirming the inauspicious yet synchronic designs of ill-fated events in that latter part of 'Uthmān's reign. Al-Māliqī, *al-Tamhīd wa'l-Bayān*, 55, 88. Al-Māliqī's account adds that Ibn Saba' settled among the 'Abd al-Qays in Basra.

46. Here it is important to draw attention to a later sectarian current that would build upon this principle of *waṣiyya* (the religious designation and investiture of a successor) as the foundation of 'Alid succession. U. Rubin, "Prophets and Progenitors in the Early Shi'a Tradition," *Jerusalem Studies in Arabic and Islam* 1 (1979): 41–65.

47. Ṭabarī, I, 2942. Ibn al-Athīr, III, 154.

48. Ṭabarī, I, 2942. Ibn al-Athīr puts it more strongly, saying: "The people of Syria drove him out [*fa-akhrajahu ahlu al-shām*]." *Al-Kāmil*, III, 154.

49. Examples of praise of *ahl al-shām* can be found in Tirmidhī (*kitāb al-fitan*), IV, 420, 431 (nos. 2192, 2217).

50. Traditional Islamicist and Judaic scholarship has tended to accept the Ibn Saba' story as reflecting a fact about how Islamic messianism emerged in connection with him (hence the group later to be known as al-Saba'iyya), and that Shī'īsm was originally related to Ibn Saba's movement as well. For a survey of this literature, see S. Wasserstrom, *Between Muslim and Jew: The Problem of Symbiosis Under Early Islam* (Princeton, 1995), 55, 64, 93, 125.

51. This profile of a deceptive Saba'iyya in Medina spearheading and coordinating a conspiracy in the provinces is laid out mostly by Ṭabarī; I, 2950–2951. 'Alī is shown discovering the role of al-Saba'iyya among the similar claims that Basrans, Kufans, and Egyptians bring to Medina. Ṭabarī, I, 2958.

52. Ṭabarī, I, 2942. The issue of "*al-amr bi'l ma'rūf* . . . [commanding right and forbidding wrong]" has been treated exhaustively by Michael Cook's famous study with the title that matches the slogan. While extensive in its gathering of information related to this pietistic call, Cook's book does not consider the polemical deployment of this religious theme in Islamic historiography across Ṭabarī's narratives on political history. The author also sometimes seems to blur the line between the extra puritanism evident in the concept of "commanding right" when applied to gray-area issues, and more clearly defined distinctions between *ḥalāl* and *ḥarām* (the permissible and the forbidden under the *sharī'a*).

53. Those who influenced 'Ammār were, in addition to Ibn Saba', Khālid b. Muljam, Sawdān b. Ḥumrān al-Sakūnī, and Kināna b. Bishr al-Laythī. It is here worth noting that if part of the message is the attraction of 'Ammār to the 'Alid

cause, 'Ammār had reportedly favored the nomination of 'Alī for succession as early as the *shūrā* occasion after 'Umar's death. Ṭabarī, I, 2785.

54. Ṭabarī, I, 2944. Humphreys, *HT,* XV, 148.

55. Ṭabarī, I, 2944. Humphreys, *HT,* XV, 149. Ibn al-Athīr, III, 155.

56. Ṭabarī, I, 2946. Humphreys, *HT,* XV, 150.

57. Ṭabarī, I, 2949.

58. See chap. 7.

59. The translation of the *ḥadīth* is: "God's curse is upon anyone who challenges the established authority of a recognized leader of the community."

60. Ṭabarī, I, 2952.

61. Ṭabarī, I, 2944.

62. This embellished synthesis of material is best preserved by Abū Mikhnaf's account. Balādhurī, *Ansāb (Banū 'Abd Shams)*, 552.

63. Ṭabarī, I, 2952–2954.

64. According to al-Aṣma'ī (citing the report of Abū 'Awāna), the leaders of the opposition who came to Medina were 'Alqama b. 'Uthmān, Kināna b. Bishr, Ḥakīm b. Jabla, al-Ashtar al-Nakha'ī, and 'Abdallāh b. Budayl. Al-Madā'inī's account states that the leaders of the opposition groups were 'Abd al-Raḥmān b. 'Adīs al-Balawī (Egypt), Ḥakīm b. Jabla al-'Abdī (Basra), al-Ashtar Mālik b. al-Ḥārith al-Nakha'ī (Kufa). Ibn 'Abd Rabbihi, *al-'Iqd*, IV, 292–293.

65. For the unflattering image of al-Sakūn, see 'Umar's comments about them in the year of al-Qādisiyya, A.H. 14/A.D. 636. Ibn al-Athīr, II, 451.

66. Ṭabarī, I, 2954–2955. Murtaḍā al-'Askarī has previously cast doubt on the historical existence of some individuals, during the Rāshidūn period. His comments, however, were mainly about Sayf b. 'Umar as having invented many significant Tamīmī characters in order to glorify his own tribe. M. al-'Askarī, *Khamsūn wa Mi'at Sahābiyy Mukhtalaq*, 2 vols. (Beirut, 1991), I, 91–176.

67. Ṭabarī, I, 2956–2957. Humphreys, *HT,* XV, 161.

68. Ṭabarī, I, 2958. Humphreys, *HT,* XV, 162.

69. The famous statement then was "I will not abandon a present king to another whose fortune I don't know [*lā ada'u malikan ḥāḍiran li-ākhar lā adrī ma yaṣīra min amrih*]." Ṭabarī, III, 772.

70. The use of the verb "*ṭalaba*" is undoubtedly a pun here on 'Alī b. Abī Ṭālib.

71. Ṭabarī, I, 2959. Humphreys, *HT,* XV, 163–164 (with variation).

72. 'Uthmān makes similar jibes later in the same narrative, when he declares in the prayer sermon, as the Egyptians had settled in the mosque, "O you enemies! Fear God, fear God! By God, the Medinese know that you have been cursed by the tongue of Muḥammad, so wipe out your errors by doing what is right. For verily Almighty God only eradicates evil with what is good [*inna allāha 'azz wa jall lā yamḥū al-sayyi' illā bi'l-ḥasan*]." Ṭabarī, I, 2960. Humphreys, *HT,* XV, 165 (with minor modification). The reader would note that the curse 'Uthmān issues against the Egyptians is identical to the curse 'Alī issued against the rebels

earlier. With the connection of 'Alī to this text established, it then becomes only a small step before discerning 'Uthmān's severe criticism of 'Alī as he says "*inna allāha lā yamḥū al-sayyi' illā bi'l-ḥasan* [God only wipes out the bad with the good]" as a reference to the replacement of 'Alī later by his son, al-Ḥasan, the latter more favored by Sunnīs generally.

73. The narrators are: Ya'qūb b. Ibrāhīm←Mu'tamir b. Sulaymān al-Taymī←Sulaymān al-Taymī←Abū Naḍra←Abū Sa'īd (*mawlā* of Abū Usayd al-Anṣārī). Ṭabarī, I, 2963.

74. Ṭabarī, I, 2965, 2989, 2995, 2996. The capture of 'Uthmān's messenger on his way to Egypt is a scene described with great dramatic slowness in Balādhurī's version, based on Abū Mikhnaf. Balādhurī, *Ansāb* (*Banū 'Abd Shams*), 555.

75. The idea that summons in the names of leading companions and mobilization letters were circulating in the provinces to rally political opposition against 'Uthmān is a central motif in the apologetic dimension of the narratives (see above). When 'Āisha was accused of having circulated a letter mobilizing opposition to 'Uthmān, she adamantly denied that she wrote anything of the sort (al-A'mash←Masrūq). Ibn 'Abd Rabbihi then adds his general commentary: "They [i.e., what the public recognized afterward] came to believe that letters were written using her name and 'Alī's, as in the case of the letter written in the name of 'Uthmān to the governor of Egypt. The fabrication of all these letters was the source of the *fitna*." Ibn 'Abd Rabbihi, *al-'Iqd*, IV, 293.

76. Ṭabarī, I, 2965. Humphreys, *HT*, XV, 169.

77. Ṭabarī, I, 2969. Humphreys, *HT*, XV, 172.

78. There are several other instances in which 'Uthmān is said to have appeared to the public from a perched position (*ashrafa 'alā al-nās*). Ṭabarī, I, 3006, 3008, 3011, 3023.

79. A secondary version by Wāqidī makes Muḥammad b. Maslama the one who convinces the Egyptians to return home. Ṭabarī, I, 2971.

80. The contradiction is even more blunt in a variant account related on the authority of Ja'far b. 'Abdallāh al-Muḥammadī, who declares that 'Uthmān sought a respite of three days in his final negotiations with 'Alī to fulfill the pledges made at home and in the provinces. "I cannot do away with the things they detest in one day," 'Uthmān claimed. 'Alī at first resisted delay, but then agreed to let 'Uthmān have this amount of time and even spoke to the public to appease them. This version somewhat foreshadows the Taḥkīm, as it portrays 'Alī keeping to his promise and addressing the public while 'Uthmān is about to dissemble. In spite of solemn oaths written in a document that 'Uthmān was going to do away with injustice and remove every governor whom the public disliked, the caliph, as it turned out wanted to use the respite of three days to prepare for war, gathering arms and forming a strong army from among the slaves acquired as part of the caliph's one-fifths share of the booty. Ṭabarī, I, 2988.

81. Ṭabarī, I, 2972. Humphreys, *HT*, XV, 175.

82. Ṭabarī, I, 2972.

83. Ṭabarī, I, 2975. Humphreys, *HT,* XV, 177–178 (with minor modification).

84. Ṭabarī, I, 2975. Humphreys, *HT,* XV, 178. Ibn al-Athīr, III, 165. Another similar version also on the authority of al-Wāqidī states that 'Uthmān stayed at home for three days, fearing to go out in public out of embarrassment over what happened. Ṭabarī, I, 2977. See also Abū Mikhnaf's account. Balādhurī, *Ansāb* (*Banū 'Abd Shams*), 554. When word of this scene came to 'Alī, the latter finally decided in anger to break off all relations with the caliph. Ṭabarī, I, 2978. Finally, it is worth noting that in Abū Mikhnaf's version of the Saqīfa story, 'Umar declares with confidence, contesting the Anṣār, "Who would attempt to wrest from us the sovereignty [*sulṭān*] of Muḥammad and his authority [*imāra*], seeing that we are his friends and kinsmen [*man dhā yunāzi'unā sulṭān Muḥammad wa imarātihi wa naḥnu awliyā'uhu wa 'ashīratuhu*], except someone advancing falsehood? . . ." Ṭabarī, I, 1841. Although at the time 'Umar was speaking in defense of the primacy of Quraysh, and his political intentions were different from those of Marwān later on, the narrative probably aimed to highlight the growth of the monopolistic albeit impious political claims of Marwān when he defended 'Uthmān's rule.

85. Ṭabarī, I, 2976.

86. Ṭabarī, I, 2975. Also Abū Mikhnaf, Balādhurī, *Ansāb* (*Banū 'Abd Shams*), 554.

87. This representation of 'Alī shows that these scenes were once made more meaningful by actually being staged rather than merely being read.

88. Ṭabarī, I, 2978.

89. The view that an aged ruler must at some point be retired in favor of a younger, more attentive leader is specifically used as an argument in A.H. 29/A.D. 649 when Abū Mūsā al-Ash'arī was replaced by 'Abdallāh b. 'Āmir b. Kurayz as governor of Basra. At the time, a certain Ghaylān b. Kharasha al-Ḍabbī was reported to have traveled from Basra to Medina and asked 'Uthmān: "Have you not a younger person to be assigned to govern Basra? How long is this old man [that is, Abū Mūsā] to rule us [*ḥattā matā yalī hādhā al-shaykh al-Baṣra*]?" Until that point, Abū Mūsā had been governor of Baṣra for six years continuously. Ṭabarī, I, 2828.

90. Writing within the apologetic frame, Ibn Shihāb al-Zuhrī places the blame on Marwān. In connection with the controversial letter sent to Egypt, al-Zuhrī declares that the companions recognized the letter brought back to Medina to be the forged writing of Marwān. The continued standoff in this account is explained this time by the fact that 'Uthmān refused to hand in Marwān for punishment. Balādhurī, *Ansāb* (*Banū 'Abd Shams*), 558.

91. Ṭabarī, I, 2999.

92. Ṭabarī, I, 2998. Humphreys, *HT,* XV, 198.

93. Ṭabarī, I, 2999. Humphreys, *HT,* XV, 198.

94. Ṭabarī, I, 2990. Humphreys, *HT,* XV, 190.

95. Ṭabarī, I, 3040–3045.

96. Ṭabarī, I, 2995. Humphreys, *HT,* XV, 195. Al-Wāqidī's version.

97. Ṭabarī, I, 2989. Humphreys, *HT,* XV, 189.

98. Ṭabarī, I, 2989. Humphreys, *HT,* XV, 189. The account of Ja'far b. 'Abdallāh al-Muḥammadī.

99. Ṭabarī, I, 3024–3025. Humphreys, *HT,* XV, 221–223.

100. See accounts in Ṭabarī, III, 780–782. Within a similar frame of seizing the initiative and forestalling future deterioration, al-Mughīra gave advice to 'Alī, "You can forestall tomorrow's loss by making a sound decision today [*inna al-ḍayā' al-yawm tuḍayyi' bihi mā fī al-ghad*]." Ṭabarī, I, 3082.

101. Balādhurī, *Ansāb (Banū 'Abd Shams)*, 547.

102. The Arabic seems reversed (*inna lanā 'alaykum ḥaqqan, al-naṣīḥatu bi'l-ghayb wa'l-mu'āwana 'alā al-khayr* rather than *inna lakum 'alaynā ḥaqqan).*

103. Ṭabarī, I, 2772. Smith, *HT,* XIV, 139. The account is narrated by 'Abd al-Ḥamīd b. Bayān←Muḥammad b. Yazīd←Ismā'īl b. Abī Khālid←Salama b. Kuhayl.

104. Ṭabarī, I, 2755–2756. Smith, *HT,* XIV, 121. The account is narrated by 'Umar (b. Shabba)←'Alī←Muḥammad b. Sāliḥ←Mūsā b. 'Uqba. Ṭabarī's version of the story does not say that 'Umar meant Mu'āwiya in his reference to the young nobleman, but several other sources state this explicitly. Ibn 'Abd Rabbihi, *al-'Iqd*, IV, 363. Also Balādhurī with slight variation. *Ansāb (Banū 'Abd Shams)*, 49. 'Abdallāh b. Ṣāliḥ←Abū Bakr b. 'Ayyāsh←al-Sha'bī. Ibn Qutayba, *'Uyūn al-Akhbār*, I, 62.

105. The events described by Ṭabarī, I, 2869. The construction of the earlier maritime story is influenced by the fact that Mu'āwiya was the one who had asked 'Umar for permission to invade Cyprus.

106. H. A. R. Gibb lecture notes. I am grateful to Richard W. Bulliet for making available Gibb's typescript lectures.

107. Ṭabarī, I, 3006, 3018.

108. Ṭabarī, I, 3012. Humphreys, *HT,* XV, 210.

109. Ṭabarī, I, 3006. Humphreys, *HT,* XV, 204.

110. Ṭabarī, I, 3006. Despite al-Ashtar's hard-line position against the caliph, his name does not surface in the final scene of 'Uthmān's murder. This is perhaps done in light of al-Ashtar's closeness to 'Alī.

111. Ṭabarī, I, 3013.

112. Matthew 26:51.

113. The metaphor was itself borrowed by the narrator from a Qur'ānic verse that describes a divinely ordained event that brought about a similar collapse of a community. The verse reads, "And when it is said to them, 'What has your Lord sent down?' they say, 'Fairy-tales of the ancients.' That they may bear their loads complete on the Day of Resurrection, and some of the loads of those that they lead astray without any knowledge. O evil the load they bear! Those that were

before them contrived [*qad makara alladhīna min qablihim*]; then God came upon their building from the foundations, and the roof fell down on them from over them [*fa-kharra 'alayhim al-saqfu min fawqihim*], and the chastisement came upon them from whence they were not aware" (Qur'ān 16:24–26 [Arberry, I, 289]). This verse describes the parable of punishment that followed a community's rejection of its prophet, which as mentioned earlier was a theme to which the plight of the third caliph was adapted.

114. Ṭabarī, I, 3020.

115. Ṭabarī, I, 3019. Humphreys, *HT,* XV, 217.

116. Qur'ān 34:53. Humphreys, *HT,* XV, 217.

117. Qur'ān 36:50. Humphreys, *HT,* XV, 217.

118. Qur'ān 59:16. Humphreys, *HT,* XV, 217.

119. Qur'ān 18:104. Humphreys, *HT,* XV, 217.

120. Ṭabarī, I, 3019.

121. Qur'ān 20:1 (Arberry, I, 339).

122. Qur'ān 3:167 (Arberry, I, 95). The standard order of *sūras* in the Qur'ān must obviously be ignored here.

123. The subject is ambiguous here, as is whether the reference is to the caliph or al-Ghāfiqī.

124. An additional detail here from Sayf's account in al-Māliqī, *al-Tamhīd wa'l-Bayān*, 139.

125. This was undoubtedly intended to evoke a connection with the title of the future caliph al-Mutawakkil.

126. All sources agree that blood was spilled on this verse. The full details of the story are preserved in al-Māliqī's *al-Tamhīd wa'l-Bayān* (138–139), which draws on reports shared by Ibn Sa'd and Ṭabarī. Ibn Sa'd, III, 74; Balādhurī, *Ansāb (Banū 'Abd Shams)*, 574, 585, 591.

## 6. 'ALĪ: IN THE IMAGE OF THE PROPHETS

1. Al-Māliqī, *Al-Tamhīd wa'l-Bayān*, 136. Yūnus al-Ṭanāfisī←Muḥammad b. Yūsuf←'Abdallāh b. Sallām. Ṭabarī omits this version of the exhortation mentioning Jesus, but includes another reported by Sayf b. 'Umar that is very similar (Ṭabarī, I, 3017). Both versions are included by al-Māliqī. *Ḥadīth* literature would preserve the prophetic connections of the story as part of *fitan* accounts. Hence the famous *ḥadīth*, "The first of the *fitan* is the murder of 'Uthmān [*yawm al-dār*], and the last of it will be the emergence of the *dajjāl*." Ibn 'Asākir, XXXIX, 447. Al-Hindī, *Kanz*, XI, 223 (no. 31306).

2. Ibn Sallām declares: "No nation ever killed its prophet and found itself reaching reconciliation until they have shed the blood of seventy thousand

people, and no nation ever killed its caliph and reconciled until forty thousand people have died." Abū'l-'Arab al-Tamīmī, *Kitāb al-Miḥan*, 82. Yaḥyā←Yaḥyā's father←Yaḥyā's grandfather←Ayyūb b. Khūṭ←Ḥumayd b. Hilāl←'Abdallāh b. Ma'qil.

3. The use of the motif of the town overturned by divine vengeance will surface in the speech attributed to Busr b. Arṭāt in A.H. 40/A.D. 660 when Mu'āwiya orders him to raid the province of Ḥijāz, which was under 'Alī's control. When he arrived in Medina, Busr made a speech from the town's mosque in which he rebuked the populace, saying, "O People of Medina, You have the parable of the wrongdoers. 'God has struck a similitude: a city that was secure, at rest, its provision coming to it easefully from every place, then it was unthankful for the blessings of God; so God let it taste the garment of hunger and of fear, for the things that they were working.' [Qur'ān 16:112 (Arberry, I, 299)]." Ya'qūbī, II, 197. Along similar lines of reading divine judgment in political events, one narrator perceives in the same light the cause of the punitive campaign that Yazīd unleashed against Medina (in the famous al-Ḥarra campaign). Ibn Sa'd quotes Mujāhid as saying, "God killed from among them [i.e., the Medinans] a crowd during the *fitnas*, and later Yazīd dispatched an army to Medina that killed twenty thousand people, and who plundered the town for three days for the complicity of its people in the murder [*li-mudāhanatihim*]." Ibn Sa'd, III, 68.

4. Ibn Sa'd, III, 80.

5. Ṭabarī, I, 2947. Humphreys, *HT*, XV, 151–152. Balādhurī does not include this important speech attributed to Mu'āwiya.

6. In fact this speech by Mu'āwiya bears a great resemblance to a declaration attributed to 'Umar that seems to have been dropped from Ṭabarī's chronicle. This declaration, which 'Umar reportedly made on his deathbed, is recounted on the authority of Mubashshir quoting Jābir, both of whom were sources for Sayf b. 'Umar on other matters (cited as Mubashshir b. al-Fuḍayl and Jābir b. 'Abdallāh; Ṭabarī, I, 2450). This account relates that after 'Umar was stabbed and he became certain of his imminent death, he exhorted the community (*awṣā fī khāṣatihi wa jam'i al-'āmma*—the usual stock phrases of Ṭabarī on such matters), saying: "O people! The succession today in the community of Muḥammad, peace be upon him, is yours [*inna al-amra fī ummati Muḥammad 'alayhi al-salām amrukum*]. You are the witnesses on affairs of the community and the people of the *shūrā* [*antum shuhūd al-umma wa ahl al-shūrā*]. Whomever you are content with, they shall be content with, and whomever you agree on, they will agree on. This success will stay with you so long as you only seek God and the hereafter as your goal. But if you seek this world and you compete among yourselves over it, God shall take it away from you and transfer it to others. And He will never again bring it back to you [*inna hādhā al-amr lā yazālu fīkum mā ṭalabtum bihi wajha allāh wa'l-dār al-ākhira, fa-idhā ṭalabtum bihi al-dunyā wa tanāza'tum salabkumūh allāh wa naqalahu 'ankum thumma lā yarudduhu 'alaykum abadān*]. [I reckon that] if you decide on

leadership in my lifetime, it is a guarantee that you will not differ after my death [*innakum ina tu'ammirū fī ḥayātin minnī ajdaru an lā takhtalifū ba'dī*]. Do you know anyone more worthy of this succession [*aḥaqqu bi-hādhā al-amr*] than this group of six whom the Prophet died while content with?" "No," they said. "Then I believe it is the sound opinion if you follow my advice and make them the ones to choose the leader for you." Al-Māliqī, *al-Tamhīd wa'l-Bayān*, 13.

7. Ṭabarī, I, 3066.

8. Ṭabarī, I, 3076.

9. Ṭabarī, I, 3066.

10. Dīnawarī, 149.

11. Ṭabarī, I, 1696. Ibn Sa'd, III, 24–25. Muslim, I, 5 (no. 2404). Bukhārī (*kitāb al-maghāzī*), *bāb ḥijjat al-wadā'*, V, 47 (no. 56); 493 (no. 700). Ibn al-Jawzī, *al-Muntaẓam*, V, 66. Qazwīnī, *al-Tadwīn*, II, 154.

12. The list of merits that surrounds the image of 'Alī in the early sources is rich and diverse. Even before the later division between Sunnism and Shī'ism that led to the redaction or embellishment of the fourth caliph's biography as caliph or *imām*, the earliest sources give praise that deserves close attention. We are told that 'Alī was the first to convert to Islam (Ṭabarī, I, 1159), the first to pray with the Prophet (Ṭabarī, I, 1160), the one with whom the Prophet established a bond of fraternity (*mu'ākhāt*) when the Muhājirūn and the Anṣār were ordered by the Prophet to establish fraternal bonds after the Hijra, 'Alī having arrived too late in Medina to find someone to establish a fraternal tie with (Ibn Sa'd, III, 22). In the military context, we read that 'Alī was the first to carry the Prophet's banner into *jihād* at the Battle of al-Abwā' (Ṭabarī, I, 1270), and at the decisive Battle of Badr (Ṭabarī, I, 1297). Other traditions say that 'Alī carried the Prophet's banner at every battle. Ibn Sa'd, III, 23. Such instances of firsts and closeness with the Prophet do not appear as random honorifics, but seem to have formed in origin an integral part of the broad narrative.

13. Ṭabarī, I, 3290. Hawting, *HT*, XVII, 37.

14. Ṭabarī, I, 3288. Both—the account of 'Alī's passionate prayer for victory and Ibn Budayl's statement drawing a parallel with Badr—are recounted on the authority of Abū Mikhnaf.

15. Ṭabarī, I, 3335. Dīnawarī, 207.

16. The account of al-Ḥudaybiyya is also in Bukhārī (*bāb kayfa yuktab hādhā mā ṣālaḥa fulān b. fulān*), III, 536–537 (nos. 862–863); (*kitāb al-khums, bāb al-muṣālaḥa*), IV, 273 (no. 408); (*kitāb al-maghāzī*), V, 388 (no. 553). Interestingly, there 'Alī is represented as refusing to erase the Prophet's title of "Messenger of God," which impels the Prophet to erase it in person in order to avail the Meccans of excuses for war. 'Alī, according to this version, would have been agreeing with 'Umar, who also took a stubborn position on that occasion.

17. W. Madelung, *The Succession to Muḥammad*, 44.

18. Ṭabarī, I, 3475–3476.

19. Although Arberry renders "'*alā ḥīni ghaflatin min ahlihā*" in religious terms as a general religious "*ghafla*" (slumber) of the populace, it can also simply refer to the "time of sleep" or "under darkness."

20. Qur'ān 28:15–17 (Arberry, II, 87) (except for phrase in brackets).

21. The Qur'ānic verse here reads: "Had the tiding of the dispute come to thee? When they scaled the Sanctuary, when they entered upon David, and he took fright at them; and they said: 'Fear not; two disputants we are—one of us has injured the other; so judge between us justly, and transgress not, and guide us to the right path.' 'Behold, this my brother has ninety-nine ewes, and I have one ewe. So he said, "Give her into my charge"; and he overcame me in the argument.' Said he, 'Assuredly he has wronged thee in asking for thy ewe in addition to his sheep; and indeed many intermixers do injury one against the other, save those who believe, and do deeds of righteousness—and how few they are!' And David thought that we had only tried him; therefore he sought forgiveness of his Lord, and he fell down, bowing, and he repented. Accordingly We forgave him that, and he has a near place in Our presence and a fair resort." Qur'ān 38:21–25 (Arberry, II, 159–160).

22. Ṭabarī, I, 3373. Hawting, *HT,* XVII, 123.

23. Ṭabarī, I, 3138. Brockett, *HT,* XVI, 80.

24. Ṭabarī, I, 3154. Brockett, *HT,* XVI, 95. Earlier in 'Umar's reign 'Alī had recommended the future of the Kufans—confirming 'Umar's dicta about them—by saying, "Commander of the Faithful, by God, *al-Kūfa* is a place to which one makes a *hijra* after the Hijra; it is the 'dome' of Islam. There will come a day when there is no believer left who does not go there out of longing. God will be made victorious through its inhabitants just as He overcame the people of Lot with stones." Ṭabarī, I, 2514 (Sayf b. 'Umar). Juynboll, *HT,* XVIII, 95.

25. Ṭabarī, I, 3269.

26. Ya'qūbī, II, 196. Another report on the authority of al-Layth b. Sa'd has 'Alī compare the replacement of the Kufans to the exchange of dinars and dirhams, one for every ten. Al-Hindī, *Kanz*, XI, 356 (no. 31727); Ibn 'Asākir, I, 320.

27. Ṭabarī, I, 3385. See below.

28. See, for instance, the debate between Ibn 'Abbās and 'Alī regarding the optimal strategy of handling Mu'āwiya's position as governor of Syria before the declaration of war between the two parties. When Ibn 'Abbās advised the caliph to keep Mu'āwiya as governor until he gave his *bay'a*, and to dismiss him later, 'Alī refused this action as a compromise. Ibn 'Abbās then commented in exasperation, "Commander of the Faithful, You are a courageous man, but you are not an expert in war. Didn't you hear the Messenger of God say, 'Warfare is a strategy of guile! [*al-ḥarb khid'a*].'" Even with this, however, 'Alī refused to bend. Ṭabarī, I, 3086. The remark, used to characterize 'Alī, would later be used by 'Abd al-Malik b. Marwān when he analyzed his opponent Muṣ'ab b. al-Zubayr. Ṭabarī, II, 805.

29. Ṭabarī, I, 3108. Brockett, *HT,* XVIII, 48–49 (with minor variations).

30. See account of the embassy below. This line of debating the past has precedents dating to interactions between 'Alī and 'Abdallāh b. 'Abbās soon after the Prophet's death and later after 'Umar's death, when the latter reportedly chided 'Alī for not having asked the Prophet where the succession should go, and for having agreed to enter in the *shūrā* after 'Umar's death.

31. Ṭabarī, I, 3294. Hawting, *HT,* XVII, 41. The identical tenor and substance of these statements, attributed variously to reports by Sayf and Abū Mikhnaf, should erase any broad confidence that these narratives belonged to these narrators. The break in Ṭabarī's *isnād* from Sayf to Abū Mikhnaf after the Battle of the Camel seems very artificial.

32. That 'Alī permitted the enemy to drink from the wells in his camp was undoubtedly meant to be read symbolically as an unwitting sanction that they would eventually inherit the caliphate. This allusive tangent ran parallel to the great anxiety surrounding the situation at the Taḥkīm when 'Alī showed his willingness to compromise by erasing his name as caliph from the document against all the warnings of his advisors that such an action reflected ominously on his future rule. Similar warnings are made about 'Alī's decision to abandon Medina as the caliphal center in favor of Kufa, predicting that if he does that he will never go back to Medina.

33. Ibn 'Asākir, XLII, 452–455.

34. The direct treachery at Ṣiffīn, for example, is attributed more to 'Amr b. al-'Āṣ, who is considered of an inferior class background in comparison with Mu'āwiya.

35. Ṭabarī, I, 3278. On a general level, Mu'āwiya would even admit that he does not command as much "*faḍl*" (merit) as 'Alī and that the community recognizes that (*lastu adda'ī annī mithlahu fī'l-faḍl*). Dīnawarī, 172.

36. 'Alī's main speech to the delegation goes as follows: "God sent Muḥammad with the truth and through him provided deliverance from error, salvation from destruction, and the overcoming of division. Then God took him to Himself after he had carried out his mission. The people appointed Abū Bakr as caliph, and Abū Bakr appointed 'Umar after him, and those two conducted themselves well and led the community with justice. We resented their ruling over us, the family of the Messenger of God, but we excused them for that. Then 'Uthmān ruled and did things that the people found reprehensible, so that they came to him and killed him. Afterward they came to me, while I was keeping out of their concerns [*wa anā mu'tazil umūrahum*], and they asked me to accept the oath of allegiance. I refused, but they insisted and said that the community would never find anyone acceptable but me, and that if I did not, they were afraid that the division would result. So I accepted the oath of allegiance from them. But then I was surprised to find dissension of two of those who had given me the oath of allegiance and the opposition of Mu'āwiya, to whom God had given neither precedence [*ṣābiqa*] in accepting the religion nor forebears of good character in Islam [*wa lā salafu*

*ṣidqin*]. He is one of those who were set free [*ṭalīq*] by the Prophet, and the son of one of them, a member of those 'parties' [*ḥizbun min hādhihi al-aḥzāb*] that persisted in enmity to God, His Prophet, and the Muslims, both he and his father, until they reluctantly entered Islam. But it is a surprise that you take part in his opposition and are led by him, abandoning the family of your Prophet, against which you must not show discord and opposition nor place anyone on the same level. I call you to the Book of God, the precedent of His Prophet, the suppression of what is false, and putting into practice the signs of the religion. That is what I have to say, and I ask God's pardon for me and for you and for every Believer." Ṭabarī, I, 3278. Hawting, *HT,* XVII, 25–26. Dīnawarī preserves only a brief two lines describing this visit, naming the same delegation, and treats it as a secondary account of the central debate between 'Alī and the enemy delegation. The more primary debate that Dīnawarī focuses on centers on the visit of the Syrian ascetic Abū Muslim al-Khawlānī, to be recounted below. Dīnawarī's abbreviated version of Ḥabīb b. Maslama's debate with 'Alī shows an angry exchange between the two, lacks the methodical debate and Qur'ānic allusion to be found in Ṭabarī, and conflates it with the account wherein 'Alī declares that he is unable to surrender the murderers of 'Uthmān because there are twenty thousand of them. Dīnawarī, 181–182.

37. 'Alī's remark at the beginning, in which he recognizes the righteous government of Abū Bakr and 'Umar even though the right of the family of the Prophet was overriden, touches on a key debate in the ninth century about the legitimacy of the caliphate of the less "excellent" (*al-afḍal wa'l-mafḍūl*). Discussion of this question not only was the basis on which a certain agreement was reached on reconciling the positions of 'Alī, Abū Bakr, and 'Umar but was extended by Sunnīs to justify even the caliphate of Mu'āwiya, since he commanded important political strategic skills.

38. Ṭabarī, I, 3279. Hawting, *HT,* XVII, 26. Naṣr b. Muzāḥim al-Minqarī, *Waq'at Ṣiffīn*, ed. A. M. Hārūn (Cairo, 1962), 202. Minqarī's account has 'Alī say only, "I do not say that [*lā aqūlu dhalika*]." On the whole, Minqarī's account redacts the accounts in favor of 'Alī.

39. Qur'ān 27:80–81.

40. Ṭabarī, I, 3279. Hawting, *HT,* XVII, 26.

41. Ṭabarī, I, 3152.

42. From there begins the negative portrayal of the expert Qurrā' in the sources, with the two main attributes ascribed to them being that they are overly proud and prone to parsing interpretation (*ta'wīl*). The caliph 'Umar tends to be the voice most often used against the extremists in this group. For a sampling of such commentaries, see al-Hindī, *Kanz*, X, 268 (no. 29404), 271 (no. 29417). The selection is placed under the topic of the drawbacks of knowledge (*āfāt al-'ilm*). The Khārijites were also prone to citing an apt Qur'ānic verse in artful response to a dispute. See the example of al-Mustwarid b. 'Ullafa in A.H. 42/A.D. 662. Ṭabarī,

II, 43. A critique of ʿAlī's erudite citation of the Qur'ān is indirectly conveyed in a different narrative that centers on the dispute between ʿAlī and Ibn ʿAbbās. After ʿAlī reportedly found out that Ibn ʿAbbās had tapped into the governorship's fund, he rebuked him in a particularly scathing letter that was filled with rhetorical flourish (the letter actually opens with ʿAlī's invocation of a Qur'ānic verse as a parable perhaps about the situation he was about to address). Although Ibn ʿAbbās usually responded effectively to such challenges, in this particular case he is not quoted defending his position as strongly as ʿAlī does. However, Ibn ʿAbbās does manage to win this debate as well by cautioning ʿAlī to refrain from further slander and stylized comparisons (with the classical texts). Ibn ʿAbbās thus alludes to ʿAlī's habit of making such boastful rhetorical citings, however in that instance referring to ancient stories. Ibn ʿAbd Rabbihi, *al-ʿIqd*, IV, 359.

43. Ṭabarī, I, 2989.

44. Ṭabarī, I, 3292.

45. Ṭabarī, I, 3318.

46. Dīnawarī, 180. Balādhurī, *Ansāb (Banū ʿAbd Shams)*, I, 510.

47. Dīnawarī, 173. Minqarī, *Waqʿat*, 85–86. Minqarī adds that the messenger commented after leaving, "Now fighting has become permissible." This line naturally changes the nature of Abū Muslim's visit and probably reflects the later embellishments of Minqarī over Dīnawarī's account. After the breakout of the war, and during a lull in the fighting, Dīnawarī redescribes a similar goodwill embassy from Syria that was undertaken by Abū Umāma al-Bāhili and Abū'l-Dardā'. This version—which bears the same structure, albeit much briefer, as the embassy of Abū Muslim al-Khawlānī—also starts out as an independent initiative put forward first to Muʿāwiya, and then, when the two mediators visit ʿAlī, we are told that they were confronted with the scene of twenty thousand people declaring that they had killed ʿUthmān. This version ends with the statement that the two men thereafter abandoned the scene of the conflict and settled on an isolated coast. Dīnawarī, 181.

48. Dīnawarī's version of ʿAlī's reaction, as this description shows, did not dwell on any ambiguity in ʿAlī's position, and the narrative did not circle around artistic features of representation as the text of Ṭabarī does. Dīnawarī's version, unlike Ṭabarī's, shows ʿAlī answering to the point and describing a situation that was already out of control before he had even assumed the caliphate. ʿAlī's letter in response to Muʿāwiya also does not digress to defame the background of Muʿāwiya, as Ṭabarī's version does. Dīnawarī's version of the letter shows disappointment on the part of ʿAlī that ʿUthmān had died and argues directly to the point that Muʿāwiya's demand is no more than a political ploy.

49. Dīnawarī, 174.

50. Dīnawarī, 175. Minqarī, *Waqʿat*, 54–55.

51. Qur'ān 28:19. This verse, along with its wider context in Sūrat al-Qaṣaṣ (15–22)—starting with "*wa dakhala al-madīnata*," until "*fa-kharaja minhā khā'ifan*

*yatraqqab*"—is extensively used in Ṭabarī's narratives about the 'Alids, Khārijites, and the 'Abbāsid *da'wa* in Khurāsān. See Ṭabarī, I, 3366 (applied to the Khārijite Sharīḥ b. Awfā); II, 222 (applied to al-Ḥusayn); II, 1987 (applied during the war between Naṣr b. Sayyār and al-Kirmānī); and II, 1990 (applied to Abū Muslim entering Marw).

52. Ṭabarī, I, 3269. 'Alī's order to his troops after they took the wells: "Take only as much water as you need from the wells then return to your camp and let them take their share, for God has made us victorious over them because of their *baghy* and *ẓulm* [aggression and oppression]."

53. Dīnawarī, 173.

54. Dīnawarī, 161. A similar comment was made at 'Uthmān's assassination, when someone said, "Can the shedding of 'Uthmān's blood be permissible but his property remain safeguarded?" Balādhurī, *Ansāb* (*Banū 'Abd Shams*), 592. This then set in motion the robbery of 'Uthmān's house.

55. 'Alī's speech went as follows: "Do not fight them unless they attack you first. You, praise be to God, have a good case and holding back from fighting them until they attack will strengthen it. If you fight them and defeat them, do not kill the fugitives, do not finish off the wounded, do not uncover their nakedness, and do not mutilate the slain. If you reach their abodes, do not tear aside a curtain, enter a dwelling without permission, or seize any of their property apart from what you find in the army camp. Do not do harm against any woman, even if they utter abuse against your honor and vilify your leaders and righteous men, for women are weak of body and soul." Ṭabarī, I, 3282. Hawting, *HT*, XVII, 30.

56. 'Alī incited his troops as follows: "God has guided you to 'a commerce that will deliver you from a bitter punishment' [Qur'ān 61:10] and bring you to the verge of good: 'belief in God and His Messenger, and *jihād* in the path of God' [Qur'ān 61:11], may His name be exalted. He has made His reward a pardon of sin 'and blessed abodes in the gardens of Eden' [Qur'ān 61:12]. Then He has informed you that 'He loves those who fight in His path in lines as if they were a tightly compact building' [Qur'ān 61:4] so make your lines even like a tightly compact building. Advance the armed man and hold back the unarmed, and grit your teeth, for it makes the swords rebound from the heads. Twist the ends of the lances, for it better preserves the points. Avert your gaze, for that is more calming for the soul and more soothing for the heart. Deaden your voices, for that is better for driving out cowardice and more dignified. As for your banners, neither lower them nor abandon them, and make sure they stay in the hands of the valiant men among you. Those who defend what it is their duty to defend and are steadfast in protecting what it is obligatory for them to protect, they are the guardians who surround their banners and protect them, fighting on both sides of them, behind and in front of them, and not abandoning them. A man has given satisfaction who strikes his opponent hard—may God have mercy on you—

and puts his brother on a level with himself, and *does not leave his opponent to his brother*, so as to acquire blame and become base. And why is it that he should not act thus, one man fighting two opponents while another who has held back his hand leaves his opponent to confront his brother, he himself fleeing or standing looking on? Whoever does that, God hates him. So do not expose yourselves to the hatred of God, praise be to Him, for your place of return is only to God. God, the mightiest of those who speak, said to a people, 'Flight will not avail you if you flee from death or slaying; in that case you will be allowed to enjoy only a little time' [Qur'ān 33:16]. And I swear by God that, if you escape from the sword of this world, you will not escape from that of the next. Ask for the assistance of sincerity and steadfastness, for after steadfastness God sends down the victory." Ṭabarī, I, 3290–3291. Hawting, *HT*, XVII, 37–38. The italicized line indicates an eventuality that would happen in the description of battle soon afterward in which al-Ḥusayn distinguishes himself but al-Ḥasan holds back and 'Alī questions him about this. Ṭabarī, I, 3293.

57. Ṭabarī, I, 3298.

58. Ṭabarī, I, 3298.

59. Ṭabarī, I, 3298. Minqarī, 245–248. Minqarī's version is a lot more elaborate than Ṭabarī's. According to Ya'qūbī, Ibn Budayl died in the Battle of the Camel in A.H. 36/A.D. 656. *Ta'rīkh*, II, 182. That version, however, also gives a dramatized description of the event.

60. Ṭabarī, I, 3297.

61. Ṭabarī, I, 3297–3298. Stressing the moral value of intention (*niyya*), 'Ammār berates 'Amr b. al-'Āṣ for having sold out his religion in exchange for gaining appointment to the governorship of Egypt from Mu'āwiya, and adds: "You should look ahead to the day when people are judged according to their *niyya* what your judgment will be [*fa-unẓur idhā u'ṭiya al-nāsu 'alā qadri niyyātihim mā niyatuka*]." Ṭabarī, I, 3319. That heroism could be accomplished for tribal honor was a phenomenon earlier associated with the Meccans at Badr, when they originally insisted on carrying through with their march so that other tribes would hear of their military might. The Qur'ān alludes to this in the verse: "Be not as those who went forth from their habitations swaggering boastfully to show off to men [*alladhīn kharajū min diyārihim baṭaran wa riyā'a al-nās*]" (Qur'ān 8:47 [Arberry, I, 202]). Ṭabarī, I, 1288. The *ḥadīth* also warns against *riyā'* in battle. Tirmidhī (*kitāb faḍā'il al-jihād*), IV, 153 (no. 1646). Muslim, V, pt. 13 (no. 1905), 50.

62. Ṭabarī, I, 3313.

63. Ṭabarī, I, 3316.

64. This evokes the Qur'ānic reference to "*ḥamiyyat al-jāhiliyya*" and its wrongful basis. Among the tribe of Tamīm the comment was even more blunt—one soldier, Zaḥr b. Nahshal, encouraged them by saying, "Woe to you! If you are not fighting for religion, then fight for your noble name [*in lam tuqātilū 'alā al-dīn fa-qātilū 'alā al-aḥsāb*]." Dīnawarī, 195.

65. The focus on Rabīʿa as steadfast supporters of ʿAlī in battle may even have been intended to carry oblique unflattery. For while the tribe of Rabīʿa was the object of praise in the Battle of Qādisiyya (dubbed there "Rabīʿat al-Asad"), it is abundantly clear in Ṭabarī's narratives that they had been a key base of Musaylima's Ridda movement before, and that some of that clique represented by al-Ashaʿth b. Qays, a key supporter of the Ridda, would later insist that the Taḥkīm not consist of two arbitrators drawn from the tribe of Muḍar (recall the famous comment, "We will not allow that both arbitrators be drawn from the tribe of Muḍar [*lā yaḥkumu fīnā muḍariyyān*]"). Yaʿqūbī, II, 189. Earlier during the Ridda war, one supporter of Musaylima, while acknowledging the latter's deceitfulness, resigned himself on tribal grounds by declaring, "The liar of Rabiʿa is more well liked to us than the truthful man of Muḍar." Ṭabarī, I, 1937. With all the fluctuation in Rabīʿa's fortunes through history, first supporting the Ridda, then joining the Muslims at Qādisiyya, and later playing a pivotal role in the ʿAbbāsid revolution, it is left unclear where the narrators intended the innuendo about ʿAlī's movement to connect. The role of tribal zeal in the Ridda wars and at Ṣiffīn, however, seems likely to form a link behind the two phases of representation.

66. Ṭabarī, I, 3284–3285. Dīnawarī's version of a similar confrontation describes a father and son who encounter one another in a duel without knowing each other's identity, since they were covered with a helmet and armor. As the two throw one another from the saddle and fall to the ground, their helmets fall off and they recognize one another and stop fighting. Dīnawarī, 184. Dīnawarī's work, to a much greater extent than Ṭabarī and others, contains numerous stories about such individual confrontations (*mubāraza*) happening before the battle. The author's focus seems to have centered not only on showing the great hesitance among the conflicting camps to fight one another but also on highlighting the ironic turns of fate these oppositions engendered. One such incident he describes is when a Syrian soldier called Ḥujr al-Sharr found himself confronted by Ḥujr b. ʿAdī; the intention here was clearly to show the confrontation of two men with a similar name. Dīnawarī, 187.

67. Ṭabarī, I, 3303. Minqarī, 262.

68. Ṭabarī, I, 3347. Hawting, *HT,* XVII, 96–97 (with minor modification). It is not clear whether ʿAlī's speech was meant as a rebuke, as a somber eulogy, or as a combined reflection on the two camps. The Arabic evokes the tragic lot of both, but puts ʿAlī on a pedestal eloquently preaching, as usual. It is important to note that this speech, like many others of ʿAlī, has minimal rhyme (*sajaʿ*) but eloquent flow. Since rhyme was frowned upon as the method of poets and pretender prophets after Muḥammad (see ʿUmar's disparagement of it), it does not feature much in the early historical tradition. Rhyme, however, would have a bonanza in later Shīʿī depictions of ʿAlī's preachings and speeches.

69. Ṭabarī, I, 3348. Hawting, *HT,* XVII, 97.

70. Ṭabarī, I, 1331–1332. Muslim, VI (pt. 17), 206 (no. 2873). Bukhārī (*kitāb al-maghāzī*), V, 211 (no. 316). Al-Nasā'ī, *Sunan*, II, 446 (nos. 1962, 1963).

71. Another instance of resemblance to the Sīra (specifically to the story of the Battle of Uḥud) has already been noted: when the followers of 'Abdallāh b. Budayl reportedly displayed zealous concern upon hearing a rumor of the Prophet's death in battle. Ṭabarī, I, 3298, 1406–1407. See above.

72. Ṭabarī, I, 3373.

73. Qur'ān 5:24 (Arberry, I, 132).

74. Ṭabarī, I, 1300.

75. Of the Anṣār, according to Ya'qūbī, only two joined the camp of Mu'āwiya: al-Nu'mān b. Bashīr and Maslama b. Mukhallad. *Ta'rīkh*, II, 188.

76. Ibn Sa'd, II, 52.

77. Ibn Sa'd, II, 151; IV, 19. During preparations for the conquest of Mecca, the Prophet also reportedly commanded Abū Hurarya to call out: "Summon the Anṣār, and let none but an Anṣārī gather." Balādhurī, *Futūḥ*, I, 44–45. When the Anṣār gathered, it was clear that a battle with the Quraysh was about to be joined. Abū Sufyan's last-minute intercession, as is well known, averted war, but apparently the Anṣār briefly grumbled that the Prophet had grown soft regarding his kinsmen. The incident was similar to the argument over distributing the booty of Ḥunayn, and the Anṣār reportedly expressed regret for having challenged the Prophet's plan.

78. Ibn Sa'd, IV, 19.

79. Ibn Sa'd, II, 253.

80. Ibn Sa'd, II, 181. This segment is omitted in Ṭabarī's version of the farewell speech, but it must have been in origin absolutely critical for understanding the unraveling of Islamic history after the deaths of the Prophet, Abū Bakr, and 'Umar.

81. His standard comment on this topic: "O People of the Muhājirūn, You have become a crowd that continues to grow in number, but the Anṣār are the same group that they used to be [*innakum aṣbaḥtum tazīdūn wa aṣbaḥat al-anṣār lā tazidu 'alā hay'tihā allatī hiya 'alayhā*]. They represent my side of weakness [*al-yawma hum 'aybatī allatī awaytu ilayhā*]. Be kind to those who do good among them, and forgive their transgressors their errors [*akrimū karīmahum wa tajāwazū 'an musī'ihim*]." Ibn Sa'd, II, 251.

82. For a survey of the legendary evidence for the descent of the Anṣār from the sons of Hārūn, Naḍīr and Qurayẓa, see M. Gil, "The Origins of the Jews of Yathrib," *JSAI* 4 (1984): 203–220.

83. The history of the Jews and the Anṣār in Medina remains caught up in factual readings that accept the purported distinctions of social groups given in the narratives, and so in the traditional references the Jews in Medina (the Banū Qurayẓa, Banū al-Naḍīr, etc.) continue to be viewed as an altogether different set of people from the tribal factions of Medina (the Anṣār). To fully appreci-

ate the foundation of an alternative interpretation one would have to describe a process of anti-Jewish polemic in the early ʿAbbāsid period that crafted a schismatic process in the Sīra and later showed how ʿAlī and Sunnism in general had to cope with these lingering zealous and schismatic trends. Examples of traditional literature that follow a factual reading for Jewish history are G. Newby, *A History of the Jews of Arabia: From Ancient Times to Their Eclipse Under Islam* (Columbia, SC, 1988), 78–96. N. Stillman, *Jews of Arab Lands*, 3–21. S. D. Goitein, *Jews and Arabs* (New York, 1974), 62–67; M. Cohen, *Under Crescent and Cross: The Jews in the Middle Ages* (Princeton, 1994), 22–24, 52–58; M. Gil, "The Medinan Opposition to the Prophet," *Jerusalem Studies in Arabic and Islam* 10 (1987): 65–67, where the author declares arbitrarily that the "Muslim traditions are most trustworthy" on these matters. A mild exception to these traditional readings is the tangential comment of P. Crone about storytellers in the early Islamic period and their instrumental role in shaping the well-known narrative about Meccan commerce during the Sīra. "They [i.e., storytellers]," she writes, "must also have invented something, possibly everything, about the position of the Jews" (*Meccan Trade*, 218–219). Also relevant is the attitude of Bernard Lewis, who seems to place little credence in the historicity of narratives about the Jews of Arabia that is ascribed in the Muslim historiographical tradition, and asserts that the Arabian Jews were probably few in number and are virtually unknown in Jewish historiography. *The Jews of Islam* (Princeton, 1984), 74, 86. J. Wansbrough, *Qur'ānic Studies* (Oxford, 1977), 51. Another scholar notes that the Jews of Ḥijāz made no contribution to the history of Talmudic discussions. A. J. Wensinck, *Muhammad and the Jews of Medina*, trans. and ed. Wolfgang H. Behn, 2nd ed. (Berlin, 1982), 37. Also, D. S. Margoliouth, *The Relations Between the Arabs and Israelites Prior to the Rise of Islam* (Oxford, 1924), 67–70.

84. In this context it is worth noting the letter that Muʿāwiya reportedly sent to Qays b. Saʿd b. ʿUbāda during the war with ʿAlī in which he calls Qays "the Jew and son of a Jew." Ibn ʿAbd Rabbihi, *al-ʿIqd*, IV, 338. Balādhurī, *Ansāb* (*Banū ʿAbd Shams*), 33 (quoting al-Madāʾinī). Ibn Qutayba, *ʿUyūn al-Akhbār*, II, 232 (quoting Ibn al-Kalbī). Generally during the Sīra, however, the Anṣār are referred to as "clients of the Jews" (*mawālī yahūd*).

85. Sayf b. ʿUmar, *Kitāb al-Ridda wa'l-Futūḥ*, I, 18; al-Hindī, *Kanz*, X, 268 (no. 29403). For the Islamic perception of the Qurrāʾ in the biblical period, see Ṭabarī, I, 592, 660. See also the relevant *ḥadīth*, which states, "The largest group of the *munāfiqūn* are the *qurrāʾ* [*inna akthara munāfiqī hādhihi al-umma la-qurrāʾuhā*]." Aḥmad, *Musnad*, XXVIII, 628. A statement of political advice also explains the unsuitability of the Qurrāʾ for holding government posts. Ibn Qutayba, *ʿUyūn al-Akhbār*, I, 71.

86. It is not coincidental that ʿUthmān is said to have been reading *sūrat al-baqara* when he was killed by the assassins (a group that foreshadows the Qurrāʾ and the Khārijites). Ṭabarī, I, 3021. Balādhurī, *Ansāb* (*Banū ʿAbd Shams*), 591. Here

one should mention the *ḥadīth* that has the Prophet declare, "No prophet has guarded my community as carefully as Moses has done." Suyūṭī, *al-Jāmiʿ al-Ṣaghīr*, 87 (no. 1407).

87. In Aḥmad's *Musnad* one tradition about the Taḥkīm describes the Khārijites as being the same group as the Qurrāʾ (*fa jāʾathu al-khawārij wa naḥnu nadʿūhum yawmidhin al-qurrāʾ*). *Musnad*, XXV, 348.

88. When they heard about the news of the Khārijite murder of ʿAbdallāh b. Khabbāb and his family, Ṭabarī says, the followers of ʿAlī declared (*fa-qāma ilayhi al-nās*): "O Commander of the Faithful, Are you going to let these people be in charge of our wealths and families when we are away? Let us first march against them and then when we are done with them we shall march against our enemy in Syria [*ʿalāma tadaʿ haʾulāʾ warāʾanā yakhlufūnanā fī-amwālinā wa ʿiyālinā? sir binā ilā al-qawm fa-idhā faraghnā mā baynanā wa baynahum sirnā ilā ʿaduwwinā min ahl al-shām*]." Ṭabarī, I, 3375.

89. Ṭabarī, I, 3385.

90. Ṭabarī, I, 3410. Hawting, *HT*, XVII, 162.

91. Ṭabarī, I, 3409–3410. Hawting, *HT*, XVII, 162.

92. Ṭabarī, I, 3411–3412. Hawting, *HT*, XVII, 163–164.

93. Qur'ān 44:30–32 (Arberry, II, 208).

94. Qur'ān 7:137 (Arberry, I, 186–187).

95. "Moses, We will not endure one sort of food; pray to thy Lord for us, that he may bring forth for us of that the earth produces—green herbs, cucumbers, corn, lentils, onions" (Qur'ān 1:57 [Arberry, I, 36]).

96. "and they came upon a people cleaving to idols they had. They said, 'Moses, make for us a god, as they have gods.' Said he, 'You are surely a people who are ignorant.' Surely this they are engaged upon shall be shattered, and void is what they have been doing" (Qur'ān 7:134 [Arberry, I, 187]).

97. "And when you said, 'Moses, we will not believe thee till we see God openly'" (Qur'ān 2:52 [Arberry, I, 35]).

98. "They said, 'Moses, there are people in it very arrogant: we will not enter it until they depart from it; if they depart from it then we will enter. . . . We will never enter it so long as they are in it. Go forth, thou and thy Lord, and do battle; we will be sitting here'" (Qur'ān 5:25–29 [Arberry, I, 131–132]).

99. Ṭabarī, I, 3331. Dīnawarī, 203.

100. If these events realistically happened on a battlefield (i.e., the conversation between ʿAlī and the dissenters), and encompassed the differentials of space and private vs. public decisions, these doubts about ʿAlī would not have been possible, since the dissenters and ʿAlī would only have seen but not heard what ʿAlī's messenger said to al-Ashtar while far away. However, ʿAlī's answer, "Didn't you hear me command him in front of you," eliminates any possibility that ʿAlī merely placated them. The conversation and the emphasis on the sincerity of ʿAlī would have been apparent only in a situation where all these events could

be compressed within a stage setting, where an audience would have seen all actors in proximity to one another and overhearing one another. Only in this context would the refusal of the dissenters in 'Alī's camp gain its full meaning as a stubborn answer reflective of the transformed followers and reminiscent of the ancient Israelites.

101. Ṭabarī, I, 3331.

102. It is important to note here that at no point are the prospective dissenters yet referred to as "Khārijites." The acceptance of the call for the Taḥkīm comes generically from his followers ("*qālū* . . ."). Ṭabarī, I, 3329–3330.

103. Ṭabarī, I, 3332. Hawting, *HT*, XVII, 81.

104. As the well-known *ḥadīth* states, "There is among you one who will fight over the interpretation of the Qur'ān as I did over its revelation." Aḥmad, *Musnad*, XVIII, 296. *Ta'wīl* was not a favored method for adducing a sound judgment, according to Sunnī Islam (Ibn 'Abd al-Barr, *Jāmi'*, II, 194). 'Umar had reportedly once told Ibn 'Abbās, "I had thought of appointing you to a provincial governorship, but I feared that you might use the revenues of the conquered lands [*al-fay'*] according to your *ta'wīl*." The account then describes how when 'Alī appointed Ibn 'Abbās to the governorship of Basra, the latter did in fact appropriate a share of the revenue as his right because of his kinship relation to the Prophet. Ibn 'Abd Rabbihi, *al-'Iqd*, IV, 354. The report is attributed to Abū Bakr b. Abī Shayba.

105. Ṭabarī, I, 2989.

106. The analogy between the situations of the two caliphs also relates to descriptions of their debates with opponents. 'Alī's debate with the Khārijites later, although partially plausible, is meant to echo the challenges of the Kufan zealots to 'Uthmān. The Kufan zealots (*al-mutasammitūn*), according to Ṭabarī's narratives, later become the Qurrā' and the Khārijites.

107. Ṭabarī, I, 3359.

108. 'Alī tried to resist the appointment, telling his followers: "You have challenged me at the start of this, so don't challenge me on this issue." However, al-Ash'ath insisted: "We don't accept anyone other than him." Ṭabarī, I, 3333.

109. The various series of episodes describing first the Kufan demand that 'Uthmān appoint Abū Mūsā al-Ash'arī as governor of Kufa in place of Sa'īd b. al-'Āṣ, and later the Khārijite challenge to 'Alī at the Taḥkīm when he sought to appoint a skilled debater as his representative finds its root in the time when the Anṣār challenged the appointment by the Prophet of Usāma b. Zayd as leader of the first Syrian campaign. Although during the Prophet's lifetime the narratives do not identify the Anṣār as the group whom the Prophet debated and silenced over this issue (the group is only identified as *al-munāfiqūn*, the hypocrites), soon after his death they are directly identified when they repeat the same line of dissent with 'Umar. Ṭabarī, I, 1796, 1849. Aḥmad, *Musnad*, IX, 450.

110. Qur'ān 6:56.

111. Ṭabarī, I, 3278. Hawting, *HT*, III, 128.

112. *Nisbas* (tribal affiliations) are included in Muslim's version of the same *ḥadīth*. Here the name of Zayd al-Khayr al-Ṭā'ī and mention of another man of Banū Nabahān and a man of Banū Kilāb are added. Muslim, III (pt. 7), 161 (no. 1062).

113. This man is identified as "dhū'l-khuwayṣira" in a *ḥadīth* that gives a variant on the same theme but under different circumstances. In that version the Prophet foretells in a story the coming of al-Mukhaddaj, the famous Khārijite leader who is killed at al-Nahrawān. Bukhārī (*bāb al-manāqib*), IV, 517 (no. 807). The *ḥadīth* is narrated on the authority of Abū Sa'īd al-Khidrī. Aḥmad, *Musnad*, XVIII, 95. The account is also in the Sīra (reported by Ibn Isḥāq), where Dhū'l-Khuwayṣira is identified as a member of the Banū Tamīm. Ibn Hishām, *Sīra*, IV, 136.

114. Bukhārī, V, 448–449 (no. 638); on the authority of Abū Sa'īd al-Khidrī. Muslim (*bāb i'ṭā' al-mu'allafa wa man yukhāfu 'alā īmānihi*), III (pt. 7), 162–163 (no. 1064). Aḥmad, *Musnad*, XVIII, 192, 227–228. There are variant versions of this *ḥadīth* (Ibn Sa'd's version reads: "*sayakūn min ba'dī min ummatī qawmun yaqra'ūna al-qur'ān lā yujāwiza ḥulūqahum yakhrujūn min al-dīn ka-mā yakhruju al-sahm min al-ramya . . . hum shirāru al-khalqi wa'l-khalīqa . . .*" [Ibn Sa'd, VII, 29–30]). In one version the zealous critic of the Prophet is reported saying, when the booty was divided, "This is a division that was not intended to please God." This made the Prophet grow very angry but just say, "May God's mercy be upon Moses. He was hassled in even worse ways but kept patient." Bukhārī, VIII, 234 (no. 348). Muslim, III (pt. 7), 158 (no. 1062). The event is set at the division of the booty after the Battle of Ḥunayn. An earlier version of this *ḥadīth* identifies the zealot as a man of the Anṣār; *Ṣaḥīḥ*, 204 (no. 306). Other versions on the authority of al-Bukhārī include: VI, *kitāb faḍā'il al-Qur'ān*, 519–520 (nos. 577, 578); IX, *kitāb al-tawḥīd*, 489 (no. 651); here the zealots are identified as coming from the east and having in common their shaving of the head. In another version, the Prophet, reportedly describing the emergent zealous faction of the Ḥarūriyya, points to Iraq and says, "They will emerge from there." Aḥmad, *Musnad*, XXV, 351. Ṭabarī's full version of the confrontation with the man from Banū Tamīm (*dhū'l-khuwayṣira*) is set in the year A.H. 8 after the Battle of Ḥunayn. Ṭabarī, I, 1682. Ibn Ḥumayd←Salama←Muḥammad b. Isḥāq←Abū 'Ubayda b. Muḥammad←Miqsam Abī'l-Qāsim mawlā 'Abdallāh b. al-Ḥārith b. Nawfal. Of related thematic relevance to this story is Ṭabarī's report about Sa'd b. 'Ubāda's direct, albeit milder, questioning of the Prophet regarding why the Anṣār were not given as much booty as they deserved. Ṭabarī, I, 1684.

115. Ṭabarī, I, 3373–3375. Ibn Sa'd, V, 246.

116. Ṭabarī, I, 3375. A variant story describes a similar Khārijite attack on a *dihqān* called Zādān Farrūkh. Ṭabarī, I, 3423.

117. This is specifically mentioned by Ibn Sa'd, V, 246.

118. Ṭabarī, I, 3361.

119. Ṭabarī, I, 3084. Here the reader would have been expected to recognize echoes from some dissident voices at the scene of the treaty of al-Ḥudaybiyya. When the Prophet conceded to establishing this treaty, we are told that 'Umar b. al-Khaṭṭāb on that occasion, ever the unbending voice in the Islamic camp, voiced criticism of the event when he told Abū Bakr, "Are we not Muslims and they are the polytheists?" When Abū Bakr said, "Yes," 'Umar answered: "Then why are we yielding to the lower position?" Abū Bakr here reprimanded 'Umar, but the latter would not budge, and then came to the Prophet and told him the same thing ("'*alāma nu'ṭī al-daniyyata fī dīninā*?"), to which the Prophet answered: "I am the servant of God and His messenger. I will not disobey His rule and He will not let me go astray [. . . *lan ukhālifa amrah wa lan yuḍayyi'anī*]." Here 'Umar reportedly felt very guilty about challenging the Prophet and humbly gave in. Ṭabarī, I, 1545–1546. Muslim, IV (pt. 12), 141 (no. 1785); Bukhārī's most detailed version of this event is given under the heading (*bāb al-shurūṭ fī'l-jihād wa'l-muṣālaḥa*), III, 568 (no. 861). Other versions given by Bukhārī, however, unlike the former, do not show 'Umar guilt-ridden over his second-guessing of the Prophet. Bukhārī (*kitāb al-tafsīr*), *bāb qawlihi 'idh yubāyi'ūnaka taḥt al-shajara'*, VI, 348 (no. 367); (*kitāb al-khums*), IV, 272 (no. 406). Aḥmad, *Musnad*, XXV, 340. This story was integrally tied to later events in the way it showed the Prophet being guided, and himself more prone, to the strategic choice, unlike the unlucky 'Alī later. Although 'Alī and 'Umar share the same puritanical language, it is shown that such "puritanism" could be at times misplaced, and that in time the Khārijites would prove to be the followers in this zealous tradition. 'Umar's presence and his comments at al-Ḥudaybiyya are consonant with his image as the initial patron of the Kufan tradition of ultra-religiosity. Wāqidī's account of 'Umar's behavior at al-Ḥudaybiyya describes a muffled beginning for Shī'ism that almost was associated with 'Umar. In an account reportedly told by 'Umar to Ibn 'Abbās (typically set at a late time, in 'Umar's reign), 'Umar states that he almost rebelled at that juncture of compromise. "Had I found anyone supporting me that day in the pursuit of this cause," 'Umar reportedly said, "I would have broken with the community [*wa law wajadtu dhalika al-yawma shī'a takhruju 'anhum raghbatan 'an al-qaḍiyya la-kharajtu thumma ja'ala allāh 'āqibatahā khayran wa rushda wa kāna rasūl allāh a'lam*]." Wāqidī, *Maghāzī*, II, 607. 'Umar's usage of the term "*shī'a*" to refer to potential partisans in the perilous context of what he deemed at the time to be a valid religious controversy was no doubt calculated in the narrative to evoke the eventual error of the Shī'ī and Khārijite positions later on. See above on 'Alī's comparison of the Taḥkīm with al-Ḥudaybiyya. The Prophet later affirmed his unwavering abidance by the treaty of al-Ḥudaybiyya much as 'Alī recognized the Taḥkīm later. Ṭabarī, I, 1548. 'Alī's adamant refusal to allow Mu'āwiya to continue serving as governor was also intended to be a repeat of 'Umar's earlier refusal to let Khālid b. al-Walīd remain in a position of military command ('Umar's comment: "*lā yalī lī 'amalan abadan*"). Ṭabarī, I, 2148. The lesson that 'Umar eventually

learned about his mistaken decision at the time, however, was clearly intended by the narrators to appear as having been lost on ʿAlī later on.

120. Ṭabarī, I, 3376.

121. Balādhurī, *Ansāb* (*Banū ʿAbd Shams*), 17. Ibn ʿAbd Rabbihi, *al-ʿIqd*, IV, 366–367; al-Jāḥiẓ, *al-Bayān wa'l-Tabyīn*, II, 115. Shihāb al-Dīn Aḥmad b. ʿAbd al-Wahhāb al-Nuwayrī, *Nihāyat al-Arab fī Funūn al-Adab*, ed. Muḥammad Rifʿat Fatḥallāh, 31 vols. (Cairo, 1923–1955), XX, 29–30.

122. A well-crafted story juxtaposing the situations in Muʿāwiya's and ʿAlī's camps describes the relationship between the leader and his followers as such: "Muʿāwiya summoned the community for a gathering in the mosque (when the hostilities with ʿAlī began), and declared to them, 'ʿAlī has mobilized against you with the people of al-ʿIraq, what do you all advise me to do?' . . . Not one of them spoke up, nor did they even look directly at him [i.e., in humility]. Amongst them, Dhū'l-Kilāʿ then spoke up, saying, 'O Commander of the Faithful, we entrust you with the sound judgment, and we act upon this with obedience [*ʿalayka al-ra'y wa ʿalaynā al-fiʿāl*].' " When ʿAlī made his summons to his followers and asked them the same as Muʿāwiya had asked of his followers, the story states, "every faction had its own opinion and they argued vehemently amid such a raucous that ʿAlī could not understand what was being said." ʿAlī then reportedly gave his reflections in the comment, "Muʿāwiya shall surely prevail over these people then." Ibn Kathīr, IV (pt. 8), 132.

123. Ṭabarī, I, 3354. Dīnawarī describes this problem in ʿAlī's camp briefly. Dīnawarī, 211.

124. After he was dismissed from office, Qays b. Saʿd reportedly traveled to Medina, where he discussed political matters with ʿAlī. Then when news of Ibn Abī Bakr's murder came to Medina, ʿAlī realized, Ṭabarī says, "that Qays had magnificent skill at strategy [*ʿarifa anna Qays b. Saʿd kāna yuwāzī umūran ʿiẓāman min al-mukāyada*]." Ṭabarī, I, 3392.

125. Ṭabarī, I, 3454.

126. Ṭabarī, I, 3438.

127. Ṭabarī, I, 3439.

128. Ṭabarī, I, 3439.

129. Ṭabarī, I, 3440.

130. Ṭabarī, I, 3441.

131. In various subtle ways the early chronicles tend to give Muʿāwiya's pretensions during the civil war some credible grounds and anticipate his regime. Later medieval chronicles continued further in that direction by commenting in apologetic terms on Muʿāwiya's challenge to ʿAlī. Ibn Kathīr is perhaps the most generous of the later orthodox writers in his interspersing the narrative with his own opinions. As he begins to describe the marauding attacks by Muʿāwiya's tribal affiliates on ʿAlī's territories in A.H. 39/A.D. 659—an action that is merely stated in the early chronicles to show the difficult situation of ʿAlī with

his followers—Ibn Kathīr seems to praise Mu'āwiya's actions. He prefaces the account of the raids by saying: "In that year, Mu'āwiya prepared many armies [*jahhaza juyūshan kathīratan*] and dispersed them to the frontier outposts of 'Alī b. Abī Ṭālib. He [i.e., Mu'āwiya] did that after he saw that 'Amr b. al-'Āṣ' agreement with Abū Mūsā to depose 'Alī had gained acceptance [*qad waqi'at al-mawqi'*], [and] thus thought himself deserving of [people's] loyalty, and because the armies of 'Alī, which were drawn from the Iraqis [*ahl al-'Irāq*], were not obeying ['Alī's] orders . . . In such a situation, [Mu'āwiya] thought himself more deserving than ['Alī] of leadership if the situation was to remain as such." Ibn Kathīr, IV (pt. 7), 331. In other words, Ibn Kathīr was saying, Mu'āwiya was doing 'Alī (and the community of Muslims) a favor in sending out these "armies" (raids) because he was allowing the opportunity for a better recentralization of the Islamic state. That 'Alī and Mu'āwiya were in conflict is not an issue for Ibn Kathīr anymore, since he considers the continuum of succession to the Umayyads in Syria acceptable and wants to use different arguments to prepare the legitimacy of Mu'āwiya. The elements of the Sunnī argument were all brilliantly deployed: 1) Mu'āwiya considered the agreement of the two arbitrators to be valid. 2) 'Alī was unable to hold together his followers and thus was a caliph without an army. 3) The situation in Iraq was leading to chaos and thus needed the Syrian army to step in to fill the security vacuum. All these factors made Mu'āwiya thus believe that he was more deserving than 'Alī of leadership [*awlā minhu idh kāna al-amru kadhalika*]. And still, with such wording, Ibn Kathīr hedges the religious sincerity of Mu'āwiya by implying that even if Mu'āwiya's opinion was a misreading of the situation, it was a carefully rationalized opinion—an *ijtihād* ["*awlā*" rather than "*aḥaqq*"]—and so Mu'āwiya was free of sin whatever the actual religious parsing of the situation was.

132. The failures in responding to Mu'āwiya's incursions were not always the result of delayed action. Sometimes they resulted from a commander dissembling to 'Alī's cause, such as when al-Musayyib b. Najba al-Fazārī allowed his opponent, a fellow tribesman ('Abdallāh b. Mas'ada al-Fazārī), to slip away from a besieged fortress after 'Abdallāh beseeched him to consider the importance of filial ties. Ya'qūbī, II, 196–197. When 'Alī heard of what had happened, he did little to punish Musayyib except to scold him for his *idhān* (duplicity), and then reassign him to a position of minor importance, that of collecting the charitable contributions (*ṣadaqa*) in Kufa.

133. The inclusion of these speeches varies among the medieval sources. A sampling can be found in the following literary works: Ibn 'Abd Rabbihi, *al-'Iqd*, IV, 66–81; al-Jāḥiẓ, *al-Bayān wa'l-Tabyīn*, II, 50–56; Ibn Qutayba, *'Uyūn al-Akhbār*, I (pt. 2), 256–258. Generally these speeches are listed among others that are attributed to Abū Bakr, Mu'āwiya, and al-Ma'mūn, and frequently the fabric of 'Alī's speeches is no different as religious exhortation from those attributed to the

other caliphs (especially al-Ma'mūn). There is little reference in most of these speeches to events or personalities that can connect their texts to the historical narrative (as for example in the famous speech of Ziyād b. Abīhi or even 'Alī's famous *khuṭbat al-jihād*). Later medieval writers such as Ibn al-Athīr and Ibn Kathīr omit nearly all of 'Alī's speeches, with the exception of the two speeches he makes after the death of Muḥammad b. Abī Bakr (it is quite telling that in these speeches 'Alī blasts the character of his followers [*ahl al-'Irāq*], which was a theme that strongly served Sunnī interest when taken out of the tragic context of the caliph's other speeches), and his final pious testament. Such later writers were clearly dubious about a component of *imāmī* philosophy in these speeches, and even more anxious about attributing to 'Alī through these profound speeches more religious wisdom than the other Rāshidūn. Earlier medieval chronicles, however, did not follow the same agenda of such strict orthodoxy. Ṭabarī, for example, while not including the whole range of wisdom sayings and speeches to be found in Ya'qūbī's *Ta'rīkh* or Ibn Abī'l-Ḥadīd's *Nahj al-Balāgha*, gives enough examples of these speeches to indicate the wider source from which they were extracted. The context of this earlier source was clearly not Shī'ī per se but parabolic and inspired by the prophetic storytelling techniques that praised 'Alī but did so within the tragic context of stories that emulated the histories of the prophets. The aim of that discourse was not simply to outline the worthiness of 'Alī for the caliphate, as Shī'ī sources would have it later, but to show the tragic turning away of 'Alī's community at key junctures in the fourth caliph's career.

134. Ya'qūbī, II, 202–204.

135. It is quite revealing that the best reply and compliment one listener, Jāriya b. Qudāma, could give to 'Alī after hearing him give one speech is to praise his eloquent style of teaching ("*fa-ni'ma al-adabi adabuka*"). Ya'qūbī, II, 198.

136. Ṭabarī, I, 3412. Hawting, *HT*, XVII, 164–165.

137. The reference here is indirectly ironic, as the narrator evokes the Sīra tradition about angelic support that the Prophet received at the Battle of Badr.

138. Ṭabarī, I, 3412–3413. Hawting, *HT*, XVII, 165.

139. One is reminded here of Muḥammad's strategy of gaining the gradual cooperation of the group described as "*al-mu'allafatu qulūbuhum*" (the tentative converts), a strategy that would have been viewed not only as a historical event dealing with a group of tentative converts but as an everyday example that confronted the ruler within his own community.

140. Qur'ān 9:33; 6:19.

141. Qur'ān 6:162–163.

142. Qur'ān 3:102–103.

143. Qur'ān 2:83.

144. Qur'ān 5:2.

145. Ṭabarī, I, 3162–3163. Hawting, *HT*, XVII, 220–222.

## 7. FROM CALIPHATE TO KINGSHIP: 'UMAR'S REIGN AND FUTURE CHANGES

1. Qur'ān 31:20.

2. Qur'ān 17:70.

3. Qur'ān 8:26.

4. Ṭabarī, I, 2761. No *isnād* is here given. Smith, *HT,* XIV, 126–127.

5. Ṭabarī, I, 2772. Smith, *HT,* XIV, 139.

6. Ibn al-Athīr, II, 404.

7. Ṭabarī, I, 2229. Friedmann, *HT,* XII, 22–23.

8. Ṭabarī, I, 2544. Juynboll, *HT,* XIII, 125.

9. 'Umār's warning regarding the potential loss of the kingdom parallels a similar cautionary message that Jesus gave to the Pharisees after concluding the parable of the vineyard and the tenants when he told them, "I tell you that the kingdom of God will be taken away from you and given to a people who will produce its fruit." Matthew 21:43.

10. Ṭabarī, I, 2751. Smith, *HT,* XIV, 117. Al-Ḥārith←Ibn Sa'd←Muḥammad b. 'Umar←Usāma b. Zayd b. Aslam←Usāma's father←Usāma's grandfather. Ibn Sa'd, III, 296. Muḥammad b. 'Umar [al-Wāqidī]←Usāma b. Zayd b. Aslam←his father←his grandfather.

11. Ṭabarī, I, 2777. Smith, *HT,* XIV, 144.

12. Ṭabarī, I, 2782.

13. Ṭabarī, I, 2781.

14. Ṭabarī, I, 2779. 'Umar declares, "If he [Ṭalḥa] comes within the three days, include him in your decision. If the three days go by and he does not come, make the decision nevertheless. Who will deal with Ṭalḥa for me?" "I shall," responded Sa'd b. Abī Waqqāṣ, "and he will not give a differing view, God willing." Ṭabarī, I, 2779. Smith, *HT,* XIV, 146.

15. This is followed up in the abbreviated version of the succession story with similar fears about Sa'd and 'Alī, but it is clear that these doubts were meant primarily for 'Uthmān and the others only to create an equitable attitude toward the companions.

16. This close coordination between some of 'Umar's statements and Jamā'ī-Sunnī ideas is also reflected in the role 'Umar gives to his son, 'Abdallāh. With full awareness of the Sunnī deference to 'Abdallāh b. 'Umar's role in transmitting *ḥadīths*, 'Umar is shown giving his son an important symbolic position as arbitrator for the assembly in case the votes are split evenly. Ṭabarī, I, 2779. Although earlier in the text of his instructions 'Umar rejects appointing his son as successor in pious humility and insists that his son should occupy the role of no more than a counselor to the group (*wa yaḥḍur 'Abdallāh mushīran wa lā shay'a lahu min al-amr*), the statement evolves in the end to make Ibn 'Umar the tilting

factor in the votes in case of division. The text reflects the methods by which the narrators tried to address a variety of interests on the part of the audience that received these narratives.

17. See appendix II for full account of the *shūrā* story.

18. Ṭabarī, I, 2784. Smith, *HT,* XIV, 151.

19. The translation of this phrase follows the version of *al-'Iqd* (IV, 278).

20. Ṭabarī, I, 2784. Smith, *HT,* XIV, 151–152. Sa'd, enacting 'Umar's prodding role at the Saqīfa, did not like the tentative nature of 'Abd al-Raḥmān's statement and/or that 'Alī may get appointed, so he asserted in clear 'Umarī decisiveness, "I am afraid that weakness has overcome you. Do as you think best. You know what 'Umar's deathbed instructions were." Ṭabarī, I, 2784. Smith, *HT,* XIV, 151. Sa'd's hints of doubt here bring to mind 'Umar's claim that the Prophet's illness had grown strong just as the latter began expressing an interest in writing down a covenant that seemed to concern the name of an official successor. 'Umar's claim is "*innahu yahjur.*"

21. There Abū Bakr declared, "I am pleased [to offer] you one of these two men [i.e., Abū 'Ubayda and 'Umar]; render your oath of allegiance to any one of them you like." Ṭabarī, I, 1823. Poonawala, *HT,* IX, 193.

22. An added clarification report on the *shūrā* scene explains that 'Amr b. al-'Āṣ met with 'Alī during the period of consultation and told him, "The more you show [your] firm resolve, the less keen he is [i.e., 'Abd al-Raḥmān] [that you be appointed]. But [the more you say you will act according to (your) effort and ability, the more keen he is (that you be appointed)." Then 'Amr b. al-'Āṣ met with 'Abd al-Raḥmān and reportedly advised him of the soundness of giving the caliphate to 'Uthmān. Ṭabarī, I, 2795. Smith, *HT,* XIV, 161.

23. Ṭabarī, I, 2783. Smith, *HT,* XIV, 150.

24. Ṭabarī, I, 2786.

25. It is not certain whether the translation of this phrase is known.

26. Qur'ān 12:18.

27. Qur'ān 55:29.

28. Ṭabarī, I, 2786. Smith, *HT,* XIV, 153.

29. Ṭabarī, I, 1524.

30. Ṭabarī, I, 2786. Smith, *HT,* XIV, 153.

31. This statement was known as an Islamic tradition (*athar*). Ibn 'Abd al-Barr, *Jāmi'*, II, 174.

32. Ṭabarī, I, 2786.

33. Ṭabarī, I, 2776–2777. Smith, *HT,* XIV, 143–144.

34. According to Ibn 'Abd Rabbihi, after Hishām b. 'Abd al-Malik completed his pilgrimage, he stopped in Medina, where he was told that Sālim b. 'Abdallāh b. 'Umar was gravely ill (the statement used to describe this situation, "*shadīd al-waja'*," is similar to 'Umar's characterization of Sālim, the *mawlā* of Abū Ḥudhayfa, as "*shadīd al-ḥubb li-allāh*)." Soon after the caliph visited him Sālim

died, and Hishām led the funeral prayer for him. Hishām then commented, "I don't know whether I feel more of a reward for having performed the pilgrimage or having led the funeral prayer for Sālim." This statement also draws on a parallel comparative phrasing from the Rāshidūn caliphate. Ibn 'Abd Rabbihi, *al-'Iqd*, IV, 447.

35. Ṭabarī, I, 2779. Smith, *HT*, XIV, 146. 'Umar's statements on the subject of succession are usually logically tendentious, such as when he shows concern that 'Uthmān might turn to appointing his kinsmen to positions of power (a summary of such statements is given in the story of 'Umar's conversation with Ibn 'Abbās about the succession). Ya'qūbī, II, 158. However, the characterization of 'Alī as someone at a disadvantage because of a sense of humor (if this expression has been transmitted and translated correctly [*dhū du'āba*]) remains the most obscure wording 'Umar ever made, since humor appears nowhere in the character of 'Alī. 'Umar's other description of 'Alī as someone who will carry the community on the firm path (*ṭarīq al-ḥaqq*) is perhaps more intelligible as an oblique criticism. What narrators were alluding to here was not 'Alī's overly confident attitude in his ability to interpret religion (such as in his statements at the *shūrā* when he declined to abide by the *sunna* of the first two caliphs), but rather his severe approach toward enforcing the letter of the law on some occasions, as he did when he flogged al-Walīd b. 'Uqba to an almost gratuitous degree for the offense of wine drinking. Balādhurī, *Ansāb* (*Banū 'Abd Shams*), 523. While 'Alī's talent as an expert religious judge was well recognized in traditionist texts, his extremist application of penalties was not always appreciated. Sunnī tradition allowed leeway for moderating sentences (such as in cases where there was reasonable doubt about the occurrence of an offense [following the principle of the famous dictum, "*idra'ū al-ḥudūd bi'l-shubuhāt*" (ward off severe penalties with the possibility of uncertainty)], a context of war for the transgression, or a plethora of methods that could be used to mitigate a sentence). Presumably negotiating such a reduced verdict also required the varied involvement of Sunnī jurists (or the collectivity of the companions during the early period) rather than the opinion of a single religious expert. This would have ultimately challenged 'Alī's monopoly on religious authority as well.

36. As 'Abd al-Raḥmān declared in his prologue to the negotiation with the companions, "A stratagem introduced into speech is more effective than swords in a wound [*inna al-ḥīlata fī al-manṭiq ablaghu min al-suyūf fī al-kalim*]." The statement in the second version of the *shūrā* continues where 'Umar b. Shabba's account stops. Ṭabarī, I, 2789. In another part of the account, the theme of political acumen is combined with praise for the 'Abbāsids. At the outset of the *shūrā*, 'Alī reportedly confides to al-'Abbās that the caliphate was about to be distanced from the Hāshimites ("'*adalat 'annā*," in 'Alī's words). When al-'Abbās inquired about what had happened, 'Alī described to him 'Umar's instructions about weighing votes in the case of a tie. Al-'Abbās then reminded 'Alī that he should

have listened to his (i.e., al-'Abbās') earlier advice not to join in the *shūrā*. That was the third political mistake 'Alī had committed by al-'Abbās' count, and it was now too late for 'Alī to do anything. Ṭabarī, I, 2781.

37. Aside from 'Uthmān's comments during the *shūrā* on this topic, one narrative attributes to him a speech announcing this. "Verily, I will be a follower, not an innovator [*innī muttabi' wa lastu bi-mubtadi'*]. Verily, you may demand three things from me, beyond [obedience to] the Book of the Almighty God and the way [*sunna*] established by His prophet. [First,] that I follow those who preceded me in matters that you have agreed upon and established [*wa inna lakum 'alayya . . . ittibā' man kāna qablī fī-mā ijtama'tum 'alayhi wa sanantum*]. [Second,] that I adhere to the path laid out by pious and virtuous men in matters that you have not established by general consensus [*wa sann sunnata ahl al-khayr fīmā lam tasunnū 'an mala'*]. [Third,] that I avoid coercion against you save in cases where you have deemed it necessary. Verily, this world is a verdant meadow that has been made to seem desirable to the people [*alā wa inna al-dunyā khaḍira qad shuhhiyat ilā al-nās*] and toward which many among them incline. Do not rely on this world and put no trust in it, for it is not a thing to be trusted. Know that it leaves nothing behind save him who has left it behind." Ṭabarī, I, 3058–3059. Humphreys, *HT*, XV, 256–257. This speech makes clear 'Uthmān's pursuit of the *sunna*, even when his innovations were considered to be problematic. The reference to the world as a verdant meadow shows that the composition of this speech was closely tied to the speeches by 'Umar and 'Abd al-Raḥmān wherein they speak of the vision of a garden and a trial.

38. One *ḥadīth* reportedly has the Prophet ask Bilāl to declare to the public that 'Uthmān would be the successor to 'Umar. Khaṭīb, *Ta'rīkh Baghdād*, VII, 429. Ibn Jurayj←'Aṭā'←Ibn 'Umar.

39. Ṭabarī, I, 2212–2213. The term "*radīf*" is explained by Ibn Manẓūr as having the meaning of "successor to the throne," in Persian kingship ("*ardāf al-mulūk hum alladhīna yakhlifūnahum fī'l-qiyām bi-amr al-mimlaka, bi-manzilat al-wuzarā' fī'l-islām*"). *Lisān al-'Arab*, IX, 117 (cited by M. Abū'l-Faḍl Ibrāhīm; Ṭabarī, IV, 480). Ibn Qutayba explains that "*al-radīf*" was an office that the kings of Ḥīra assigned to an individual from the tribe of Banū Tamīm who substituted for the king while the latter was on military campaign. Ibn Qutayba, *al-Ma'ārif*, 651.

40. Ṭabarī, I, 2948. Humphreys, *HT*, XV, 152.

41. Ṭabarī, I, 2947. Humphreys, *HT*, XV, 152.

42. Ṭabarī, I, 2558. Juynboll, *HT*, XIII, 138.

43. The similarity to 'Umar's words of caution is again worth stressing. Also remarkable here is the great similarity of this discourse with the famous cultural swipes of the Shu'ūbiyya (nationalist Persian movement) against the Arabs. Shu'ūbī writers, it will be recalled, narrowed the Arab contribution in history to the gift of prophecy, and argued otherwise for the more preeminent secular role of Persian writers in Islamic civilization (Ibn 'Abd Rabbihi, *al-'Iqd*, III, 405).

Thus what is couched in 'Umar's and Mu'āwiya's words as a pious Sunnī self-deprecation and admonition against pride seems to mesh with the Shu'ūbī cultural view in the ninth century.

44. It is worth noting that traditions on the authority of al-Zuhrī attributed in a tendentious way prior monarchal qualities to Abū Sufyān. This originates in an encounter with the Byzantine emperor, Heraclius, when the latter reportedly inquired of Abū Sufyān about the habits of the Prophet and especially if he broke his agreements during disputes with the Meccans. Abū Sufyān (in an aside told to the narrator) reportedly said that he was tempted to twist the truth on this issue but found that lying was not part of his honorable style. This type of explanation is consistent with the general lore of Ṭabarī and other chroniclers about the central quality of truthfulness in the code of behavior of kings. Abū Nu'aym, *Dalā'il al-Nubuwwa*, 343–346. Ḥabīb b. al-Ḥasan←Muḥammad b. Yaḥyā al-Marwazī←Aḥmad b. Muḥammad b. Ayyūb←Ibrāhīm b. Sa'd←Ṣāliḥ b. Kaysān←Ibn Shihāb al-Zuhrī←'Ubaydallāh b. 'Utba←'Abdallāh b. 'Abbās.

45. This secular perspective on hierarchy and definition of rank was also something that Islam eventually accommodated with the *ḥadīth* that states, "The elect in the Jāhiliyya are also the elect in the Islamic period if they become religiously knowledgeable [*al-nāsu ma'ādin, khiyāruhum fī'l jāhiliyya khiyāruhum fī'l-Islām idhā faqīhū*]." Bukhārī (*kitāb aḥādīth al-anbiyā'*), IV, 508 (no. 787); 388 (no. 593); 390 (no. 597); 461 (no. 700). The same *ḥadīth* is set in the context of a story referring to the generosity of Sa'd b. 'Ubāda. Wāqidī, *Maghāzī*, III, 1095. Another version of this *ḥadīth*, however, adds, "People should follow Quraysh in this matter [i.e., political leadership] [*al-nāsu taba'un li-Quraysh fī hādhā al-sha'n*]." Muslim (*bāb faḍā'il Yūsuf*), V (pt. 14), 134 (no. 2378).

46. Of relevance here is the formerly mentioned *ḥadīth* that declares, "*al-a'imma junna*." Mu'āwiya's full comment here is: "I have been told, however, that you are angry with Quraysh. But were it not for Quraysh, you would have returned to being lowly, like you were before. [The community leaders] are a shield for you [*al-a'imma junna*], so don't break with your *a'imma*, for they bear the burden of providing for you [*wa qad balaghanī annakum naqamtum qurayshan wa inna qurayshan in lam takun 'udtum adhillatan kamā kuntum. Inna a'immatakum lakum ilā al-yawmi junna*]." Ṭabarī, I, 2910.

47. Another example of this, one that created major controversy, was Mu'āwiya's declaration that tax revenues are "God's wealth" (*al-māl māl allāh*). As is well known, Abū Dharr was adamant that Mu'āwiya should not use this phrase even though Mu'āwiya claimed that his intention from the statement was in harmony with religion. "Aren't we the servants of God, and doesn't all wealth belong to God?," Mu'āwiya would reportedly ask Abū Dharr. However, the possibility that Mu'āwiya was referring to the caliph as "God's deputy" and that the wealth belonged to the caliph was indirectly the implication of this controversy.

'Uthmān also argued with the opposition over a similar controversy, according to the account of Abū Mikhnaf.

48. Ṭabarī, I, 2947.

49. Mu'āwiya can be seen as preparing the way for 'Uthmān's resistance when he rebukes the Kufans, saying, "If affairs were decided according to your opinion and wishes, things would not go well for the people of Islam either day or night [*law kānat al-umūr tuqḍā 'alā ra'iykum wa amānīkum ma istaqāmat al-umūr li-ahl al-Islām yawman wa lā laylatan*]." Ṭabarī, I, 2919. Humphreys, *HT,* XV, 123–125. In light of this, 'Uthmān's reluctance to bend to the challenges in Medina form the logical sequel when he tells the opposition, "I don't find myself any more in charge if I name officials whom you desire, and remove those hateful to you [*mā arānī idhan fī shay'in in kuntu asta'milu man hawaytum wa a'zilu man karihtum*]." Ṭabarī, I, 2989.

50. Ṭabarī, I, 3042. Humphreys, *HT,* XV, 242.

51. Ṭabarī, III, 780–782.

52. Ṭabarī, I, 2945.

53. Ṭabarī, I, 2945. Humphreys, *HT,* XV, 149.

54. It is worth noting that 'Umar is reported to have advised a similar policy when writing to none other than Mu'āwiya. 'Umar wrote to Mu'āwiya, "There is no better way for governing your subjects than to start out tough on both those close to you or distant, for easiness after a stern policy lends more immunity to the security of the subject population and general pardon after penalties makes them more loyal." 'Umar b. Shabba, *Ta'rīkh al-Madīna*, I, 411.

55. Ṭabarī, I, 2946.

56. In spite of his advocacy for the values of humility and equality, it is often overlooked that 'Umar also provided the tendentious, later 'Abbāsid argument of obedience to caliphal authority, which was styled as divinely sanctioned. The concept of "God's caliph," or "*sulṭān allāh*," although not a widespread element in Rāshidūn discourse (with the exception of 'Uthmān's caliphate, where the title is shown being misused by the caliph to appropriate authority), also appears occasionally in 'Umar's usages. In several instances 'Umar has confrontations with leading companions for being audacious in demanding things without proper permission or deference to the office of the caliph. Ibn Sa'd, III, 287, 309. Balādhurī, *Ansāb* (*Sā'ir*), 399, 424. Ṭabarī, I, 2754. Also relevant in this context is the *ḥadīth* that states, "The leader [or leadership in general, "*al-sulṭān*"] is the shadow of God on earth that provides a haven for those experiencing injustice. If the leader is just then he will be worthy of religious reward and the subjects have [*al-ra'iyya*] to show him gratitude. If he is unjust then he carries the religious blame ['*alayhi al-iṣr*] while the subjects must be patient [*wa 'alā al-ra'iyya al-ṣabr*]." Ibn Zanjawayh, *Kitāb al-Amwāl*, I, 77; Ibn Qutayba, '*Uyūn al-Akhbār*, I, 55 (the *ḥadīth* is related on the authority of Ibn Mas'ūd). This ideological position was no doubt

also formulated in response to the revolt against 'Uthmān. A pious saying attributed to Ḥudhayfa b. al-Yamān declares, "Those who strive to humiliate God's ruler on earth will be humiliated before their death comes." Ibn Qutayba, *'Uyūn al-Akhbār*, I, 78; Ibn Zanjawayh, *Kitāb al-Amwāl*, I, 85; Ibn 'Abd Rabbihi, *al-'Iqd*, I, 7; 'Umar b. Shabba, *Ta'rīkh al-Madīna*, II, 206 (related on the authority of Abū Nu'aym); Sayf b. 'Umar, *Kitāb al-Ridda*, I, 76. Aḥmad, *Musnad*, XXIV, 135 (Aḥmad also includes a simplified version of this statement). Ḥudhayfa's statement was no doubt crafted in light of the history of 'Uthmān's overthrow. The saying is attributed to Ibn 'Abbās in *Ta'rīkh Baghdād*, and couched within a wider statement of advice about necessary religious duties. Khaṭīb, *Ta'rīkh Baghdād*, VI, 76.

57. One such example can be found in Ziyād's first, and still somewhat lenient, speech, when he assumed the governorship of Kufa in A.H. 51/A.D. 671 after the death of al-Mughīra b. Shu'ba. Continuing for a while the same approach to ruling, Ziyād made a speech in which he declared, "Now then, indeed, we have been put to the test and we have tested. We have ruled and rulers have ruled us, and we have found that this matter would only be set right in the end by that which set it right at the beginning: tractable obedience, the same in secret as openly, when people are absent as when they are present, and [in] their hearts as [on] their tongues. We have found that only flexibility without weakness and strength without violence would reform the people [*ammā ba'd fa-innā qad jarrabnā wa jurribnā wa susnā wa sāsanā al-sā'isūn fa-wajadnā hādhā al-amr lā yaṣluḥ ākhiruhu illā bi-mā ṣaluḥa awwaluhu, bi'l-ṭā'ati al-layyina al-mushabbah sirruhā bi-'alāniyatihā wa ghaybi ahlihā bi-shāhidihim wa qulūbihim bi-alsinatihim wa wajadnā al-nās lā yaṣliḥuhum illā līnun fī ghayri ḍa'f wa shiddatun fī ghayri 'unf*]. I shall not undertake a matter with you unless I carry it out to its smallest detail. There is no lie to which God and the people are witness greater than the lie of an *imām* upon the pulpit." Ṭabarī, II, 114–115. Balādhurī, *Ansāb* (*Banū 'Abd Shams*), 244. Trans. M. Morony, *The History of al-Ṭabarī: Between Civil Wars, The Caliphate of Mu'āwiya* (Albany, 1987), XVIII, 125. The line about "*līn fī ghayri ḍa'f wa shiddatun fī ghayri 'unf*" comes clearly from the political language of 'Umar before. Ibn Sa'd, III, 344. Balādhurī, *Ansāb* (*Sā'ir*), 405. Sometimes, however, it is the speech of Ziyād that sets the standard, and is emulated earlier. An example of this is 'Umar's warning statement: "But [now] show us the best of your character, and we shall leave your secrets to God. For those who show us what is bad, yet claim that what they keep secret is good, will not be believed by us; as for those who show us something good openly, we shall think good of them [*aẓhirū lanā aḥsana akhlāqikum, wa allāh a'lamu bi-sarā'irikum, fa-innahu man aẓhara lanā 'alāniyyatan ḥasanatan ẓananā bihi ḥusnan wa man aẓhara lanā sū'an wa za'ama anna sarīratahu ḥasanatun lam nuṣaddiqhu*]." Balādhurī, *Ansāb* (*Sā'ir*), 417. Ṭabarī, I, 2759. Smith, *HT*, XIV, 125 (with some modification in the excerpted translation). A variant account given by Ibn 'Abd al-Ḥakam includes a statement with a similar message attributed to 'Umar. Ibn 'Abd al-Ḥakam; *Futūḥ Miṣr*, 167.

58. The most glaring example of this is a report given by Ibn Sa'd. His narrator states that he had happened to be visiting 'Umar with a group of three other Syrians (*min ahl al-shām*) after the group had performed the pilgrimage when news came to the caliph that the Iraqis (*ahl al-'Irāq*) had pelted their governor. This came after the caliph had already replaced their previous *imām* (i.e., the governor) with a new one. The narrator then describes how 'Umar became so distracted and preoccupied with this matter that he lapsed in the proper performance of the community prayer. 'Umar afterward addressed the crowd, saying, "O People of Syria [*yā ahl al-shām*], prepare to march against the Iraqis [*tajahhazū li-ahl al-'Irāq*], for Satan has come to thrive amongst them." Then he prayed, "O Lord, these people [i.e., the Iraqis] have made things impossible. Hasten the arrival among them of the Thaqafī man who will rule them by the law of the *jahīliyya*, who will neither reward the helpful amongst them, nor overlook the error of their wrongdoer." Ibn Sa'd, VII, 442. Abū'l-Yamān←Jarīr b. 'Uthmān←'Abd al-Raḥmān b. Maysara←Abū 'Adhaba al-Ḥaḍramī. Also, Ibn Qutayba, *al-Ma'ārif*, 397. That 'Umar was addressing his congregation in Medina as "*ahl al-shām*" gives a clear indication of the pro-Syrian tendentiousness of the account. It is also significant that later, in A.H. 94/A.D. 713, Ṭabarī gives an account that confirms this anti-Iraqi message. This occurs as he recounts the speech of 'Uthmān b. Ḥayyān al-Murrī when the latter was appointed governor of Medina and set about persecuting the Iraqis. The speech reiterates the words of 'Umar b. al-Khaṭṭāb toward Kufa, and recounts the troubles they presented throughout the Rāshidūn and early Umayyad periods. 'Uthmān's speech is presented in a way that captures not only the infamous political treachery of the Iraqis, but also their polemical and argumentative potency, which was as much a source of dissent and *fitna* within the community as their political prejudice. Of particular significance is an excerpt of the speech that quotes 'Umar b. al-Khaṭṭāb as saying, "Syria is dearer to me. I think that Iraq is an incurable disease; in it Satan has hatched [his brood] and they [i.e., the Iraqis] have made things difficult for me. I can see myself scattering them in the [various] territories. [But] then I say, 'If I were to scatter them, they would corrupt those into whose presence they enter by [using] argument and contention, [saying,] "How?" and "Why?" and by [their] swiftness of entering into sedition.'" Ṭabarī, II, 1257–1260. Trans. M. Hinds, *History of al-Ṭabarī: The Zenith of the Marwanid House*, (Albany, 1990), XXIII, 207–208. The account is narrated on the authority of al-Wāqidī.

59. The resemblance in some of the political language and authoritarian style of Ziyād b. Abīhi to 'Umar in the depictions of the historical narratives was something that narrators considered to reflect in part a deliberate emulation of the second caliph by Ziyād. A famous remark characterizing the career of Ziyād states, "Ziyād sought to emulate 'Umar and in doing this went to excess, and when al-Ḥajjāj emulated Ziyād, he brought ruin on the people." Ibn Qutayba, *'Uyūn al-Akhbār*, I, 451; al-Hindī, *Kanz*, XVI, 163.

60. Note the resemblance of Abū Sufyān's advice to Mu'āwiya, after the latter was appointed as governor of Syria by 'Umar, to the parallel situation of wise counsel from al-'Abbās to his son, 'Abdallāh, when he became an important member of 'Umar b. al-Khaṭṭab's entourage. Ibn 'Abd Rabbihi, *al-'Iqd*, IV, 365. Balādhurī, *Ansāb* (*Banū 'Abd Shams*), 11. Ibn Kathīr, IV (pt. 8), 122.

61. One telling assessment of the secular virtues of the Umayyads that eventually holds religious importance is given by the scholar Abū Bakr ibn 'Ayyāsh on the occasion when the caliph Hārūn al-Rashīd asked him, "You have caught up with the time of our rule, and you have experienced the days of Banū Umayya. Whose do you find better?" Ibn 'Ayyāsh replied, "Truly you keep up the ritual, but they were more beneficial to the people [*antum aqwam bi'l-ṣalāt wa ulā'ika kānū anfa' li'l-nās*]." Dhahabī, *Siyar*, VIII, 498. Another religious ascetic would stress the need for equity to the caliph al-Manṣūr by reminding him of the secret of success in Umayyad rule. The ascetic tells the caliph how the Umayyads used to address the grievances of a man treated unjustly for no interest in gaining religious reward, and only in pursuit of attaining the honorable name (*laysa fī dhalika ṭalabu thawāb illā iltimāsa makārim al-dunyā*). Ibn Bakkār, *al-Akhbār al-Muwaffaqiyyāt*, 328.

62. As he put it to the envoys of 'Alī in A.H. 37/A.D. 657 just before the Battle of Ṣiffīn, "You have summoned us to obedience and to rejoin the community. As for the community unity to which you have called us, we have it among ourselves [*fa-innakum da'awtum ilā al-ṭā'a wa'l-jamā'a, fa-ammā al-jamā'a allatī da'awtum ilayhā fa-ma'anā hiya*]." Ṭabarī, I, 3275.

63. Hence the title that Ibn 'Asākir would bestow on Mu'āwiya, "*khāl al-mu'minīn wa kātib waḥy rabb al-'ālamīn*" (the uncle of the believers and the scribe of divine revelation). Ibn 'Asākir, LIX, 55. Although the reference to Mu'āwiya as "the uncle of the believers" does not seem to be widely attested in the historical narratives about the first and second *fitnas*, it does appear to have been well understood within the fabric of the later narratives. When Ziyād b. Abīhi declared in his famous speech in A.H. 45/A.D. 665, upon assuming the governorship of Basra, "O people, we have become your rulers and protectors. We rule you by the authority of God which He gave us, and protect you with the wealth which He bestowed on us [*nadhūdu 'ankum bi-fay' allāh alladhī khawwalanā*]," he was most likely referring to the aforementioned maternal kinship or title attributed to Mu'āwiya (who was also Ziyād's alleged half-brother). Ṭabarī, II, 73–76.

64. Later traditions that exaggerate the religious merits of Mu'āwiya are varied. They include mentions that the Prophet predicted Mu'āwiya would rule, that Mu'āwiya used to pour the ablutions of the Prophet, and that he was the scribe of revelation. For a range of such *ḥadīths*, see Ibn Kathīr, IV (pt. 8), 126. Ibn 'Abd Rabbihi, *al-'Iqd*, IV, 364. As for Mu'āwiya's role as a scribe to the Prophet, Ṭabarī states that Mu'āwiya was a scribe for mundane matters, as was Khālid b. Sa'īd b. al-'Āṣ, but that the ones who wrote the *waḥy* were 'Alī, 'Uthmān, Ubayy

b. Ka'b, and Zayd b. Thābit. Ṭabarī, II, 836. As if to anticipate Mu'āwiya's role in leading Syria, he is also said to have been present on one occasion when the Prophet received the envoy of Heraclius, and to have read the Byzantine emperor's letter. Ibn Zanjawayh, *Kitāb al-Amwāl*, II, 585. Umayyad lore would later add the myth that it was Mu'āwiya who killed Musaylima, the leader of the apostate movement. Balādhurī, *Futūḥ*, I, 107. One report also claims that Mu'āwiya had converted relatively early during the year of al-Ḥudaybiyya, but that he kept his conversion secret from his father. Ibn Sa'd, VII, 406.

65. Other signals of 'Umar's endorsement of Mu'āwiya as a credible governor can be recognized in an extant document in which 'Umar advises Mu'āwiya about the proper manner for administering justice (especially notable is his statement, "seek to establish reconciliation among contenders when the case does not have a clear verdict [*wa uḥruṣ 'alā al-ṣulḥ bayn al-nās mā lam yastabin laka al-qaḍā'*])." Ibn 'Abd Rabbihi, *al-'Iqd*, I, 84–85; Wakī', *Akhbār al-Quḍāt*, ed. A. M. al-Murāghī, 3 vols. (Cairo, 1950), I, 74–75.

66. The same statement is attributed to 'Umar in his biography. Balādhurī, *Ansāb* (*Sā'ir*), 366. Ibn Sa'd, III, 275.

67. Although the verbal structure of the next clause is in the singular and thus refers more clearly to 'Umar, the Arabic syntax can allow that in this sentence 'Umar and the community are two different subjects (*wa law ra'ā dhalika amīr al-mu'minīn wa jamā'at al-muslimīn, la-katab ilayya*). This unusual reading is also plausible because 'Umar is never referred to as "*amīr jamā'at al-muslimīn*."

68. Ṭabarī, I, 2919. Humphreys, *HT*, XV, 123. This is Wāqidī's version of Mu'āwiya's declaration. Sayf b. 'Umar's version is even stronger, where it has Mu'āwiya saying to the opposition, "I reiterate to you that the Messenger of God was protected [from sin], and he bestowed authority upon me and brought me into his affairs [*kāna ma'ṣūman fa-wallānī wa adkhalanī fī amrihi*]. Then Abū Bakr was named his successor, and he bestowed authority upon me. 'Umar and 'Uthmān did the same upon their succession. I have not acted on behalf of any of them, nor did any of them put me in authority, without his being satisfied with me [*fa-lam ali li-aḥadin minhum wa lam yuwallinī illā wa huwa rāḍin 'annī*]. The Messenger of God sought for office only men fully capable of acting on behalf of Muslims [*wa innamā ṭalaba rasūl allāh li'l-a'māl ahla al-jazā'i 'an al-muslimīn wa al-ghanā' wa lam yaṭlub lahā ahla al-ijtihād wa al-jahl bihā wa al-ḍa'f 'anhā*]." Ṭabarī, I, 2913. Humphreys, *HT*, XV, 118.

69. It should be noted here that this networking of contentious discourse for political legitimation is not fully clarified until the reign of al-Ḥasan b. 'Alī, for it was then that Mu'āwiya was finally represented articulating the full extent of his grounds for ascent to rule (i.e., the tendentious parabolic argument on behalf of his rule). In an exchange of correspondence with al-Ḥasan over their competing claims to the caliphate, Mu'āwiya writes a significant letter debunking the 'Alid political demands. As he had done before when debating delegations from 'Alī,

Mu'āwiya does not deny the excellence of the Hāshimites and the superiority of the Prophet's position. What is different this time, however, is that Mu'āwiya, after the absence of 'Alī, takes advantage of the generational difference between him and al-Ḥasan to stress the issue of political experience. Mu'āwiya writes: "I have understood your summons to me for political agreement [*al-ṣulḥ*], but the situation between the two of us today is similar to that you [i.e., the 'Alids] had with Abū Bakr after the Prophet's death. Had I believed that you are more capable to control the subject population, more attentive to the community of believers, and better skilled in government than I, and more capable to collect the tax revenues and confront the enemy [*aḍbaṭ li'l-ra'iyya, wa aḥwaṭ 'alā hādhihi al-umma, wa aḥsanu siyāsa, wa aqwā 'alā jam' al-amwāl wa akyadu li'l-'aduww*], I would have conceded to your demands and admitted your better suitability for these tasks. But I have come to know that my duration in rule is longer than yours, and that I am more experienced in this matter, better at politics and older than you, therefore it is more incumbent upon you to give allegiance to me [*qad 'alimtu annī aṭwalu minka wilāyatan wa aqdamu minka li-hādhihi al-umma tajruba wa aktharu minka siyāsatan wa akbaru minka sinnan fa-anta aḥaqqu an tujībanī ilā hādhihi al-manzila allatī sa'altanī*]. If you declare your loyalty to me, then you can become the ruler after me [*fa-udkhul fī ṭā'atī wa la-ka al-amru ba'dī*]." Mu'āwiya then adds the well-known offer that he would grant al-Ḥasan the tax revenues of Iraq if he conceded his title to the caliphate. Al-Iṣfahānī, *Maqātil al-Ṭalibiyyīn*, ed. al-Sayyid Aḥmad Ṣaqr (Beirut, 1987), 66–67. The aforementioned letter is additionally remarkable for summarizing what would later be viewed as an essentially Sunnī argument about the *tafḍīl* (preference) of Mu'āwiya over al-Ḥasan; more noteworthy still is its inclusion in a well-known Shī'ī source.

70. In a famous quote when Aḥmad b. Ḥanbal was asked about the caliphs, he named the four Rāshidūn. Then when asked about Mu'āwiya, Ibn Ḥanbal replied, "No one was more worthy for the caliphate in 'Alī's time than 'Alī, and may God have mercy on Mu'āwiya." By not diminishing Mu'āwiya's credentials as a rebel or a later king, the story implied that Mu'āwiya would be qualified to succeed after 'Alī. Ibn Kathīr, IV (pt. 8), 132, quoting al-Bayhaqī.

71. Later medieval sources would go farther in admiring the reign of Mu'āwiya. Summarizing the history of the early period with the use of a narrative line from the Ayyubid and Mamluk periods, Ibn Kathīr describes Mu'āwiya's accession to rule and reign as follows: "Mu'āwiya was the deputy of the caliph over Syria [*nā'iban 'alā al-shām*] during the reigns of 'Umar and 'Uthmān [*al-dawla 'al-'Umarriyya wa'l-'Uthmāniyya*] . . . The community agreed to have him lead in A.H. 41/A.D. 661 [*fa-in'aqadat al-kalima 'alā Mu'āwiya wa ajma'at al-ra'āyā 'alā bay'atihi*]. He then held power exclusively for the rest of his reign, during which *jihād* in the enemy lands was underway, and the word of God kept high. The booty of conquests came to him from the extremities of the empire, and Muslims enjoyed the peace, justice, and forbearance of his rule [*wa'l-muslimūn ma'ahu fī*

*rāḥatin wa ʿadl wa ṣafḥin wa ʿafw*]." Ibn Kathīr, IV (pt. 8), 122. Ibn Kathīr later adds an apology for the protagonists (ʿAlī and Muʿāwiya) in the conflict by saying, "Disputes happened between him [i.e., Muʿāwiya] and ʿAlī, after the murder of ʿUthmān, due to their variant interpretations [*ʿalā sabīl al-ijtihād wa'l-ra'y*]. A great war happened between the two, as we described earlier. The position of correctness and righteousness was with ʿAlī, but Muʿāwiya is excused among the majority of scholars in ancient times and in the present." Ibn Kathīr, IV (pt. 8), 129.

72. Ibn ʿAbd Rabbihi, *al-ʿIqd*, IV, 365. Al-ʿUtbī←his father. Ṭabarī's version of the same story is similar but less clear in the dialogue's conclusion. Ṭabarī, II, 207. Aḥmad b. Zuhayr←ʿAlī b. Muḥammad←Abū Muḥammad al-Umawī. The additional excerpt is from Ṭabarī. Balādhurī, *Ansāb* (*Banū ʿAbd Shams*), 147. Balādhurī's version, closer to Ṭabarī's though still slightly varied, is related on the authority of Hishām b. ʿAmmār.

73. ʿUmar's comment: "You speak of the skill [*dahā'*] of Khusraw and Caesar, but you have Muʿāwiya." Ṭabarī, II, 206.

74. See chap. 5, n. 104.

75. Some narrators established a direct comparison between ʿUmar's and Muʿāwiya's models of rule, and concluded with the assessment, "Muʿāwiya was the more successful sovereign, but ʿUmar was better than him." This account is usually recounted after an assertion that states that no one was more successful in rule after the Prophet than Muʿāwiya. Ibn Kathīr, IV (pt. 8), 137. Dhahabī, *Siyar*, III, 152. (where the report is attributed to Ibn Isḥāq).

76. ʿAbd al-Malik reportedly outlined this viewpoint when he commented to a pious sage, Thaʿlaba b. Abī Mālik al-Quraẓī, "[The caliph] ʿUthmān did not change ways from the path of ʿUmar except in being lenient towards people. He was so lenient towards them that they took advantage of him. Had he been rough like ʿUmar, they would not have treated him the way they did . . . And where would one find today a community of subjects like those over whom ʿUmar ruled. O Thaʿlaba, it is my view that the ruler must adjust to the way the subjects are [*innī ra'aytu sīrata al-sulṭān tadūru maʿ al-nās*]. If someone today were to rule in the same way [as ʿUmar did], people would be robbed in their homes, and raids would happen on the roads; and people would exploit each other and sedition would happen. The ruler must therefore govern in a manner that adjusts to his times." Ibn Saʿd, V, 232. Al-Wāqidī←Ibn Abī Sabra←al-Miswar b. Rifāʿa←Thaʿlaba.

77. Ṭabarī, II, 211–212. ʿAbdallāh←ʿAbdallāh's father←Sulaymān←ʿAbdallāh b. al-Mubārak←Jarīr b. Ḥāzim←Muḥammad b. al-Zubayr←ʿAbdallāh b. Masʿada b. Ḥakma al-Fazārī (a man reportedly from the clan of Badr, *min banī āl Badr*). Also, Ibn ʿAbd Rabbihi, *al-ʿIqd*, IV, 364–365 (related by al-Qadhḥamī). An abbreviated and slightly varied account of the story is reported by al-Madā'inī. Balādhurī, *Ansāb* (*Banū ʿAbd Shams*), 110. Also, *Akhbār al-Dawla al-ʿAbbāsiyya*, 83. Ibn ʿAsākir, XLIV, 287. In another report also involving the examples of the first two caliphs, Muʿāwiya declares to the community, "I have sought the path of Abū

Bakr and 'Umar but could not bear it, so I have applied with you a path that has some personal gain [*'alā ba'ḍ al-athra*]. Accept what I give you even when it is scarce, for the bounty in its scarcity can become a source of wealth [*inna al-khayr idhā tatāba'a wa in qall aghnā*]. Balādhurī, *Ansāb* (*Sā'ir*), 49. Ibn 'Abd Rabbihi, *al-'Iqd*, IV, 81–82. The comparison with Abū Bakr and 'Umar will later become a stock theme of monarchal apology by other rulers. 'Abd al-Malik, for example, would declare to his subjects, "Be just toward us, you ask us to rule you like Abū Bakr and 'Umar did, but you are not toward us [i.e., obedient] like the community of Abū Bakr and 'Umar was towards them." Ibn Qutayba, *'Uyūn al-Akhbār*, I, 62. Al-Jāḥiẓ, *al-Bayān wa'l-Tabyīn*, I, 265; al-Ṭurṭūshī, *Sirāj al-Mulūk*, 348. When an asectic named Abū Naṣr admonished Hārūn al-Rashīd in the mosque of Medina to be more caring in his rule, the caliph reportedly sought to defend himself by also stating that his times and community were different from those in the reign of 'Umar (*inna ra'iyyatī wa dahrī ghayru ra'iyyati 'Umar wa dahrihi*). This reponse did not avail al-Rashīd of continued ascetic admonition. Although this exchange is significant for its idealized portrayal of the relations between rulers and religious scholars in general, it is the 'Abbāsid provenance of such an apologetic response about the first two caliphs that is here more noteworthy, and shows the shaping of Umayyad historiography through the narrative lens of 'Abbāsid times. Ibn Bakkār, *al-Akhbār al-Muwaffaqiyyāt*, 131 (this tradition is part of a wider cluster of reports narrated on the authority of Aḥmad b. Sa'īd al-Dimashqī). Finally, a spinoff variant on 'Abd al-Malik's statement also shows al-Ma'mūn expressing similar expediency and doubt that the policies of Abū Bakr and 'Umar could continue to be applicable. Al-Bayhaqī, *al-Maḥāsin wa'l-Masāwi'*, 495. Ibn al-Ṭiqṭiqā would also assert the more secularist view that the rule of the first caliphs was not to be taken as a model for kings, because the lifestyle of the first caliphs was closer to that of the prophets. Ibn al-Ṭiqṭiqā, *al-Fakhrī*, 29, 73.

78. I have elsewhere noted a number of anecdotes in this genre that show Ibn al-Mubārak and other prominent ascetics having the upper hand in rebuking the caliphs and awakening their religiosity, but at the same time alerting the community to its duty to obey rulers and avoid seditious challenges to the caliphs. Mu'āwiya here seems to be having his moment in these stories when Ibn al-Mubārak is featured in the *isnād* to underscore admiration for Mu'āwiya's contrition over having competed for power. The *isnād* of this account underscores the orthodox shaping of the anecdote, with the redundant use of the name 'Abdallāh at the outset, clearly referring through a stress of Ibn al-Mubārak's first name to his singular importance in the chain of narration, and through the reference to one narrator as a man from the children of the clan of Badr, an allusive reference to the fighters at Badr no doubt rather than to any particular family by that name. A key example of a debating story between the caliph and a pious figure has Mu'āwiya admonish al-Miswar b. Makhrama for dwelling only on the short-

comings of the caliph. "Do you not know that a good deed receives its reward in tenfold, or do you only count the misdeeds," Mu'āwiya tells al-Miswar. "The tasks that I perform for the well-being of the people are greater than what you are in charge of. . . . I always choose God's way when I am given a choice between two paths, and I am of a faith where God accepts deeds, and rewards them [*wa anā 'alā dīnin yaqbal allāh fīhi al-'amal wa yujzī bi'l-ḥasanāt*] . . . I am entrusted with many tasks that I don't even count, including keeping up the congregational prayer for the Muslims, the defense of the community, ruling according to God's law, and a great many other acts which bring benefit to you personally, so ponder this sometime." Khaṭīb, *Ta'rīkh Baghdād*, I, 208–209 (reported by al-Zuhrī). Balādhurī, *Ansāb* (*Banū 'Abd Shams*), 36, 47 (reported by al-Madā'inī).

79. While narrators sought to distance Mu'āwiya (and later 'Abd al-Malik) from 'Umar's idealistic practices, they also found it essential that the Umayyads be viewed as continuators of certain key governmental policies that were purportedly developed by 'Umar. Thus although there is no firm historical evidence before the year A.H. 45/A.D. 665 (during the governorship of Ziyād b. Abīhi) about a substantial organization of the *diwān* (government departments) that dispensed military stipends and the tax revenues of the conquered lands, the early 'Abbāsid narrators consistently began the story of the organization of the *diwān* as the innovation of 'Umar. This historical claim was established and embellished because of the legalistic implications of such an action (for instance, toward land tax policy, relations with non-Muslim subjects, and a host of polemical purposes), not because of its historicity. In other words, what may have been a secular Umayyad economic and administrative policy was reshaped in a legalistic 'Abbāsid discourse, and back-projected onto the reign of 'Umar. F. Donner has noted that most of the accounts about 'Umar's organization of the *dīwān* in Ṭabarī's history are reported on the authority of Wāqidī. F. Donner, *Narratives*, 169. Ṭabarī, I, 2749–2757.

80. Ibn 'Asākir, XXXVII, 151 (the statement is conveyed through a report by 'Umar b. Shabba). Ibn Kathīr, V (pt. 9), 71.

81. Ibn Sa'd, V, 233. Al-Wāqidī←Ibn Abī Sabra←Abū Mūsā al-Ḥannāṭ←Ibn Ka'b. Ibn Kathīr, V (pt. 9), 68. Al-Zuhrī would elsewhere phrase his motive for writing down the *sunna* in similar terms, stating, "Were it not for certain lore that has come to us from the east [*lawlā aḥādīth sālat 'alaynā min al-mashriq*], I would not have written down [the *sunna*], nor commanded others to write it." Ibn 'Asākir, LV, 319. It is also notable that 'Abd al-Malik's declaration confirms what 'Umar b. al-Khaṭṭāb reportedly said to the crowd visiting the Prophet during his final illness: "The Prophet has been weakened by illness. You should all now abide by the Qur'ān. The Book of God shall suffice us."

82. Balādhurī, *Ansāb*, IV, pt. 2, 496. Ibn 'Asākir, XXXVII, 135 (reported on the authority of Ibn Jurayj). Ibn Kathīr, V (pt. 9), 68. 'Abd al-Malik's cautioning statement to the public after the downfall of 'Amr b. Sa'īd b. al-'Āṣ strongly resembles

in dramatic tone and some of its reworked content a statement that al-Manṣūr gave after the overthrow of Abū Muslim al-Khurāsānī. Dhahabī, *Siyar*, VII, 89.

83. Qur'ān 3:26 (Arberry, I, 76).

84. Suyūṭī, *Ta'rīkh*, 13.

85. Ibn Kathīr, IV (pt. 8), 134. Dhahabī, *Siyar*, III, 143.

86. Qur'ān 4:59.

87. Ibn al-Ṭiqṭiqā, *al-Fakhrī*, 28.

88. In spite of the modesty of this early political office, believers were strongly discouraged from seeking to aspire to political leadership. This was the message of the famous *ḥadīth* in which the Prophet reportedly tells 'Abd al-Raḥmān b. Samra, "O 'Abd al-Raḥmān, do not seek leadership. If it comes to you from the offer of the people, then God will help you in handling the matter [government]." Khaṭīb, *Ta'rīkh Baghdād*, II, 268, 400–401; VII, 161. It was probably in light of this *ḥadīth* that much of the contrast between the history of Abū Bakr's and 'Uthmān's caliphates was understood by a medieval audience. Abū Bakr had been disinterested in ruling, but when the caliphate was reportedly pushed upon him, he was largely aided in ruling as 'Abd al-Raḥmān and 'Umar volunteered their services for subsidiary tasks such as the judgeship (Ibn Sa'd, III, 184). In contrast, 'Uthmān was known to have been very eager to rule, and thus found himself challenged and abandoned by the companions, some of whom had served him as officials. The example of the treasurer, Ibn al-Arqam, throwing the keys of the state treasury to the caliph during the crisis of 'Uthmān's reign illustrates the contrast. Balādhurī, *Ansāb (Banū 'Abd Shams)*, 518, 548.

89. Ṭabarī, II, 854–855.

90. Ṭabarī, II, 869.

91. This was the message of 'Abd al-Malik's statement "*lastu bi'l-khalīfa al-mustaḍ'af wa lā bi'l-khalīfa al-mudāhin wa lā bi'l-khalīfa al-ma'fūn.*" Ibn 'Abd Rabbihi, *al-'Iqd*, IV, 90–91; al-Jāḥiẓ, *al-Bayān*, II, 85. Ibn 'Asākir, XXXVII, 151. Balādhurī, *Ansāb al-Ashrāf*, ed. 'Abd al-'Azīz al-Dūrī and 'Iṣām 'Uqla (Wiesbaden, 2001), IV, pt. 2, 496. Abū Ṣāliḥ al-Anṭākī←al-Ḥajjāj b. Muḥammad←Ibn Jurayj←Ismā'īl b. Muḥammad. The statement is excerpted and simplified in another version. *Ansāb*, IV, pt. 2, 486. Al-Madā'inī←Maslama b. Muḥārib. 'Abd al-Malik's extremist position of avenging 'Uthmān by forbidding any religious critique of power, however, did not put an end to the historical polemic with the Umayyads. Later it will be the 'Abbāsids who are represented as providing the final balance between affirming political order while remaining within the juridical limits of the faith. The caliph al-Manṣūr, whose biography is shaped in a way that provides a complete mix of secular wisdom and pious deference, ultimately repudiates the example of 'Abd al-Malik's resort to pure force. In a speech that is crafted in a way that responds to the Umayyad arrogance of power, al-Manṣūr states, after being interrupted during his sermon at the Friday prayer by an ascetic who exhorted him to be pious ("*Ittaqi allāh*"), "You have spoken of a great matter, and

reminded us of the fear of the Sublime. I seek refuge with God that I become like the one [i.e., 'Abd al-Malik] who, when advised with the same invocation, would show an arrogance on top of his transgression [*akhadhathu al-'izzatu bi'l-ithm*]." The caliph then goes on to appropriate the pious platform by asserting that religious advice began with the Hāshimite or 'Abbāsid household ("*al-maw'iẓatu minnā bada'at wa min 'indinā kharajat*"), and then rebukes the religious zealot as an opportunist seeking to elicit a punishment against himself that would make him a revered victim. The caliph concludes by warning the public against using such religious provocations. Khaṭīb, *Ta'rīkh Baghdād*, X, 55. Ibn 'Asākir, XXXII, 312. A similar version given by Ṭabarī (replacing, however, the phrase about "*al-maw'iẓa*" [instructive advice] with the statement "*inna al-ḥikma 'alaynā nazalat wa min 'indinā faṣalat*" [wisdom descended on us and we imparted it to others]). Ṭabarī, III, 427. A simplified version of this story is also given by Ibn Rabbihi, *al-'Iqd*, IV, 98. The 'Abbāsid response was therefore not the idealistic reaction of 'Umar when he was told by a zealot "*Ittaqi allāh*" (fear God in your actions) (when someone chided the man for challenging 'Umar, the latter rejected this suppression and encouraged the public to make pious exhortation, stating, "Shame on them if they don't say it, and we would be unjust if we didn't accept criticism"). But neither was it the militant reaction of political power, as in the case of the Umayyads. With the 'Abbāsids, the caliphate had established rules for critique set within the jurisprudential rules that it laid out as the legal code of the faith, and had finally ended the discordant tendencies of zealotry (or messianism) that had begun with the famous example of the proto-Khārijite who had once challenged the Prophet's division of the booty at Ḥunayn as inequitable.

92. Hence the clearly fabricated reports about the voluntary agreement of 'Abdallāh b. 'Umar to offer the *bay'a* to 'Abd al-Malik. Ibn al-'Arabī, *al-'Awāṣim min al-Qawāṣim*, 251 (citing a tradition of Bukhārī). According to a report given by Ibn 'Abd Rabbihi, 'Abdallāh b. 'Umar sent a concise statement of his *bay'a*, as well as a *bay'a* on behalf of his *mawlā*, Nāfi', to 'Abd al-Malik. Ibn 'Abd Rabbihi, *al-'Iqd*, IV, 400. Balādhurī, *Ansāb*, IV, pt. 2, 484 (excluding, however, the *bay'a* of Nāfi'). A followup report describes how—when he was asked, "Do you accept that he [i.e., Ibn 'Umar] write to you like this [partly in reference to the blunt reference to the caliph by his first name]—'Abd al-Malik said, "This much [loyalty] from Abū 'Abd al-Raḥmān is indeed a lot." Al-Madā'inī←Muḥammad b. Ṣāliḥ←Ismā'īl b. Abī Khālid←al-Sha'bī. Other accounts relating to the Umayyads are clearly modeled after an antecedent 'Abbāsid tradition. The seemingly Sunnī obedience to authority that some scholars, such as Ibn Shihāb al-Zuhrī and Sa'īd b. al-Musayyib, displayed toward the Umayyad caliphs is crafted in light of an 'Abbāsid shaping of traditions about caliphs as well as 'ulamā'. Examples of this include the feisty defiance shown by Sa'īd b. al-Musayyib toward 'Abd al-Malik when he visited Medina. Dhahabī, *Siyar*, IV, 226–227. Ibn 'Asākir, LV, 322–324 (where the account is related on the authority of al-Wāqidī and Ibn Sa'd, but is not found in

the *Ṭabaqāt*). This was meant to be similar to Mālik b. Anas' disinterest in interacting with Hārūn al-Rashīd when he came on pilgrimage. Another story, about al-Zuhrī's awkward first attempt to be introduced to the court of 'Abd al-Malik in a search for patronage, is highly similar in drama (although different in details) to al-Wāqidī's equally botched first audience with the Barmakids, seeking to gain the patronage of Hārūn al-Rashīd. Dhahabī, *Siyar*, V, 330–331. Ibn Sa'd, V, 425–430. Also, about Yaḥyā al-Barmakī's patronage for al-Wāqidī. Bayhaqī, *al-Maḥāsin wa'l-Masāwi'*, 196. Other means of representation from the 'Abbāsid period were sometimes used out of their original context to describe personalities in the Umayyad period.

93. Ya'qūbī, II, 261. Oleg Grabar's skepticism about the validity of the reason Ya'qūbī gave for the construction of the Dome of the Rock (as a temporary pilgrimage site while Mecca was under the control of the rival caliph 'Abdallāh b. al-Zubayr during his war with 'Abd al-Malik) has been stated and restated over the years by art historians and historians alike. This skepticism has helped to privilege Grabar's own theory of reading the structure as a monument for Islamic monotheistic propaganda against Christians and Jews. Oleg Grabar, *The Formation of Islamic Art* (New Haven, 1972), 49–50, 62–64. Beyond a reading of the Qur'ānic inscriptions inside the monument in a search for verification of such an interpretation, there has never been any proof from the classical sources (either Muslim or non-Muslim) that such was the aim for the structure. Indeed, Ya'qūbī's explanation remains the only plausible theory for the original motive for the ambitious and unusual design of the Dome of the Rock. That the Qur'ānic inscriptions underscored the monotheistic message was a feature of enhancement but not the original purpose for building the commemorative structure.

94. It seems to have been only an earlier, different cultural sensibility during the Rāshidūn caliphate that prevented including Islamic slogans on the coinage. This can partly be inferred from a report of Ibn Sa'd's that 'Umar had banned the inscription of seals with Arabic, and another report of Wahb b. Munabbih that compares coinage to seals. Ibn Sa'd, IV, 176; Dhahabī, *Siyar*, IV, 548.

95. Ya'qūbī states that "Mu'āwiya did in Syria, al-Jazīra, and Yemen what he did in Iraq, which was to extract the former crown lands in these territories for his own personal wealth [*istaṣfā mā kāna li al-mulūk min al-ḍiyā' wa taṣyīrihā khāliṣātan li-nafsihi*], which he bequeathed to his family and his protégés [*wa aqṭa'ahā ahla baytihi wa khāṣatihi*]." *Ta'rīkh*, II, 234.

96. Goldziher, *Muslim Studies*, II, 45–46, 123–124.

97. It is thus not a coincidence that al-Zuhrī reported hardly any historical information about the Umayyads, but gave abundant reporting about the Rāshidūn. This was mainly Wāqidī's way of continuing the Sīra project established by Ibn Isḥāq, and it also proposed an early picture of cooperation between some Umayyad caliphs and religious scholars that was modeled on the 'Abbāsid patronage of Sunnī knowledge compilation, and the Arabization of this project.

I. Goldziher had a crucial role in cultivating the credulous attitude in anecdotes about al-Zuhrī and al-Zuhrī's relation to the Umayyads. He concluded, after recounting one account about al-Zuhrī's permission for the Umayyad Ibrāhīm b. al-Walīd to write and recite *ḥadīths*, by saying, "This account fully confirms the willingness of al-Zuhrī . . . to promote the interests of the dynasty by religious means." Goldziher, *Muslim Studies*, II, 46.

98. See 'Umar's comments above about the danger of the spread of the *ra'y* method and its association with the non-Arabs. Other famous statements of 'Umar's criticizing those who pose hypothetical questions or debate too much were indirectly used by *ahl al-ḥadīth* (the traditionist scholars) against the *ahl al-ra'y* (scholars who used reasoned interpretation in addition to traditionist texts) and more specifically the Iraqi school of jurisprudence (*ahl al-'Irāq*). Khaṭīb, *Kitāb al-Faqīh*, II, 11–14. Ibn 'Abd al-Barr, *Jāmi' Bayān al-'Ilm*, II, 53.

99. Ibn 'Asākir, II, 290–291, 296–207, 334–341. The *ḥadīth* about the *abdāl* is mainly attributed to 'Alī b. Abī Ṭālib, who reportedly narrated it to his followers in order to discourage them from cursing the followers of Mu'āwiya. Also, Aḥmad, *Musnad*, XXVIII, 129. Mu'āwiya is also quoted as narrating the *ḥadīth* that states, "When the *fitan* break out, the faith shall remain [steadfast] in Syria." Ibn 'Abd al-Ḥakam, *Futūḥ Miṣr*, 267.

100. The Prophet reportedly counted the heavenly cities as four: Mecca, Medina, Jerusalem, and Damascus. *Al-Buldān*, 37. In another tradition, when one of the companions declares his intention to migrate to Iraq, the Prophet reportedly advises him to emigrate to Syria instead, asserting that "God has guaranteed the blessing of its land and its people." Wakī', *Akhbār al-Quḍāt*, I, 324; al-Hamadānī, *al-Buldān*, 103.

101. Various traditions interpret the Qur'ānic description of where Mary and Jesus settled after his birth (*wa awaynāhumā ilā rabwatin dhāta qarārin wa ma'īn*) as the locale of Syria. Ibn 'Asākir, *Ta'rīkh*, II, 203–213.

102. Ibn Sa'd, I, 360. Ibn 'Asākir, I, 183–184. A slightly variant version of this *ḥadīth* is provided by Bukhārī, *Ṣaḥīḥ*, *kitāb al-tafsīr*, VI, 345 (no. 362). 'Abdallāh b. Salama←'Abd al-'Azīz b. Abī Salama←Hilāl b. Abī Hilāl←'Aṭā' b. Yasār←'Abdallāh b. 'Amr b. al-'Āṣ. Another declaration, with a similar articulation of concepts and a parallel chiliastic tenor, attributed to Zayd b. Khārija, carries the prediction to a comparison of the qualities of the first caliphs and the emergence of *fitna*, and then declares that this path of events is a result of fate (*wa kāna amru allāh qadaran maqdūran*). Ibn Bakkār, *al-Akhbār al-Muwaffaqiyyāt*, 394–396.

103. Ibn 'Asākir, I, 185, 188. Another *ḥadīth* reportedly transmitted by Abū Hurayra simply states, "The caliphate will be in Medina, and the kingdom in Syria [*al-khilāfa bi'l-madīna wa'l-mulk bi'l-shām*]." Ibn 'Abd al-Barr, *Jāmi'*, II, 186.

104. Ṭabarī, I, 2523.

105. Ṭabarī, I, 2524. Juynboll, *HT*, XIII, 104.

106. Ṭabarī, I, 2525.

## 8. CONCLUSION

1. As he put it, "*al-ārā' al-marwiyya fī faḍā'ilihim mut'āriḍa.*" *Kitāb al-Irshād*, 431.

2. This political foundation for the historical narration is so central that if one were to backtrack into reading the standoff between Moses and Pharaoh anew, one would find that the story in Islam was not just about Pharaoh's blasphemy and the beginnings of salvation history for the Israelites, but that it was equally about the political-moralistic problematic of tyrannical rule and its detrimental effect on the relation between leadership and society.

3. Ṭabarī, III, 445.

4. Ṭabarī, III, 446–447: *al-sulṭān, ya bunayy, ḥablu allāh al-matīn wa 'urwatuhu al-wuthqā wa dīn allāh al-qayyim fa-iḥfaẓhu wa ḥuṭhu wa ḥaṣṣinhu wa dhub 'anhu wa awqi' bi'l-mulḥidīn fīhi wa iqma' al-māriqīn minhu . . . wa lā tujāwiz mā amara allāh bihi fī muḥkami al-qur'ān wa uḥkum bi'l-'adl wa lā tushṭiṭ.*

5. Ṭabarī, III, 446–448. Trans. J. A. Williams, *al-Ṭabarī: The Early 'Abbāsī Empire*, II, 48–49.

6. Al-Manṣūr states about the support of Khurāsān: "Then the Sons of Umayya fell upon us [i.e., the 'Abbāsids] and put our leading men to death and took away our power, although by God there was no revenge due them from our family that they should seek . . . they drove us out of the land, and we fled now to Ṭā'if, now to Syria, and now to al-Sharrāt, until God sent you to us as partisans and helpers and revived our honor and gave us power through you, the people of Khurāsān, and made your fidelity overcome the people of falsehood, and caused our right to prevail, and caused our heritage from our Prophet to come to us. Then Truth settled in its place and its beacon became manifest and its helpers became mighty and those who had oppressed were exterminated; and praise be to God, the Lord of all being [*ḥattā ibta'athakum allāh lanā shī'atan wa anṣāran fa-aḥyā sharafanā wa 'azzanā bi-kum ahlu khurāsān wa damagha bi-ḥaqqikum ahla al-bāṭil wa aẓhara ḥaqqanā wa aṣāra ilaynā mirāthanā 'an nabiyyinā, fa-qarra al-ḥaqqu maqarrahu wa aẓhara manārahu wa a'azza anṣārahu*]." Ṭabarī, III, 430–432. Trans. Williams, II, 35. According to al-Haytham b. 'Adī's account, al-Manṣūr exhorts al-Mahdī to honor the Khurāsānīs (ahl Khurāsān), and puts this advice in terms that are similar to the Prophet Muḥammad's exhortation during his final sermon that the community safeguard the Anṣār and ignore their lapses. Ṭabarī, III, 443–444.

## APPENDIX 1. ABŪ MIKHNAF'S ACCOUNT OF THE SAQĪFA OF BANŪ SĀ'IDA

1. Ṭabarī, I, 1837–1844. Donner, *HT*, X, 1–10.

2. Lit. "the people are in your shade and shadow."

3. Abū Mikhnaf's account of events here is undoubtedly the fullest and most cogent in the positioning of actors and various positions and reactions. This text, however, can be found heavily redacted and its various statements shifted in more orthodox versions. Ibn Sa'd, for example, attributes the statement *"minnā amīr wa minkum amīr,"* and later *"anā judhayluhā al-muḥakkak,"* to Sa'd b. 'Ubāda rather than al-Ḥubāb b. al-Mundhir. The account is given a clearly contrived *isnād*: Muḥammad b. 'Umar (al-Wāqidī)←Ma'mar and Muḥammad b. 'Abdallāh←al-Zuhrī←'Ubaydallāh b. 'Abdallāh b. 'Utba←Ibn 'Abbās←'Umar b. al-Khaṭṭāb. Ibn Sa'd, III, 615–616.

4. The situation presumes that Sa'd was still seated.

## APPENDIX 2. THE SUCCESSION TO 'UMAR

1. *"alā a'riḍū 'an hādhā ajma'ūn."* The statement may be referring to Ibn 'Umar, in which case 'Umar's comment would mean: "All of you, don't listen to this one [i.e., Ibn 'Umar]."

2. This reference to 'Alī (*fa-fīhi du'āba*) has been one of the most obscure and yet crucial comments made about 'Alī by 'Umar. A sense of humor was certainly not a quality of 'Alī's personality, as all the narratives of his biography show, so the word must have had an archaic meaning that is now lost to readers.

3. *"wa aymu allāh lā yanāluhu illā bi-sharr lā yanfa'u ma'ahu khayr."*

4. *"lam tura' yā abā al-Ḥasan."* More likely, it is possible that the Arabic is: *"li-ma tura' yā abā al-Ḥasan"* (what are you afraid of, O Abū'l-Ḥasan?), as if anticipating 'Alid dissent in the future.

5. *"arjū an af'al wa a'mal bi-mablagh 'ilmī wa ṭāqatī."* The phrasing is ambiguous, making it unclear whether 'Alī was promising to abide by the rulings of his predecessors, add to their practice, or simply govern according to his own independent expertise.

6. Ṭabarī, I, 2776–2786. Trans. G. Rex Smith, *HT,* XIV, 143–154.

## APPENDIX 3. MANŪSHIHR'S DECLARATION

1. Ṭabarī, I, 436–440. Trans. W. Brinner, *HT,* III, 24–28.

# Glossary

*BAY'A*. The oath of political allegiance given to the caliph.
*BID'A*. An innovation in religious practice usually viewed as unorthodox.
*DA'WA*. A religious or political call by a leader or a new social movement.
*FAY'*. The immovable portion of the spoils of war (mainly agricultural lands).
*FITNA* (PL. *FITAN*). Trial or temptation; originally a religious reference to discord, but more commonly applied in the chronicles to political sedition or civil war.
*ḤADĪTH* (PL. *AḤĀDĪTH*). The sayings or traditions of the Prophet. *ḥadīth* is sometimes used in the plural sense to refer to the genre.
*HĀSHIMITES*. Descendants of Hāshim, the ancestor of the Prophet. The term referred to various branches of the family of the Prophet, including the 'Abbāsids (descended from al-'Abbās, the Prophet's uncle) and the 'Alids (decendants of 'Alī b. Abī Ṭālib, the Prophet's cousin and son-in-law).
*ḤIMĀ*. A certain type of economic reserve in the early caliphate pertaining to agricultural surplus or grazing pastures for horses or camels of the military.
*ḤIZB*. A group or faction.
*IMĀM*. In basic terms a leader of a congregation in prayer, but in wider terms also an inspired religious guide or a leader in comprehensive terms (both secular and religious).
*IQṬĀ'*. A proto-feudal type of land assignment to a conquering army or a political elite.
*ISNĀD*. Chain of transmitters of *ḥadīth* texts.
JĀHILIYYA. The period preceding the coming of Islam in Arabia.

*JAMĀʻA*. The community of believers or the concept of a collectivity or unanimity.

QURRĀʼ. The Qur'ān reciters.

*RA'Y*. LIT. "opinion," but in classical usage often referring to sound judgment. In juristic terms it also applied to the method of exercising reason to interpret a canonical religious text.

RIDDA. The war against a movement of apostasy from Islam that occurred during the reign of Abū Bakr, mainly in central Arabia.

SAWĀD. The rich agricultural land in central and southern Iraq.

*SHĪʻA*. One of several terms referring to a group of followers or a faction. Eventually the term came to refer mainly to the followers of ʻAlī.

*SULṬĀN ALLĀH*. A reference in abstract terms to divine authority on earth (e.g., the purview of the law); less commonly in the early Islamic period it referred to a caliph as the symbol of divine authority. This latter usage did not gain currency until well after the ninth century.

*SUNNA*. LIT. "the well-trodden path," referring to the practices of the Prophet, and very often including the practices of his most important companions, especially Abū Bakr and ʻUmar.

TAHKĪM. LIT. "the Arbitration." This reference in early Islam is to the culmination of the standoff between the armies of ʻAlī and Muʻāwiya at the Battle of Ṣiffīn with a political arbitration between their respective representatives (Abū Mūsā al-Ashʻarī and ʻAmr b. al-ʻĀṣ). Dissatisfaction with having such an arbitration between a caliph and a governor caused the secession of the Khārijites from ʻAlī's camp.

*TA'WĪL*. One of several terms that referred to religious interpretation. The term was applied to an indirect explanation of a religious text, to a less common and often individualistic interpretation, or to a gnostic interpretation by a Shīʻī *imām* or a Ṣūfī scholar.

WAṢIYYA. LIT. "a testament for a successor." The term refers more specifically to the Shīʻī principle of formal religious designation from one *imām* to the next within the line of twelve *imām*s who succeeded ʻAlī.

# Bibliography

## ABBREVIATION

*HT* = *The History of al-Ṭabarī*. 40 vols. Albany: State University of New York Press, 1986–2007.

## PRIMARY SOURCES

Abū Nuʻaym al-Iṣbahānī, Aḥmad b. ʻAbdallāh (d. 430/1038). *Dhikr Akhbār Iṣbahān*. Ed. Sven Dedering. 2 vols. Leiden, 1931–1934.

——. *Ḥilyat al-Awliyā'*. 10 vols. Cairo, 1932–1938.

——. *Dalā'il al-Nubuwwa*. Ed. Muḥammad Rawwās Qalʻajī et al. 2 vols. Beirut, 1986.

Abū Dāwūd, Sulaymān b. al-Ashʻath al-Sijistānī al-Azdī (d. 275/888). *Sunan Abī Dāwūd*. 4 vols. Beirut, 1988.

Abū Yūsuf, Yaʻqūb b. Ibrahīm (d. 182/798). *Kitāb al-Kharāj* (in *Mawsūʻat al-Kharāj*). Beirut, 1979.

*ʻAhd Ardashīr*. Ed. I. Abbas. Beirut, 1967.

*Akhbār al-ʻAbbās wa-Wildihi* (anonymous). *Akhbār al-dawla al-ʻAbbāsiyya*. Ed. ʻAbd al-ʻAzīz al-Dūrī and ʻAbd al-Jabbār al-Muṭṭalibī. Beirut, 1971.

Al-ʻAskarī, Abū Hilāl al-Ḥasan b. ʻAbdallāh b. Sahl (d. ca. 395/969). *al-Awā'il*. Ed. M. al-Maṣrī et al. 2 vols. Damascus, 1975.

al-Azraqī, Muḥammad b. ʻAbdallāh (d. 222/837). *Akhbār Makka*. Ed. F. Wüstenfeld. Leipzig, 1858.

al-Baghdādī, Abū Bakr Aḥmad b. ʿAlī al-Khaṭīb (d. 463/1071). *Taʾrīkh Baghdād.* 14 vols. Cairo, 1931.

——. *al-Kifāya fī ʿIlm al-Riwāya.* Ed. Ahmad ʿUmar Hāshim. Beirut, 1986.

——. *Kitāb al-Faqīh waʾl-Mutafaqqih.* Ed. ʿAdil b. Yusuf al-ʿAzzāzī. 2 vols. Riyad, 1996.

——. *Taqyīd al-ʿIlm.* Ed. Yusuf al-ʿUsh. Beirut, 1974.

al-Baghdādī, Abū Jaʿfar Muḥammad b. Ḥabīb (d. 246/860). *Kitāb al-Muḥabbar.* Ed. I. Lichtenstädter. Beirut, 1967.

al-Balādhurī, Aḥmad b. Yaḥyā (d. 279/892). *Ansāb al-Ashrāf,* vol. I: *Banū ʿAbd Shams.* Ed. ʿAbd al-ʿAzīz al-Dūrī. Wiesbaden, 1979.

——. *Ansāb al-Ashrāf,* vol. II: *ʿAlī wa Banūh.* Ed. W. Madelung. Wiesbaden, 2003.

——. *Ansāb al-Ashrāf,* vol. III: *al-ʿAbbās b. ʿAbd al-Muṭṭalib wa waladuhu.* Ed. A. al-Dūrī. Wiesbaden, 1987.

——. *Ansāb al-Ashrāf,* vol. IV. Ed. ʿAbd al-ʿAzīz al-Dūrī and ʿIṣām ʿUqla. Wiesbaden, 2001.

——. *Ansāb al-Ashrāf,* vol. V: *Sāʾir Furūʿ Quraysh.* Ed. I. ʿAbbās. Wiesbaden, 1996.

——. *Futūḥ al-Buldān.* Ed. Ṣalāḥ al-Dīn al-Munajjid. 2 vols. Cairo, 1956–1957.

al-Baqillānī, Abū Bakr (d. 403/1012). *Manāqib al-Aʾimma al-Arbaʿa.* Ed. Samīra Farḥāt. Beirut, 2002.

al-Bayhaqī, Ibrāhīm b. Muḥammad (d. ca. 320/932). *al-Maḥāsin waʾl-Masāwiʾ.* Beirut, n.d.

al-Bukhārī, Abū ʿAbdallāh Muḥammad b. Ismāʿīl (d. 256/870). *Ṣaḥīḥ.* Ed. Muḥammad Muḥsin Khan. 9 vols. Riyad, 1997.

al-Dhahabī, Shams al-Dīn Muḥammad b. Aḥmad (d. 748/1348). *Taʾrīkh al-Islām wa Wafayāt al-Mashāhīr waʾl-Aʿlām.* Ed. ʿUmar Tadmurī. 29 vols. in 26. Beirut, 1990.

——. *Siyar Aʿlām al-Nubalāʾ.* Ed. S. al-Arnaʾūṭ et al. 24 vols. Beirut, 1994–1998.

——. *al-Khulafāʾ al-Rāshidūn.* Ed. Ḥusām al-Dīn al-Qudsī. Beirut, 1992.

al-Dimashqī al-Ḥanafī, Ḥāmid b. ʿAlī b. Ibrāhim b. ʿImād al-Dīn b. Muḥibb al-Dīn al-ʿImādī (d. 1171/1756). *al-Durr al-Mustaṭāb fī Muwāfaqāt ʿUmar b. al-Khaṭṭāb wa Abī Bakr wa ʿAlī Abī Turāb.* Ed. Muṣṭafā ʿUthmān Ṣumayda. Beirut, 1996.

al-Dīnawarī, Abū Ḥanīfa Aḥmad b. Dāwūd (d. 282/895). *Kitāb al-Akhbār al-Ṭiwāl.* Ed. V. Guirgass. Leiden, 1888.

*al-Fitna wa Waqʿat al-Jamal, Riwāyat Sayf b. ʿUmar.* Ed. Aḥmad Rātib ʿArmūsh. Beirut, 1972.

al-Ghazalī, Abū Ḥāmid Muḥammad b. Muḥammad (d. 505/1111). *al-Tibr al-Masbūk fī Naṣīḥat al-Mulūk.* Ed. Muḥammad Aḥmad Damaj. Beirut, 1996.

al-Hindī, ʿAlāʾ al-Dīn al-Muttaqī b. Husām al-Dīn (d. 975/1567). *Kanz al-ʿUmmāl fī Sunan al-Aqwāl waʾl-Afʿāl.* Ed. Ṣafwat al-Saqqā and Bakrī al-Ḥayyānī. 16 vols. Beirut, 1985.

al-Ḥuṣarī, Abū Isḥāq Ibrāhīm b. ʿAlī (d. 453/1061). *Zahr al-Adāb wa Thamar al-Albāb.* Ed. A. M. al-Bijāwī. 2 vols. Cairo, 1953.

Ibn 'Abd al-Barr, Yūsuf b. 'Abdallāh al-Namarī, *al-Istī'āb fī Ma'rifat al-Aṣḥāb*, Abū 'Umar Yūsuf b. 'Abdallāh al-Qurṭubī (d. 463/1070). Ed. 'Alī Muḥammad Mu'awwaḍ et al. 4 vols. Beirut, 1995.

Ibn 'Abd al-Ḥakam, Abū'l-Qāsim 'Abd al-Raḥmān b. 'Abdallāh (d. 214/829). *Futūḥ Miṣr wa Akhbāruhā*. Ed. C. Torrey. New Haven, 1922.

Ibn 'Abd Rabbihi, Abū 'Umar Aḥmad b. Muḥammad (d. 328/940). *Kitāb al-'Iqd al-Farīd*. Ed. A. Amīn et al. 8 vols. Cairo, 1940–1953.

Ibn Abī al-Shaykh, Abū Muḥammad 'Abdallāh b. Muḥammad (d. 369/979). *Ṭabaqāt al-Muḥaddithīn bi-Iṣbahān wa al-Wāridīn 'alyahā*. 4 vols. in 2. Beirut, 1989.

Ibn al-'Arabī, Abū Bakr Muḥammad b. 'Abdallāh (d. 543/1148). *al-'Awāṣim min al-Qawāsim fī Taḥqīq Mawāqif al-Ṣaḥāba ba'd Wafāt al-Nabī*. Ed. Muḥibb al-Dīn al-Khaṭīb. Cairo, 1968.

Ibn 'Asākir, Abū'l-Qāsim 'Alī b. al-Ḥasan (d. 571/1176). *Ta'rīkh Madīnat Dimashq*. Ed. 'Umar b. Gharāma al-'Amrawī. 80 vols. Beirut, 1995–2000.

Ibn al-Athīr, 'Izz al-Dīn 'Alī b. Aḥmad (d. 630/1233). *al-Kāmil fī'l-Ta'rīkh*. 13 vols. Beirut, 1965–1967.

——. *Usd al-Ghāba fī Ma'rifat al-Ṣaḥāba*. Ed. 'Alī Muḥammad Mu'awwaḍ and Aḥmad 'Abd al-Mawjūd. 7 vols. Beirut, 1994.

Ibn al-Faqīh, Abū Bakr Aḥmad b. Muḥammad (d. 365/975). *Mukhtaṣar Kitāb al-Buldān*. Ed. M. J. de Goeje. Leiden, 1885.

Ibn al-Farrā' al-Andalusī, Abū Bakr 'Atīq (d. 698/1298). *Nuzhat al-Abṣār fī Faḍā'il al-Anṣār*. Ed. 'Abd al-Razzāq b. Muḥammad Marzūq. Riyad, 2004.

Ibn Ḥajar al-'Asqalānī, Abū'l-Faḍl Aḥmad b. Nūr al-Dīn 'Alī (d. 852/1449). *Fatḥ al-Bārī fī Sharḥ Ṣaḥīḥ al-Bukhārī*. 18 vols. Beirut, 2003.

——. *al-Iṣāba fī Tamyīz al-Ṣaḥāba*. Ed. 'Alī Muḥammad al-Bījāwī. 8 vols. Beirut, 1992.

Ibn Ḥamdūn, Maḥmūd b. al-Ḥasan (d. 562/1166). *al-Tadhkira al-Ḥamdūnīyya*. ed. Iḥsān and Bakr 'Abbās. 10 vols. Beirut, 1996.

Ibn Ḥanbal, Aḥmad (d. 241/855). *Musnad*. Ed. Shu'ayb al-Arna'ūṭ. 50 vols. Beirut, 1993–2001.

Ibn Ḥazm, Abū Muḥammad 'Alī b. Aḥmad al-Andalusī (d. 456/1064). *Jamharat Ansāb al-'Arab*. Ed. A. M. Hārūn. Cairo, 1962.

Ibn Hishām, 'Abd al-Malik (d. 218/834). *al-Sīra al-Nabawiyya*. Ed. 'Umar Tadmurī. 4 vols. Beirut, 1993.

Ibn al-Jawzī, Abū'l Faraj 'Abd al-Raḥmān b. 'Alī (d. 597/1201). *al-Miṣbāḥ al-Muḍī' fī Khilāfat al-Mustaḍī'*. Ed. Nājiya 'Abdallāh Ibrāhīm. 2 vols. Baghdad, 1976–1977.

——. *al-Muntaẓam fī Ta'rīkh al-Mulūk wa'l-Umam*. Ed. M. A. 'Aṭā. 18 vols. in 16. Beirut, 1992.

——. *Kittāb al-Quṣṣāṣ wa'l-Mudhakkirīn*. Ed. M. Schwartz. Beirut, 1971.

——. *Ṣifat al-Ṣafwa*. Ed. Ibrahīm Ramaḍān et al. 2 vols. Beirut, 1989.

——. *Talqīḥ Fuhūm Ahl al-Athar fī 'Uyūn al-Ta'rīkh wa'l-Siyar*. Cairo, n.d.

——. *Ta'rīkh 'Umar b. al-Khaṭṭāb*. Beirut, 1985.

Ibn Kathīr, ʻImād al-Dīn Ismāʻīl b. ʻUmar (d. 774/1373). *al-Bidāya wa'l-Nihāya.* 14 parts in 8 vols. Beirut, 1985.

——. *al-Nihāya fī'l-Fitan wa'l-Malāḥim.* Ed. Ahmad ʻAbd al-Shāfī. Beirut, 1988.

——. *Qiṣaṣ al-Anbiyā'.* Ed. al-Sayyid al-Jamīlī. Beirut, 1985.

Ibn Khallikān, Aḥmad b. Muḥammad (d. 681/1282). *Wafayāt al-Aʻyān wa Anbā' Abnā' al-Zamān.* Ed. I. ʻAbbās. 8 vols. Beirut, 1968–1972.

Ibn Khayyāṭ, Khalīfa b. Khayyāṭ (d. 240/854). *Ta'rīkh.* Ed. A. al-ʻUmarī. al-Najaf, 1967.

Ibn Māja, Abū ʻAbdallāh Muḥammad b. Yazīd (d. 273/887). *Sunan.* Ed. Muḥammad Fu'ād ʻAbd al-Bāqī. 2 vols. Beirut, 1980.

Ibn Miskawayh, Abū ʻAlī Aḥmad b. Muḥammad Miskawayh al-Rāzī (d. 421/1030). *Tajārib al-Umam.* Ed. M. J. De Goeje. Leiden, 1871.

——. *Tajārib al-Umam.* Ed. Abū'l-Qāsim Emāmī. 2 vols. Tehran, 1987.

Ibn al-Muqaffaʻ (d. 139/756). *Āthār ibn al-Muqaffaʻ.* Ed. Umar Abū'l-Naṣr. Beirut, 1966.

Ibn al-Nadīm, Abū'l-Faraj Muḥammad b. Abī Yaʻqūb Isḥāq al-Warrāq (d. 380/990). *Kitāb al-Fihrist.* Ed. G. Flügel. 2 vols. Leipzig, 1871–1872. Repr. Beirut, 1966.

Ibn Qudāma al-Maqdisī, Muwaffaq al-Dīn ʻAbdallāh (d. 620/1223). *al-Istibṣār fī Nasab al-Ṣaḥāba min al-Anṣār.* Ed. ʻAlī Nuwayhiḍ. Beirut, 1972.

Ibn Qutayba, Abū Muḥammad ʻAbdallāh b. Muslim (d. 276/889). *Kitāb al-Maʻārif.* Ed. T. ʻUkāsha. Cairo, 1969.

——. *Kitāb ʻUyūn al-Akhbār.* Ed. Mufīd Muḥammad Qumayḥa. 4 parts in 2 vols. Beirut, n.d.

Ibn Saʻd, Abū ʻAbdallāh Muḥammad b. Saʻd (d. 230/845). *al-Ṭabaqāt al-Kubrā.* 9 vols. Beirut, 1957–1968.

Ibn Sallām, Abū ʻUbayd al-Qāsim (d. 224/838). *Kitāb al-Amwāl.* Beirut, 1981.

Ibn Shabba, Abū Zayd ʻUmar b. Shabba al-Numayrī al-Baṣrī (d. 262/876). *Kitāb Ta'rīkh al-Madīna al-Munawwara (Akhbār al-Madīna al-Nabawiyya).* Ed. ʻAlī Muḥammad Dandal. 2 vols. Beirut, 1996.

Ibn Taghrībirdī, Abū al-Maḥāsin Yūsuf al-Atābikī (d. 874/1470). *al-Nujūm al-Zāhira fī Mulūk Miṣr wa'l-Qāhira.* 16 vols. Cairo, 1963–1972.

Ibn al-Ṭiqṭiqā, Muḥammad b. ʻAlī b. Ṭabāṭabā (d. 709/1309). *Kitāb al-Fakhrī.* Beirut, 1966.

Ibn Zanjawayh, Aḥmad (d. 251/865). *Kitāb al-Amwāl.* Ed. Shākir Dīb Fayyāḍ. 3 vols. Riyad, 1986.

al-ʻIṣāmī al-Makkī, ʻAbd al-Malik b. Ḥusayn (d. 1111/1700). *Simṭ al-Nujūm al-ʻAwālī fī Anbā' al-Awā'il wa'l-Tawālī.* 4 vols. Cairo, 1961.

al-Iṣfahānī, Abū'l-Faraj ʻAlī b. al-Ḥusayn (d. 356/967). *Maqātil al-Ṭālibiyyīn.* Ed. M. Ṣaqr. Beirut, 1987.

al-Iṣfahānī, Ḥamza b. al-Ḥasan. *Ta'rīkh Sinī Mulūk al-Arḍ.* Beirut, n.d.

al-Jāḥiẓ, ʻAmr b. Baḥr (d. 255/869). *al-Bayān wa'l-Tabyīn.* Ed. ʻAbd al-Salām Muḥammad Hārūn. 4 vols. Cairo, 1948.

——. *Rasā'il al-Jāḥiẓ*. Ed. A. M. Hārūn, Cairo, 1963–1965.
——. *al-'Uthmāniyya*. Ed. A. M. Hārūn. Cairo, 1955.
——. *Kitāb al-Tāj* (attrib.). Ed. A. Zakī. Cairo, 1914.
al-Juwaynī, Abū'l-Ma'ālī 'Abd al-Malik b. 'Abdallāh (d. 478/1085). *Kitāb al-Irshād*. Ed. Muḥammad Yūsuf Mūsā and 'Alī 'Abd al-Mun'im 'Abd al-Ḥamīd. Cairo, 2002.
al-Kindī, Muḥammad b. Yūsuf (d. 350/961). *Kitāb al-Wulāt wa'l-Quḍāt*. Ed. R. Guest. London, 1912.
——. *Wulāt miṣr*. Ed. H. Naṣṣār. Beirut, 1959.
al-Kutubī, Muḥammad b. Shākir (d. 764/1363). *Fawāt al-Wafayāt*. Ed. I. 'Abbās. Beirut, 1974.
Mālik b. Anas (d. 179/795). *Kitāb al-Muwaṭṭa*. Ed. M. F. 'Abd al-Bāqī. Cairo, 1951. Repr. Beirut, 1988.
al-Māliqī, Muḥammad b. Abī Bakr Yaḥyā al-Ash'arī al-Andalusī (d. 741/1340). *al-Tamhīd wa'l-Bayān fī Maqtal al-Shahīd 'Uthmān*. Ed. Maḥmūd Yūsuf Zāyed. Beirut, 1964.
al-Marwazī, Nu'aym b. Ḥammād (d. 229/844). *al-Fitan*. Ed. Suhayl Zakkār. Beirut, 1993.
al-Mas'ūdī, 'Alī b. al-Ḥusayn (d. 345/956). *Murūj al-Dhahab*. Ed. C. Pellat. Beirut, 1973.
——. *al-Tanbīh wa'l-Ishrāf*. Ed. M. J. de Goeje. Leiden, 1894.
al-Maqdisī, Muṭahhar b. Ṭāhir (d. 355/965). *al-Bad' wa'l-Ta'rīkh*. Ed. C. Huart. 6 vols. Paris, 1899.
al-Maqrīzī, Taqī al-Dīn Aḥmad b. 'Alī (d. 854/1442). *Kitāb al-Nizā' wa'l-Takhāṣum fī-mā bayn Banī Umayya wa Banī Hāshim*. Ed. Ḥusayn Mu'nis. Cairo, 1988.
al-Māwardī, Abū'l-Ḥasan 'Alī b. Muḥammad (d. 450/1058). *al-Aḥkām al-Sulṭāniyya*. Beirut, 1985.
al-Minqarī, Naṣr b. Muzāḥim (d. 212/827). *Waq'at Ṣiffīn*. Ed. 'Abd al-Salām Muḥammad Hārūn. Cairo, 1962.
al-Mubarrad, Abū'l-'Abbās Muḥammad b. Yazīd (d. 285/898). *al-Kāmil*. Ed. Muḥammad Abū'l-Faḍl Ibrāhīm and al-Sayyid Shaḥāta. 4 vols. Cairo, n.d.
Muslim b. al-Ḥajjāj al-Qurashī al-Nīsābūrī (d. 261/875). *Ṣaḥīḥ*. Ed. M. M. 'Abd al-Laṭīf. 18 vols. in 9. Repr. Beirut.
al-Nasā'ī, Abū 'Abd al-Raḥman Aḥmad b. al-Ash'ath (d. 303/915). *Sunan*. Ed. Zuhayr al-Shāwīsh. 3 vols. Riyad, 1988.
al-Nuwayrī, Shihāb al-Dīn Aḥmad b. 'Abd al-Wahhāb (d. 733/1331). *Nihāyat al-'Arab fī Funūn al-Adab*. Ed. Muḥammad Rif'at Fatḥallāh. 31 vols. Cairo, 1923–1955.
al-Qazwīnī, 'Abd al-Karīm b. Muḥammad al-Rāfi'ī (d. 622/1225). *al-Tadwīn fī Akhbār Qazwīn*. Ed. 'Azīz allāh al-'Uṭāridī. 4 vols. Beirut, 1987.
al-Qazwīnī, Abū 'Abdallāh Zakariyya b. Muḥammad (d. 682/1283). *Āthār al-Bilād wa Akhbār al-'Ibād*. Beirut, 1960.

al-Qurtubī, Abū 'Abdallāh Muḥammad b. Aḥmad al-Anṣārī (d. 671/1272). *Jāmi' al-Bayān li-Aḥkām al-Qur'ān*. 20 parts in 10 vols. Beirut, 1993.
al-Sahmī, Abū al-Qāsim Ḥamza (d. 427/1035). *Ta'rīkh Jurjān*. Beirut, 1987.
Sayf b. 'Umar al-Tamīmī (d. 194/810). *Kitāb al-Ridda wa al-Futūḥ and Kitāb al-Jamal wa Masīr 'Āisha wa 'Alī*. Ed. Qāsim al-Sāmarrā'ī. Leiden, 1995.
Ṣibṭ Ibn al-Jawzī, Yūsuf b. Qizgalū (d. 654/1256). *al-Jalīs al-Ṣāliḥ wa'l-Anīs al-Nāṣiḥ*. Ed. Fawwāz Fawwāz. London, 1989.
al-Sijistānī, Abū Bakr 'Abdallāh b. Abī Dāwūd Sulaymān (d. 316/928). *Kitāb al-Maṣāḥif*. Cairo, 1936.
al-Suyūṭī, Abū al-Faḍl 'Abd al-Raḥmān (d. 911/1505). *Ta'rīkh al-Khulafā'*. Cairo, 1964.
——. *al-Khaṣā'iṣ al-Kubrā aw Kifāyat al-Ṭālib al-Labīb fī Khaṣā'iṣ al-Ḥabīb*. Ed. Muḥammad Khalīl Harrās. 3 vols. Cairo, 1967.
al-Ṭabarī, Abū Ja'far Muḥammad b. Jarīr (d. 310/923). *Ta'rīkh al-Rusul wa'l-Mulūk*. Ed. M. J. De Goeje. 3rd ser. Leiden, 1879–1901.
——. *Ta'rīkh al-Rusul wa'l-Mulūk*. Ed. M. Abū'l-Faḍl Ibrāhīm. 10 vols. Cairo, 1960–1969.
——. *Jāmi' al-Bayān fī Ta'wīl Āy al-Qur'ān*. 12 vols. Beirut, 1992.
al-Ṭabarī, Muḥibb al-Dīn Aḥmad b. 'Abdallāh (d. 694/1295). *al-Riyāḍ al-Naḍira fī Manāqib al-'Ashara*. 2 vols. in 1. Cairo, 1953.
——. *Dhakhā'ir al-'Uqbā fī Manāqib Dhawī al-Qurbā*. Beirut, n.d.
al-Tamīmī, Abū'l-'Arab Muḥammad b. Aḥmad (d. 333/944). *Kitāb al-Miḥan*. Ed. Y. al-Jubūrī. Beirut, 1983.
al-Tanūkhī, Abū 'Alī al-Muḥassin b. 'Alī (d. 384/994). *al-Faraj ba'd al-Shidda*. Ed. A. al-Shāljī. 5 vols. Beirut, 1978.
al-Tha'ālibī, Abū Manṣūr 'Abd al-Malik b. Muḥammad (d. 429/1038). *Ghurar Akhbār Mulūk al-Furs*. Ed. and trans. H. Zotenberg, *Histoire des rois Perses*. Repr. Tehran, 1963.
——. *Laṭā'if al-Ma'ārif*. Ed. P. de Jong. Leiden, 1867.
al-Tha'labī, Aḥmad b. Muḥammad (d. 427/1035). *Qiṣaṣ al-Anbiyā'*, known as *'Arā'is al-Majālis*. Beirut, n.d.
al-Thaqafī, Abū Isḥāq Ibrāhim b. Muḥammad (d. 283/896). *al-Ghārāt*. Beirut, 1987.
Tirmidhī, Abū 'Isā Muḥammad b. 'Isā (d. 279/892). *al-Jāmi' al-Ṣaḥīḥ wa huwa al-Sunan*. Ed. Aḥmad Muḥammad Shākir. 5 vols. Beirut, 1987.
al-Ṭurṭūshī, Abū Bakr Muḥammad b. al-Walīd (d. 520/1126). *Kitāb al-Ḥawādith wa'l-Bida'*. Ed. A. M. Turkī. Beirut, 1990.
——. *Sirāj al-Mulūk*. Ed. Ja'far al-Bayyātī. London, 1990.
——. *al-'Uyūn wa'l-Ḥadā'iq fī Akhbār al-Ḥaqā'iq*. Ed. M. de Goeje. Leiden, 1869.
al-Wāḥidī, Abū'l-Ḥasan 'Alī b. Aḥmad (d. 468/1076). *Asbāb al-Nuzūl*. Ed. Kamāl Basyūnī Zaghlūl. Beirut, 1990.
al-Wāqidī, Muḥammad b. 'Umar (d. 207/823). *Kitāb al-Maghāzī*. Ed. Marsden Jones. Oxford, 1966.

Wakī', Muḥammad b. Khalaf b. Ḥayyān (d. 306/918). *Akhbār al-Quḍāt*. Ed. A. M. al-Murāghī. 3 vols. Cairo, 1950.

al-Yāfi'ī, Abū Muḥammad 'Abdallāh b. As'ad (d. 768/1367). *Mir'āt al-Janān wa 'Ibrat al-Yaqẓān fī mā Yu'tabar min Ḥawādith al-Zamān*. 4 vols. Beirut, 1970.

al-Ya'qūbī, Aḥmad b. Abī Ya'qūb b. Wāḍiḥ (d. 284/897). *Kitāb al-Buldān*. Ed. M. J. de Goeje. Leiden, 1892.

——. *Ta'rīkh*. 2 vols. Beirut, 1960.

——. *Mushākalat al-Nās li-Zamānihim*. Ed. W. Millward. Beirut, 1962.

Yāqūt b. 'Abdallāh al-Ḥamawī (d. 626/1229). *Mu'jam al-Buldān*. 5 vols. Beirut, 1957.

al-Zamakhsharī, Abū'l-Qāsim Maḥmūd b. 'Umar (d. 538/1144). *Rabī' al-Abrār wa Fuṣūṣ al-Akhbār*. Ed. 'Abd al-Majīd Diyāb. Cairo, 1992.

al-Zubayr b. Bakkār (d. 256/870). *al-Akhbār al-Muwaffaqiyyāt*. Ed. S. M. al-'Ānī. Baghdad, 1972.

al-Zuhrī, Muḥammad b. Muslim b. 'Ubaydallāh b. Shihāb (d. 124/742). *al-Maghāzī al-Nabawiyya*. Ed. Suhayl Zakkār. Damascus, 1980.

## SECONDARY WORKS

Abbott, Nabia. *'Aisha, the Beloved of Mohammed*. Chicago, 1942.

——. *Studies in Arabic Literary Papyri I: Historical Texts*. University of Chicago Oriental Institute Publications 75. Chicago, 1957.

——. *Studies in Arabic Literary Papyri II: Qur'ānic Commentary and Tradition*. University of Chicago Oriental Institute Publications 76. Chicago, 1976.

Afsaruddin, Asma. *Excellence and Precedence: Medieval Islamic Discourse on Legitimate Leadership*. Leiden, 2002.

——. "In Praise of the Caliphs: Recreating History from the Manāqib Literature." *International Journal of Middle Eastern Studies* 31 (1999): 329–350.

Alter, Robert. *The Art of Biblical Narrative*. New York, 1981.

Āl 'Ukla, Ṭāhir. *al-Anṣār, Ramz al-Īthār wa Ḍaḥiyyat al-Athra*. Beirut, 2001.

Ankersmit, F. R., and H. Kellner. *A New Philosophy of History*. Chicago, 1995.

Arberry, A. J. *The Koran Interpreted*. 2 vols. London, 1955.

al-'Askarī, Murtaḍā. *'Abdallāh ibn Saba' wa Asāṭīr Ukhrā*. 2 vols. in 1. Baghdad, n.d.

——. *Khamsūn wa Mi'at Ṣaḥābiyy Mukhtalaq*. Baghdad, 1969. Repr. Beirut, 1991.

'Athamina, Khalil. "Al-Qaṣaṣ: Its Emergence, Religious Origin, and Socio-Political Impact on Early Muslim Society." *Studia Islamica* 76 (1992): 53–74.

——. "The Sources of al-Balādhurī's *Ansāb al-Ashrāf*." *Jerusalem Studies in Arabic and Islam* 5 (1984): 237–262.

——. "The Tribal Kings in Pre-Islamic Arabia: A Study of the Epithet *malik* or *dhū al-tāj* in Early Arabic Traditions." *Qantara* 19 (1998): 19–37.

'Aṭwān, Husayn. *Al-Riwāya al-Ta'rīkhiyya fī Bilād al-Shām fī al-'Aṣr al-Umawī*. Beirut, 1986.

al-Bakay, Latifa. *Ḥarakāt al-Khawārij, Nash'atuhā wa taṭawwuruhā ilā nihāyat al-'ahd al-Umawī, 37–132* A.H. Beirut, 2001.

Bashear, Suliman. *Muqaddima fī al-Tārīkh al-Ākhar: Naḥwa Qirā'a Jadīda li'l-Riwāya al-Islāmiyya*. Jerusalem, 1984.

——. "The Title 'Fārūq' and Its Association with 'Umar I." *Studia Islamica* 72 (1990): 47–70.

——. *Arabs and Others in Early Islam*. Princeton, 1997.

Berg, Herbert. "Competing Paradigms in the Study of Islamic Origins: Qur'ān 15:89–91 and the Value of *Isnāds*." In *Method and Theory in the Study of Islamic Origins*, ed. H. Berg (Leiden, 2003), 259–290.

——. *The Development of Exegesis in Early Islam: The Authenticity of Muslim Literature from the Formative Period*. London, 2000.

——. "The Implications of, and Opposition to, the Methods and Theories of John Wansbrough." *Method and Theory in the Study of Religion* 9.1 (1997): 3–22.

Blankinship, Khalid Yahya, trans. *The History of al-Ṭabarī*, XI: *The Challenge to Empires*. Albany, 1993.

Brinner, William, trans. *The History of al-Ṭabarī*, III: *The Children of Israel*. Albany, 1991.

Brockett, Adrian, trans. *The History of al-Ṭabarī*, XVI: *The Community Divided*. Albany, 1997.

Brooks, Peter. *Reading for the Plot, Design, and Intention in Narrative*. Cambridge, Mass., 1984.

Browne, E. G. "Some Account of the Arabic Work Entitled 'Niháyatu'l-irab fī akhbári'l-Furs wa'l-'Arab.'" *Journal of the Royal Asiatic Society* (1900): 195–259.

Brunschvig, Robert. "Ibn 'Abdalḥakam et la conquête de l'Afrique du Nord par les Arabes." *Annales de l'Institut des Études Orientales de l'Université d'Alger* (1942–1947).

Bulliet, Richard. *Conversion to Islam in the Medieval Period: An Essay in Quantitative History*. Cambridge, Mass., 1979.

Burton, John. *An Introduction to Hadith*. Edinburgh, 1994.

Caetani, L. *Annali dell'Islam*. 10 vols. Milan, 1905–1926. Repr. Hildesheim, 1972.

Cameron, Averil. *Christianity and the Rhetoric of Empire*. Berkeley, 1991.

Christensen, A. *L'Iran sous les Sassanides*. Copenhagen, 1936.

Cohen, Mark. *Under Crescent and Cross: The Jews in the Middle Ages*. Princeton, 1994.

Conrad, Lawrence. "Seven and the Tasbī': On the Implications of Numerical Symbolism for the Study of Medieval Islamic History." *Journal of the Economic and Social History of the Orient* 31 (1988): 42–73.

——. "The Conquest of Arwād: A Source-Critical Study in the Historiography of the Medieval Near East." In *The Byzantine and Early Islamic Near East*, I: *Problems in the Literary Source Material*, ed. Averil Cameron and Lawrence Conrad (Princeton, 1992), 317–401.

Cook, Michael. "The Opponents of the Writing of Tradition in Early Islam." *Arabica* 44 (1997): 437–530.

Coulson, N. *A History of Islamic Law*. Edinburgh, 1964.

Cox-Miller, Patricia. *Dreams in Late Antiquity*. Princeton, 1996.

Crone, Patricia, *Meccan Trade and the Rise of Islam*. Princeton, 1987.

——. *Roman, Provincial, and Islamic Law*. Cambridge, 1987.

——. "Shūrā as an Elective Institution." *Quaderni di Studi Arabi* 19 (2001): 3–39.

——. *Slaves on Horses*. Cambridge, 1980.

Crone, Patricia, and Michael Cook. *Hagarism: The Making of the Islamic World*. Cambridge, 1977.

Crone, Patricia, and Martin Hinds. *God's Caliph: Religious Authority in the First Centuries of Islam*. Cambridge, 1986.

Davis, D. *Epic and Sedition: The Case of Ferdowsi's Shahnameh*. Fayetteville, 1992.

Dentan, R. ed. *The Idea of History in the Ancient Near East*. New Haven, 1955.

Djaït, Hichem. *Al-Kufa: Naissance de la ville islamique*. Paris, 1986.

——. *La Grande Discorde: Religion et politique dans l'Islam des origines*. Paris, 1989.

Donner, Fred, trans. *The Early Islamic Conquests*. Princeton, 1981.

——. "The Formation of the Islamic State." *Journal of the American Oriental Society* 106 (1986): 283–296.

——, trans. *The History of al-Ṭabarī, X: The Conquest of Arabia*. Albany, 1993.

——. *Narratives of Islamic Origins: The Beginnings of Islamic Historical Writing*. Princeton, 1998.

——. "Uthmān and the Rāshidūn Caliphs in Ibn 'Asākir's *Ta'rīkh madīnat Dimashq*: A Study in Strategies of Compilation." In *Ibn 'Asākir and Early Islamic History*, ed. J. Lindsay (Princeton, 2001), 44–62.

Duri, 'Abd al-'Aziz. *Baḥth fī Nash'at 'ilm al-Ta'rīkh 'inda al-'Arab*. Beirut, 1960.

——. *The Rise of Historical Writing Among the Arabs*. Trans. L. Conrad. Princeton, 1983.

——. "Al-Zuhrī: A Study of the Beginnings of History Writing in Islam." *Bulletin of the School of Oriental and African Studies* 19 (1957): 1–12.

Eagleton, T. *Literary Theory*. Minneapolis, 1983.

El-Hibri, Tayeb. "The Redemption of Umayyad Memory by the 'Abbāsids." *Journal of Near Eastern Studies* 61 (2002): 241–265.

——. *Reinterpreting Islamic Historiography: Hārūn al-Rashīd and the Narrative of the 'Abbāsid Caliphate*. Cambridge, 1999.

Eliade, M. *Myth and Reality*. New York, 1963.

——. *Images and Symbols*. Princeton, 1991.

Fahd, Toufic. *La divination arabe: Études religieuses, sociologiques et folkloriques sur le milieu natif de l'Islam*. Leiden, 1966.

Faizer, Rizwi. "Muhammad and the Medinan Jews: A Comparison of the Texts of Ibn Ishaq's *Kitab Sirat Rasul Allah* with al-Waqidi's *Kitab al-Maghazi*." *International Journal of Middle East Studies* 78 (1996): 463–489.

Forand, P. G. "The Status of the Land and Inhabitants of the *Sāwad* During the First Two Centuries of Islam." *Journal of the Economic and Social History of the Orient* 14 (1971): 25–37.

Freedman, David N. *The Unity of the Hebrew Bible*. Ann Arbor, 1991.

Friedmann, Y., trans. *The History of al-Ṭabarī*, XII: *The Battle of al-Qādisiyya and the Conquest of Syria and Palestine*. Albany, 1992.

Frye, Northrop. *The Secular Scripture: A Study in the Structure of Romance*. Cambridge, 1976.

Frye, R. N. *The Golden Age of Persia*. London, 1975.

Gibb, H. A. R. "The Evolution of Government in Early Islam." *Studia Islamica* 4 (1955): 1–17.

——. "An Interpretation of Islamic History." *Journal of World History* 1 (1953): 39–62 (repr. in his *Studies on the Civilization of Islam*, ed. Stanford J. Shaw and William R. Polk [London, 1962], 3–33).

Gil, M. "The Medinan Opposition to the Prophet." *Jerusalem Studies in Arabic and Islam* 10 (1987): 65–96.

——. "The Origin of the Jews of Yathrib." *Jerusalem Studies in Arabic and Islam* 4 (1984): 203–220.

Goitein, S. D. "The Place of Balādhurī's Ansāb al-Ashrāf in Arabic Historiography." *International Congress of Orientalists* 19 (1935): 603–606.

Goldziher, Ignaz. *Muhammedanische Studien*. Halle, 1889–90. = *Muslim Studies*. Trans. C. R. Barber and S. M. Stern. 2 vols. London, 1967–1971.

Guillaume, Alfred. *The Traditions of Islam: An Introduction to the Study of Hadith Literature*. Oxford, 1924.

Hawting, G. R. *The First Dynasty of Islam: The Umayyad Caliphate,* A.D. *661–750*. London, 1986.

——, trans. *The History of al-Ṭabarī*, XVII: *The First Civil War*. Albany, 1996.

——. *The Idea of Idolatry and the Emergence of Islam: From Polemic to History*. Cambridge, 1999.

Hillenbrand, C., trans. *The History of al-Ṭabarī*, XXVI: *The Waning of the Umayyad Caliphate*. Albany, 1989.

Hinds, Martin. "Kufan Political Alignments and Their Background in the Mid-Seventh Century A.D." *International Journal of Middle East Studies* 2 (1971).

——. "The Murder of the Caliph 'Uthmān." *International Journal of Middle East Studies* 3 (1972): 450–469.

——. "Sayf b. 'Umar's Sources on Arabia." In *Sources for the History of Arabia*, part II. Riyad, 1979. Repr. in *Studies in Early Islamic History*, ed. J. Bacharach, L. Conrad, and P. Crone (Princeton, 1995).

——. "The Ṣiffīn Arbitration Agreement." *Journal of Semitic Studies* 17 (1972): 450–469.

Hodgson, M. G. S. *The Venture of Islam*. 3 vols. Chicago, 1974.

Horovitz, Josef. *The Earliest Biographies of the Prophet and Their Authors.* Ed. L. Conrad. Princeton, 2002.

Hoyland, Robert. "New Documentary Texts and the Early Islamic State." *Bulletin of the School of Oriental and African Studies* 69 (2006): 395–416.

Humphreys, R. S., trans. *The History of al-Ṭabarī*, XV: *The Crisis of the Early Caliphate.* Albany, 1990.

——. *Islamic History: A Framework for Inquiry.* Princeton, 1991.

Jabalī, Fu'ād. *The Companions of the Prophet: A Study of Geographical and Political Alignments.* Leiden, 2003.

Jeffery, Arthur. *Materials for the History of the Text of the Qur'ān* (includes an edition of Sijistānī's *Kitāb al-Maṣāḥif*). Leiden, 1937.

Johns, Jeremy. "Archaeology and the History of Early Islam: The First Seventy Years." *Journal of the Economic and Social History of the Orient* 46 (2003): 411–436.

Jones, J. M. B. "The Maghāzī Literature." In *The Cambridge History of Arabic Literature to the End of the Umayyad Period*, ed. A. F. L. Beeston, T. M. Johnstone, R. B. Serjeant, and G. R. Smith (Cambridge, 1983), 344–351.

Juynboll, G. H. A. "Early Islamic Society as Reflected in Its Use of *isnāds*." *Le Museon* 107 (1994): 151–194.

——, trans. *The History of al-Ṭabarī*, XIII: *The Conquest of Iraq, Southwestern Persia, and Egypt.* Albany, 1989.

——. *Muslim Tradition: Studies in Chronology, Provenance, and Authorship of Early Ḥadīth.* Cambridge, 1983.

——. "On the Origins of Arabic Prose: Reflections on Authenticity." In *Studies on the First Century of Muslim Society*, ed. G. H. A. Juynboll, 161–175. Papers on Islamic History 5. Carbondale, 1982.

——. "The Position of Qur'ān Recitation in Early Islam." *Journal of Semitic Studies* 19 (1974): 240–251.

——. "The Qurrā' in Early Islamic History." *Journal of the Economic and Social History of the Orient* 16 (1973): 113–129.

——. "Some Thoughts on Early Muslim Historiography." *Bibliotheca Orientalis* 49 (1992): 685–691.

Katibi, Ghayda Khazna. *al-Kharāj mundhu al-Fatḥ al-Islāmī ḥattā Awāṣiṭ al-Qarn al-Thālith al-Hijrī.* Beirut, 1997.

Keaney, Heather. "The First Islamic Revolt in Mamluk Collective Memory: Ibn Bakr's (d. 1340) Portrayal of the Third Caliph 'Uthmān." In *Ideas, Images, and Methods of Portrayal: Insights Into Classical Arabic Literature and Islam*, ed. Sebastian Günther (Leiden, 2005), 375–400.

Kennedy, Hugh. *The Prophet and the Age of the Caliphate.* London, 1986.

Khalīfa, Ḥāmid Muḥammad. *al-Anṣār fī al-'Aṣr al-Rāshidī.* Cairo, 2002.

Kinberg, Leah. *Morality in the Guise of Dreams.* Leiden, 1994.

Kister, M. J. "Ḥaddithū 'an banī isrā'ila wa lā ḥaraj." *Israel Oriental Studies* 2 (1972): 215–239. Repr. in *Studies in Jahiliyya and Early Islam*, XIV (London, 1980).

Lambton, Ann. *State and Government in Medieval Islam*. London Oriental Series 36. London, 1981.

Lammens, Henri. *Études sur le régne du Calife Omaiyade Mo'awiya Ier*. Paris, 1908.

——. "Le Tirumvirat Abou Bakr, 'Omar et Abou 'Obaida." *Mélanges de la Faculté Orientale de l'Université St Joseph de Beyrouth* 4 (1910): 113–144.

Landau-Tasseron, Ella. "Sayf b. 'Umar in Medieval and Modern Scholarship." *Der Islam* 67 (1990): 1–26.

——. "From Tribal Society to Centralized Polity: An Interpretation of Events and Anecdotes of the Formative Period of Islam." *Jerusalem Studies in Arabic and Islam* 24 (2000): 180–216.

Lassner, Jacob. *Islamic Revolution and Historical Memory*. American Oriental Society series. New Haven, 1986.

Lecker, Michael. "Biographical Notes on Ibn Shihāb al-Zuhrī." *Journal of Semitic Studies* 61 (1996): 21–63.

——. "The Death of the Prophet Muhammad's Father: Did Wāqidī Invent Some of the Evidence?" *Zeitschrift der Morgendeutschen Gesellschaft* 145 (1995): 9–27.

Leder, Stefan. "Conventions of Fictional Narration in Learned Literature." In *Storytelling in the Framework of Non-Fictional Arabic Literature* (Berlin, 1998), 34–60.

——. "The Literary Use of the Khabar: A Basic Form of Historical Writing." In *The Byzantine and Early Islamic Near East, 1: Problems in the Literary Source Material*, ed. Averil Cameron and L. I. Conrad, 277–315. Studies in Late Antiquity and Early Islam 1. Princeton, 1992.

——. "The Paradigmatic Character of Madā'inī's *shūrā*-Narration." *Studia Islamica* 88 (1998): 35–54.

Leemhuis, Fred. "Origins and Early Development of the *Tafsīr* Tradition." In *Approaches to the History of the Interpretation of the Qur'ān*, ed. A. Rippin (Oxford, 1988), 12–30.

Le Strange, G. *The Lands of the Eastern Caliphate*. London, 1905.

Lindsay, James. "'Ibn 'Asākir, His *Tār'īkh madīnat Dimashq*, and Its Usefulness for Understanding Early Islamic History." In *Ibn 'Asākir and Early Islamic History*, ed. J. Lindsay (Princeton, 2001), 1–24.

Lokkegaard, F. *Islamic Taxation in the Classical Period with Special Reference to Circumstances in Iraq*. Copenhagen, 1950.

Madelung, Wilferd. *The Succession to Muhammad: A Study of the Early Caliphate*. Cambridge, 1997.

Margoliouth, D. S. *The Early Development of Mohammedanism*. London, 1913.

——. *Lectures on Arabic Historians*. New York, 1929.

——. *The Relations Between the Arabs and Israelites Prior to the Rise of Islam*. Oxford, 1924.

Ma'rūf, Nayef. *al-Khawārij fī al-'Aṣr al-Umawī*. Beirut, 1977.

Milḥim, ʻAdnān Muḥammad. *al-Mu'arrikhūn al-ʻArab wa'l-Fitna al-Kubrā*. Beirut, 1998.

Mitchell, W. J. T. *On Narrative*. Chicago, 1980.

Morony, Michael G., trans. *The History of al-Ṭabarī*, XVII: *Between Civil Wars, the Caliphate of Muʻāwiya*. Albany, 1987.

———. *Iraq after the Muslim Conquest*. Princeton, 1984.

Motzki, Harald. "The Collection of the Qur'ān: A Reconsideration of Western Views in Light of Recent Methodological Developments." *Der Islam* 78 (2001): 1–34.

———. "The *Muṣannaf* of ʻAbd al-Razzāq al-Ṣanʻānī as a Source of Authentic *aḥādīth* of the First Century A.H." *Journal of Near Eastern Studies* 50 (1991): 1–21.

———. *The Origins of Islamic Jurisprudence: Meccan Fiqh Before the Classical Schools*. Trans. Marion Katz. Leiden, 2002.

———. "The Question of the Authenticity of Muslim Traditions Reconsidered: A Review Article." In *Method and Theory in the Study of Islamic Origins*, ed. H. Berg (Leiden, 2003), 211–257.

———. "The Role of Non-Arab Converts in the Development of Early Islamic Law." *Islamic Law and Society* 6 (1999): 1–25.

Muir, William, *The Caliphate: Its Rise, Decline, and Fall*. 2nd ed. London, 1892. New ed. revised by T. H. Weir. Edinburgh, 1915.

Nagel, Tilman. "Some Considerations Concerning the Pre-Islamic and the Islamic Foundations of the Authority of the Caliphate." In *Studies on the First Century of Islamic Society*, ed. G. H. A. Juynboll (Carbondale, Ill., 1982), 177–198.

Newby, Gordon. *A History of the Jews of Arabia: From Ancient Times to Their Eclipse Under Islam*. Columbia, 1988.

Noth, A., and L. Conrad. *The Early Arabic Historical Tradition: A Source-Critical Study*. Princeton, 1994.

Pedersen, Johannes. "The Islamic Preacher, wāʻiẓ, mudhakkir, qāṣṣ." In *Ignace Goldziher Memorial Volume*, part 1, ed. S. Lowinger and J. Somogyi (Budapest, 1948), 226–251.

Petersen, E. L. *ʻAlī and Muʻāwiya in Early Arabic Tradition: Studies on the Genesis and Growth of Islamic Historical Writing Until the End of the Ninth Century*. Trans. P. L. Christensen. Copenhagen, 1964.

Poonawala, Ismail R., trans. *The History of al-Ṭabarī*, IX: *The Last Years of the Prophet*. Albany, 1990.

Powers, David. *Studies in Qur'ān and Ḥadīth: The Formation of the Islamic Law of Inheritance*. Berkeley, 1987.

Qalʻajī, Muḥammad Rawwās. *Mawsūʻat Fiqh ʻUmar b. al-Khaṭṭāb, ʻAṣruhu wa Ḥayātuh*. Beirut, 1986.

———. *Mawsūʻat Fiqh ʻUthmān b. ʻAffān*. Beirut, 1991.

Rippin, Andrew, ed. *Approaches to the History of the Interpretation of the Qur'ān*. Oxford, 1988.

——. "Interpreting the Bible Through the Qur'ān." In *Approaches to the Qur'ān*, ed. G. R. Hawting and Abdul-Kader A. Shareef, 249–259. London, 1993.
——. "Literary Analysis of the *Qur'ān, tafsīr* and *sīra*: The Methodologies of John Wansbrough." In *Approaches to Islam in Religious Studies*, ed. Richard C. Martin (Tucson, 1985), 151–163.
Rosenthal, Franz. *A History of Muslim Historiography*. 2nd ed. Leiden, 1968.
——. "The Influence of Biblical Tradition on Muslim Historiography." In *Historians of the Middle East*, ed. B. Lewis and P. Holt (Oxford, 1962), 35–45.
Rubin, Uri. "Prophets and Progenitors in Early Shī'a Tradition." *Jerusalem Studies in Arabic and Islam* 1 (1975): 41–65.
Sachedina, A. A. *Islamic Messianism: The Idea of the Mahdi in Twelver Shiism*. Albany, 1981.
Ṣafwat, Aḥmad Zakī, *Jamharat Khuṭab al-'Arab fī 'Uṣūr al-'Arabiyya al-Zāhira*. 3 vols. Cairo, 1933.
——. *Jamharat Rasā'il al-'Arab fī 'Uṣūr al-'Arabiyya al-Zāhira*. Cairo, 1937.
Sayyid, Radwan. "al-Khilāfa wa'l-Mulk, Dirāsa fī al-Ru'ya al-Umawiyya li'l-Sulṭa." In *The Fourth International Conference on the History of Bilad al-Sham During the Umayyad Period: Proceedings of the Third Symposium*, ed. 'Adnan al-Bakhit and Robert Schick (Amman, 1989), 96–142.
Schacht, Joseph. *An Introduction to Islamic Law*. Oxford, 1964.
——. "On Mūsā b. 'Uqba's *Kitāb al-Maghāzī*." *Acta Orientalia* 21 (1953): 288–300.
——. *The Origins of Muhammadan Jurisprudence*. Oxford, 1950.
——. "A Revaluation of Islamic Traditions." *Journal of the Royal Asiatic Society* (1949): 143–154.
Schoeler, G. "Character and Authenticity of the Muslim Tradition on the Life of the Prophet." *Arabica* 48 (2002): 360–366.
Serjeant, R. B. "Early Arabic Prose." In *Arabic Literature to the End of the Umayyad Period*, ed. A. F. L. Beeston et al. (Cambridge, 1983), 114–146.
Shaban, M. A. *Islamic History: A New Interpretation*, I: A.D. *600–750* (A.H. *132)*, Cambridge, 1971.
Shoufani, Elias. *al-Riddah and the Muslim Conquest of Arabia*. Toronto, 1973.
Smith, G. Rex, trans. *The History of al-Ṭabarī*, XIV: *The Conquest of Iran*. Albany, 1994.
Spellberg, Denise. "Nizam al-Mulk's Manipulation of Tradition: 'Aisha and the Role of Women in the Islamic Government." *Muslim World* 77 (1988): 111–117.
——. *Politics, Gender, and the Islamic Past: The Legacy of 'A'isha bint Abi Bakr*. New York, 1994.
States, Bert. *Dreaming and Storytelling*. Ithaca, 1993.
Tayob, 'Abdelkader I. "Ṭabarī on the Companions of the Prophet: Moral and Political Contours in Islamic Historical Writing." *Journal of the American Oriental Society* 119 (1999): 203–219.
Tottoli, Roberto. *Biblical Prophets in the Qur'an and Muslim Literature*. London, 2002.

Van Ess, Josef. "Political Ideas in Early Islamic Religious Thought." *British Journal of Middle Eastern Studies* 28 (2001): 151–164.

Waldmann, Marilyn. *Toward a Theory of Historical Narrative: A Case Study in Perso-Islamicate Historiography*. Columbus, 1980.

Wansbrough, J. *Qur'anic Studies: Sources and Methods of Scriptural Interpretation*. Oxford, 1977.

——. *The Sectarian Milieu: Content and Composition of Islamic Salvation History*. Oxford, 1978.

Wasserstrom, S. M. *Between Muslim and Jew: The Problem of Symbiosis Under Early Islam*. Princeton, 1995.

Watt, W. Montgomery. *Bell's Introduction to the Qur'ān*. Edinburgh, 1970.

——. "The Early Development of the Muslim Attitude to the Bible." *Transactions of the Glasgow University Oriental Society* 16 (1957): 50–62 (repr. in his *Early Islam* [Edinburgh, 1990], 77–85).

——. *The Formative Period of Islamic Thought*. Edinburgh, 1973.

——. "God's Caliph: Qur'ānic Interpretations and Umayyad Claims." In *Iran and Islam*, ed. C. Bosworth (London, 1971), 565–574 (repr. in his *Early Islam* [Edinburgh, 1990], 57–63).

——. *Islamic Political Thought*. Edinburgh, 1968.

Wellhausen, Julius. *The Arab Kingdom and Its Fall*. Trans. M. G. Weir. Calcutta, 1927.

——. *The Religio-Political Factions in Early Islam*. Trans. R. C. Ostle et al. Amsterdam, 1974.

Wensinck, A. J. *Muhammad and the Jews of Medina (with an excursus on Muhammad's Constitution of Medina by Julius Wellhausen)*. Trans. and ed. Wolfgang H. Behn. 2nd ed. Berlin, 1982.

White, Hayden. *Tropics of Discourse: Essays in Cultural Criticism*. Baltimore, 1978.

——. *The Content of the Form*. Baltimore, 1987.

Yazigi, Maya. "*Ḥadīth al-ʿashara*; or, The Political Uses of a Tradition." *Studia Islamica* 86 (1997): 159–167.

Zaman, Muhammad Qasim. "*Maghazi* and *Muhaddithun*: Reconsidering the Treatment of 'Historical' Materials in Early Collections of Hadith." *International Journal of Middle East Studies* 28 (1996): 1–18.

# Index